The Cumulated Indexes
to the
Public Papers of the Presidents
of the
United States

DWIGHT D. EISENHOWER
1953–1961

kto press

A U.S. Division of Kraus-Thomson Organization Ltd.
Millwood, New York
1978

First Printing
Printed in the United States of America

Library of Congress Cataloging in Publication Data
    Main entry under title:

    The Cumulated indexes to the public papers of the Presidents of
        the United States, Dwight D. Eisenhower, 1953-1961.

        1.   United States—Politics and government—1953-1961
—Addresses, essays, lectures—Indexes.   2.   Eisenhower,
Dwight David, Pres. U.S., 1890-1969—Indexes.
I.   Eisenhower, Dwight David. Pres. U.S., 1890-1969.
II.   KTO Press.
J82.D8 1978   016.973921   78-135
ISBN 0-527-20753-5

PREFACE

Although the words spoken by a president during the course of his administration are directed to the citizens of his own time, they become invaluable to future generations of Americans who look to the past for help in understanding their present world. *The Cumulated Indexes to the Public Papers of the Presidents of the United States* provide, for the first time in one volume, full access to the papers of each presidential administration published in the government series, the *Public Papers of the Presidents*. The *Public Papers* offer a remarkable view of the American presidents and of American history. The character of a president, the individuals with whom a president interacts, the historical events that are shaped by a president and that, in turn, shape his presidency, are all to be found within the pages of the *Public Papers*.

A resolution passed by the United States Congress on July 17, 1894, provided that a compilation of "all the annual, special, and veto messages, proclamations, and inaugural addresses" of all the presidents from 1789 to 1894 be printed. The publication was to be prepared by James D. Richardson, a representative from Tennessee, under the direction of the Joint Committee on Printing, of which Richardson was a member. The official set was issued in two series of ten volumes each. A joint resolution of May 2, 1896, provided for the distribution of the set to members of Congress, with the remainder to be delivered to the compiler, James Richardson. An act passed about a year later provided that the plates for *A Compilation of the Messages and Papers of the Presidents* be delivered to Richardson "without cost to him." Representative Richardson then made arrangements for the commercial publication of the set. Several other compilations of presidential papers were commercially published in the first half of the nineteenth century; these usually contained only selected documents.

The Richardson edition of the *Messages and Papers*, however, was the only set authorized by Congress and published by the government until 1957, when the official publication of the public messages and statements of the presidents, the *Public Papers of the Presidents of the United*

States, was initiated based on a recommendation made by the National Historical Publications Commission (now the National Historical Publications and Records Commission). The Commission suggested that public presidential papers be compiled on a yearly basis and issued in a uniform, systematic publication similar to the *United States Supreme Court Reports* and the *Congressional Record*. An official series thus began in which presidential writings and statements of a public nature could be made promptly available. These presidential volumes are compiled by the Office of the Federal Register of the General Services Administration's National Archives and Record Service.

As might be expected, the "public papers" vary greatly in importance and content; some contain important policy statements while others are routine messages. They include, in chronological order, texts of such documents as the president's messages to Congress, public addresses, transcripts of news conferences and speeches, public letters, messages to heads of state, remarks to informal groups, etc. Executive orders, proclamations, and similar documents that are required by law to be published in the *Federal Register* and *Code of Federal Regulations* are not reprinted, but are listed by number and subject in an appendix in each volume.

The *Public Papers of the Presidents* are kept in print, and are available from the Superintendent of Documents, United States Government Printing Office. The *Papers* of each year are published in single volumes, with each volume containing an index for that calendar year. *The Cumulated Indexes to the Public Papers of the Presidents* combines and integrates the separate indexes for a president's administration into one alphabetical listing.

References to all of the volumes of a president's public papers can thus be found by consulting this one-volume cumulated index. *See* and *see also* references have been added and minor editorial changes have been made in the process of cumulating the separate indexes.

References in *The Cumulated Indexes to the Public Papers of the Presidents* are to item numbers. Individual volumes are identified in the *Index* by year, as are the actual volumes of the *Papers*. The year identifying the volume in which a paper is located appears in boldface type. When page references are used, they are clearly noted in the entry.

Other volumes in the set of *The Cumulated Indexes to the Public Papers of the Presidents* include Richard M. Nixon, 1969–1974; Lyndon B. Johnson, 1963–1969; John F. Kennedy, 1961–1963; and Harry S. Truman, 1945–1953. Forthcoming volumes will index the papers of Herbert C. Hoover and Gerald R. Ford, as well as those of future presidents when their administrations are completed.

KTO PRESS

DWIGHT D. EISENHOWER
1953–1961

Abaca fiber production program, **1954:** 14 (p. 180)

Abbot, Mary, **1959:** 167

Abbott, Harold W., and others, tax refund claim, disapproval, **1959:** 237

Abdul Aziz Ibn al Saud, **1953:** 18
Death of, **1953:** 245

Abel, Elie, **1954:** 311; **1955:** 47, 62, 81, 90, 95; **1956:** 32, 78, 88

Abel, Col. Rudolf I., **1960–61:** 143, 268

Abilene, Kans., **1953:** 225, 252; **1956:** 242n., 268; **1957:** 68, 134; **1959:** 177, 186; **1960–61:** 45, 290

Eisenhower Library, **1959:** 179; **1960–61:** 21, 118
Ground-breaking ceremony, **1959:** 258, 259
Eisenhower Museum, **1954:** 167n.
Dedication, remarks, **1954:** 331
Reflector-Chronicle, **1954:** 149

ABMA.
See Army Ballistic Missile Agency.

Abraham, **1954:** 325; **1959:** 347

Abraham Lincoln, U.S.S., **1960–61:** 360

Abrams, Capt. Bernard, **1953:** 17

Acapulco, Mexico, **1959:** 39n., 40n., 41n., 254, 256n., 257; **1960–61:** 334
Joint statement with President Lopez Mateos, **1959:** 38
News conference remarks, **1959:** 21, 36, 42
Remarks at airport, **1959:** 37

Accelerated depreciation allowances, **1957:** 80, 92, 115, 124, 145

Accelerators
High-energy, AEC, **1958:** 5 (p. 33)
Linear, **1960–61:** 414 (p. 960)
Construction of, **1959:** 89, 107

Accident compensation benefits, budget message, **1958:** 5 (p. 72)

Accidents
Aircraft, **1958:** 135
La Guardia Airport, New York, **1959:** 26 and ftn. (p. 156)
Near London, **1959:** 36 and ftn. (p. 191)

Accidents — *continued*
Aircraft — *continued*
Troop transport, Germany, **1955:** 204
U. S. military transport in Soviet Armenia, **1958:** 310
U.S. plane in Bering Sea, **1955:** 146
Highway traffic, **1955:** 39, 243; **1958:** 45
Statement on safe driving, **1955:** 111
Holidays, **1954:** 157, 161, 255
Industrial, **1954:** 100
Occupational, **1954:** 288; **1956:** 55, 104; **1958:** 55
Traffic, **1954:** 37, 255, 336, 351; **1956:** 2, 12 (p. 139), 19, 36, 37, 316; **1957:** 14 and n., 118; **1959:** 129, 185
U.S. Navy transport over Brazil, **1960–61:** 55, 64

Accountants, Certified Public, American Institute of, address, **1960–61:** 304

Accounting and budget practices, **1956:** 100
Approval of bill, **1956:** 156
Hoover Commission report, letter, **1956:** 89

Accra, Ghana, **1957:** 43n.; **1960–61:** 248
African conference, **1958:** 180

Acheson, Dean, **1953:** 37; **1954:** 125, 126; **1956:** 216; **1958:** 74, 288
Berlin situation, **1959:** 48
News conference remarks on, **1954:** 33, 157; **1959:** 48, 148

Acker, Achille Zan, **1957:** 153 and n.

Acreage allotments, **1954:** 4; **1955:** 90; **1956:** 6; **1957:** 16; **1958:** 12; **1959:** 23
Budget message, **1958:** 5 (p. 65)
Cotton, **1954:** 24
Durum wheat, bill approved, **1957:** 59
Tobacco, **1959:** 140
Veto of farm "freeze" bill, **1958:** 56
Broadcast, **1958:** 60
Wheat, **1954:** 4, 24; **1959:** 108, 132, 139; **1960–61:** 32

Acreage controls, **1955:** 4, 17 (p. 150)

Acreage reserve.
See Soil bank.

Actuaries, International Congress of, remarks to, **1957:** 222
Adams, Abigail, **1956:** 106
Adams, Avery C., **1959:** 211n.
Adams, Francis L., **1955:** 146 and ftn. (p. 658)
Adams, John, **1954:** 128, 136; **1956:** 106; **1959:** 107
Adams, John G., **1954:** 115
Adams, John Quincy, **1959:** 219
Adams, Lt. Gen. Paul D., **1960–61:** 396
Adams, Sherman, **1953:** 37; **1954:** 50, 57, 143, 192, 311; **1955:** 131, 133, 134, 135; **1956:** 78, 171; **1958:** 166
   Chairman, Federal fund-raising campaign for health agencies, **1957:** 18
   News conference remarks on, **1955:** 119, 146, 176; **1957:** 17, 28, 72; **1958:** 28, 37, 141, 153, 198, 274
   Resignation, letter, **1958:** 266
   Statement on, **1958:** 141
Adamson, Herbert A., **1959:** 109
Adamy, Clarence G., **1955:** 51n.
Addis Ababa, **1957:** 50
Addresses or remarks, election.
   See Election campaign addresses or remarks.
Addresses or remarks on commemorative or dedicatory occasions
   Aerial Fire Depot, dedication, **1954:** 270
   AFL-CIO, dedication of new building, **1956:** 119
   AFL cornerstone-laying ceremony, **1955:** 84
   Alfred E. Smith memorial dinner, **1954:** 301
   Allied landings, 10th anniversary
      Normandy, **1954:** 133
      Southern France, **1954:** 198
   American Forces Network, 15th anniversary, **1958:** 158
   American Hereford Association, dedication of building, **1953:** 218
   American Jewish tercentenary dinner, **1954:** 297
   American University School of International Service, **1957:** 109
   Anthony Wayne Library of American Study, Defiance College, cornerstone-laying ceremony, **1953:** 215
   Anti-Defamation League of B'nai B'rith, 40th anniversary, **1953:** 252
   Armed Forces Institute of Pathology, dedication, **1955:** 108
   Atomic Energy Commission headquarters building, **1957:** 231
   Boy Scouts of America
      43d anniversary, **1953:** 9
      50th anniversary, **1960–61:** 35, 166
   Capitol rotunda frieze, dedication, **1954:** 106
   Carpenters and Joiners Brotherhood, 75th anniversary, **1956:** 265
   Coast and Geodetic Survey anniversary, **1957:** 27
   Columbia University National Bicentennial Dinner, **1954:** 128

Addresses or remarks — *continued*
   Columbus, ceremony honoring, **1958:** 284
   Edmund A. Walsh School of Foreign Service, **1958:** 286
   Eisenhower Museum, dedication, **1954:** 331
   Eisenhower Park (Newport, R.I.), dedication, **1960–61:** 239
   Ellsworth Air Force Base, dedication, **1953:** 103
   Export-Import Bank, 25th anniversary, **1959:** 33
   Falcon Dam, dedication, **1953:** 222
   Federal Housing Administration, 25th anniversary, **1959:** 133
   Fort Ligonier bicentennial, **1958:** 269
   Fort Randall Dam, dedication of first power unit, **1954:** 53
   Francis Scott Key Memorial Auditorium, St. John's College, dedication, **1959:** 116
   Freedom Celebration Day, **1954:** 114
   Garrison Dam, closure ceremonies, **1953:** 100
   General Motors Research Center, dedication, **1956:** 107
   George C. Marshall Space Flight Center, dedication, **1960–61:** 287
   Hiawatha Bridge, Red Wing, Minn., dedication, **1960–61:** 330
   Incandescent lamp, 75th anniversary, **1954:** 305
   Indiana University, tablet honoring Ernie Pyle, dedication, **1953:** 204
   Industrial College of the Armed Forces, new building, dedication, **1960–61:** 283
   Interchurch Center, cornerstone laying ceremony, **1958:** 285
   International Atomic Energy Agency, ratification, **1957:** 144
   International Chamber of Commerce, 40th anniversary, **1959:** 84
   International Christian Leadership, dedicatory prayer breakfast, **1953:** 8
   Islamic Center, opening, **1957:** 120
   Japan, centennial of first diplomatic mission to U.S., **1960–61:** 134
   Labor Day, stamp in honor of American labor, **1956:** 194
   Louisiana Purchase, 150th anniversary, **1953:** 219
   McNary Dam, dedication, **1954:** 271
   Memorial Press Center, dedication, **1954:** 350
   Mount Saint Mary's College, sesquicentennial commencement, **1958:** 123
   National Broadcasting Company, dedication of radio-TV facilities, **1958:** 111
   National Bureau of Standards laboratories, dedication, **1954:** 267
   National Education Association centennial, **1957:** 68
   National 4-H Club Center, dedication, **1959:** 131
   National Lincoln Sesquicentennial, **1959:** 31

Addresses or remarks — *continued*
  NATO
    4th anniversary, **1953:** 42
    10th anniversary, **1959:** 70
  Netherlands, 15th anniversary of liberation,
    1960–61: 138
  Old Man cf the Mountain, 150th anniversary of
    discovery, **1955:** 136
  Powered flight, 50th anniversary, **1953:** 267
  President Magsaysay Champion of Liberty
    Stamp, issuance, **1957:** 166
  Red Cross Chapter House, District of Columbia,
    dedication, **1953:** 201
  Robert A. Taft Memorial Bell Tower, dedica-
    tion, **1959:** 77
  SEATO, 6th anniversary, **1960–61:** 286
  Shippingport atomic power plant, dedication,
    1958: 113
  Smith-Mundt Act, 10th anniversary, **1958:** 23
  St. Lawrence Seaway, dedication, **1959:** 141
  State University of New York Medical Center,
    dedication, **1954:** 300
  Statue of Simon Bolivar, dedication, **1959:** 44
  Theodore Roosevelt Home at Sagamore Hill,
    dedication, **1953:** 105
  Trans-Atlantic Cable, centenary, **1958:** 209
  Transylvania College, 175th anniversary, **1954:**
    89
  U.N. 10th anniversary meeting, **1955:** 126
  Veterans of Foreign Wars Memorial Building,
    dedication, **1960–61:** 31
  Washington Hebrew Congregation Temple, ded-
    ication, **1955:** 92
  Women's suffrage amendment, 40th anniversary,
    1960–61: 269
  Woodrow Wilson, ceremonies honoring memory
    of, **1960–61:** 340
  World Health Organization, 10th anniversary,
    1958: 116
Addresses or remarks to national groups
  Advertising Council Conference, **1955:** 58; **1956:**
    75; **1957:** 60; **1958:** 95; **1959:** 76; **1960–61:**
    94
  AFL, **1953:** 193; **1954:** 275
  AFL-CIO merger meeting, **1955:** 245
  American Assembly, **1960–61:** 86
  American Bankers Association, **1953:** 189
  American Bar Association, **1955:** 210; **1959:** 185;
    1960–61: 276
  American Council on Education, **1953:** 207
  American Council To Improve Our Neighbor-
    hoods, **1954:** 333
  American Forest Congress, **1953:** 234
  American Helicopter Society, **1960–61:** 145
  American Institute of Certified Public Account-
    ants, **1960–61:** 304
  American Junior Red Cross, **1958:** 144
  American Legion, **1954:** 225; **1955:** 38

Addresses or remarks — *continued*
  American Management Association, **1958:** 110
  American Medical Association, **1953:** 29; **1959:**
    129
  American Newspaper Publishers Association,
    1954: 87
  American Red Cross, **1953:** 117; **1957:** 89
  American Retail Federation, **1953:** 23
  American Society of Newspaper Editors, **1953:**
    50; **1956:** 87; **1958:** 80
  Anti-Defamation League of B'nai B'rith, **1953:**
    252
  Associated Press, **1955:** 79
  Association of American Colleges, **1955:** 11
  Association of Junior Leagues of America, **1958:**
    94
  Association of Land-Grant Colleges and Uni-
    versities, **1954:** 335
  Association of Retail Grocers, **1954:** 144
  Association of State Planning and Development
    Agencies, **1959:** 8
  Big Brothers of America, **1960–61:** 404
  Boy Scouts of America, **1953:** 9, 137; **1954:** 127;
    1955: 28; **1960–61:** 35, 166
  Boys Nation, **1957:** 142
  Carpenters and Joiners Brotherhood, **1956:** 265
  Chamber of Commerce, U.S., **1958:** 90
  Citizens for Eisenhower-Nixon, **1958:** 306
  Civil Service Assembly of the United States and
    Canada, **1956:** 238
  Council of Christian Leadership, **1956:** 28
  Daughters of the American Revolution, **1954:** 86
  4-H Club, **1954:** 146; **1959:** 131
    Conference, **1955:** 128; **1957:** 113; **1958:** 142;
    1960–61: 123
  Future Farmers of America, **1953:** 216; **1954:**
    169
  Girls Nation, **1957:** 146
  Governors' Conference, **1957:** 118
  League of Women Voters, **1954:** 91
    National Council, **1957:** 79
  Masonic breakfast, **1955:** 43
  Military Chaplains National Association, **1956:**
    98
  National Association for the Advancement of
    Colored People, **1954:** 51
  National Association of Manufacturers, **1959:** 83
  National Association of Radio and Television
    Broadcasters, **1955:** 105
  National Association of Real Estate Boards,
    1960–61: 19
  National Association of Television and Radio
    Farm Directors, **1955:** 127; **1957:** 114
  National Cartoonists Society, **1954:** 151
  National Conference of Catholic Charities,
    1960–61: 306
  National Conference of Christians and Jews,
    1955: 40

[References are to items except as otherwise indicated]

Addresses or remarks — *continued*
  National Conference of Republican Women,
    1954: 77
  National Council of Catholic Women, **1954:** 325
  National Council of Churches, **1953:** 250; **1959:**
    212
  National Council of the United Service Organ-
    izations, **1956:** 57
  National Editorial Association, **1954:** 149
  National Education Association, **1957:** 68
  National Food Conference, **1958:** 35
  National Fund for Medical Education, **1957:** 223
  National Junior Chamber of Commerce, **1953:**
    98
  National Newspaper Publishers Association,
    1958: 102
  National Press Club, **1959:** 7
  National Rivers and Harbors Congress, **1954:**
    120
  National Rural Electric Cooperative Associa-
    tion, **1959:** 30
  National Rural Letter Carriers Association,
    1959: 177
  National Safety Council, **1958:** 297
  National Security Industrial Association, **1954:**
    308
  National Urban League, **1958:** 315
  National Women's Advisory Committee on Civil
    Defense, **1954:** 310
  National Young Republican Organization, **1953:**
    101
  Polish-American Congress, **1960–61:** 310
  President's Conference on Occupational Safety,
    1956: 104; **1958:** 55
  Republican National Committee, **1955:** 35;
    1956: 84; **1958:** 26, 223; **1960–61:** 246, 395
  Republican National Conference, **1957:** 108
  Republican Women's Conference, **1953:** 57;
    1955: 94; **1956:** 50; **1957:** 63; **1958:** 49;
    1959: 75; **1960–61:** 107 .
  Small Business Conference, **1957:** 196
  Society for Personnel Administration, **1954:** 108
  Spiritual Foundations of American Democracy
    Conference, **1954:** 327
  United Church Women, **1953:** 205
  United Daughters of the Confederacy, **1953:** 240
  United Service Organizations, **1955:** 27
  U.S. Chamber of Commerce, **1954:** 90; **1955:** 85;
    1959: 87; **1960–61:** 131
  White House Conference on Education, **1955:**
    242
  Young Republican National Conference, **1957:**
    116
Addresses or remarks at presentation ceremonies
  "Aloha State" medal, acceptance, **1960–61:** 206
  American Helicopter Society citation, accep-
    tance, **1960–61:** 145

Addresses or remarks — *continued*
  America's Democratic Legacy Award, accep-
    tance, **1953:** 252
  AMVETS World Peace Award, acceptance,
    1959: 92
  Army flag, acceptance, **1957:** 127
  Atoms for Peace Award, Professor Niels H. D.
    Bohr, **1957:** 225
  Big Brother of the Year Award, acceptance,
    1960–61: 404
  Bust of Lincoln, acceptance, **1960–61:** 246
  Churchill, Winston, medallion on 81st birthday,
    1955: 244
  Department of State honor awards, **1954:** 294
  "Dinner with Ike" Rally, acceptance of medal,
    1960–61: 23
  Discoverer XIII flag, acceptance, **1960–61:** 261
  Distinguished Civilian Service Citation, Pres.
    Herbert Hoover, **1957:** 26
  Distinguished Service Medal
    Carney, Adm. Robert B., **1955:** 188
    Greunther, Gen. Alfred M., **1956:** 317
    Radford, Adm. Arthur W., **1957:** 151 and n.
    Ridgway, Gen. Matthew B., **1955:** 144
  Eisenhower Exchange Fellowships, acceptance
    of plans for, **1953:** 212
  Fawn from Rangeley, Maine, acceptance, **1955:**
    141
  Football Hall of Fame Medal, acceptance, **1958:**
    307
  Foreign gifts and awards, acceptance
    Chile, **1960–61:** 70, 74
    Italy, **1956:** 45
    Montevideo, **1960–61:** 79
    The Philippines, **1960–61:** 188
    Uruguay, **1960–61:** 81
  Forrestal Memorial Award, acceptance, **1954:**
    308
  4-H tie clasp, acceptance, **1960–61:** 123
  Frank H. Lahey Award, acceptance, **1954:** 334
  Honorary degrees, acceptance, **1953:** 79, 104,
    251; **1954:** 136, 204n., 295; **1955:** 70, 121;
    1956: 114; **1958:** 123, 130, 286; **1959:** 314;
    1960–61: 174, 186
  Hoover Medal Award, acceptance, **1960–61:** 405
  Keys to cities, acceptance
    Buenos Aires, **1960–61:** 57
    Ciudad Acuna, **1960–61:** 334
    Detroit, **1960–61:** 326
    Mar del Plata, **1960–61:** 61
  Laboring Youth Statue, acceptance, **1955:** 22
  Lafayette Gold Medal Award, Gen. Alfred M.
    Greunther, **1958:** 118
  Legion of Merit
    See main heading, Legion of Merit.
  Medal of Freedom
    See under Medals, remarks on presentation or
    acceptance.

Addresses or remarks — *continued*
  Medal of Honor, seven Korean war veterans,
    1953: 229
    See also under Medals, remarks on presenta-
      tion or acceptance; Congressional Medal
      of Honor.
  Military Chaplains Association citation, accep-
    tance, **1954:** 103
  National Cartoonist Society, acceptance of T-
    square, **1954:** 151
  National Editorial Association, acceptance of
    plaque, **1954:** 149
  National Foundation for Infantile Paralysis,
    1955: 78
  National Geographic Society Medal, Prince
    Philip, **1957:** 221
  National Press Club, acceptance of membership,
    1959: 7
  National Security Medal, J. Edgar Hoover, **1955:**
    110
  Pan American Society, Golden Insignia, accep-
    tance, **1957:** 64 and n.
  Portrait by Sir Oswald Birley, acceptance, **1954:**
    167
  Presidential Unit Citation, Comdr. W. R. An-
    derson, **1958:** 201
  Red oak tree from District of Columbia, accep-
    tance, **1960–61:** 325
  Salk, Dr. Jonas E., citation, **1955:** 77
  Simon Bolivar statue, acceptance, **1959:** 44
  "Spirit of Detroit" Statue, acceptance, **1960–61:**
    326
  United Defense Fund citation, Gen. J.H.
    Doolittle, **1954:** 93
  United Jewish Appeal, citation, acceptance,
    1955: 115
  U.S. Junior Chamber of Commerce, acceptance
    of plaque, **1954:** 338
  U.S.S. *Nautilus*, citation to crew, **1958:** 201
  Vice President Richard Nixon, 48th birthday
    presentation, **1960–61:** 403
Adenauer, Konrad, **1959:** 190; **1960–61:** 147, 362
    ftn. (p. 864)
  Conversations with, **1959:** 179
  East German food shortage, **1953:** 134
  Exchange of toasts, **1957:** 98 and n.; **1960–61:** 91
  Hospital visit, **1956:** 125n.
  Invitation to visit U.S.S.R., **1955:** 119
  Joint statement with, **1954:** 314; **1955:** 122; **1957:**
    100; **1959:** 192; **1960–61:** 92
  Joint statements with Western leaders, **1959:** 335,
    336
  Letters, **1953:** 135, 138, 146; **1954:** 189; **1955:** 190
  Meeting with, **1954:** 214
  Messages, **1953:** 121, 188; **1955:** 204; **1956:** 129;
    1958: 210

Adenauer, Konrad — *continued*
  News conference remarks on, **1953:** 126, 141,
    225; **1954:** 50, 311; **1959:** 173, 179, 191,
    271; **1960–61:** 38, 93, 143
  Tenth anniversary as Chancellor, message, **1959:**
    220
  Visit to United States, **1955:** 119
Adkins, Bertha, **1954:** 77n.; **1955:** 94; **1956:** 50;
    1957: 45, 63; **1958:** 49
Adler, Julius Ochs
  Letter, **1954:** 7
  Nomination to National Security Training Com-
    mission, **1953:** 144
Administrative Procedure, President's Conference
    on, **1953:** 59; **1960–61:** 275
Administrative Vice President, news conference
    remarks on, **1956:** 16
Admissions tax on motion picture performances,
    repeal, disapproval, **1953:** 157
Advanced Research Projects Agency, **1958:** 64, 65,
    321; **1959:** 102
  Director (Roy W. Johnson), **1959:** 277
  Space projects, **1958:** 57n.
Advertising
  Along highways, **1957:** 72, 169; **1958:** 77
    Budget message, **1958:** 5 (p. 53)
    Letter to Gen. Grant, **1958:** 14
  Bureau of, **1954:** 87
  News conference remarks, **1958:** 56, 83
Advertising Council, **1955:** 96; **1958:** 109
  Conference, remarks, **1955:** 58; **1956:** 75; **1957:**
    60; **1958:** 95; **1959:** 76; **1960–61:** 94
Advisory Board on Economic Growth and Stabil-
    ity, **1953:** 93
Advisory Commission on Intergovernmental Re-
    lations, **1960–61:** 115, 208, 415n.
  Budget messages, **1960–61:** 13 (p. 105), 414 (p.
    1022)
Advisory Committee on Government Operations,
    1955: 74
Advisory Committee on Voluntary Foreign Aid,
    1953: 92
AEC.
  See Atomic Energy Commission.
Aerial Fire Depot, Missoula, Mont., dedication,
    remarks, **1954:** 270
Aerial inspection, **1956:** 2, 143, 251, 266; **1957:** 3, 8
  See also Inspection and control of nuclear weap-
    ons; Disarmament.
  Budget message, **1956:** 12 (p. 108)
  Letters to Premier Bulganin, **1956:** 23, 52, 166,
    262
  News conference remarks, **1956:** 20, 78; **1957:**
    92, 150
Aerial photography, Italy, **1956:** 264
Aerial reconnaisance, **1956:** 2

Aerial sentinels, **1957:** 8
Aerial surveillance
    Open skies proposal, **1960–61:** 143, 163, 209
    United Nations, proposed, **1960–61:** 154, 163
Aerodynamic missiles, **1957:** 210
Aerodynamics, research on, **1958:** 64
Aeronautical research, **1955:** 17 (p. 92); **1958:** 64,
    105, 135, 185, 246
    Budget message, **1958:** 5 (p. 60)
Aeronautical Research and Development, NATO
    Advisory Group for, General Assembly,
    1957: 238
Aeronautics, National Advisory Committee for,
    1954: 14 (p. 174); **1955:** 17 (p. 170); **1958:**
    64, 105, 185
    Budget message, **1958:** 5 (pp. 20, 48, 60)
    Report, **1959:** 85
Aeronautics, scientific research, **1954:** 14 (p. 174)
Aeronautics and space activities, reports, **1959:** 25;
    1960–61: 47, 424
Aeronautics and Space Board, National, proposed,
    1958: 64
Aeronautique Internationale, Federation, remarks,
    1958: 71
Afghanistan.
    See also Kabul.
    Ambassador Henry A. Byroade, **1959:** 306n.
    Assistance, **1959:** 308
    Cultural agreement with (1958), **1958:** 150
    Maiwandwal, M. H., **1959:** 306n.
    Sardar Mohammed Daud, **1959:** 306
        Joint statement with, **1958:** 150
    Visit to, **1959:** 277, 306, 307, 308, 309
    Zahir, Mohammad, **1959:** 306, 307, 308
AFL.
    See American Federation of Labor.
AFL-CIO, **1956:** 265n.; **1958:** 70, 288; **1959:** 186
    Code of ethical conduct, **1957:** 45, 56, 87
    Dedication of new building, remarks, **1956:** 119
    Merger, **1955:** 47, 245
    News conference remarks, **1956:** 193, 198, 229
    Opening of Union-Industries Show, remarks,
        1960–61: 139
    Political alignment, **1956:** 193, 198
    Position on Berlin, **1959:** 163
    Testimonial dinner for Secretary Mitchell,
        remarks, **1960–61:** 215
Africa, **1957:** 6, 35, 56; **1960–61:** 271, 272
    See also specific countries.
    Allied landings (1942), **1960–61:** 355
    Assistance, **1953:** 66; **1954:** 14 (p. 139), 150;
        1955: 17 (p. 130), 76; **1956:** 58, 62, 87;
        1958: 36, 96, 198; **1959:** 55, 71, 269n.;
        1960–61: 13 (p. 63), 36, 242, 263, 302, 414
        (pp. 961, 967, 968)
    Bases in, **1956:** 96; **1958:** 32
    Campaign remarks, **1956:** 206, 210

Africa — *continued*
    Communist activities, **1956:** 62
    Foreign service posts, **1958:** 5 (p. 41)
    French Africa, **1959:** 214
    Industrial revolution, **1959:** 55
    Joint statements with
        Premier Mollet, **1957:** 38
        President Bourguiba, **1959:** 329
        President De Gaulle, **1959:** 202
        Prime Minister Nkrumah, **1958:** 180
    New nations, **1960–61:** 36, 410
        U.N. delegation, remarks to, **1960–61:** 324
    News conference remarks, **1956:** 62, 96; **1958:**
        74, 120, 198; **1960–61:** 263, 284
    North Africa, **1958:** 80, 120
    Program for, proposed, address before U.N.
        General Assembly, **1960–61:** 302
    Soviet activities, **1958:** 96
    U.S. diplomatic posts and information centers,
        1960–61: 414 (p. 968)
    Visit of President Eisenhower.
        See Visit of the President to Europe, Asia, and
        Africa; Visits, foreign.
    Visit of Vice President Nixon, **1957:** 28, 43, 50,
        56, 84 and n.
    World War II, **1955:** 10; **1956:** 206
Afro-Asian Conference.
    See also Bandung conference of Asian-African
        countries.
    Cairo, letter to Premier Bulganin, **1958:** 31
Agadir, Morocco, earthquake disaster, **1960–61:** 99
Age as factor in choosing President, comment on,
    1960–61: 222
Aged persons, **1956:** 2
    See also Older persons.
    Housing, **1957:** 13
    Medical care for indigent, **1956:** 21
Aggression.
    See also Communist aggression and expansion.
    Far East, **1958:** 261
    Middle and Near East, **1958:** 172, 173
        Letter to Senator Green, **1958:** 277
        United Nations address, **1958:** 207
    News conference remarks, **1958:** 120, 198, 213
    Retaliation in case of, comment on, **1954:** 9, 57,
        63, 72, 353; **1960–61:** 24
    Statement, **1959:** 186
Aging, Federal Council on, **1956:** 63
    Memorandum on, **1956:** 74
Agra, India, visit to, **1959:** 317
Agreements, international.
    See International agreements.
Agricultural Act of 1954, approval, **1954:** 221
Agricultural Act of 1956.
    See also Farm bill.
    Approval, statement, **1956:** 115
    Veto, **1956:** 82, 83

Agricultural Adjustment Act, **1959:** 267 ·
   Amendment, approval, **1954:** 24
Agricultural Advisory Commission, National,
   1953: 6, 153, 216; **1954:** 196
   News conference remarks, **1953:** 12, 225, 230,
      238
   Statement, **1953:** 227
Agricultural advisory committee, **1956:** 211
Agricultural Conservation Program Service, **1960–
   61:** 13 (p. 81)
Agricultural conservation reserve program, **1960–
   61:** 32
   Budget messages, **1960–61:** 13 (pp. 77, 81, 82),
      414 (pp. 987, 991)
Agricultural Marketing Act amendment, veto,
   1955: 147
Agricultural production, **1958:** 16
Agricultural Products, Commission on Increased
      Industrial Use of, **1958:** 12
   Budget message, **1958:** 5 (p. 67)
Agricultural research, **1953:** 95; **1954:** 4, 221, 291;
      1955: 17 (pp. 94, 155); **1956:** 6, 214, 250;
      1958: 12, 49; **1960–61:** 32, 391, 410
   Budget messages, **1954:** 14 (p. 163); **1956:** 12 (pp.
      125, 130, 132); **1959:** 10 (p. 92); **1960–61:**
      13 (p. 82), 414 (p. 992)
   Campaign remarks, **1958:** 292, 295
Agricultural resources, **1956:** 12 (pp. 125–131)
   Budget message, **1958:** 5 (pp. 24, 41, 63–68)
   Table, **1958:** 5 (p. 64)
Agricultural science and technology, **1958:** 12
Agricultural subsidies, **1957:** 72
Agricultural Surplus Disposal, Interagency Com-
      mittee on
   Letter to Chairman, **1954:** 262
   Letter to members, **1954:** 263
Agricultural Surplus Disposal Administrator, ap-
      pointment, **1956:** 6
Agricultural surpluses, **1953:** 6, 68, 69, 95, 153;
      1954: 3, 4, 35n., 139, 144, 146, 150, 195,
      209, 221, 308, 323; **1955:** 4, 7; **1956:** 2, 6,
      19, 35, 58, 83; **1958:** 2, 12, 26, 110; **1959:**
      6, 116; **1960–61:** 4, 32, 133, 242n., 246,
      255, 279, 410
   See also specific commodities.
   Approval of amendment to Public Law 480,
      1955: 202
   Bolivian relief, **1953:** 213
      Memorandum, **1953:** 206
   Brannan plan, **1958:** 56
   Budget messages, **1954:** 14 (pp. 139, 140, 144,
      158, 160, 162); **1955:** 17 (pp. 103, 130, 152,
      153); **1956:** 12 (pp. 102, 103, 109, 124,
      127–130); **1958:** 5 (pp. 36, 64, 65); **1959:**
      10 (p. 89); **1960–61:** 13 (pp. 77, 79, 80, 82,
      107), 414 (pp. 967, 987–989)
   Campaign remarks, **1954:** 273, 286, 318; **1956:**
      190, 214, 241, 250, 268

Agricultural surpluses — *continued*
   Cotton, **1956:** 82, 115
   Dairy products, **1954:** 25, 39, 50, 196
   Disaster relief program, **1956:** 236
   Disposal, **1954:** 162, 261, 262, 263; **1956:** 6, 20,
      83, 214, 236; **1958:** 2, 12, 56, 163; **1959:** 23
   Joint statement with Prime Minister Suhra-
      wardy, **1957:** 131
   Messages, **1957:** 8, 13, 16
   News conference remarks, **1957:** 45, 72, 115
   Distribution in Kentucky, **1959:** 67 ftn. (p. 297)
   Export, **1956:** 6, 12 (pp. 102, 103, 109, 129), 42,
      58, 214, 241
   Farm "freeze" bill, veto, **1958:** 59, 60
   Food for Peace program, **1959:** 226
   Food stamp plan, **1959:** 226
   Foreign emergency relief, message, **1953:** 125
   Industrial use, bipartisan commission on, **1956:**
      187
   News conference remarks, **1953:** 12, 31, 41, 109;
      1954: 9, 25, 39, 50, 157, 172; **1955:** 90;
      1956: 16, 20, 62, 78, 216; **1958:** 56, 153,
      222
   Overseas relief, **1954:** 175, 195
   Relief of poor in U.S., **1960–61:** 127 and ftn. (p.
      362), 414 (p. 989)
   Rice, **1955:** 148
   Sale for foreign currencies, **1955:** 76
   Sale to Japan, joint statement, **1954:** 330
   Sale to Soviet Union, question of, **1954:** 9, 50
   School lunch program, **1956:** 12 (p. 124), 214
   State and local distribution, **1959:** 226
   Storage costs, **1956:** 12 (p. 128), 83, 214, 268
   Welfare distribution, **1956:** 236
   Wheat, **1954:** 4; **1958:** 163; **1959:** 102, 104, 108,
      122, 132, 139
      U.S.-Canadian discussions, **1958:** 153
Agricultural Trade Development and Assistance
      Act, **1954:** 221, 261n., 262, 263, 323; **1955:**
      76; **1956:** 6, 12 (p. 129); **1958:** 5 (p. 65),
      12, 59; **1960–61:** 136n.
   Amendment, approval, **1955:** 202
   Approval, **1954:** 162
   Budget message, **1959:** 10 (pp. 88, 89)
   Extension, approval, **1959:** 226
   Reports, **1955:** 7, 150
   Title I, proposed extension, **1957:** 16
Agricultural workers, migratory, **1956:** 190
   Education of children, **1954:** 14 (p. 153)
   Employment, **1954:** 14 (p. 184)
   Social and economic status, improvement, **1954:**
      14 (p. 184)
Agriculture, **1953:** 6, 95, 101, 158, 216, 264, 268;
      1954: 3, 67, 139, 162, 201, 221, 226, 291,
      349; **1955:** 4, 6, 221; **1956:** 2, 3, 6, 19, 169;
      1958: 12, 18; **1959:** 6, 23, 169, 225, 288;
      1960–61: 4, 23, 133, 255, 410

Agriculture — *continued*
> *See also* Farm bill; Farm economy; Farm programs; Farms; Price supports; Soil bank; *specific programs.*
> Addresses, **1957:** 8, 13, 16, 86
> Budget
>> Messages, **1954:** 14 (pp. 156–164); **1955:** 17 (pp. 93, 94, 148–155); **1956:** 12 (pp. 77, 82, 125–131); **1958:** 5 (pp. 24, 41, 63–68); **1959:** 10 (pp. 49, 88–92); **1960–61:** 13 (pp. 77–82), 414 (pp. 985–993)
>> Tables, **1954:** 14 (pp. 156, 157); **1955:** 17 (p. 151); **1958:** 5 (p. 64); **1959:** 10 (p. 90); **1960–61:** 13 (p. 78), 414 (p. 986)
>> Statement, **1958:** 324
> Campaign remarks, **1956:** 190, 214, 224, 250; **1958:** 292, 294, 295, 296
>> *See also* Campaign remarks *under* Agricultural Surpluses.
> Census of, **1954:** 14 (p. 155)
> Drought and other disasters, **1957:** 11, 12, 41, 145
> Durum wheat acreage allotments, **1957:** 59
> Expenditures for, **1957:** 13
> Farm "freeze" bill, veto, **1958:** 59, 60
> Legislative recommendations, **1956:** 6
> Messages to Congress, **1954:** 4; **1960–61:** 32
> News conference remarks, **1953:** 12, 225, 249 and ftn. (p. 780); **1954:** 9, 18, 143; **1955:** 33, 90; **1956:** 88; **1957:** 17, 45, 72, 124, 169; **1958:** 213, 310
> 9-point program, **1956:** 6, 83
> Relation to world trade, **1954:** 261, 262, 263
> Soviet Union, **1955:** 33
> Use of atomic energy, **1957:** 231
Agriculture, Department of, **1954:** 4, 270; **1955:** 147; **1958:** 43, 217; **1959:** 6, 267; **1960–61:** 32, 217, 358
> Assistant Secretary of (Earl L. Butz), **1957:** 115
> Award for Distinguished Federal Civilian Service
>> Hendricks, Sterling B., **1958:** 13
>> McArdle, Richard E., **1960–61:** 389n.
>> Stiebeling, Hazel K., **1959:** 9n.
> Budget messages, **1954:** 14 (pp. 144, 157, 162, 163); **1955:** 17 (pp. 144, 155); **1956:** 12 (pp. 102, 126); **1960–61:** 13 (pp. 77, 80, 81, 96), 414 (pp. 987, 989–992, 996–998, 1012)
> Drought and other natural disasters, **1957:** 11, 12, 41, 145
> Emergency feed for drought areas, **1954:** 14 (p. 162)
> Farm lands for lease by Federal agencies, **1956:** 111
> Great Plains problems, studies of, **1956:** 6, 7
> Ladejinsky, Wolf, **1955:** 10, 18
> Meat purchases from drought-stricken farmers, **1954:** 14 (p. 162)

Agriculture, Department of — *continued*
> Meeting with Prime Minister Kishi, **1957:** 117
> Morse, True D., Under Secretary of, **1956:** 217n.; **1959:** 18n., 67 ftn. (p. 297); **1960–61:** 322
> News conference remarks, **1953:** 15, 22, 41, 225; **1957:** 17, 145, 157; **1958:** 37, 274, 288
> REA loan approval, supervision of, **1959:** 86
> Reorganization, **1959:** 35, 153; **1954:** 14 (p. 157); **1959:** 101
> Reports on cotton production, **1958:** 142
> Rural development program, **1957:** 156; **1959:** 273
> Sugar imports, **1960–61:** 374
> Supplemental appropriation proposed, **1953:** 136
> Trade promotion activities, **1960–61:** 95
> Upstream dams for soil conservation, authority re, **1953:** 15, 22
> Water conservation, **1954:** 14 (pp. 162, 163)
> Wool production study, **1953:** 131
Agriculture, Secretary of (Ezra Taft Benson), **1953:** 6, 25, 13, 6, 268; **1954:** 146, 256, 291, 349; **1955:** 90 ftn. (p. 475), 127; **1956:** 6, 83, 84, 241; **1957:** 156; **1958:** 12, 49, 60, 100; **1959:** 122, 131; **1960–61:** 32, 418
> Administration of certain Oregon lands, **1954:** 152
> Agricultural commodities for Bolivian relief, memorandum, **1953:** 206
> Agricultural Surplus Disposal Administrator, appointment of, **1956:** 6
> Appraisal by the President, **1958:** 37
> Beef prices, investigation, **1953:** 227, 249
> Broadcast with the President, **1953:** 95
> Drought relief, **1953:** 227; **1956:** 236
>> Meeting with Governors, **1953:** 216
> European storm disaster relief, **1953:** 7n.
> Federal Council on Aging, **1956:** 74
> Flood relief in Europe, memorandum, **1954:** 195
> Foreign aid, memorandum, **1954:** 323
> Great Plains program, **1956:** 7, 169
> Low income farmers, 15-point program, **1955:** 82
> Milk consumption, **1954:** 115
> News conference remarks on, **1953:** 15, 41, 128, 225, 249; **1954:** 39, 92, 115, 143, 172; **1955:** 10, 18; **1956:** 47, 78, 216; **1957:** 50, 150; **1958:** 37, 213, 222; **1959:** 132, 223; **1956:** 127, 256, 268
> Price supports, **1954:** 4, 39, 143, 172, 196; **1959:** 23
> REA construction programs, **1958:** 51
> Reorganization of Department, functions re, **1953:** 35, 153
> Resignation, letter, **1960–61:** 391
> Rural development
>> Program report, letter, **1958:** 313
>> Recommendations, **1956:** 217
> Water resources, report, **1956:** 13

Agriculture, Secretary of — *continued*
  Wheat acreage allotment authority, **1954:** 24
  Wichita conference on drought and other natural disasters, **1957:** 11, 12, 41 and n.
  Wool production, **1953:** 131; **1954:** 49
Agriculture Fair, World, New Delhi, **1959:** 315; **1960–61:** 136
Agronsky, Martin, **1953:** 31, 109; **1954:** 50, 68, 73, 165; **1955:** 90, 95, 149, 185; **1958:** 310
Aguinaldo, Emilio, **1958:** 140
Aiken, Sen. George D., **1953:** 187, 268; **1954:** 196; **1955:** 131; **1956:** 35; **1957:** 134
  News conference remarks on, **1954:** 143, 192
Air-to-air missiles, **1957:** 210, 230
Air alert, **1959:** 48
Air attack, **1959:** 26
Air bases, U.S., **1954:** 25
  See also Bases; Bases, U.S., in foreign countries.
  Budget message, **1958:** 5 (p. 30)
  Campaign remarks, **1958:** 292, 296
  Lackland Air Force Base, Texas, **1957:** 124
Air bases, U. S., in foreign countries, **1956:** 12 (p. 96), 96
  Dhahran Airfield, Saudi Arabia, **1957:** 31
  Morocco, **1958:** 32; **1959:** 345
  Libya, **1958:** 32
  Saudi Arabia, **1956:** 94, 96
Air cadet exchange group, international, remarks, **1958:** 200
Air carriers, **1956:** 255
  Large irregular air carrier investigation, memorandum, **1960–61:** 408
  Service to Regina, Saskatchewan, **1960–61:** 281
  Trans-Pacific route case, **1960–61:** 436
  U. S.-Alaska, certification, **1957:** 162
Air Command, Strategic.
  See Strategic Air Command.
Air Coordinating Committee, **1955:** 17 (p. 169)
  Budget message, **1954:** 14 (p. 173)
  Letter to Chairman, **1953:** 194
  Replacement, **1959:** 74
  Report on U.S. aviation policy, **1954:** 123, 200
Air defense, **1953:** 31; **1954:** 92; **1959:** 57
  Budget messages, **1959:** 10 (pp. 60, 61); **1960–61:** 13 (p. 54), 414 (pp. 949, 952–954)
  U.S.-Canada, **1953:** 246, 247; **1958:** 163; **1960–61:** 13 (p. 54)
Air Defense Command, **1955:** 13, 17 (p. 116)
Air Force, **1953:** 98; **1954:** 225; **1955:** 50; **1959:** 10 (pp. 59–62)
  Accident to troop transport, Germany, **1955:** 204
  Budget, **1953:** 82 (pp. 311, 312); **1954:** 14 (pp. 123, 124); **1955:** 17 (pp. 113, 114, 117); **1960–61:** 13 (pp. 48, 50, 56), 414 (pp. 950–952, 954, 956)
  Chief of Staff (Gen. Thomas D. White), **1960–61:** 7, 261n.

Air Force — *continued*
  Contract with Graphic Arts Corp. of Ohio, **1954:** 232
  MIT survey on civil and air defense, **1953:** 31
  News conference remarks, **1953:** 31, 54, 62, 88; **1954:** 25, 345; **1960–61:** 7, 38
  Personnel, **1954:** 345; **1955:** 3
  Reduction in, **1953:** 88
  Resignation of Gen. Quesada, **1958:** 272
Air Force, Department of the, **1957:** 80, 92, 194, 230
  See also Armed forces, U. S.; Military personnel.
  Award for Distinguished Federal Civilian Service, Doyle L. Northrup, **1959:** 9n.
  Bombers.
    See main heading Bombers.
  Budget messages, **1958:** 5 (pp. 28, 29); **1959:** 10 (p. 65)
  Career incentives and service credits for medical and dental officers, **1956:** 91
  Chief of Air Staff (General Nathan F. Twining), **1956:** 121
    Visit to U.S.S.R., **1956:** 121
  Civil Air Patrol, **1957:** 87
  Housing at military installations, **1956:** 141
  Manual on communism and the churches, **1960–61:** 38
  News conference remarks on, **1958:** 28, 288, 310
  Officers ceiling, **1956:** 81n.
  Reorganization.
    See Defense reorganization.
  Reorganization Plan 6, message, **1953:** 61
  ROTC, Baylor University, remarks, **1956:** 114
  Security risk case, **1956:** 96
Air Force, Secretary of the (Donald A. Quarles), **1956:** 96
Air Force, Secretary of the (Dudley C. Sharp), **1960–61:** 38
Air Force, Secretary of the (Harold E. Talbott), **1955:** 90, 112, 119, 176, 185
Air Force Academy, **1957:** 170
  Appointment of son of Capt. Kincheloe, **1958:** 314
  Comment on proposal, **1953:** 31
  Remarks on establishment, **1955:** 117
Air-to-ground missiles, **1957:** 210
Air navigation facilities, **1955:** 17 (p. 92); **1956:** 38; **1957:** 71 and n.
  Budget message, **1956:** 12 (pp. 140, 141)
  User charges, **1957:** 75
Air pollution, **1955:** 25; **1956:** 21; **1960–61:** 410, 413
  Budget messages, **1956:** 12 (p. 121); **1960–61:** 13 (p. 94), 414 (p. 1008)
Air power, U.S., **1953:** 82, 83, 98, 267, 272; **1954:** 14 (pp. 86, 117), 25; **1955:** 100
  See also Military strength, U.S.
  News conference remarks, **1956:** 94, 96

Air power, Soviet, **1955:** 100
Air safety, **1959:** 26
   Regulations, **1958:** 135
   Budget message, **1958:** 5 (p. 60)
Air traffic control, **1956:** 38; **1957:** 71 and n.
   Budget message, **1956:** 12 (pp. 140, 141)
Air traffic management, **1958:** 135
   Budget message, **1958:** 5 (p. 60)
Aircraft, **1956:** 38; **1958:** 64, 105, 135
   See also Air carriers; Aircraft, military; Aviation.
   Accidents
      Mid-air collisions, **1958:** 135
      Soviet Armenia, **1958:** 310
   Air carriers, U. S.-Alaska, certification, **1957:** 162
   Alleged flights over Cuba from United States, **1959:** 271
   Bombers, **1956:** 12 (p. 96), 88, 94, 96, 113; **1957:** 17, 86, 169, 230
   Budget messages, **1956:** 12 (pp. 96, 97, 140, 141); **1958:** 5 (p. 60)
   C-47 missing in Germany, **1960–61:** 162
   Chinese Communist attack on transport plane, **1954:** 172
   Columbine, **1956:** 257
   Equipment investment program, report on, **1958:** 194
   Hostile, **1957:** 105
   Interceptors, **1957:** 230
   Jet planes, **1959:** 53
   Jet tankers, **1957:** 230
   Naval carriers, **1957:** 230
   News conference remarks, **1958:** 310
   Nuclear-powered, **1956:** 2, 12 (p. 97); **1959:** 10 (p. 63)
      Soviet, **1958:** 318
   Trans-Pacific certificate renewal case, **1956:** 14, 56
   U. S. plane shot down by Communist China, **1956:** 193
   U.S.-U.K. trade discussions, **1959:** 67
   U-2 incident, **1960–61:** 143, 154, 162, 163, 231n., 263
Aircraft, military, **1953:** 267; **1958:** 2, 135; **1959:** 6
   See also Aircraft; Aviation.
   Accidents
      Bering Sea, U.S. plane, **1955:** 146
      Brazil, U.S. Navy Transport, **1960–61:** 55, 64
      Germany, U.S. troop transport, **1955:** 204
   Allies, **1959:** 55
   Attack on Navy patrol plane over Sea of Japan, **1959:** 132
   Bombers, **1954:** 63, 353; **1955:** 3, 149; **1958:** 2, 5 (p. 29); **1959:** 7, 48, 57; **1960–61:** 13 (pp. 52–54, 56), 24, 42, 414 (pp. 938, 949, 951, 952, 954, 956)
      See also Aircraft; Bombers.
      B-29, **1960–61:** 245

Aircraft, military — *continued*
   Bombers — *continued*
      B-36, **1955:** 100, 112; **1960–61:** 245
      B-47, **1960–61:** 13 (p. 53), 245, 255
      B-52, **1955:** 100; **1959:** 10 (pp. 57, 60); **1960–61:** 13 (p. 53), 245, 410, 414 (p. 951)
      B-58, **1959:** 10 (p. 60), 288; **1960–61:** 13 (p. 53), 245, 410, 414 (p. 951)
      B-70, **1959:** 10 (p. 63); **1960–61:** 7, 13 (p. 52), 255, 256, 414 (pp. 938, 951)
      F-105, **1960–61:** 13 (p. 56), 414 (p. 956) Soviet, 21
      Withdrawal from France, **1959:** 154
   Budget messages, **1954:** 14 (pp. 123, 124, 174); **1955:** 17 (pp. 116, 117, 121); **1958:** 5 (pp. 18, 20, 29, 30); **1960–61:** 13 (pp. 52–54, 56), 414 (pp. 938, 949, 951, 952, 954–957, 959)
   Fighter escorts, comment on use of, **1954:** 328
   Fighters, **1958:** 5 (p. 29); **1959:** 7
   Indochina, servicing by U.S. technicians, **1954:** 25, 33
   News conference remarks, **1955:** 100, 112, 146, 149; **1958:** 83, 88, 222, 318
   Nuclear, **1955:** 17 (p. 121); **1959:** 10 (p. 63); **1960–61:** 414 (p. 959)
   Research and development, **1954:** 14 (p. 174); **1959:** 288
   Soviet, **1955:** 112
      Attacks, **1953:** 31
      Attack on U.S. plane over Habomal Islands, **1954:** 328, 345
      Attack on U. S. transport plane in Soviet Armenia, **1959:** 94 and ftn. (p. 361)
      Attack on USAF RB-47 plane, **1960–61:** 231, 232, 255, 284, 302, 313
      Nuclear-powered, **1958:** 318
   Tactical, **1958:** 292
   Turkish border incidents, **1959:** 29
   Use by members of Congress, **1958:** 88
   X-15 research plane, **1960–61:** 264
Aircraft industry dispersal, comment on, **1955:** 90
Airlift of armed forces, **1958:** 120
Airlift of Ghanaian forces to the Congo, **1960–61:** 248
Airline subsidies, message, **1953:** 94; **1955:** 17 (p. 169), 30, 33, 106; **1956:** 12 (pp. 82, 141); **1958:** 5 (p. 60), 246; **1960–61:** 13 (p. 68), 414 (p. 974)
Airlines
   Alaska Airlines, **1955:** 106
   Northwest Airlines, **1955:** 30, 33
   Pacific Northern Airlines, **1955:** 106
   Pan American World Airways, **1955:** 30, 33
Airmail, Government subsidies, **1954:** 14 (pp. 173, 174)
   News conference remarks, **1955:** 18, 41, 62, 81, 112, 176

Airmail, Government subsidies — *continued*
    Prisoners in Communist China, **1955:** 4, 16, 148
    Release from Communist China, **1955:** 112, 179;
        1956: 2
    Shot down in Soviet Armenia, **1959:** 94 and ftn.
        (p. 361)
    Soviet detention of RB-47 fliers, **1960–61:** 284
    U.N. action on, **1955:** 156
Airplane, invention, subject of frieze in Capitol
        rotunda, **1954:** 106n.
Airport bill, **1959:** 26, 29
Airport construction, Federal aid, **1960–61:** 414
        (pp. 973, 974)
Airports
    Budget message, **1956:** 12 (p. 141)
    Chantilly, Va., recommended site, **1958:** 9
    Elkins, W. Va., RFC loan, **1956:** 163
    Federal aid, **1955:** 146; **1959:** 10 (p. 78)
    Federal Airport Act,
        Amendment, **1959:** 143
        Disapproval, **1958:** 246
    La Guardia, N.Y., plane crash, **1959:** 26
    Question of location, **1959:** 26
    Surplus military facilities, **1958:** 246
Airspace over United States, **1958:** 135
Airways, **1958:** 246
    Budget messages, **1958:** 5 (pp. 53, 60); **1959:** 10
        (p. 45)
    Letter to Secretary Weeks, **1958:** 299
Airways Modernization Board, **1957:** 71
    Budget message, **1958:** 5 (p. 60)
    Message on Federal Aviation Agency, **1958:** 135
Airways modernization program, **1960–61:** 255
Airways system, **1956:** 12 (pp. 140, 141)
Akihito, Crown Prince, **1960–61:** 140, 209, 294n.
    Exchange of toasts, **1960–61:** 308
Akron, Ohio, **1956:** 90
Alabama, **1954:** 143
    Bankhead (William B.) National Forest, **1954:**
        156
    Hill, Sen. Lister, **1955:** 33
    Huntsville, **1960–61:** 287
    Montgomery, **1956:** 62; **1959:** 31
        Appeal of Negro leaders, **1957:** 17
    Patterson, Gov. John, **1960–61:** 287
    Sparkman, Sen. John, **1959:** 42
    Voting rights investigation, **1958:** 318
Alaska, **1954:** 125, 126; **1956:** 50; **1958:** 163;
        1960–61: 42, 80, 261n.
    Admission into Union (1959), **1960–61:** 4, 13 (p.
        104), 402, 410
    Aliens from, **1956:** 33; **1957:** 25
    Anchorage, **1960–61:** 178
    Bartlett, Sen. E. L., **1959:** 3n.
    Budget message, **1959:** 10 (pp. 65, 109, 110)
    Certification of certain air carriers, **1957:** 162
    Communication facilities, **1960–61:** 13 (p. 50),
        414 (p. 956)

Alaska — *continued*
    Control over schools, **1959:** 21
    Defense needs, **1956:** 205; **1958:** 159
    Egan, Gov. William A., **1959:** 150; **1960–61:** 178
    Election, **1954:** 311
    Federal communications facilities, sale pro-
        posed, **1959:** 10 (p. 65)
    Funds under amended Federal Airport Act,
        1959: 143
    Gruening, Sen. Ernest, **1959:** 3n.
    Hemtzleman, Gov. B. Frank, **1954:** 73
    International Boundary Commission, **1953:** 41
    Mental health problem, **1956:** 12 (p. 120)
    News conference remarks, **1953:** 15, 41, 77;
        1955: 56, 95; **1958:** 28, 42, 120, 274, 318
    Oil and gas leases, veto, **1959:** 182
    Rivers, Repr. Ralph J., **1959:** 3n.
    Statehood, **1953:** 15, 77; **1954:** 9, 33, 50, 73, 165,
        311; **1955:** 4, 247; **1956:** 2, 205; **1957:** 13;
        1958: 5 (p. 73), 28, 42, 120, 292; **1959:** 174
        Admission ceremony, remarks, **1959:** 3
        Approval of act, **1958:** 159
        Letter to Gov. Stepovich, **1958:** 160
    Visit of President, **1960–61:** 177, 178
        Comment on, **1958:** 274, 318
    Wildlife ranges, **1960–61:** 414 (p. 999)
Alaska Airlines, certification, **1955:** 106; **1957:** 162
Alaska Housing Corporation **1954:** 14 (p. 150)
Alaska Railroad, **1959:** 10 (p. 53)
    Budget message, **1960–61:** 414 (p. 1023)
    Economic regulation under Interstate Commerce
        Act, disapproval, **1960–61:** 225
Alba, Duke of, **1959:** 100
Albania, **1953:** 233n.
    Offer of food supplies, statement, **1955:** 49
Albany, N. Y., **1958:** 306
Alberdi, Juan, **1960–61:** 58
Albert, Rep. Carl, bipartisan meeting on Suez
        Canal, **1956:** 184
Albert, Irene, **1955:** 90
Albert, Prince, exchange of toasts, **1960–61:** 317
Alberta, Canada, Mount Eisenhower, dedication,
        1958: 220
Albrecht, E. J., Co., relief of, disapproval, **1955:**
        196
Albright, Horace M., letters, **1953:** 25; **1956:** 285
Albright, Robert C., **1953:** 225
Alcohol butadiene plant, **1956:** 90
Alcoholic beverage tax, **1960–61:** 414 (p. 940)
Alcorn, Meade, **1957:** 63, 108n., 214; **1958:** 96, 223,
        287; **1959:** 21, 75
    News conference remarks on, **1957:** 28, 50, 105;
        1958: 83, 274, 310
Aldrich, Winthrop, **1953:** 34n.; **1955:** 244n.
Alessandri Rodriguez, Jorge, **1960–61:** 69, 73, 77,
        87, 228
    Joint statement with, **1960–61:** 76
    Message, **1960–61:** 175

[References are to items except as otherwise indicated]

Alessandri Rodriguez, Jorge — *continued*
    Toasts to, **1960–61:** 71, 75
Alex, Ralph, **1960–61:** 145
Alexander I, **1957:** 124; **1959:** 132, 219
Alexander, G. Harold, **1956:** 278n.
Alexander the Great, **1957:** 235; **1960–61:** 58
Alexander, Field Marshal Harold R., **1954:** 167
Alexander, Henry C., **1954:** 78n.
Alexander, Holmes, **1958:** 310; **1960–61:** 143
Alexander, J. Don, tax refund claim, veto, **1953:**
    107
Alexander, Jake, conveyance of lands to, veto,
    1954: 156
Alexander Industries, Inc., **1953:** 107
Alger, Horatio, **1954:** 293
Algeria, **1956:** 62
    De Gaulle program for, **1959:** 223
    De Gaulle policy on, **1960–61:** 127
    Earthquake, message, **1954:** 265
    Joint statements
        King Mohamed V, **1959:** 345
        King of Morocco, **1957:** 240
        Premier Mollet, **1957:** 38
        President Bourguiba on, **1959:** 329
    News conference remarks, **1957:** 22, 28, 124;
        1958: 42, 103
    Timgad, **1953:** 234
Algerian citizen, charge against Army specialist in
    killing of, **1957:** 124
Algiers, **1960–61:** 124
Alien Property, Office of, **1958:** 124
Aliens
    Deportation cases
        Engelbert, Wilhelm, veto, **1954:** 58
        Makeef (Berberova), Nina, disapproval, **1954:**
            212
        Pantelas, George, disapproval, **1954:** 215
        Sheepherders, nonquota immigrant visas, **1954:**
            250
        Subversives, **1954:** 130
        Weigand, Margareth, estate, relief of, veto, **1954:**
            59
Al-Khayyal, Sheikh Abdullah, **1957:** 120 and n.
Allegheny Ludlum Steel Corporation, **1959:** 211n.
Allen, Douglass M., **1957:** 50
Allen, Ethan, **1955:** 131
Allen, George V., **1954:** 44; **1958:** 23, 63; **1960–61:**
    143
    See also United States Information Agency,
        Director (George V. Allen).
Allen, Repr. John J., Jr., **1958:** 294
Allen, Repr. Leo E., **1956:** 214
    Bipartisan meeting on Suez Canal, **1956:** 184
Allies, weapons for, **1958:** 5 (p. 20)
Alloys, imports, **1953:** 69
Almond, Gov. J. Lindsay, Jr., **1959:** 17
    Meeting with, comment on, **1958:** 198, 213, 222
Alphand, Herve, **1959:** 332n.

Alsace-Lorraine, **1957:** 235
Alsop, Joseph, **1955:** 119
Alsop, Stewart, **1955:** 119
Aluminum manufacturing, Ghana, **1958:** 180
Ambassadorial appointments, **1957:** 17, 70; **1959:**
    29
    Gluck, Maxwell H., **1957:** 145
    McLeod, Scott, **1957:** 70, 72
    Science attaches, **1957:** 230
    Taylor, Henry J., **1957:** 70
Ambassadors, U.S., **1959:** 130
American Aeronautical Association, **1958:** 71
American Assembly, **1954:** 182; **1960–61:** 29, 30n.
    Remarks, **1960–61:** 86
American Association for the Advancement of
    Science, **1959:** 107
American Bankers Association, remarks, **1953:** 189
American Bar Association, **1956:** 216; **1959:** 42;
    1960–61: 275
    See also under Addresses or remarks to national
        groups
    News conference remarks, **1955:** 47, 112
American Battle Monuments Commission, **1956:**
    102
American College of Surgeons, message to Clinical
    Congress of, **1957:** 216
American Colonization Society, colonization of
    Liberia, **1954:** 293
American Council on Education, remarks, **1953:**
    207
American Council To Improve Our Neighbor-
    hoods, remarks, **1954:** 333
American Council on NATO, Inc., **1959:** 204n.
American Democracy, Spiritual Foundations of,
    Conference on, remarks, **1954:** 327
American Education Week, **1953:** 237; **1954:** 328
American Federation of Labor, **1953:** 128, 130;
    1954: 107, 161 ftn. (p. 622), 274n.; **1955:**
    41
    Convention, remarks, **1954:** 275
    Cornerstone-laying ceremonies, remarks, **1955:**
        84
    Message, **1953:** 193
American Field Service students, remarks, **1955:**
    151; **1957:** 137; **1958:** 168; **1959:** 164
American Forces Network, 15th anniversary, mes-
    sage, **1958:** 158
American Forest Congress, remarks, **1953:** 234
American Helicopter Society, remarks, **1960–61:**
    145
American Hereford Association, dedication of
    building, remarks, **1953:** 218
American Heritage Foundation, **1955:** 32n.
American Institute of Certified Public Account-
    ants, address, **1960–61:** 304
American Jewish tercentenary dinner, address,
    1954: 297
American Junior Red Cross, remarks, **1958:** 144

American-Korean Foundation, **1953:** 159, 258; **1954:** 78n.
  Campaign, **1953:** 65
American Legion, **1954:** 200; **1955:** 119, 169; **1957:** 146
  Address, **1954:** 225
  Americanism program, remarks, **1955:** 38
  "Back to God" program, remarks, **1953:** 5; **1954:** 32
American Library Association, **1953:** 120
American Management Association, address, **1958:** 110
American Meat Institute, **1959:** 161
American Medical Association, **1953:** 29; **1954:** 334n.; **1955:** 34n.; **1958:** 109; **1959:** 129; **1960–61:** 263
  Action on polio vaccine, **1955:** 112, 113
American Mission for Aid to Greece, **1954:** 80
American National Cattlemen's Association, meeting, **1953:** 230
American Nationalities for Nixon-Lodge, remarks, **1960–61:** 298
American Newspaper Publishers Association, address, **1954:** 87
American Patent Law Association, **1958:** 28
American Planning and Civic Association, **1958:** 14
American Relief for Korea, **1953:** 258
American Republics, **1955:** 76; **1959:** 6; **1960–61:** 42, 49, 58, 86, 87, 183
  See also American States, Organization of; Inter-American; Latin America; *specific countries.*
  Assistance, **1954:** 14 (p. 127)
  Caracas conference.
    See Inter-American conference.
  Declaration of Solidarity (1954), **1958:** 133
  Economic problems, letter, **1958:** 164
  Foreign ministers meeting (1958), **1959:** 98
  Heads of government meeting, question of, **1960–61:** 268
  News conference remarks, **1960–61:** 228, 256, 268
  Representation at heads of government meeting, **1958:** 181
American Retail Federation, remarks, **1953:** 23
American Revolution, **1955:** 10; **1956:** 208, 282
American Royal Livestock and Horse Show, **1953:** 218n.
American Samoa, **1954:** 125, 126; **1956:** 172
American Society of Chile, **1960–61:** 72n.
American Society of Newspaper Editors, **1953:** 50; **1955:** 79, 99n.; **1956:** 87; **1958:** 80; **1960–61:** 80n.
  News conference remarks, **1956:** 88
American States
  See also Inter-American; Latin America; *specific countries.*
  Campaign remarks, **1956:** 210, 278

American States — *continued*
  Declaration against international Communist intervention (1954), **1956:** 146
  Declaration of Principles (1956), **1956:** 146
  Inter-American Treaty of Reciprocal Assistance (1947), **1956:** 146
  Panama meeting of Presidents.
    See Panama.
American States, Organization of.
  See Organization of American States.
American University, Beirut, **1958:** 173
American University, Washington, D.C., remarks at, **1957:** 109 and n.
America's Democratic Legacy Award, acceptance, remarks, **1953:** 252
Amerika, U.S.-Russian language magazine, **1960–61:** 410
Ames, Iowa, visit by Premier Khrushchev, **1959:** 186
Amistad Dam, Rio Grande, **1960–61:** 303, 334
  Budget messages, **1960–61:** 13 (p. 83), 414 (p. 995)
  Joint declaration with President Lopez Mateos, **1960–61:** 335
  Joint statement on, **1959:** 257
Amortization of facilities.
  See Tax write-off allowances.
Amory, Robert, Jr., **1953:** 33
Amsterdam, **1960–61:** 279
Amtorg, **1955:** 10
Amusement industry employees, **1954:** 5
AMVETS, **1955:** 169
  Presentation of 1958 World Peace Award to the President, remarks, **1959:** 92
Anchorage, Alaska, remarks on arrival, **1960–61:** 178
Anders, Lt. Gen. Wladyslaw, letter, **1954:** 112
Anderson, Sen. Clinton P., **1953:** 58; **1954:** 33, 50; **1956:** 230; **1957:** 134
  Clean bombs, **1956:** 88
  NATO cooperation re atomic information letter, **1955:** 71
  News conference remarks on, **1955:** 10
  Peaceful uses of atomic energy, panel report, letter, **1956:** 30
Anderson, Gov. C. Elmer, **1953:** 98
Anderson, Dillon, **1953:** 33n.; **1955:** 146 ftn. (p. 644)
Anderson, Lt. Gov. Emmett T., **1956:** 251, 253
Anderson, Vice Adm. George W., Jr., **1959:** 331
Anderson, Hurst R., **1957:** 109
Anderson, J. Merrill, **1956:** 211n.
Anderson, Jack, *U.S.A.: Second-Class Power?*, **1959:** 167
Anderson, Robert B., **1954:** 111; **1957:** 80, 102 and n.
  See also Treasury, Secretary of the.
  Medal of Freedom, citation, **1955:** 183

Anderson, Samuel W., **1953:** 213n.
Anderson, Gov. Sigurd, **1953:** 101, 103; **1954:** 53
Anderson, Gov. Victor E., **1957:** 138
Anderson, Comdr. W. R.
    Legion of Merit, citation, **1958:** 201
    Message, **1958:** 15
Andrea Doria, statement, **1956:** 149
Andresen, Repr. August H., death of, statement,
    1958: 10
Andrews, T. Coleman, **1954:** 107
Anglo-American Financial Agreement of 1945,
    amendment, **1957:** 44 and n.
Animal Agriculture, National Institute of, address,
    1954: 291
Ankara, Turkey, **1958:** 174
    Arrival, remarks, **1959:** 295
    Dinner given by President Bayar, toast, **1959:**
    296
    Joint statement with President Bayar, **1959:** 297
    Remarks on departure, **1959:** 298
Ann Arbor, Mich., **1958:** 138n.
Annapolis, Md., U.S. Naval Academy, **1953:** 80,
    81; **1956:** 128n., 241; **1958:** 125; **1959:** 116
Antarctic, **1958:** 123; **1960–61:** 414 (p. 1004)
    Conference on, **1959:** 284
    Expedition, **1957:** 122
    Mission of U.S.S. *Atka*, **1955:** 47
    Scientific expeditions, message, **1959:** 135
    Use for peaceful purposes, proposed conference
    on, **1958:** 92
    U.S. exploration, **1954:** 200
Antarctic Treaty, **1960–61:** 4, 302, 410
    Ratification, proposed, **1960–61:** 255
    Statement, **1959:** 284
Anthony, Prince, birth of, statement, **1960–61:** 40
Anthony, Susan B., **1960–61:** 269
Anti-American demonstrations, comment on,
    1958: 101, 103, 107, 189
Anti-Defamation League of B'nai B'rith, **1954:** 18
    40th anniversary, remarks, **1953:** 252
Anti-Semitism
    Factor in Secretary Strauss' confirmation dif-
    ficulties, **1959:** 123
    Soviet Union, **1953:** 22
Anti-aircraft guns, **1957:** 230
Antietam, Battle of, **1960–61:** 370
Anti-intellectualism, comment on, **1954:** 328
Anti-segregation amendments to legislation, **1955:**
    119
Antitrust
    Automobile industry, review of conditions, **1956:**
    174
    Campaign remarks, **1956:** 234, 241, 268
    Cases, **1958:** 293
    Laws, **1954:** 21, 67; **1956:** 118, 263; **1957:** 16,
    132; **1960–61:** 410
        Budget messages, **1960–61:** 13 (p. 76), 414 (p.
        984)
    Study, **1955:** 56

Anzio, Italy, **1956:** 102, 113; **1959:** 7
    Battle of (1944), **1954:** 63
ANZUS organization, **1954:** 129
ANZUS treaty (Australia, New Zealand, U.S.),
    1958: 96; **1958:** 410
Apaloo, Lawrence K., **1958:** 23
Appeasement, **1955:** 79
    Aggressor nations, **1957:** 261, 274, 288, 292
    Indochina, question of, **1954:** 168
    News conference remarks, **1955:** 26, 100
Appel, Jule, **1956:** 226
Apple price predictions, prohibition of Govern-
    ment publication, veto, **1955:** 147
Appointees, political, tasks, **1956:** 22
Appointments
    AEC, news conference remarks, **1957:** 145
    Ambassadorial, **1957:** 70, 72, 145, 230; **1959:** 29
    Assistant Attorney General, news conference
    remarks, **1956:** 56
    Bevis, Howard L., Chairman, National Commit-
    tee on Development of Scientists and
    Engineers, **1956:** 77
    Board of Consultants on Foreign Intelligence
    Activities, **1956:** 9, 10
    Bragdon, Maj. Gen. John S., Special Assistant to
    the President, **1955:** 203
    Burgess, Carter L. Chairman, Citizens Advisory
    committee on Fitness of American Youth,
    1957: 104
    Burns, Arthur F., Chairman, Committee on
    Small Business, **1956:** 118
    Committee on Education Beyond the High
    School, **1956:** 85
    Congressional action on, **1959:** 102
    Curtis, Edward P., Special Assistant to the
    President for Aviation Facilities Planning,
    1956: 38
    Cutler, Robert, U.S. member, Board of Execu-
    tive Directors, Inter-American Develop-
    ment Bank, **1959:** 261
    Dodge, Joseph M., Special Assistant, and Chair-
    man, Council on Foreign Economic Pol-
    icy, **1954:** 348
    Federal Highway Administrator, news confer-
    ence remarks, **1956:** 235
    Federal members of Joint Federal-State Action
    Committee, **1957:** 138
    Francis, Clarence, Chairman, Interagency Com-
    mittee on Agricultural Surplus Disposal,
    1954: 262
    George, Walter F., President's personal repre-
    sentative and special ambassador to At-
    lantic Community, **1956:** 97, 114
    Hearst, William Randolph, Jr., Committee for
    Traffic Safety, **1955:** 124
    Hoover Commission, **1953:** 145
    Lodge, Henry Cabot, Jr., President's personal
    representative at Pulaski Day parade,
    1956: 227

Appointments — *continued*
  News conference remarks, **1959:** 21, 29, 102
  Petersen, T. S., Committee for Traffic Safety,
    1955: 125
  Political pressures, **1959:** 29
  President's Commission on Veterans Pensions,
    1955: 51
  Procedures on, **1953:** 37
  Quesada, E. R., Administrator, Federal Aviation
    Agency, **1958:** 272
  Randall, Clarence B., Special Assistant to the
    President, **1956:** 139
  Reed, Harry J., Rural Development Program,
    1957: 156
  Rockefeller, Nelson, Special Assistant to the
    President, **1954:** 354
  Stassen, Harold E., Special Assistant to the
    President, **1955:** 57
  TVA board member, news conference remarks,
    1957: 22, 56, 62, 80, 105, 124
  Wright, Adm. Jerauld, Supreme Allied Com-
    mander, Atlantic, **1954:** 36
Appropriation policy, budget message, **1957:** 13
Appropriations
  Annual budget message, **1957:** 13
  Atomic Energy Commission, **1957:** 159; **1958:**
    193
  Civil functions, **1957:** 161
  Department of Defense Appropriation Act,
    1956, **1955:** 155
  Department of Defense Appropriation Act,
    1959, **1958:** 218
  Departments of Labor, and Health, Education,
    and Welfare, **1959:** 181
  Development Loan Fund, statement, **1959:** 65
  Independent offices, **1958:** 192; **1960–61:** 229
  Mutual security
    Letters, re, **1960–61:** 271, 272
    Statement, **1960–61:** 270
  Mutual Security Appropriation Act, **1955:** 182;
    1956: 152; **1957:** 173
  Public Works Appropriation Act, **1955:** 157;
    1956: 136; **1958:** 244
  Public works bills, vetoes, **1959:** 194, 213
  Supplemental Appropriation Act, **1956:** 109;
    1957: 124; **1959:** 197
  Treasury-Post Office, 1958, **1957:** 99
Appropriations and authorization bills, veto of
    specific items proposed, **1959:** 6
Approval of acts of Congress.
  See also Legislation, statements or messages
    upon approval.
  Agricultural Act of 1956, **1956:** 115
  Air carriers, certification, **1957:** 162
  American Samoa labor standards, **1956:** 172
  Atomic Energy Commission, appropriations,
    1957: 159
  Automobile dealers, suits by, **1956:** 174
  Bank Holding Company Act of 1956, **1956:** 99

Approval of acts of Congress — *continued*
  Brucellosis eradication program, **1956:** 72
  Budget and accounting methods and procedures,
    1956: 156
  Career incentives, medical and dental officers,
    1956: 91
  Civil functions, appropriations for, Army and
    Interior Departments, **1957:** 161
  Cotton, long-staple, sale of, **1957:** 128
  Customs Simplification Act of 1956, **1956:** 162
  Durum wheat, additional acreage allotments,
    1957: 59
  Farm Credit Act of 1956, **1956:** 147
  Federal Flood Insurance Act of 1956, **1956:** 167
  Fish and Wildlife Act of 1956, **1956:** 173
  Gasoline for farm use, tax relief, **1956:** 72
  Great Plains conservation program, **1956:** 169
  Health Amendments Act of 1956, **1956:** 161
  Health Research Facilities Act of 1956, **1956:**
    151
  Housing Act of 1957, **1957:** 129 and n.
  Immigration and Nationality Act, amendment,
    1957: 187
  Jackson School Township, Ind., relief of, **1957:**
    174
  Kawar, Irfan, relief of, **1956:** 59
  Library services, **1956:** 127
  Middle East, joint resolution on, **1957:** 46
  Muscatine Bridge Commission, creation of,
    1956: 148
  Mutual Security Appropriation Act, **1956:** 152;
    1957: 173
  National Music Council, incorporation, **1956:**
    159
  Ovens, Michael D., relief of, **1957:** 181
  Panama, conveyance of property to, **1957:** 167
  Public Works Appropriation Act, 1957, **1956:**
    136
  Railroad Retirement Act of 1937, amendment,
    1956: 168
  Savings bonds, increase of interest rates on,
    1957: 76
  School construction aid in areas affected by
    Federal activities, **1957:** 170
  School milk program, **1956:** 72
  Second Supplemental Appropriation Act, 1956,
    1956: 109
  Service-connected disability compensation and
    dependency allowances, **1957:** 163
  Servicemen's and Veterans' Survivor Benefits
    Act, **1956:** 157
  Sibley Memorial Hospital and Nurses Home,
    1957: 175
  Small reclamation projects, Federal aid, **1956:**
    165
  Social Security Amendments of 1956, **1956:** 158
  Sugar Act of 1948, amendment and extension,
    1956: 116

[References are to items except as otherwise indicated]

Approval of acts of Congress — *continued*
  Treasury-Post Office Appropriation Act, 1958,
    1957: 99
  Washita River Basin reclamation project, Okla-
    homa, **1956:** 44
  Water Pollution Control Act Amendments of
    1956, **1956:** 137
  Watershed Protection and Flood Prevention Act,
    amendment, **1956:** 170
  Wright, Mr. and Mrs. Derfery William, relief of,
    1956: 24
Aqaba, Gulf of, **1957:** 34, 35 and n.
  Joint statement with Prime Minister Macmillan,
    1957: 55
  News conference remarks, **1957:** 45, 56, 62, 72,
    87
  U.S. shipping in, **1957:** 72
Arab-Israeli hostilities, **1954:** 297; **1955:** 76, 239;
    1956: 143, 268, 282; **1958:** 293
  Joint statement with Prime Minister Eden, **1956:**
    26
  News conference remarks, **1954:** 68, 157, 172;
    1956: 20, 198, 298
  Statement, **1955:** 234
Arab States, **1953:** 18; **1956:** 2, 282; **1957:** 6, 91;
    1958: 207, 293
  Assistance, **1954:** 14 (p. 139)
  Conditional guarantee of borders, **1956:** 298
  Cultural contributions, **1958:** 207
  Dispute with Israel, **1953:** 230; **1960–61:** 38, 332
  Joint statement
    King Mohamed V on, **1959:** 345
    Prime Minister Eden, **1956:** 26
  Jordan River development, **1953:** 217, 230; **1956:**
    198, 298
  Letter to Premier Khrushchev, **1958:** 177
  News conference remarks, **1956:** 298; **1957:** 70,
    207; **1958:** 213
  Refugees, **1953:** 89, 217; **1955:** 17 (p. 131); **1956:**
    12 (p. 107), 26, 58, 298; **1957:** 6
  Regional development association, **1958:** 207,
    213
  Soviet arms for, **1960–61:** 38
Aram, Abbas, **1959:** 322
Aramburu, Pedro Eugenio, **1957:** 233
Aramco, taxes, **1957:** 72, 80
Aranha, Oswaldo, **1960–61:** 51
Architect of the Capitol (J. George Stewart), **1959:**
    151
Archives, National.
  See National Archives.
Arctic, **1957:** 87
  Inspection to prevent surprise attack, **1958:** 86,
    88, 112, 163
    Soviet protest, **1958:** 83
  Nautilus cruise, **1958:** 15, 201, 210, 211
  News conference remarks, **1958:** 83, 88

Arctic Wildlife Range, establishment, proposed,
    1960–61: 133
Area assistance.
  See Unemployment.
Area Development, Office of, **1960–61:** 5
Area redevelopment, **1956:** 2, 3; **1960–61:** 133, 255
  Bill for relief of depressed areas, **1958:** 120
    Veto, **1958:** 258
  Budget message, **1956:** 12 (pp. 148, 149); **1959:**
    10 (p. 87)
  Campaign remarks, **1958:** 294, 308
  Meeting on, **1956:** 318
Area Redevelopment Bill, veto, **1960–61:** 146
Arends, Repr. Leslie C., **1955:** 41; **1956:** 214
  Bipartisan meeting on Suez Canal, **1956:** 184
Argentina
  Air Force, **1957:** 233
  Aramburu, Pedro Eugenio, **1957:** 233 and n.
  Assistance, **1960–61:** 58
  Atomic research agreement, **1955:** 121
  Aviation Week, **1957:** 233 and n.
  Barros Hurtado, Cesar, **1958:** 164
  Beaulac, Willard L. (U.S. Ambassador), **1960–
    61:** 56n., 57n.
  Buenos Aires.
    See main heading Buenos Aires.
  Economy, **1960–61:** 58
  Frondizi, Arturo, (President), **1958:** 164; **1959:**
    13, 14, 16, 17, 26, 28; **1960–61:** 56, 57n.,
    58, 59, 60, 61, 62, 63, 66, 67, 87, 228
  Loan to, **1956:** 216, 251, 272, 278
  Mar del Plata, **1960–61:** 60n., 61
  Patagonia, **1960–61:** 62
  Peron, Juan D., **1956:** 216, 251, 272, 278
  Press associations, **1956:** 216
  San Carlos de Bariloche.
    See main heading San Carlos de Bariloche.
  Steel mill, **1956:** 216
  Toboada, Diogenes (Foreign Minister), **1960–61:**
    56n.
  Vice Pres. Nixon's return from, remarks, **1958:**
    107
  Visit to, **1960–61:** 42, 56, 57, 58, 59, 60, 61, 62, 63,
    64, 66, 67, 87
Argonne, the, **1957:** 91
Argonne National Laboratory, foreign students,
    remarks, **1955:** 53
Argonza, Nieves G., **1960–61:** 224
Argus project, **1959:** 67 and ftn. (p. 294)
Arias Espinosa, Ricardo M., **1956:** 101, 145
Arizona
  Sen. Barry Goldwater, **1954:** 101; **1957:** 70;
    1959: 127
  Tucson, **1957:** 10n.
  Weather research, **1957:** 92
Arkabutla Reservoir project, Mississippi, mineral
    interest, **1956:** 154

Arkansas
  Closing of public schools, **1958:** 267
  4-H Club, gift to President, **1954:** 146
  Fryingpan-Arkansas power project, **1957:** 13
  Faubus, Gov. Orval, **1957:** 169, 178, 188 and n.,
    205 and n., 207, 210; **1958:** 11
  Fulbright, Sen. J. W., **1957:** 132; **1958:** 23; **1959:**
    89, 123; **1960–61:** 80, 103, 132
  Harris, Repr. Oren, **1957:** 72, 115; **1958:** 37
  Hays, Repr. Brooks, **1957:** 210
  Little Rock.
    See main heading Little Rock.
  McClellan, Sen. John L., **1954:** 12n., 120n.; **1957:**
    150; **1958:** 56, 216, 292; **1959:** 6, 21, 89,
    123, 167, 176, 180
  Mills, Repr. Wilbur D., **1958:** 58, 132
Arkansas National Guard
  News conference remarks, **1957:** 205, 207, 210
  Statements and telegram, **1957:** 193, 200, 205n.
Arkansas River Basin, navigation development,
    1956: 12 (p. 143), 136
Arlington, Va., **1958:** 222; **1959:** 130n.; **1960–61:**
    138n.
Arlington National Cemetery, **1958:** 122n.; **1959:**
    105n.; **1960–61:** 91n.
Armaments industry, **1960–61:** 421
Armas, Carlos Castillo, **1957:** 143, 145
Armco Steel Corporation, **1959:** 211n.
Armed forces, Canada, **1958:** 163
Armed forces, NATO, **1956:** 78; **1957:** 17, 22, 28,
    34, 72, 91, 119, 226
Armed forces, Philippines, joint statement, **1958:**
    143
Armed forces, U.N.
  Dispatched to Egypt, **1956:** 295
  United States contribution to, **1959:** 55
Armed forces, UNEF, **1958:** 8, 148
Armed forces, U.S., **1953:** 4, 6, 11, 13, 61, 248;
    1955: 4; **1957:** 87, 115, 234; **1958:** 38, 125;
    1959: 145; **1960–61:** 4, 135, 163, 348, 397,
    410
  See also Military personnel; Veterans; World
    War II.
  Absentee voting rights, **1954:** 3; **1955:** 29
  Addresses, messages, statements, **1956:** 2, 33, 39,
    58, 98, 141, 232, 244, 275; **1957:** 6, 25, 86,
    139, 235
  Adopted foreign-born children, admission to
    U.S., **1956:** 275
  Airlift, **1958:** 120
  Armed robbery case, damage claim, **1958:** 254
  Army reserves, minimum strength, **1958:** 218
  Balanced forces, **1954:** 9
  Beef supply, **1953:** 12
  Budget messages, **1954:** 14 (pp. 122–124); **1958:** 5
    (pp. 31, 73); **1959:** 10 (pp. 43, 63, 65, 66);
    1960–61: 13 (pp. 46, 48–50, 52, 54–57),
    414 (pp. 947–956)

Armed forces, U.S. — *continued*
  Campaign remarks, **1954:** 273, 286; **1956:** 190,
    210, 224, 226, 228, 241; **1958:** 292, 295,
    296, 303
  Chaplains Corps, **1956:** 98
  Code of conduct, **1955:** 207
  Congressional investigation, **1954:** 57
  Cordiner report, **1957:** 115
  Decline in re-enlistment rate, **1955:** 13
  Doctors, quota of, **1953:** 15
  Enlistments, voluntary, **1956:** 232
  Equality of opportunity, **1956:** 206
  Foreign countries
    Caribbean, **1958:** 103
    Egypt, Soviet proposal, **1956:** 291n.
    Europe, **1954:** 84; **1956:** 78; **1960–61:** 362
      Aid to storm damaged areas, **1953:** 7n., 8
      Withdrawal from, **1957:** 17, 105; **1959:** 36
    Far East, **1953:** 272; **1954:** 14 (pp. 122, 123), 68
    Formosa area, **1955:** 21, 24n.; **1958:** 261, 263,
      277
      Secretary Dulles statement, **1958:** 257
    Germany, **1955:** 119; **1960–61:** 362 ftn. (p.
      864), 365
    Greece, aid to earthquake disaster area, **1953:**
      172n.
    Haiti, aid to hurricane damaged area, **1954:**
      289
    Japan, withdrawal from, **1957:** 119
    Korea, **1953:** 12; **1960–61:** 202
      Reduction of ground forces, **1953:** 272; **1954:**
        14 (pp. 122, 123), 33, 48
      Withdrawal from, in 1950, **1957:** 86
    Lebanon, **1958:** 172, 173, 174n., 176, 182n.,
      198, 207, 213
      Letter to Premier Khrushchev, **1958:** 177
      Withdrawal, message, **1958:** 291
    Morocco, withdrawal, **1959:** 345
    Tachen Islands, **1955:** 36
  Housing, **1955:** 4, 13, 17 (p. 118); **1956:** 2, 12 (p.
    146), 81n., 141, 232; **1958:** 49, 62; **1959:**
    10 (p. 63), 153
    Overseas, **1956:** 241
  Immigration laws affecting, **1956:** 33, 275; **1957:**
    25
  Infantry, **1958:** 295
  Integration in, **1954:** 3, 51; **1956:** 190, 210, 224,
    226, 229, 241
  Joint statements
    Chancellor Adenauer, **1957:** 100
    King of Morocco, **1957:** 240
    Prime Minister Kishi, **1957:** 117
  Letter to Secretary Wilson re, **1955:** 3
  Medical care of dependents, **1956:** 2, 21, 81n.,
    232, 244
  Medical Corps, **1955:** 108
  Military construction, **1959:** 10 (pp. 65, 66)
  Milk program for, **1955:** 17 (p. 152); **1958:** 59
  Morale, **1954:** 93, 97, 103

[References are to items except as otherwise indicated]

Armed forces, U.S. — *continued*
   National Security Training Corps, **1957:** 57
   News conference remarks, **1953:** 12, 15, 37, 41,
      62, 230; **1954:** 9, 18, 33, 48, 57, 68, 107,
      138, 200, 345, 353; **1955:** 26, 119, 149;
      1956: 16, 78, 113, 171, 229; **1957:** 17, 22,
      45, 105, 119, 134; **1958:** 11, 63, 103, 120,
      198, 213; **1960–61:** 93, 362
   Nondiscrimination, **1958:** 102
   Nuclear weapons, use of, **1953:** 256
   Olympic Games assistance, **1958:** 5 (p. 73)
   Passport letter, **1957:** 141
   Pay and incentive increases, **1958:** 2, 120
   Personnel turnover, **1954:** 345
   Power to use in peacetime, **1957:** 17
   Publicity campaigns and Congressional hearings,
      1958: 80, 96
   Racial discrimination, elimination, **1953:** 6;
      1960–61: 410
   Red Cross services for, **1960–61:** 37, 65
   Reduction, **1953:** 37, 41; **1954:** 353; **1955:** 26,
      119; **1956:** 52, 143, 155, 171, 229, 232;
      1957: 134, 165; **1958:** 7, 148; **1959:** 53, 271
   Reenlistment in, **1954:** 166
   Remaining in Communist China, comment on,
      1954: 18
   Reserve bill, **1955:** 90, 100, 119, 146, 149, 176,
      192
   Reserve program, **1955:** 3, 4, 12, 17 (p. 91); **1956:**
      51
   Reserves, **1953:** 144; **1954:** 7, 14 (p. 124), 200,
      225, 351, 353; **1956:** 12 (p. 97); **1958:** 5 (p.
      31), 218
   Roles and missions, **1956:** 113; **1958:** 63, 65
   Selective Service.
      See main heading Selective Service.
   Service rivalries, **1958:** 2, 65, 80, 96, 121
   Status of forces abroad, **1957:** 92, 105, 134, 139
   Status of Forces Agreement, comment on, **1954:**
      18
   Subversives in, question re, **1954:** 48
   Unification, **1958:** 11, 63, 65, 122; **1959:** 10 (p.
      43)
      See also Defense reorganization.
   Use to enforce court orders, **1958:** 103
   Use in event of attack on Quemoy or Matsu,
      1956: 16
Armed forces, U.S.S.R., **1955:** 119; **1956:** 58; **1958:**
   295; **1959:** 53, 55
   Egypt, proposed intervention, **1956:** 291n.
   Hungary, **1956:** 270, 282, 283, 287, 291
   Poland, **1956:** 260, 282
   Reduction, **1956:** 113
   Rumania, **1956:** 282
Armed Forces Day, remarks, **1954:** 111; **1955:** 97;
   1956: 93

Armed Forces Industrial College, dedication of
   new building, remarks, **1960–61:** 283
Armed Forces Institute of Pathology, dedication
   remarks, **1955:** 108
Armistice Day, **1953:** 243
   See also Missiles; Weapons.
   Illegal exportation of, **1954:** 25
   Supplied to Near East, **1958:** 207
Arms limitation and reduction, **1953:** 1, 50; **1955:**
   4; **1956:** 2, 143
   See also Disarmament.
   Joint statement with President Gronchi, **1956:** 49
   Letters to Premier Bulganin, **1956:** 52, 166, 262
   Statement at Geneva, **1955:** 164
   Western European Union, **1955:** 54
Arms shipments, U.S.
   Chinese Republic, **1956:** 56
   Israel, **1956:** 56
   Middle East, **1956:** 53
   Saudi Arabia, **1956:** 113
Arms shipments, U.S.S.R.
   Egypt, **1956:** 282, 298
   Joint statement with Prime Minister Eden, **1956:**
      26
   Middle East, **1956:** 26, 53, 298; **1957:** 134
Army, **1954:** 225; **1955:** 3; **1957:** 75, 92, 230; **1958:**
   43; **1959:** 57, 267; **1960–61:** 245, 284, 287,
   410
   See also Armed forces, U.S.; Military personnel.
   Appropriations for civil functions, **1957:** 161
   Army-McCarthy hearings, **1954:** 63, 92, 101, 107,
      115
   Assistant Secretary for Research and Devel-
      opment, reorganization plan, **1956:** 105
   Budget messages, **1954:** 14 (p. 123); **1955:** 17 (pp.
      112-114, 116); **1959:** 10 (pp. 60, 61, 64,
      65); **1960–61:** 13 (pp. 4850, 56), 414 (pp.
      938, 947, 949, 955, 956)
   Camp Blanding Military Reservation, Fla., con-
      veyance of land, veto, **1954:** 121
   Career incentives, medical and dental officers,
      1956: 91
   Chief of Staff (Gen. Lyman L. Lemnitzer),
      1960–61: 135
   Chief of Staff (Gen. Matthew B. Ridgway),
      award of Distinguished Service Medal,
      1955: 144
   Chief of Staff (Gen. Maxwell D. Taylor)
      Army flag presentation ceremony, **1957:** 127
         and n.
      Award of Distinguished Service Medal, **1959:**
         145
   Congressional investigation, **1954:** 57
   Demonstration of new equipment, remarks,
      1960–61: 135
   Fifth Division, deactivation, **1953:** 62
   Hearings, Congressional, news conference
      remarks, **1956:** 216

Army — *continued*

Hinman, Wilbur S., Jr., Award for Distinguished Federal Civilian Service, **1960–61:** 389n.

Housing at military installations, veto, **1956:** 141

Integration in schools on Army posts, **1953:** 31, 101; **1956:** 229

Korean reconstruction, aid for, **1954:** 78

Memorandum, **1953:** 36

Mitchell. James P., Assistant Secretary for Manpower and Reserve Affairs, **1953:** 208

Modernization, **1955:** 4; **1960–61:** 255, 414 (p. 938)

News conference remarks, **1953:** 31, 62, 254; **1957:** 80; **1958:** 74, 288

Officers, regular and reserve, **1956:** 81

Peress (Irving) case, **1955:** 48

Procurement and production, **1957:** 75

Public works appropriation
  Approval, **1956:** 136
  Vetoes, **1959:** 194, 213

Reduction, **1953:** 254; **1955:** 119

Reorganization.
  See Defense reorganization.

Reorganization Plan 6, message, **1953:** 61

Reserves, **1959:** 10 (pp. 64, 65); **1960–61:** 13 (pp. 48, 49), 414 (p. 950)

Reservoir projects in Mississippi, mineral interests, **1956:** 154

Space programs, **1958:** 288

Secretary of the (Wilber M. Brucker), **1958:** 85; **1960–61:** 135
  Army flag presentation ceremony, **1957:** 127 and n.
  Little Rock, conduct of troops, **1957:** 200
  Memorandum, **1960–61:** 382

Secretary of the (Robert T. Stevens), **1953:** 36
  Meeting on release of loyalty records to Congress, **1954:** 115
  News conference remarks on, **1954:** 48, 57, 92, 101, 115
  Resignation, rumor of, **1955:** 33

Weapons display, **1960–61:** 143

Army Ballistic Missiles Agency, **1958:** 74; **1959:** 9n., 266, 267
  Space vehicle development operations, transfer to NASA, **1960–61:** 10, 13 (p. 66)
  Von Braun, Wernher, **1959:** 9n., 266, 267

Army Industrial College, **1960–61:** 283

Army National Guard, **1960–61:** 13 (p. 48), 414 (p. 950)

Arn, Gov. Edward F., 85n., 99, 143, 331

Arndt, Robert and Thelma, mining claim, disapproval, **1956:** 179

Arnold, Mary I., message, **1954:** 342

Aronson, Albert H., **1956:** 238n.

Aronson, Gov. J. Hugo, **1954:** 270, 271; **1960–61:** 208

ARPA.
  See Advanced Research Projects Agency.

Arrowsmith, Marvin L., **1953:** 31, 37, 41, 54, 62, 88, 109, 128, 141, 198, 238, 249, 254, 265; **1954:** 9, 18, 25, 33, 50, 57, 63, 73, 92, 101, 115, 129, 143, 172, 192, 200, 311, 322, 341, 345, 347, 353; **1955:** 10, 18, 26, 33, 41, 47, 56, 59, 62, 81, 90, 95, 100, 112; **1956:** 5, 16, 20, 32, 53, 56, 62, 78, 88, 94, 96, 113, 121, 155, 171, 189, 193, 198, 205, 235, 298; **1957:** 17, 28, 45, 50, 56, 62, 70, 72, 80, 87, 105, 119, 124, 157, 169, 210, 228; **1958:** 11, 28, 37, 56, 63, 70, 74, 83, 88, 103, 120, 141, 153, 198, 213, 222, 274, 288, 310, 318; **1959:** 17, 21, 29, 36, 42, 48, 53, 67, 89, 94, 102, 123, 132, 148, 154, 161, 167, 186, 191, 223, 243, 267, 271, 277; **1960–61:** 7, 21, 24, 34, 38, 93, 103, 127, 143, 222, 228, 284

Art, works of, restored to Italy, **1956:** 45n.

Art exhibit in Moscow, U.S., **1959:** 148

Arth, Carol R., **1953:** 101n.

Articles of Confederation, **1954:** 9

Artigas, José, **1960–61:** 79, 80

Arts, encouragement of, **1956:** 12 (p. 153)

Arts, Federal Advisory Commission on, proposed, **1955:** 4; **1957:** 13

Arvada, Colo., **1960–61:** 23

Asbestos
  Imports, **1958:** 96
  Purchase program, veto, **1958:** 206

Asgeirsson, Asgeir, exchange of greetings, **1955:** 162

Ashby, Jack L., **1959:** 211n.

Asia, South Asia, and Southeast Asia, **1953:** 50, 70, 98, 156, 256; **1954:** 89, 90, 128, 148n., 149, 209, 273, 286, 319; **1955:** 4, 99, 248; **1956:** 2; **1957:** 6, 8, 35, 90, 91; **1958:** 32, 36; **1959:** 302; **1960–61:** 164

See also specific countries.

Assistance, **1953:** 66, 143; **1954:** 3, 14 (p. 139), 150, 347; **1955:** 17 (pp. 123, 129, 130), 41, 47, 48, 69, 76; **1956:** 58, 87, 121; **1958:** 5 (p. 35), 36; **1959:** 55, 71; **1960–61:** 4, 36, 132, 193, 242, 302

Bandung conference, **1955:** 26

Budget message, **1954:** 14 (p. 139)

Colombo Plan for economic development, **1955:** 76; **1956:** 26, 27; **1958:** 207, 312

Communist aggression in, **1954:** 73 and ftn. (p. 384), 101, 115, 297, 316, 330

Editors, visit to United States, **1954:** 157

Industrial revolution, **1959:** 55

Joint statements
  President Bourguiba, **1959:** 329
  President Diem, **1957:** 83
  President Garcia, **1958:** 143; **1960–61:** 189
  Prime Minister Churchill on, **1954:** 154
  Prime Minister Eden, **1956:** 26, 27

Asia — *continued*
  Joint statements — *continued*
    Prime Minister Huh Chung, **1960–61:** 203
    Prime Minister Karamanlis, **1959:** 327
    Prime Minister Kishi, **1957:** 117; **1960–61:** 16
    Prime Minister Macmillan, **1957:** 55
    Prime Minister Nu, **1955:** 148
    Prime Minister Suhrawardy, **1957:** 131
    Prime Minister Yoshida on, **1954:** 330
    Western leaders, **1953:** 255
  Luncheon given by King Paul, toast, **1959:** 326
  Mission of hospital ship proposed, **1959:** 29
  News conference remarks, **1953:** 54, 77, 254, 265;
    1954: 57, 63, 73 and ftn. (p. 384), 101, 115,
    129, 165, 347; **1955:** 18, 26, 41, 47; **1959:**
    29, 179
  Parliament, address to, **1959:** 325
  Rubber and tin resources, **1958:** 36
  SEATO.
    See Southeast Asia Treaty Organization.
  Soviet activities, **1958:** 96
  Visit of Secretary Dulles, **1953:** 101
  Visit of President Eisenhower.
    See Visit of the President to Europe, Asia, and
    Africa.
  Visit of Vice President Nixon, **1953:** 254, 265;
    1954: 57
Asian spouses, immigration, **1956:** 33
Asiatic flu vaccine, **1957:** 157
Assistant President, duties and functions, comment
  on, **1958:** 141
Associated Press, address, **1955:** 79
Associated States of Indochina.
  See Cambodia; Laos; Vietnam.
Association of American Colleges, remarks, **1955:**
  11
Association of American Medical Colleges, **1954:**
  334n.
Association of American Railroads, **1954:** 78n.;
  1956: 237; **1957:** 12
Association of American Women in Chile, **1960–
  61:** 72n.
Association of Graduates of the United States
  Military Academy, **1958:** 52
Association of Junior Leagues of America,
  remarks, **1958:** 94
Association of Land-Grant Colleges and Univer-
  sities, remarks, **1954:** 335
Association of State Planning and Development
  Agencies, remarks, **1959:** 8
Astin, A. V., **1953:** 41; **1954:** 267
Aswan Dam, Egypt, **1957:** 50, 70, 157; **1959:** 94;
  1960–61: 7
Ataturk, Mustafa Kemal, **1954:** 20; **1959:** 296
Athens, Greece, **1953:** 232; **1958:** 93; **1960–61:** 284
  Arrival, remarks, **1959:** 324
Atherton, Warren H., **1957:** 57n.
  Nomination to National Security Training Com-
    mission, **1953:** 144

Athletics for young people, news conference
  remarks, **1956:** 96, 121
Atka, U.S.S., Antarctic mission, **1955:** 47
Atl, Dr. (Gerardo Murillo), **1959:** 256
Atlanta, Ga., bombing of synagogue, **1958:** 285,
  288
Atlantic alliance, joint statement with Chancellor
  Adenauer, **1957:** 100
Atlantic Charter, **1953:** 14
Atlantic City, N.J., **1953:** 205, 208; **1959:** 129
  Clinical Congress of American College of Sur-
    geons, message to, **1957:** 216 and n.
  Regional conference on traffic safety, **1958:** 45n.
Atlantic Community, **1956:** 87, 114
Atlantic Missile Range, **1958:** 321
Atlantic Treaty.
  See North Atlantic Treaty.
Atlantic Treaty Association, message, **1959:** 204
Atlas (ICBM).
  See Missiles.
Atlas satellite (Score), **1958:** 321, 322; **1959:** 10 (p.
  57)
Atomic attack, highways for evacuation purposes,
  1955: 39
Atomic bomb, **1953:** 256; **1954:** 38, 89; **1957:** 230
  See also Nuclear weapons; Nuclear weapons
    tests.
  Cablegram to Prime Minister Nehru, **1957:** 244
  French explosion of, **1960–61:** 38
  Nevada test, **1953:** 31
  News conference remarks, **1953:** 12, 31; **1954:**
    25, 57, 73, 165, 341; **1956:** 16, 62, 78, 113;
    1957: 105, 119, 145
Atomic community, European, **1957:** 8, 80, 245
  Joint statements
    Chancellor Adenauer, **1957:** 100
    Premier Mollet, **1960–61:** 38
Atomic depth bomb, **1957:** 230
Atomic development, broadcast on cost of Gov-
  ernment, **1957:** 86
Atomic energy, **1955:** 17 (pp. 108, 119); **1956:** 190;
  1958: 2
  Budget messages **1956:** 12 (pp. 81, 99–101); **1958:**
    5 (pp. 18, 20, 26)
  Geneva conference, **1956:** 2
  Information exchange, U. S.-U. K., **1956:** 26
  International control of, **1956:** 191
  Letter to Premier Bulganin, **1958:** 31
  Meeting on, **1956:** 318
Atomic Energy Act, **1953:** 265; **1959:** 120
  Amendments **1953:** 268; **1954:** 223
    Budget message, **1954:** 14 (pp. 127, 129)
    Message to Congress, **1954:** 38
    News conference remarks, **1954:** 39, 115, 168,
      172, 192, 200
  Violations, **1953:** 264
Atomic Energy Agency, International.
  See International Atomic Energy Agency.

Atomic Energy Commission, **1953:** 143, 263; **1954:** 193; **1955:** 79, 89, 123, 146 ftns. (pp. 646, 658), 223; **1957:** 56, 105, 134, 234; **1959:** 102; **1960–61:** 116, 358
   Acting Chairman (Willard F. Libby), **1958:** 156, 157
   Announcement of Soviet nuclear tests, statement, **1958:** 311
   Appropriations, **1955:** 157; **1958:** 193
   Argonne National Laboratory, **1955:** 53
   Authority re atomic energy program, proposals, **1954:** 38
   Budget messages, **1954:** 14 (pp. 86, 128, 169); **1955:** 17 (pp. 119, 121, 143, 161, 162); **1956:** 12 (pp. 80, 100, 101); **1958:** 5 (pp. 33, 48); **1959:** 10 (pp. 55, 66–68); **1960–61:** 13 (pp. 47, 58, 59, 94), 414 (pp. 948, 959, 960)
   Building made available to Clinton, Tenn., for school, **1958:** 288
   Chairman (John A. McCone) **1958:** 239; **1959:** 68, 119, 121, 243; **1960–61:** 116, 420
      International Atomic Energy Agency, conference, **1960–61:** 301
      U.S. agreements with Canada, France, Greece, U.K., **1959:** 119n., 120n.
   Chairman (Lewis L. Strauss), **1953:** 268; **1954:** 111n.; **1955:** 10, 53, 177, 228n.; **1956:** 43; **1957:** 105; **1958:** 21, 145n.
      Bipartisan conference, **1957:** 2
      Geneva conference on atomic energy, **1955:** 191
      Joint study with Sir Edwin Plowden on nuclear cooperation, **1957:** 226n.
      Labor dispute at atomic energy plants, **1954:** 161 ftn. (p. 622)
      Labor-management panel, memorandum, **1956:** 95
      Memorandum, **1953:** 273
      News conference remarks on, **1953:** 12, 265; **1954:** 63, 68 and ftn. (p. 364), 73, 92, 115, 311; **1956:** 78, 193; **1958:** 11, 37, 74, 103
      Nuclear-powered merchant ship, **1956:** 243
      Reappointment, comment on, **1958:** 103
      Soviet nuclear tests, **1956:** 191, 193
      Statement on nuclear power development abroad, **1956:** 299
      Statement on nuclear weapons tests in Pacific, **1954:** 68n.
      Visit of King Leopold, **1957:** 153
   Conference on Statute of International Atomic Energy Agency, **1956:** 274
   Congressional meeting, **1956:** 318
   Dedication of headquarters building at Germantown, Md., **1957:** 231
   Dixon-Yates contract, **1954:** 157, 161, 168, 200, 311, 328

Atomic Energy Commission — *continued*
   "Effects of High-Yield Nuclear Explosions," **1955:** 41, 56
   Expenditures for, **1957:** 13
   Facilities at Hanford, Wash., **1957:** 88, 171
   Filling of vacancy, **1955:** 62, 119
   Floberg, John F., **1957:** 145; **1959:** 18n.
   General Advisory Committee, **1959:** 107
   Graham, John S., **1957:** 145
   International Atomic Energy Agency, **1957:** 144, 204
   Libby, Willard F., **1955:** 89n., 191n.
   Murray, Thomas E., **1954:** 328; **1956:** 78
   News conference remarks, **1953:** 54, 208, 265; **1954:** 18, 63, 73, 129, 143, 157, 161, 168, 200, 311, 328, 341; **1955:** 10, 41, 56, 62, 119; **1956:** 5, 78, 88, 198; **1958:** 42, 88, 288
   Nuclear reactor for merchant ship, **1956:** 243
   Oppenheimer (J. Robert) case, **1954:** 92, 129, 143, 157
   Panel report on work of, **1956:** 30
   Radioactive fallout research, **1959:** 68
   Salary payment to interim appointee, **1955:** 193
   Semiannual report, **1956:** 43n.
   Technical libraries, **1955:** 228
   U-235 for peaceful uses, **1956:** 43, 299; **1957:** 13, 124, 125
   Weapons responsibility, **1956:** 230
Atomic Energy Commission, International, proposed, **1953:** 256
Atomic Energy Labor-Management Panel, Chairman (Cyrus Ching), memorandum, **1956:** 95
Atomic energy development and control, budget message, **1954:** 14 (pp. 107, 118, 128)
Atomic energy facilities, labor dispute
   Letter to Attorney General Brownell, **1954:** 193
   Letter to T. Keith Glennan, **1954:** 281
   News conference remarks, **1954:** 161 and ftn. (p. 622), 192
Atomic energy for military purposes, **1958:** 5 (pp. 32, 33), 157
Atomic energy for mutual defense, **1954:** 14 (pp. 85, 86); **1959:** 55
   U.S. agreement with Italy, **1960–61:** 420
   U.S. agreements with Canada, France, Germany, Greece, Netherlands, Turkey, U.K., **1959:** 119 and n., 120
   U. S.-U. K. agreement
      Memorandum to Secretary of Defense and Acting Chairman, Atomic Energy Commission, **1958:** 156
Atomic energy for peaceful uses, **1953:** 50, 268; **1954:** 3, 128, 286, 308; **1955:** 4, 53n., 121, 126; **1956:** 2, 114, 143, 190, 266; **1958:** 207; **1959:** 55, 189, 217n., 243; **1960–61:** 36, 301, 409, 410

Atomic energy for peaceful uses — *continued*
  See also International Atomic Energy Agency;
    Power projects.
  Address at United Nations, **1953:** 256; **1960–61:**
    209
  News conference remarks, **1953:** 265
  Bilateral agreements on, **1954:** 260; **1958:** 113
  Budget messages, **1954:** 14 (pp. 128–130); **1955:**
    17 (p. 91); **1956:** 12 (pp. 81, 99–101, 106,
    108, 155); **1958:** 5 (pp. 32, 43); **1959:** 10
    (pp. 44, 55, 67, 68); **1960–61:** 13 (pp. 47,
    58, 59), 414 (pp. 948, 959, 960)
  Citation to Dr. Lawrence for work on, **1958:** 52
  Euratom.
    See European Atomic Energy Community.
  Exchange of messages with Prime Minister
    Kishi, **1957:** 208
  Federal-State Action Committee recommenda-
    tions, **1958:** 106
  Fissionable materials, **1954:** 14 (p. 128), 38, 260;
    1955: 79, 156, 164, 165
    See also Disarmament, Uranium.
  Geneva conference (1955), **1955:** 100, 123, 149,
    156, 165, 176, 177n., 191, 228
  Geneva conterence (1958), **1958:** 188, 240; **1959:**
    10 (p. 67)
  International agreements on civil uses.
    See International agreements.
  International atomic pool, President's proposal,
    1953: 265; **1954:** 3, 9, 18, 23n., 25, 38, 39,
    57, 115, 129, 138, 165, 182, 200, 223, 225,
    297, 322, 325, 337, 347
  Joint declaration with Prime Minister Churchill,
    1954: 155
  Joint statement with Prime Minister Yoshida,
    1954: 330
  Letters to Premier Khrushchev, **1958:** 67, 86
  Memorandum on, **1956:** 266n.
  Merchant ship **1955:** 79; **1956:** 243
  Messages, statements, etc., **1955:** 228; **1957:** 8,
    13, 90, 96, 125, 153, 165, 231
  News conference remarks, **1953:** 54, 208, 243,
    265; **1954:** 9, 18, 25, 39, 57, 63, 73, 115,
    129, 138, 165, 172, 182, 200, 311, 322, 347;
    1955: 59, 81, 100, 146, 149, 176; **1956:** 78,
    251, 256, 272; **1957:** 80, 115, 119, 124, 158
  Pakistan, **1959:** 302
  Plutonium, **1956:** 299
  Power projects, **1954:** 38, 172
  President's address at United Nations (1953),
    1954: 38, 63, 129, 223, 322, 337, 347;
    1955: 191; **1959:** 302
  Project Plowshare, **1959:** 10 (p. 68); **1960–61:** 143
  Report on, letter, **1956:** 30
  Shippingport atomic power plant, **1954:** 260
  Special Assistant to President on, **1958:** 166
  State responsibility, **1958:** 5 (p. 43); **1960–61:** 116

Atomic energy for peaceful uses — *continued*
  Statement on British and American contribu-
    tions, **1958:** 21
  U.N. activities, **1955:** 156; **1958:** 8
  U.N. address, **1956:** 52n.
  U.N. conference (1955), **1958:** 240
  Uranium-233, **1956:** 299
  Uranium-235 available for, **1956:** 43, 52, 274,
    299; **1957:** 13, 124, 125
Atomic energy project, Hanford, Wash., **1957:** 88,
    171
  See also Joint Committee on Atomic Energy.
Atomic explosions, **1957:** 55, 208n.
  See also Nuclear weapons tests.
  Radioactive fallout, **1957:** 55, 105, 124, 208 and
    n., 230
Atomic information, agreement with Australia,
    1957: 130 and n.
Atomic information exchange, **1953:** 128, 265;
    1954: 38, 223, 260; **1958:** 83, 145, 236;
    1960–61: 24
  News conference remarks, **1954:** 39, 73, 138, 168
  Technical cooperation with Great Britain, joint
    statement, **1954:** 154
Atomic isotopes, use in charting underground
    rivers, **1958:** 207
Atomic monopoly, **1957:** 245
Atomic power projects.
  See Power projects.
Atomic-powered ships.
  See Ships.
Atomic Radiation, United Nations Scientific Com-
    mittee on the Effect of, **1958:** 56
Atomic reactors.
  See Reactors.
Atomic stockpile for NATO countries, **1957:** 134
Atomic warheads, **1956:** 32; **1957:** 56, 230
  U.S.S.R., **1957:** 245
Atomic weapons.
  See Bombs; Nuclear weapons.
Atoms-for-Peace program, **1957:** 2, 13, 54, 245;
    1959: 121; **1960–61:** 330
  Award to Professor Bohr, **1957:** 225 and n.
  Distribution of Uranium 235 for purposes of,
    1957: 13, 124, 125
  Funds for **1958:** 32
  Postage stamp, remarks on issuance, **1955:** 177
Attlee, Clement R., **1953:** 77
Attorney General, **1958:** 222
  See also Justice, Department of.
  Adopted orphans, admission to U. S., **1956:** 275
  Authority concerning paroling certain refugees
    into U.S., **1960–61:** 233
  Civil rights cases, **1956:** 16, 32
  Deportation of aliens, **1956:** 33
  Immigration hardship cases, **1956:** 33
  News conference remarks, **1956:** 16, 32, 53, 96

Attorney General — *continued*
　Power to inspect election records, proposed,
　　1959: 27
　Security program, responsibility for, **1956:** 96
　Waiver of fingerprinting requirement for foreign
　　visitors, **1956:** 33, 53
Attorney General, Acting, regulations re, **1953:** 51
Attorney General, Assistant, for civil rights, **1957:**
　119, 133
Attorney General (Herbert Brownell, Jr.), **1953:**
　269; **1954:** 12n., 72; **1955:** 110n.
　See also Justice, Department of.
　Action on subversives, **1954:** 129, 130, 209
　Antitrust laws, **1957:** 132
　Broadcast with the President, **1953:** 95
　Civil rights cases, **1957:** 45, 119, 134, 150, 178n.
　Congressional meeting, **1956:** 318
　Hoover Commission, representation on, **1953:**
　　145n.
　Hungarian refugees, admission, **1957:** 1, 25
　Immigration hardship cases, **1957:** 25
　Immigration study, **1956:** 33
　Injunction in maritime strike, letter, **1953:** 203
　Interdepartmental Committee on Narcotics,
　　letter, **1954:** 343
　Investigation of FHA, **1954:** 302
　Labor dispute at atomic energy facilities, letters,
　　1954: 193; **1957:** 88 and n.
　Labor disputes in maritime industry, letter, **1956:**
　　300
　Little Rock case, **1957:** 178n.
　Meeting on release of Loyalty Board records to
　　Congress, **1954:** 115
　Memorandum on authority of President to with-
　　hold information from Congress, **1954:**
　　113n.
　Mexican migratory labor program, **1954:** 168
　News conference remarks on, **1953:** 22, 109, 126,
　　243, 249, 254; **1954:** 9, 18, 115, 129, 168,
　　311, 341; **1955:** 81, 149; **1956:** 16, 94, 96,
　　235; **1957:** 28, 45, 56, 62, 86, 119, 134, 150
　News conferences with, question of, **1954:** 9
　Opinion on Department of Defense Appropri-
　　ation Act, **1955:** 155
　Opinion (1954) re encroachment on Executive
　　powers, comment on, **1959:** 172
　Presidential disability study, **1957:** 56
　President's Conference on Administrative Pro-
　　cedure, **1953:** 59
　Public school integration, recommendations re,
　　1953: 249
　Resignation, **1957:** 224 and n.
　Security information, new procedures, **1953:** 110
　Security program, **1953:** 6, 254
　Statement on separation of powers of Govern-
　　ment, **1954:** 129
　Swing, J. M., trip to Mexico, **1956:** 235
　Visit to Texas, **1956:** 94

Attorney General (Brownell) — *continued*
　White (Harry Dexter) case, **1953:** 243
　Witnesses, immunity from self-incrimination,
　　recommendation re, **1953:** 249
　"Your Government and You" broadcasts, **1956:**
　　246
Attorney General (William P. Rogers), **1957:**
　224n.; **1960–61:** 233
　Chairman, U.G.F. campaign, **1958:** 136
　Civil rights proposals, **1960–61:** 21
　Deceptive practices in broadcasting media,
　　letter, **1960–61:** 1
　Maritime strike injunction, **1959:** 250
　News conference remarks on, **1958:** 28; **1959:**
　　267, 271, 288; **1960–61:** 21, 143
　Opinion on disallowance of use of certain mu-
　　tual security funds, **1960–61:** 380n.
　Resignation, letter, **1960–61:** 411
　Statement on school integration, **1958:** 267n.
　Steel strike injunction, **1959:** 265, 267
　Taft-Hartley Act study, **1960–61:** 21
Atwood, Frank, **1955:** 127
Atwood, Robert, **1959:** 3n.
Auchincloss, Repr. James C., letter, **1955:** 20
Auditorium Commission, District of Columbia,
　1957: 21 and n., 28
Augusta, Ga., **1953:** 249, 253; **1954:** 82, 83, 185,
　186, 342; **1955:** 1n., 26 ftn. (p. 231), 71n.,
　72n., 73n., 74n.; **1956:** 80n., 304n., 305n.,
　306n., 307n., 308n., 309n., 310n.; **1957:** 17,
　72, ftn. (p. 286), 76, 77, 80, 236, 237; **1958:**
　27n., 85n., 316n., 317n.; **1959:** 73n., 74n.,
　76, 78, 80n., 81n., 89, 266n., 267, 268n.,
　271, 277, 279n., 281n., 282n., 283n., 348n.,
　349n., 350n., 351n.; **1960–61:** 2, 116, 118,
　119, 358–361, 363, 365, 396
　Mayor Millard Beckum, **1960–61:** 396n.
Augusta National Golf Club, **1957:** 236 and n.
Aurand, Capt. E. P., **1957:** 151; **1958:** 201n.;
　1960–61: 142n.
Austin, Rev. J. C., **1956:** 241
Australia, **1954:** 115, 129; **1957:** 45; **1959:** 96n.;
　1960–61: 36, 410
　Agreement on atomic information, **1957:** 130
　　and n.
　Armed forces in Korea, **1960–61:** 202
　Defense treaty with United States, **1953:** 96
　Escapees settling in, **1953:** 257n.
　Federated Iron Workers Association, **1954:** 77
　Menzies, Robert G. **1956:** 205; **1960–61:** 312
　SEATO membership, **1960–61:** 286
　See also Southeast Asia Treaty Organization.
　U.N. committee on Hungary, **1958:** 8
　Wheat for Pakistan relief, **1953:** 97
Austria, **1957:** 25; **1958:** 80, 261; **1960–61:** 23, 410
　Ambassador Llewellyn E. Thompson, **1955:** 146
　　ftn. (p. 644)

Austria — *continued*
    Campaign remarks, **1956:** 210, 224; **1958:** 287,
        290, 293, 302
    Death of President Koerner, **1957:** 5
    Decrease in immigrants from, **1956:** 2
    Exchange visitor, Kurt Glaser, **1955:** 116
    Flood relief, **1954:** 175, 182, 195
    Four-power conference on, proposed, **1953:** 238,
        254
    Gruber, Dr. Karl, **1957:** 204n.
    Hungarian refugees, **1956:** 304, 306; **1957:** 70, 85,
        250
    Koerner, Theodor, **1955:** 98
    News conference remarks, **1953:** 238, 254; **1955:**
        81, 100; **1956:** 198; **1958:** 274
    Neutralization, **1955:** 100
    Peace treaty, **1957:** 111
    Proposed treaty, **1953:** 50, 255, 256
    Raab, Julius, **1957:** 5, 186
    Vienna, **1955:** 81, 95, 98n., 114; **1959:** 121;
        1960–61: 301n.
Austrian State Treaty, **1954:** 68, 128, 225, 297, 341;
    1955: 99
    Message to President Koerner upon signing,
        1955: 98
    News conference remarks, **1955:** 59, 81, 95, 100
    Transmittal to Senate, **1955:** 114
Automation, **1959:** 67
    Comment on, **1955:** 56
    Wheelbarrow anecdote, **1958:** 63
Automobile Dealers, suits by, approval of bill,
    1956: 174
    Free importation for show purposes, approval,
        1958: 76
    Industry, threatened strike, **1955:** 112
    News conference remarks, **1958:** 56, 83, 120
    Prices, **1959:** 53
    Production, **1960–61:** 256
    Tax, **1954:** 3, 14 (pp. 88, 99); **1955:** 41; **1957:** 13;
        1958: 56; **1959:** 104, 187; **1960–61:** 414
        (pp. 940, 977)
    Travel, first crossing from San Francisco to New
        York, **1960–61:** 332
Automobile Manufacturers Association, **1960–61:**
    328
Automobile Show, National, dinner, address,
    1960–61: 328
Averoff-Tossizza, Evanghelos, **1959:** 40
Aviation, **1955:** 17 (pp. 169, 170)
    See also Air carriers; Aircraft; Aircraft, military.
    Budget messages, **1958:** 5 (pp. 45, 54, 60); **1959:**
        10 (pp. 78, 79); **1960–61:** 13 (pp. 65, 68,
        69), 414 (pp. 973–975)
    Federal Airport Act, disapproval, **1958:** 246;
        1959: 143
    50th anniversary of powered flight, **1953:** 267
    Fuel tax.
        See Gasoline taxes.

Aviation — *continued*
    Joint statement with Prime Minister of Afghan-
        istan, **1958:** 150
    Message on Federal Aviation Agency, **1958:** 135
    Progress in, **1959:** 169; **1960–61:** 185
    Promotion of, **1956:** 12 (pp. 140, 141)
    Service charges, **1958:** 5 (p. 45)
    Speed, progress, **1953:** 267
    U.K.-Soviet talks on air safety over Germany,
        1953: 41
Aviation, civil, **1954:** 123, 200
    See also Aircraft.
    Budget message, **1954:** 14 (pp. 171, 173, 174)
    Industry, **1956:** 257
    Policy review, letter to Robert B. Murray, Jr.,
        1953: 194
    U.S. policy report, statement, **1954:** 123
Aviation facilities planning
    Budget message, **1956:** 12 (pp. 140, 141)
    Reports, **1957:** 71; **1958:** 135; **1959:** 74
    Special Assistant to President for, appointment,
        1956: 38
Aviation Week, Argentina's, **1957:** 233
Avocations of the President, news conference
    remarks, **1956:** 20
Awards and citations
    American Helicopter Society Citation, accep-
        tance, **1960–61:** 145
    America's Democratic Legacy Award, accep-
        tance, **1953:** 252
    AMVETS World Peace Award, acceptance,
        1959: 92
    Atoms for Peace Award, Professor Bohr, **1957:**
        225 and n.
    Award in memory of Ernest O. Lawrence, letter,
        1958: 239
    Big Brother of the Year Award, acceptance,
        1960–61: 404
    Citation, Gen. Melvin J. Maas, **1960–61:** 417
    Department of State honor awards, **1954:** 294
    Distinguished Civilian Service Award
        President Hoover, **1957:** 26 and n.
        Rechnitzer, Andreas B., **1960–61:** 25
    Distinguished Federal Civilian Service Awards,
        1958: 13; **1959:** 9; **1960–61:** 68, 389
    Distinguished Public Service Award, Jacques
        Piccard, **1960–61:** 25
    Distinguished Service Medal
        Carney, Adm. Robert B., **1955:** 188
        Greunther, Gen. Alfred M., **1956:** 317
        Radford, Adm. Arthur W., **1957:** 151
        Ridgway, Gen. Matthew B., **1955:** 144
        Taylor, Gen. Maxwell D., **1959:** 145
        Van Flect, Gen. James A., **1953:** 19
    Football Hall of Fame Award, acceptance, **1958:**
        307
    Forrestal Memorial Award, acceptance, **1954:**
        308

Awards and citations — *continued*
  Honorary degrees, acceptance, **1955:** 70, 121;
    1956: 114; **1957:** 109n.; **1958:** 123, 130,
    286
  Hoover Medal Award, acceptance, **1960–61:** 405
  Lafayette Gold Medal Award, General Gruen-
    ther, **1958:** 118
  Lahey, Frank H., Award, acceptance, **1954:** 334
  Lake, Mrs. Louise, and essay winners, **1958:** 99
  Legion of Merit
    Anderson, Comdr. W. R., **1958:** 201
    President Bayar of Turkey, **1954:** 20
    Beach, Capt. Edward L., **1960–61:** 142
    Bhumibol Adulyadej, **1960–61:** 212
    King Paul of Greece, **1953:** 233
    Field Marshal Pibulsonggram, **1955:** 87
    Walsh, Lt. Don, **1960–61:** 25
  Medal of Freedom
    Anderson, Robert B., **1955:** 183
    De Galard-Terraube, Genevieve, **1954:** 176
    Douglas, James H., **1960–61:** 425
    Dulles, John Foster, **1959:** 114
    Gates, Thomas S., Jr., **1960–61:** 426
    Goodpaster, Gen. Andrew J., **1960–61:** 430
    Gray, Gordon, **1960–61:** 427
    Herter, Christian A., **1960–61:** 428
    Kistiakowsky, George B., **1960–61:** 429
    McElroy, Neil H., **1959:** 286
    Strauss, Lewis L., **1958:** 166
    Von Neumann, Dr. John, **1956:** 40
    Wilson, Secretary Charles E., **1957:** 212
  Medal of Honor
    Bleak. David B., **1953:** 122, 229n.
    Charette, William R., **1954:** 8
    Dewey, Duane E., **1953:** 27
    McLaughlin, Alford L., **1953:** 174, 229n.
    Miyamura, Hiroshi H., **1953:** 229n.
    Mize, Ola L., **1954:** 61
    Murphy, Lt. Raymond G., **1953:** 226, 229n.
    O'Brien, Lt. George H., Jr., **1953:** 170, 229n.
    Schowalter, Edward R., Jr., **1954:** 8
    Simanek, Robert E., **1953:** 175, 229n.
    Stone, Lt. James L., **1953:** 229n.
    West, Ernest E., **1954:** 8
    Wilson, Benjamin F., **1954:** 79
  Medallion, Winston Churchill, **1955:** 244
  Medals, acceptance, **1960–61:** 23, 74, 79, 81,
    178n., 206, 405
  Military Chaplains Association citation, accep-
    tance, **1954:** 103
  National Foundation for Infantile Paralysis,
    1955: 78
  National Geographic Society Medal, Prince
    Philip, **1957:** 221
    Donovan, Maj. Gen. William J., **1957:** 66
    Hoover, J. Edgar, **1955:** 110
    Murphy, Robert, **1960–61:** 375

Awards and citations — *continued*
  Navy Commendation Ribbon with Metal Pen-
    dant, Lt. Lawrence A. Shumaker, **1960–
    61:** 25
  Order of Sikatuna, Rajah, acceptance, **1960–61:**
    188
  Pan American Society Golden Insignia, accep-
    tance, **1957:** 64 and n.
  Posthumous citation, James Forbis Brownlee,
    1960–61: 377
  Presidential Unit Citation, U. S. S. *Nautilus*,
    1958: 201
  Salk, Dr. Jonas E., Citation, **1955:** 77
  Sylvanus Thayer Award, Dr. Lawrence, **1958:** 52
  United Defense Fund citation, Gen. Doolittle,
    1954: 93
  United Jewish Appeal, Citation, Acceptance,
    1955: 115
  U.S. Mint modal, Prime Minister Kishi, **1960–
    61:** 15n.
  Young Republican National Federation citation,
    1957: 116 and n.
Axelroad, Col. Benjamin, veto of bill for relief of,
    1957: 123
Ayres, Representative William H., **1957:** 145; **1959:**
    92n.
Ayub Khan, Mohammed, **1959:** 299, 302, 305;
    1960–61: 284, 297
  Joint statement with, **1959:** 303
  Toast to, **1959:** 304
Ayyangar, M.A., **1959:** 311n.
Azerbaijan, Iran, **1959:** 320
Azikiwe, Nnamdi, letter, **1960–61:** 361

B-36 bomber, **1957:** 86, 230, 234
B-47 bomber, **1956:** 94
B-52 jet bomber, **1956:** 12 (p. 96), 94, 113; **1957:** 17,
    86, 230, 234
Ba, Ousmane, **1960–61:** 324n.
Bacher, Robert F., telegram, **1958:** 149n.
"Back to God" program of American Legion,
    remarks, **1953:** 5; **1954:** 32
Baghdad, Iraq, outbreak in, **1958:** 171, 172
Baghdad Pact, **1956:** 2; **1958:** 32
  See also Central Treaty Organization.
  Joint statements
    Prime Minister Eden, **1956:** 26
    Prime Minister Macmillan, **1957:** 55, 226
    Prime Minister Suhrawardy, **1957:** 131
  Military Committee, **1957:** 55
  Ministerial Council, meeting in Karachi, mes-
    sage, **1959:** 19
  News conference remarks, **1956:** 78
Bailey, Charles W., **1956:** 94, 198, 205; **1957:** 17, 45,
    50, 72, 115, 124, 210; **1958:** 37; **1959:** 42,
    132; **1960–61:** 127, 222

Bailey, Repr. Cleveland M., **1957:** 150, 228
Bailey, Clyde A., mining claim, disapproval, **1956:** 179
Baker, Edward L., **1959:** 270
Baker, Repr. Howard H., **1957:** 80, 124
Baker, Milton G., **1954:** 304n.; **1960–61:** 341
Baker, Russell, **1956:** 155, 216, 229; **1957:** 115
Balafrej, Ahmed, **1957:** 84
Balance of payments deficit, **1960–61:** 4, 415, 423
  Anderson-Dillon mission to Europe, **1960–61:** 362 and ftn. (p. 864), 365
  Budget message, **1960–61:** 414 (pp. 936, 962)
  Directive, **1960–61:** 362 ftn. (p. 862), 434
  Discussion with President-elect Kennedy, **1960–61:** 369
Balatbat, Marcelo, **1960–61:** 187
Balboa, Canal Zone, bridge construction, **1957:** 167
Balkans, joint statement on, **1959:** 327
"Ballistic blackmail," **1958:** 207
Ballistic missiles.
  See Missiles.
Ballistic Missile Agency, Army.
  See Army Ballistic Missile Agency.
Ballistic Missile Early Warning System (BMEWS), **1959:** 10 (p.57); **1960–61:** 414 (p. 953)
Balmoral Castle, Scotland, **1959:** 193n., 198n.
Baltic countries, incorporation into U.S.S.R., **1957:** 6
Baltimore, Md., campaign remarks, **1958:** 308; **1960–61:** 290
Bandaranaike, S. W. R. D., death of, **1959:** 241
Bandaranaike, Mrs. S. W. R. D., **1959:** 241
Bandung conference of Asian-African countries, **1955:** 26 and ftn. (p. 231)
Bandung meeting, **1956:** 87
Bane, Frank, **1957:** 124
Banff National Park, dedication of Mount Eisenhower, **1958:** 220
Bangkok, Thailand
  SEATO conference, **1955:** 41
  SEATO Day ceremonies, **1960–61:** 286
  Trade fair (1954), **1955:** 6
Bangor, Maine, remarks at Dow Air Force Base, **1955:** 143
Bank Holding Company Act of 1956, **1956:** 99
Bankers Association, American.
  See American Bankers Association.
Bankhead (William B.) National Forest, **1954:** 156
Bankruptcy Act, amendment, disapproval, **1960–61:** 289
Banks
  Cooperatives, **1956:** 12 (p. 131)
  Federal intermediate credit, **1956:** 147
Bannow, Rudolph F., **1960–61:** 127 and ftn. (p. 368)
Bao Dai, **1954:** 83, 105; **1955:** 48
Barbara Anne, (President's yacht), **1957:** 201; **1960–61:** 244n.

Barbosa, Luis, **1960–61:** 50
Barkley, Sen. Alben W., death of, statement, **1956:** 92
Barkout, Raymond, relief of, disapproval, **1960–61:** 288
Barksdale, A.D., **1957:** 50
Barnard, Chester I., letter, **1954:** 153
Barnes, Bert V., President's Award for Distinguished Federal Civilian Service, **1960–61:** 389n.
Barnes, Stanley N., **1955:** 56; **1956:** 56
Barnes, Wendell B.
  See Small Business Administator.
Barr, Andrew, President's Award for Distinguished Federal Civilian Service, **1960–61:** 68n.
Barr, Beverly, **1956:** 268
Barr, Frank Stringfellow, **1959:** 116
Barriault, Art, **1959:** 267
Barros, Adhemar de, **1960–61:** 52
Barros Hurtado, Cesar, **1958:** 164
Barry, Commodore John, statue, **1956:** 208
Barry, Repr. Robert R., **1960–61:** 346
Bartelt, Edward F., **1954:** 15; **1955:** 187
Barter of agricultural commodities, **1958:** 163
Bartlett, Charles L., **1953:** 208, 265; **1954:** 33, 115, 192, 200; **1955:** 146, 149; **1956:** 16, 216; **1957:** 45, 56, 62, 80, 124; **1958:** 288; **1959:** 172; **1960–61:** 256
Bartlett, Sen. E. L., **1959:** 3n.
Barton, Clara, **1959:** 45
Baruch, Bernard, **1960–61:** 38, 283
  Disarmament plan (1946), **1956:** 266; **1958:** 63
  Expansion of National Security Council, **1958:** 213
  News conference remarks on, **1958:** 63, 213
  Recession, **1958:** 63
Baseball
  Little league, **1960–61:** 199
  Scout, the President as, **1958:** 88
  Team, Washington, D.C., **1953:** 41; **1956:** 229
  World series, **1960–61:** 284, 319
Baseball Club, Washington, D.C., **1958:** 222
Basel, Switzerland, **1960–61:** 279
Bases, U.S., **1954:** 25, 57, 63; **1958:** 2, 32, 96; **1959:** 55, 179, 288
  See also Air bases, U.S.
Bases, U. S., in foreign countries, **1956:** 12 (p. 96); **1957:** 50, 72, 86, 90, 230, 234
  Communist China, area near, **1957:** 150
  Morocco, **1959:** 345
  News conference remarks, **1956:** 78, 94, 96; **1957:** 50, 72, 150, 169
  Nuclear weapons bases, **1960–61:** 24
  North Africa, **1956:** 96
  Philippines, **1960–61:** 189
  Reduction, **1959:** 271
  Saudi Arabia, **1956:** 94, 96; **1957:** 31
  Spain, **1953:** 198; **1959:** 200

Basic research, **1954:** 14 (pp. 151–153, 155); **1956:** 12 (pp. 122, 123); **1957:** 234; **1958:** 5 (pp. 30, 33, 46, 48); **1959:** 10 (p. 98); **1960–61:** 393, 410

Budget messages, **1960–61:** 13 (pp. 39, 87, 89, 91), 414 (pp. 939, 959, 1004)

Symposium on, address, **1959:** 107

Bass, Repr. Perkins, **1955:** 139

Bastian, Judge Walter M., **1953:** 59

Bataan, fall of, 12th anniversary, **1954:** 73

Bataan Day Messages, **1954:** 75; **1956:** 80; **1957:** 69; **1958:** 69; **1959:** 73; **1960–61:** 112

Battle, Gov. John Stewart, **1953:** 79; **1958:** 318; **1959:** 271

Battle Act, amendments proposed, **1960–61:** 13 (p. 64)

Battle of the Bulge, **1956:** 155; **1958:** 310

Baudouin I, **1955:** 208n.

Exchange of toasts, **1959:** 100, 105

Letter, **1958:** 79

Message, **1953:** 7

Remarks of welcome, **1959:** 99

Bauer, Dr. Louis H., **1953:** 29

Bausch & Lomb scholarship award, **1958:** 141

Bauxite imports, **1958:** 58, 96; **1959:** 55

Baxter, James Phinney, **1956:** 3d, 265

Bayar, Celal, **1954:** 18; **1955:** 89; **1957:** 49; **1959:** 295, 298

Exchange of toasts, **1954:** 20, 23

Joint statement with, **1959:** 297

Legion of Merit, citation, **1954:** 20

Letter, **1958:** 174

Message, **1959:** 282

Remarks of welcome, **1954:** 19

Toast to, **1959:** 296

Bayar, Madame, **1954:** 18, 19, 20, 23

Baylor University, **1956:** 121

Commencement, **1956:** 114

Beach, Comdr. Edward L., **1953:** 229n., 254 ftn. (p. 800); **1954:** 8n.; **1955:** 183, 188; **1956:** 208n.

Legion of Merit citation, **1960–61:** 142

Beach erosion control, **1956:** 12 (pp. 134, 135)

Beach erosion projects, **1958:** 155

Beale, Betty, **1956:** 47

Beale, W. L., Jr., **1953:** 126

Beall, Senator J. Glenn, **1957:** 231 and n.; **1958:** 123, 308

Beam, Jacob, **1958:** 261

Bear Mountain State Park, N.Y., **1960–61:** 173

Beard, Dr. George Miller, **1959:** 129

Beardsley, Gov. William S., **1954:** 226

Death of, statement, **1954:** 339

Beardsley, Mrs. William S., **1954:** 339

Beaudoin, Louis, **1953:** 246n.

Beaulac, Willard L., **1960–61:** 56n., 57n.

Beck, Dave, telegram, **1955:** 232; **1957:** 50, 87

Beckley, Mrs. Dorothy, **1956:** 241

Beckley, Harold, death of, **1955:** 62

Beckum, Millard, **1960–61:** 396n.

Beebe, Brig. Gen. R. E., **1953:** 71

Beef

Consumption, **1953:** 30, 216, 230

News conference remarks, **1953:** 12, 230, 249

Prices, **1953:** 12, 249

Beeson, Albert C., nomination to National Labor Relations Board, **1954:** 25

Beirut, Lebanon, **1958:** 173, 174n.

Belair, Felix, Jr., **1953:** 31; **1958:** 37, 83, 88, 222; **1959:** 42, 53, 102, 132, 173, 179, 191, 243, 267, 271; **1960–61:** 7, 21, 24, 34, 38, 93, 143, 222, 228, 256, 263, 268, 362

Belgium, **1954:** 84n.; **1955:** 54n., 112 ftn. (p. 548); **1959:** 214; **1960–61:** 216, 256

Agreement with U.S. on civil uses of atomic energy, **1954:** 260; **1955:** 123

Baudouin I

See main heading, Baudouin I.

Brussels, **1959:** 100

Brussels Universal and International Exhibition, 1958, **1958:** 79

Euratom.

See European Atomic Energy Community.

European Defense Community Treaty, ratification, statement, **1954:** 52

King Leopold, **1957:** 153 and n.

Passchendaele, **1959:** 7

Storm disaster, **1953:** 7

Visit of Prince Albert and Princess Paola to U.S., **1960–61:** 317

Ypres, **1959:** 7

Zan Acker, Achille, **1957:** 153 and n.

Bell, Daniel W., **1953:** 22 and ftn. (p. 86)

Bell, Jack L., **1953:** 62; **1954:** 25, 39; **1956:** 47; **1958:** 74; **1960–61:** 256, 263, 268

Bell, Repr. John J., **1955:** 95

Bell Telephone Laboratory, Holmdel, N.J., **1960–61:** 258n.

Beltran, Pedro G., **1960–61:** 247

Ben Slimane (Boulhaut), U.S. air base, Morocco, withdrawal from, **1959:** 345

Bender, Repr. George H., **1954:** 317

Bender, Sen. George H., **1956:** 224, 229

Ben-Gurion, David, **1956:** 276; **1957:** 34, 35 and n., 62

Letter to, **1957:** 40

Message, **1956:** 295

Bennett, James V., Award for Distinguished Federal Civilian Service, **1959:** 9n.

Bennett, Richard Bedford, **1959:** 141

Bennett, Sen. Wallace F., **1955:** 119; **1960–61:** 167

Benson, Ezra Taft.

See Agriculture, Secretary of.

Bentley, Elizabeth T., **1953:** 243

Berckemeyer, Fernando, **1959:** 244n.
Bering Sea, **1958:** 201
    U.S. plane accident, **1955:** 146
Berkner (Lloyd) Panel on Seismic Improvement,
    1959: 132 and ftn. (p. 463); **1960–61:** 143
    ftn. (p. 410)
Berlin, Germany, **1956:** 26, 58, 125; **1957:** 134;
    1959: 6, 67 ftn. (p. 292), 71, 190, 214;
    1960–61: 23, 302
    Allied policy on, **1960–61:** 38, 93
    Anti-Communist uprisings in East Berlin, **1953:**
        109, 130, 146, 159
      Message to Chancellor Adenauer, **1953:** 121
    Assistance, statement, **1953:** 113; **1955:** 76
    Blockade, **1958:** 207; **1959:** 57, 167
    Broadcasts on, **1959:** 57, 196
    Camp David discussions, **1959:** 271
    Campaign remarks, **1960–61:** 348, 355
    Communist threat to West Berlin, **1960–61:** 24,
        127, 222, 256, 348, 410
    Corridor proposal, rumor of, **1959:** 186
    Declaration of North Atlantic Council (1958),
        1959: 336
    Economic assistance, **1959:** 55
    Employment, **1953:** 185
    Five-year interim agreement on, **1959:** 172
    Flight ceilings, **1960–61:** 93
    Food shortage in East Berlin, **1953:** 135 and n.,
        141, 159, 185, 188
    Foreign ministers meeting, **1954:** 18, 25, 39, 128,
        225, 297, 314
    Four-power council (1945), **1953:** 128
    Imprisoned workers in East Berlin, U.S. position
        on, **1953:** 130
    Information withheld from press by U.S. offi-
        cials, **1960–61:** 7
    Joint statements with
      Chancellor Adenauer, **1959:** 192; **1960–61:** 92
      Premier Khrushchev, **1959:** 242
      President de Gaulle, **1959:** 202
      Western leaders, **1959:** 336
    Letter to George Meany re, **1959:** 163
    Mayor Brandt of West Berlin, **1959:** 195
    Mayor Ernst Reuter, **1953:** 185, 197
    Message to K. E. Voroshilov re, **1959:** 1
    Negotiations on, **1959:** 243
    News conference remarks, **1953:** 109, 128, 141;
        1955: 33; **1959:** 17, 21, 26, 29, 36, 42, 48,
        53, 89, 123, 132, 148, 154, 161, 167, 172,
        186, 191, 223, 243, 271; **1960–61:** 7, 24, 38,
        93, 127, 222, 256
    Refugees in, **1953:** 53
    Secretary Dulles report, **1959:** 29
    Soviet inspection of U.S. army truck convoy,
        1959: 26
    Summary of events leading to division, **1958:** 318
    Western rights in, **1959:** 36, 123, 172; **1960–61:**
        93

Berlin, N.H., remarks at Hansen Ski Jump area,
    1955: 139
Bermuda, **1957:** 52n.
    Field hockey team, **1960–61:** 319n.
    Governor, Lt. Gen. Sir John Woodall, **1957:** 53n.
Bermuda Conference with Prime Minister
    Macmillan, **1957:** 53
    Joint statement, **1957:** 55
    News conference remarks, **1957:** 28, 50, 56, 70,
        72
Bermuda Meeting of Western leaders, **1953:** 95,
    256
    Joint statement, **1953:** 255
    News conference remarks, **1953:** 88, 126, 198,
        243, 249, 254, 265
    Postponement, message to Prime Minister
        Churchill, **1953:** 123
    Statement, **1953:** 85
Bernalillo County, N. Mex., payments for hospi-
    talization of Indians, disapproval, **1960–**
    61: 235
Berney, E. S. relief of, disapproval, **1954:** 242
Bernhard, Prince, **1953:** 53
Berry, Repr. E. Y., **1953:** 101
Berry, Walter H., veto of bill for relief of, **1957:** 155
Berwind, Charles G., **1960–61:** 404n.
Betancourt, Romulo, (President of Venezuela),
    1956: 323; **1959:** 44; **1960–61:** 122, 267
Bethlehem Steel Corporation, **1959:** 211n.
Beverley, Marshall, **1956:** 241
Beverly Hills, Calif., **1956:** 258
Bevis, Howard L., **1956:** 77; **1957:** 241; **1958:** 327
Bhumibol Adulyadei, **1960–61:** 209
    Exchange of toasts, **1960–61:** 213
    Joint statement with, **1960–61:** 218
    Legion of Merit citation, **1960–61:** 212
    Remarks of welcome, **1960–61:** 211
Big Brother of the Year Award, acceptance,
    remarks, **1960–61:** 404
Big Dam Foolishness (Peterson), **1955:** 56
Big Four Conference.
    See Heads of state and governments, meeting.
Bilbo, Theodore G., **1953:** 37
Bill of Rights, **1954:** 72; **1956:** 241; **1957:** 56; **1958:**
    285; **1959:** 151; **1960–61:** 127
    News conference remarks, **1955:** 56, 59
Bill of Rights Day, statement, **1955:** 249
Billboards along Federal highways, **1957:** 72, 169;
    1958: 77
    Letter to Maj. Gen. U.S. Grant, 3d, **1958:** 14
Bingham, Hiram, **1955:** 10
Binns, Joseph P., **1954:** 12n.
Biology, use of atomic energy, **1957:** 231
Bipartisan action, **1955:** 185
    Foreign affairs and national defense, **1955:** 248
    Report on Geneva heads of government con-
        ference, **1955:** 174

Bipartisan Commission on Civil Rights, **1957:** 8, 133
  Stanley F. Reed, withdrawal from, **1957:** 242 and n.
Bipartisan Commission on Foreign Economic Policy, **1957:** 32
Bipartisan conferences, **1954:** 337, 347, 351; **1957:** 2
  Domestic legislative programs, White House statement, **1956:** 318
  Foreign affairs, news conference remarks, **1956:** 62
  Suez Canal, White House statement, **1956:** 184
Bipartisan support of program, comment on, **1954:** 33
Bipartisanship in foreign affairs, **1953:** 6, 249; **1954:** 92, 107, 209, 273, 316, 320; **1960–61:** 7, 103, 268
Birely, Victor M., **1959:** 31n.
Birley, Oswald, **1954:** 167
Birth control information, distribution by Government, comment on, **1959:** 288
Birthday, the President's, **1953:** 211, 212; **1958:** 320; **1960–61:** 284
  Campaign remarks, **1956:** 241
  Celebrations, **1957:** 214, 215; **1958:** 287
  Tree-planting ceremony, remarks, **1960–61:** 325
  TV program on eve of, remarks, **1956:** 242
Birthplace of the President, Texas, **1956:** 293; **1959:** 179, 186
Bisar, Mohamed, **1957:** 120 and n.
Bismarck, Otto von, **1953:** 187
Black, Eugene R., **1960–61:** 284, 297
Black, James B., **1953:** 33n.
Black market, **1959:** 17
Blaik, Earl, comment on, **1959:** 7
Blair, William M., **1954:** 138, 161, 168, 192, 311, 328; **1955:** 62, 90, 95, 119, 176; **1956:** 78; **1959:** 123, 167
Blake, Robert O., **1959:** 328n.
Blankenship, R. B., **1956:** 226
Blaushild, David, **1958:** 83
Bleak, David B., Medal of Honor award, **1953:** 122, 299n.
Bleriot, Louis, **1960–61:** 100
Blind persons, **1954:** 14 (p. 153); **1956:** 21, 158
  Budget messages, **1956:** 12 (p. 118); **1960–61:** 13 (p. 95), 414 (p. 1010)
  Federal aid, **1960–61:** 127 ftn. (p. 362), 410
  Medical care, **1955:** 25
  Services of Post Office Department, **1955:** 9
Bliss, Ray C, **1956:** 224n.
Block, Joseph L., **1959:** 211n.
Blockade, theory of, comment on, **1954:** 345
Blood Program, National, **1953:** 4
Bloomingdale Bros., Inc., **1953:** 208
Blough, Roger M., **1958:** 120; **1959:** 211n.; **1960–61:** 7
Bluecher, Franz, **1955:** 208n.

Blum, David, **1960–61:** 290
Blumenthal, Hermann, **1955:** 22n.
B'nai B'rith, Anti-Defamation League, **1954:** 18
  40th anniversary, remarks, **1953:** 252
Board of Inquiry on labor dispute at atomic energy facilities, **1957:** 88
Bogota, Colombia, **1956:** 75n.; **1958:** 137
  OAS economic conference, **1960–61:** 228 and ftn. (p. 569), 255, 256
Boggs, Gov. J. Caleb, **1960–61:** 208
Bohlen, Charles E., **1953:** 22, 31, 37, 41, 265; **1954:** 328, 345, 353; **1955:** 146 ftn. (p. 644)
  Reassignment, comment on, **1959:** 161, 167
Bohr, Niels Henrik David, Atoms for Peace award, **1957:** 225
Boland, Frederick H., **1960–61:** 302n.
Boldocsky, Janos, **1954:** 182 ftn. (p. 678)
Bolivar, Simon, **1956:** 146
  Statue, **1959:** 44
Bolivia
  Assistance, **1955:** 17 (p. 129), 76
    Letter to President Paz Estenssoro, **1953:** 213
    Memorandum, **1953:** 206
    Visit of Milton S. Eisenhower, **1953:** 213
  Economic problems, **1958:** 103
  Time article on, **1959:** 89
Bolton, Repr. Frances P., **1960–61:** 350
Bomarc missile (anti-aircraft).
See Missiles.
Bombers, **1956:** 12 (p. 96); **1957:** 86, 230, 234
  See also Aircraft, military.
  News conference remarks, **1956:** 88, 94, 96, 113; **1957:** 17, 28, 119, 169
  Soviet, **1956:** 94
Bombing of Germany in World War II, **1957:** 28, 119
Bombing of Israeli Cabinet, **1957:** 228
Bombings of schools or churches, **1959:** 27; **1960–61:** 137
Bombing of synagogues and Jewish community centers, **1958:** 285, 288
Bombs, **1957:** 28
  See also Nuclear tests; Nuclear weapons.
  Atomic, **1953:** 12, 31, 256; **1954:** 25, 38, 57, 73, 89, 165, 341; **1956:** 16, 62, 78; **1957:** 105, 119, 145, 230, 244; **1959:** 132, 154; **1960–61:** 38
    See also main heading, Atomic Bomb.
  Clean, **1956:** 229; **1957:** 105, 119, 124, 150
  Clean and "dirty," **1958:** 70, 88
  Exchange of information with allies, **1958:** 83
  Hydrogen, **1953:** 198, 208, 256; **1954:** 57, 63, 72, 73, 89, 157, 165, 192, 341; **1958:** 21, 88, 296, 300; **1959:** 102, 132; **1960–61:** 422
    See also main heading, Hydrogen bomb.
  News conference remarks, **1955:** 33, 41, 47, 56; **1956:** 32, 53, 62, 229; **1958:** 70, 83, 88
Bonaparte, Napoleon, **1955:** 59, 118; **1956:** 84

Bond, Jay D., **1953:** 59
Bond, Virginia, relief of, veto, **1960–61:** 114
Bonds, Federal
   Interest rates, **1959:** 36, 123, 124, 126, 144n., 161,
      167, 179, 186, 223, 230, 231; **1960–61:** 6,
      13 (pp. 41, 42, 100, 101), 17, 133, 255, 414
      (p. 942), 423
   Long-term vs. short-term financing, **1959:** 186,
      223
   News conference remarks, **1959:** 36, 102, 123,
      161, 167, 179, 186, 223
   Purchase by Federal Reserve banks, **1959:** 124
   Treasury bonds, **1959:** 126, 188; **1960–61:** 6, 133,
      255, 414 (p. 942), 423
   Savings, **1953:** 189; **1954:** 14 (p. 187); **1955:** 186,
      187; **1958:** 43, 126, 188, 225, 230, 231
   School construction, **1956:** 8
   TVA construction, **1956:** 109; **1958:** 5 (p. 70)
Bonin, Repr. Edward J., **1954:** 341
Bonin Islands
   Compensation for displaced residents, **1960–61:**
      13 (p. 65)
   Joint statement with Prime Minister Kishi, **1957:**
      117
   Joint statement with Prime Minister Yoshida,
      1954: 330
Bonn, Germany, **1954:** 307; **1957:** 100; **1959:**
      192n.; **1960–61:** 91n., 362 ftn. (p. 864),
      365
   Conventions (1952), **1954:** 154, 189n., 332
   News conference in, **1959:** 191
   Remarks on arrival, **1959:** 190
   Visit to, remarks re, **1959:** 179, 214
Bonnell, Rev. John Sutherland, **1953:** 132
Bonnet, Henri, **1953:** 219; **1954:** 176n.
Bonnet, Madame, **1954:** 176n.
Bonneville Dam, **1960–61:** 419
Bonneville Power Administration, **1954:** 14 (p.
      168); **1956:** 12 (p. 136); **1959:** 10 (p. 95)
Bonsal, Philip W., **1960–61:** 22
   News conference remarks on, **1960–61:** 21, 103
"Book burning," comment on, **1953:** 109, 126
Books in U.S. libraries overseas, **1953:** 109, 126,
      128
Books for use abroad, **1956:** 12 (p. 108)
Boone, Iowa, **1956:** 212
Booth, Lt. Gen. Donald P., **1960–61:** 197
Boston, Mass., **1954:** 325; **1956:** 293; **1959:** 191 ftn.
      (p. 611); **1960–61:** 309n.
   Address, **1953:** 187
   Campaign remarks (via TV), **1956:** 292
   Tax protest, **1957:** 80
   Wage rates, **1960–61:** 230
Boston Tea Party, **1955:** 92; **1959:** 196
Boulder, Colo., dedication of National Bureau of
      Standards laboratories, **1954:** 267
Boulhaut, Morocco.
   See Ben Slimane.

Boundary and Water Commission, International,
      1959: 38; **1960–61:** 335
   Budget message, **1960–61:** 13 (p. 83), 414 (p. 996)
   United States and Mexico, **1953:** 222
Bourgholtzer, Frank, **1953:** 31; **1959:** 67, 161, 186,
      271; **1960–61:** 103
Bourguiba, Habib, **1958:** 74; **1959:** 328, 330
   Joint statement with, **1959:** 329
Boutwell, William A., tax refund claim, **1958:** 228
Bowie, Robert R., **1953:** 254 ftn. (p. 800); **1955:** 146
      ftn. (p. 644)
Bowles, Chester, *American Politics in a Revolu-*
      tionary World, **1956:** 171
Boxing incident, **1958:** 287
Boy Scout Week, **1955:** 28
Boy Scouts, **1955:** 28; **1956:** 122; **1957:** 203; **1958:**
      270, 307; **1959:** 156; **1960–61:** 153, 210
   43d anniversary, message, **1953:** 9
   50th anniversary, remarks, **1960–61:** 35, 166
   National Council, remarks, **1954:** 127
   National Jamboree, message, **1953:** 137
Boycotts, **1954:** 5; **1958:** 20, 216; **1959:** 6, 22, 176
Boys Nation, remarks to delegates, **1957:** 142
   News conference remarks, **1959:** 36, 89, 172, 179
Boyer, Col. C. M., letter, **1953:** 11
Braddock, Daniel M. (U.S. Charge d'Affaires ad
      interim of U.S. Embassy, Havana),
      1960–61: 388
Braden, Spruille, **1957:** 64n.
Bradley, Gen. Omar N., **1953:** 109 ftn. (p. 439);
      1955: 135; **1956:** 267n.; **1959:** 7; **1960–61:**
      135, 405
   Chairman, United Defense Fund, **1954:** 55, 93
   Letter, **1955:** 51
Bradley Commission, **1956:** 267
Bradley University, broadcast, **1956:** 214
Bragdon, Maj. Gen. John S., **1957:** 138; **1959:** 42
   Appointment as Special Assistant to the Pres-
      ident, **1955:** 203
   Coordinator of public works planning
   Interstate highway study, **1959:** 227; **1960–61:** 93
   Letter, **1956:** 309
   News conference remarks on, **1956:** 16
Brandon, O. Henry, **1956:** 189
Brandt, Raymond P., **1953:** 12, 15, 31, 77, 88, 109,
      126, 198, 243; **1954:** 9, 18, 73, 101, 107,
      138, 165, 168, 172, 182, 192, 311, 322, 328,
      353; **1955:** 26, 41, 47, 56, 59, 62, 81, 95;
      1956: 16, 47, 56, 88, 113, 155, 171, 205,
      216, 229, 235, 298; **1957:** 17, 28, 45, 50, 56,
      62, 70, 92, 105, 124, 145, 157, 207, 210,
      228; **1958:** 11, 28, 37, 56, 63, 74, 103, 141,
      153, 274; **1959:** 17, 21, 26, 29, 36, 53, 67,
      123, 132, 148, 154, 161, 167, 172, 186, 223,
      243, 288; **1960–61:** 7, 21, 38, 143, 222, 268,
      422
Brandt, Willy, message, **1959:** 195

Brannan (Charles F.) plan, **1954:** 172; **1956:** 224; **1958:** 56

Branscomb, Harvie, **1953:** 230

Brasilia, Brazil, **1958:** 197; **1960–61:** 42n., 49, 55
Inauguration as new capital, message to President Kubitschek, **1960–61:** 119
Joint statement with President Kubitschek, **1960–61:** 46
Remarks at civic reception, **1960–61:** 45

Brazil, **1955:** 112 ftn. (p. 548); **1959:** 89
Airplane collision over Guanabara Bay, **1960–61:** 55, 64
Assistance, **1960–61:** 49, 53
Atomic research agreement, **1955:** 121
Brasilia.
See main heading, Brasilia, Brazil.
Ceremonies honoring dead of World War II, **1960–61:** 379
Goulart, Joao, **1960–61:** 49n.
Kubitschek de Oliveira, Juscelino, **1958:** 133, 181, 197, 319; **1959:** 287; **1960–61:** 45, 48, 49n., 50, 51, 53, 54, 55, 87, 228
Joint statement with, **1960–61:** 46
Messages, **1960–61:** 64, 119, 379
Lafer, Horacio, **1960–61:** 46n.
Muniz, Joao Carlos, **1956:** 273, 274
Rio de Janeiro.
See main heading, Rio de Janeiro.
Sao Paulo.
See main heading, Sao Paulo.
Trade with U.S., **1960–61:** 54
U.S. Ambassador John M. Cabot, **1960–61:** 45n.
U. S. mission, **1956:** 20
U.S. price increase on Brazilian coffee, **1954:** 39
Visit to, **1960–61:** 42, 45, 46, 48, 49, 50, 51, 52, 53, 54, 55, 87, 119

Brennan, John William, **1957:** 73

Brennan, Mrs. John William, veto of bill for relief of, **1957:** 73

Brennan, William J., Jr., **1957:** 28

Brenner Pass, **1956:** 113

Brentano, Heinrich von, **1956:** 20

Brenton, W. Harold, **1953:** 189n.

Bretton Woods Agreements Act, **1959:** 32

Breuninger, Lewis T., **1959:** 127n.

Bricker, Sen. John W., **1953:** 215, 269; **1955:** 59; **1956:** 78, 224; **1957:** 50; **1958:** 310
Amendment, **1953:** 31, 37, 126; **1954:** 9, 18, 25, 33, 48, 50, 168, 353; **1955:** 59, 81; **1956:** 53, 56, 78, 96; **1957:** 50; **1958:** 310
News conference remarks on, **1953:** 31, 126

Bridge commissions
Muscatine commission, **1956:** 148, 182
Ohio River commission, disapproval, **1956:** 182
White County commission, investigation, **1956:** 182

Bridges, Sen. Styles, **1953:** 37, 187; **1955:** 134, 135, 139; **1958:** 63

Bridges, Sen. Styles — *continued*
Bipartisan meeting on Suez Canal, **1956:** 184
Investigation of report of Communist infiltration into Italian aircraft plants, **1954:** 39
Letter, **1953:** 143
News conference remarks on, **1956:** 78, 216

Bridwell, Lowell K., **1959:** 94; **1960–61:** 93

Briggs, Ellis O., **1953:** 141; **1959:** 324n., 327

Briggs, Maj. Gen. James E., **1959:** 109

Briscoe, Vice Adm. Robert P., **1953:** 159

Bristow, Joseph L., **1960–61:** 18
Appointment of Dwight D. Eisenhower to Military Academy, **1956:** 241

British Commonwealth, **1959:** 198

British Empire Service League, **1955:** 119

British Open Golf Championship, **1953:** 140n.

British West Indies, **1958:** 208

Broadcasting media, deceptive practices, letter to Attorney General Rogers, **1960–61:** 1

Broadcasts
American people.
See Messages to the American people.
Interviews with Communist leaders, **1957:** 105, 124
Leaving New Delhi, **1959:** 318
Prime Minister Macmillan, **1959:** 196

Bronk, Detlev W., **1955:** 191n.; **1959:** 107

Brookhaven Medical Center, nuclear reactor for medical research, **1959:** 10 (p. 68)

Brooklyn, New York, **1957:** 184

Brooks, George, **1954:** 231

Brooks, Repr. Overton, **1954:** 120n.; **1955:** 100

Bronzini, Todoro, **1960–61:** 61n.

Brookhaven National Laboratory, **1960–61:** 13 (p. 59), 414 (p. 959)

Brose, Lambert, **1959:** 123, 154, 172, 186, 223; **1960–61:** 34, 38, 263

Brosio, Manlio, **1955:** 61; **1959:** 294n.

Brossard, Edgar B. (Chairman, Tariff Commission), **1953:** 131

Brotherhood Week, **1955:** 40

Brotzman, Donald G., **1956:** 259

Brown, Repr. Clarence J., **1953:** 238; **1954:** 12n.; **1959:** 77n.

Brown, Edgar A., **1954:** 311

Brown, George R., **1960–61:** 336

Brown, John R., **1955:** 112

Brown, R. Fay, **1953:** 100n.

Brown, Bishop Robert B., **1957:** 207, 228

Brown, Mrs. Rollin, **1960–61:** 100

Brown Swiss Dairy Cattle Association, remarks, **1955:** 131

Browne, Mary M., tax refund claim, **1958:** 230

Brownell, Herbert, Jr.
See Attorney General.

Brownell, Mrs. Herbert, Jr., **1957:** 224n.

Brownell, Samuel M., **1955:** 96

Brownlee, James Forbis, posthumous citation,
    1960–61: 377
Brownlee, Mrs. James Forbis, **1960–61:** 277n.
Brownsville, Tex., **1959:** 250
Broyhill, Repr. Joel T., **1954:** 313; **1958:** 198
Bruce, David K. E., **1953:** 111n.; **1954:** 107
Bruce, Preston (White House usher and son), **1958:**
    88
Brucellosis control, **1955:** 17 (p. 155); **1956:** 72, 83;
    1958: 59
Bruces Eddy reservoir, Idaho, **1956:** 12 (p. 136)
Brucker, Wilber M.
    See Army, Secretary of.
Brundage, Percival F.
    See Budget, Bureau of the, Director.
Brundage, Mrs. Percival F., **1958:** 46
Brunsdale, Gov. Norman, **1953:** 100
Brussels compact, **1956:** 114
Brussels Treaty, **1954:** 332; **1955:** 54
Brussels Universal and International Exhibition,
    1958, **1958:** 5 (p. 41), 79; **1959:** 100
Bryan, Maj. Gen. Blackshear M., **1955:** 117, 118
Bryan, D. Tennant, **1959:** 274n.
Bryce, James, **1959:** 129
Bryson, Lyman, **1954:** 128n.
Buchanan, James, **1958:** 209
Buchanan, Scott, **1959:** 116
Buchanan, Wiley T., Jr., **1957:** 106n.
Buck Rogers cartoon, **1958:** 295
Buckley, Repr. Charles A., letter, **1958:** 190
Budapest, Hungary, **1957:** 15
Buddhist Synod, **1955:** 148
Budget, **1953:** 6, 30, 84, 95, 98, 187; **1954:** 21; **1959:**
        43, 63, 83, 129, 144n., 188, 225, 244;
        1960–61: 19, 133, 174, 415
    Campaign remarks, **1958:** 293, 295
    Fiscal 1954, **1953:** 82, 83, 84, 159
        News conference remarks, **1953:** 12, 15, 31, 62
        Review, **1954:** 169
        White House release, **1953:** 12 ftn. (p. 53)
    Fiscal 1955, **1953:** 266; **1954:** 3
        Annual message, **1954:** 14
        Comparison with previous administration,
            1954: 18
        News conference remarks, **1954:** 18, 192, 347
        Tables, **1954:** 14 (pp. 82, 84, 85, 101, 102,
            104–106, 107, 109–116, 120, 121, 125, 131,
            135–137, 141, 145, 147, 152, 156, 157, 165,
            172, 177, 179, 183, 185, 186, 191)
    Fiscal 1956, **1955:** 247
        Annual message, **1955:** 17
        News conference remarks, **1955:** 18, 41, 112
        Tables, **1955:** 17 (pp. 89, 90, 96, 102.105, 107,
            110, 111, 115, 123, 127, 135, 140, 142, 146,
            151, 157, 165, 166, 178, 180, 184)
    Fiscal 1957, **1955:** 247; **1956:** 2, 3, 58, 226, 318
        Annual message, **1956:** 12
        Meeting on, **1956:** 318

Budget — *continued*
    Fiscal 1957 — *continued*
        News conference remarks, **1956:** 20, 113
        Tables, **1956:** 12 (pp. 75, 81, 82, 85, 87–90, 92)
    Fiscal 1958, **1956:** 318; **1959:** 48
        Messages, **1957:** 13, 75, 80, 86
        News conference remarks, **1957:** 17, 45, 50, 56,
            62, 70, 72, 80, 87, 92, 105, 169, 207, 228
    Fiscal 1959, **1958:** 2
        Annual message, **1958:** 5
        News conference remarks, **1957:** 87, 169;
            1958: 11, 37, 74, 222, 288
        Tables, **1958:** 5 (pp. 18, 24, 25, 26, 28, 34, 37,
            41, 47, 54, 62, 64, 69, 70, 72)
    Fiscal 1960, **1959:** 6, 15, 225, 300n.; **1960–61:** 222
        Annual message, **1959:** 10
        Broadcast, **1959:** 11
        Criticism of, **1959:** 17
        News conference remarks, **1958:** 153, 222;
            1959: 7, 17, 42, 48, 148
        Statement, **1958:** 324
        Surplus, **1960–61:** 237
        Tables, **1959:** 10 (pp. 40–42, 45–47, 50, 55, 56,
            70, 72, 76, 81, 90, 93, 97, 102, 103, 106,
            108, 109)
        Unbalance for political reasons, **1959:** 48
    Fiscal 1961, **1959:** 288, 300n.; **1960–61:** 4, 17,
            133, 255n.
        Annual message, **1960–61:** 13
        News conference remarks, **1960–61:** 7, 34, 222
        Tables, **1960–61:** 13 (pp. 42, 44–47, 61, 62, 67,
            78, 84, 88, 98, 101, 102, 109)
    Fiscal 1962, **1960–61:** 410, 422
        Annual message, **1960–61:** 414
        Tables, **1960–61:** 414 (pp. 940, 941, 943, 947,
            948, 963, 964, 971, 986, 994, 1000, 1001,
            1014, 1016, 1018)
    News conference remarks, **1953:** 31, 208, 249;
            1959: 36, 53, 102, 288; **1960–61:** 34, 222,
            256
Budget, Bureau of the, **1953:** 12 ftn. (p. 54), 55, 228;
        1955: 222; **1960–61:** 376
    Assistant Director for Accounting, **1956:** 89n.
    Budget and accounting practices, **1956:** 89
    Budget message, **1954:** 14 (p. 84); **1958:** 5 (p. 32);
            1959: 10 (pp. 53, 54); **1960–61:** 13 (p. 102)
    Career and political Government personnel,
            tasks, **1956:** 22
    Dixon-Yates contract, **1955:** 146, 149
    Employment of Adolphe Wenzell, **1955:** 146 and
            ftn. (pp. 657, 658)
    Expansion, **1956:** 89n.
    Farm lands for lease by Federal agencies, **1956:**
            111
    Findings on operation of Panama Steamship
            Line, **1960–61:** 382
    Hungarian refugees, funds for, **1956:** 307

Budget, Bureau of the — *continued*
Interagency cooperation in aviation matters, analysis, **1959:** 74
Jones, Roger W., Award for Distinguished Federal Civilian Service, **1958:** 13
Memorandum on conduct of Government employees, **1954:** 311
News conference remarks, **1957:**2
Office of Accounting, **1957:** 13
Report, **1960–61:** 406
Small business report and statistics, **1957:** 132
Staats, Elmer B., **1959:** 18n.
Water resources, report, **1956:** 13
Development projects, standards and procedures review, **1953:** 153
Budget, Bureau of the, Director (Percival F. Brundage), **1956:** 100; **1957:** 138, 207; **1958:** 43
Advisory Council on Federal Reports, **1956:** 110
Airways Modernization Board, **1957:** 71
Aviation facilities planning, **1956:** 38
Budget and accounting, letter, **1956:** 89
Government reporting requirements, letter, **1956:** 110
Memorandum on Hoover Commission recommendations, **1957:** 112 and n.
Resignation, **1958:** 46
Staff Office of Accounting, **1956:** 89n.
Budget, Bureau of the, Director (Joseph M. Dodge), **1953:** 12 ftn. (p. 53), 15, 57, 95, 136, 266
See also Dodge, Joseph M..
Agricultural commodities for Bolivian relief, memorandum, **1953:** 206
News conference remarks on, **1954:** 50, 68
Resignation, letter, **1954:** 65
Budget, Bureau of the, Director (Rowland R. Hughes), **1954:** 169, 348, 349, 351; **1955:** 74, 90 ftn. (p. 475), 146 ftns. (pp. 646, 657)
Death of, statement, **1957:** 65
Flood relief in Europe, memorandum, **1954:** 195
News conference remarks on, **1955:** 56, 176
Resignation, **1956:** 17
Budget, Bureau of the, Director (Maurice H. Stans), **1959:** 288; **1960–61:** 304
Government operations, reports, **1960–61:** 435
Interstate highway study, **1959:** 227
Letters, **1959:** 62, 74
Report on improvements in budgeting, **1959:** 300
Resignation, letter, **1960–61:** 406
Summary of effect of Congressional actions on 1960 budget, **1959:** 225n.
Summary of effect of congressional action on 1961 budget, **1960–61:** 255n.
Surplus budget details, **1960–61:** 237
Budget and accounting practices, **1956:** 100
Approval of bill, **1956:** 156
Hoover Commission report, letter, **1956:** 89

Budget policies, **1955:** 17 (pp. 88, 89); **1956:** 12 (pp. 77.79)
Budget system, improvements in, **1959:** 10 (pp. 53, 54)
Letter to Erwin D. Canham, **1959:** 300
Buencamino, Delfin, **1960–61:** 224
Buenos Aires, **1960–61:** 42n., 61
Address to Congress of Argentina, **1960–61:** 58
Mayor Herman M. Giralt, **1960–61:** 57n.
Remarks on arrival, **1960–61:** 56
Remarks to Supreme Court, **1960–61:** 60
Remarks at U.S. embassy, **1960–61:** 57
Toast to President Frondizi, **1960–61:** 59
Buenos Aires Economic Conference, **1957:** 157, 177; **1959:** 98
Buildings, Federal, **1959:** 10 (p. 108); **1960–61:** 13 (pp. 101, 102), 414 (pp. 1017, 1019)
See also Property, Federal.
Budget message, **1958:** 5 (p. 72), 70
Post Office, **1958:** 29, 33, 43, 49, 70, 110, 117
Bulganin, Nikolai A., **1955:** 161, 164, 166n.; **1956:** 287; **1957:** 3, 226; **1958:** 1, 165
Letter released in Moscow, **1956:** 291n.
Letters, **1955:** 220; **1956:** 23, 52, 166, 262, 291; **1958:** 7, 17, 31
News conference remarks on, **1955:** 62, 95, 146, 185; **1956:** 16, 32, 53, 56, 78, 88, 96; **1958:** 11, 28, 37
Visit, rumor of, **1956:** 88
Bulgaria
Compensation claims of U.S. nationals, **1954:** 94
Gueorgui Nadjakov, **1960–61:** 301n.
Bull Elephants Club, remarks, **1955:** 181
Bullis, Harry, letter, **1954:** 217
Bunche, Ralph, **1957:** 50
Bunker, Ellsworth, **1959:** 310n., 312, 313
Bunker Hill, Battle of, **1955:** 118
Bunn, Rev. Edward B., **1958:** 286
Burbank, Calif., **1958:** 257
Burd, Laurence H., **1953:** 12, 31, 62, 254; **1954:** 25, 50, 101, 115, 129, 200, 322; **1955:** 18, 33, 41, 62, 81, 90, 95, 112, 149; **1956:** 5, 16, 20, 32, 47, 53, 96, 121, 189, 198, 235; **1957:** 50, 62, 87, 150, 152, 157, 210; **1958:** 28, 37, 42, 63, 88, 198, 288, 310, 318; **1959:** 42, 67, 89, 123, 154, 179, 243, 267, 271, 288; **1960–61:** 24, 38, 127, 143, 222, 228, 256
Burdick, Eugene, *The Ugly American*, **1960–61:** 184
Burdine, Dr. Winston E., **1959:** 92
Bureau of Advertising.
See Advertising, Bureau of.
Bureau of Engraving and Printing.
See Engraving and Printing, Bureau of.
Bureau of Foreign Commerce.
See Foreign Commerce, Bureau of.
Bureau of Indian Affairs.
See Indian Affairs, Bureau of.
Bureau of Land Management.
See Land Management, Bureau of.

Bureau of Mines.
  See Mines, Bureau of.
Bureau of Public Roads.
  See Public Roads, Bureau of.
Bureau of Public Debt.
  See Public Debt, Bureau of.
Bureau of Reclamation.
  See Reclamation, Bureau of.
Bureaucracy, **1957:** 118
Burgess, Carter L., **1954:** 351, 353; **1957:** 104
Burgess, Randolph, **1957:** 102n.
Burke, Adm. Arleigh A., **1958:** 125; **1959:** 42
Burke, Comdr. Julian T., **1953:** 118
Burlap imports, **1958:** 58, 96
Burma
  Gift to children of U.S. veterans, **1955:** 169
  Gift to the President, **1956:** 60
  Nu (U), **1955:** 146, 148, 169
  Rangoon, **1955:** 148
Burnham, David B., **1958:** 222
Burns, Arthur F., **1954:** 107, 129
  See also Council of Economic Advisers, Chair-
    man (Arthur F. Burns).
Burns, Maj. Gen. Eedson L. M., **1956:** 26
Burton, Harold H., retirement, letter, **1958:** 279
Burton, Mrs. Harold H., **1958:** 279
Bush, Sen. Prescott, **1956:** 272; **1957:** 87; **1960–61:**
    127
Bush, Vannevar, **1954:** 311 **1957:** 87, 228; **1960–61:**
    132
Business
  Action to aid economy, **1958:** 110
  News conference remarks, **1958:** 63, 103, 120,
    198, 213
  Responsibility re inflation, **1956:** 298; **1957:** 8,
    16, 119, 124
  Responsibility for wage-price stability, **1958:** 16,
    63, 103, 120, 198, 213, 303, 308; **1959:** 15,
    17, 67, 123
Business Advisory Council, **1953:** 31; **1960–61:** 13
    (p. 64)
  Recommendation on wage-price increases, **1958:**
    103
  Remarks, **1953:** 30
Business cycles, **1958:** 296
Business and Defense Services Administration,
    1954: 14 (p. 181)
Business Economics, Office of, **1954:** 14 (p. 181)
Business leaders and Government positions, **1957:**
    145
Business loans, **1955:** 17 (pp. 176, 177)
  RFC program, liquidation, **1954:** 14 (p. 181)
  Small business loans, **1954:** 14 (p. 181)
Business magazine editors, remarks to, **1959:** 124
Businessmen in Government, **1956:** 241
Butler, Sen. Hugh, **1953:** 268
Butler, Sen. John M., **1957:** 210; **1958:** 83, 308
Butler, Karl D., **1956:** 187n.

Butler, Paul, **1954:** 347; **1959:** 161; **1960–61:** 93
Butler, Richard Austen, **1953:** 128
Butler University, **1954:** 291
Butter
  Consumption, **1954:** 165
  Prices, **1953:** 41
  Price supports, **1954:** 25, 39, 143, 165
  Surpluses, **1953:** 12, 41, 109; **1954:** 25, 39, 50
  Surplus disposal, **1956:** 6
Butterfat, price supports, **1960–61:** 295
Butz, Earl L.
  See Agriculture, Department of.
"Buy," to stimulate economy
  News conference remarks, **1958:** 37, 56, 70, 83
  Question of President's purchases, **1958:** 83
Buy American Act, **1953:** 54; **1954:** 67, 115;
    1960–61: 13 (p. 50)
  Applicability to spun silk yarn for cartridge
    cloth, **1955:** 155
  Memorandum, **1955:** 67
  Requirement for foreign aid, **1959:** 267, 271
Buzzanca, Sam J., relief of, disapproval, **1960–61:**
    226
Byer, George H., **1960–61:** 178
Byg, Mrs. Violet, **1956:** 268
Byrd, Sen. Harry Flood, **1953:** 78; **1954:** 115; **1955:**
    81, 90 ftn. (p. 471); **1956:** 280; **1957:** 56,
    80, 92; **1959:** 138; **1960–61:** 340
  Government spending, **1959:** 67
Byrd, Rear Admiral Richard E., statement on
    death of, **1957:** 47 and n.
Byrnes, Gov. James F., **1953:** 15; **1954:** 115, 164;
    1955: 73
Byroade, Henry A., **1959:** 306n.

Cabbages for unemployed coal miners, **1959:** 67
    and ftn. (p. 297)
Cabell, Lt. Gen. C. P., **1956:** 197
Cabell, Royal E., Jr., **1956:** 280
Cabinet, **1960–61:** 246, 309
  Meetings with Republican congressional leaders
    and chairmen of standing committees,
    1953: 266, 268, 269
  Members, pay adjustments, **1958:** 169
  Report of Secretary Dulles on negotiations in
    Europe, **1954:** 307
  Role of, **1953:** 68, 101
Cabinet Committee on Minerals Policy, estab-
    lishment, **1953:** 228
Cabinet Committee on Price Stability for Econom-
    ic Growth, report, statement, **1960–61:**
    117
Cabinet Committee on Small Business, **1957:** 13
  Budget message, **1958:** 5 (p. 23)
  Recommendations, **1957:** 132 and n.
Cabinet Committee on Water Resources Policy,
    1957: 8

Cabot, John M., **1953:** 48, 213n.; **1960–61:** 45n.
Caccia, Sir Harold, **1957:** 44
Caesar, Claudia V., **1958:** 245
Caesar, George P. E., Jr., tax refund claim, **1958:** 245
Caesar, Julius, **1955:** 118; **1959:** 100
Caffery, Jefferson, **1955:** 47; **1956:** 65
Cain, Harry P., **1956:** 96, 113, 155
  Criticism of Government employee security program, **1955:** 18
Cairo, Egypt, **1956:** 205, 235; **1957:** 70, 72
  Afro-Asian Conference, **1958:** 31
California, **1954:** 39; **1956:** 84, 193, 206
  Allen, Repr. John J., Jr., **1958:** 294
  Beverly Hills, **1956:** 258
  Burbank, **1956:** 257
  Campaign remarks, **1958:** 294
  Candidates for public office, **1956:** 258; **1958:** 288, 292, 294
  Central Valley Project, San Luis Unit, approval, **1960–61:** 168
  Chula Vista, **1960–61:** 333n.
  Condon, Repr. Robert L., **1954:** 18
  Cypress Point, **1956:** 191n.
  Edwards Air Force Base, **1958:** 314n.
  Goldstone, **1960–61:** 258n.
  Gubser, Repr. Charles S., **1954:** 161; **1958:** 294
  Hanford, **1954:** 14 (p. 128)
  Hillings, Repr. Patrick J., **1958:** 292, 294
  Holifield, Repr. Chet, **1954:** 12n.
  Hollywood, **1956:** 242n.
  Knight, Gov. Goodwin J., **1954:** 274; **1956:** 188, 189, 258; **1958:** 288, 292, 294
  Knowland, Sen. William F., **1953:** 31, 126, 142, 230; **1954:** 9, 33, 48, 129, 157, 161, 168, 172, 273, 274, 341, 345; **1955:** 26, 41, 59; **1956:** 16, 20, 56, 78, 184, 189; **1957:** 28, 87, 92, 157; **1958:** 36, 42, 43, 83, 85, 221, 288, 292, 294
  Kuchel, Sen. Thomas H., **1954:** 273; **1956:** 189, 258; **1960–61:** 333
  La Quinta, **1959:** 249n., 250n.
  Los Angeles, **1954:** 273, 274, 275; **1958:** 71, 288, 292, 305; **1960–61:** 23
  Mailliard, Repr. William S., **1958:** 294
  Newport Harbor, **1953:** 137n.
  Palm Springs, **1960–61:** 331n.
  Primary election, **1956:** 47
  Sacramento, **1959:** 270
  San Diego, **1960–61:** 333
  San Francisco, **1954:** 14 (p. 134); **1955:** 47, 81, 112, 126, 131, 156; **1956:** 143, 188, 189, 190, 193; **1958:** 7, 45n., 288, 293, 294; **1959:** 24, 89; **1960–61:** 332
  Utt, Repr. James B., **1960–61:** 333
  Warren, Gov. Earl, **1953:** 109 ftn. (p. 439), 198
  Wilson, Repr. Bob, **1960–61:** 333
  Younger, Repr. J. Arthur, **1958:** 294

California and Oregon Railroad grant lands, **1954:** 152
Calumet-Sag Waterway, Ill., **1955:** 17 (p. 169)
Cambodia, **1960–61:** 422
  Assistance, **1955:** 17 (p. 129); **1959:** 55
  Communist aggression in, **1954:** 280
  Indochina war, U.S. assistance, **1953:** 66
  Joint statement with Western leaders, **1953:** 255
  Membership in defense alliance, question of, **1954:** 107
  News conference remarks, **1954:** 101, 107, 168
  Norodom Sihanouk, message, **1954:** 280
  U.S. Ambassador Robert M. McClintock, **1954:** 280n.
Cambridge, England, **1956:** 102
Camden, N. J., **1958:** 11
Cameroun, Republic of, Charles Okala, **1960–61:** 324n.
Camp Blanding Military Reservation, Fla., conveyance of lands within, veto, **1954:** 121
Camp David, **1953:** 126; **1954:** 50, 192; **1960–61:** 102n., 296n.
  Discussions with President Lleras, **1960–61:** 111
  Editor's note, **1955:** p. 822
  Meeting with Premier Khrushchev, **1959:** 218, 223, 242, 271, 277; **1960–61:** 222
  Meeting with Prime Minister Macmillan, **1959:** 67; **1960–61:** 101, 103
  Meeting with President Lopez Mateos, **1959:** 257
  News conference remarks, **1959:** 67, 179, 223, 271, 277; **1960–61:** 24, 93, 103, 222
  "Spirit of Camp David," comment on, **1959:** 277; **1960–61:** 24
Camp Feldafing, **1955:** 115n.
Camp Kilmer, N. J., refugee reception center, **1956:** 301; **1957:** 25, 250
Campaign, election.
  See Election campaign.
Campbell, Boyd, letter, **1955:** 214
Campbell, Joseph, **1955:** 62; **1959:** 161
  Letter, **1959:** 342
Canada, **1955:** 43, 112 ftn. (p. 548); **1957:** 230; **1959:** 93n., 96n.; **1960–61:** 92
  Address before Parliament, **1953:** 246; **1958:** 163
  Agreement with U.S. on civil uses of atomic energy, **1954:** 260; **1955:** 123
  Air defense agreement, **1958:** 163
  Air Defense Command, **1959:** 10 (p. 61); **1960–61:** 13 (p. 54)
  Alberta, **1958:** 220
  Armed forces, **1958:** 163
  Armed forces in Korea, **1960–61:** 202
  Arms inspection, news conference remarks, **1957:** 87, 131
  Assistance to new nations, **1960–61:** 36
  Atomic energy for mutual defense, U.S. Canada agreement, **1959:** 119n., 120n.
  Beaudoin, Louis, **1953:** 246n.

Canada — *continued*
  Big Brothers of Canada, **1960–61:** 404n.
  Broadcast in London re, **1959:** 196
  Chamber of Commerce, remarks, **1954:** 338
  Civil Service Assembly of U.S. and, remarks, **1956:** 238
  Columbia River Basin development, **1960–61:** 410
    Treaty with U.S., **1960–61:** 331, 414 (p. 994), 416, 419
  Continental air defense, **1953:** 246, 247
  Diefenbaker, John, **1958:** 153, 163; **1959:** 125, 141, 196; **1960–61:** 171, 208, 331, 416
    Joint statement with, **1960–61:** 172
  Disarmament proposal, **1957:** 124, 158, 165, 208 and n., 210, 226, 244
  Distant early warning system, **1956:** 2
  Drouin, Mark, **1958:** 163
  Escapees settling in, **1953:** 257n.
  Gas from, **1959:** 288
  Great Lakes water level discussion, **1956:** 177
  Heeney, A. D. P., **1954:** 110n.
  Highways to, **1955:** 39
  International Boundary Commission, **1953:** 41
  International Joint Commission, **1954:** 165, 271
  Joint Committee on Trade and Economic Affairs, **1953:** 246, 247
  Massey, Vincent, **1954:** 101
  Meetings of U.S. and Canadian Cabinet members, **1958:** 153
  Michener, Roland, **1958:** 163
  Montreal, **1959:** 36, 141n.
  News conference remarks, **1953:** 22, 31, 41, 77, 208, 243; **1958:** 56, 153
  Niagara Falls project.
    See main heading Niagara Falls power project.
  Norman, E. H., **1957:** 70, 72
  Nuclear weapons, **1953:** 256
  Ogdensburg Declaration (1940), **1953:** 70, 247
  Oil, discussions on, **1959:** 51
  Ontario, **1953:** 22, 31, 77; **1959:** 141n.
  Ottawa, **1953:** 208, 246; **1959:** 141
  Pearson, Lester B., **1953:** 70, 104
  Permanent Joint Board on Defense, **1953:** 70, 246, 247
  Position on Great Lakes water diversion, **1954:** 253
  Prince Albert Radar Laboratory, Saskatchewan, **1959:** 125
  Robertson, Wishart, **1953:** 246n.
  Royal Canadian Air Force, **1954:** 159
  St. Laurent, Louis S., **1953:** 208, 246; **1956:** 53, 71
    Joint statements with, **1953:** 70, 247
  St. Lawrence River projects.
    See St. Lawrence power project; St. Lawrence Seaway project.
  Seed wheat from, **1958:** 217

Canada — *continued*
  Trade with, **1953:** 70; **1959:** 141
  United Community Campaigns, **1957:** 203
  U.S. relations with **1953:** 70, 246, 247; **1957:** 70; **1960–61:** 131, 171, 172
  U.S. tariffs on Canadian clover, **1954:** 172
  Visit to, **1953:** 208, 243
  Wheat for Pakistan relief, **1953:** 97
Canal Zone.
  See Panama Canal.
Canali, Paolo, **1955:** 61
Cancer, **1958:** 2
Candidacy of Earl Warren for President, **1956:** 20, 32
Candidacy for second term, the President's, **1953:** 15; **1954:** 9, 143, 192, 322, 347, 353; **1955:** 10, 47, 56, 62, 146, 149, 185; **1956:** 15, 84
  See also Election campaign.
  Announcement of, **1956:** 47, 48
  Attitude prior to illness, **1956:** 47
  Election victory remarks, **1956:** 294
  News conference remarks, **1956:** 5, 16, 20, 32, 47, 53, 94, 155
  Nomination, acceptance address, **1956:** 190
Candidacy for second term, the Vice President's
  Attitude of Stassen, **1956:** 155, 189
  Campaign remarks on, **1956:** 190, 206, 241, 258
  Close of election campaign, **1956:** 293, 294
  "Dump Nixon" rumor, **1956:** 53, 155
  News conference remarks, **1956:** 20, 47, 53, 56, 94, 155, 216, 229, 258
  To "chart own course," **1955:** 53, 56, 88
Candidates for Presidency
  Attitude of President on, **1959:** 42, 179
  Democratic, comment on, **1959:** 172
  News conference remarks, **1958:** 88, 222, 310; **1959:** 7, 42, 67, 94, 148, 154, 167, 172, 179
  President's role, **1959:** 7, 148, 167
  Question of religion, **1959:** 154
  Selection of, **1958:** 310
Candidates for public office, **1954:** 177; **1956:** 54; **1957:** 50, 56, 62, 72, 87, 92, 124, 150; **1960–61:** 93, 246, 278
  Campaign remarks, **1954:** 304, 317, 318, 319, 320; **1956:** 212, 214, 224, 226, 234, 249, 250, 251, 253, 255, 256, 258, 259, 272, 278, 280, 283, 292; **1958:** 292, 294, 302, 303, 306, 308; **1960–61:** 290, 309, 341, 344, 345, 346, 347, 348, 350, 353, 354, 355
  Equal time on radio and television, **1954:** 50; **1959:** 216; **1960–61:** 268 and ftn. (p. 647)
  News conference remarks on, **1954:** 50, 172, 192, 200, 311; **1956:** 20, 62, 78, 94, 121, 155, 171, 198, 205, 298; **1958:** 28, 56, 153, 213, 222, 288
  President's support of, **1954:** 172, 192, 200
  Remarks to group of Republican candidates, **1954:** 197

Candidates for Vice Presidency,
   Milton S. Eisenhower, question of, **1959:** 179
   News conference remarks, **1956:** 47, 56, 155
Canham, Erwin D., **1959:** 300; **1960–61:** 30n., 131
Cannelton Bridge Commission, disapproval, **1956:** 182
Cannon, Cavendish W., **1957:** 84
CAP.
   See Civil Air Patrol.
Cape Canaveral, Fla., **1958:** 322n.; **1959:** 17
   Launching of "Score," statement, **1958:** 321
   Missile Test Center, inspection, **1960–61:** 34
   Remarks, **1960–61:** 33
Capehart, Sen. Homer E., **1953:** 266; **1959:** 42
   Letter, **1954:** 302
   News conference remarks on, **1954:** 138, 165
Capetown, South Africa, visit of U.S.S. *Midway*, **1955:** 18
Capital Transit Co., termination of franchise, **1955:** 206
Capitalism, **1959:** 21; **1960–61:** 328
Capitalism, People's, **1956:** 75
Capitol, U.S., **1956:** 12 (p. 150)
   Cornerstone laying ceremony, remarks, **1959:** 151
   Rotunda frieze, dedication, remarks, **1954:** 106
Capitol Hill Club, message, **1955:** 20
Capone, Al, **1953:** 109
Captive nations
   News conference remarks, **1959:** 167, 172, 186
   Proclamation, **1959:** 167 and ftn. (p. 536), 172
Caracas, Venezuela, **1953:** 260; **1958:** 323
Caracas conference.
   See Inter-American conference.
Caracas Resolution against Communist infiltration
   into Western Hemisphere, **1954:** 115, 143,
   203, 209, 225, 273, 297, 304; **1957:** 111;
   1960–61: 222
Carbaugh, Harry C., **1954:** 63
CARE, **1953:** 258; **1954:** 204
Career Executive Development Program, memo-
   randums, **1960–61:** 26, 27, 28
Career incentives for military personnel, **1955:** 17
   (pp. 91, 109); **1956:** 2, 81, 91
Career service, Federal personnel, **1956:** 22
Carey, Archibald J., Jr., report, letter, **1960–61:** 394
Carey, James B., letters to members of Congress on
   labor bill, **1959:** 186
Carey, Walter F., **1958:** 297n.
Carignan, Norman, **1954:** 18, 143, 157, 200; **1955:** 10
Carillon, gift from Netherlands, message to Queen
   Juliana, **1960–61:** 138
Carlbach, William D., **1959:** 8n.
Carlson, Sen. Frank, **1953:** 8, 269; **1954:** 39; **1955:** 62; **1956:** 28n.
Carlson, Theodore W., relief of, veto, **1954:** 134
Carlson, William S., **1954:** 300

Carlton, Doyle Elam, **1958:** 318
Carlyle, Thomas, **1956:** 119, 194
Carmichael, Leonard, **1955:** 22
Carmichael, Omer, **1956:** 205
Carnahan, Rep. A. S. J., bipartisan meeting on
   Suez Canal, **1956:** 184
Carnegie, Andrew, **1956:** 283
Carney, Adm. Robert B., **1954:** 129, 138
   Comment on, **1955:** 62
   Distinguished Service Medal, citation, **1955:** 188
   Nomination as Chief of Naval Operations, **1953:** 71, 72, 76
Carnoustie, Scotland, **1953:** 140n.
Carpenter, Elizabeth, **1953:** 141; **1956:** 155; **1957:** 207, 210; **1958:** 11
Carpenters and Joiners of America, United Broth-
   erhood of, **1953:** 224
Carr, Edward R., **1956:** 315n.; **1957:** 248 and n.
Carraway, Gertrude S., **1954:** 86n.
Carriers, common, finality of contracts with Fed-
   eral Government, disapproval, **1954:** 246
Carrillo Flores, Antonio, **1956:** 218n.
Carroll, Coleman F., bishop of Miami, **1960–61:** 371
Cartier, Jacques, **1959:** 141n.
Cartoonists Society, National, remarks, **1954:** 151
Cartoons, aid in selling savings bonds, **1954:** 151
Caruso, Enrico, **1956:** 283
Carvalho Pinto, Carlos A., **1960–61:** 52, 53, 54
Carver, George Washington, **1957:** 4
Casablanca, Morocco, **1960–61:** 124
   Arrival, remarks, **1959:** 343
   Joint statement with King Mohamed V, **1959:** 345
   Luncheon honoring President, remarks, **1959:** 344
Case, Repr. Clifford, **1954:** 165, 192; **1957:** 87; **1958:** 70
Case, Sen. Francis, **1953:** 101, 269; **1954:** 138
Case, Frank, Jr., **1959:** 204n.
Casey, Dr. C. Brewer, **1960–61:** 333
Cash, Elba H., indemnity claim, disapproval, **1959:** 236
Casper, Wyo., remarks at airport, **1954:** 257
Cassels, Louis, **1956:** 171; **1957:** 92
Casson, Dollier de, **1959:** 141n.
Castiella, Fernando Maria, **1959:** 200
Castillo Armas, Carlos, telegram, **1955:** 230
Castillo Armas, Senora, **1955:** 230
Castle, Lewis G., **1959:** 141
Castries, Col. Christian de, French commander at
   Dien Bien Phu, **1954:** 63, 83
Castro, Fidel, **1960–61:** 368n., 388
   Attacks on U.S., **1960–61:** 21, 22, 103
   News conference remarks on, **1959:** 21, 161, 271;
      1960–61: 21, 93, 103, 127, 268
   Soviet support for regime, **1960–61:** 227

Cater, S. Douglass, Jr., **1953:** 243; **1954:** 63, 107,
    115, 138, 165, 347; **1955:** 26, 119; **1956:**
    62, 94, 113, 171, 198; **1957:** 28, 50, 124,
    150; **1958:** 310; **1959:** 94; **1960–61:** 256
Cathey, Sam M., **1955:** 103
Catholic Charities, National Conference, Golden
    Jubilee Dinner, address, **1960–61:** 306
Catholic Church, position on birth control infor-
    mation, **1959:** 288
Catholic University, acceptance of honorary de-
    gree, remarks, **1953:** 251
Catholic Welfare Conference, National, **1960–61:**
    371
Catholic Women National Council of, address,
    1954: 325
Catt, Carrie Chapman, **1960–61:** 269
Cattle, **1958:** 60
    See also Livestock.
    Prices, unsupported, **1958:** 59
Cattlemen's Association, American National,
    meeting, **1953:** 230
Caudle, T. Lamar, **1954:** 115; **1958:** 141
Cease and desist orders under Clayton Act, **1957:**
    132
Cedar Rapids, Iowa, **1958:** 305
    Campaign remarks, **1958:** 290
Censorship, **1954:** 128; **1959:** 267
Census of agriculture, **1954:** 14 (p. 155)
Census, Bureau of the, **1954:** 311; **1955:** 17 (p. 148);
    1956: 12 (pp. 123, 124); **1960–61:** 5
    Budget message, **1954:** 14 (pp. 153, 155)
    Employment statistics, **1958:** 88
    Population statistics, **1957:** 223
Census, decennial, **1960–61:** 13 (p. 91), 414 (p.
    1005)
Census, 1950, proposed basis for immigrant quotas,
    1956: 2, 33
Centaur space project, **1960–61:** 13 (p. 68), 414 (p.
    972)
CENT.
    See Central Treaty Organization.
Central African Republic
    Dacko, David, message, **1960–61:** 259
    Gallin-Douathe, Michel, **1960–61:** 324n.
    Independence, **1960–61:** 259
Central America.
    See Latin America.
Central Intelligence Agency, **1954:** 161; **1955:** 59;
    1956: 53; **1957:** 194
    Acting Director (Lt. Gen. C. P. Cabell), **1956:**
        197
    Amory, Robert, Jr., **1953:** 33
    Briefings for Senators Kennedy and Johnson,
        proposed, **1960–61:** 236
    Budget message, **1956:** 12 (p. 151)
    Cornerstone laying ceremony, remarks, **1959:**
        276

Central Intelligence Agency — *continued*
    Director (Allen W. Dulles), **1954:** 161; **1959:**
        82n., 89, 276; **1960–61:** 236
    Discussion on Hungary, **1956:** 287
    Foreign intelligence activities, Board of Con-
        sultants on, **1956:** 9, 10
    Donovan, Maj. Gen. William J., **1957:** 66
Central Treaty Organization, **1959:** 243, 251, 296,
    320; **1960–61:** 410
    Budget messages, **1960–61:** 13 (p. 58), 414 (p.
        959)
    Joint statements
        President Ayub Khan on, **1959:** 303
        President Bayar on, **1959:** 297
        Shah Mohammad Reza Pahlavi on, **1959:** 322
Central Valley Project, San Luis Unit, approval,
    1960–61: 168
Centralization of government, **1960–61:** 336, 340
Centre College, **1960–61:** 395
Ceylon
    Bandaranaike, S. W. R. D., death of, **1959:** 241
    Goonetilleke, Oliver E., **1959:** 241
    U.S. Ambassador Maxwell H. Gluck, **1957:** 145
    U.N. committee on Hungary, **1958:** 8
Chad, Republic of
    Independence, message to Prime Minister
        Tombalbaye, **1960–61:** 257
    Toura Gaba, Jules, **1960–61:** 324n.
Chagla, M.C., **1960–61:** 136n.
Challenges in civil cases, **1958:** 250
Chamber of Commerce, Canadian, remarks, **1954:**
    338
Chamber of Commerce, International, 40th anni-
    versary, remarks, **1959:** 84
Chamber of Commerce, U.S., **1954:** 90; **1957:** 45,
    80
    Action on flood disaster, letter, **1955:** 214
    Annual meeting, remarks, **1959:** 87; **1960–61:**
        131
    Cleveland meeting, remarks, **1956:** 223
    Convention, remarks, **1958:** 90
    Improvements in Federal budgeting, letter, **1959:**
        300
Chamber of Commerce, U.S., Junior, remarks,
    1954: 338
Chamberlain Water Co., relocation claim, **1958:**
    225
Chambers, Stuart M., **1954:** 87
Chambers, Whittaker, **1953:** 243
Chamoun, Camille, **1956:** 61; **1958:** 171, 172, 173,
    174n, 176, 177, 182
Champagne, France, **1957:** 235
Chancellorsville, battle of, **1953:** 240
Chandler, Gov. Albert B., **1956:** 225
Chandler, Alvin Duke, **1953:** 79
Chandler, Herbert A., **1953:** 218n.
Chang Myon, message, **1960–61:** 274
Chantilly, Va., recommended airport site, **1958:** 9

Chaplains, NATO Naval, remarks to, **1957:** 213 and n.

Chaplains Association, Military, **1954:** 103; **1956:** 98

Chaplains Corps, **1956:** 98

Chaplains who died in sinking of *Dorchester*, **1953:** 5

Charette, William R., Medal of Honor, citation, **1954:** 8

Charges, special Government services, budget message, **1958:** 5 (pp. 42, 44–46)

Charitable contributions, income tax deductions for, **1960–61:** 169

Charleston, S.C., **1959:** 13
  Remarks at The Citadel, **1955:** 70

Charleston, W. Va., campaign remarks, **1958:** 302

Charlotte, N.C., **1954:** 92, 114, 115

Charlottesville, Va., **1958:** 267

Chatterjee, D. N., **1960–61:** 315n.

Chavez, Sen. Dennis, **1953:** 22; **1954:** 63; **1956:** 113; **1958:** 88

Chemical warfare, **1960–61:** 7

Chemistry and wonder drugs, **1957:** 231

Chen Cheng, **1960–61:** 192n.

Chequers, **1959:** 196, 198n.

Cherbourg, France, **1954:** 131

Cherington, Paul W., **1958:** 194n.

Cherne, Leo, **1953:** 185n.

Chestertown, Md., **1954:** 136

Chi-Com.
  See China, Communist.

Chiang, Joseph, **1953:** 208; **1954:** 63, 101, 157; **1955:** 56, 81, 176

Chiang Ching-kuo, **1953:** 208

Chiang Kai-shek, **1953:** 208; **1954:** 63, 328; **1957:** 62, 80, 105; **1960–61:** 192, 193, 196
  See also under China, Republic of.
  Exchange of messages, **1955:** 36
  Joint statement with, **1960–61:** 195
  Message, **1958:** 282
  News conference remarks on, **1955:** 18, 26, 47; **1958:** 274, 288, 310
  Toast to, **1960–61:** 194

Chiang Kai-shek, Madame, **1960–61:** 194

Chicago, Ill., **1954:** 119; **1955:** 47; **1957:** 14n.; **1958:** 11, 18, 288, 297, 305; **1959:** 7, 36; **1960–61:** 23n., 246, 310, 320n.
  Campaign remarks, **1958:** 295, 296; **1960–61:** 309
  Governors Conference (1955), **1955:** 90
  Lake Michigan water diversion, disapproval, **1956:** 177
  Regional conference on traffic safety, **1958:** 45n.
  Republican National Committee meeting, remarks, **1958:** 223
  Republican National Convention, **1960–61:** 245

Chickamauga, Battle of, **1960–61:** 370

Chief Justice of the United States, annual address to Congress, proposed, **1957:** 13

Chief Justice of the United States (Fred M. Vinson), **1953:** 1n., 198
  Conference on administrative procedure, recommendations re, **1953:** 59
  Death of, statement, **1953:** 182

Chief Justice of the United States (Earl Warren), **1954:** 48, 273, 308; **1955:** 210; **1956:** 20, 47, 87, 106, 202n.; **1958:** 36; **1959:** 8, 21, 255; **1960–61:** 171n., 275, 276
  Administration of oath of office to the President, **1957:** 15n.
  Bill of Rights, **1955:** 56, 59

Chiefs of Police, International Association, remarks, **1960–61:** 314

Chiefs of Staff of the Armed Services, **1960–61:** 283

Child Health Day, change of date, statement, **1958:** 175

Child welfare, **1956:** 2, 158; **1958:** 234
  Budget message, **1956:** 12 (pp. 118, 121)
  U.N., contributions to, **1956:** 88; **1957:** 90

Children
  Adopted foreign-born, admission of, **1956:** 33, 275
  Dependent, aid to, **1956:** 2, 12 (p. 118), 21, 158; **1960–61:** 127 ftn. (p. 362), 410
    Budget messages, **1960–61:** 13 (p. 95), 414 (p. 1010)
  Health program, **1955:** 25
  Immigration, **1957:** 25
  Indian, **1956:** 2
  Mentally retarded, **1956:** 2
  Migratory workers, education, **1954:** 14 (p. 153)
  Orphans, recommendations under Refugee Relief Act, **1955:** 109
  Salk vaccine for, **1956:** 303
  U.S. veterans, gift from Burma, **1955:** 169

Children and youth, White House conference on (1960), **1958:** 119, 320; **1959:** 10 (p. 104); **1960–61:** 103
  Address, **1960–61:** 100
  Budget messages, **1960–61:** 13 (p. 96), 414 (p. 1012)

Children's Bureau, **1955:** 25

Children's Fund, United Nations, **1953:** 143; **1955:** 76, 156; **1956:** 58; **1958:** 5 (p. 140), 32; **1960–61:** 279

Chile
  American Society of Chile, **1960–61:** 72n.
  Assistance, **1960–61:** 255, 414 (p. 966)
  Association of American Women in Chile, **1960–61:** 72n.
  Del Campo, Carlos Ibanez, **1958:** 81
  Earthquake disaster, **1960–61:** 175, 214
  Economic development, **1960–61:** 73, 75
  Jorge, Alessandri Rodriguez, **1960–61:** 69, 71, 73, 75, 76, 77, 87, 175, 228
  Santiago.
    See main heading Santiago, Chile.

Chile — *continued*
   Students Federation of Chile, **1960–61:** 72n.
   U.S. Ambassador Walter Howe, **1960–61:** 69n., 72n., 75n.
   Vergara, German, **1960–61:** 73n.
   Visit to, **1960–61:** 42, 69, 70, 71, 72, 73, 74, 75, 76, 77, 86, 87
Chilean-American Chamber of Commerce, **1960–61:** 72n.
Chilean-American Cultural Institute, presentation of scroll to the President, **1960–61:** 70
China, **1958:** 124, 173
China, Communist, **1953:** 6; **1955:** 21; **1957:** 90; **1959:** 71; **1960–61:** 36, 193, 196, 209, 410
   Admission to United Nations, question of, **1953:** 77, 88, 254; **1954:** 161, 182; **1960–61:** 410
   Aggression in India, **1959:** 94
   Aggression in North Korea, **1955:** 185
   Aggression in Tibet, **1960–61:** 410
   Agricultural communes, **1960–61:** 193
   American fliers, release of, **1956:** 2, 143, 193
   Appeasement, **1958:** 274, 288
   Armed forces, **1960–61:** 93
   Attack on transport plane, **1954:** 172
   Blockade, question of, **1953:** 12
   Border dispute with India, **1959:** 288
   Campaign remarks, **1958:** 302, 303; **1960–61:** 351
   Chinese Peoples Liberation Army, **1958:** 257
   Chou En-lai, **1958:** 257n., 261
   Disarmament, **1957:** 115; **1960–61:** 34, 93
   Embargo on trade with, **1954:** 67
   Entry of American newsmen, **1956:** 193; **1957:** 17, 45, 80, 134
   Evacuation of North Korea, **1958:** 302, 303
   Formosa Strait situation.
     See Formosa (Taiwan) Strait situation.
   Geneva conference on Indochina.
     See main heading, Geneva conferences.
   Invasion of Formosa, question of, **1954:** 200
   Japan, trade agreement, **1958:** 70
   Joint statement with President Chiang Kai-shek on, **1960–61:** 195
   Joint statement with President Garcia on, **1960–61:** 189
   Mao Tse-tung, **1958:** 198, 213, 261
   Military strength, **1959:** 55
   Missiles, comment of Premier Khrushchev re, **1959:** 154
   News conference remarks, **1953:** 12, 41, 77, 88, 238, 254; **1954:** 18, 73, 101, 157, 161, 172, 182, 200, 328, 341, 345, 347; **1955:** 18, 33, 41, 47, 59, 62, 81, 112, 176, 185; **1958:** 11, 70, 213, 274, 288, 310; **1959:** 7, 94, 154, 186, 243, 267, 271, 277, 288; **1960–61:** 34, 93, 103, 222, 284, 422
   Participation in Big Five conference, question of, **1954:** 18

China, Communist — *continued*
   Participation in nuclear ban agreement, comment on, **1958:** 213
   Peaceful coexistence with, **1954:** 157
   Peiping, **1955:** 16
   Recognition of, comment on, **1958:** 310
   Recognition by Cuba, **1960–61:** 284
   Recognition by Egypt, **1956:** 113
   Refugees from, assistance, **1953:** 257n.
   Sino-Soviet bloc, **1958:** 7, 32
   Soviet Union, relations with, **1955:** 33
   Trade with, **1956:** 53; **1957:** 70, 105
   U.S. bases in area near, **1957:** 150
   U.S. negotiations with, **1955:** 176, 185; **1958:** 257, 261, 263
   U.S. plane shot down, **1956:** 193
   U.S. prisoners, **1954:** 161, 345, 347; **1955:** 4, 16, 18, 41, 62, 81, 148, 176; **1956:** 96, 193; **1957:** 28; **1958:** 274, 310; **1959:** 243, 267, 271, 277
     Message to relatives of, **1954:** 342
     Release of, **1955:** 112, 179
     U.N. action on, **1955:** 156
   U.S. servicemen choosing to remain in, **1954:** 18
   Vietnam, **1957:** 83
China, Republic of, **1953:** 6; **1959:** 132; **1960–61:** 133,410
   See also Formosa (Taiwan); Formosa (Taiwan) Strait situation.
   Assistance, **1954:** 3; **1955:** 17 (p. 129), 21; **1957:** 90, 91, 136; **1958:** 32; **1959:** 10 (p. 69), 55; **1960–61:** 36, 195, 341
   Campaign remarks, **1958:** 293
   Chen Cheng, **1960–61:** 192n.
   Chiang Ching-kuo, **1953:** 208
   Chiang Kai-shek, **1953:** 208; **1954:** 63, 328; **1955:** 18, 26, 36, 47; **1957:** 80, 105; **1958:** 274, 288, 310; **1960–61:** 192, 193, 194, 196
     See also main heading, Chiang Kai-shek
     Exchange of letters, **1958:** 282
     Joint statement with, **1960–61:** 195
   Defense treaty with **1958:** 96, 261, 277, 282
   Economy, **1960–61:** 193, 195
   Inclusion in Southeast Asia security pact, **1954:** 168
   Invasion of mainland, question of, **1955:** 47
   Land reform, **1960–61:** 193
   Letter to Premier Khrushchev on, **1958:** 263
   Message to Vice President Nixon on, **1958:** 289
   Military assistance, **1955:** 76
   Mutual defense treaty, **1954:** 345, 351; **1955:** 4, 5, 21, 35; **1960–61:** 194, 195
   News conference remarks, **1954:** 168, 328, 345; **1955:** 18, 26, 47, 81; **1958:** 222, 274, 310
   Relations with U.S., **1960–61:** 194, 195
   Statement by Secretary Dulles, **1958:** 257
   Taipei.
     See main heading, Taipei.

China, Republic of — *continued*
  U.S. Ambassador Everett F. Drumright, **1960–61:** 192n.
  U.S. Ambassador Karl L. Rankin, **1954:** 168
  U.S. arms shipments, **1956:** 56
  Visit to, **1960–61:** 177, 192, 193, 194, 195, 196, 209
  Yeh, George K. C., **1954:** 345
China policy, State Department mail on, **1958:** 274
China trade, **1957:** 70, 105
Chinese overseas, question of return to mainland, **1955:** 56
Chinese students in United States, question of return to Communist China, **1954:** 192
Ching, Cyrus, Chairman, Atomic Energy Labor-Management Panel, memorandum, **1956:** 95
Chiperfield, Repr. Robert B., **1953:** 268
  Bipartisan meeting on Suez Canal, **1956:** 184
  Letter, **1953:** 111
Chittenden, Vt., remarks to women representatives of dairy and agricultural organizations, **1955:** 132
Cholera in Southeast Asia, **1960–61:** 286
Chotiner, Murray M., **1956:** 94
Chou En-lai, **1958:** 257n., 261
Christian Endeavor Convention, World, remarks, **1954:** 170
Christian Leadership, International, remarks, **1953:** 8; **1956:** 28
Christians and Jews, National Conference of, message, **1953:** 132
Christmas mail, statement, **1955:** 246
Christmas Tree, National Community, **1953:** 271; **1954:** 355; **1955:** 250; **1956:** 315; **1957:** 248; **1958:** 325; **1959:** 347; **1960–61:** 381
Christopher, George E., **1960–61:** 332
Chula Vista, Calif., Mayor Robert R. McAllister, **1960–61:** 333
Chungang University, Seoul, Korea, **1960–61:** 250n.
Church, Rep. Marguerite Stitt, **1956:** 214
Church Women, United, address, **1953:** 205
Church World Service, **1953:** 258
Churches
  Air Force manual on alleged Communist infiltration, **1960–61:** 38
  Communism in, question re, **1953:** 31, 132
  Our Lady of the Lake Church, relief of, veto, **1960–61:** 179
Churches, National Council of
  General Board meeting, remarks, **1953:** 250
  United Church Women, address, **1953:** 205
Churchill, Winston, **1953:** 187; **1954:** 148, 164, 297; **1956:** 78, 216; **1959:** 196; **1960–61:** 21, 287
  Comment on, **1955:** 47
  Decision on Germany, **1958:** 318
  Dinner honoring, remarks, **1959:** 96

Churchill, Winston — *continued*
  80th birthday, message, **1954:** 344
  Joint statements with, **1953:** 255; **1954:** 154, 155
  Medallion, presentation letter, **1955:** 244
  News conference remarks on, **1953:** 22, 77, 88, 126, 128, 198, 208, 230, 254; **1954:** 50, 63, 73, 143, 157, 161, 192, 311, 345; **1958:** 288, 318; **1959:** 7, 94
  Remarks of welcome to, **1959:** 93
  Retirement as Prime Minister of United Kingdom, statement, **1955:** 65
  World War II, **1958:** 288
CIA.
  See Central Intelligence Agency.
Cigarette tax, **1960–61:** 414 (p. 940)
Cincinnati, Ohio, Taft Sanitary Engineering Center, **1954:** 301
CIO.
  See Congress of Industrial Organizations.
Circuit Court of Appeals, Fourth, filling vacancies on, **1956:** 20
Cisler, Walker L., **1960–61:** 405n.
Citadel, The, commencement remarks, **1955:** 70
Citations.
  See Awards and citations.
Citizens, new, remarks, **1954:** 326
Citizens Commission for the Public Schools, National, **1955:** 96
Citizens Committee for the Hoover Report, **1957:** 26n.
Citizens for Eisenhower, **1954:** 197; **1956:** 121, 281n., 290; **1958:** 94
  Congressional Committee, National
    Meeting of district chairmen, address, **1954:** 139
    News conference remarks on, **1954:** 138, 347
  Congressional Committee, Washington, D.C., address, **1954:** 316
  Executive Campaign Conference, National, remarks, **1956:** 117
Citizens for Eisenhower-Nixon, remarks, **1956:** 241; **1958:** 306
Citizens for Eisenhower of Southern California, **1954:** 273
Citizens for Good Government, **1956:** 290
Citizens for Rockefeller, **1958:** 306
Citizens travelling or serving abroad, **1957:** 141
Citizenship, loss of, for conspiring to overthrow Government, **1954:** 9
Ciudad Acuna, Mexico, **1960–61:** 333
  Broadcast to Mexican people, **1960–61:** 334
  Joint declaration with President Lopez Mateos, **1960–61:** 335
  Mayor Lucina Sanchez Martinez, **1960–61:** 334
Ciudad Trujillo, Dominican Republic, **1953:** 260
Civil Aeronautics Administration, **1954:** 14 (p. 173); **1955:** 146; **1958:** 135
  Airport, Chantilly, Va., **1958:** 9

Civil Aeronautics Administration — *continued*
  Budget messages, **1956:** 12 (p. 141); **1958:** 5 (p. 60)
  Elkins, W. Va., airport, **1956:** 163
Civil Aeronautics Board, **1954:** 14 (p. 178); **1956:** 94; **1959:** 10 (pp. 78, 79)
  Airline subsidies, **1953:** 94
  Budget messages, **1955:** 17 (p. 169); **1960–61:** 13 (p. 68), 414 (pp. 974, 984)
  Certification of Northern Airlines and Alaska Airlines, **1957:** 162
  Chairman, filling of position, **1955:** 10
  Code of ethics, **1958:** 74
  Investigation of aircraft accidents, **1958:** 135
  Large irregular air carrier investigation, **1960–61:** 408
  News conference remarks, **1958:** 37, 74
  States-Alaska case, **1955:** 106
  Trans-Pacific certificate renewal case, **1956:** 14, 56
  Trans-Pacific route case, memorandum, **1960–61:** 436
  West Coast-Hawaii case, **1955:** 30, 33
Civil Aeronautics Board, Chairman (Whitney Gillilland)
  Letter, **1960–61:** 281
  Memorandums, **1960–61:** 408, 436
Civil Aeronautics Board, Chairman (Ross Rizley), letters, **1955:** 106; **1956:** 14
Civil Air Patrol, **1957:** 87
  14th anniversary, statement, **1955:** 224
Civil Air Patrol Cadets, remarks, **1958:** 200
"Civil Air Policy," **1954:** 123n., 200
Civil aviation, **1954:** 123
  Monopolistic trend, **1954:** 200
Civil benefits, **1958:** 5 (pp. 24, 41–70)
  Budget message, **1955:** 17 (pp. 96, 101–103)
  Expenditures for, **1957:** 13, 86
  Funds for, **1956:** 12 (pp. 81–84, 99)
  Tables, **1955:** 17 (p. 103); **1956:** 12 (p. 82)
Civil defense, **1953:** 6, 21, 31, 82; **1954:** 3, 72, 225; **1955:** 4; **1956:** 21, 56; **1960–61:** 410
  Budget messages, **1954:** 14 (pp. 119–121, 151); **1955:** 17 (pp. 119, 175); **1956:** 12 (pp. 80, 150); **1958:** 5 (p. 61); **1959:** 10 (pp. 70, 87, 88); **1960–61:** 13 (p. 76), 414 (pp. 961, 984, 985)
  Fallout shelters, **1960–61:** 13 (p. 76), 229, 384, 414 (p. 985)
  Governors' conference committee, **1959:** 277
  Letter to Civil Defense Administrator, **1956:** 142
  Letter to Leo A. Hoegh, **1958:** 146
  News conference remarks, **1955:** 56, 112, 149
  Relocation of Federal agencies (Operation Alert), **1955:** 149 and ftn. (p. 672)
  Remarks to State directors, **1953:** 202; **1959:** 103
  Reorganization Plan 1 of 1958, **1958:** 84
  Responsibility of individuals, **1953:** 156

Civil defense — *continued*
  Role of women, **1954:** 310
  Test exercise, memorandums, **1953:** 195; **1954:** 98; **1955:** 101
  White House meeting, **1960–61:** 229
Civil Defense, National Women's Advisory Committee, remarks, **1954:** 310
Civil Defense Administration.
  See Federal Civil Defense Administration.
Civil Defense Administrator (Val Peterson).
  See Federal Civil Defense Administrator (Val Peterson).
Civil Defense Advisory Council, Reorganization Plan 1 of 1958, **1958:** 84
Civil Defense Coordinating Board, **1956:** 142
Civil and Defense Mobilization, Office of, **1958:** 146n., 327n.; **1960–61:** 386
  Budget messages, **1959:** 10 (pp. 70, 87, 88); **1960–61:** 13 (p. 49)
  Letter re, **1958:** 146, 147
  Patterson, John S., **1959:** 18n.
  Report, **1960–61:** 384
  Reorganization Plan 1 of 1958, message, **1958:** 84
Civil and Defense Mobilization, Office of, Director (Leo A. Hoegh), **1959:** 29, 47, 103
  Oil import program, **1959:** 51
  Resignation, letter, **1960–61:** 384
Civil Defense Week, National, statements, **1956:** 203; **1957:** 190
Civil rights, **1953:** 6, 101, 159, 187; **1955:** 247; **1956:** 2, 190; **1957:** 8, 13, 133, 147; **1958:** 26, 123, 285; **1959:** 6; **1960–61:** 4, 137, 410
  See also Integration.
  Biracial conferences proposed, **1960–61:** 93, 143
  Budget messages, **1960–61:** 13 (p. 105), 414 (pp. 1021–1023)
  Campaign remarks, **1956:** 210, 224, 226, 241, 251, 258, 272
  Consultation with religious and educational leaders, **1957:** 207
  Discrimination, **1956:** 2, 190, 210, 224, 226, 229, 241, 251
  District of Columbia, **1953:** 6, 101; **1960–61:** 410
  Equal Opportunity Day, statement, **1957:** 237
  Equal rights for women, **1957:** 13
  Fair employment practices, **1954:** 48, 92
  Federal conciliation service on, **1959:** 17
  Government employment, **1960–61:** 410
  Housing, **1954:** 101, 182; **1959:** 26
  Interstate travel, **1954:** 143, 161
  Legislation, question of, **1953:** 265
  Little Rock situation.
    See Little Rock, Ark.
  Meeting on, **1956:** 318
  Meeting of Negro leaders, remarks, **1958:** 102, 153
  Message to Congress, **1959:** 27

Civil rights — *continued*
  Montgomery, Ala., situation, **1956:** 62
  New legal provisions proposed, comment on,
    1959: 288
  News conference remarks, **1954:** 48, 57, 63, 92,
    101, 143, 161, 182, 347; **1956:** 32, 121, 171,
    193, 198, 229; **1957:** 28, 45, 56, 87, 92, 105,
    115, 119, 124, 134, 145, 150, 157, 207;
    1958: 56, 103, 153, 318; **1959:** 7, 17, 26,
    154, 167, 223, 288; **1960–61:** 7, 21, 93, 103,
    143, 256
  Non-discrimination in Federal Government,
    1958: 102
  Non-discrimination in Federal Government and
    District of Columbia, **1954:** 3, 347
  Public school education.
    See Integration, public schools; Little Rock,
      Ark.
  Role of Administration re problem, **1958:** 56
  School integration, **1954:** 115, 192, 341
  "Sit-in" demonstrations, comment on, **1960–61:**
    93, 103, 143
  Voting right, **1956:** 2, 32; **1958:** 102, 295, 308;
    1959: 17; **1960–61:** 4, 7, 13 (p. 105), 24, 93,
    137, 410, 414 (p. 1021)
Civil rights, Commission on, **1956:** 2, 16, 56, 69;
    1959: 128; **1960–61:** 4, 410
  Budget messages, **1960–61:** 13 (p. 105), 414 (p.
    1022)
  Continuation, **1958:** 318
  Extension proposed, **1959:** 7, 17, 27
  Filling of vacancy, **1959:** 271
  Investigation in Alabama, **1958:** 318
  News conference remarks, **1957:** 119, 124, 228;
    1958: 56, 213, 318; **1959:** 7, 17, 26, 223,
    288; **1960–61:** 7, 21
  Reed, Stanley F., withdrawal from, **1957:** 242
    and n.
  Report, **1959:** 288
  Wilkins, J. Ernest, **1958:** 213
Civil Rights, National Conference on, remarks,
    1959: 128
Civil Rights Act (1957), **1960–61:** 137, 410
  Budget message, **1960–61:** 414 (p. 1022)
Civil Rights Act (1960), **1960–61:** 7, 93, 133, 410
  Approval, **1960–61:** 137
  Budget message, **1960–61:** 414 (p. 1022)
Civil rights bill, **1959:** 7, 179, 186
  Jury trial amendment, **1957:** 45, 87, 105, 133,
    145, 147, 150, 157
  News conference remarks, **1957:** 45, 87, 105, 134
    and n., 145, 150, 157
  Objectives, statement, **1957:** 133
  Senate action, statement, **1957:** 147
Civil rights division, Justice Department, proposed,
    1957: 8
Civil rights legislation, **1959:** 7

Civil service.
  See also Government employees.
  Merit system, **1954:** 14 (p. 188)
  Retirement system, financing of, **1954:** 14 (p.
    189)
  Status, **1954:** 313
Civil Service Act, 75th anniversary, **1958:** 6, 13
Civil Service Assembly, U.S.-Canada, **1956:** 238
Civil Service Commission, **1953:** 31 ftn. (pp. 112,
    113); **1954:** 38, 116; **1960–61:** 26, 27, 28
  Budget messages, **1954:** 14 (p. 188); **1955:** 17 (p.
    181); **1960–61:** 13 (p. 102), 414 (p. 1019)
  Fair Employment Board, **1954:** 92
  Federal employees training program, report,
    1960–61: 149
  Government employees incentive awards pro-
    gram, **1955:** 1
  Lawton, Frederick J., **1960–61:** 389n.
  News conference remarks, **1954:** 9, 18, 39, 48, 92,
    107
  Security clearance program, **1954:** 9, 18, 39, 48
Civil Service Commission, Chairman (Harris
    Ellsworth), letter, **1958:** 6
Civil Service Commission, Chairman (Roger W.
    Jones), memorandum, **1960–61:** 28
Civil Service Commission, Chairman (Philip
    Young), **1953:** 269
  Federal Council on Aging, **1956:** 74
  Meeting on pay for Federal employees, **1954:**
    349
  News conference remarks on, **1954:** 18, 48, 92,
    107
  Oath of office ceremony, statement, **1953:** 32
  Resignation, **1957:** 33 and n.
Civil Service Retirement Act, amendment, disap-
    proval, **1955:** 201
Civil service retirement fund, **1955:** 17 (pp. 96,
    106); **1958:** 192
Civil service system, **1953:** 32, 238
  Statement, **1953:** 31 ftn. (pp. 112, 113)
Civil War, **1954:** 22, 31; **1956:** 113; **1959:** 129, 255,
    333; **1960–61:** 171n.
  Centennial, **1960–61:** 370, 392
  Subject of frieze in Capitol rotunda, **1954:** 106n.
Civil works.
  See Public works.
Civilian Employee Compensation, Commission on,
    proposed, **1959:** 10 (p. 109)
Civilian-Military Liaison Committee, **1960–61:** 11
Civilian-training corps, **1957:** 57
Clague, Ewan, **1955:** 18
Claims against the United States, **1954:** 14 (p. 190)
Claims and relief acts, **1955:** 17 (p. 183)
Clapp, Gordon R.
  See Tennessee Valley Authority, Chairman
    (Gordon R. Clapp).
Clark, Clarence Don, **1954:** 113n.

Clark, Grenville, *World Peace Through World Law*, **1958:** 153

Clark, Mayor Joseph S., Jr., (Philadelphia), Civil defense, **1955:** 56
Message, **1954:** 160

Clark, Gen. Mark W., **1953:** 159; **1954:** 107, 161, 192; **1955:** 70; **1959:** 96
News conference remarks on, **1953:** 41, 77

Clark, Robert E., **1953:** 15, 54, 77, 109, 128, 198, 225, 238, 249, 265; **1954:** 9, 18, 25, 73, 92, 101, 115, 165, 168, 172, 182, 192, 200, 311, 328, 341, 345, 347; **1955:** 18, 26, 33, 41, 47, 59, 62, 81, 90, 100, 112, 146, 176, 185; **1956:** 5, 16, 20, 32, 47, 53, 62, 88, 94, 96, 113, 121, 189, 193, 198, 205, 216, 229, 235, 298; **1957:** 17, 22, 28, 45, 50, 56, 62, 72, 80, 92, 105, 115, 119, 145, 150, 157, 169, 207, 210, 228

Clark, William, **1956:** 107

Class struggle doctrine of Karl Marx, **1955:** 245

Classified information.
See Information.

Clausewitz, Karl von, **1953:** 31

Clay, Henry, **1954:** 89, 106

Clay, Gen. Lucius D., **1954:** 346; **1955:** 39, 146; **1956:** 45n.; **1957:** 89

Clayton Act, **1957:** 132

Clean bombs, **1956:** 229; **1957:** 105, 119, 124, 150; **1958:** 70, 88

Clemenceau, Georges, **1958:** 94

Clement, Gov. Frank G., **1953:** 208, 225; **1954:** 161; **1956:** 198; **1957:** 205n., 207

Clements, Sen. Earle C., **1955:** 33
Bipartisan meeting on Suez Canal, **1956:** 184

Clergymen
Attacks on loyalty of, **1953:** 132
Social security coverage, **1953:** 155

Cleveland, Grover, use of veto, **1959:** 161

Cleveland, Richard, **1959:** 116

Cleveland, Ohio, **1954:** 130, 320; **1956:** 223; **1957:** 236; **1958:** 83
Campaign remarks, **1954:** 317; **1956:** 224; **1960–61:** 350, 351, 352
Pan-American games, **1957:** 45

Cliburn, Van, **1958:** 78

Clifford, Clark, **1960–61:** 369

Clinchy, Everett R., **1955:** 40

Clinics, construction of, Federal aid, **1960–61:** 414 (p. 1008)

Clinton, Tenn., **1958:** 288

Clover, Canadian, U.S. tariffs on, **1954:** 172

Coal, commission on rehabilitation of Pennsylvania hard coal region, **1954:** 168

Coal industry, **1956:** 279

Coal mines, automation in, **1959:** 67

Coal Research and Development Commission, creation, disapproval, **1959:** 221

Coal research programs, **1960–61:** 13 (p. 85), 133, 402, 414 (p. 998)

Coal and Steel Community, **1958:** 145; **1959:** 7, 94

Coal and Steel Community, European, **1953:** 109, 265 ftn. (p. 843); **1957:** 245

Coast and Geodetic Survey, **1954:** 137
Remarks on 150th anniversary, **1957:** 27

Coast Guard, **1954:** 137; **1955:** 17 (p. 169); **1960–61:** 414 (p. 976)
Budget messages, **1954:** 14 (p. 175); **1959:** 10 (p. 80)
Functions under Federal Boating Act, **1959:** 228
Nuclear-powered ice breaker, veto, **1958:** 204

Cobo, Albert E., **1954:** 318n.

Cochran, Carlos M., estate, relief of, disapproval, **1954:** 230

Cochrane, Lord, **1960–61:** 73

COCOM.
See Coordinating Committee on Trade with Communist Areas.

Code of conduct for members of armed forces, statement, **1955:** 207

Code of ethics, Civil Aeronautics Board, **1958:** 74

Code of ethics in Government, **1956:** 32, 94, 117

Codification of laws affecting personnel systems and procedures, **1956:** 22

Coexistence, comment on use of term, **1955:** 26

Coffee
Imports, **1960–61:** 54
International agreement on, **1959:** 257
Joint statement with President Lemus, **1959:** 54
Joint statements with President Lopez Mateos, **1959:** 38, 257
Prices, **1953:** 30; **1960–61:** 111n.
Federal Trade Commission investigation, **1954:** 18, 25, 39, 50, 57

Coffee Study Group, International, **1959:** 38, 54

Coffee and Sugar Exchange, **1954:** 18

Coggeshall School (Newport, R.I.), **1960–61:** 239

Cohn, Roy M., **1954:** 115

Coinage of 50-cent pieces for commemorative events, vetoes
Louisiana Purchase, sesquicentennial, **1954:** 29
New York City, tercentennial, **1954:** 28
Northampton, Mass., tercentennial, **1954:** 27

Colbert, L. L., **1960–61:** 328

Cold war, **1959:** 21

Cole, Albert M.
See Housing and Home Finance Agency, Administrator (Albert M. Cole).

Cole, Benjamin R., **1955:** 26, 47, 81; **1956:** 121, 298; **1957:** 157; **1958:** 74; **1960–61:** 263

Cole, W. Sterling, **1953:** 268; **1954:** 57, 129; **1958:** 148

Coleman, Governor James P., **1957:** 138; **1959:** 88

Coleman, John S., **1957:** 110 and n.

Collective bargaining, **1953:** 6, 77, 248; **1954:** 5; **1955:** 245; **1958:** 20, 210, 234, 242; **1959:** 6, 22, 142, 160, 209, 211, 250, 253, 264, 290; **1960–61:** 343, 410
  News conference remarks, **1959:** 67, 161, 179, 223, 243, 288
Collective defense system (Western), joint statement with Chancellor Adenauer, **1957:** 129
Collective security, **1953:** 1, 6, 26, 50, 61, 66, 89, 98, 101, 143, 187; **1954:** 6, 38, 45, 72, 73 ftn. (p. 384), 84, 91, 297, 329; **1955:** 3, 4; **1956:** 2, 87; **1958:** 32, 96, 163, 171, 173, 207; **1959:** 6, 55, 57, 87, 116, 119, 120, 152, 204, 251, 302; **1960–61:** 4, 36, 42, 58, 87, 164, 183, 188, 193, 209, 409, 410
  See also North Atlantic Treaty Organization; Organization of American States; Southeast Asia Treaty Organization.
Asia
  See Southeast Asia Treaty Organization.
Baghdad Pact, CENTO, NATO, SEATO, OAS. *See specific organization.*
Budget messages, **1956:** 12 (pp. 80, 81); **1958:** 5 (p. 19)
Campaign remarks, **1956:** 190, 283; **1958:** 292, 294; **1960–61:** 348
Defense treaties, **1956:** 58; **1957:** 6, 13, 55, 90, 91, 129, 226
Europe.
  See North Atlantic Treaty Organization.
Expenditures for, **1957:** 13
Joint statements
  Chancellor Adenauer, **1959:** 192
  King Bhumibol Adulyadej, **1960–61:** 218
  Prime Minister Eden, **1956:** 27
  Prime Minister Macmillan, **1957:** 55, 226
Letter to Premier Bulganin, **1958:** 7
News conference remarks, **1953:** 54, 62, 88, 141, 254; **1954:** 101, 115, 157, 168, 311; **1957:** 119, 228
Role of Secretary McElroy, **1959:** 286
Security pacts, **1958:** 28
South America.
  See Organization of American States; Rio Treaty.
White House statement, **1956:** 121 ftn. (p. 556)
Colfax, Iowa, campaign remarks, **1956:** 211
College student, Karen Cornell, letter, **1955:** 277
College of Surgeons, **1957:** 223; **1959:** 129
Colleges and universities, **1957:** 28
  Agricultural and technical training, **1955:** 222
  Air Force Academy, **1957:** 170
  American University, **1957:** 109
  American University, Beirut, **1958:** 173
  Association of American Colleges, **1955:** 11
  Association of American Medical Colleges, **1954:** 334n.

Colleges and universities — *continued*
  Association of Land-Grant Colleges and Universities, **1954:** 335
  Baylor University, **1956:** 114, 121
  Bradley University, **1956:** 214
  Budget message, **1958:** 5 (pp. 46, 48, 51, 53, 54, 59)
  Butler University, **1954:** 291
  Catholic University, **1953:** 251
  Centre College, **1960–61:** 395
  Chungang University, Seoul, Korea, **1960–61:** 250n.
  Citadel, The, **1955:** 70
  College of William and Mary, **1953:** 79
  Columbia University, **1953:** 15, 109, 126, 215, 238; **1954:** 39, 118, 128, 300, 347; **1955:** 62, 151; **1956:** 88, 96, 235; **1957:** 33n., 105, 134, 223; **1958:** 168; **1959:** 164, 196, 259, 311; **1960–61:** 29n., 30n., 86, 143, 186, 187
  Cornell University, **1954:** 12n., 200; **1956:** 211
  Counseling and guidance training, **1958:** 24
  Dartmouth College, **1953:** 104, 109, 126; **1958:** 138n.; **1959:** 7
  Defiance College, **1953:** 214, 215; **1957:** 251 and n.
  Duke University, **1954:** 33
  Emory University, **1954:** 33
  Federal aid, **1960–61:** 13 (pp. 75, 90, 91), 133, 255, 410, 414 (pp. 939, 1002)
  Federal aid for medical research, **1954:** 14 (p. 143)
  Federal student loan program, **1959:** 288
  Fordham University, **1959:** 21, 106
  Foreign language teaching, **1958:** 24
  Gettysburg College, **1955:** 242n., 250n.; **1959:** 71, 172
  Georgetown University, **1957:** 109; **1958:** 286
  Georgia Institute of Technology, **1957:** 207
  Grants, **1956:** 222
  Harvard University, **1954:** 129; **1956:** 201n.; **1958:** 194n.
  Health research facilities construction, **1956:** 151
  Housing, **1954:** 14 (pp. 87, 151); **1955:** 17 (pp. 174, 175); **1956:** 2, 12 (p. 147), 85n.; **1957:** 19, 56, 75, 129; **1958:** 5 (pp. 53, 54, 59), 50, 96, 110, 224; **1959:** 10 (pp. 82, 86), 26, 94, 153, 208; **1960–61:** 13 (p. 75), 414 (pp. 982, 983)
  Howard University, **1954:** 14 (pp. 153, 154), 33; **1956:** 12 (p. 120); **1960–61:** 23, 414 (p. 1009)
  Illinois University, **1956:** 85n.
  Increased enrollment, **1956:** 85n.
  Indiana University, **1953:** 204; **1959:** 148 ftn. (p. 490)
  Johns Hopkins University, **1958:** 130; **1959:** 129; **1960–61:** 349
  Junior colleges, **1958:** 320

Colleges and universities — *continued*
  Land grants, **1957:** 68
  Loan fund, **1958:** 162; **1959:** 10 (p. 99)
  Mary Baldwin College, **1960–61:** 340
  Massachusetts Institute of Technology, **1953:** 31;
    1959: 125n.
  Medical and dental facilities, **1956:** 12 (p. 120),
    21, 151; **1958:** 5 (p. 51)
  Mount Saint Mary's College, **1958:** 123
  Naval Academy, **1957:** 207
  North American Ecclesiastical College, Rome,
    1959: 294n.
  Northwestern University, **1954:** 192, 204
  Occidental College, **1956:** 298
  Ohio State University, **1956:** 77
  Pennsylvania State College, **1953:** 48, 101
  Pennsylvania State University, **1955:** 121, 149;
    1957: 196
  Princeton University, **1960–61:** 21
  Puget Sound, College of, **1956:** 253
  Purdue University, **1953:** 97; **1954:** 291n., 335n.;
    1957: 156; **1958:** 128n.
  Rice University, **1960–61:** 336
  St. John's College, **1959:** 116
  Scholarships, **1958:** 162, 195
  Science education and training grants, **1958:** 5
    (pp. 46, 48, 49)
  Scientific research, **1956:** 12 (p. 123); **1958:** 5 (p.
    48)
  SEATO Graduate School of Engineering, **1960–
    61:** 286
  Southern Methodist University, **1954:** 12n.
  Stanford University, **1959:** 89, 107
  State University of New York, **1954:** 300
  Swarthmore College, **1959:** 116
  Teachers, **1957:** 234n.; **1958:** 24; **1956:** 85n.
    Science teaching, **1956:** 12 (p. 123)
  Transylvania College, **1954:** 89
  Trinity College, **1954:** 295
  University of Alabama, **1956:** 32
  University of California, **1958:** 52
  University of Chicago, **1959:** 36, 144n.
  University of Delhi, India, **1959:** 314, 317
  University of Kentucky, **1956:** 226; **1959:** 29
  University of Louisville, International Center,
    1955: 116
  University of Maryland, **1960–61:** 100
  University of Michigan, **1955:** 113n.
  University of Notre Dame, **1959:** 26; **1960–61:**
    174
  University of the Philippines, **1960–61:** 186
  University of Pittsburgh, **1955:** 11n.
  U.S. Military Academy, **1960–61:** 135, 173, 319,
    340
  Vanderbilt University, **1953:** 230
  Williams College, **1956:** 265n.
  Yale University, **1956:** 255
Collins, Frederic W., **1953:** 54, 141, 265; **1960–61:**
  228

Collins, Gen. J. Lawton, **1954:** 341; **1955:** 48, 81
Collins, Gov. LeRoy, **1956:** 69; **1957:** 205n.; **1958:**
  103; **1960–61:** 103
Collins, Seaborn P., Jr., **1955:** 119
Colombia, **1955:** 112 ftn. (p. 548)
  Agricultural and industrial production, **1960–61:**
    111
  Assistance, **1960–61:** 109n., 111n.
  Atomic research agreement, **1955:** 121
  Bogota, **1956:** 75n.; **1958:** 137
    OAS economic conference, **1960–61:** 228 and
      ftn. (p. 569), 255, 256
  Lleras Camargo, Alberto, **1958:** 137; **1960–61:**
    108, 109, 110
    Discussions with, statement, **1960–61:** 111
  Participation in Korean war, **1960–61:** 108, 109
Colombo plan for economic development of South
  and Southeast Asia, **1955:** 76; **1956:** 26,
  27; **1958:** 207, 312
Colonialism, **1959:** 158n., 196; **1960–61:** 183
  Indochina, **1954:** 39
Colorado, **1953:** 62; **1959:** 75
  Air Force Academy, **1957:** 170
    Appointment of son of Capt. Kincheloe, **1958:**
      314
  Arvada, **1960–61:** 23
  Boulder, **1954:** 267
  Candidates for public office, **1956:** 259
  Colorado Springs, **1956:** 210; **1959:** 109
  Denver, **1953:** 169; **1954:** 101, 165, 182, 200,
    209n., 260, 286, 287; **1955:** 207n., 208,
    211n., 212n., 213n., 214n., 215n., 216n.,
    217n., 219n., 220n., 221n., 222n., 223n.,
    224n., 225n., 226n., 227n., 228n., 229n.,
    230n., 231n., 232n., 233n., 234n., 235;
    1956: 259, 260n.; **1958:** 288, 305; **1959:**
    109n., 110n., 133n., 232; **1960–61:** 12n.,
    247n.
    Releases from, **1954:** 210–222, 227–232, 234–
      255, 259, 261–266, 268, 269, 276–285, 288,
      289
  Editor's note on President's illness, **1955:** p. 822
  Fraser, **1954:** 233n., 270
  Grand Junction, **1954:** 256
  Johnson, Sen. Edwin C., **1953:** 77; **1956:** 259
  Millikin, Sen. Eugene D., **1954:** 33; **1955:** 81;
    1956: 184
  News conference remarks, **1956:** 121, 189, 216
  Radioactive waste disposal, **1959:** 161
  Releases from, **1953:** 165–186
  State flower, **1956:** 257
  Thornton, Gov. Dan, **1953:** 62, 77; **1954:** 35, 39,
    85n., 99, 165, 256, 286
  U.S. District Court, **1953:** 107
Colorado Fuel and Iron Corporation, **1959:** 211n.
Colorado River storage project, **1960–61:** 410
Colorado River Project, Upper, **1954:** 101, 172;
  1955: 4, 56; **1956:** 2, 251, 256

Colorado River Project, Upper — *continued*
Ceremony marking beginning, remarks, **1956:** 245
News conference remarks, **1956:** 47, 53
Recommendations on, statement, **1954:** 62
Colt, S. Sloan, **1954:** 334; **1957:** 223 and n.
Colts, football team, **1960–61:** 290
Columbia Broadcasting System interview of Khrushchev, **1957:** 105
Columbia Institution for the Deaf, **1954:** 14 (p. 155)
Columbia Republican Club, Indianapolis, remarks, **1954:** 290
Columbia River, **1954:** 271
Columbia River Basin development, **1960–61:** 410
Treaty with Canada, **1960–61:** 414 (p. 994)
Message to Congress, **1960–61:** 419
Proposed, statement, **1960–61:** 331
Remarks on signing, **1960–61:** 416
Columbia University, **1953:** 215; **1954:** 118, 300, 347; **1955:** 151; **1956:** 88, 96, 235; **1957:** 33n., 105, 134, 223; **1958:** 168; **1959:** 164, 196, 259, 311; **1960–61:** 29n., 30n., 86, 143, 186, 187
See also under Colleges and Universities.
Bicentennial celebration, **1953:** 238; **1954:** 39, 128
News conference remarks, **1953:** 15, 109, 126, 238
Columbine, the President's airplane, **1956:** 257
Columbus, Christopher, **1955:** 219; **1959:** 338; **1960–61:** 332
Ceremony honoring, remarks, **1958:** 284
Columbus Citizens' Committee, letter, **1955:** 219
Cominform, **1956:** 78
Commemorative or dedicatory occasions.
See Addresses or remarks on commemorative or dedicatory occasions.
Commerce, Department of, **1957:** 169; **1958:** 14, 29, 68, 258; **1959:** 167; **1960–61:** 143, 146
Anderson, Samuel W., **1953:** 213n.
Aviation facilities planning, **1956:** 38
Budget messages, **1954:** 14 (pp. 178, 181, 182); **1956:** 12 (pp. 140, 141, 142); **1958:** 5 (pp. 45, 53); **1959:** 10 (pp. 65, 73, 87, 100); **1960–61:** 13 (pp. 64, 68, 69, 75, 91), 414 (pp. 968, 969, 973, 975, 977, 979, 983, 984, 992)
Bureau of Public Roads, **1956:** 186n.
Business Advisory Council, **1959:** 10 (p. 73)
Remarks, **1953:** 30
Recommendation on wage-price increases, **1958:** 103
Business programs, reorganization, **1954:** 14 (p. 181)
Conference for benefit of small business, **1957:** 132
Employment and unemployment information, **1954:** 39, 107, 308

Commerce, Department of — *continued*
Management counseling, **1956:** 263
Merchant marine, study of, **1954:** 67
Moore, George T., **1959:** 18n.
Ray, Philip A., **1960–61:** 170n.
Reports, **1958:** 283; **1960–61:** 387
Rural development program, **1956:** 6; **1957:** 156
Small business purchases, **1956:** 263
Statistics on construction, **1959:** 10 (p. 100)
Trade promotion services, **1960–61:** 95
Transportation programs, **1954:** 163
Transportation study, **1960–61:** 13 (p. 68), 414 (p. 973)
Water resources, report, **1956:** 13
Commerce, Secretary of, **1955:** 222; **1956:** 12 (p. 149); **1959:** 148
Commerce, Secretary of (Frederick H. Mueller), **1959:** 167; **1960–61:** 131
Interstate highway study, **1959:** 227
Letters, **1960–61:** 358, 376, 387
Reports, **1960–61:** 358, 387
Resignation, **1960–61:** 387
Taft-Hartley Act study, **1960–61:** 21
U.S. participation in New York World's Fair (1964–65) study, **1960–61:** 358, 376
Commerce, Secretary of (Lewis L. Strauss), **1959:** 112
See also Strauss, Lewis L.
Congressional action on appointment, **1959:** 89, 94, 102, 123, 132
Statement, **1959:** 134
Letter, **1959:** 113
Resignation, letter, **1959:** 147
Transportation study, **1959:** 10 (pp. 76, 79)
Commerce, Secretary of (Sinclair Weeks), **1953:** 187, 266, 268, 269; **1954:** 37, 267, 311; **1955:** 39n., 90 ftn. (p. 475), 137; **1957:** 27, 235; **1958:** 14, 25, 93
Bipartisan conference, 2
Campaign remarks on, **1956:** 241
Chairman, Red Cross campaign, **1954:** 356
Chairman, Trade Policy Committee, **1958:** 5 (p. 38)
Commerce Department budget, recommendations re, **1953:** 31
Committee on Small Business, member, **1956:** 118
Discussions with Prime Minister Kishi, **1957:** 117
European visit, **1955:** 59
Federal Council on Aging, representation on, **1956:** 74
Foreign aid, memorandum, **1954:** 323
General Chairman, Conference on Highway Safety, **1953:** 261
Highway, study, **1954:** 102
Highways, progress report, **1956:** 186
Letters, **1954:** 163; **1958:** 82
News conference remarks on, **1953:** 31, 41, 128; **1956:** 94; **1958:** 70, 83

Commerce, Secretary of — *continued*
  Nuclear-powered merchant ship, **1956:** 243
  Oil supply study, **1956:** 239
  Organization for Trade Cooperation, **1957:** 61
  Recession, **1958:** 83
  Recommendations on railroads and transportation industry, **1958:** 82n.
  Resignation, **1958:** 299
  Small business, report on conference for benefit of, letter, **1957:** 227 and n.
  Telegram on construction quoted, **1958:** 308
Commerce, Under Secretary of (Walter Williams)
  Rural development committee, **1956:** 217n.
  Visit to Japan, **1958:** 70
Commerce and housing, **1958:** 5 (pp. 24, 41, 53–61); **1959:** 10 (pp. 76–88)
Commerce and manpower, budget message, **1955:** 17 (pp. 163–178)
Commissary and post exchange privileges, **1955:** 100
Commission on Civil Rights, **1957:** 8, 133, 242 and n.; **1959:** 128; **1960–61:** 4, 410
  Budget messages, **1960–61:** 13 (p. 105), 414 (p. 1022)
  Chairman (John A. Hannah), **1959:** 128n.
  Extension proposed, **1959:** 7, 17, 27
  News conference remarks on, **1959:** 7, 17, 26, 223, 288; **1960–61:** 7, 21
  Proposed, **1956:** 16, 56, 69
  Report, **1959:** 288
Commission on Civilian Employee Compensation, Joint, proposed, **1959:** 10 (p. 109)
Commission on the Civilian Employee Compensation Policy of the Federal Government, establishment proposed, **1958:** 169
Commission for Construction of Ohio River Bridges, disapproval, **1956:** 182
Commission on Equal Job Opportunity, proposed, **1960–61:** 414 (p. 1023)
Commission on Equal Job Opportunity under Government Contracts, proposed, **1959:** 27
Commission on Financial System, **1957:** 8, 16
Commission on Fine Arts, **1955:** 17 (p. 141); **1956:** 4n.; **1960–61:** 243
Commission on Foreign Economic Policy (Randall Commission), **1953:** 176, 246, 249; **1958:** 56, 318
  Bipartisan, **1957:** 32
  Establishment, **1953:** 161
  Letter to Chairman, **1953:** 177
  News conference remarks on, **1954:** 18, 68, 101, 138, 157, 353
  Proposed, **1953:** 63, 70, 131
  Recommendations, **1956:** 162
  Remarks, **1953:** 190
  Report, **1954:** 16, 18, 67, 68, 90, 101, 209, 349, 351, 353

Commission on Government Security, **1956:** 12 (p. 153)
Commission on Increased Industrial Use of Agricultural Products, **1958:** 12
  Budget message, **1958:** 5 (p. 67)
  Statement, **1956:** 187
Commission on Intergovernmental Relations, **1953:** 159, 169; **1954:** 3, 102, 222, 273, 346; **1955:** 4; **1956:** 2; **1957:** 418; **1960–61:** 208
  Budget message, **1954:** 14 (p. 190)
  Civil defense recommendations, **1955:** 149
  News conference remarks, **1953:** 37, 54, 198, 225; **1955:** 47, 146, 149
  Proposed, **1953:** 6, 16, 37, 54, 67, 156
    Message to Congress, **1953:** 39
  Report, **1955:** 145; **1958:** 106
  Statements, **1953:** 16, 186
Commission on Intergovernmental Relations, Advisory, **1960–61:** 115, 208, 415n.
  Budget messages, **1960–61:** 13 (p. 105), 414 (p. 1022)
Commission on International Rules of Judicial Procedure, **1960–61:** 13 (p. 105)
Commission on Judicial and Congressional Salaries, **1958:** 169
Commission on National Goals, **1960–61:** 21
  Letters to Chairman, **1960–61:** 29, 240
  Memorandum, **1960–61:** 30
Commission on Naval Vessels, **1957:** 112n.
Commission on Organization of the Executive Branch of the Government.
  See Hoover Commission.
Commission on Presidential Office Space, **1956:** 131; **1960–61:** 414 (p. 1017)
Commission on Postal Rates, proposed, **1954:** 3
Commission on Religious Organizations, National Conference of Christians and Jews, message, **1953:** 132
Commission on Renovation of the Executive Mansion, **1956:** 131
Commission on Telecommunications, proposed, **1959:** 47
Commission on Veterans Pensions, **1956:** 2, 267n.
  Budget messages, **1955:** 17 (p. 134); **1956:** 12 (p. 111)
  Letter, **1955:** 51
Commissioner of Education, **1953:** 28
Commissioner of Indian Affairs, vacancy in office, **1953:** 128
Commissioner of Indian Affairs (Glenn L. Emmons), letter, **1953:** 180
Commissioner for Social Security, **1953:** 28
Commissions, Presidential, comment on, **1960–61:** 268
Committee, Fairless, **1957:** 45, 50
Committee for Aeronautics, National Advisory, **1956:** 12 (p. 141)

Committee on Children and Youth,
  Interdepartmental, **1958:** 119
Committee on Civilian Compensation and Pay
  Systems, Interdepartmental, **1958:** 169
Committee to Coordinate Federal Area Assistance
  Programs, Interdepartmental, **1960–61:** 5,
  176n.
Committee on Department of Defense Organiza-
  tion, **1953:** 61
Committee for Development of Scientists and
  Engineers, National, **1956:** 76, 77, 277
  Chairman, Howard L. Bevis, appointment, **1956:**
  77
Committee on Disarmament, Ten-Nation, **1960–
  61:** 241
Committee for Economic Development, remarks,
  1954: 118
Committee on Education, proposed, **1959:** 7
Committee on Education Beyond High School,
  1956: 85, 222, 277; **1957:** 19
Committee on Education and Utilization of Sci-
  entists and Engineers, Interdepartmental,
  1956: 76, 77
Committee on Employment of the Physically
  Handicapped, President's, remarks, **1953:**
  192; **1954:** 96; **1958:** 99; **1960–61:** 417
Committee on Energy Supplies and Resources
  Policy (Flemming Committee), report,
  1955: 33 and ftn. (p. 259), 41, 56
Committee for European Migration, Intergovern-
  mental, **1953:** 53, 89; **1956:** 58, 213n., 306
  Contributions to, **1956:** 12 (p. 107)
Committee on the Fitness of American Youth,
  1956: 96, 128; **1957:** 104
Committee on Foreign Economic Policy, **1956:** 198
Committee on Government Activities Affecting
  Prices and Costs, establishment, state-
  ment, **1959:** 18
Committee on Government Contracts, President's,
  1959: 27; **1960–61:** 410
  Budget message, **1960–61:** 414 (p. 1023)
  Report, statement, **1960–61:** 407
Committee on Government Contract Compliance,
  1953: 41, 54, 88
Committee on Government Employment Policy,
  President's, **1960–61:** 410
  Report, **1960–61:** 217 ftn. (p. 545), 394
Committee on Government Operations, **1955:** 74
Committee on Government Organization, Presi-
  dent's Advisory, **1953:** 6; **1954:** 163, 348;
  1960–61: 349
  News conference remarks, **1953:** 37, 62
  Report, letter, **1960–61:** 433
  Study of Federal civil defense, **1956:** 142
Committee for the Hoover Report, **1957:** 26n.
Committee on Housing Policies and Programs,
  1954: 17
  Budget message, **1954:** 14 (p. 146)

Committee for Hungarian Refugee Relief, report,
  1957: 85
Committee on Information Activities Abroad,
  President's, **1960–61:** 332 ftn. (p. 789)
Committee on Inter-American Affairs, National
  Advisory, **1960–61:** 42 and ftn. (p. 205),
  51, 69, 228, 349
  Message to President Kubitschek, **1959:** 287
Committee for International Economic Growth,
  address, **1960–61:** 132
Committee for International Geophysical Year,
  1957: 211
Committee on International Information Activi-
  ties, President's, **1953:** 230n.
  Establishment, statement, **1953:** 2
  Report, **1953:** 126, 128 and ftn. (p. 472)
Committee to Investigate Crude Oil Imports, **1957:**
  145, ftn. (p. 581); **1958:** 54; **1959:** 51n.
Committee on Juvenile Crime, **1954:** 207
Committee on Minerals Policy, Cabinet, **1953:** 228;
  1954: 14 (p. 170); **1955:** 17 (p. 163); **1956:**
  12 (p. 138)
Committee on the Mutual Security Program, Pres-
  ident's Citizens Advisers, **1957:** 45
Committee on Narcotics, report, **1956:** 31
Committee on National Goals, **1959:** 6
  News conference remarks on, **1959:** 36, 89, 154,
  179, 271
  Selection of members, **1959:** 271
Committee on a National Highway Program (Clay
  Committee), **1954:** 346n., 349; **1955:** 4,
  146
  Report, **1955:** 39
Committee for a National Trade Policy, **1955:** 83;
  1957: 110
Committee for the 1960 White House Conference
  on Children and Youth, remarks, **1958:**
  320
Committee on Poliomyelitis Vaccine, National Ad-
  visory, **1955:** 81, 90
Committee of Presidential Representatives, Inter-
  American, report, **1957:** 96
Committee on Price Stability for Economic
  Growth, **1959:** 6
  News conference remarks on, **1959:** 17, 36 and
  ftn. (p. 197), 67
  Report, statement, **1959:** 144
Committee on Professional and Technical Com-
  pensation, Defense Advisory, **1957:** 13;
  1958: 169; **1959:** 10 (p. 59)
  Budget message, **1958:** 5 (p. 31)
Committee for Public Education, Charlottesville,
  Va., Letter to chairman, **1958:** 267
Committee on Radioactive Fallout, U.N., **1957:**
  208
Committee on Recent Social Trends, **1959:** 6, 29
Committee for Refugees, **1959:** 91

Committee on Religion in American Life, radio and television program, recorded statement, **1953:** 236

Committee on Retirement Policy for Federal Personnel, **1954:** 10, 43, 145
Budget message, **1954:** 14 (p. 189)
Report, **1955:** 17 (p. 181)

Committee for Rural Development Program, **1959:** 273; **1960–61:** 5
Budget message, **1960–61:** 414 (p. 993)

Committee on Scientists and Engineers
Letter, **1958:** 327
Report, **1957:** 241
Study of pay problems, **1958:** 169

Committee on Small Business, Cabinet, **1956:** 118, 176, 263; **1957:** 13, 132 and n.
Budget message, **1958:** 5 (p. 23)

Committee to Strengthen the Frontiers of Freedom, address, **1960–61:** 132

Committee to Study the U.S. Military Assistance Program (Draper Committee), **1959:** 6, 55; **1960–61:** 36
Budget messages **1959:** 10 (p. 69); **1960–61:** 13 (p. 57), 414 (p. 962)
Letter to Chairman, **1958:** 316
News conference remarks on, **1959:** 53, 94, 154, 288
Reports, **1959:** 53, 90, 136, 137, 170, 183, 288

Committee on Telecommunications, report, **1959:** 47

Committee on Trade with Communist Areas, **1956:** 53

Committee on Trade and Economic Affairs, U.S.-Canada, **1953:** 246
Joint statement with Prime Minister St. Laurent, **1953:** 247

Committee for Traffic Safety, **1954:** 37n.; **1955:** 111, 243; **1956:** 36, 37, 305
Hearst, William Randolph, Jr., letter re appointment, **1955:** 124
Petersen, T. S., letter re appointment, **1955:** 125
Regional conference, message, **1958:** 45
Report, **1957:** 14

Committee on Transport Policy and Organization, **1957:** 13
Establishment, **1954:** 163
Reports, **1955:** 33, 62, 90 and ftn. (p. 475); **1960–61:** 21

Committee of Under Secretaries on rural Development, report of, statement, **1956:** 217

Committee for United Nations Day, United States, remarks, **1953:** 191

Committee on Voluntary Foreign Aid, Advisory, **1953:** 92

Committee on Water Resources Policy, **1954:** 120, 122; **1956:** 12 (p. 133), 13, 16, 170; **1957:** 8

Committee for the White House Conference on Education, **1955:** 96; **1956:** 103

Committees (Federal and State) on Public Works Planning, **1956:** 309n.

Commodity Credit Corporation, **1953:** 35, 97, 206, 213; **1954:** 4, 168 ftn. (p. 646), 195; **1955:** 17 (pp. 126, 130, 149, 150, 152, 155); **1956:** 6; **1958:** 59, 60; **1959:** 10 (pp. 89–91); **1960–61:** 32
Agricultural commodities for foreign emergency relief, authority re, **1953:** 125
Budget messages, **1954:** 14 (pp. 139, 158, 159); **1956:** 12 (pp. 127, 128, 129); **1958:** 5 (pp. 21, 63); **1960–61:** 13 (pp. 79, 107), 414 (pp. 938, 986, 988, 989, 1012)
News conference remarks, **1953:** 225 and ftn. (p. 699), 249
Surplus stocks, **1954:** 3

Commodity Credit Corporation Advisory Board, **1958:** 12

Common market, European, **1956:** 278; **1957:** 8
See also European Economic Community.
Campaign remarks, **1956:** 278
Joint statements
Chancellor Adenauer, **1957:** 100
Premier Mollet, **1957:** 38
Prime Minister Macmillan, **1957:** 55, 226

Common market for Central American, joint statement on, **1959:** 54
Bulwark against aggression, **1957:** 226
Establishment of Republic of Pakistan, **1956:** 65

Commonwealth Club of California, address, **1960–61:** 332

Communication services, budget message, **1954:** 14 (pp. 171, 172, 176–178)

Communications
Alaska, **1960–61:** 13 (p. 50), 414 (p. 956)
Budget messages, **1960–61:** 13 (pp. 50, 68), 414 (pp. 956, 970, 972, 973, 977, 978)
Earth satellites, **1960–61:** 261, 264, 410, 414 (pp. 970, 972), 424
Commercial use, statement, **1960–61:** 386
Message recorded for transmission via Echo I, **1960–61:** 258

Communications Act, amendment, approval, **1959:** 216

Communications between heads of state or governments, disclosure of, **1958:** 74

Communications facilities, Alaska, **1959:** 10 (p. 65)

Communiques, comment on, **1955:** 146

Communism, **1953:** 6, 79, 98, 104, 120, 181, 187; **1954:** 72, 77, 86, 89, 128, 160, 170, 318, 319, 320; **1955:** 13, 35, 43, 48, 57, 58, 64, 79, 85, 94, 99, 175; **1956:** 2, 3, 87, 114, 283; **1958:** 32, 35, 36, 58, 95, 102, 123, 154, 161, 173, 261, 263, 277; **1959:** 6, 63, 76, 79, 83, 84, 87, 90, 128, 158n., 296; **1960–61:** 4, 22, 30, 36, 42, 53, 160, 171n., 183, 186, 188, 191, 192, 193, 194, 209, 250, 359, 409, 410, 420

Communism — *continued*
  Campaign remarks, **1958:** 287, 290; **1960–61:** 345, 347, 348, 354
  Cuba, **1959:** 277; **1960–61:** 227, 256, 410, 431
  Declaration of American States against Communist intervention (1954), **1956:** 146
  Exploitation of unrest, **1958:** 103
  Hungary, **1954:** 30; **1956:** 296
  Iraq, **1959:** 36, 89
  Joint statements
    President Chiang Kai-shek, **1960–61:** 195
    Prime Minister Eden, **1956:** 27
  Letters to Premier Bulganin, **1958:** 7, 31
  Moscow Manifesto (1957), **1958:** 31
  News conference remarks, **1953:** 109, 126, 225, 243, 254; **1954:** 33, 48, 92, 138, 143, 157, 192, 341, 345, 347, 353; **1955:** 26, 81, 119; **1956:** 16, 78; **1959:** 36, 89, 223, 271, 277; **1960–61:** 24, 127, 222, 256
  Subject in educational curriculum, **1956:** 201
  Threat to American freedom, **1954:** 3
  Uncommitted areas, **1958:** 35
Communism, Commission on Education and, **1956:** 201n.
Communism, international
  Addresses and messages, references in, **1957:** 6, 15, 37, 91
  Joint statements
    Prime Minister Kishi, **1957:** 117
    Prime Minister Macmillan, **1957:** 226
    Prime Minister Suhrawardy, **1957:** 131
  News conference remarks, **1957:** 134, 157
Communist activities in Italy, **1954:** 39
Communist activities in United States, **1953:** 95; **1954:** 72, 139, 210, 211, 225, 273, 275, 286, 291; **1959:** 172
  Churches, question re, **1953:** 31, 132; **1960–61:** 38
  Department of Justice record of action re, **1954:** 129, 130, 209
  Education, **1953:** 15
  News conference remarks, **1953:** 15, 31, 109, 126, 243, 249, 254; **1954:** 18, 48, 92, 129
  Norwalk, Conn., question of, **1954:** 18
Communist aggression and expansion, **1953:** 6, 50, 82, 101; **1954:** 3, 71, 72, 87, 104, 105, 209, 225, 226, 286, 297, 319, 320, 325, 337; **1955:** 4, 12, 21, 24; **1958:** 2, 8, 32, 36, 80, 96, 125, 163, 261, 289; **1959:** 57, 70, 71; **1960–61:** 36, 38, 133, 164, 200, 201, 202, 203, 209, 245, 286, 422
  See also Aggression.
  Asia, **1954:** 73 and ftn. (p. 384), 101, 115, 297, 316
    Joint statement with Prime Minister Yoshida, **1954:** 330
  Budget messages, **1955:** 17 (p. 129); **1959:** 10 (pp. 69, 70)

Communist aggression and expansion — *continued*
  Cambodia, **1954:** 280
  Campaign remarks, **1958:** 290, 292, 293, 294, 295, 296
  Economic activities in foreign countries, **1958:** 16, 25, 32, 58, 290; **1959:** 55
  Economic offensive, **1955:** 6
  Greece, **1953:** 66, 233n.
  India, **1959:** 94
  Indochina, **1954:** 33, 203
  Iran, **1953:** 22; **1954:** 192, 203, 209, 273, 286, 316, 317, 318, 353
  Joint statement with President Garcia on, **1958:** 143
  Korea, **1953:** 96; **1954:** 171n.
  Laos, **1959:** 214
  Latin America
    Caracas Resolution against, **1954:** 115, 143, 203, 209, 225, 273, 297, 304
    Guatemala, **1954:** 115, 143, 157, 203, 209, 225, 226, 273, 286, 297, 304, 316, 317; **1960–61:** 368
  Letter to Senator Green, **1958:** 277
  News conference remarks, **1954:** 63, 73 and ftn. (p. 384), 101, 115, 311; **1958:** 153, 213, 274, 288; **1959:** 94, 172, 179, 186
  SEATO council of ministers action re, **1960–61:** 286
  Tibet, **1960–61:** 410
  White House release, **1958:** 257n.
Communist areas, **1956:** 87, 230
  Trade with, **1956:** 53
Communist attitude on international agreements, **1954:** 128; **1959:** 6
Communist bloc, **1954:** 73 ftn. (p. 384); **1955:** 4; **1958:** 7, 58; **1960–61:** 174, 183, 341, 342, 409, 422
  See also Satellite countries, Soviet; *specific countries.*
  Budget message, **1958:** 5 (p. 39)
  Economic offensive, **1959:** 55
  Economic and technical aid to foreign countries, **1958:** 16, 25, 32, 58, 290
  Food production, **1958:** 290
  Joint statement with President Ayub Khan on, **1959:** 303
  Military strength, **1959:** 55
  Peaceful coexistence with, **1954:** 157
  Trade with, **1953:** 88; **1954:** 9, 67, 138, 143; **1955:** 18
    Cuba, **1960–61:** 223
    Embargo, Congressional committee discussions re, **1953:** 41
    U.S. policy, **1954:** 149; **1959:** 48
Communist Control Act
  Approval, **1954:** 210
  Remarks, **1954:** 211

Communist doctrine, **1960–61:** 328
  Premier Khrushchev on, **1959:** 243
Communist-front and Communist-infiltrated organizations, **1954:** 210
Communist imperialism, **1954:** 150, 308; **1955:** 4; **1959:** 53, 290; **1960–61:** 286, 422
Communist infiltration, **1957:** 17, 87
  Western Hemisphere, Caracas Resolution against, **1957:** 111
Communist membership affidavit by employers, **1959:** 22
Communist Party in United States, outlawing of, **1954:** 48, 200
  Approval of act, **1954:** 210
Communist propaganda, **1957:** 87
Communist territorial expansion.
  See Communist aggression and expansion
Communists, **1956:** 2, 75, 87, 117, 190, 248
  French armed forces, handling of, **1954:** 48
  News conference remarks, **1956:** 62, 78, 210
Community Chest campaigns, **1954:** 132, 183, 276; **1955:** 130; **1956:** 138, 185; **1957:** 140, 154, 203; **1958:** 184; **1959:** 159; **1960–61:** 293
  Memorandums, **1953:** 115, 179; **1960–61:** 210
  Message, **1953:** 196
  National Capital area, **1953:** 127
Community development, budget messages, **1954:** 14 (pp. 146–151); **1959:** 10 (pp. 47, 48, 82–86)
Community facilities bill, news conference remarks, **1958:** 74
Commuter services, unprofitable, recommendations on, **1958:** 82n.
Compensation.
  See Pay.
Compensation and Pay Systems, Interdepartmental Committee on, **1958:** 169
Compton, Karl T., nomination to National Security Commission, **1953:** 144
Compton, Mr. and Mrs. Thomas V., relief of, **1956:** 126
Comptroller General of the United States, **1957:** 72
  Filling of vacancy, comment on, **1954:** 311
Comptroller General of the United States (Joseph Campbell), **1955:** 62; **1959:** 161
  Letter, **1959:** 342
  View on disallowance of use of certain mutual security funds, **1960–61:** 380n.
Comptroller General of the United States (Lindsay C. Warren), **1954:** 73
  Retirement, letter, **1954:** 69
Conant, James B., **1953:** 138n.; **1960–61:** 30n.
  Food shortage in East Germany, **1953:** 135
Concord, Mass., **1956:** 87
Concord, N. H., remarks, **1955:** 133
Condemnation of realty, procedure, Declaration of Taking Act, amendment, **1958:** 250

Condon, Repr. Robert L., **1959:** 18
Conduct of elected officials, **1958:** 141
Conduct of Government employees, **1954:** 92, 302, 311, 353
Conduct of Government officials.
  See Government officals.
"Confederate underground," **1958:** 288
Conference on Administration Procedure, President's, letter to Chairman, **1960–61:** 275
Conference of Christians and Jews, National, message, **1953:** 132
Conference on Equal Job Opportunity, letter, **1955:** 225
Conference on Fitness of American Youth, message, **1955:** 217
Conference of the Inter-Parliamentary Union, greetings to delegates, **1953:** 209
Conference of Mayors, White House, remarks, **1953:** 262
Conflict of interest case, Gen. W. W. White, **1955:** 185
Conflict-of-interest statutes
  Effect on President, **1957:** 145
  News conference remarks, **1957:** 62, 145
Congo, Republic of
  News conference remarks, **1960–61:** 256, 263, 284
  Soviet action in, **1960–61:** 284
  U.N. action in, **1960–61:** 263, 284, 302, 304
    Airlift of Ghanaian forces, **1960–61:** 248
    Malayan support, **1960–61:** 339
Congo, Republic of (Brazzaville)
  Tchichelle, Stephane, **1960–61:** 324n.
  Youlou, Fulbert, **1959:** 214; **1960–61:** 260
Congo, Republic of (Leopoldville), **1960–61:** 245, 270, 410
  Assistance, **1960–61:** 263
  Independence from Belgium, **1960–61:** 216
  Joint statement with Prime Minister Macmillan on role of U.N., **1960–61:** 307
  Kasavubu, Joseph, **1960–61:** 216, 364
  Lumumba, Patrice, **1960–61:** 263, 284
Congress
  Address by Premier Khrushchev, question of, **1959:** 186
  Address by President de Gaulle, **1960–61:** 124
  Address by President Lleras, **1960–61:** 111
  Adjournment, statement, **1959:** 225
  Committee investigations, comments on, **1953:** 15, 22, 243, 249; **1954:** 48, 57, 63, 72, 92, 101, 107, 113, 115, 129, 302, 347
    Immunity of witnesses, **1954:** 139
  85th, fixing date of meeting, disapproval, **1956:** 175
  House Rules Committee membership increase, **1960–61:** 422
  Meetings with leaders of, **1960–61:** 246
  Pay increase, question of, **1953:** 77

Congress — *continued*
 Power to declare war, **1954:** 57, 92
 Privileged information of executive, disclosure to Congress forbidden by President, **1960–61:** 380
 Record of, **1954:** 192, 200, 322; **1960–61:** 263, 284
  Broadcast, **1953:** 159; **1954:** 209
 Relations with, **1953:** 30, 101, 159; **1954:** 33, 273, 286, 322, 347; **1959:** 154, 161, 179, 223; **1960–61:** 422
 Republican leaders and chairmen of standing committees, legislative conference, **1953:** 249, 265, 266, 268, 269
 Special session, question of, **1959:** 186
Congress, letters to Members of
See also Congress, messages to.
 Aiken, Sen. George D.
  Farm bill, **1954:** 196
  Soil bank, **1956:** 35
 Anderson, Sen. Clinton P.
  NATO cooperation re atomic information, **1955:** 71
  Peaceful uses of atomic energy, **1956:** 30
  Submerged lands bill, **1953:** 58
 Bennett, Sen. Wallace F., sugar quotas, **1960–61:** 167
 Bridges, Sen. Styles, mutual security appropriations, **1953:** 143
 Broyhill, Repr. Joel T., Federal employees benefits, **1954:** 313
 Buckley, Repr. Charles A., National Cultural Center, **1958:** 190
 Capehart, Sen. Homer E., Federal Housing Administration investigation, **1954:** 302
 Chiperfield, Repr. Robert B., European Coal and Steel Community, **1953:** 111
 Cooper, Repr. Jere, Organization for Trade Cooperation, **1955:** 160
 Cooper, Sen. John Sherman, Federal aid to chronic labor surplus areas, **1960–61:** 5
 Dirksen, Sen. Everett McK., mutual security appropriations, **1960–61:** 271
 Gore, Sen. Albert, highway program, **1959:** 252
 Green, Sen. Theodore F., Formosa Strait situation, **1958:** 277
 Halleck, Repr. Charles A.
  Government spending, **1959:** 34
  Mutual security appropriations, **1960–61:** 272
 Hope, Repr. Clifford R., farm bill, **1954:** 196
 House Ways and Means Committee, Chairman
  Duties on lead and zinc, **1957:** 160
  Small business, **1957:** 132
 Hyde, Repr. DeWitt S., Federal employees benefits, **1954:** 313
 Johnson, Sen. Lyndon B.
  Briefings by CIA, **1960–61:** 236

Congress, letters to Members of — *continued*
 Johnson, Sen. Lyndon B. — *continued*
  Congratulations on election victory, **1960–61:** 356
  Mutual security appropriations, **1960–61:** 271
  Reports of Killian and Gaither panels, **1958:** 19
 Joint Committee on Atomic Energy, Chairman, proposed agreement with Australia, **1957:** 130
 Keating, Rep. Kenneth B., refugees, **1956:** 213
 Kennedy, Sen. John F.
  Briefings by CIA, **1960–61:** 236
  Congratulations on Presidential election victory, **1960–61:** 356
 Knowland, Sen. William F.
  Election campaign, **1958:** 221
  Measures to aid economy, **1958:** 43
  Water resources development projects, **1958:** 85
 Mansfield, Sen. Michael J., ICA report on Vietnam program, **1959:** 278
 Martin, Repr. Joseph W., Jr.
  Measures to aid economy, **1958:** 43
  Status of forces overseas, **1957:** 139
  Water resources development projects, **1958:** 85
 Mills, Repr. Wilbur D., trade agreements bill, **1958:** 132
 Powell, Adam C., **1957:** 191 and n.
 President of the Senate
  Air carriers equipment investment program, **1958:** 194
  Assistance to Yugoslavia, **1956:** 248
  Congressional election campaign, efforts toward, **1954:** 312
  Corporate and excise taxes, **1958:** 114
  Debt limit increase, **1958:** 183
  Defense reorganization, draft bill, **1958:** 75
  Foreign economic policy, **1953:** 63
  Great Plains program, **1956:** 7
  Hoover Commission recommendations, **1957:** 112
  Inter-American highway, **1955:** 64
  Military assistance program, **1959:** 90, 136, 170, 183
  Military career incentives, **1956:** 81
  Mission 66, National Park Service, **1956:** 29
  Philippine trade agreement revision, **1955:** 91
  Post election telegram, **1960–61:** 357
  Presidential office space, **1956:** 131; **1957:** 135
  Refugees, admission to United States, **1953:** 52
  Resolution on subjugated peoples, **1953:** 14
  Telecommunication systems, **1959:** 47
  Transportation survey of Washington area, **1959:** 157
  Virgin Islands Corporation, **1955:** 14
  Water resources policy, **1956:** 13

Congress, letters to Members of — *continued*
  Russell, Richard B., **1957**: 200 and n.
  Small, Repr. Frank, Jr., Federal employees ben-
     efits, **1954**: 313
  Smith, Sen. H. Alexander, older persons, **1956**:
     63
  Speaker of the House of Representatives
     Air carriers equipment investment program,
        1958: 194
     Assistance to Yugoslavia, **1956**: 248
     Budget, **1957**: 75
     Corporate and excise taxes, **1958**: 114
     Debt limit increase, **1958**: 183
     Defense reorganization, draft bill, **1958**: 75
     Federal-State Action Committee recommen-
        dations, **1958**: 106
     Foreign economic policy, **1953**: 63
     Great Plains program, **1956**: 7
     Hoover Commission recommendations, **1957**:
        112
     Inter-American highway, **1955**: 64
     Military assistance program, **1959**: 90, 136,
        170, 183
     Military career incentives, **1956**: 81
     Mission 66, National Park Service, **1956**: 29
     Mutual security appropriations, **1960–61**: 272
     Philippine trade agreement revision, **1955**: 91
     Presidential office space, **1956**: 131; **1957**: 135
     Refugees, addmission to United States, **1953**:
        52
     Resolution on subjugated peoples, **1953**: 14
     Supplemental appropriation for Department
        of Agriculture, **1953**: 136
     Telecommunication systems, **1959**: 47
     Transportation survey of Washington area,
        1959: 157
     Virgin Islands Corporation, **1955**: 14
     Water resources policy, **1956**: 13
  Vinson, Repr. Carl, defense reorganization,
     1958: 108
  Wainwright, Repr. Stuyvesant, education, **1958**:
     162
  Wiley, Sen. Alexander
     European Coal and Steel Community, **1953**:
        111
     St. Lawrence Seaway project, **1953**: 56
  Zablocki, Repr. Clement J., arrest of Cardinal
     Wyszynski of Poland, **1953**: 235
Congress, Members of, pay adjustments, **1958**: 169
Congress, messages to.
  See also Congress, letters to Members of.
  Act to stimulate residential construction, **1958**:
     62
  Aeronautics and space activities, **1959**: 25;
     1960–61: 47, 424
  Agricultural Trade Development and Assistance
     Act (P.L. 480, 83d Cong.), reports, **1955**:
     7, 150

Congress, messages to — *continued*
  Agriculture, **1954**: 4; **1956**: 6; **1958**: 12; **1959**: 23;
     1960–61: 32
     Commodities for foreign emergency relief,
        1953: 125
     Surpluses, **1959**: 104
  Airport, Chantilly, Va., report, **1958**: 9
  Anglo-American financial agreement of 1945,
     1957: 44
  Atomic Energy Act, amendment, **1954**: 38
  Atomic energy for mutual defense agreements
     U. S.-Germany, Netherlands, and Turkey,
        1959: 119
     U.S.-Italy, **1960–61**: 420
     U.S.-U.K., **1958**: 157
  Austrian State Treaty ratification, **1955**: 114
  Aviation facilities planning, report on, **1957**: 71
     and n.
  Budget, **1955**: 17; **1956**: 12; **1957**: 13; **1958**: 5;
     1959: 10; **1960–61**: 13, 414
  Budget and accounting, **1956**: 100
  Civil rights, **1959**: 27
  Columbia River Basin Treaty, **1960–61**: 419
  Commission on Intergovernmental Relations,
     1953: 39; **1955**: 145
  Debt limit, **1953**: 152
  Debt management, **1959**: 126, 188
  Defense reorganization, **1958**: 65
  Department of Defense Appropriation Act,
     1955: 155
  Drought and other natural disasters, **1957**: 41
  Economic reports, **1954**: 21; **1955**: 19; **1956**: 19;
     1957: 16; **1958**: 16; **1959**: 15; **1960–61**: 17,
     423
  Education, **1956**: 8; **1957**: 19; **1958**: 24
  Export trade, **1960–61**: 95
  Federal Aviation Agency, **1958**: 135
  Federal employees training program, report,
     1960–61: 149
  Federal personnel management, **1955**: 8
  FHA mortgage insurance authority, **1959**: 187
  Foreign affairs, organization of executive branch
     for conduct of, **1953**: 89
  Foreign economic policy, **1954**: 67; **1955**: 6
  Formosa Strait situation, **1955**: 21
  Freedom Monument, proposed, report, **1960–61**:
     152
  German-U.S. agreements on settlement of debts
     and claims, **1953**: 46
  Germany, protocols to treaties re, **1954**: 332
  Group life insurance for Federal employees,
     1954: 116
  Health program, **1954**: 11; **1955**: 25; **1956**: 21
  Highway program, **1955**: 39; **1959**: 104, 187
  Housing, **1954**: 17; **1959**: 104
  ILO conventions and recommendations, **1955**:
     107
  Immigration, **1956**: 33; **1957**: 25; **1960–61**: 96

Congress, messages to — *continued*
  Increase in funds for International Monetary
    Fund and World Bank, **1959:** 32
  Inter-American Development Bank, U.S. partic-
    ipation in, **1959:** 98
  Interest rates on Federal bonds, **1960–61:** 6
  International Atomic Energy Agency, **1957:** 54
    U.S. participation, report, **1959:** 189
  International Development Association, U.S.
    participation, **1960–61:** 39
  International Finance Corporation, U.S. partic-
    ipation in, **1955:** 86
  International Labor Organization
    Convention on social security standards, **1954:**
      126
    Recommendations on collective agreements
      and voluntary conciliation and arbitra-
      tion, **1954:** 125
  Joint Commission on the Civilian Employee
    Compensation Policy of the Federal Gov-
    ernment, establishment, **1958:** 169
  Korea, assistance for, **1953:** 148
  Labor-management relations, **1954:** 5; **1958:** 20;
    1959: 22
  Lebanon, assistance to, **1958:** 172
  Legislative program, **1960–61:** 133
  Low income farmers, **1955:** 82
  Middle East, report, **1957:** 149; **1958:** 41
  Middle East situation, **1957:** 6
  Military personnel, **1955:** 13
  Mutual Defense Treaties, U.S.-China, **1955:** 5
    U.S.-Korea, **1954:** 6
  Mutual security program, **1953:** 66; **1954:** 150;
    1955: 76; **1956:** 58; **1957:** 90; **1958:** 32;
    1959: 55; **1960–61:** 36
  National Advisory Committee for Aeronautics,
    report, **1959:** 85
  National Aeronautics and Space Act, amend-
    ments, **1960–61:** 11
  National Aeronautics and Space Administration,
    transfer of certain Department of Defense
    functions, **1960–61:** 10
  Natural resources, **1953:** 153
  National security, **1955:** 12
  Organization for Trade Cooperation, **1957:** 61
    U.S. membership, **1955:** 72
  Pakistan famine relief, **1953:** 97
  Passports, **1958:** 161
  Peace and stability in the Middle East, report,
    1957: 149
  Postal pay and rates, **1955:** 9
  Postal rate increase, **1960–61:** 89
  Public assistance programs, **1954:** 10
  Reclamation projects, approval of act, **1955:** 180
  Reconvening of Congress, **1960–61:** 255
  Refugee Relief Act, recommendations, **1955:** 109
  Renegotiation Act, extension, **1955:** 50

Congress, messages to — *continued*
  Reorganization Plans
    No. 1, Department of Health, Education, and
      Welfare, establishment, **1953:** 28
    No. 1 of 1954, **1954:** 94
    No. 1 of 1956, **1956:** 105
    No. 1 of 1957, **1957:** 78
    No. 1 of 1958, **1958:** 84
    No. 1 of 1959, **1959:** 101
    No. 2, Department of Agriculture, **1953:** 35
    No. 2 of 1954, **1954:** 95
    No. 2 of 1956, **1956:** 108
    No. 3, Executive Office, organization, **1953:** 40
    No. 4, Department of Justice, **1953:** 51
    No. 5, Export-Import Bank, **1953:** 60
    No. 6, Department of Defense, **1953:** 61
    No. 7, Foreign Operations Administration,
      establishment, **1953:** 90
    No. 8, United States Information Agency,
      establishment, **1953:** 91
    No. 9, Council of Economic Advisers, **1953:** 93
    No. 10, Air carriers, payments to, **1953:** 94
    Period for transmitting, **1957:** 58
  School construction, **1955:** 31
  Social security program, **1953:** 155; **1954:** 10
  Southeast Asia Collective Defense Treaty, **1954:**
    329
  Space science and exploration, **1958:** 64
  State of the Union, **1953:** 6; **1954:** 3; **1955:** 4;
    1956: 2; **1957:** 8; **1958:** 2; **1959:** 6;
    1960–61: 4, 410
  Sugar quota of Dominican Republic, **1960–61:**
    267
  Synthetic rubber facilities disposal, **1953:** 49
  Taxes, **1953:** 84
  Trade Agreements Act, renewal proposed, **1953:**
    44
  Trade agreements program, **1956:** 123; **1957:** 32;
    1958: 25
  Unemployment compensation, **1958:** 53
  United Nations, U.S. participation, reports,
    1955: 156; **1958:** 8, 148
  U.S.-Euratom international agreement, **1958:**
    145
Vetoes
  Alaskan oil and gas leases, **1959:** 182
  Alexander, J. Don, tax refund claim, **1953:** 107
  Alexander, Jake, conveyance of lands to,
    1954: 156
  Apple price predictions, prohibition of Gov-
    ernment publication, **1955:** 147
  Area redevelopment bill, **1958:** 258; **1960–61:**
    146
  Axelroad, Col. Benjamin, relief of, **1957:** 123
  Berry, Walter H., relief of, **1957:** 155
  Board of Commissioners, Sedgwick County,
    Kans., relief of, **1956:** 112
  Bond, Virginia, relief of, **1960–61:** 114

Congress, messages to — *continued*
  Vetoes — *continued*
    Brennan, Mrs. John William, relief of, **1957:** 73
    Camp Blanding Military Reservation, Fla., conveyance of lands within, **1954:** 121
    Carlson, Theodore W., relief of, **1954:** 134
    Compton, Mr. and Mrs. Thomas V., relief of, **1956:** 126
    Continental Hosiery Mills, Inc., relief of, **1958:** 187
    Court of Claims jurisdiction in overtime compensation case, **1954:** 41
    Cowan, Roy, and others, relief of, **1956:** 79
    Crow Indian Tribe, payment to, **1956:** 124
    Dew Hong-to, relief of, **1958:** 124
    District of Columbia, certain gasoline filling stations, **1953:** 149
    District of Columbia, election of delegates to national political conventions, **1954:** 206
    Eber Brothers Wine and Liquor Corp., relief of, **1959:** 215
    Engelbert, Wilhelm, relief of, **1954:** 58
    Farm bill, **1956:** 82
    Farm "freeze" bill, **1958:** 59
    Federal employees, salary increase, **1960–61:** 217
    Federal employees operating Government motor vehicles, defense of suits against, **1960–61:** 180
    Federal National Mortgage Association, income tax treatment of nonrefundable capital contributions, **1960–61:** 151
    Federal Water Pollution Control Act, amendment, **1960–61:** 44
    Glaser, Kurt, relief of **1955:** 116
    Grand Lodge of North Dakota, relief of, **1960–61:** 181
    Gruhl, Helmuth W., relief of, **1953:** 108
    Hanzal, Alfred, relief of, **1958:** 34
    Harry, Ralston E., relief of, **1954:** 159
    Haun, Cale P. and Julia Fay, relief of, **1955:** 48
    Hines, Fred P., relief of **1953:** 139
    Holder, Anna, relief of, **1954:** 42
    Housing bills, **1959:** 153, 208
    Importation of seed wheat, **1958:** 217
    Income tax deductions for certain charitable contributions, **1960–61:** 169
    Independent Offices Appropriation Act, **1958:** 192
    Kaczmarczyk, Rose, relief of, **1954:** 141
    Kaiser, William J., relief of, **1960–61:** 113
    Kilpatrick, Shirley Leeke, relief of, **1958:** 61
    Klyce Motors, Inc., relief of, **1954:** 181
    Laney, D. S. and Elizabeth, relief of, **1958:** 205
    Louisiana Purchase, sesquicentennial, coinage of 50-cent pieces in commemoration, **1954:** 29

Congress, messages to — *continued*
  Vetoes — *continued*
    Military installations, housing, **1956:** 141
    Minerals program, **1958:** 206
    Nakamura, Harry H., relief of, **1959:** 155
    Natural Gas Act, amendment, **1956:** 41
    New York City, tercentennial, coinage of 50-cent pieces in commemoration, **1954:** 28
    Northampton, Mass., tercentennial, coinage of 50-cent pieces in commemoration, **1954:** 27
    Nuclear-powered ice breaker, **1958:** 204
    Our Lady of the Lake Church, relief of, **1960–61:** 179
    Postal field service compensation bill, **1955:** 102
    Public Health Service Act, amendment, **1954:** 137
    Public work appropriation bills, **1959:** 194, 213
    Rivers and harbors bill, **1958:** 73
    Roach, Lucian, relief of, **1958:** 212
    Rural Electrification Administration, loan approval authority, **1959:** 86
    St. Marie, Josette L., relief of, **1954:** 142
    Spencer, Susie Lee, estate, relief of, **1956:** 134
    Stone, William E., claim of, **1956:** 135
    Thomson Contracting Co., Inc., relief of, **1958:** 208
    Tobacco price support bill, **1959:** 140
    Unemployment tax credits of successor employers, **1960–61:** 170
    Universal Trades, Inc., relief of, **1960–61:** 150
    Wage rates, Portsmouth naval shipyard, **1958:** 191
    Weigand, Margareth, estate, relief of, **1954:** 59
    Wheat bill, **1959:** 139
Congress, reports to, list, Appendix C, **1953:** p. 885; **1954:** p. 1138; **1955:** p. 884; **1956:** p. 1155; **1957:** p. 874; **1958:** p. 889; **1959:** p. 908; **1960–61:** p. 1091
Congress, reports to, messages transmitting.
    See also Congress, letters to Members of.
    Aeronautics and space activities, **1959:** 25; **1960–61:** 47, 424
    Agricultural Trade Development and Assistance Act (Public Law 480, 83d Cong.), **1955:** 7, 150
    Air carriers equipment investment program, **1958:** 194
    Airport, Chantilly, Va., **1958:** 9
    Aviation facilities planning, **1957:** 71
    Commission on Intergovernmental Relations, **1955:** 145
    Economic reports, **1955:** 19; **1957:** 16; **1958:** 16; **1959:** 15; **1960–61:** 17, 423
    Federal employees training program, **1960–61:** 149

Congress, reports to — *continued*
  Freedom Monument, proposed, **1960–61:** 152
  Great Plains program, **1956:** 7
  International Atomic Energy Agency, U.S. participation, **1959:** 180
  Middle East, **1957:** 149; **1958:** 41
  Military assistance program, letters, **1959:** 90, 136, 170, 183
  National Advisory Committee for Aeronautics, **1959:** 85
  National Advisory Council on International Monetary and Financial Problems, **1959:** 98
  Presidential office space, **1957:** 135
  Rubber requirement and resources, **1956:** 90
  Trade Agreements Program, operation, **1957:** 32
  Transportation survey of Washington area, letter, **1959:** 157
  United Nations, U.S. participation, **1955:** 156; **1956:** 143; **1958:** 8, 148
  Water resources policy, **1956:** 13
Congress, special session, **1957:** 152
Congress of Industrial Organizations, **1953:** 128, 130; **1954:** 161 ftn. (p. 622)
  15th Constitutional Convention, **1953:** 248
  News conference remarks on, **1954:** 107, 347
Congressional election campaign.
  See Election campaign.
Congressional investigations, **1957:** 56, 87
  Army-McCarthy hearing, **1956:** 216
  Testimony by Federal employees on nonsecurity matters, **1956:** 216
Congressional Medal of Honor, remarks to holders of, **1958:** 122
  See also Medal of Honor *under* Medals, remarks on presentation or acceptance.
Congressional obstructionist practices, **1954:** 316
Congressional support of program, **1954:** 139; **1958:** 292; **1959:** 67
  Campaign remarks, **1956:** 268
  News conference remarks, **1955:** 41, 95, 185; **1956:** 47, 62, 78, 88, 155; **1957:** 87, 119, 150, 157, 169; **1958:** 11, 70, 198, 222, 310
  Party responsibility, **1956:** 47, 268, 298
  Priority list, **1955:** 146
  Relations with Democratic members, **1958:** 310
  Score board, **1956:** 62
Congressmen.
  See also Congress, letters to Members of.
  Appointment by Governors under certain wartime conditions, proposed, **1960–61:** 24
  Honored by Veterans of Foreign Wars, **1953:** 13
  Meetings with the President, comment on, **1954:** 341
  Pay raise and term of office, comment on, **1955:** 47
  Picture taking with the President, comment on, **1954:** 172

  Relations with, **1959:** 21
  Term of four years, proposed, **1960–61:** 24
Connally Reservation on U.S. participation in World Court, **1960–61:** 276 ftn. (p. 665)
Connecticut
  Bush, Sen. Prescott, **1956:** 272; **1957:** 87; **1960–61:** 127
  Greenwich, **1956:** 289
  Hartford, **1954:** 295, 296; **1955:** 209; **1956:** 293
  Kowalski, Repr. Frank, **1959:** 102
  Lodge, Gov. John, **1953:** 296; **1954:** 296
  Norwalk, **1954:** 18
Connell, Arthur J., **1954:** 225
Connelly, Matthew, **1958:** 141
Connole, William R., **1960–61:** 127
Conolly, Adm. Richard L., **1956:** 10n.
Conservation of natural resources, **1953:** 6, 25, 153, 234; **1954:** 3, 4, 201, 308; **1955:** 4; **1956:** 2, 3, 170, 256, 318; **1958:** 12, 49, 59; **1960–61:** 133, 410
Conservation reserve.
  See also Soil bank.
  Budget messages, **1954:** 14 (pp. 162–171); **1955:** 17 (pp. 155–163); **1956:** 12 (pp. 125, 131–138); **1958:** 5 (pp. 63, 64, 66, 68); **1959:** 10 (pp. 92–96); **1960–61:** 13 (pp. 82–86), 414 (pp. 939, 993–999)
  Disapproval of certain projects, **1956:** 180
  Great Plains, **1956:** 169
  Letter, **1956:** 285
  Mineral lands, **1955:** 172
  Sea resources, **1959:** 257
  Theodore Roosevelt centennial ceremony, remarks, **1958:** 100
Conservation reserve program.
  See also Soil bank.
  Agricultural, **1960–61:** 32
  Budget messages, **1960–61:** 13 (pp. 77, 81, 82), 414 (pp. 987, 991)
Conspiracy to overthrow Government by force, **1954:** 210, 211, 286
  Loss of citizenship for, comment on, **1954:** 9
Constantine, Prince, **1959:** 324n.
Constantinople Convention of 1888 on Suez Canal, **1956:** 184, 192, 205, 216
Constitution, U.S., **1953:** 8, 81, 89, 96; **1954:** 274; **1955:** 40, 70, 81, 118, 131, 145, 155, 249; **1956:** 141, 165; **1957:** 178, 216, 223; **1958:** 123; **1959:** 6, 128, 151; **1960–61:** 4, 58, 163, 165, 276, 336
  Amendments
    Bill of Rights, **1954:** 72; **1960–61:** 127
    5th amendment, **1953:** 249; **1954:** 210
    15th amendment, **1960–61:** 137
    Presidential term of office, **1956:** 229
    22d amendment, comment on **1960–61:** 422
    Women's suffrage amendment, 40th anniversary, statement, **1960–61:** 269

Constitution, U.S. — *continued*
  Amendments, proposed
    Bricker Amendment, curbing treaty-making
      powers, **1953:** 31, 37, 126
    Curbing treaty-making powers, **1954:** 9, 18, 25,
      33, 48, 50, 353
    District of Columbia, voting rights, **1960–61:**
      24, 414 (p. 1021)
    Equal rights for women, **1957:** 13
    Knowland Amendment, curbing treaty-mak-
      ing powers, statement, **1953:** 142
    Limitation on income taxes, **1956:** 94
    Lowering of voting age, **1954:** 3, 129, 146, 149
    Poll tax abolishment, **1960–61:** 24
    Presidential election and inauguration, **1960–
      61:** 422
    Representatives, appointment by Governors
      under certain wartime conditions, **1960–
      61:** 24
    Representatives, term of four years, **1960–61:**
      24
    Voting age in Federal elections, **1957:** 13
  Article VI, **1960–61:** 127
  Foreign affairs, Presidential authority, **1956:** 62;
    1960–61: 246
  News conference remarks, **1953:** 41, 126, 249;
    1954: 9, 18, 25, 33, 48, 50, 57, 92, 129, 138,
    341, 353; **1956:** 20, 32, 47, 198; **1957:** 22,
    56, 70, 134, 207; **1959:** 7, 17, 29, 94, 102,
    123; **1960–61:** 24, 93, 127, 143, 268, 284,
    422
  Presidential authority until end of term, **1960–
    61:** 369
  Presidential disability, **1957:** 56; **1958:** 37, 40, 42
  Question of change to provide for parliamentary
    government, **1959:** 123
Constitutional Convention (1787), **1953:** 8, 215;
  1954: 47; **1956:** 265
Construction
  Equipment exports, **1958:** 58
  Industry, **1958:** 308
    Employees, **1954:** 5
  Projects, public, **1959:** 15
  Starts, **1955:** 157
Consumer
  Dissatisfaction with manufactured products,
    1958: 70
  Installment credit, **1956:** 19, 32, 205; **1957:** 95
  Price Index, **1959:** 10 (p. 100), 76; **1960–61:** 217
    Budget message, **1960–61:** 414 (p. 1005)
  Spending, **1954:** 318; **1955:** 4, 18, 19; **1959:** 15
  Urged to buy, **1958:** 37, 56, 70, 83
Continental Congress, **1957:** 216
Continental defense, **1953:** 246, 249; **1954:** 14 (pp.
  119, 120); **1957:** 230; **1960–61:** 245
  Joint statements with Prime Minister St.
    Laurent, **1953:** 70, 247
Continental Hosiery Mills, Inc., tax refund claim,
  veto, **1958:** 187

Continental Shelf, Outer, **1955:** 17 (p. 162)
  See also Tidelands, Federal vs. State claims.
  Mineral leases, **1956:** 12 (pp. 133, 138); **1958:** 5
    (p. 68)
Contracts, Government, **1960–61:** 410
  Air Force, **1953:** 54
  Commission on Equal Job Opportunity, pro-
    posed, **1959:** 27
  Committee on, President's, **1960–61:** 407, 410,
    414 (p. 1023)
  Committee on Government Contract Compli-
    ance, **1953:** 41, 54 ftn. (p. 205), 88
  Common carriers, **1954:** 246
  Cooper Tire and Rubber Co., claim for losses,
    disapproval, **1958:** 252
  Cuban nickel plant, sub-contracting, **1956:** 20
  Defense, **1954:** 9, 18
    Foreign bids, **1958:** 5 (p. 38)
    Procurement, **1958:** 16, 29, 33, 43, 303
    Procurement by Government employees,
      1959: 132
  Depressed areas, **1960–61:** 5
  Discrimination ban, **1956:** 2, 190, 210, 224, 226,
    229, 241, 251
  Dixon-Yates contract, **1954:** 157, 161, 168, 200,
    311, 328
  Graphic Arts Corp. of Ohio, Claim, **1954:** 232
  Kramer, Lawrence F., claim, **1954:** 231
  Labor-management, **1954:** 5
  News conference remarks, **1959:** 102, 132
  Renegotiation, **1958:** 5 (p. 32)
    Extension of Renegotiation Act, **1955:** 50
  Small business concerns, **1956:** 118, 263; **1957:**
    132
  Southwest Research Institute, claim, **1958:** 247
  Tankers, **1956:** 239
  Thomson Contracting Company, Inc., relief of,
    veto, **1958:** 208
Controlled thermonuclear reactions, **1956:** 12 (p.
  101)
Controls, Government, **1953:** 6, 159, 187, 216;
  1954: 273, 286, 290; **1960–61:** 410
  Budget messages, **1960–61:** 13 (p. 77), 414 (p.
    987)
  Campaign remarks, **1960–61:** 346, 351, 352
  Economic, **1955:** 18, 26, 112, 146; **1958:** 18, 26,
    96, 298; **1959:** 17, 29, 94
    Campaign remarks, **1958:** 292, 293, 295, 308
    News conference remarks, **1958:** 11, 120, 198,
      213
  Scarce materials, **1958:** 5 (p. 33)
    News conference remarks, **1953:** 12 and ftn. (p.
      46), 22
Convention, income tax (U.S.-U.K.), **1956:** 181
Conversations between officials and advisers, com-
  ment on investigation of, **1955:** 149
Conway, Leo J., **1958:** 83
Cook, Glenn F., **1958:** 269n.
Cook, Winfield C., **1960–61:** 337n.

Cooley, Repr. Harold D., **1957:** 45

Coolidge, Calvin, **1953:** 31; **1955:** 131

Coolidge, Charles A., **1958:** 37; **1959:** 191 ftn. (p. 611)
  See also Joint Disarmament Study Group.
  News conference remarks on, **1959:** 186, 243

Coolidge, Mrs. Grace Goodhue, death of, statement, **1957:** 126

Coon, Repr. Sam, **1956:** 256

Cooper, Repr. Jere, **1954:** 57, 322; **1955:** 90 ftn. (p. 471)
  Lead and zinc duties, **1957:** 160
  Letter, **1955:** 160
  Small business, **1957:** 132

Cooper, Sen. John Sherman, **1954:** 88, 89, 319; **1956:** 155, 171, 226; **1957:** 87, 124; **1959:** 29; **1960–61:** 176
  Letter, **1960–61:** 5
  News conference remarks on, **1954:** 168, 172, 182, 328
  State Department consultant (1950), **1954:** 328

Cooper Dam and Reservoir, Texas, approval, **1955:** 184

Cooper Tire and Rubber Co., bill for relief of, disapproval, **1958:** 252

Cooperatives, farmer-owned and controlled, **1958:** 12

Cooperatives, taxes on, **1960–61:** 414 (p. 943)

Cooperman, Philip, bill for relief of, **1957:** 184

Coordinating Committee on Trade with Communist Areas, **1956:** 53

Coosa River, Ala., **1955:** 4

Copenhagen, University of, **1957:** 225n.

Copin, Margaret P., relief of, disapproval, **1960–61:** 234

Copper
  Imports, **1958:** 58, 96
  Industry, labor dispute, **1955:** 176
  Prices, **1953:** 22
  Surplus, expenditures for, **1957:** 169

Coppers, George Henry, **1956:** 187n.

Corbett, Repr. Robert J., **1956:** 234

Corcoran, Thomas G., **1959:** 288; **1960–61:** 127

Cordiner, Ralph J., report, **1957:** 115
  See also Defense Advisory Committee on Professional and Technical Compensation.

Cordon, Sen. Guy, **1954:** 34, 152, 271, 272

Corn, **1958:** 12, 60
  Acreage reserve (soil bank), **1956:** 6
  Export program, **1958:** 59
  Price supports, **1954:** 4; **1956:** 6, 12 (p. 128), 82, 83, 88; **1957:** 13, 16, 17, 169; **1959:** 23; **1960–61:** 32
  Surpluses, **1960–61:** 414 (p. 987)

Corn Picking Contest, National, remarks, **1958:** 290

Cornell, Douglas B., **1953:** 22, 109; **1954:** 157; **1956:** 216, 229; **1957:** 228; **1959:** 179

Cornell, Karen, letter, **1956:** 277

Cornell University, **1954:** 12n., 200; **1956:** 211

Coronado, Francisco, **1959:** 338

Corporal missile (short range).
  See Missiles.

Corporate taxes, **1953:** 84, 254; **1954:** 3, 54, 67, 353; **1955:** 4, 6, 41; **1956:** 2, 183, 268; **1957:** 13; **1958:** 114, 120; **1959:** 10 (pp. 39, 41)
  Budget messages, **1954:** 14 (pp. 88, 94–99); **1955:** 17 (pp. 87, 97, 98); **1958:** 5 (p. 22); **1960–61:** 13 (pp. 39, 42), 414 (pp. 937, 940, 943, 944)
  Depreciation allowances, **1960–61:** 414 (p. 944)

Corporations, Government, budget message, **1958:** 5 (p. 44)

Corporations, small business, **1956:** 263; **1957:** 132

Corps of Engineers.
  See Engineers, Corps of.

Corregidor, **1959:** 73

Corruption in Administration, answer to charge of, **1956:** 258

Corsi, Edward, **1954:** 188; **1955:** 62

Cortney, Philip, **1959:** 84n.

Cosmetics, drugs, and food, revision of laws, disapproval, **1954:** 254

Cost of Government, broadcast, **1957:** 86

Cost of living, **1955:** 41, 119; **1956:** 263, 269, 289; **1957:** 119, 124, 169, 228; **1959:** 172; **1960–61:** 217
  Campaign remarks, **1956:** 224, 234, 241, 251; **1958:** 293, 296, 308
  News conference remarks, **1956:** 193, 235; **1958:** 70, 120, 213
  Statement, **1958:** 298

Costa Rica
  Conflict in, **1955:** 10
  OAS foreign ministers meeting at San Jose, **1960–61:** 228, 263, 267, 268
  U.S. embassy in **1958:** 288

Costello, John A., visit to U.S., **1956:** 57

Cothran, James W., letter, **1953:** 13

Cotten, Felix, **1953:** 141

Cotton, Sen. Norris, **1955:** 139

Cotton, **1958:** 60
  Acreage allotments, **1954:** 24; **1955:** 90; **1958:** 12, 59
  Acreage reserve (soil bank), **1956:** 6
  Acreage reserve (1957), **1958:** 12
  Exports, **1954:** 4; **1955:** 6, 185; **1956:** 82, 115; **1958:** 58, 59; **1960–61:** 132
  Import restrictions, **1956:** 115
  Joint statement with President Lopez Mateos on, **1959:** 38, 257
  Long-staple, act authorizing sale, **1957:** 128
  Price supports, **1954:** 4; **1956:** 6, 12 (p. 128), 82, 83, 88; **1958:** 12, 59; **1959:** 23, 257
  Production increase, **1958:** 142
  Surpluses, **1960–61:** 414 (p. 987)
  Textiles, imports from Japan, **1956:** 198

Cotton Association, El Paso, Tex., **1953:** 265
Cotton Council of America, National, **1959:** 267
Cottonseed oil and meal, surplus, **1956:** 6
Coty, René, **1954:** 157; **1957:** 243 and n., 247 and n.
  Messages, **1953:** 270; **1954:** 83, 104, 148, 265;
    1957: 103 and n.
Coue, Emile, **1960–61:** 350
Cougar Dam, Oreg., **1954:** 50; **1955:** 17 (p. 158);
    1956: 12 (p. 134)
Council on Aging, Federal, **1956:** 63
Council of Economic Advisers, **1953:** 230; **1954:**
    21, 26; **1955:** 4, 19; **1956:** 19; **1957:** 16,
    119; **1959:** 15; **1960–61:** 17, 263, 410
  Budget message, **1960–61:** 414 (p. 944)
  Chairman (Arthur F. Burns), **1953:** 128, 249
    News conference remarks on, **1956:** 94, 235
    Resignation, **1956:** 297
    Small business, letters, **1956:** 118, 176
  Chairman (Raymond J. Saulnier), **1959:** 18n., 53,
    133, 161, 167, 186; **1960–61:** 21
    News conference remarks on, **1956:** 37
    Telegram from, **1958:** 296
  Consumer installment credit, **1957:** 95
  Davis, Joseph S., rural development committee,
    1956: 217n.
  Economic report, **1958:** 16
  Reorganization Plan 9, message, **1953:** 93
  Rural development program, **1957:** 156
Council for Europe, **1956:** 114
Council on Federal Reports, Advisory, **1956:** 110
Council on Foreign Economic Policy, **1954:** 354;
    1955: 76
  Chairman (Clarence B. Randall), letter, **1956:**
    139
  Letter to Chairman, **1954:** 348
Council on Foreign Relations, **1960–61:** 86
Council on Group Insurance, proposed, **1954:** 116
Council on International Monetary and Financial
    Problems, National Advisory, **1960–61:**
    39
Council on Law Enforcement of the District of
    Columbia, **1954:** 207
Council for Science and Technology, Federal,
    1958: 326; **1960–61:** 349
Council of State Governments, **1957:** 14n.
Council on Youth Fitness, **1956:** 128
Counseling and guidance service, **1958:** 5 (p. 49), 24
Counterpart funds, **1958:** 5 (p. 36)
  Use for foreign travel, **1956:** 205
Courier communications satellite, **1960–61:** 424
  Budget message, **1960–61:** 414 (p. 970)
Court buildings, construction, **1960–61:** 243
Court of Claims.
  See Courts, Federal.
Court of Customs and Patent Appeals, filling of
    vacancy, **1958:** 28
Court of Justice, International, **1953:** 129n.; **1959:**
    6, 314; **1960–61:** 73

Court of Justice, International — *continued*
  U.S. acceptance of jurisdiction, **1960–61:** 4, 13
    (p. 65), 276 and ftn. (p. 665), 414 (p. 968)
Courts
  School integration cases, **1959:** 27
  Traffic, **1959:** 185
Courts, Federal.
  See also Judiciary; Supreme Court, U.S.
  Appointment of Simon Sobeloff to Court of
    Appeals, **1956:** 113
  Circuit Court of Appeals, Fourth
    Filling of vacancy, **1955:** 149, 176
    Knipp, Howard F., tax claim, **1959:** 240
    Nomination to, **1956:** 20
  Circuit Court of Appeals, Fifth, nomination of
    John R. Brown, **1955:** 112
  Circuit Court of Appeals, Sixth, filling of vacan-
    cy, **1959:** 29
  Circuit Court of Appeals, Seventh
    Decision on taxation of disability payments,
      1958: 232; **1959:** 234; **1960–61:** 291
    Filling of vacancy, **1958:** 103
    McQuilkin, Anna K., insurance claim, **1954:**
      228
  Circuit Court of Appeals, Eighth, school inte-
    gration case, **1958:** 214
  Circuit Court of Appeals, Tenth, **1953:** 107
  Civil rights, orders re, **1960–61:** 137
  Court of Claims, **1954:** 244, 251; **1960–61:** 224
    Jurisdiction in overtime compensation case,
      veto, **1954:** 41
    North Counties Hydro-Electric Co., claim,
      1958: 229
    Stone, William E., disability retirement claim,
      1956: 135
    Whitaker, D. A., and others, pay claim, **1958:**
      255
  District Courts
    Challenges in civil cases, **1958:** 250
    Colorado, **1953:** 107
    District of Columbia, **1953:** 116
    Eastern Tennessee, **1954:** 193n., 281
    New Mexico, **1954:** 243
    Northern Illinois, **1954:** 228
    Northern Texas court, filling of vacancy, **1955:**
      47
    School integration cases, **1955:** 149; **1956:** 32,
      47, 171, 198, 205; **1958:** 98, 274
    Southern New York, **1953:** 203n.; **1959:** 250n.
    Texas, **1956:** 198, 205
    Western Pennsylvania, **1959:** 265n.
  Judgeships, additional, proposed, **1960–61:** 13 (p.
    105), 133, 255, 268, 414 (p. 1023)
  News conference remarks, **1955:** 47, 112, 149,
    176
  Pending cases, reduction, **1956:** 12 (p. 84)
  Royalty tax paid in United Kingdom, cases re,
    1956: 181

Courts, Federal — *continued*
  Tax Court of the United States, **1960–61:** 150,
      414 (p. 1021)
  Voting rights case, Alabama, **1958:** 318
Couve de Murville, Maurice, **1959:** 123 ftn. (p.
      425), 202
Cowan, Roy, and others, relief of, **1956:** 79
Cowen, Myron M., letter, **1953:** 239
Cowles, Mrs. Gardner, **1953:** 109 ftn. (p. 439)
Cowles, John, **1953:** 33n.
Cox, Allyn, **1954:** 106n.
Cox, J. Earl, **1953:** 59
Craft, Scott, **1956:** 226
Craig, Gov. George N., **1954:** 203, 290
Craig, May, **1953:** 12, 15, 22, 31, 37, 41, 54, 62, 77,
      88, 109, 128, 230, 243, 249, 254, 265; **1954:**
      18, 25, 33, 39, 48, 50, 57, 63, 73, 92, 101,
      107, 115, 157, 168, 172, 311, 322, 341, 347,
      353; **1955:** 10, 18, 26, 41, 81, 95, 112, 146,
      149, 176; **1956:** 16, 20, 53, 56, 62, 88, 96,
      113, 155, 189, 193, 205, 216, 235; **1957:** 17,
      28, 45, 50, 62, 72, 80, 87, 105, 119, 124,
      145, 150, 169, 210; **1958:** 42, 56, 63, 74,
      103, 141, 198, 213, 222, 288, 310, 318;
      1959: 17, 26, 29, 36, 42, 48, 53, 67, 89, 102,
      123, 148, 154, 167, 172, 173, 186, 243, 271,
      277, 288; **1960–61:** 7, 21, 24, 127 and ftn.
      (p. 362), 143, 256, 263, 284, 422
Creagh, Edward F., **1953:** 88; **1954:** 161, 165; **1957:**
      145
Creasy, Maj. William M., **1959:** 132
Crecy, Battle of, **1956:** 113
Credit controls, **1957:** 16, 169
  Consumer installment credit, **1957:** 95
  Study by National Monetary and Financial
      Commission, **1957:** 16
Credit outflow, **1960–61:** 362
Credit policies, **1957:** 13
Credit programs, Federal, **1959:** 6, 15
  Budget message, **1958:** 5 (pp. 43, 44)
  Interest rates, **1959:** 10 (pp. 50, 51)
Crespo, Daniel Fernandez, **1960–61:** 79n.
Cressy, Ferne and Frank, mining claim, disap-
      proval, **1956:** 179
Crime, organized, **1960–61:** 13 (p. 105)
Crime rate, **1958:** 213
Criminal aliens, deportation, **1956:** 33
Criminal offenses of members of armed forces.
  See also Status of Forces agreements.
  Allied troops in U.S. in World War II, **1957:** 132
  Foreign countries, **1957:** 139
  Girard, William S., **1957:** 92, 105, 115, 134, 150
  McOsler, William, **1957:** 124
Crippled children, **1955:** 25
Criticism of the President, **1958:** 42
  News conference remarks, **1956:** 189; **1957:** 28,
      70, 72
  Retaliation, comment on, **1958:** 70

Crittenberger, Lt. Gen. Willis D., **1958:** 52
Cromley, Allan W., **1955:** 146
Cromwell, Oliver, **1954:** 86, 103, 304; **1955:** 213;
      1959: 127
Croneis, Carey, **1960–61:** 336
Crop insurance, **1960–61:** 414 (p. 989)
Crops, reports on, **1959:** 36
Crosby, Gov. Robert B., **1954:** 258
Cross, Gov. Burton M., **1953:** 187
Crow Indian Tribe claim, veto, **1956:** 124
Crude Oil Imports, Special Committee to Inves-
      tigate, report, **1958:** 54
Crusade in Europe (Eisenhower), **1954:** 182; **1958:**
      37, 153
Crusade for Freedom campaign, **1955:** 32
  Fund-raising **1956:** 66
  Participation of newspaper boys, **1955:** 79
Crusades, comment on, **1954:** 204
Cuaderno, McGill, **1957:** 195n.
Cuba, **1960–61:** 245, 255
  Alleged illegal flights over, **1959:** 271
  Castro, Fidel, **1959:** 21, 161, 271; **1960–61:** 21,
      22, 93, 103, 127, 227, 268, 368n., 388
  Communism in, **1959:** 277; **1960–61:** 227, 256,
      410, 431
  Embargo on exports to, **1960–61:** 332
  Guantanamo naval base, **1960–61:** 228, 342
  Havana, **1953:** 260; **1960–61:** 388
  Illegal exportation of arms to, comment on,
      1954: 25
  Independence, **1955:** 69
  News conference remarks, **1959:** 21, 148, 161,
      271, 277; **1960–61:** 7, 21, 38, 93, 103, 222,
      228, 256, 263, 268, 284
  OAS action on, **1960–61:** 263
  Recognition of Communist China, **1960–61:** 284
  Refugees from, **1960–61:** 410
    Letter to Cardinal Spellman on aid, **1960–61:**
      371
    Report, statement, **1960–61:** 431
  Relations with U.S., **1960–61:** 22, 268
  Roa, Raul, **1960–61:** 268
  Seizure of U.S. property, **1960–61:** 7, 222
  Soviet bases in, question of, **1960–61:** 222
  Sugar quotas, **1960–61:** 21, 38, 93, 167n., 222, 267
    Approval of bill, **1960–61:** 223
    Proclamation, statement, **1960–61:** 374
  Trade with Communist bloc, **1960–61:** 223
  U.S. Ambassador Philip W. Bonsal, **1960–61:** 22
  U.S. and Canadian prisoners, **1958:** 153
  U.S. nickel plant, **1956:** 20, 96, 113
  U.S. policy, **1958:** 310; **1960–61:** 22
  U.S. relations with, **1959:** 271
  U.S. termination of diplomatic relations, state-
      ment, **1960–61:** 388
Cuban-American Sugar Co., tax refund claim,
      disapproval, **1954:** 244
Culin, Curtis J., **1956:** 253; **1960–61:** 405

Cullman, Howard S., **1958:** 79
Cultural agreement with Afghanistan (1958), **1958:** 150
Cultural agreement with Guinea, joint statement with President Toure, **1959:** 272
Cultural Center, National, **1958:** 190; **1960–61:** 414 (p. 1023)
Cultural exchange, **1954:** 146, 335; **1958:** 58, 114, 204; **1960–61:** 98, 286, 319
  Budget message, **1956:** 12 (p. 109)
  Smith-Mundt Act anniversary, remarks, **1958:** 23
  U.S.-Pakistan, **1959:** 302
  U.S.-Soviet Union, **1958:** 22; **1959:** 223; **1960–61:** 410, 414 (p. 969)
Cultural presentations abroad, **1956:** 12 (p. 109)
Cultural programs, budget message, **1958:** 5 (pp. 40, 41)
Culzean Castle, Turnberry, Scotland, visit to, **1959:** 198
Cummings, Reuben, letter, **1956:** 288
Cunningham, Col. Harry F., relief of, disapproval, **1953:** 168
Currencies, foreign.
  See Foreign currencies.
Currency, U.S., prevention of debasement.
  See Dollar, sound.
Curry, Ralph, **1955:** 47
Curtice, Harlow H., **1954:** 37; **1955:** 111, 124, 125; **1956:** 37; **1957:** 14 and n.
  Traffic safety, letters, **1956:** 36, 305
Curtis, Repr. Carl T., **1953:** 268
Curtis, Edward P., **1957:** 71 and n.; **1959:** 74
  Letter on aviation facilities planning, **1956:** 38
  Report, **1958:** 135
Curtis, Rep. Laurence, **1956:** 292
Cushing, Ned, **1955:** 18n.
Cushing, Archbishop Richard J., **1954:** 325
Custer State Park, S. Dak., **1953:** 102n.
Customs, Bureau of, **1956:** 162; **1960–61:** 179, 181, 285
Customs duties, refund claims, vetoes
  Grand Lodge of North Dakota, **1960–61:** 181
  Our Lady of the Lake Church, **1960–61:** 179
Customs simplification, **1953:** 6, 70, 187; **1955:** 6; **1956:** 2, 19
  Approval of act, **1956:** 162
  Approval of bill, **1953:** 164
Customs procedures, **1954:** 67
Cutler, Robert, **1953:** 2n., 33, 266; **1957:** 60 and n., 216; **1958:** 95
  Appointment, U.S. member, Board of Executive Directors, Inter-American Development Bank, **1959:** 261
Cutrer, Lewis, **1960–61:** 336n.
Cutter, John L., **1954:** 9, 107, 129, 161, 328, 341; **1955:** 59, 81, 90
Cutter Laboratories, licensing to produce Salk vaccine, **1955:** 95

Cyclone in Mexico, letter to President Lopez Mateos, **1959:** 275
Cyclotron, **1958:** 52
Cypress Point, Calif., **1956:** 191n.
Cyprus, **1956:** 56
  Foot, Sir Hugh, **1959:** 39
  Greece-Turkey-United Kingdom agreement, **1959:** 39, 40, 41
  Joint statement with Prime Minister Karamanlis on, **1959:** 327
  Settlement of dispute, **1959:** 326
Cyprus, Republic of
  Independence, **1960–61:** 262
  Kutchuck, Fazil, **1960–61:** 262
  Makarios, archbishop, message, **1960–61:** 262
  Rossides, Zenon, **1960–61:** 324n.
  U.N. delegation, remarks to, **1960–61:** 324
Cyrus the Great of Persia, **1959:** 321
Czechoslovakia, **1958:** 173, 261
  Anti-Communist demonstrations, **1953:** 146
  Flood relief, **1954:** 175, 182 ftn. (p. 678), 200
  Letter to Premier Bulganin re, **1958:** 7
  News conference remarks, **1958:** 56, 274
  Technical conference, Geneva, **1958:** 131
  Representation at foreign ministers conference, question of, **1959:** 102

D-Day anniversary, **1956:** 121, 122
Dabney, Virginius, **1958:** 80n.
Dacko, David, message, **1960–61:** 259
Da Gama, Vasco, **1960–61:** 160
D'Agostino, Mary, relief of, disapproval, **1959:** 235
Dahl, Lt. Gov. C.P., **1953:** 100n.
Dahlberg, Rev. Edwin T., **1959:** 212
Dahomey, Republic of
  Maga, Hubert, message, **1960–61:** 249
  Pinto, Ignacio, **1960–61:** 324n.
Dail, Charles C., **1960–61:** 333
Dairy products, **1956:** 6; **1958:** 59
  Butter, **1953:** 12, 109; **1954:** 25, 39, 50, 143, 165
  Milk, **1954:** 115, 347
  News conference remarks, **1954:** 25, 39, 50, 115, 143, 165, 172, 192, 347
  Prices, **1953:** 12; **1954:** 347
  Price supports, **1954:** 4, 25, 39, 143, 165, 172, 196; **1956:** 12 (p. 128), 83; **1958:** 12, 37, 56, 60
  Surpluses, **1954:** 25, 39, 50, 196
Dakar, **1958:** 309
Dake, Marietta, **1953:** 265; **1954:** 48
Dale, Edwin L., Jr., **1954:** 200; **1956:** 88, 171, 229; **1958:** 70
Dallas, Tex., **1955:** 10
Dalton, John N., **1953:** 79n.
Dalton, Theodore R., **1953:** 230
Dalton, Ted, **1957:** 50

Dalton, Mrs. William H., **1954:** 325n.
Da Maia, José Joaquim, **1960–61:** 45
Dams.
  See also specific projects.
  Hydroelectric vs. multiple purpose, **1953:** 77
Danaher, John A., **1953:** 59
Daniel, Dewey, **1956:** 226n.
Daniel, James M., **1954:** 101
Daniel, Governor Price, **1957:** 138
Daniel, Sen. Price, **1953:** 54; **1955:** 47
  News conference remarks on, **1954:** 161, 168
Darby, Harry, **1953:** 218; **1959:** 258, 259; **1960–61:** 118n.
Dardanelle lock and dam, **1956:** 12 (p. 143)
Darden, Colgate W., Jr., **1959:** 271; **1960–61:** 30n.
Darius the Great of Persia, **1959:** 321
Darlington, Brig. Gen. Henry, **1954:** 103n.
Darrison, F. Gibson, **1955:** 181n.
Dartmouth College, **1958:** 138n.; **1959:** 7
  Commencement exercises, remarks, **1953:** 104
  News conference remarks, **1953:** 109, 126
Daud, Sardar Mohammed, joint statement with
      President, **1958:** 150
Daud Khan, Mohammed, **1959:** 306
Daughters of the American Revolution, National
      Society of the, remarks, **1954:** 86
Daughters of the Confederacy, United, remarks,
      1953: 240
Davidson, Eugene, **1954:** 347
Davidson, Jean, **1953:** 54
Davies, John Paton, **1954:** 341
Davies, Joseph E., **1957:** 105
Davies, Lawrence, **1956:** 189
Davies, Ronald N., **1957:** 178 and n.
Davis, Clarence A.
  See Interior, Under Secretary of.
Davis, Elmer, **1953:** 128; **1954:** 25
Davis, Repr. Glenn R., **1955:** 56
Davis, Harold, **1960–61:** 362, 422
Davis, Harold J., disability compensation claim,
      disapproval, **1953:** 167
Davis, Jefferson, **1954:** 89; **1959:** 31
Davis, John W., **1957:** 28
Davis, Joseph S., Council of Economic Advisers,
      1956: 217n.
Davis, Richard Harding, **1958:** 88
Davis, Roy T., **1954:** 289
Davis, Spencer, **1957:** 70, 92, 105, 119, 145, 150,
      157; **1958:** 37, 42, 70, 83, 103, 213, 288;
      1959: 36, 53, 94, 132, 148, 154, 167, 173,
      179, 277; **1960–61:** 21, 34, 93, 127, 222,
      256, 263
Dawson, Donald, **1954:** 18
Day, John, water resources project, **1956:** 2
Deaf, Columbia Institution for the, **1954:** 14 (p. 155)
Deaf persons, **1954:** 14 (p. 153)
Deakin, James, **1956:** 5, 193

Dean, Gordon E., **1953:** 128
Dean, Maj. Gen. William F., **1953:** 225, 265
Dear, Joseph A., **1954:** 73; **1955:** 149
Deaths, statements, etc.
  Abdul Aziz Ibn al Saud, **1953:** 245
  Beardsley, Gov. William S., **1954:** 339
  De Gasperi, Alcide, **1954:** 205
  Dulles, John Foster, **1959:** 117
  Freeman, Douglas S., **1953:** 106
  Griswold, Sen. Dwight P., **1954:** 80
  Hansen, H. C., **1960–61:** 41
  Hazza al-Majali, **1960–61:** 277
  Hoey, Sen. Clyde R., **1954:** 109
  Hutcheson, William L., **1953:** 224
  Kestnbaum, Meyer, **1960–61:** 372
  Leahy, Adm. William D., **1959:** 166
  Marshall, Gen. George C., **1959:** 262
  Maybank, Sen. Burnet R., **1954:** 233
  McKay, Douglas, **1959:** 168
  Meyer, Eugene, **1959:** 165
  Quarles, Donald A., **1959:** 97
  Queen Mother Mary, **1953:** 34
  Reuter, Ernst, **1953:** 197
  Rockefeller, John D., Jr., **1960–61:** 144
  Sibley, Harper, **1959:** 87
  Simpson, Repr. Richard M., **1960–61:** 3
  Stalin, Joseph, **1953:** 24
  Taft, Sen. Robert A., **1953:** 154
  Vandenberg, Gen. Hoyt S., **1954:** 70
  Vinson, Fred M., **1953:** 182
  Wilkins, J. Ernest, **1959:** 12
  Williams, Walter W., **1959:** 333
De Barros, Adhemar, **1960–61:** 52
Debre, Michel, **1959:** 202, 207
Debt, national, **1953:** 6, 159; **1954:** 15, 209; **1956:** 2, 3, 19, 20, 113, 224, 279; **1957:** 13, 86; **1959:** 63, 126, 129, 144n., 188, 274; **1960–61:** 4, 17, 23, 89
  Budget messages, **1954:** 14 (pp. 86, 89, 190, 191); **1955:** 17 (pp. 99–101, 106, 183, 184); **1956:** 12 (pp. 90, 91, 153, 154); **1958:** 5 (pp. 23, 70, 71); **1960–61:** 13 (pp. 38, 40–42, 45, 100), 414 (pp. 935, 938, 942, 1016)
  Campaign remarks, **1960–61:** 344, 350, 354
  Interest on, **1954:** 14 (pp. 190, 191); **1959:** 10 (pp. 107, 108), 43, 102, 124, 288, 290; **1960–61:** 4, 13 (pp. 41, 42, 100), 414 (pp. 938, 1016)
  Limit on, **1953:** 6, 159, 198, 249; **1954:** 14 (p. 89), 57, 165, 168, 172; **1958:** 183; **1959:** 123, 126; **1960–61:** 13 (p. 41), 133, 414 (p. 942)
    Approval of bill, **1954:** 219
    Statement, **1953:** 152
  Management, **1954:** 21; **1959:** 124, 186, 223, 225, 274; **1960–61:** 4, 6, 13 (pp. 41, 42), 344, 414 (p. 942), 415
  Messages to Congress, **1959:** 126, 188

Debt, national — *continued*
  News conference remarks, **1953:** 198, 249; **1954:**
    18, 57, 165, 168, 172; **1955:** 33; **1958:** 74,
    222; **1959:** 102, 123, 148, 167, 223, 288;
    1960–61: 7, 34
  Reduction, **1960–61:** 13 (pp. 38, 40, 41), 414 (p.
    942)
Decentralization, governmental.
  See Federal-State-local governmental
    responsibilities.
De Casson, Dollier, **1959:** 141n.
De Castries, Col. Christian, French commander at
    Dien Bien Phu, **1954:** 63, 83
Decatur, Stephen, **1958:** 125
Decatur House (Washington, D.C.), **1960–61:** 243
Decennial census, **1960–61:** 13 (p. 91), 414 (p. 1005)
Decentralization of government, **1954:** 346
Declaration of American States against interna-
    tional Communist intervention (1954),
    1956: 146
Declaration of Independence, **1953:** 8, 69, 78, 250;
    1954: 51, 72, 86, 89, 160, 204, 341; **1955:**
    40, 136; **1957:** 216; **1958:** 125, 320; **1959:**
    151, 152, 214, 290; **1960–61:** 4, 58, 73,
    171n., 183, 284
Declaration of Principles, Panama, address on
    signing, **1956:** 146
Declaration of Santiago, joint statement with Pres-
    ident Alessandri, **1960–61:** 76
Declaration of Solidarity, inter-American confer-
    ence (1954), **1956:** 133
Declaration of Soviet Government (Oct. 30, 1956),
    1956: 291
Declaration U.S.-U.K., Bermuda, 1957, letter to
    Premier Khrushchev, **1958:** 67
Declaration of Washington, joint declaration with
    Prime Minister Eden, **1956:** 27
DeCoursey, Brig. Gen. Elbert, **1955:** 108
Dedicatory occasions.
  See Addresses or remarks., on commemorative
    or dedicatory occasions.
Defender project, **1960–61:** 414 (pp. 953, 954)
Defense, continental, **1954:** 3
Defense, Assistant Secretary of (Gordon Gray),
    bipartisan meeting on Suez Canal, **1956:**
    184
Defense, Assistant Secretary of (Murray Snyder),
    1957: 70
Defense, Department of, **1953:** 40; **1954:** 12n.;
    1955: 3, 24n., 74, 207n.; **1959:** 191 ftn. (p.
    611), 267; **1960–61:** 5, 10, 36, 148, 255,
    386, 410
  See also Joint Chiefs of Staff.
  Adams, John G., **1954:** 115
  Addresses and messages, **1957:** 13, 90, 230
  Advanced Research Projects Agency, **1958:** 57n.,
    64, 321
  Advisory Committee on Professional and Tech-
    nical Compensation, **1957:** 13

Defense, Department of — *continued*
  Agreement with Australia on atomic informa-
    tion, **1957:** 130
  Air traffic management, message on Federal
    Aviation Agency, **1958:** 135
  Anderson, Robert B., **1954:** 111
  Appropriation Act, 1956, **1955:** 155
  Appropriation Act, 1959, **1958:** 218
  Authority re atomic energy program, proposals,
    1954: 38
  Aviation facilities planning, **1956:** 38
  Budget messages, **1954:** 14 (pp. 85, 86, 107, 118,
    119, 120–126, 155, 175, 190); **1955:** 17 (pp.
    91, 107, 111, 115, 119, 121, 169, 183);
    1956: 12 (pp. 80, 81, 93–99, 123, 141, 146);
    1958: 5 (pp. 18, 19, 21, 25–32, 48, 71);
    1959: 10 (pp. 38, 43, 55–66, 85); **1960–61:**
    13 (pp. 38, 46–58, 60, 65, 108), 414 (pp.
    944, 948–959, 970, 1019)
  Budget (1960), **1958:** 75
  Burgess, Carter L., **1954:** 351, 353
  Campaign remarks, **1958:** 293, 308
  Central procurement, **1957:** 87, 124
  Claims against U.S. resulting from Department
    activities, **1954:** 14 (p. 190)
  Committee on Department of Defense Organi-
    zation, **1953:** 61
  Coolidge, Charles A., **1958:** 37
  Defense Supply Management Agency, **1953:** 61
  Director of Defense Research and Engineering,
    proposed, **1958:** 65
  Director of Installations, abolishment of office,
    1953: 61
  Douglas, James H., **1960–61:** 425
  Expenditures for, **1957:** 13
  Flood relief in Italy, **1954:** 315
  Hensel, H. Struve, **1954:** 351
  Hoover Commission recommendations, **1956:**
    62, 64
  Housing at military installations, **1956:** 141
  Hungarian refugees, funds for, **1956:** 307
  Information, release of, **1955:** 81
  Kyes, Roger M., **1953:** 2n., 266; **1954:** 68
  McGuire, Perkins, **1959:** 18n.
  McNeil, W. J., **1954:** 351
  Manpower and reserve program, **1954:** 200, 353
  Meeting with Prime Minister Kishi, **1957:** 117
  Military assistance responsibilities, **1959:** 136,
    137
  Military and defense support assistance appro-
    priation, **1957:** 90
  Missiles
    Development, **1957:** 80, 210, 230
    Duplication, **1959:** 102
    Programs, effect of steel strike, **1959:** 268
  Munitions Board, **1953:** 61
  Nash, Frank C., **1953:** 33, 254 ftn. (p. 800)

Defense, Department of — *continued*
News conference remarks, **1953:** 54, 88, 198;
1954: 107, 200, 311, 353; **1955:** 81, 176,
185; **1956:** 32, 62, 78, 113, 171, 205, 229;
1957: 87, 92, 124, 134, 157, 169; **1958:** 37,
310; **1960–61:** 21, 34, 284, 422
Ocean weather stations, **1955:** 14 (p. 175)
Officials, attendance at Republican dinners,
comment on, **1960–61:** 34
Overseas personnel, reduction, **1960–61:** 434
Overseas supply activities, **1957:** 13
Plutonium for military purposes, **1958:** 193
Procurement practices, **1958:** 5 (p. 32)
Quarles, Donald A., death of, **1959:** 97
Radioactive fallout, report, **1959:** 68
Reduction of armed forces, **1956:** 232
Reorganization (1947), **1958:** 65; **1959:** 6, 10 (pp.
58, 59), 102; **1960–61:** 350, 414 (pp. 944,
957), 433
See also Defense reorganization.
Report, **1960–61:** 397n.
Research and development, **1953:** 61; **1956:** 105;
1957: 17, 80, 210, 211, 234
Satellite development, **1957:** 211
Security risk problems, handling of, **1955:** 107
Service rivalries, **1958:** 2, 65, 80, 96, 121
Settlement of certain damage claims, disap-
proval, **1958:** 259
Small business purchases, **1956:** 263
Space activities, **1958:** 28, 64, 105; **1960–61:** 11
Surplus funds, use for Korean assistance, pro-
posed, **1953:** 148
Task force on, **1958:** 134n.
Transfer of certain research functions to Na-
tional Science Foundation, proposed,
1954: 14 (p. 155)
Travel expenses of personnel, **1960–61:** 414 (p.
950)
U-235 available for peaceful uses, **1957:** 125
Unification, **1957:** 87, 169
See also Defense reorganization.
Wage board employees, **1958:** 191
Whitte, Gen. W. W., Staff Director of Petroleum
Logistics, **1955:** 176, 185
Defense, Deputy Secretary of (Donald Quarles),
1957: 226n.
Defense, Guided Missiles Director for Secretary of
(William M. Holaday), **1957:** 80, 210, 230
Defense, national.
See National security.
Defense, Permanent Joint Board on, United States
and Canada, **1953:** 246
Joint statements with Prime Minister St.
Laurent, **1953:** 70, 247
Defense, Secretary of, **1955:** 12; **1958:** 74, 80
Acting Secretary, designation of Secretary of
Navy to act as, **1959:** 111

Defense, Secretary of — *continued*
Authority, **1958:** 63, 65, 70, 80, 88, 95, 134; **1959:**
6, 10 (p. 62)
Prestige of office, **1959:** 53
Review of National Guard programs, **1955:** 192
Defense, Secretary of (Thomas S. Gates, Jr.), **1959:**
351; **1960–61:** 132, 135, 261n., 365, 369,
420
Balance of payments directive, letter, **1960–61:**
434
Medal of Freedom, citation, **1960–61:** 426
Military readiness, order re, **1960–61:** 163
News conference remarks on, **1960–61:** 21, 24
Resignation, letter, **1960–61:** 397
Soviet strength, **1960–61:** 21
Vice Chairman, United Community campaigns,
1960–61: 210
Defense, Secretary of (Neil H. McElroy), **1957:** 206
and n., 228; **1958:** 2, 90, 121, 316; **1959:**
55, 276
Alaskan defense needs, **1958:** 159
Atomic energy for defense, U.S.-U.K. agreement
memorandum, **1958:** 156
Defense spending, **1958:** 120
Medal of Freedom, citation, **1959:** 286
Memorandum, **1959:** 119
Missiles, **1959:** 102, 123, 172
News conference remarks on, **1958:** 28, 37, 83,
213; **1959:** 36, 48, 53, 102, 123
Oath of office, **1957:** 212n.
Preventive war, **1959:** 48
Resignation, **1959:** 48, 102, 285
U.G.F. campaign, Chairman, **1959:** 156
Vice Chairman, United Community Campaigns,
1958: 184; **1959:** 159
Defense, Secretary of (Charles E. Wilson), **1953:** 6,
57, 71; **1954:** 337; **1955:** 29, 71n., 90 ftn.
(p. 475), 108
Administration of foreign military assistance,
proposed, **1954:** 3
Arkansas National Guard, **1957:** 205n.
Army-McCarthy hearings, letter of May 17,
1954, **1956:** 216
Bipartisan conference, **1957:** 2
British machinery, decision on purchase of,
1953: 54
Campaign remarks on, **1956:** 241, 246
Civil defense, **1956:** 142
Committee on Small Business, member, **1956:**
118
European storm disaster relief, **1953:** 7n.
Foreign aid programs, **1954:** 323
Great Lakes water level report, **1956:** 177
Guided missiles, **1956:** 53
Hoover Commission recommendations, letter,
1956: 64
Letters to, **1954:** 113, 343; **1955:** 3, 154
Medal of Freedom, citation, **1957:** 212 and n.

Defense, Secretary of (Wilson) — *continued*
  Meeting with Marshal Zhukov, proposed, **1957:**
     134, 210
  Meeting with Prime Minister Suhrawardy, **1957:**
     131
  Memorandums, **1953:** 36, 273
  Military career incentives, proposals, **1956:** 81
  Military dependents medical care regulations,
     approval, **1956:** 244
  Military personnel, benefits for, **1954:** 349
  Military training for all citizens, **1954:** 200
  Mutual security appropriations, **1953:** 143
  NATO, report on, **1953:** 265 ftn. (p. 843)
  News conference remarks on, **1953:** 37, 41, 54,
     62, 77, 208, 254, 265; **1954:** 18, 25, 92, 107,
     115, 200, 353; **1955:** 18, 81; **1956:** 16, 53,
     216; **1957:** 17, 22, 125, 134, 210, 228
  Presidential order on information to be released
     to Congress, **1954:** 113, 115
  Reorganization Plan 6, functions re, **1953:** 61
  Resignation, **1957:** 206 and n.
  Trade with Communist bloc, **1955:** 18
  Water resources, report, **1956:** 13
  "Your Government and You" broadcasts, **1956:**
     246
Defense Advisory Committee on Prisoners of War,
     report, **1955:** 207n.
Defense Advisory Committee on Professional and
     Technical Compensation, **1958:** 169
  Budget message, **1958:** 5 (p. 31)
Defense Advisory Committee on Women in the
     Services, remarks, **1954:** 97
Defense agreement, U.S.-Spain, **1953:** 198
Defense and Civilian Mobilization, Office of
  See Civil and Defense Mobilization, Office of.
Defense Education Act, National, **1960–61:** 410,
     413
  Budget messages, **1960–61:** 13 (p. 89), 414 (pp.
     1002, 1003)
  Loyalty affidavit, repeal proposed, **1960–61:** 13
     (p. 89), 414 (p. 1003)
Defense establishment, **1953:** 61, 62; **1955:** 12, 248;
     1960–61: 410, 421
  Expenditures, reduction of, **1955:** 4
Defense Homes Corporation, **1954:** 95
Defense mobilization, **1956:** 76
Defense Mobilization, Office of, **1953:** 41; **1957:**
     194; **1958:** 147
  Ad Hoc Rubber Committee, **1956:** 90
  Defense procurement contracts, **1954:** 9
  Elliott, William Y., **1953:** 33
  Manpower, report, **1953:** 144
  Reorganization Plan 1 of 1958, **1958:** 84
  Reorganization Plan 3, **1953:** 40
  Reserve forces, plans for, **1954:** 7
  Rusk, Dr. Howard A., **1953:** 15 and ftn. (p. 59)
  Science Advisory Committee, **1957:** 228, 230n.

Defense Mobilization, Office of, Director (Arthur
     S. Flemming); **1954:** 7, 12n.; **1955:** 90 ftn.
     (p. 475), 119; **1956:** 90; **1957:** 28, 115
  Assistance to depressed areas, **1953:** 273
  Bipartisan meeting on Suez Canal, **1956:** 184
  Civil defense report, **1955:** 149 ftn. (p. 672)
  Committee on Small Business, member, **1956:**
     118
  Federal Council on Aging, representation on,
     1956: 74
  Foreign aid programs, **1954:** 323
  Memorandum, **1955:** 67
  Oil supply study, memorandum, **1956:** 239
  Representation on Hoover Commission, **1953:**
     145n.
  Resignation, **1957:** 29 and n.
  Tanker construction, memorandum, **1956:** 239
  Texas City tin smelter, sale, **1956:** 62 ftn. (p. 336)
Defense Mobilization, Office of, Director, (Gordon
     Gray), **1957:** 28, 115; **1958:** 147
Defense Mobilization Board, **1954:** 345; **1957:** 194
Defense procurement, **1955:** 26, 76, 95; **1958:** 16,
     29, 33, 43, 303; **1959:** 10 (p. 63), 15
  Budget messages, **1954:** 14 (pp. 119, 124); **1960–
     61:** 13 (p. 50), 414 (pp. 955–957)
  Chronic unemployment areas, **1954:** 9, 18, 33;
     1960–61: 5
  Policies, assistance in depressed areas, **1953:** 273
  Reorganization message, **1958:** 65
Defense production, **1954:** 14 (p. 180); **1955:** 17
     (pp. 175, 176); **1956:** 12 (pp. 80, 101, 102)
  Budget message, **1958:** 5 (p. 26)
Defense Production Act, extension, **1955:** 4, 17 (p.
     175), 112; **1956:** 2; **1958:** 5 (p. 33)
Defense program.
  See also National security.
  Bipartisan meeting, **1956:** 318
  Criticism of, comment on, **1960–61:** 38
  News conference remarks, **1960–61:** 7, 21, 34, 38,
     256
Defense reorganization, **1953:** 159; **1958:** 2, 18, 26,
     80, 90, 95, 96, 110, 122
  Campaign remarks, **1958:** 287, 292, 296, 308
  Letter to President Hoover, **1958:** 134
  Letter to Repr. Vinson, **1958:** 108
  Letters sent by the President re, **1958:** 287
  Message to Congress, **1958:** 65
  News conference remarks, **1953:** 54, 62; **1958:**
     11, 37, 63, 70, 74, 88, 120
  Reorganization Plan 6, message, **1953:** 61
  Statement, **1958:** 178
  Testimony and public speeches on, **1958:** 74
Defense reorganization bill
  Approval of act, **1958:** 199
  Danger of personal army under, **1958:** 83
  Draft bill, transmittal letter, **1958:** 75
  News conference remarks, **1958:** 83, 198, 213
  Objectionable features, **1958:** 121
  Statement, **1958:** 121

Defense spending, **1953:** 95, 98, 159; **1954:** 351; **1958:** 80; **1959:** 6, 42, 71; **1960–61:** 4, 36, 410

  Budget messages, **1959:** 10 (pp. 38, 43, 55–57); **1960–61:** 13 (pp. 38, 46–58), 414 (pp. 938, 948–961)

  News conference remarks, **1953:** 31, 37, 54, 62, 88, 126, 198, 208, 254; **1954:** 92, 138, 353; **1958:** 120, 213, 310; **1959:** 148, 243, 271; **1960–61:** 7, 24, 34, 222, 256

  Reduction, **1955:** 19

  Talk with Premier Khrushchev on, **1959:** 243

Defense Supply Management Agency, **1953:** 61

Defense support.

  See Military assistance and defense support.

Defense treaties, **1957:** 6, 13, 55, 90, 91, 129, 226, 228

Deffner, Hugo, **1957:** 94n.

Defiance, Ohio, **1953:** 215

Defiance College, **1953:** 214

  Anthony Wayne Library of American Study, cornerstone-laying ceremony, remarks, **1953:** 215

  Letter to President of, **1957:** 251 and n.

Deficit (fiscal 1958, 1959), **1958:** 56, 153

Deficit spending, **1953:** 6, 57, 84, 95; **1954:** 209; **1956:** 235; **1956:** 11, 153, 222; **1959:** 6, 43, 63; **1960–61:** 255, 336, 410

  Budget message, **1960–61:** 414 (p. 935)

  Campaign remarks, **1960–61:** 341, 344, 346, 350, 354

  Comments on, **1955:** 18, 41

  News conference remarks, **1953:** 12, 37, 109, 249; **1954:** 165, 347, 353; **1959:** 7, 26, 29, 36, 53, 288

Definitive Treaty of Peace of **1955:** 1783, 81

De Galard-Terraube, Genevieve, Medal of Freedom, citation, **1954:** 176

De Gasperi, Alcide, death of, **1954:** 205

De Gasperi, Madame, message, **1954:** 205

De Gaulle, Charles, **1959:** 199, 201, 207, 214, 271 and ftn. (p. 748), 332, 349; **1960–61:** 147, 154, 162, 163, 313

  Algerian policy, **1960–61:** 127

  East-West summit conference, agreement with Western leaders on, **1959:** 337

  Inauguration, message, **1959:** 5

  Joint statement with, **1959:** 202, 335, 336; **1960–61:** 125, 155

  Message, **1958:** 273

  News conference remarks on, **1958:** 120, 141; **1959:** 7, 132, 154, 191, 223, 271; **1960–61:** 24, 127

  Program for Algeria, comment on, **1959:** 223

  Remarks of welcome to, **1960–61:** 120

  Toasts to, **1960–61:** 121, 124

De Gaulle, Madame, **1960–61:** 120, 121, 124

De Gomez, Carmen Vda, **1960–61:** 224

De La Salle, Robert, **1959:** 141n.

Delaware

  Boggs, Gov. J. caleb, **1960–61:** 208

  Candidates for public office, **1954:** 320

  Warburton, Repr. Herbert B., **1954:** 320

  Wilmington, **1954:** 320

  Williams, Sen. John J., **1954:** 92, 192, 320, 353; **1957:** 92

Delaware River channel, dredging of, **1955:** 17 (p. 168), 18

Delhi University, India, acceptance of honorary degree, remarks, **1959:** 314

Del Rio, Sotero, **1960–61:** 77

Del Rio, Tex., **1959:** 257

Del Sesto, Gov. Christopher, **1959:** 113

  Letter, **1959:** 112

De Luz Dam, Calif., **1954:** 173

Demagogue defined, **1958:** 26

DeMaioribus, A. L., **1960–61:** 350n.

De Malo France, Afranio, **1960–61:** 51

Democracy, American, Spiritual Foundations of, Conference on, remarks, **1954:** 327

Democracy, comment on, **1960–61:** 24

"Democrat" Party, comment on use of term, **1956:** 193

Democratic Congress, **1959:** 17

Democratic Convention, news conference remarks, **1956:** 198

Democratic Digest, **1953:** 128

Democratic leaders

  Consultation on proposed legislation, comment on, **1955:** 26

  Meetings with, comment on, **1959:** 26

Democratic Legacy Award, America's, acceptance, remarks, **1953:** 252

Democratic National Committee

  Chairman (Paul Butler), **1954:** 347; **1960–61:** 93

  Chairman (Stephen A. Mitchell), **1954:** 200

  News conference remarks on, **1954:** 101, 347

Democratic Party

  Consultation with leaders of, comment on, **1954:** 50

  News conference remarks on, **1954:** 33, 50; **1960–61:** 21, 93

  Presidential nomination, **1960–61:** 93

Democratic platform, campaign remarks, **1956:** 251

Democrats, comment on, **1954:** 107

Democrats for Eisenhower, **1954:** 273; **1956:** 281n.

De Montcalm de Saint-Veran, Louis, **1959:** 141n.

Dempsey, Jack, **1954:** 290, 298

Denby, Edwin, **1954:** 115

Denfeld, Adm. Louis E., **1955:** 112

Denison, Tex., birthplace of the president, **1956:** 242n.; **1959:** 179, 186

Denmark

  Atomic research agreement, **1955:** 121

  Frederik IX, **1960–61:** 41, 209, 320, 321

  Hansen, H. C., death of, **1960–61:** 41

Denmark — *continued*
  Payment for loan of vessels, **1958:** 129
  Queen Ingrid, **1960–61:** 209, 320, 321
  U.N. committee on Hungary, **1958:** 8
  U.S.-Denmark defense alliance, **1960–61:** 321n.
Denninger, Mary B., estate, indemnity claim, disapproval, **1954:** 216
Denninger, Robert W., **1954:** 216
Dennison, Adm. Robert L., **1959:** 350, 351
Dent, Harry C., **1954:** 92, 115, 143, 192, 311, 322, 341, 347
Dental care, veterans, **1954:** 14 (p. 134)
Dental officers
  Military career incentives, **1956:** 2, 81n., 91
  Service credits, **1956:** 91
Dental schools
  Federal aid, **1960–61:** 414 (p. 1008)
  Teaching and research facilities, **1958:** 5 (p. 51)
Dentists, **1956:** 2, 12 (p. 120)
  Induction, **1955:** 12
  Social security coverage, **1956:** 158
  Traineeships and research fellowships, **1956:** 21
Denver, Colo., **1954:** 209n., 260; **1955:** 207n., 208, 211n., 212n., 213n., 214n., 215n., 216n., 217n., 219n., 220n., 221n., 222n., 223n., 224n., 225n., 226n., 227n., 228n., 229n., 230n., 231n., 232n., 233n., 234n.; **1956:** 259, 260n.; **1958:** 288, 305; **1959:** 109n., 110n., 133n., 232; **1960–61:** 12n., 247n.,
  Campaign remarks, **1954:** 286
  Editor's note on President's illness, **1955:** p. 822
Denver, Colo.
  Federal payments for street improvements, disapproval, **1953:** 169
  National Security Council meeting, statement, **1954:** 266
  News conference remarks on, **1954:** 101, 165, 182, 200
  Releases from, **1953:** 165–186; **1954:** 210–222, 227–232, 234–255, 259, 261–266, 268, 269, 276–285, 288, 289
  Remarks on departure, **1955:** 235
  Remarks to Olympic Committee, **1955:** 287
Dependent children, **1955:** 25; **1956:** 2, 12 (p. 118), 21, 158
Deportation, judicial review, **1956:** 33
Deportation of aliens, **1957:** 25
Depressed areas, assistance to, **1956:** 2, 3, 19, 121, 155, 226, 279, 318
  Budget message, **1956:** 12 (pp. 117, 139)
Depressed areas (chronic unemployment), **1955:** 56; **1959:** 167
  Area development bill, **1958:** 120; **1960–61:** 143
    Vetos, **1958:** 258; **1960–61:** 146
  Budget messages, **1960–61:** 13 (pp. 75, 76), 414 (pp. 939, 983)
  Campaign remarks, **1958:** 294, 308
  Defense procurement, **1953:** 273; **1954:** 9, 18, 33

Depressed areas — *continued*
  Detroit, **1954:** 33
  Federal aid, **1960–61:** 5, 13 (pp. 75, 76), 127 and ftn. (p. 362), 133, 43, 146, 176, 414 (pp. 939, 983)
  Letter to Senator Cooper, **1960–61:** 5
  Letter to Governor Underwood, **1960–61:** 176
  New England, **1954:** 9
Depression, rumor of, **1956:** 268
Depressions, **1958:** 70
Depth bomb, atomic, **1957:** 230
De Rio Branco, Baron, **1960–61:** 51
De San Martin, Jose, **1960–61:** 58, 60, 69
DeSapio, Carmine, **1957:** 22
Deshmukh, Panjabrao S., **1959:** 315n.
Des Moines, Iowa, **1954:** 226; **1956:** 212, 216; **1959:** 69
  Republican meeting, **1959:** 21
  Visit by Premier Khrushchev, **1959:** 186
Des Moines, U.S.S., **1959:** 327n., 328n., 330n.
  Remarks to ship's company, **1959:** 331
Deseret (Utah) *News*, **1958:** 99
De Soto, Hernando, **1959:** 338
De Sreitas, C. Arreiro, **1960–61:** 157n.
D'Estaing, Edmond G., **1959:** 84n.
Destroyers in Mediterranean, **1956:** 88
De Tassigny, Marshal Jean de Lattre, **1954:** 133, 198
Detection of aircraft and missiles, **1958:** 163, 292
  Budget message, **1958:** 5 (pp. 19, 30)
Detection of nuclear tests, technical conference on. *See* Geneva conferences.
De Tocqueville, Alexis, **1959:** 214
  Journey to America, **1959:** 107
De Toledano, Ralph, **1960–61:** 256
Detroit, Mich., **1954:** 130, 320; **1956:** 107, 198; **1957:** 183; **1958:** 138n.; **1960–61:** 326, 327, 328
  Automobile industry, threatened strike, **1955:** 112
  Campaign remarks, **1954:** 318
  Cobo, Mayor Albert E., **1954:** 318n.
  Mirani, Mayor Louis C., **1960–61:** 326n., 328
  Refusal to meet with Kozlov, **1959:** 154
  Unemployment, **1954:** 33
"Development of Agriculture's Human Resources," report on problems of low income farmers, **1955:** 82
Development Association, International, **1958:** 222, 312; **1959:** 223, 244
  Arab States, **1958:** 207, 213
Development Loan Fund, **1958:** 2, 32, 36, 312; **1959:** 55, 98; **1960–61:** 36, 39, 148, 245, 247, 410
  Appropriations for, statement, **1959:** 65
  Budget messages, **1959:** 10 (pp. 44, 74); **1958:** 5 (pp. 34, 36, 37, 39); **1960–61:** 13 (pp. 38, 60), 414 (pp. 961, 965, 966)

Development Loan Fund — *continued*
 "Buy American" policy, **1959:** 267, 271
 Funds for, comment, **1959:** 123
 Joint statement with President Garcia, **1958:** 143
 Joint statement with President Toure on, **1959:** 272
 Sen. Fulbright's proposal, **1959:** 89
 U.S. aid to South America, documents re, **1960–61:** 380
Development loans, **1960–61:** 39, 279
 See also Development Loan Fund; Economic assistance; Inter-American Development Bank.
 Foreign, **1957:** 90, 91, 131, 152n.
 Latin America, **1959:** 6; **1960–61:** 247n.
 Organization for Economic Cooperation and Development, **1960–61:** 414 (p. 965)
Devereux, Repr. James P. S., **1958:** 308
Devers, Gen. Jacob L., **1954:** 198n.
De Visale, Antonio, **1960–61:** 53n.
Devraigne, Pierre, **1959:** 201
D'Ewart, Repr. Wesley A., **1954:** 270
Dewey, Duane E., Medal of Honor, citation, **1953:** 27
Dewey, George, **1958:** 125
Dewey, Gov. Thomas E., **1953:** 68, 69, 105; **1954:** 298, 300, 301; **1955:** 10, 56; **1956:** 32, 56, 94, 189; **1957:** 28
 Letter, **1954:** 188
 News conference remarks on, **1953:** 128, 230, 265; **1954:** 18, 115, 143 and ftn. (p. 568)
Dew Hong-to, relief of, veto, **1958:** 124
DEW Line.
 See Distant Early Warning (DEW) Line.
Dhahran Airfield, Saudi Arabia, **1957:** 31
Diablo Dam, Rio Grande River, joint statement with President Lopez Mateos on, **1955:** 38
Diary, the President's, **1960–61:** 21
Diaz Lanz, Pedro L., testimony on Fidel Castro, **1959:** 161
Dickenson, Edward S., court-martial, **1954:** 18
Dickey, John, **1953:** 104
Dickinson, William B., **1954:** 33
Dickinson County, Kansas, **1954:** 331
Diefenbaker, John G., **1958:** 153, 163; **1959:** 141, 196; **1960–61:** 208, 331, 416
 Exchange of toasts, **1960–61:** 171
 Joint statement with, **1960–61:** 172
 Message, **1959:** 125
Diefenbaker, Mrs. John G., **1960–61:** 171
Diem, Ngo Dinh, **1955:** 48, 81; **1957:** 80
 Exchange of greetings, **1957:** 81 and n.
 Exchange of toasts, **1957:** 82 and n.
 Joint statement with, **1957:** 83
 Letters, **1954:** 306; **1956:** 271
 Messages, **1957:** 97 and n.; **1959:** 158; **1960–61:** 338

Dien Bien Phu, battle of, **1954:** 89, 176
 French commander, Col. Christian de Castries, **1954:** 63, 83
 French defeat, messages, **1954:** 104, 105
 Messages, **1954:** 83, 104, 105
 News conference remarks, **1954:** 57, 63, 107, 138, 168
Dies, Repr. Martin, **1954:** 143
Dillon, C. Douglas, **1956:** 62; **1957:** 177; **1959:** 82n., 121, 130, 174, 243, 261n.
 Mission to Germany on U.S. balance of payments, **1960–61:** 362 and ftn. (p. 864), 365
 News conference remarks on, **1960–61:** 127, 203, 263, 362
Dillon, James, **1953:** 216n.
Diori, Hamani, message, **1960–61:** 251
Diplomatic code, **1957:** 157
Diplomatic missions, U.S., **1953:** 92
Diplomatic personnel, reduction, **1960–61:** 362
Diplomatic posts, U.S., **1960–61:** 13 (p. 64), 414 (p. 968)
Dirksen, Sen. Everett McK., **1956:** 78, 94, 214, 216, 229; **1958:** 296; **1959:** 127, 151n.; **1960–61:** 132, 272
 Letter, **1960–61:** 271
 News conference remarks on, **1958:** 83, 103; **1960–61:** 143, 263
Disability compensation claim of Harold J. Davis, disapproval, **1953:** 167
Disability compensation for Government employees, **1955:** 4
 Budget message, **1955:** 17 (p. 106)
Disability fund, civil service, veto message, **1958:** 192
Disability insurance, **1954:** 10; **1958:** 234
 Budget messages, **1958:** 5 (pp. 45, 51, 52); **1959:** 10 (pp. 102, 104, 105)
 District of Columbia, **1956:** 2
 Longshoremen, **1958:** 5 (p. 45)
 Tax refund claim of Lourene O. Estes, **1959:** 234
 Tax refund claim of Marion S. Symms, **1958:** 232
Disability of President, **1956:** 16
 Agreement with Vice President Nixon on procedures, **1958:** 37, 40, 42
 Constitutional provision in event of, **1956:** 47
 News conference remarks, **1957:** 56, 62, 115; **1958:** 11, 28, 37, 42
Disability trust fund, **1956:** 158
Disabled persons, **1955:** 25; **1956:** 12 (pp. 118, 124), 21, 158
 See also Handicapped persons.
 Federal aid, **1960–61:** 127 ftn. (p. 362), 410
 Budget messages, **1960–61:** 13 (p. 95), 414 (pp. 1010–1012)
Disabled veterans, **1956:** 12 (p. 113)
Disapproval of bills.
 See Memorandums of Disapproval.

Disarmament, **1954:** 139, 341; **1955:** 94, 164, 166; **1956:** 2, 114, 191; **1957:** 86; **1958:** 2, 32, 80, 148; **1959:** 6, 70, 290, 302, 320; **1960–61:** 2n., 4, 49, 63, 75, 80, 85, 91n., 163, 209, 245, 421

See also Aerial inspection; Inspection and control of nuclear weapons; Nuclear tests.

Address before U.N. General Assembly, **1960–61:** 302

Aerial inspection (open skies) proposal, **1955:** 166, 175, 176, 185, 220, 248; **1956:** 2, 12 (p. 108), 20, 23, 52, 78, 143, 166, 251, 262, 266; **1958:** 67, 86

Arms inspection and control, **1960–61:** 23, 73, 76, 188, 302, 332

Arms limitation and reduction, **1953:** 1, 50; **1955:** 4, 41, 166, 211; **1956:** 2, 49, 52, 143, 166, 262; **1958:** 7, 148, 163; **1959:** 10 (p. 67), 214, 258

Ban on fissionable materials for weapons purposes, **1956:** 52, 53, 166

Ban or suspension of nuclear tests.
  See Nuclear tests.

Baruch plan, **1956:** 266; **1958:** 63

Budget messages, **1958:** 5 (pp. 33, 40); **1960–61:** 13 (pp. 46, 64)

Cablegram to Prime Minister Nehru, **1957:** 244 and n.

Campaign remarks, **1956:** 210, 251, 272

Conference.
  See Disarmament conference, London.

Deadlock on discussion, **1957:** 169

Effect on U.S. economy, comment on, **1960–61:** 127

Exchange of information on military establishments, **1955:** 164, 166, 176, 185, 220

Exchange of messages with Prime Minister Kishi, **1957:** 208 and n.

Exchange of military blueprints with U. S. S. R., **1956:** 2, 23, 166, 266

Fissionable materials, production ban and conversion of weapons stocks, **1958:** 7, 21, 31, 56, 63, 67, 86, 148, 219, 222

Fund for world aid and reconstruction, **1956:** 210

Geneva conferences on.
  See Geneva conferences.

Ground inspection, Soviet proposal, **1956:** 2, 52, 78, 166, 266

Inspection and control systems, **1956:** 198, 230, 266; **1958:** 63, 67, 86, 219; **1959:** 271
  Arctic inspection zone, **1958:** 88, 163
  Inspection zones to prevent surprise attack, **1958:** 70, 148

Joint statements
  Chancellor Adenauer, **1957:** 100; **1959:** 192
  King Mohammad Zahir, **1959:** 308
  Premier Khrushchev, **1959:** 242

Disarmament — *continued*
  Joint statements — *continued*
    President Bayar, **1959:** 297
    President de Gaulle, **1959:** 202
    President Gronchi, **1956:** 49; **1959:** 293
    Prime Minister Churchill, **1954:** 155
    Prime Minister Diefenbaker, **1960–61:** 172
    Prime Minister Eden, **1956:** 27
    Prime Minister Kishi, **1957:** 117; **1960–61:** 16
    Prime Minister Macmillan, **1957:** 55, 226
    Prime Minister Segni, **1959:** 203, 248
    Shah Mohammad Reza Pahlavi, **1959:** 322
    Western leaders, **1959:** 336

Khrushchev, Nikita S., TV interview, **1957:** 105

Letters to
  Premier Bulganin, **1955:** 220; **1956:** 23, 52, 166, 262; **1957:** 3; **1958:** 7, 31
  Frederick M. Eaton, **1960–61:** 9, 10, 241
  Premier Khrushchev, **1958:** 67, 86, 112
  James J. Wadsworth, **1958:** 39

London conference proposals, **1958:** 88

Memorandum on disarmament negotiations, **1956:** 266n.

News conference remarks, **1955:** 33, 41, 47, 62, 95, 146, 149, 176, 185; **1956:** 20, 78, 88, 94, 96, 198; **1957:** 92, 115, 119, 124, 150, 169; **1958:** 63, 213; **1959:** 132, 186, 191, 223, 243, 271; **1960–61:** 34, 93, 103, 127, 143, 222, 284, 422

Nuclear vs. general, **1959:** 191

Open skies proposal, **1960–61:** 143, 163, 209

Peaceful and scientific uses of outer space, **1958:** 148

Proposals by
  Eisenhower, **1953:** 50; **1954:** 297; **1959:** 311
  Premier Khrushchev at U.N., **1959:** 223, 243
  United Kingdom in U.N., **1959:** 243
  Soviet, **1955:** 95, 156; **1958:** 148; **1960–61:** 93
  Stassen, comment on, **1958:** 37
  U.S., **1960–61:** 93

Statement, **1959:** 186

Summit conference discussion re, comment on, **1959:** 271

Ten-nation disarmament committee meeting (1960), 248, 293

Ten-Nation Disarmament Conference, **1960–61:** 13 (p. 64), 34, 90, 92, 209, 222, 238, 241n., 255, 302, 313

Disarmament, Special Assistant to the President on.
  See Stassen, Harold E.

Disarmament Administration, **1960–61:** 414 (p. 968)

Disarmament Commission and subcommittee, U.N., **1955:** 57, 156, 166; **1958:** 8, 148; **1960–61:** 302
  London meeting, **1955:** 41
  Need for meeting, statement, **1960–61:** 238
  New York meeting, statement, **1955:** 211

Disarmament Commission — *continued*
  News conference remarks, **1955:** 41, 95, 185
  Soviet disarmament plan, **1955:** 95
Disarmament conference, London
  Japanese proposal, **1957:** 208n.
  Joint statement with Prime Minister Kishi, **1957:** 117
  Joint statements with Prime Minister Macmillan, **1957:** 55, 226
  News conference remarks, **1957:** 28, 72 and n. (p. 286), 80, 87, 105, 115, 119, 134, 150
  Western Powers proposal, **1957:** 158, 165, 208 and n., 210, 226, 244
Disarmament Study Group, Joint (Department of State), **1959:** 191 and ftn. (p. 611), 243
Disarmament Subcommittee, U. N., London, **1956:** 2
  Letters to Bulganin, **1956:** 52, 166, 262
  News conference remarks, **1956:** 78, 88, 94
Disaster insurance, **1955:** 222; **1958:** 37
  Budget message, **1958:** 5 (p. 54)
Disaster loan program, **1954:** 14 (p. 162)
Disaster Loan Revolving Fund, **1957:** 11, 12
Disaster relief, **1955:** 4, 95, 208n.; **1956:** 2, 214, 235, 236, 237; **1958:** 106; **1960–61:** 279
  Budget messages, **1955:** 17 (p. 175); **1956:** 12 (pp. 139, 149, 150); **1958:** 5 (pp. 43, 54, 64, 66)
Disaster Relief Fund, President's, **1954:** 99
Disasters, natural, **1954:** 192; **1956:** 241; **1958:** 12, 38
  Addresses and messages, **1957:** 16, 41, 75, 118
  Cyclone in Mexico, **1959:** 275
  Drought, **1953:** 95, 97, 119, 124, 128, 136, 141, 159, 216, 225, 230, 249; **1954:** 9, 14 (p. 162), 168 and ftn. (p. 646), 291; **1955:** 4, 95; **1956:** 2, 235, 236, 237
  Dust storms, **1954:** 85, 99
  Earthquake, **1953:** 172, 173; **1954:** 265; **1959:** 224
    Chile, **1960–61:** 175, 214
    Greece, **1956:** 140
    Iran, **1960–61:** 126
    Lebanon, **1956:** 61
    Morocco, **1960–61:** 99
  Fire, **1953:** 258
  Floods, **1953:** 53n.; **1954:** 158, 175, 182 and ftn. (p. 678), 195, 200; **1956:** 12 (pp. 135, 139, 140, 149, 150), 47; **1959:** 45, 95
    See also Floods.
  Hurricanes, **1954:** 264, 289
    Hurricane Audrey, statement, **1957:** 121
  News conference remarks, **1957:** 17, 50, 62, 145
  Snow-stricken areas of Italy, telegram, **1956:** 39
  Storms, **1953:** 7
  Tornado, **1953:** 117
    St. Louis, Mo., **1959:** 29
  Western Europe crop damage, statement, **1956:** 42
Wichita conference, **1957:** 11, 12, 41

Discoverer earth satellite, **1960–61:** 261, 424
Discrimination.
  See also Civil rights; Integration.
  Civil Air Patrol, **1957:** 87
  Women, equal rights for, **1957:** 13, 150
Discus Thrower, presentation of statue to President, **1956:** 45n.
Disease, campaigns against, **1958:** 2, 36, 207
Diseases, decline in, **1959:** 129
Diseases, prevention and correction, **1954:** 301
Dispersal of U.S. industry, **1955:** 90
  Commission to study, comment on proposal, **1955:** 119
Displaced families, housing for, **1958:** 5 (p. 58)
Displaced persons, **1955:** 115n.
  Immigration policies, **1956:** 33
  Visas, **1957:** 25
Disraeli, Benjamin, **1953:** 187
  Sybil or *The Two Nations*, **1959:** 196
Distant Early Warning (DEW) Line, **1958:** 163, 292
  Budget message, **1958:** 5 (p. 30)
Distant early warning system, **1954:** 14 (p. 120); **1956:** 2, 12 (p. 97), 58, 148; **1959:** 6, 57
  See also Warning systems for missile and aircraft detection.
  Budget message, **1959:** 10 (pp. 60, 61)
Distinguished civilian achievement awards, **1957:** 13
Distinguished Civilian Service, citation to President Hoover, **1957:** 26 and n.
Distinguished Civilian Service Award, presentation to Andreas B. Rechnitzer, **1960–61:** 25
Distinguished Federal Civilian Service Awards, **1959:** 9; **1960–61:** 68, 389
  See also under Medals, remarks on presentation or acceptance.
Distinguished Public Service Award, presentation to Jacques Piccard, **1960–61:** 25
Distinguished Service Award, Chaplains Association, presentation to Secretary of Navy, **1956:** 98n.
Distinguished Service Cross recipients, remarks, **1955:** 52
Distinguished Service Medal
  See under Medals, remarks on presentation or acceptance.
District of Columbia, **1954:** 136
  American University, **1957:** 109
  Baseball team, **1953:** 41; **1956:** 229; **1958:** 222
  Board of Commissioners
    Filling of vacancy on, **1953:** 15, 22, 31
    Increase in membership, proposed, **1953:** 6
    President of Board, **1953:** 261n., 269
  Budget messages, **1954:** 14 (p. 189); **1955:** 17 (pp. 182, 183); **1956:** 12 (p. 153); **1958:** 5 (pp. 72, 73); **1960–61:** 13 (p. 104), 414 (p. 1021)

District of Columbia — _continued_
  Campaign remarks, **1956:** 190, 210, 226
  Citizens for Eisenhower Congressional Committee, address, **1954:** 316
  Community Chest and United Defense Fund campaigns, **1953:** 127
  Conference of mayors, remarks, **1954:** 346
  Council on Law Enforcement, **1954:** 207
  Election of delegates to national political conventions, regulation of, veto, **1954:** 206
  Gasoline filling stations, improvement, vetos, **1953:** 149; **1956:** 153
  Georgetown University, **1957:** 109
  Highway program, **1959:** 138
  Home rule, **1953:** 6; **1956:** 2, 32, 62, 318; **1957:** 13; **1958:** 5 (p. 73); **1959:** 10 (p. 109), 36; **1960–61:** 13 (p. 104), 414 (p. 1021)
  Increase in benefits for retired policemen and firemen, disapproval, **1959:** 239
  Integration, **1954:** 3, 51, 347
  Judicial conference, **1960–61:** 275
  Lincoln Day box supper, incident at, **1954:** 33
  McLaughlin, Robert E., **1960–61:** 325n.
  March of unemployed, **1959:** 36
  Mass transportation survey, report, **1959:** 157
  Murray, Robert V., **1960–61:** 314
  Narcotics users, treatment for, approval, **1953:** 116
  National Cultural Center, **1958:** 190
  News conference remarks, **1954:** 33, 345, 347; **1956:** 32, 62, 121, 229
  Non-occupational disability insurance, **1956:** 2
  Police arrest books, inspection, **1954:** 207
  Police force, **1955:** 149
  Potomac River bridge construction, **1954:** 224
  Presentation of tree to President, **1960–61:** 325
  Public transportation bill, approval, **1955:** 206
  Public transportation commission, disapproval, **1954:** 252
  Public works, construction, **1954:** 3, 14 (p. 189)
  Racial discrimination, elimination, **1953:** 6, 101; **1956:** 2, 190, 210, 224, 226, 229; **1960–61:** 410
  Red Cross Chapter House, dedication, remarks, **1953:** 201
  Redevelopment of Southwest Washington, **1954:** 345; **1955:** 55; **1956:** 4
  Republican Women's Finance Committee, remarks, **1955:** 104
  Self-government, **1955:** 4
  Sibley Memorial Hospital site, **1957:** 175
  Spencer, Samuel, President, Board of Commissioners, letter, **1956:** 37n.
  Stadium, **1956:** 121; **1957:** 45
  Suffrage and self-government, proposed, **1954:** 3, 349
  Transit strike, **1955:** 149, 176, 206
  Transportation, **1960–61:** 13 (p. 104)

District of Columbia — _continued_
  Unemployment compensation, **1955:** 4; **1956:** 2
  Unemployment insurance, approval, **1954:** 227
  United Givers Fund campaign, **1960–61:** 153
  U.S. Capitol, cornerstone laying ceremony, remarks, **1959:** 151
  U.S. District Court, **1953:** 116
  Voting rights, **1956:** 2, 32, 318; **1959:** 36; **1960–61:** 24, 414 (p. 1021)
  Water, **1957:** 45
District of Columbia Auditorium Commission, report, **1957:** 21 and n.
District of Columbia Young Republicans, leadership training school, **1956:** 122n.
Dixon, Edgar, **1955:** 149 ftn. (p. 669)
Dixon-Yates contract, **1957:** 124
  News conference remarks, **1954:** 157, 161, 168, 200, 311, 328; **1955:** 26, 41, 56, 146 and ftn. (p. 646), 149, 176
  White House releases, **1955:** 146 ftn. (pp. 657, 658), 149 ftn. (p. 669)
Djermakoye, Issofou, **1960–61:** 324
Docking, Governor George, **1957:** 138; **1959:** 258, 259; **1960–61:** 113n.
Doctors in armed forces, **1953:** 15; **1955:** 12
Dodds, Harold W., **1954:** 12n.
Dodge, Joseph M., **1955:** 74, 176; **1956:** 17n.
  See also Budget, Bureau of the, Director (Joseph M. Dodge).
  Appointment as Special Assistant to the President and Chairman, Council on Foreign Economic Policy, letter, **1954:** 348
Dodge Committee, **1956:** 94
Dole, **1958:** 83
Dollar
  Canadian, **1958:** 163
  Integrity of, **1957:** 8, 28, 50
  Purchasing power, **1957:** 13, 119
  Sound, **1953:** 82, 84; **1954:** 21, 308, 353; **1955:** 4; **1956:** 263; **1958:** 110, 293, 298; **1959:** 6, 15, 43, 75, 76, 83, 87, 124, 127, 188, 212, 274; **1960–61:** 19, 23, 131, 268, 341, 410, 415
    Budget message, **1960–61:** 414 (pp. 935, 936)
    Campaign remarks, **1956:** 224, 234, 255, 258; **1960–61:** 344, 350, 354
    Discussions with President-elect, **1960–61:** 369
    News conference remarks, **1955:** 41, 119, 185; **1956:** 171, 235, 298; **1958:** 120; **1959:** 17, 29, 36, 48, 288
"Dollar gap," **1954:** 67
Domestic workers, social security coverage, **1953:** 155
Dominican Republic, **1959:** 148
  Ciudad Trujillo, **1953:** 260
  OAS action on, **1960–61:** 263, 267
  Sugar quota, **1960–61:** 267, 374, 418
  Trujillo y Molina, Hector, **1956:** 88; 0 263

Dondero, Repr. George A., **1953**: 128, 268; **1954**: 110n.

Donegan, Bishop Horace W., **1957**: 223 and n.

Donnelly, Gov. Phil M., **1953**: 216, 225

Donnelly, Walter J., **1959**: 287n.

Donovan, Robert J., **1953**: 12, 15, 31, 54, 77, 88, 109, 225, 230; **1954**: 25, 57, 63, 92, 157, 200, 311, 322; **1955**: 18, 33, 81, 90, 100, 112, 185; **1956**: 205, 235; **1957**: 17, 45, 50, 56, 92, 105, 115, 228; **1958**: 11, 28, 37, 42, 153, 274, 318; **1959**: 89, 132, 161, 167, 173, 223; **1960–61**: 7, 127, 143, 422

Donovan, William J., **1955**: 51n.; **1956**: 102; **1957**: 66 and n.

Dooley, Dr. Thomas A., **1960–61**: 174

Doolittle, Gen. James H., **1953**: 267; **1956**: 10n.
  United Defense Fund citation, **1954**: 93

Dorado, P. R., **1960–61**: 86

Dorchester, U.S.S., **1953**: 5; **1954**: 32

Dormitzer, Mrs. Helen, **1956**: 268

Doty, Foster W., **1956**: 292

Doud, Mrs. John Sheldon (Mrs. Eisenhower's mother), **1958**: 288; **1959**: 105n.

Editor's note on President's illness, **1955**: p. 822

Douglas, James H., Medal of Freedom, citation, **1960–61**: 425

Douglas, James M., **1954**: 12n.

Douglas, Lewis, **1956**: 241; **1957**: 92

Douglas (Lewis W.) study of foreign economic policy, **1953**: 31

  Financial and economic mission to United Kingdom, report
    Letter to Lewis W. Douglas, **1953**: 176
    Letter to Clarence Randall, **1953**: 177

Douglas, Sen. Paul H., **1957**: 92; **1959**: 36
  Bill for relief of depressed areas, **1958**: 120
  Limit on gifts, **1958**: 141

Downs, R. B., letter, **1953**: 120

Doyle, Arthur Conan, *White Company*, **1954**: 192

Doyle, Richard S., **1953**: 59

Do Yun Kim, **1960–61**: 201n.

Draft.
  See also Selective Service.
  Commission for study of, **1953**: 15
  Extension, comment on proposal, **1953**: 22

Draguignan, France, **1956**: 102

Draheim, Erwin D., **1954**: 108n.

Draper, William H., Jr., **1953**: 71; **1960–61**: 36
  Letters, **1958**: 316; **1959**: 137
  News conference remarks on, **1959**: 53, 89, 288

Draper Committee.
  See President's Committee to Study the U.S. Military Assistance Program.

Drees, Willem, **1957**: 56

Driscoll, Gov. Alfred E., **1953**: 15, 205

Drought and other natural disasters.
  See also Disasters, natural.
  Hurricane Audrey, statement, **1957**: 121
  Messages, **1957**: 16, 41, 75

Drought and other natural disasters — *continued*
  News conference remarks, **1957**: 17, 59, 145
  Wichita conference, **1957**: 11, 12, 41

Drought relief, **1953**: 136, 159, 216, 227, 268; **1954**: 9, 14 (p. 162), 168 and ftn. (p. 646), 291; **1955**: 4, 95
  See also under Federal aid to States.
  Governors' meeting on, **1953**: 216, 225
  News conference remarks, **1953**: 128, 141, 225 and ftn. (p. 699), 230, 249 and ftn. (p. 780)
  Pakistan, **1953**: 95, 97, 159
    Approval of bill, **1953**: 119
    Message to Prime Minister Mohammed Ali, **1953**: 124

Drouin, Mark, **1958**: 163n.

Drug control and addiction, report, **1956**: 31n.

Drugs, food, and cosmetics, revision of laws, disapproval, **1954**: 254

Drugs, wonder, **1957**: 231

Drummond, Roscoe, **1953**: 15, 22, 88, 109, 126, 128, 141, 230, 243, 249; **1954**: 33, 50, 57, 101, 115, 129, 157, 200, 345, 347, 353; **1955**: 18, 26, 33, 41, 81, 119; **1956**: 20, 53, 88, 155; **1957**: 22, 50; **1958**: 42, 120, 213; **1959**: 48, 89, 154, 186; **1960–61**: 7, 222

Drumright, Everett F., **1960–61**: 192n.

Drury, Ill., **1956**: 148, 182

Dryden, Hugh L., **1960–61**: 287
  President's Award for Distinguished Federal Civilian Service, **1960–61**: 68n.

DuBois, Father John, **1958**: 123

Dudman, Richard, **1959**: 173

Duff, Harry N., disability retirement claim, **1958**: 248

Duff, Sen. James H., **1953**: 128; **1954**: 341; **1956**: 234, 283

Duff, O'Dair, **1958**: 302

Duke University glee club, **1954**: 33

Dulles, Allen W.
  See Central Intelligence Agency, Director.

Dulles, John Foster, **1959**: 123 ftn. (p. 425), 130, 200n.; **1960–61**: 91n., 194, 209, 410
  See also State, Secretary of (John Foster Dulles).
  Death of, statement, **1959**: 117
  Discussions on possible Khrushchev visit, **1959**: 179
  Illness, **1959**: 89, 102
  Medal of Freedom, citation, **1959**: 114
  News conference remarks on, **1959**: 89, 102, 123, 179; **1960–61**: 7, 21, 24
  Official papers in Eisenhower Library, **1959**: 258; **1960–61**: 21
  Special Consultant to the President, remarks at oath of office ceremony, **1959**: 82
  State Department consultant (1950), **1954**: 328

Dulles, Mrs. John Foster, **1959**: 82n., 114n., 117

Dulles International Airport, **1959**: 117n.; **1960–61**: 414 (pp. 974, 1021)
  Sewage disposal, **1959**: 197

Dunbar, Arthur B., Jr., **1958:** 42, 70
Dunne, Irene, **1956:** 242
Dunnigan, Alice A., **1953:** 31, 54, 88, 198, 265; **1954:** 48, 92; **1955:** 18; **1956:** 32; **1958:** 213
Duquesne Light Co., **1958:** 113n.
Durham, Repr. Carl T., **1957:** 231 and n.
 Letter re agreement with Australia, **1957:** 130 and n.
Durkin, Martin P., **1953:** 193
 See also Labor, Secretary of (Martin P. Durkin).
 Death of, letter, **1955:** 238
 News conference remarks on, **1953:** 198, 208, 230
Durkin, Mrs. Martin P., letter, **1955:** 238
Durum Wheat
 Acreage allotments, **1957:** 59
 Exemption from controls, proposed, **1956:** 6
"Dust bowl," campaign remarks, **1956:** 214
Dust storms
 Governors' conference on, **1954:** 85, 92, 99
 Statement, **1954:** 99
 Telegram to Governors, **1954:** 85
Dwinell, Gov. Lane, **1955:** 133, 135, 136, 139; **1957:** 138
Dworshak, Sen. Henry, **1959:** 154

Eagan, Col. P. F., **1960–61:** 319
Eagle Gorge Reservoir, Wash., **1955:** 17 (p. 160)
Eaker, Lt. Gen. Ira C., **1953:** 192
Early warning radar, **1957:** 17, 230, 234
Early warning systems.
 See Warning systems for missile and aircraft detection.
Earthquakes
 Algeria, **1954:** 265
 Chile, **1960–61:** 175, 214
 Greece, **1953:** 172, 173
 Iran, **1960–61:** 126
 Morocco, **1960–61:** 99
 Western United States, **1959:** 224
Earth satellites.
 See Satellites, earth.
East Germany, **1957:** 118
East-West contacts, **1955:** 175, 176; **1956:** 96, 190, 204; **1958:** 2, 36; **1959:** 214; **1960–61:** 4, 127, 209
 Agreement with Soviet Union on cultural, technical, and educational exchanges, **1958:** 22
 Broadcast with Prime Minister Macmillan, **1959:** 196
 Letters to Premier Bulganin, **1956:** 23, 166; **1958:** 7
 Joint statement with Premier Khrushchev, **1959:** 242
 News conference remarks, **1959:** 7, 17, 123
 Statements at Geneva conference, **1955:** 164, 167

East-West relations, **1960–61:** 163
 Joint statement with Chancellor Adenauer, **1960–61:** 92
 Joint statement with Western leaders, **1959:** 336
East-West trade, **1955:** 100
Easter egg rollers, remarks, **1955:** 68
Eastland, Sen. James O., **1958:** 103
Easton, Pa., IRS District Office, **1960–61:** 288
Eaton, Frederick M., letters, **1960–61:** 90, 241
Eaton, William J., **1959:** 172, 173, 243; **1960–61:** 21, 362, 422
Eban, Abba, **1960–61:** 21, 24
Ebenezer Home for the Aged, remarks, **1953:** 99
Eber Brothers Wine and Liquor Corp., tax refund claim, veto, **1959:** 215
Echegoyen, Martin R., letter, **1955:** 95
Echeverria, Esteban, **1960–61:** 58
Echo communications satellite, **1960–61:** 261, 264, 410, 424
 Budget message, **1960–61:** 414 (p. 970)
 Message recorded for transmission via, **1960–61:** 258
Echo Park Dam, **1954:** 62; **1956:** 47
Economic Advisers, Council of.
 See Council of Economic Advisers.
Economic assistance, **1953:** 92, 206, 213, 254; **1954:** 67, 139, 150; **1955:** 76; **1956:** 2, 282; **1957:** 6, 86, 91; **1958:** 35, 36, 49, 95, 96, 207; **1959:** 32, 55, 302; **1960–61:** 36, 132, 133, 203, 279, 362
 See also Foreign assistance; Mutual security program; Technical assistance to less developed countries.
 Asia, statement, **1955:** 69
 Budget messages, **1954:** 14 (pp. 86, 137–139); **1955:** 17 (pp. 91, 92); **1958:** 5 (pp. 20, 26, 36, 37, 39); **1959:** 10 (pp. 44, 69, 74); **1960–61:** 13 (pp. 60–64), 414 (pp. 962, 964–967)
  Table, **1958:** 5 (p. 34)
 Campaign remarks, **1958:** 290, 294
 Colombo Plan meeting, remarks, **1958:** 312
 Defense support.
  See Military assistance and defense support.
 Development loans, **1956:** 2, 20, 58, 87; **1957:** 90, 91, 131, 152n.; **1958:** 2, 5 (pp. 34, 36, 37, 39), 32, 36, 143, 312
 International Development Association, **1958:** 222
 Joint statements
  General Franco, **1959:** 340
  King of Morocco, **1957:** 240
  King Saud, **1957:** 31
  President Bayar, **1959:** 297
  President Garcia, **1958:** 143
  President Gronchi, **1956:** 49
  Prime Minister Kishi, **1957:** 117
  Prime Minister Nkrumah, **1958:** 180
  Prime Minister Suhrawardy, **1957:** 131

Economic assistance — *continued*
 Letter to Secretary of State, **1955:** 74
 Long-range commitments, **1956:** 20, 88, 94
 Meeting of World Bank and International Monetary Fund, message, **1958:** 278
 News conference remarks, **1954:** 92, 347; **1955:** 47; **1956:** 20, 53; **1957:** 62, 152 and n., 157; **1958:** 42, 213, 222; **1959:** 94, 148, 288
 Report on, **1959:** 170, 288
 Statement, **1958:** 151
 U.N. activities, report, **1958:** 148
 U.N. program, contributions to, **1955:** 126
 Use of agricultural surpluses, **1954:** 4
Economic conference, remarks, **1959:** 274
Economic controls.
 See Controls, Government economic.
Economic cooperation, international, **1956:** 114
Economic Cooperation and Development, Organization for, **1960–61:** 414 (p. 965)
Economic Declaration of Buenos Aires, **1957:** 177 and n.
Economic Development, Committee for, remarks, **1954:** 118
Economic development of South and Southeast Asia, Colombo Plan, **1958:** 207, 312
Economic growth, **1954:** 4, 139, 144; **1959:** 6, 15, 43, 76, 84, 87, 126, 127, 144
 See also Economy, national.
 Budget message, **1959:** 10 (pp. 37, 39)
 Incentives, **1959:** 271
 Latin America, **1959:** 98
 News conference remarks, **1959:** 17, 36
 Soviet Union, **1959:** 55
Economic Growth, Committee on Price Stability for, **1959:** 6
 News conference remarks on, **1959:** 17, 36 and ftn. (p. 198), 67
 Reports, statements, **1959:** 144; **1960–61:** 117
Economic Growth and Stability, Advisory Board on, **1953:** 93
Economic humanism, **1959:** 21
Economic integration of Central America, joint statement on, **1959:** 54
Economic Mission, Belgian, **1960–61:** 317n.
Economic Mobilization Conference, address, **1958:** 110
Economic policy, foreign, **1955:** 72
 Message, **1955:** 6
 Soviet, **1956:** 53, 58, 87
Economic report to the Congress, **1954:** 21; **1955:** 19; **1956:** 19; **1957:** 16; **1958:** 16, 37; **1959:** 15; **1960–61:** 17, 423
 News conference remarks on, **1954:** 25
Economic sanctions in case of Israel, **1957:** 28
Economic situation, international, joint statement with Western leaders, **1959:** 335
Economic and Social Council, Inter-American, **1959:** 98

Economy, farm.
 See Farm economy.
Economy, Government, **1957:** 75
Economy, Mexican, joint statement on, **1959:** 257
Economy, national, **1953:** 6, 61, 82, 93, 98, 101, 159, 189, 190, 219, 227; **1954:** 3, 4, 10, 54, 67, 72, 169, 199, 203, 221, 275, 291, 308; **1955:** 3, 4, 12, 19, 20, 128; **1956:** 2, 3, 12 (pp. 154, 155), 19; **1957:** 8, 13, 16, 195; **1958:** 2, 16, 35, 90, 95, 102, 223, 312; **1959:** 6, 15, 30, 43, 55, 63, 87, 116, 124, 126, 127, 129, 188, 244, 290; **1960–61:** 4, 5, 17, 23, 53, 245, 283, 410, 423
 See also Economic growth.
 Budget messages, **1955:** 17 (p. 87); **1956:** 12 (pp. 154, 155); **1958:** 5 (pp. 22, 23); **1959:** 10 (pp. 37, 39); **1960–61:** 13 (pp. 38, 40, 76, 91, 100), 414 (pp. 934–937)
 "Buy" to stimulate economy, **1958:** 37, 56, 70, 83
 Campaign remarks, **1954:** 273, 286, 316, 318, 320; **1956:** 210, 258, 268, 279, 280; **1958:** 292, 293, 295, 296, 302, 303, 308; **1960–61:** 348, 350, 351, 354, 355
 Economic conference, remarks, **1959:** 274
 Economic Mobilization Conference, address, **1958:** 110
 Economic Report, **1956:** 19
 Effect of disarmament on, **1960–61:** 127
 Effect of steel strike, **1959:** 246, 253, 288
  Statement, **1959:** 268
 Executive responsibility, **1960–61:** 255
 Fact paper, statement, **1958:** 29
 Federal activities in aid of, **1958:** 43, 49, 50, 51, 96, 103, 110, 303; **1959:** 7
 Letters to
  Secretary Benson, **1958:** 51
  Administrator Cole, **1958:** 50
  Minority leaders, **1958:** 43
  Walter Reuther, **1954:** 26
  Secretary Weeks, **1958:** 299
 "Make-work, pump priming," **1958:** 43, 49
 Need for confidence, **1958:** 83
 News conference remarks, **1953:** 12, 22, 37, 62, 109, 128, 230; **1954:** 18, 25, 39, 63, 73, 101, 129, 192, 200, 311, 347, 353; **1955:** 18, 41, 56, 81, 119, 185; **1957:** 17, 119, 124, 169, 228; **1958:** 11, 28, 37, 42, 56, 63, 70, 83, 88, 103, 120, 213; **1959:** 7, 17, 29, 42, 102, 267, 271, 288; **1960–61:** 21, 93, 127, 222, 256, 263, 284, 362, 422
 Residential construction act, message, **1958:** 62
 Statements, **1954:** 194; **1958:** 283
 Statistics on, **1954:** 192, 194, 200
 Telegram to Gov. Averell Harriman, **1958:** 33
Economy, world, **1960–61:** 38
Ecuador, U.S. Embassy, **1958:** 101n.
EDC.
 See European Defense Community.

[References are to items except as otherwise indicated]

Edelweiler, Germany, **1955:** 204n.
Eden, Anthony, **1953:** 22, 254; **1954:** 148; **1955:**
    208n.; **1957:** 7, 62, 80
  Appointment as Prime Minister of United King-
    dom, statement, **1955:** 66
  Comment on, **1955:** 41
  Joint statements with, **1956:** 26, 27
  News conference remarks on, **1954:** 143, 157;
    1956: 32, 53, 78, 155; **1960–61:** 7, 21
  Suez invasion (1956), comment on, **1960–61:** 21
  U.S. foreign policy, comment on, **1960–61:** 7
Eden, Lady, **1957:** 7
Edgerton, Glen E.
  See Export-Import Bank, Chairman of the Board
    of Directors (Glen E. Edgerton).
Edison, Thomas, **1954:** 305
Editorial Association, National, remarks, **1954:** 149
Editors, National Society of, **1959:** 271
Editors of business magazines, remarks to, **1959:**
    124
Edson, Peter, **1953:** 238; **1959:** 161
Education, **1953:** 95, 215; **1954:** 308; **1955:** 4, 11,
    121; **1956:** 2, 8; **1958:** 2, 12, 18, 24, 320;
    1959: 71; **1960–61:** 4, 94, 363, 410
  Addresses, messages, etc., **1957:** 16, 19, 68, 86,
    118, 222, 223, 230, 234
  Advisory Committee on, proposed, **1954:** 14 (p.
    154)
  Agricultural, **1956:** 222; **1958:** 12
  Beyond high school, **1956:** 8, 85, 222, 277
  Budget messages, **1954:** 14 (pp. 132, 140, 151–
    155); **1955:** 17 (pp. 94, 140–148); **1956:** 12
    (pp. 121–124); **1958:** 5 (pp. 18, 20, 42, 43,
    46–50); **1959:** 10 (pp. 46, 98, 99); **1960–61:**
    13 (pp. 87, 89), 414 (pp. 1001–1003)
    Tables, **1954:** 14 (p. 152); **1955:** 17 (p. 142)
  Campaign remarks, **1956:** 241, 253, 256; **1958:**
    295, 296
  Civil rights.
    See main headings, Civil rights; Integration,
      public schools; Little Rock.
  Committee on, proposed, **1953:** 28; **1959:** 7
  Communism, study of, **1956:** 201
  Communist activities in, **1953:** 15
  Conference on at Defiance, Ohio, **1957:** 251n.
  Deaf and blind, **1954:** 14 (p. 153)
  Federal aid, **1953:** 6; **1954:** 14 (p. 153); **1955:** 31,
    33, 47, 119; **1956:** 2, 8, 222; **1958:** 5 (pp.
    42, 48–50), 24, 203, 222, 295; **1959:** 6, 10
    (p. 99), 29, 123; **1960–61:** 13 (pp. 89, 90),
    23, 34, 133, 255, 410, 414 (pp. 939, 1001–
    1003)
  School construction.
    See main heading, School construction.
  Federal personnel training at public or private
    facilities, **1957:** 112
  Federally affected areas, **1956:** 2, 8, 12 (p. 122),
    222

Education — *continued*
  Fellowships, **1958:** 5 (pp. 46, 48), 24, 28
  Fiscal vs. human values, comment on, **1959:** 29
  Foreign exchange programs, **1953:** 89; **1954:** 14
    (p. 140), 128
  Hoover Commission recommendations, **1957:**
    112
  Integration in public schools.
    See main heading, Integration, public schools.
  International teacher development program,
    1959: 222
  Institution of higher learning, definition, **1953:**
    79
  Institutions of learning, province of, comment
    on, **1954:** 295
  Junior colleges, **1958:** 320
  Land-grant colleges, **1954:** 335
  Language teaching, **1958:** 5 (p. 49), 24
  Loan fund, **1955:** 162
  Medical and dental, **1956:** 2, 12 (p. 120), 21;
    1957: 13, 223
  National defense education bill, **1958:** 153
    Approval, **1958:** 243
    Letter to Repr. Wainwright, **1958:** 162
    Statement, **1958:** 195
  News conference remarks, **1955:** 33, 47, 95, 119;
    1958: 28, 153; **1959:** 7, 17, 29, 123
  Religion, teaching of, **1956:** 241
  Research, **1956:** 8, 12 (p. 122), 222, 277
  Rural development program, **1956:** 12 (pp. 131,
    132)
  School construction.
    See main heading, School construction.
  School districts in Federally affected areas, **1953:**
    6, 95; **1954:** 14 (pp. 153, 154); **1959:** 10
    (pp. 98–100), 17, 27, 181
  Schools abroad, American, **1959:** 55
  Science, **1954:** 328; **1956:** 12 (p. 122); **1958:** 2, 5
    (pp. 18, 20, 42, 46, 48, 49), 24, 223;
    1960–61: 13 (p. 89), 414 (p. 1002)
  Science, engineering, and mathematics, **1956:** 12
    (p. 122), 76, 77, 277; **1957:** 230, 234 and
    n., 251 and n.; **1959:** 6, 10 (pp. 46, 98, 99),
    107, 118
  Science Advisory Committee report, **1959:** 118
  Smith-Mundt Act anniversary, remarks, **1958:** 23
  Soviet system, **1958:** 295
  State and community conferences on, **1954:** 3, 14
    (p. 153), 268; **1955:** 33, 95, 96
  Teachers, **1954:** 308; **1956:** 8, 103, 222, 277;
    1957: 19, 68, 230, 234 and n., 251 and n.;
    1958: 5 (pp. 46, 48), 24, 28, 320; **1959:** 6,
    7, 10 (p. 99), 118, 222
  Testing and counseling service, **1958:** 5 (p. 49),
    24
  U.S.S.R., scientific education, **1957:** 234
  Veterans, **1954:** 14 (p. 132); **1956:** 12 (p. 112)

Education — *continued*
   Vocational, **1954:** 14 (p. 153); **1956:** 222; **1958:** 5
      (pp. 43, 46), 12, 106, 313; **1959:** 10 (p. 98);
      1960–61: 13 (p. 89), 414 (p. 1015)
   White House Conference on (1955), **1954:** 14
      (pp. 152, 153), 268, 273; **1955:** 17 (pp. 141,
      147), 31, 96, 242; **1956:** 2, 8, 103, 222, 234,
      253, 277; **1957:** 68
   News conference remarks, **1955:** 18, 33, 95
Education, American Council on, remarks, **1953:**
   207
Education, Commissioner of, **1953:** 28
   Samuel M. Brownell, **1955:** 96
Education, Office of, **1953:** 28, 54, 95; **1954:** 14 (pp.
   153, 154); **1955:** 31; **1956:** 2; **1958:** 24
   Budget messages, **1955:** 17 (pp. 141, 148); **1956:**
      12 (p. 122)
   Educational research, funds for, **1956:** 8, 277
   International educational exchange service,
      1959: 222n.
Education Act, National Defense, **1960–61:** 410,
   413
   Budget messages, **1960–61:** 13 (p. 89), 414 (pp.
      1002, 1003)
   Loyalty affidavit, repeal proposed, **1960–61:** 13
      (p. 89), 414 (p. 1003)
Education Association, National, **1954:** 182; **1956:**
   222
Education beyond high school, **1956:** 8, 222, 277
   Committee on, **1956:** 85, 222; **1957:** 19
Education Week, American, statement, **1953:** 237
Educational exchange, **1955:** 4; **1956:** 58, 114, 204;
   1958: 23; **1959:** 222n.
   Budget message, **1956:** 12 (pp. 108, 109)
   Less developed areas, **1955:** 17 (p. 132)
   Soviet Union, **1958:** 22
Educational TV, news conference remarks, **1957:**
   28
Educators, consultation on civil rights, **1957:** 207
Edward VII of England, **1959:** 141n.
Edwards, John, **1959:** 179, 191
Egan, Charles E., **1955:** 62, 112, 149
Egan, Gov. William A., **1959:** 150; **1960–61:** 178
Egg-rolling, White House grounds, remarks, **1958:**
   66
Egypt, **1955:** 4, 18, 234; **1956:** 164, 192, 282, 295;
   1957: 34; **1958:** 177
   See also Arab-Israeli dispute and hostilities;
      United Arab Republic.
   Agreement with United Kingdom on Suez Ca-
      nal, **1954:** 172, 192, 226, 297, 316
   Ancient civilization, **1960–61:** 328
   Assistance, **1955:** 17 (p. 130)
   Cairo, **1956:** 205, 235
      Afro-Asian Conference, **1958:** 31
   Campaign remarks, **1956:** 241, 268, 283, 290
   Israeli hostilities, **1956:** 276, 282, 295, 298
   Lebanon, broadcasts to, **1958:** 173

Egypt — *continued*
   Nasser, Gamal Abdel, **1956:** 164, 192, 205; **1957:**
      62
   News conference remarks, **1956:** 16, 113, 171,
      193, 205, 235; **1957:** 28, 45, 50, 62, 70, 72,
      87, 124, 134, 157, 228
   Recognition of Communist China, **1956:** 113
   Soviet arms shipments, **1956:** 282, 298
   Soviet proposal to U. S. on use of military force,
      1956: 291n.
   Suez Canal.
      See main heading, Suez Canal.
   Suez crisis (1956), **1960–61:** 21, 410
   U. N. action on, **1957:** 6
Eight-hour law, Federal, **1957:** 13
Einaudi, Luigi, message, **1954:** 283
Einstein, Albert, **1956:** 283; **1959:** 107, 116
   Death of, statement, **1955:** 75
Eisendrath, Maurice N., **1953:** 132
Eisenhower, Mrs. David J., President's mother,
      1953: 78, 79; **1956:** 280; **1960–61:** 340
Eisenhower, Dwight D., personal reminiscences
   Address to Chaplains of SHAPE (1952), **1954:**
      103
   American Assembly, **1960–61:** 86
   Anti-American demonstration (1951), **1958:** 103
   Appointment to Military Academy, **1956:** 241
   Argentina, plans to visit as youth, **1960–61:** 57
   Argument with foreign diplomat, **1954:** 294
   Army Industrial College assignment, **1960–61:**
      283
   Association with Rev. Edmund A. Walsh, **1958:**
      286
   Athletic teams, **1960–61:** 395
   Berlin four-power council, **1953:** 128
   Birthplace, **1960–61:** 336
   Boxing at West Point, **1958:** 287
   Boy Scout training of John Eisenhower, **1960–**
      61: 166
   Boyhood, game of "shinny," **1960–61:** 319
   Boyhood in Kansas, **1953:** 216, 218, 252; **1954:**
      291; **1959:** 7, 258
      Blood-poisoning, **1956:** 268
      Effect of drought, **1956:** 236
      Grocery stores, **1954:** 144
      Missouri River flood (1903), **1953:** 100
      Plowing, **1956:** 211
      Raising and selling vegetables, **1953:** 150
      Rural mail delivery, **1959:** 177
      Work experience, **1956:** 241; **1959:** 179
   Boyhood visit to South, **1958:** 142
   Brazil, visit to (1946), **1960–61:** 48
   Canada, visits to, **1953:** 246; **1958:** 163
   China, visit to (1946), **1960–61:** 194
   Columbia University, **1953:** 109; **1958:** 168;
      1960–61: 186, 187
   Congressional hearings on appropriations, **1959:**
      29

Eisenhower, D.D., reminiscences — *continued*
  Decision to run for Presidency, **1960–61:** 290
  De Gaulle, Charles, **1958:** 120
  Dempsey-Firpo prize fight, **1954:** 290
  Early military career and experiences, **1954:** 111;
      1958: 80
    Gettysburg command, **1958:** 123
    Lt. Gen. Troy Middleton, **1959:** 36
    Panama, **1958:** 287; **1960–61:** 24
    Pantelleria, capture of, **1955:** 59
    Philippines, **1958:** 71, 139; **1959:** 36; **1960–61:**
        182, 185, 186, 187, 188
    War College, **1958:** 286
  Election campaigns (1952, 1956), **1959:** 127
  England, first visit to, **1953:** 30
  First insurance policy, **1959:** 124
  First meeting with wife, **1960–61:** 336
  First trans-Atlantic crossing, **1959:** 222
  Football coaching, **1958:** 286
  Fort Leavenworth, **1954:** 120
  French handling of Communists in armed
      forces, **1954:** 48
  Friendship with Winston Churchill, **1959:** 96
  Gettysburg College, **1959:** 71
  High school athletic contest, **1958:** 83
  Korea, visits to, **1960–61:** 198, 201
  Language study, **1958:** 144
  Lobbyists in defense matters, **1958:** 70
  Marching in Woodrow Wilson inaugural parade,
      1960–61: 340
  McKinley torch parade (1896), **1959:** 177; **1960–
      61:** 327
  Meeting with Mikoyan (1945), **1959:** 17
  Member of board on establishment of Air Force
      Academy, **1955:** 117
  Mexican border incident, **1956:** 87
  NATO, **1956:** 78; **1959:** 70; **1960–61:** 362
  Paris, **1958:** 1928, 74
  Patton, Gen. George S., **1955:** 81
  Pearl Harbor day, **1960–61:** 336
  Portugal, visit to (1951), **1960–61:** 157, 161
  Red Cross meeting in London (1942), **1953:** 117,
      201
  Religion of parents, **1954:** 161
  Resignation of commission, **1958:** 288
  SHAEF, **1953:** 88
  Soldier's oath, **1954:** 111
  Soviet Union, visit to (1945), **1959:** 271
    Visit to Soviet collective farm, **1955:** 47
  Spanish-American War, **1954:** 111
  Spring (1945), **1953:** 50
  Start of military career, **1960–61:** 336
  State loyalties, **1959:** 75
  Study of wage-price controls, **1955:** 26
  Sturgis, Maj. Gen. S. D., Jr., first meeting with,
      1954: 271
  Suggestion re presidency, **1955:** 10
  Turkey, visit to (1952), **1959:** 296

Eisenhower, D.D., reminiscences — *continued*
  TV appearances, **1956:** 229
  V-E Day, **1955:** 81
  Vice President, choice of (1952), **1960–61:** 38
  West Point, **1955:** 70, 118; **1960–61:** 57, 173, 319
  Work on U. N. peace force (1947), **1958:** 213
  Work week, **1955:** 84
  World War I, **1953:** 105, 192, 246; **1954:** 72
    Draft, **1959:** 53
    Gas warfare, **1955:** 118
  World War II, **1954:** 103, 290; **1955:** 4, 22, 59,
      100; **1958:** 288, 318; **1959:** 96
    Achievement of integration in combat units,
        1956: 229
    African campaign, **1953:** 234; **1959:** 330; **1960–
        61:** 355
    Armistice, **1956:** 78
    Association with allied leaders, **1954:** 133;
        1959: 7
    Association with General Doolittle, **1953:** 267
    Battle of Anzio, **1954:** 63; **1956:** 113
    Battle of Normandy, **1954:** 9, 131; **1956:** 253;
        1960–61: 405
    Concentration camps, **1953:** 22
    D-Day, **1953:** 88; **1954:** 57; **1956:** 122; **1960–
        61:** 354
    Feelings on Germany, **1953:** 128
    Japanese-American unit, **1960–61:** 205
    Operation Overlord, **1959:** 7, 8; **1960–61:** 405
    Rhine River crossing, **1960–61:** 405
    Sacrifices of soldiers, **1960–61:** 318
    Ste. Mere Eglise incident, **1956:** 96
    Visits to troops, **1956:** 206
    Yalta conference, **1955:** 59
    Zhukov, Marshal Georgi, **1955:** 33
Eisenhower, Dwight D., writings, **1958:** 11
  Crusade in Europe, **1958:** 37, 153
Eisenhower, Mrs. Dwight D., **1953:** 78, 79, 80, 106,
    154, 211, 230, 232, 233, 246, 253; **1954:** 19,
    20n., 23n., 31, 86, 109, 124n., 171n., 174n.,
    176n., 205, 226, 290, 291, 293n., 303, 304,
    316, 321, 339, 355; **1955:** 20, 23n., 42, 45,
    61, 63, 68, 88, 90, 133, 152, 163, 195, 230,
    235, 236, 237, 238, 250; **1956:** 25, 47, 66n.,
    92, 122, 129, 188, 190, 199, 206, 211, 212,
    216, 226, 234, 240, 241, 247, 249, 250, 254,
    257, 259, 268, 280, 292, 293, 315; **1957:** 7,
    47, 52, 65, 102 and n., 103, 116, 126, 143,
    148, 150, 157, 176, 201, 224n., 248; **1958:**
    2, 10, 11, 30, 46, 66, 81, 94, 115, 138,
    140n., 163, 221, 233, 279, 288; **1959:** 12,
    16n., 50n., 52n., 59n., 64n., 97, 100n.,
    105n., 127, 141n., 165, 166, 168, 200, 210,
    219n., 247, 255, 262, 269n.; **1960–61:** 3,
    51, 109n., 110n., 121n., 129n., 187, 213n.,
    239, 245, 308, 317n., 320n., 321n., 327,
    336, 367, 371, 372, 381
  Editor's note on President's illness, **1955:** p. 822

Eisenhower, Mrs. Dwight D. — *continued*
   News conference remarks on, **1959:** 21, 48, 223,
     277; **1960–61:** 38, 143, 222
   Visit to Soviet Union, question of, **1959:** 223
Eisenhower, Dwight David, II, **1957:** 234
Eisenhower, Edgar, **1956:** 268; **1957:** 72; **1958:** 220;
   1960–61: 276n.
Eisenhower, General, use of term by press, **1958:**
   288
Eisenhower, John S., **1953:** 253; **1956:** 190; **1959:**
   114n., 277 ftn. (p. 768), 308; **1960–61:** 118,
   166, 355, 430
Eisenhower, Mrs. John S., **1953:** 253; **1956:** 190;
   1959: 277 ftn. (p. 768), 308; **1960–61:** 355
Eisenhower, Milton S., **1955:** 10, 121; **1957:** 62, 72,
   96, 217; **1958:** 130
   American-Korean Foundation, **1953:** 65n.
   Candidacy in 1960, question of, **1959:** 179
   Latin American visits, **1953:** 48 and ftn., 101,
     141, 198 and ftn., 213, 265; **1956:** 146, 216
   News conference remarks on, **1953:** 141, 198,
     265; **1956:** 5, 32, 216; **1959:** 148, 179, 186
   Political plans, **1956:** 32
   Report on U.S.-Latin American relations, **1959:**
     261n., 287n.
   Resignation from committees, letter, **1960–61:**
     349
   Visit to Central America, **1958:** 197
   Visit to Soviet Union, **1959:** 148
   White House meeting on Latin America, **1954:**
     18
   World Health Organization, President's repre-
     sentative at meeting, **1958:** 116n.
Eisenhower Cracker Barrel, **1957:** 236 and n.
Eisenhower Doctrine.
   See Middle East Joint Resolution.
Eisenhower Exchange Fellowships, **1953:** 212;
   1957: 222; **1960–61:** 98n., 305
Eisenhower family, **1954:** 331
   Members present at nomination acceptance,
     1956: 190
Eisenhower Foundation, **1960–61:** 118
Eisenhower Library.
   See Abilene, Kansas.
Eisenhower Museum.
   See Abilene, Kansas.
Eisenhower Park (Newport, R.I.), dedication,
   remarks, **1960–61:** 239
Ekra, Mathieu, **1960–61:** 324n.
ElAlamein, Egypt, **1959:** 96
Elbe River, **1954:** 133
Elbrick, C. Burke, **1960–61:** 157n.
Eleazer, Frank, **1960–61:** 263
Election campaign, Congressional (1954); **1955:** 10
   Addresses or remarks
     September 23, Los Angeles, Calif., **1954:** 273
     September 24, Los Angeles, Calif., **1954:** 274
     October 8, Denver, Colo., **1954:** 286

Election campaign, Congressional (1954) — *continued*
     October 15, Indianapolis, Ind., **1954:** 290
     October 21, New York City, **1954:** 298
     October 23, Gettysburg, Pa., **1954:** 304
     October 28, Washington, D.C., **1954:** 316
     October 29, Cleveland, Ohio, **1954:** 317
     October 29, Detroit, Mich., **1954:** 318
     October 29, Louisville, Ky., **1954:** 319
     October 29, Wilmington, Del., **1954:** 320
     November 1, Washington, D.C., **1954:** 321
   News conference remarks, **1953:** 41, 225, 230,
     238; **1954:** 33, 63, 92, 157, 172, 182, 192,
     200, 311, 322, 341
   Post election remarks, **1954:** 322, 341
   President's participation in campaign, **1953:** 225,
     230
Election campaign, Congressional (1958), **1958:** 26,
   307
   Addresses or remarks
     October 14, Washington, D.C., **1958:** 287
     October 17, Cedar Rapids, Iowa, **1958:** 290
     October 20, Los Angeles, Calif., **1958:** 292
     October 21, San Francisco, Calif., **1958:** 293,
     294
     October 22, Chicago, Ill., **1958:** 295, 296
     October 27, Charleston, W. Va., **1958:** 302
     October 27, Pittsburgh, Pa., **1958:** 303
     October 28, New York City, **1958:** 305, 306
     October 31, Baltimore, Md., **1958:** 308
   News conference remarks, **1958:** 11, 37, 42, 70,
     213, 222, 274, 288, 310, 318
   Post campaign remarks, **1958:** 310, 318
Election campaign, Presidential (1952), **1953:** 57,
   238; **1954:** 91, 139, 174n., 197; **1959:** 127
   News conferences remarks, **1954:** 92, 138, 143,
     165
   Remarks on, **1954:** 286, 290, 316, 319, 320
   Remarks on the budget, quoted, **1955:** 18
Election campaign, Presidential (1956), **1954:** 143,
   347, 353; **1958:** 42; **1959:** 127; **1960–61:**
   7
   Addresses or remarks
     September 12, Gettysburg, Pa., **1956:** 206
     September 18, Washington National Airport,
     1956: 209
     September 19, White House, **1956:** 210
     September 21, Colfax, Iowa, **1956:** 211
     September 21, Des Moines, Iowa, **1956:** 212
     September 25, Peoria, Ill., **1956:** 214
     October 1, Cleveland, Ohio, **1956:** 224
     October 1, Lexington, Ky., **1956:** 225, 226
     October 9, Pittsburgh, Pa., **1956:** 233, 234
     October 12, Washington, D.C., **1956:** 241
     October 15, Washington, D.C., **1956:** 246
     October 16, Minneapolis, Minn., **1956:** 247,
     250
     October 16, St. Paul, Minn., **1956:** 249
     October 17, Seattle, Wash., **1956:** 251

Election campaign, Presidential — *continued*
    October 18, Portland, Ore., **1956:** 254, 255, 256
    October 18, Tacoma, Wash., **1956:** 253
    October 19, Beverly Hills, Calif., **1956:** 258
    October 19, Burbank, Calif., **1956:** 257
    October 20, Denver, Colo., **1956:** 259
    October 24, Washington, D.C., **1956:** 268
    October 25, New York City, **1956:** 272
    October 29, Jacksonville, Fla., **1956:** 279
    October 29, Miami, Fla., **1956:** 278
    October 29, Richmond, Va., **1956:** 280
    November 1, Philadelphia, Pa., **1956:** 283
    November 5, Boston, Mass. (via TV), **1956:** 292
    November 25, Washington, D.C., **1956:** 290, 293
    Cancellation of meetings, Tex., Okla., Tenn., **1956:** 281
    Comment on, **1955:** 10, 47
    National Citizens for Eisenhower Executive Campaign Conference, **1956:** 117
    News conference remarks, **1956:** 20, 32, 47, 53, 62, 78, 94, 121, 193, 198, 205, 216, 229, 235
    Nomination, acceptance broadcast, **1956:** 190
    Type of, **1956:** 47, 48, 53, 62; **1956:** 32, 48, 53, 62, 193, 216
    Victory remarks, **1956:** 294
Election campaign, Presidential (1960), **1960–61;** 107, 245, 337
    Addresses or remarks
      September 12, Baltimore, Md., **1960–61:** 290
      September 29, Chicago, Ill., **1960–61:** 309
      October 18, Minneapolis, Minn., **1960–61:** 329
      October 28, Philadelphia, Pa., **1960–61:** 341
      November 1, Washington, D.C., **1960–61:** 344
      November 2, Garden City, N.Y., **1960–61:** 345
      November 2, New York City, **1960–61:** 347, 348
      November 2, Westchester County, N.Y., **1960–61:** 346
      November 4, Cleveland, Ohio, **1960–61:** 350, 351, 352
      November 4, Pittsburgh, Pa., **1960–61:** 353, 354
      November 7, Washington, D.C., **1960–61:** 355
    News conference remarks, **1959:** 7, 123, 148, 179; **1960–61:** 93, 103, 222, 256, 263, 268, 284, 422
    Post election remarks, **1960–61:** 422
    Post election telegrams, **1960–61:** 356, 357
    Role of President, **1959:** 179; **1960–61:** 93, 222, 256, 263, 268, 422
Election campaigns, Presidential.
    See also Candidacy for second term, the President's; Election campaign addresses or remarks.
Election contributions, **1956:** 32, 121

Election expenditures, **1956:** 94
Election of union officers, **1959:** 22
Elections, Presidential, constitutional amendment proposed, **1960–61:** 422
Elections, primary.
    See Primary elections.
Elections, split tickets, **1959:** 123
    Electoral college, **1955:** 47
Electric power, policy on, statement, **1953:** 171
Electrical machinery, U.S.-U.K. trade discussions, **1959:** 67
Electricity, REA loans, **1957:** 157
Elephant, gift to the President, **1959:** 214; **1960–61:** 260n.
Elephant Butte Dam construction, claims, disapproval, **1954:** 243
Elizabeth, Queen Mother, **1954:** 39, 311, 322
Elizabeth II, **1955:** 208n.; **1957:** 50; **1958:** 163, 318; **1959:** 96, 141, 193, 196, 198n., 214; **1960–61:** 40, 171
    Coronation, **1953:** 109 and ftn. (p. 439)
    Messages, **1953:** 7, 34; **1958:** 209
    Toast to, **1957:** 220 and n.
    Welcoming remarks, **1957:** 218 and n.
Elkins, W. Va., relief of, **1956:** 163
Ellender, Sen. Allen J., Sr., **1954:** 143
Eller, Dr. Joseph J., **1953:** 260
Elliott, T. C., relief of, disapproval, **1954:** 247
Elliott, William Y., **1953:** 33; **1956:** 201n.
Ellsworth, Repr. Harris, **1954:** 34, 152; **1956:** 256; **1958:** 6
Ellsworth, Brig. Gen. Richard, **1953:** 103
Ellsworth, Mrs. Richard, **1953:** 103
Ellsworth Air Force Base, dedication, remarks, **1953:** 103
El Paso, Tex., cotton association, **1953:** 265
El Salvador, Jose Maria Lemus, **1959:** 50, 52
    Joint statement with, **1959:** 54
Elson, Rev. Edward L. R., letter to, **1956:** 68; **1957:** 74
Emancipation Proclamation, **1954:** 22; **1956:** 84
Embassies, representation allowances, **1957:** 50
Emergency assistance to friendly nations, **1957:** 90
Emergency feed program, **1954:** 14 (p. 162)
Emerson, Ralph Waldo, **1956:** 87
Emmitsburg, Md., **1958:** 123
Emmons, Glenn L., letter, **1953:** 180
Emory, Alan S., **1953:** 12, 22, 37, 41, 77, 88, 126, 225, 238, 249, 265; **1954:** 33, 39, 63, 107, 115, 143, 165, 168, 172, 192, 311, 322, 347; **1955:** 10, 26, 33, 41, 47, 56, 62, 90, 100, 146, 176; **1956:** 32, 56, 94, 96, 155, 216; **1957:** 50; **1958:** 37, 213, 288; **1959:** 36, 42; **1960–61:** 24
Emory University glee club, **1954:** 33
Employee Compensation Policy of the Federal Government, Joint Commission on, establishment proposed, **1958:** 169
Employees, Government, **1955:** 8, 186, 187

Employment, **1953:** 93, 249; **1954:** 21, 26, 67, 72, 194, 308, 318; **1955:** 4, 19; **1956:** 2, 19; **1958:** 2, 49; **1959:** 15, 76; **1960–61:** 17, 23, 410, 423

See also Unemployment.

Amusement, construction, and maritime industries, **1954:** 5

Campaign remarks, **1956:** 224, 226, 234, 251, 268, 279; **1958:** 292, 296, 303, 308

Conference on Equal Job Opportunity, **1955:** 225

Disabled and handicapped, **1956:** 158, 226; **1958:** 99

Equal opportunity, **1960–61:** 407, 410

Fair employment practices, **1954:** 92

Government, **1953:** 12 ftn. (p. 53), 101, 159; **1954:** 273, 286, 291, 316; **1956:** 2, 94, 226; **1957:** 13, 62; **1958:** 96, 169, 292, 296, 308; **1959:** 9, 10 (pp. 108, 109), 36; **1960–61:** 410

Information, **1956:** 12 (p. 131)

Migratory workers, **1954:** 14 (p. 184)

News conference remarks, **1954:** 92, 107, 311; **1955:** 119, 185; **1958:** 37, 88; **1960–61:** 143, 222, 256, 263

Older persons, **1956:** 12 (p. 117), 226

Report on, **1954:** 107

Services, **1956:** 12 (p. 117); **1958:** 5 (p. 50)

Statements, **1958:** 68, 283

Women, **1958:** 320

Employment Act, amendment proposed, **1960–61:** 423

Budget messages, **1960–61:** 13 (p. 105), 414 (p. 1022)

Employment of the Physically Handicapped, President's Committee on, remarks, **1953:** 192; **1954:** 96; **1955:** 103; **1958:** 99; **1960–61:** 417

Empress of Britain, **1955:** 146

Energy Supplies and Resources Policy, President's Advisory Committee on (Flemming Committee), report, **1955:** 33 and ftn. (p. 259), 41, 56

Engebretsen, Toley, tax refund claim, **1958:** 249

Engelbert, Wilhelm, relief of, veto, **1954:** 58

Engels, Friedrich, **1956:** 265; **1960–61:** 328

Engineers, **1956:** 85n.; **1958:** 24

Budget message, **1958:** 5 (pp. 19, 46, 49)

Committee on Scientists and Engineers, **1958:** 169, 327

European, contacts with, **1958:** 145

Interdepartmental committee on education and utilization, **1956:** 76

National committee for development of, **1956:** 76, 77, 277

Engineers, Corps of, **1953:** 37; **1954:** 34; **1955:** 4; **1957:** 105; **1958:** 37; **1959:** 194; **1960–61:** 410

Engineers, Corps of — *continued*

Appropriations for civil functions, **1957:** 161

Budget messages, **1954:** 14 (pp. 167, 168, 175); **1955:** 17 (pp. 158–160, 168); **1956:** 12 (pp. 134, 135, 136, 142); **1958:** 5 (pp. 68, 69); **1959:** 10 (pp. 94, 95); **1960–61:** 13 (pp. 38, 83), 414 (pp. 947, 993, 994, 996, 997)

Civil water resources functions, **1960–61:** 414 (p. 947)

Civil works projects, **1958:** 43

Approval, **1958:** 155

Veto, **1958:** 73

Flood control study **1953:** 153; **1955:** 222

Great Lakes water level report, **1956:** 177

New construction starts, **1955:** 157; **1956:** 136; **1957:** 161

Spending authority reduction, **1957:** 75

Water resources projects, land management, **1953:** 153

Engineers from India participating in education program, remarks, **1960–61:** 315

England.

See United Kingdom.

English Channel, **1956:** 122

Engraving and Printing, Bureau of, fair employment practices, **1954:** 92

Enid Reservoir project (Miss.), mineral interests, **1956:** 154

Enlistments in armed services, **1956:** 232

Enterprise system, **1953:** 29, 100; **1954:** 21, 87; **1955:** 19; **1956:** 12 (pp. 78, 82), 19, 32, 298; **1958:** 2, 12, 16, 18, 25, 26, 46, 49, 62, 110, 163, 208; **1959:** 6, 76, 84, 133, 244, 290; **1960–61:** 17, 23, 53, 215, 343, 355, 410

Abroad, **1955:** 76

Campaign remarks, **1958:** 295, 296, 303

News conference remarks, **1953:** 109, 225; **1954:** 39, 168, 353; **1958:** 274, 310; **1959:** 21, 53; **1960–61:** 24, 143

Epinal, France, **1956:** 102

Eqbal, Manuchehr, **1959:** 251, 320, 322

Equal Job Opportunity under Government Contracts, Commission on, proposed, **1959:** 27; **1960–61:** 414 (p. 1023)

Equal opportunity.

See also Civil rights; Integration, public schools.

Equal Opportunity Day, statement, **1957:** 237

Equal pay for equal work, **1956:** 2, 190, 253, 272; **1958:** 5 (p. 50); **1959:** 10 (p. 101); **1960–61:** 13 (p. 93)

Equal rights.

See Civil rights; Integration.

Equal rights for women, **1957:** 13, 150

Erhard, Ludwig, **1958:** 70

Erosion control claim, Madeira Beach, Fla., approval, **1959:** 232

Escalator clause in price support law, **1958:** 12, 59
"Escape clause," Trade Agreements Extension Act, **1957:** 160
Escapee program, U. S., **1957:** 1, 250
Escapees.
   See Refugees and escapees.
Esenbel, Melih, **1959:** 297
Espionage.
   See Subversive activities.
Essex, U.S.S., **1959:** 331
Esso Export Corp., **1955:** 176, 185
Estes, Lourene O., tax refund claim, disapproval, **1959:** 234
Ethiopia, **1957:** 50; **1958:** 261
   Armed forces in Korea, **1960–61:** 202
   Haile Selassie, **1954:** 129; **1955:** 231
     Exchange of toasts, **1954:** 124
   Richards mission, **1957:** 72
Etzel, Franz, **1953:** 111n.
Etzell, George F., **1956:** 249n., 250n.
Eufaula Reservoir, **1956:** 12 (p. 143)
Eugene, Oreg., **1954:** 34; **1956:** 12 (p. 134)
EURATOM.
   See European atomic community.
Europe, **1958:** 7, 31, 32, 144, 189
   See also specific countries.
   Assistance, **1954:** 150; **1958:** 5 (p. 35)
   Flood relief (1954), **1955:** 37, 47, 49
   Report of Secretary Dulles on, **1954:** 307, 318
Europe, Central and Eastern, **1956:** 282, 298
   See also Satellite countries, Soviet; *specific countries.*
   Denuclearization proposal for central Europe, **1958:** 7, 28
   Flood relief, **1954:** 182 and ftn. (p. 678), 200
     Memorandum, **1954:** 195
     Statement, **1954:** 175
Europe, Council for, **1956:** 114
Europe, Western, **1953:** 98, 159; **1954:** 209, 273
   See also specific countries.
   Assistance, **1953:** 66; **1959:** 271, 335
     Countries of Africa and Asia, **1960–61:** 4, 36, 362
     Following World War II, **1960–61:** 80, 132, 133
   Communist objectives in, **1954:** 345
   Defense of, **1953:** 50; **1960–61:** 13 (pp. 57, 58), 36, 414 (pp. 958, 959)
     Atomic, **1954:** 353
   Economic integration, **1960–61:** 92
   Economic recovery, **1959:** 244
   Economic and trade communities, **1960–61:** 16
   Economy, **1960–61:** 362
   EDC.
     See European Defense Community.
   Joint statement with Chancellor Adenauer on, **1959:** 192

Europe, Western — *continued*
   Joint statement with Prime Minister Churchill, **1954:** 154
   Missile squadrons, **1960–61:** 245
   Need for unity, comment on, **1959:** 94
   News conference remarks, **1953:** 54, 77, 265; **1959:** 36, 48, 94, 191; **1960–61:** 103, 263, 362
   Reduction of U.S. troops, question of, **1960–61:** 362
   Refugees in, U.S. assistance, **1953:** 257n.
   Storm disasters, **1953:** 7, 8
   Unity, question of, **1953:** 1, 6, 26, 50, 111, 255, 265; **1954:** 307, 317, 319, 320
   U.S. armed forces in, **1954:** 84
   Visits to.
     See Visits, foreign.
   Western European Union, **1955:** 54, 61, 100
   Withdrawal of U.S. troops, comment on, **1959:** 36, 48
   Meeting in London (1944), **1955:** 59
   Work in 1944 on Berlin division, **1958:** 318
European atomic community, **1956:** 2, 43, 299; **1957:** 8, 80, 245; **1958:** 188
   Agreement for cooperation with U. S., **1958:** 145
   Budget message, **1959:** 10 (p. 68)
   Euratom Cooperation Act of 1958, **1958:** 236
   Joint statement with Chancellor Adenauer, **1957:** 100
   Joint statement with Premier Mollet, **1957:** 38
   News conference remarks, **1959:** 7, 94
European Coal and Steel Community, **1953:** 6, 109, 265 ftn. (p. 843); **1956:** 114; **1957:** 245; **1958:** 145; **1959:** 7, 94
   Joint statement with Rene Mayer, **1956:** 34
   Letter, **1953:** 111
European Defense Community, **1953:** 6, 50, 146; **1954:** 3, 282, 307, 332; **1955:** 54
   Budget message, **1954:** 14 (p. 127)
   Joint statement with Western leaders, **1953:** 255
   News conference remarks, **1953:** 128, 225, 238, 265 and ftn. (p. 843); **1954:** 68, 165, 172, 200, 345; **1955:** 41, 62
   Statement, **1954:** 84
European Defense Community Treaty, **1954:** 84, 154
   Ratification
     Belgium, statement, **1954:** 52
     Germany, statement, **1954:** 66
     Luxembourg, statement, **1954:** 74
     The Netherlands, statement, **1954:** 13
   Rejection by France, **1954:** 226, 297
European Economic Commission, joint statement with Chancellor Adenauer, **1960–61:** 92
European Economic Community, **1957:** 8, 245; **1958:** 25, 58, 145; **1959:** 7, 214; **1960–61:** 16, 80, 103
   See also Common market, European.

European Economic Community — *continued*
  Budget message, **1958:** 5 (p. 37)
  Joint statements
    President Bayar, **1959:** 297
    Western leaders, **1959:** 335
  News conference remarks, **1959:** 7, 94
European Economic Cooperation, Organization
    for, **1956:** 114; **1959:** 200; **1960–61:** 4, 263
  Budget message, **1960–61:** 414 (p. 965)
  Joint statements
    Chancellor Adenauer, **1960–61:** 92
    General Franco, **1959:** 340
    Prime Minister Eden, **1956:** 26
    Western leaders, **1959:** 335
European Free Trade Area, **1956:** 278; **1957:** 38,
    55, 226
European Free Trade Association, **1960–61:** 80,
    103
  Joint statement with Western leaders on, **1959:**
    335
European Migration, Intergovernmental Commit-
    tee for, **1953:** 53, 89; **1955:** 17 (p. 131), 76;
    1956: 12 (p. 107), 58, 213n., 306
European Payments Union, **1954:** 67
European Recovery Program (1947), **1953:** 50;
    1955: 76
European security, **1955:** 175
  Letter to Premier Bulganin, **1956:** 23
European Union.
  See Western European Union.
European unity, **1956:** 2, 34, 46; **1957:** 55
Evans, Rowland, Jr., **1956:** 32, 62, 78, 88, 94, 113,
    229; **1957:** 17, 56, 62, 72, 80, 87, 119, 134,
    150; **1958:** 83, 288; **1959:** 17, 26, 67, 102,
    161; **1960–61:** 24, 103, 222, 250
Evanston, Ill., address to World Council of
    Churches, **1954:** 204
Evins, Repr. Joe L., **1955:** 112
Exchange Fellowships, Eisenhowever, **1960–61:**
    98n., 305
Exchange of persons, **1954:** 14 (p. 140), 128; **1955:**
    17 (p. 132); **1959:** 223; **1960–61:** 58, 87
  See also East-West contacts; Exchange of stu-
    dents; People-to-people program.
  Budget messages, **1958:** 5 (pp. 37, 40, 41);
    1960–61: 414 (p. 969)
  Conference on, remarks, **1959:** 24
  News conference remarks, **1959:** 223
  Students, **1960–61:** 38, 80
  Teachers, **1960–61:** 80
Exchange of persons, international, **1956:** 114, 204
  See also East-West contacts.
Exchange of scientific and technical information,
    1956: 2, 83
  With Soviet Union, **1958:** 22
  U.S.-Euratom agreement, **1958:** 145, 236
Exchange of students, **1954:** 14 (p. 140), 128; **1955:**
    4; **1957:** 222; **1958:** 23; **1959:** 222; **1960–**
    61: 80

Exchange of students — *continued*
  American Field Service, **1958:** 168; **1959:** 164
  Budget message, **1958:** 5 (p. 41)
  International air cadets, **1958:** 200
  U.S.-Soviet, **1960–61:** 38
    Letter to Premier Bulganin, **1958:** 31
Exchange of teachers, **1959:** 222
Exchange visitors, **1955:** 116
Excess profits tax, **1953:** 82, 84, 95, 157, 268; **1954:**
    3, 68, 290
  News conference remarks, **1953:** 12, 31
Excise taxes.
  See Taxes.
Executive Branch.
  See also Separation of powers of Government.
  Organization for conduct of foreign affairs
    Memorandum, **1953:** 92
    Message to Congress, **1953:** 89
  Reorganization, Presidential powers, **1960–61:**
    133, 255
Executive Management, Office of, proposed,
    1960–61: 422
  Budget message, **1960–61:** 414 (pp. 945. 946)
Executive Office of the President, **1953:** 40; **1960–**
    61: 243, 414 (pp. 945, 946, 1017–1019)
Executive orders, **1953:** 12 ftn. (p. 46), 31 ftn. (pp.
    112, 113), 40, 41, 54 ftn. (p. 205), 110, 128
    ftn. (p. 472), 203; **1954:** 15, 18, 57, 60, 107,
    115, 161 ftn. (p. 622), 176, 193, 234, 261n.,
    262, 263, 323; **1955:** 67, 74n., 186, 187,
    192n., 207n.; **1956:** 9n., 128, 180, 300;
    1957: 47n., 88n., 104n., 198n.; **1959:** 3, 18,
    56, 68n., 97n., 111, 117n., 166n., 184, 250,
    253, 265, 273; **1960–61:** 8, 268, 343n.
  List, Appendix B, **1953:** p. 880; **1954:** p. 1133;
    1955: p. 877; **1956:** p. 1151; **1957:** p. 868;
    1958: p. 884; **1959:** p. 904; **1960–61:** p.
    1087
Executive privilege.
  See Privileged documents and information.
Executive Reserve Conference, National Defense,
    remarks, **1957:** 235 and n.
Explorer earth satellites, **1960–61:** 287, 424
Explorer rockets, **1958:** 308
  Explorer I in orbit, statement, **1958:** 27
Explorer IV, information on Argus project, **1959:**
    67
Export Control Act, extension, **1958:** 5 (p. 53)
Export-Import Bank, **1953:** 129n., 213; **1954:** 67,
    95, 150; **1955:** 86; **1957:** 90; **1958:** 2, 32,
    145, 312; **1959:** 6, 98; **1960–61:** 39, 53, 73,
    86, 245, 247
  Budget messages, **1955:** 17 (pp. 128, 129); **1956:**
    12 (pp. 107, 108); **1958:** 5 (pp. 21, 36, 38,
    39); **1959:** 10 (pp. 71, 74); **1960–61:** 13 (p.
    64), 414 (pp. 938, 965, 966)
  "Buy American" policy, **1959:** 267
  Credit program, **1960–61:** 95

Export-Import Bank — *continued*
  Joint statement with President Toure on, **1959:** 272
  Letter to minority leaders re, **1958:** 43
  Loans to Latin American countries, **1955:** 76
  Mexican credit, **1959:** 257
  Mexican livestock purchase loan, **1956:** 235, 236
  Mutual security loans, **1956:** 58
  News conference remarks, **1959:** 223, 267, 271
  Philippines development loan, **1958:** 143
  Reorganization Plan 5, message, **1953:** 60
  25th anniversary, remarks, **1959:** 33
Export-Import Bank, Chairman of the Board of Directors (Glen E. Edgerton), foreign aid programs, **1954:** 323
Export-Import Bank, President (Samuel C. Waugh), **1959:** 33
  Meeting with Prime Minister Kishi, **1957:** 117
Exports, U.S., **1954:** 67, 226; **1955:** 79; **1958:** 25, 95, 96; **1960–61:** 4, 279, 410, 423
  Agricultural commodities, **1953:** 5; **1954:** 146; **1955:** 4, 6, 7, 72; **1956:** 6, 12 (pp. 102, 103, 109, 129), 42, 58, 214, 241; **1957:** 8, 13, 16, 45, 115, 131; **1958:** 12, 35, 49, 59, 60, 290, 292, 295, 296
  Budget message, **1960–61:** 414 (pp. 968, 984)
  Canada, **1958:** 163
  Conference on trade policy, address, **1958:** 58
  Cotton, **1954:** 4; **1955:** 6, 185; **1956:** 82, 115; **1960–61:** 132
  Cuba, embargo, **1960–61:** 332
  Increase proposed, **1960–61:** 362, 387
  Japan, **1959:** 71
  Joint statement with Prime Minister Kishi, **1957:** 117
  Less developed and new countries, **1958:** 32, 49
  Message to Congress, **1960–61:** 95
  Oil for Europe, **1957:** 8, 13, 16, 45, 115, 131
  Under Public Law **1959:** 480, 226
  Wheat, **1953:** 12, 95, 101; **1954:** 14 (p. 160); **1955:** 6, 17 (p. 152); **1956:** 12 (p. 129); **1960–61:** 132
Extension Service, **1956:** 12 (p. 131)

F-8U fighter, **1956:** 12 (p. 96)
F-101, F-104, interceptors, **1956:** 12 (p. 96)
Fact paper on national economy, **1958:** 29
Fair Employment Board (Civil Service Commission), **1954:** 92
Fair employment practices, **1954:** 92
Fair Labor Standards Act, **1957:** 13
  Extension of coverage, **1954:** 349; **1956:** 2; **1959:** 10 (p. 101); **1960–61:** 133, 255
    Budget message, **1960–61:** 13 (p. 93)
Fairless, Benjamin F., **1956:** 10n.; **1957:** 45, 50; **1959:** 258

Faisal, Prince, meeting with, statement, **1953:** 18
Falcon Dam, **1953:** 221; **1960–61:** 335
  Dedication
    Address, **1953:** 222
    Remarks following, **1953:** 223
Fall, Albert B., **1954:** 115
Fallout, radioactive.
  See Radioactive fallout.
Fallout shelters, **1960–61:** 384
  Budget messages, **1960–61:** 13 (p. 76), 414 (p. 985)
  Government buildings, construction proposed, **1951:** 229
Family Service Associations, **1960–61:** 153
Fanfani, Amintore
  Exchange of messages, **1956:** 207; **1958:** 211
  Joint statement with, **1958:** 186
FAO.
  See Food and Agriculture Organization.
Far East, **1954:** 3, 35, 148n.; **1957:** 8; **1958:** 32, 36, 261, 277; **1959:** 55, 57, 71; **1960–61:** 191, 209, 348, 410
  See also Asia, South Asia, and Southeast Asia; *specific countries.*
  Assistance, **1953:** 66; **1956:** 12 (p. 105)
  Budget messages, **1955:** 17 (p. 112); **1958:** 5 (p. 41)
  Defense alliance.
    See Southeast Asia Treaty Organization.
  Escapees and refugees, U.S. assistance program, **1953:** 257n.
  Joint statements
    President Diem, **1957:** 83
    President Garcia on, **1958:** 143
    Prime Minister Eden, **1956:** 26
    Prime Minister Kishi, **1957:** 117
    Prime Minister Macmillan, **1957:** 55
    Western leaders, **1953:** 255
  News conference remarks, **1953:** 37, 109; **1954:** 63, 68, 157; **1958:** 83, 198
  U.S. military forces in, **1953:** 272; **1954:** 14 (pp. 122, 123)
    Policy on, **1954:** 68
Faraday, Michael, **1959:** 107
Farewell address, **1960–61:** 421
Faricy, William T., **1956:** 237; **1957:** 12
Farley, James A., **1954:** 12n.
  Appointment to Hoover Commission, **1953:** 145
Farm, the President's, **1955:** 127; **1956:** 20; **1957:** 150, 157
Farm bill, **1959:** 167, 186
  See also Agricultural act of 1956.
  Approval, statement, **1956:** 115, 250
  Letters to Sen. Aiken and Repr. Hope, **1954:** 196
  News conference remarks, **1954:** 157, 165, 172, 192, 200; **1956:** 47, 53, 56, 62, 78, 88, 171
  Veto message, **1956:** 82
    Broadcast on, **1956:** 83

Farm Bureau Federation, **1958:** 35n.
Farm bureaus, **1956:** 20, 250
Farm-City Week, statement, **1955:** 221
Farm committees, **1954:** 196
Farm Cooperative Service, **1954:** 291
Farm credit, **1954:** 14 (p. 160); **1956:** 20, 83, 147, 214, 224, 250; **1958:** 59
  Budget message, **1956:** 12 (p. 130)
Farm Credit Act, approval, **1953:** 158
Farm Credit Administration, **1953:** 35, 158; **1954:** 291; **1955:** 147; **1956:** 147; **1960–61:** 410
  Budget messages, **1954:** 14 (p. 160); **1955:** 17 (p. 153); **1956:** 12 (pp. 126, 131)
  Federal land-bank loans, **1956:** 6
Farm Credit Board, Federal, **1953:** 158; **1954:** 14 (p. 160)
Farm credit system, **1953:** 158, 159
Farm Director, National Association of Radio and Television, **1957:** 114 and n.
Farm economy, **1953:** 6, 95, 216; **1954:** 4, 209, 261, 291, 317; **1955:** 4, 62, 127, 128; **1956:** 6, 19, 83; **1958:** 26, 49, 59, 60, 223; **1959:** 10 (p. 49), 23; **1960–61:** 4, 23, 32, 410
  See also Agriculture; Rural development program.
  Budget messages, **1955:** 17 (pp. 150–153); **1956:** 12 (p. 127); **1960–61:** 13 (pp. 79–81), 414 (p. 988)
  Campaign remarks, **1956:** 190, 214, 226, 250, 251, 268; **1958:** 292, 296, 308
  News conference remarks, **1953:** 12, 230, 249; **1956:** 47, 198, 216
Farm "freeze" bill, **1958:** 56
  Veto, **1958:** 59, 60
Farm income and prices.
  See Farm economy.
Farm lands, Government, leasing policies, **1956:** 111
Farm program, **1953:** 6, 101, 216, 227, 268; **1954:** 3, 4, 139, 144, 209, 291, 308; **1955:** 127, 247; **1956:** 2, 3, 19; **1958:** 12, 26, 295; **1959:** 10 (p. 49), 116, 288; **1960–61:** 350
  See also specific programs; Agriculture.
  Budget message, **1955:** 17 (p. 103); **1958:** 5 (pp. 63–68)
  Campaign remarks, **1954:** 273, 286, 316, 318
  Meeting on legislation, **1956:** 318
  News conference remarks, **1953:** 12, 225, 230, 238; **1954:** 9, 18, 92, 101, 129, 157, 161, 165, 172, 200, 322, 341; **1955:** 18, 62, 90; **1956:** 5, 20, 62, 205; **1957:** 45, 70, 124; **1958:** 37, 56, 310; **1960–61:** 34, 38, 93, 222, 256, 268
Farm surpluses.
  See Agricultural surpluses.
Farm workers, migratory.
  See Agricultural workers, migratory.
Farmer, Guy, **1957:** 88n.

Farmers, **1957:** 72; **1960–61:** 255
  Disaster loans, **1954:** 14 (p. 162), 221
  Drought relief.
    See main heading Drought relief.
  Farm ownership loans, **1954:** 14 (p. 161)
  Low-income, **1955:** 4, 82
  Payments for conservation measures, **1957:** 11, 12
  Social security coverage, **1953:** 155; **1954:** 291, 308; **1956:** 158, 250
  Soil conservation and development, **1953:** 153
  Tax deductions, **1954:** 14 (p. 96), 291
  Water facilities, loans for, **1954:** 14 (p. 161)
Farmers Home Administration, **1954:** 168 ftn. (p. 646); **1955:** 17 (pp. 149, 153); **1958:** 5 (p. 67); **1959:** 10 (pp. 53, 91, 92); **1960–61:** 13 (pp. 81, 108), 414 (pp. 990, 1025)
  Budget message, **1954:** 14 (p. 161); **1956:** 12 (pp. 130, 131)
  Credit program, **1954:** 221
  Loans, **1956:** 6
Farmers Union, **1956:** 250
Farms, **1958:** 12, 290
  See also Agriculture.
  Campaign remarks, **1956:** 190, 211, 224, 250
  Commercial, **1956:** 6, 20
  Family-size or small, **1956:** 6, 12 (p. 131), 20, 193, 224, 250; **1958:** 12, 60, 274
  Gasoline for farm use, tax refund, **1956:** 6, 12 (p. 127), 20, 72, 83, 214, 250
  News conference remarks, **1956:** 20, 88, 205
  1952 statement, **1956:** 88
  Rural development program, report, **1958:** 313
Farnam, C. Eugene, **1956:** 292
Farragut, David G., **1958:** 125
Fascism, **1954:** 128, 160; **1960–61:** 355
Faubus, Governor Orval E., **1957:** 178, 188, 189, 193, 205; **1958:** 11
  News conference remarks, **1957:** 207, 210
Faure, Edgar, **1955:** 170n.
Fawn, gift to the President, **1955:** 141
Fay, Joseph S., **1953:** 230
FBI.
  See Federal Bureau of Investigation.
FCC.
  See Federal Communications Commission.
Federal Advisory Commission on the Arts, **1955:** 4; **1957:** 13
Federal Aid Highway Act, approval, **1959:** 227
Federal aid to States, **1953:** 39; **1956:** 2; **1957:** 86, 118; **1960–61:** 410
  Agricultural research, **1954:** 14 (p. 163)
  Airports, **1955:** 146; **1959:** 10 (p. 78), 143
  Budget messages, **1954:** 14 (pp. 86, 142–144, 151, 153, 161–163, 170, 176); **1955:** 17 (pp. 94, 103, 106, 167); **1956:** 12 pp. 82, 82, 115 ff.; **1958:** 5 (pp. 42, 46, 48–50, 56–58); **1959:** 10 (pp. 48, 49, 78, 99, 100, 103, 104, 110);

Federal aid to States — *continued*
  Budget messages — *continued*
    1960–61: 13 (pp. 70–73, 75, 76, 87, 89, 90,
      92, 95), 414 (pp. 939, 1001–1003, 1021,
      1022)
  Depressed areas, **1960–61:** 5, 13 (pp. 75, 76), 127
    and ftn. (p. 362), 133, 143, 146, 176, 414
    (pp. 939, 983)
  Desegregation costs, **1959:** 27
  Disaster relief, **1954:** 192; **1957:** 11, 41
  Drought relief, **1954:** 14 (p. 162); **1957:** 11, 41
    See also main heading, Drought relief.
  Education, **1953:** 6; **1954:** 14 (p. 153); **1955:** 31,
    33, 47, 119; **1956:** 2, 8, 222; **1957:** 19, 116,
    223; **1958:** 5 (pp. 42, 48–50), 24, 203, 222,
    295; **1959:** 6, 10 (p. 99), 29, 123; **1960–61:**
    13 (pp. 89, 90), 23, 34, 133, 255, 410, 414
    (pp. 939, 1001–1003)
  Employment services, **1959:** 10 (p. 100)
  Fish and wildlife restoration, **1954:** 14 (p. 170)
  Health programs, **1954:** 11; **1955:** 25; **1956:** 21,
    151, 161
  Highway program, **1954:** 3, 14 (p. 176), 33, 102,
    165; **1955:** 17 (p. 167), 39, 146; **1956:** 2,
    305; **1958:** 43, 49, 77; **1959:** 6, 10 (p. 50),
    227; **1960–61:** 13 (pp. 70, 71), 255, 330,
    414 (p. 977)
  Hospital and health center construction, **1955:**
    17 (p. 94)
  Hospitals and medical care facilities, **1954:** 14 (p.
    143)
  News conference remarks, **1957:** 22, 145; **1960–
    61:** 34, 127 and ftn. (p. 362), 422
  Public assistance, **1954:** 14 (pp. 142, 143); **1955:**
    17 (p. 103)
  Public works, **1954:** 14 (p. 151)
  Reclamation projects, **1956:** 165
  School construction, **1954:** 182; **1958:** 5 (pp. 42,
    46, 50), 203
    See main heading, School construction.
  School lunch program, **1954:** 14 (p. 144)
  Social Security Amendments of 1956, **1958:** 234
  Unemployment insurance, **1954:** 73; **1958:** 53;
    1959: 10 (pp. 48, 49)
  Urban renewal, **1954:** 17; **1958:** 5 (pp. 56–58)
Federal-Aid Highway Act, approval, **1954:** 102
Federal Airport Act, disapproval, **1958:** 246
  Amendment, approval, **1959:** 143
Federal airway facilities, user charges, **1957:** 75
Federal Aviation Agency, **1960–61:** 349, 410, 433
  Budget messages, **1959:** 10 (p. 78); **1960–61:** 13
    (pp. 50, 68, 109), 414 (pp. 944, 945, 956,
    973)
  Campaign remarks, **1958:** 292, 308
  Dulles International Airport, sewage disposal,
    1959: 197
  Establishment, message, **1958:** 135
  Pyle, James T., **1959:** 18n.

Federal Aviation Agency, Administrator (Elwood
    R. Quesada), **1959:** 26
  Appointment, statement, **1958:** 272
  Aviation facilities planning, report, **1959:** 74
  Discretion re grants under Federal Airport Act,
    1959: 143
Federal Bar Association, **1960–61:** 275
Federal Boating Act, amendment, disapproval,
    1959: 228
Federal Bureau of Investigation, **1953:** 6; **1954:** 38,
    72, 139, 275, 291; **1955:** 4, 17 (pp. 95,
    182); **1956:** 12 (p. 153), 16; **1957:** 232 and
    n.; **1958:** 213; **1959:** 271
  Atomic Energy Act, violations, **1953:** 263
  Budget message, **1954:** 14 (p. 189)
  Campaign remarks, **1954:** 273, 286
  Cases involving destruction of schools or
    churches, **1959:** 27; **1960–61:** 137
  Communist subversion, investigation of, **1953:**
    95; **1954:** 130, 209
  FBI Badge, presentation to President, **1957:** 232
  Files, comment on, **1954:** 63
  Little Rock investigation, **1957:** 210
  National Academy, remarks at graduation ex-
    ercises, **1957:** 232 and n.
  News conference remarks, **1953:** 88, 243; **1954:**
    18, 63, 107, 200
  Parker (Mack Charles) case, **1959:** 88, 94, 123
  Records, availability of, **1957:** 134, 169
  Reports, availability of, **1953:** 243
  Security information given to Sen. McCarthy,
    1954: 107
  White (Harry Dexter) case, **1953:** 243
Federal Bureau of Investigation, Director of (J.
    Edgar Hoover), **1953:** 95; **1957:** 232;
    1960–61: 38
  Award for Distinguished Federal Civilian Serv-
    ice, **1958:** 13
  National Security Medal, citation, **1955:** 110
  Premier Khrushchev's 1959 visit to U.S.,
    1960–61: 38
Federal City Council of Washington, D.C., **1955:**
    55
Federal Civil Defense Administration, **1955:** 17 (p.
    119); **1956:** 2, 21, 142, 203
  Budget messages, **1956:** 12 (p. 135); **1958:** 5 (p.
    54)
  Disaster relief, **1957:** 145
  Katherine G. Howard, **1954:** 310n.
  Reorganization Plan 1 of 1958, **1958:** 84
Federal Civil Defense Administrator (Leo
    A.Hoegh), letter, **1958:** 146
Federal Civil Defense Administrator (Val
    Peterson), **1953:** 216, 262; **1955:** 209
  Oath of office ceremony, statement, **1953:** 21
  Operation Alert 1956, letter, **1956:** 142
Federal Communications Commission, **1954:** 14 (p.
    178), 50; **1955:** 41; **1958:** 42; **1959:** 267

Federal Communications Commission — *continued*
  Budget messages, **1960–61:** 13 (p. 76), 414 (pp. 946, 984)
  Mack, Richard A., **1958:** 37
  Study of ultrahigh frequency television, **1960–61:** 13 (p. 76)
  Utilization of communication satellites, **1960–61:** 386
Federal Conciliation Service on Civil Rights Matters, **1959:** 17
Federal Council on Aging, **1956:** 63; **1959:** 49
  Memorandum on, **1956:** 74
  Report, letter, **1959:** 280
Federal Council for Science and Technology, **1958:** 326; **1959:** 56; **1960–61:** 349
  Budget messages, **1960–61:** 13 (p. 91), 414 (p. 1004)
Federal courts, **1957:** 8, 133, 134, 178, 197, 198, 200, 205, 207
  See also Judiciary; Supreme Court.
  U. S. District Court, Little Rock, Ark., **1957:** 134, 169, 178, 197, 198, 205
Federal Crop Insurance Corporation, **1960–61:** 414 (p. 989)
Federal Deposit Insurance Corporation, **1960–61:** 414 (p. 1025)
Federal eight-hour law, **1957:** 13
Federal employees.
  See Government employees.
Federal Employees' Group Life Insurance Act, approval, **1954:** 202
Federal Farm Credit Board, **1953:** 158; **1954:** 14 (p. 160)
Federal Highway Administrator, appointment, news conference remarks, **1956:** 235
Federal Highway Administrator (Bertram D. Tallamy), report, **1959:** 138
Federal highways, **1957:** 13, 105
  Advertising along, **1957:** 72, 169
  Home mortgage funds, **1958:** 49
  Independent agency, **1955:** 194
  Letter to minority leaders re, **1958:** 43
  Reorganization, **1956:** 108
Federal Homestead Act, **1957:** 108
Federal Housing Administration, **1954:** 273; **1955:** 17 (pp. 171, 172), 26; **1956:** 2, 12 (p. 145); **1958:** 43, 62; **1959:** 104, 146; **1960–61:** 410
  Budget messages, **1954:** 14 (pp. 148, 149); **1958:** 5 (pp. 54, 59); **1959:** 10 (pp. 46, 51, 84, 85); **1957:** 13 (pp. 73, 74), 414 (pp. 980, 981)
  Downpayment provision, **1957:** 129n.
  Investigation of, **1954:** 92, 311, 349
    Letter to Senator Capehart, **1954:** 302
    Memorandum to Administrator Cole, **1954:** 81
  Mortgage insurance authority, **1954:** 14 (pp. 148, 149), 17; **1959:** 102, 153, 186, 208
    Message, **1959:** 187

Federal Housing Administration — *continued*
  News conference remarks, **1954:** 92, 101, 107, 311; **1959:** 102, 186
  25th anniversary, remarks, **1959:** 133
Federal Kidnapping Act, **1959:** 88n.
Federal lands, surplus, restoration to States, **1957:** 75
Federal Maritime Board, construction and sale of superliner passenger vessels, approval, **1958:** 171
Federal Mediation and Conciliation Service, **1953:** 203n.; **1954:** 5, 193n.; **1955:** 95; **1959:** 160
  Maritime industry dispute, **1956:** 300n.
  Negotiations in steel strike, **1959:** 142, 161, 211, 265n., 290
  News conference remarks, **1959:** 161, 179
Federal Mediation and Conciliation Service, Director (Joseph F. Finnegan)
  Atomic Energy Labor-Management Panel, memorandum, **1956:** 95
  Consultation in steel strike, **1956:** 150
Federal National Mortgage Association, **1954:** 17, 95, 179; **1955:** 17 (pp. 166, 172, 173); **1956:** 2; **1957:** 16, 182; **1958:** 224; **1959:** 153
  Budget messages, **1954:** 14 (pp. 148, 149); **1956:** 12 (pp. 146, 147); **1958:** 5 (p. 58); **1959:** 10 (pp. 46, 76, 85); **1960–61:** 13 (p. 74), 414 (p. 982)
    Table, 5 (p. 54)
  Housing Act of 1957, **1957:** 129 and n.
  Income tax treatment of nonrefundable capital contributions, veto, **1960–61:** 151
  Letter to minority leaders re, **1958:** 43
  Mortgage purchases, **1958:** 62
  Mortgages on housing for older persons, **1956:** 252
  Spending authority reduction, **1957:** 75
Federal Old-Age and Survivors Insurance Program, relief of Michael D. Ovens, **1957:** 181
Federal personnel.
  See Government employees.
Federal personnel management, message, **1955:** 8
Federal police power, **1957:** 17, 232
Federal Power Commission, **1953:** 246; **1954:** 271; **1955:** 4; **1956:** 96; **1959:** 288; **1960–61:** 127
  Adams, Francis L., **1955:** 146 and ftn. (p. 658)
  Budget message, **1958:** 5 (p. 69)
  Connole, William R., **1960–61:** 127
  Natural gas regulation, **1957:** 13
  News conference remarks, **1953:** 22, 128; **1954:** 311, 328; **1955:** 10, 33
  Regulation of natural gas rates, **1954:** 64
  River basin surveys, **1960–61:** 414 (pp. 947, 996)
  St. Lawrence power project, **1953:** 70

Federal Radiation Council, **1959:** 68n.; **1960–61:** 410
   Report, **1960–61:** 268 and ftn. (p. 654)
Federal Republic of Germany.
   See Germany.
Federal Reserve Act, amendment, **1959:** 161
Federal Reserve Board, **1955:** 81
Federal Reserve System, **1953:** 6; **1954:** 21, 67; **1955:** 19; **1956:** 19, 268; **1960–61:** 17, 344
   Budget message, **1954:** 14 (p. 88); **1956:** 12 (p. 91)
   Campaign remarks, **1958:** 303
   Consumer installment credit, **1957:** 95
   Credit controls, **1957:** 169
   Easing of credit, **1958:** 42, 43, 49, 110
   Interest rates, **1956:** 88, 94, 171, 229, 235
   News conference remarks, **1956:** 88, 94, 229, 235; **1957:** 119, 228; **1958:** 11, 42, 70
   Purchase of Federal bonds, **1959:** 124
   Riefler, Winfield W., **1954:** 39
Federal Reserve System, Chairman of Board of Governors (William McC. Martin, Jr.), **1959:** 186
   Chairman, Red Cross campaign, **1953:** 4
Federal Safety Council, **1954:** 288; **1960–61:** 410
Federal Savings and Loan Insurance Corporation, **1955:** 194
   Premium rate increase proposed, **1960–61:** 13 (p. 73), 414 (p. 980)
   Reorganization, **1956:** 108
Federal Security Administrator (Oveta Culp Hobby), **1953:** 15, 28
   See also Health, Education, and Welfare, Secretary of.
   News conference remarks, **1953:** 12, 22
   Transfer of functions to Department of Health, Education, and Welfare, **1953:** 28
Federal-State Action Committee, **1957:** 138 and n.; **1959:** 10 (pp. 68, 98); **1960–61:** 116
   Budget message, **1958:** 5 (pp. 43, 46)
   Recommendations, letter, **1958:** 106
   Report, letter, **1960–61:** 115
Federal-State Joint Action Board, recommendations, budget message, **1958:** 5 (p. 57)
Federal-State-local governmental responsibilities, **1953:** 39, 67, 100, 101, 153, 156, 171, 262; **1954:** 201, 258, 273, 346; **1955:** 4, 19, 31, 43, 242; **1956:** 2, 8, 12 (pp. 83, 155), 142; **1957:** 8, 11, 19, 75, 118, 223; **1958:** 12, 24, 96; **1959:** 29; **1960–61:** 5, 23, 44, 103, 127 ftn. (p. 362), 208, 245, 333, 336, 340, 372, 410
   See also Commission on Intergovernmental Relations.
   Atomic energy for peaceful uses, **1960–61:** 116
   Budget messages, **1955:** 17 (pp. 93, 94, 140, 147, 156, 158, 161); **1958:** 5 (pp. 42, 43, 49, 52, 56, 68); **1959:** 10 (pp. 96, 98); **1960–61:** 13 (pp. 94–96), 414 (pp. 939, 985, 1022)

Federal responsibilities — *continued*
   Campaign remarks, **1956:** 190, 214, 224, 255, 256; **1958:** 287, 292, 294
   Civil defense, **1955:** 149
   Federal Highway Act of 1958, approval, **1958:** 77
   Flood prevention, **1955:** 17 (p. 94)
   Governors' conference, **1953:** 15, 16n.
   Health services, **1954:** 301
   Interstate highway system, **1959:** 227; **1960–61:** 330
   Medical care for older persons, **1960–61:** 133
   Narcotics problem, **1954:** 343
   News conference remarks, **1953:** 15, 31, 37, 54, 265; **1954:** 33, 39, 192; **1955:** 18, 33, 47, 149; **1956:** 235; **1957:** 70, 145, 207
   Rehabilitation program for disabled, **1954:** 301
   Report of Commission on Intergovernmental Relations, **1955:** 145
   School construction, **1960–61:** 133
   Statement, **1953:** 16
   Taxes, **1954:** 144
   Water, power, and soil resources, development, **1954:** 308
Federal Trade Commission, **1960–61:** 285
   Budget messages, **1956:** 12 (p. 149); **1960–61:** 13 (p. 76), 414 (p. 984)
   Cease and desist orders, **1957:** 132
   Information given Sherman Adams, **1958:** 141
   Investigation of coffee prices, **1954:** 18, 25, 39, 50, 57
   Kern, William C., **1955:** 95
   Mead, James M., **1955:** 95
   Small business problems, **1956:** 263
   TV quiz investigation, **1955:** 267, 277
Federal Trade Commission, Chairman (Edward F. Howrey), **1953:** 37
Federal troops in Little Rock, Ark.
   See Little Rock.
Federal Unemployment Tax Act, **1958:** 53
Federal Water Pollution Control Act, amendment, veto, **1960–61:** 44
Federated Iron Workers Association of Australia, **1954:** 77
Federation Aeronautique de Belgique, **1958:** 71n.
Federation Aeronautique Internationale, remarks, **1958:** 71
Feed grains, **1958:** 60
   Export program, **1958:** 59
   Price supports, **1953:** 225; **1958:** 12
Fees, special service.
   See Charges.
Feldmann, Louis G., **1960–61:** 31
Fellows, Harold E., **1955:** 105
Fellowships, **1958:** 24, 28
   See also Scholarships.
   Budget message, **1958:** 5 (pp. 46, 48)
   Eisenhower, **1957:** 222; **1960–61:** 98n., 305
   Federal, to increase output of teachers, **1957:** 234
   Health personnel, **1956:** 21

Felt, Adm. Harry D., **1960–61:** 205, 206
Fenton, Brig. Gen. Chauncey L., **1955:** 117
Ferdinand, King, **1959:** 338
Ferguson, Sen. Homer, **1954:** 12n., 110n., 318
    Constitutional amendment on treatymaking
        power, **1954:** 33
Fermi, Enrico, **1959:** 107
Fernsworth, Lawrence, **1954:** 311, 341; **1955:** 47,
    62, 100; **1956:** 88, 216
Ferre, Luis A., **1960–61:** 93
Fertilizer production costs (TVA), **1954:** 14 (p. 169)
    TVA, **1957:** 112n.
FFA Clubs.
    See Future Farmers of America Clubs.
FHA.
    See Federal Housing Administration.
Field hockey international festival, remarks to
    participants, **1960–61:** 319
Fifth amendment, **1957:** 56
Fifteenth amendment, **1957:** 134
Fillmore, Millard, **1959:** 151
Finance, international, **1960–61:** 13 (pp. 59–64),
    414 (pp. 961–968)
    Tables, **1960–61:** 13 (p. 61), 414 (p. 963)
Financial system, study by independent commis-
    sion, **1957:** 8, 16
Fine, Gov. John, **1954:** 35n., 304
Fine Arts, Commission of, **1956:** 4n.; **1960–61:** 243
Finland, **1957:** 230
    Kekkonen, Urho K., **1956:** 311
    Paasikivi, Juho Kusti, death of, **1956:** 311
Finnegan, Joseph F.
    See Federal Mediation and Conciliation Service,
    Director.
Finney, Nat S., **1953:** 37, 54, 77, 128, 225, 238, 249,
    265; **1954:** 9, 25, 39, 48, 63, 92, 115, 143,
    157, 168, 192, 200, 341, 353; **1955:** 10, 18,
    26, 33, 59, 90, 112, 149; **1956:** 32, 94;
    1957: 56
Fire Depot, Aerial, Missoula, Mont., dedication,
    remarks, **1954:** 270
Fire prevention, forests, statement, **1953:** 112
Fire in Pusan, Korea, statement, **1953:** 258
Firearms, restrictions on ownership, **1958:** 213
Firemen, Washington, D.C., increase in benefits,
    disapproval, **1959:** 239
Firestone, Harvey S., Jr., letter, **1954:** 276; **1955:** 80
Firpo, Luis, **1954:** 290, 298
First automobile crossing, San Francisco to New
    York, **1960–61:** 332
First Boston Corporation, **1955:** 146
First Continental Congress, **1956:** 265
First War Powers Act of 1941, title II, extension,
    1955: 4
Fiscal integrity, **1956:** 2, 3
    Campaign remarks, **1956:** 255

Fish and wildlife resources, **1953:** 153; **1954:** 3, 14
    (pp. 87, 164); **1955:** 4; **1958:** 5 (p. 69);
    1959: 10 (p. 95); **1960–61:** 13 (p. 86), 410,
    414 (pp. 998, 999)
    Approval of act, **1956:** 173
    Budget message, **1956:** 12 (p. 133)
    Fish hatcheries, **1956:** 12 (p. 138)
    International actions on, **1956:** 173
Fish and Wildlife Service, **1953:** 153; **1960–61:** 414
    (p. 996)
Fisher, Archbishop Geoffrey F., **1954:** 204
Fisher, Mary Elizabeth, **1957:** 123
Fishing, **1958:** 288
Fisk, James Brown, telegram, **1958:** 149
Fissionable materials, **1953:** 12, 256, 263; **1954:** 14
    (p. 128), 38, 260
    Ban on production for weapons, **1956:** 53; **1957:**
        80, 115, 119, 158, 165, 245
        Letters to Premier Bulganin, **1956:** 52, 166
    International Atomic Energy Agency, **1959:** 189
    News conference remarks, **1957:** 115, 134
    Uranium 235, distribution of, **1957:** 13, 124, 125
Fissionable materials for peaceful uses, **1955:** 79,
    156, 164, 165; **1958:** 86, 148, 219
    See also Uranium.
    Address before U.N. general Assembly, **1960–**
      61: 302
    Letters to Premier Bulganin, **1958:** 7, 31, 67
    News conference remarks, **1958:** 56, 222
Fitzgerald, Rufus H., **1955:** 11n.
Fitzsimons Army Hospital, **1955:** 235
    Editor's note on President's illness, **1955:** p. 822
Flag, Army, presentation, **1957:** 127 and n.
Flag, U.S., **1959:** 97n., 117n., 166n., 262n., 333n.
    Display, approval, **1953:** 133
    Letter to Gov. William A. Egan, **1959:** 150
    New design, remarks, **1959:** 3, 184
    Panama Canal Zone, **1959:** 288
    Pledge of allegiance, amendment, **1954:** 140
Flag from capsule of Discoverer XIII, gift to the
    President, **1960–61:** 261
Flag carriers, U.S., on routes to Orient, **1960–61:**
    436
Flag of Panama in Canal Zone, **1960–61:** 24 and
    ftn. (p. 150)
Flag of United Nations, **1953:** 133
Flaherty, Edward L., **1960–61:** 354
Flake, Wilson C., **1958:** 44
Flaming Gorge dam, **1956:** 235, 256
Flanders, Sen. Ralph E., **1953:** 77, 187; **1955:** 131,
    149
    News conference remarks on, **1954:** 50, 165, 168,
      182
    Resolution of censure against Sen. McCarthy,
      1954: 165, 168, 182
Flannery, Harry, **1954:** 345
Flaxseed, price support, **1956:** 20
Fleeson, Doris, **1953:** 77, 238; **1954:** 168

Fleming, Robert H., **1959:** 267, 271
Fleming, Robert V., **1957:** 15n.
Flemming, Arthur S.
    See Defense Mobilization, Office of, Director;
        Health, Education, and Welfare, Secre-
        tary of.
Flissler, Joyce, **1958:** 78
Floberg, John F., **1957:** 145; **1959:** 18n.
Floete, Franklin.
    See General Services Administrator.
Flood control, **1953:** 100, 153; **1954:** 3, 53, 201;
        1956: 12 (p. 131), 44, 170; **1960–61:** 419
    Amistad Dam, joint statement on, **1959:** 257
    Appropriation, **1958:** 244
    Authorization of certain projects, disapproval,
        1956: 180
    Budget messages, **1954:** 14 (pp. 164, 167, 169);
        1955: 17 (pp. 94, 156–160); **1956:** 12 (pp.
        133, 134); **1958:** 5 (p. 68); **1959:** 10 (pp.
        45, 94); **1960–61:** 13 (p. 85), 414 (pp. 994,
        996, 997)
    Floods resulting from hurricanes, **1958:** 73, 85,
        155
    Letter to minority leaders, **1958:** 43
    Letter to Gov. Roberts, **1955:** 222
    McKenzie River project, **1954:** 34
    News conference remarks, **1957:** 105
    Projects, **1956:** 12 (p. 135)
Flood Control Act, approval, **1954:** 249; **1958:** 155
Flood-damage indemnities
    Bill for relief of Roy Cowan, **1956:** 79
    Proposed, **1956:** 2, 3, 19
Flood insurance, **1956:** 2, 3, 12 (p. 149)
    Approval of bill, **1956:** 167
    News conference remarks, **1957:** 169
Flood relief
    Central and Eastern Europe, **1954:** 182 and ftn.
        (p. 678), 200; **1955:** 37, 47, 49
    Memorandum, **1954:** 195
    News conference remarks, **1954:** 168, 182 and
        ftn. (p. 678), 200
    Statement, **1954:** 175
    Pakistan, **1954:** 195n.
Floods, **1956:** 12 (p. 139); **1959:** 45
    Missouri River (1903), **1953:** 100
    Netherlands, **1953:** 53n.
    1955, **1956:** 12 (pp. 135, 140, 149), 47
    1956, **1956:** 12 (p. 150)
    Northeastern States, **1955:** 208, 209, 210, 214,
        222
    Rio Grande River, message to President Ruiz
        Cortines, **1954:** 158
    Tampico, Mexico, **1955:** 229
    Uruguay, **1959:** 95
Florida, **1955:** 210n.
    Camp Blanding Military Reservation, convey-
        ance of lands within, veto, **1954:** 121
    Candidates for public office, **1956:** 278

Florida — *continued*
    Cape Canaveral, **1958:** 321, 322n.; **1959:** 17;
        1960–61: 33, 34
    Collins, Gov. LeRoy, **1956:** 69; **1957:** 205n.;
        1958: 103; **1960–61:** 103
    Illegal flights to Cuba from, **1959:** 271
    Inter-American Cultural and Trade Center,
        1956: 278
    Jacksonville, **1956:** 279
    Key West, **1956:** 1, 3, 5, 16, 32
    Madeira Beach, **1959:** 232
    Mayport, **1957:** 107n.
    Miami, **1956:** 278; **1958:** 120; **1960–61:** 431
    Miami Beach, **1958:** 45n.; **1959:** 185
    Naval maneuvers, **1957:** 107n.
    Smathers, Sen. George A., **1955:** 62; **1958:** 82
        and n.
    Supreme Court, **1954:** 245
Fluorspar purchase program, veto, **1958:** 206
Flying saucers, comment on, **1954:** 353
Flythe, William P., Jr., **1953:** 198; **1954:** 33, 57, 63
FNMA.
    See Federal National Mortgage Association.
Fogarty, Repr. John E., **1957:** 62
Folger, John C., **1953:** 201; **1957:** 153
Folliard, Edward T., **1953:** 12, 22, 37, 54, 62, 77,
        141, 198, 208, 249, 265; **1954:** 48, 50, 57,
        92, 107, 157, 161, 168, 172, 182, 200, 322,
        328, 345, 353; **1955:** 10, 18, 26, 33, 47, 56,
        59, 81, 112, 146, 149, 176, 185; **1956:** 16,
        20, 47, 94, 96, 155, 189, 235, 298; **1957:** 17,
        50, 56, 105, 145, 150; **1958:** 11, 28, 37, 42,
        70, 74, 83, 88, 198, 310, 318; **1959:** 21, 29,
        42, 48, 53, 67, 148, 173, 179, 186, 191, 223,
        243, 267, 271; **1960–61:** 7, 93, 143, 263,
        268
Folsom, Frank M., **1954:** 308
Folsom, Marion B., **1960–61:** 263
    See also Health, Education, and Welfare, Sec-
        retary of (Marion B. Folsom).
    Rumor of appointment as Secretary of Health,
        Education, and Welfare, **1955:** 112
Fong, Sen. Hiram, **1959:** 184n.
Food
    Irradiation, **1956:** 12 (p. 101)
    Prices, **1954:** 172
        News conference remarks, **1958:** 56, 70
        Statement, **1958:** 298
    Revision of laws, disapproval, **1954:** 254
    Shortage in East Germany.
        See Germany, East.
    Stamp plan, **1959:** 226
    U.S. offer to flooded areas of Europe, **1954:** 182
        and ftn. (p. 678), 200
        Memorandum, **1954:** 195
        Statement, **1954:** 175
Food and Agriculture Organization, **1959:** 189;
        1960–61: 221, 279, 302

Food Conference, National, remarks, **1958:** 35
Food and Drug Act, amendment proposed, **1953:** 95
Food and Drug Administration, **1955:** 25; **1956:** 12 (p. 121), 21; **1959:** 10 (p. 46); **1960–61:** 410
  Budget messages, **1960–61:** 13 (p. 94), 414 (pp. 1008, 1009)
  Factory inspections, **1953:** 6, 95
  Seizure of food, drugs, and cosmetics, authority re, **1954:** 254
Food for Peace program, **1959:** 226; **1960–61:** 32, 221, 246, 279, 302, 391, 410
  Budget messages, **1960–61:** 13 (pp. 79, 80), 414 (p. 988)
  Report, statement, **1960–61:** 242
  U.S.-Indian agreement, statement, **1960–61:** 136
Foodstuffs, imports, **1958:** 96
Foot, Sir Hugh, **1959:** 39
Football, **1958:** 286, 307; **1960–61:** 319
Football Foundation, National, remarks, **1958:** 307
Football Hall of Fame, remarks, **1958:** 307
Foote, Comdr. Ovid, **1956:** 241
Forbes, Malcolm S., **1957:** 87, 228
Force, international renunciation of, **1958:** 31
Forced labor, **1956:** 96, 121
  U.N. Ad Hoc Committee on, **1955:** 156
  U.S.S.R., **1957:** 245
Ford, Henry, 2d, **1953:** 15; **1959:** 154
Ford, William C., **1957:** 225n.
Ford Foundation, **1960–61:** 315n.
Ford Motor Co., **1955:** 119; **1957:** 225n.
Fordham University, **1959:** 21, 106
Foreign affairs, **1953:** 6, 57, 61, 68, 69, 101, 241; **1954:** 3; **1955:** 185; **1956:** 12 (p. 109); **1959:** 130, 212, 225; **1960–61:** 148, 163, 245, 332, 341, 410
  Bipartisanship in, **1953:** 6, 249; **1954:** 92, 107, 157, 209, 273, 311, 319, 320, 328; **1955:** 248; **1960–61:** 7, 103, 268
    Conferences, **1954:** 337, 351
  Briefing for next President, proposed, **1960–61:** 222
  Budget messages, **1954:** 14 (pp. 135–140); **1955:** 17 (pp. 126–132); **1959:** 10 (pp. 71–75); **1960–61:** 13 (pp. 59, 60, 64, 65), 414 (pp. 961–969)
    Tables, **1954:** 14 (p. 137); **1955:** 17 (p. 127); **1959:** 10 (p. 72); **1960–61:** 13 (p. 61), 414 (p. 963)
  Campaign remarks, **1954:** 273, 286, 319, 320
  Conduct of, **1954:** 323; **1958:** 5 (p. 41)
  Discussions with President-elect Kennedy, **1960–61:** 369
  Leadership of the President, comment on, **1959:** 179
  News conference remarks, **1953:** 37, 41, 208, 249; **1954:** 92, 107, 115, 157, 311, 322, 328, 341; **1960–61:** 7, 103, 222, 268, 422

Foreign affairs — *continued*
  Organization of executive branch for conduct of
    Memorandum, **1953:** 92
    Message to Congress, **1953:** 89
  Policies, **1953:** 231
  Presidential authority, **1953:** 41, 142; **1960–61:** 246
  Responsibility of Secretary of State, **1953:** 92
Foreign agents, registration of, **1953:** 95
Foreign Agricultural Service, **1954:** 14 (p. 160)
Foreign aid program.
  See Mutual security program.
Foreign Aid, Advisory Committee on Voluntary, **1953:** 92
Foreign aspects of national security, conference on, **1958:** 42
  Letter to Eric Johnston, **1958:** 4
  Remarks, **1958:** 36
Foreign assistance, **1953:** 89, 101, 141; **1954:** 3, 139, 209, 297, 323; **1955:** 4, 248; **1956:** 2; **1957:** 91; **1958:** 32; **1959:** 152; **1960–61:** 362
  See also Economic assistance; Military assistance and defense support; Mutual security program; Technical assistance to less developed countries.
  Advisory board, **1956:** 88
  Afghanistan, **1958:** 150; **1959:** 308
  Africa, **1953:** 66; **1954:** 14 (p. 139), 150; **1955:** 17 (p. 130), 76; **1956:** 58, 62, 87; **1958:** 36, 96, 198; **1959:** 55, 71, 269n.; **1960–61:** 13 (p. 63), 36, 242, 263, 302, 414 (pp. 961, 967, 968)
  American Republics, **1954:** 14 (p. 127)
  Arab States, **1954:** 14 (p. 139)
  Argentina, **1960–61:** 58
  Asia, South Asia, and Southeast Asia, **1953:** 66, 143; **1954:** 14 (p. 139), 150, 347; **1955:** 17 (pp. 123, 129, 130), 41, 47, 48, 69, 76; **1956:** 12 (p. 105), 58, 87, 121; **1958:** 5 (p. 35), 36; **1959:** 55, 71; **1960–61:** 4, 36, 132, 193, 242, 302
  Berlin, **1953:** 113; **1956:** 58; **1959:** 55
  Bolivia, **1953:** 206, 213; **1955:** 17 (p. 129), 76
  Brazil, **1960–61:** 49, 53
  "Buy American" requirement, **1959:** 267, 271
  Cambodia, **1955:** 17 (p. 129); **1959:** 55
  Chile, **1960–61:** 255, 414 (p. 966)
  China, Republic of, **1954:** 3, 14 (pp. 127, 139); **1955:** 17 (p. 129), 21; **1957:** 90, 91, 136; **1958:** 32; **1959:** 10 (p. 69), 55; **1960–61:** 36, 195, 341
  Colombia, **1960–61:** 109n., 111n.
  Congo, **1960–61:** 263
  Contingency fund, **1958:** 32
  Continuance, legislative recommendation on, **1957:** 16
  Developing countries, **1958:** 49, 123; **1959:** 55, 186, 214, 296

Foreign assistance — *continued*
  Distribution through U.N., **1956:** 12 (p. 106), 58,
      88, 94
  Egypt, **1955:** 17 (p. 130)
  Europe, **1954:** 150; **1958:** 5 (p. 35); **1960–61:** 80,
      132, 133
  Far East, **1956:** 12 (p. 105)
  France, **1953:** 66
  Germany, **1955:** 17 (p. 124), 76
  Greece, **1953:** 66, 233n.; **1955:** 76; **1957:** 6, 90,
      91, 152, 169; **1958:** 36; **1959:** 55; **1960–61:**
      132, 133
  Guatemala, **1955:** 17 (p. 129), 76; **1957:** 90;
      1960–61: 368
  Haiti, **1955:** 23n.
  India, **1953:** 143; **1954:** 14 (p. 139), 44; **1955:** 17
      (p. 129); **1959:** 94; **1960–61:** 36, 136, 410
  Indochina, **1953:** 66, 156; **1954:** 3, 14 (pp. 127,
      139), 92
  Iran, **1953:** 129, 178; **1954:** 14 (p. 139); **1955:** 17
      (p. 130), 76; **1957:** 90; **1958:** 36; **1959:** 55,
      342; **1960–61:** 341
  Iraq, **1954:** 92
  Israel, **1953:** 225, 230; **1954:** 14 (p. 130) 139), 92;
      1955: 17 (p. 130)
  Jordan, **1955:** 17 (p. 130); **1959:** 55
  Korea, **1953:** 96, 148, 159; **1954:** 3, 14 (p. 139),
      35, 150, 171n.; **1955:** 17 (pp. 104, 124,
      129); **1956:** 12 (p. 104), 20; **1957:** 90, 91,
      136, 152; **1958:** 32; **1959:** 10 (p. 69), 55;
      1960–61: 36, 203
  Laos, **1955:** 17 (p. 129); **1959:** 55, 186; **1960–61:**
      256
  Latin America, **1953:** 66, 143; **1954:** 14 (p. 139),
      150; **1955:** 17 (pp. 129, 130), 76; **1956:** 12
      (p. 104), 58; **1959:** 55, 94; **1960–61:** 36, 42,
      49, 72, 80, 86, 87, 228, 242, 247, 255, 256,
      263, 302, 380, 414 (pp. 961, 966, 968)
  Lebanon, **1955:** 17 (p. 130); **1959:** 55
  Legislation, **1954:** 157, 182
  Less developed countries, **1954:** 150; **1955:** 6;
      1958: 120, 198, 312; **1959:** 10 (pp. 71, 72,
      74, 75), 55, 87, 186, 189, 191, 196, 223,
      244, 248, 258, 267, 269n., 293, 297, 329;
      1960–61: 4, 13 (pp. 60–64), 16, 19, 39, 58,
      80, 209, 362 ftn. (p. 864), 365, 414 (pp.
      961, 964, 965)
  Libya, **1955:** 17 (p. 130); **1958:** 32; **1959:** 55
  Middle East, **1953:** 66, 143; **1954:** 14 (p. 139);
      1955: 17 (pp. 125, 130); **1956:** 12 (pp. 104,
      105), 53, 58, 298; **1957:** 6, 17, 31, 90, 91;
      1958: 5 (p. 35), 198; **1959:** 55; **1960–61:** 7,
      302
  Morocco, **1957:** 240; **1958:** 32; **1959:** 55
  NATO members, **1956:** 12 (p. 104), 58; **1959:** 55
  Near East, **1954:** 150
  Nepal, **1960–61:** 130
  Netherlands, **1960–61:** 138n.

Foreign assistance — *continued*
  Newly emerging countries, **1960–61:** 4, 36, 163,
      302
  News conference remarks, **1955:** 41, 47, 119;
      1956: 20, 88, 94, 121, 235, 298; **1957:** 45,
      50, 56, 80, 157
  Pakistan, **1953:** 95, 97, 109, 119, 124, 143, 249;
      1954: 14 (p. 139), 44, 45; **1956:** 12 (p.
      104); **1957:** 131; **1959:** 55, 94, 302, 303;
      1960–61: 36
  Philippines, **1954:** 14 (pp. 127, 139); **1958:** 143;
      1959: 55; **1960–61:** 189, 341
  Poland, **1956:** 282; **1958:** 141
  SEATO countries, **1956:** 58
  Spain, **1955:** 76; **1956:** 58; **1959:** 55, 200, 340
  Special assistance, funds for, **1958:** 32
  Study by commission proposed, **1956:** 94
  Sudan, **1959:** 55
  Taiwan, **1956:** 12 (p. 104)
  Thailand, **1954:** 14 (p. 127); **1957:** 36 and n.;
      1959: 55, 342
  Tunisia, **1959:** 55
  Turkey, **1955:** 76; **1956:** 12 (p. 104); **1957:** 6, 90,
      136, 152; **1958:** 32; **1959:** 55, 297; **1960–
      61:** 132, 133
  Vietnam, **1954:** 306; **1955:** 17 (p. 129), 48; **1957:**
      83, 90, 91, 136, 152; **1958:** 32, 36; **1959:** 10
      (p. 69), 55, 71, 278; **1960–61:** 36, 341
  Voluntary, **1956:** 58; **1957:** 250
  Western Europe, **1953:** 66
  Yugoslavia, **1955:** 76, 119; **1956:** 58, 121, 235,
      248; **1958:** 141
Foreign assistance funds, Presidential power to
      transfer, **1954:** 3, 14 (p. 126).
Foreign Claims Settlement Commission, estab-
      lishment, **1954:** 94
Foreign Commerce, Bureau of, **1954:** 14 (p. 181)
Foreign currencies, **1953:** 6; **1955:** 6
  Budget messages, **1960–61:** 13 (pp. 80, 82, 107),
      414 (pp. 988, 1025, 1026)
  Convertibility, **1954:** 67
  Sale of agricultural surpluses for, **1955:** 17 (p.
      130), 76; **1959:** 10 (pp. 54, 74), 226;
      1960–61: 13 (pp. 80, 82, 107), 414 (p. 988)
Foreign economic policy, **1953:** 44, 161, 246; **1955:**
      72
  Douglas (Lewis W.) Study, **1953:** 31
  Financial and economic mission to United
      Kingdom, report, **1953:** 176, 177
  Letter, **1953:** 63
  Letter to Harry Bullis, **1954:** 217
  Letter to Joseph M. Dodge, **1954:** 348
  Letter to Charles H. Percy, **1954:** 119
  Message, **1955:** 6
  To Congress, **1954:** 67
Foreign Economic Policy, Commission on
      (Randall Commission), **1953:** 176, 246,
      249; **1956:** 139; **1958:** 56, 318

Foreign Economic Policy, Comm. on — *continued*
  Establishment, **1953:** 161
  Letter to Chairman, **1953:** 177
  Meeting with, **1956:** 198
  News conference remarks on, **1954:** 18, 68, 101, 138, 157, 353
  Proposed, **1953:** 63, 70, 131
  Recommendations, **1956:** 162
  Remarks, **1953:** 190
  Report, **1954:** 16, 18, 67, 68, 90, 101, 209, 349, 351, 353
Foreign Economic Policy, Council on, **1954:** 354; **1955:** 76
  Letter to Chairman, **1954:** 348
Foreign educators, remarks, **1959:** 222
Foreign firms, competitive bidding on military supply items, **1959:** 10 (p. 65)
Foreign information activities, budget message, **1956:** 12 (pp. 80, 81, 108, 109)
Foreign intelligence activities, Board of Consultants on
  Appointment of Chairman, **1956:** 10
  Letter to Director of Central Intelligence re, **1956:** 9
Foreign intelligence reports (1952), **1956:** 198
Foreign investments.
  See Investments, abroad.
Foreign languages.
  See Languages, foreign.
Foreign markets, **1958:** 16
Foreign ministers meetings, **1958:** 42
  American Republics (1958), **1959:** 98
  Berlin (1954), **1954:** 18, 25, 39, 128, 225, 297
  Four-power meeting, proposed, **1953:** 146, 254, 255, 256
  Geneva.
    See also main heading, Geneva Conferences.
  Geneva (1954), **1954:** 92 101, 128, 143, 157, 165, 168, 225, 297
  Geneva (1955), **1955:** 170, 185, 226; **1958:** 7; **1959:** 7
    Statement re, **1955:** 227
  Geneva (1959), **1959:** 29, 36, 42, 48, 57, 67 and ftn. (p. 292), 78, 89, 94, 102, 123 and ftn. (p. 425), 132, 148, 154, 161, 167, 172, 173, 179, 192
  Letter to Premier Khrushchev, **1958:** 177
  London (1954), **1954:** 282, 332, 337
  News conference remarks, **1954:** 18, 25, 39, 50, 92, 101, 143, 157, 165, 168, 341
  North Atlantic Council, remarks, **1959:** 70
  Organization of American States
    San Jose (1960), **1960–61:** 228, 263, 267, 268
    Santiago (1959), **1960–61:** 73, 76, 228
  Paris (1954), **1954:** 297, 332, 337
  Santiago, Chile (1959), **1959:** 172
  Southeast Asia Treaty Organization, **1960–61:** 164, 189, 286

Foreign ministers meetings — *continued*
  Vienna (1955), **1955:** 95
  Washington, D.C., **1953:** 126, 146
Foreign Operations Administration, **1953:** 89, 92; **1954:** 150
  See also Mutual Security Agency.
  Assistance for escapees and refugees, **1953:** 257n.
    Palestine, **1953:** 89
  Establishment under Reorganization Plan 7, message, **1953:** 90
  Flood relief for Europe, **1955:** 49
  Ladejinsky, Wolf, **1955:** 10, 18
  News conference remarks, **1955:** 10, 18, 62
  Termination in 1955, **1955:** 76
  Transfer of functions, **1955:** 62, 74
Foreign Operations Administration, Director (Harold E. Stassen), **1953:** 217, 266, 268; **1954:** 349, 351; **1955:** 57, 60n., 94; **1958:** 30n.
  See also Mutual Security, Director for.
  Bolivian relief, **1953:** 213
    Memorandum, **1953:** 206
  Flood relief in Central and Eastern Europe, memorandum, **1954:** 195
  Flood relief in Italy, **1954:** 315
  Foreign aid programs, **1954:** 323
  Meeting with Prime Minister Yoshida, **1954:** 330
  NATO, report on, **1953:** 265 ftn. (p. 843)
  News conference remarks on, **1955:** 10, 47, 62, 146, 185
  Visit to New Delhi, **1955:** 47
Foreign policy, **1954:** 91, 128, 139, 225, 316; **1959:** 6, 116
  Advisory board, proposed, **1956:** 87
  Bipartisan meetings on, **1956:** 318; **1957:** 2
  News conference remarks, **1956:** 62, 113; **1958:** 110, 120, 288, 310
  Partisan debate opposed, **1958:** 288
  President's responsibility, **1954:** 341
  Relationship between executive and legislative branches, **1956:** 62
  Telegram to Vice President Nixon, **1958:** 289
Foreign Relations, Council on, **1960–61:** 86
Foreign service, **1955:** 47; **1958:** 286; **1960–61:** 95
  Budget message, **1955:** 17 (p. 126)
  Improvements, **1955:** 17 (p. 132)
  Pay adjustments, **1955:** 8
  Pay system, **1958:** 169
Foreign Service Institute, graduation exercises, remarks, **1959:** 130
Foreign Service officers
  Deportment, **1958:** 120
  Language requirements, **1958:** 32, 120
Foreign service posts, Africa, **1958:** 5 (p. 41)
Foreign students
  American Field Service students, remarks to, **1957:** 137
  Atomic studies in U.S., **1955:** 165
  Exchange students, **1957:** 222

Foreign visitors.
  See Joint statements with heads of state and governments; Visitors, foreign.
Forest Congress, American, remarks, **1953:** 234
Forest fire prevention, statement, **1953:** 112
Forest highway program, **1954:** 14 (pp. 170, 176)
Forest resources, **1955:** 4; **1958:** 5 (p. 69)
  Conservation and development, **1953:** 234
Forest Service, **1953:** 153; **1954:** 270; **1958:** 5 (p. 67); **1960–61:** 13 (p. 85), 414 (p. 997)
  Budget message, **1954:** 14 (p. 170)
Forests, national, **1953:** 153; **1954:** 3; **1955:** 17 (pp. 162, 163); **1956:** 12 (pp. 133, 137); **1960–61:** 410
  Bankhead (William B.) National Forest, **1954:** 156
  Budget messages, **1954:** 14 (pp. 164, 169, 170); **1960–61:** 13 (pp. 85, 86), 414 (pp. 997, 998)
  Conservation, **1958:** 100; **1959:** 10 (p. 95)
  Functions re, under Reorganization Plan 1 of 1959, **1959:** 101
  Lands in Oregon, **1954:** 152
  Management of grazing lands, **1954:** 196
  Tongass National Forest, **1959:** 101
Formosa Declaration of 1955, **1957:** 111
Formosa (Taiwan), **1953:** 6; **1956:** 210, 283; **1957:** 6, 152, 157; **1958:** 80, 124, 295; **1959:** 6, 94, 132; **1960–61:** 143, 245, 341
  See also China, Republic of.
  Assistance, **1956:** 12 (p. 104)
  Chinese Communist invasion, question of, **1954:** 200
  Defense treaty and Joint Resolution on, **1955:** 21, 26, 47, 62; **1958:** 222, 257, 261, 274, 277, 293
    Joint Resolution, approval, **1955:** 24
  Letter to Premier Khrushchev, **1958:** 263
  Military Assistance Advisory Group (MAAG), **1955:** 90
  News conference remarks, **1955:** 18, 26, 33, 47, 62, 81, 90, 185; **1956:** 16, 56, 235; **1958:** 120, 274
  Statement by Secretary Dulles, **1958:** 257
  U.S. armed forces in, **1955:** 21, 24n.
  U.S. military base, comment on, **1955:** 90
  Visit of Secretary Dulles, **1955:** 47
Formosa (Taiwan) Strait Situation, **1958:** 207, 261
  Campaign remarks, **1958:** 293, 296
  Letter to Sen. Green, **1958:** 277
  Letter to Premier Khrushchev, **1958:** 263
  Message to Congress, **1955:** 21
  News conference remarks, **1955:** 18, 26, 33, 41, 59, 62, 81, 90, 100, 112; **1958:** 222, 274, 288
  Resolution on, **1956:** 62
  Soviet bloc position, comment on, **1959:** 267
  Statement by Secretary Dulles, **1958:** 257

Formosa (Taiwan) Strait Situation — *continued*
  U.N. truce, comment on proposal, **1955:** 18
  U.S.-Communist China negotiations, **1955:** 81; **1958:** 257, 261, 263
  U.S.-Soviet Union negotiations, **1955:** 90
Forrestal, James, **1954:** 308; **1955:** 117
Forrestal Memorial Award Dinner of the National Security Industrial Association, remarks, **1954:** 308; **1958:** 110
Fort Benning, Ga., **1960–61:** 135
Fort Gordon, troop review ceremonies, remarks, **1960–61:** 396
Fort Knox, **1955:** 52
Fort Leavenworth, Kans., **1954:** 120
Fort Lewis, Wash., **1956:** 253
Fort Ligonier, bicentennial celebration, address, **1958:** 269
Fort McNair, dedication of new building, remarks, **1960–61:** 283
Fort Myer, Va., **1953:** 150
Fort Peck dam, power plant, **1956:** 12 (p. 135)
Fort Pemberton, Miss., **1958:** 226
Fort Randall Dam and Reservoir project, **1958:** 225
  Dedication of first power unit, remarks, **1954:** 53
Fort Sumter, **1959:** 31
Foster, Paul F., U.S. Representative to International Atomic Energy Agency, statement re, **1959:** 121
Foster, William C., **1958:** 310
Foundation for Religious Action in the Social and Civil Order, **1954:** 327n.; **1956:** 201
4-H Club Center, National, dedication, remarks, **1959:** 131
4-H Clubs, **1954:** 127; **1955:** 128; **1958:** 307; **1959:** 164
  Remarks to campers, **1954:** 146
4-H Conference, National, remarks, **1957:** 113; **1958:** 142; **1960–61:** 123
Fourteenth amendment to Constitution, **1957:** 134
Fox, Joseph A., **1953:** 12, 31, 62, 77, 109, 225, 230, 249
France, **1953:** 6, 256, 265 ftn. (p. 843); **1954:** 84n., 128; **1955:** 54n.; **1957:** 91, 235; **1958:** 8, 32, 80, 118; **1960–61:** 207, 249, 253, 254, 257, 259, 260, 265
  See also, Paris.
  African colonies, **1958:** 74; **1959:** 214
  Agreement with Germany on Saar, **1954:** 307, 337
  Algeria, **1956:** 62; **1957:** 28, 124; **1958:** 42, 103; **1959:** 223, 329, 345
  Allied landings, World War II, 10th anniversary Normandy invasion, **1954:** 131, 133
    Southern France, ceremonies, message, **1954:** 198
  Alphand, Herve, **1959:** 332n.
  American cemeteries for World War II dead, **1956:** 102

France — *continued*
  Armed forces in Korea, **1960–61:** 202
  Atomic bomb explosion, **1960–61:** 38
  Atomic energy for mutual defense, U.S.-France agreement, **1959:** 119n., 120n.
  Bermuda conference.
    See Bermuda meeting of Western leaders.
  Bonnet, Henri, **1953:** 219; **1954:** 176n.
  Campaign remarks, **1958:** 287, 293
  Cherbourg, **1954:** 131
  Communists in armed forces, handling of, **1954:** 48
  Coty, Rene.
    See main heading, Coty, Rene.
  Couve de Murville, Maurice, **1959:** 123 ftn. (p. 425), 202
  Debre, Michel, **1959:** 202, 207
  Declaration of the Rights of Man. **1953:** 250
  De Gaulle, Charles, **1958:** 120, 141, 273; **1959:** 5, 7, 132, 154, 191, 199, 201, 207, 214, 271, 332, 349; **1960–61:** 24, 120, 121, 124, 127, 147, 154, 162, 163, 313
    East-West summit conference, agreement with Western leaders on, **1959:** 337
    Joint statements with, **1959:** 202; **1960–61:** 125, 155
    Joint statements with Western leaders, **1959:** 335, 336
  Disarmament proposal, **1957:** 158, 165, 208 and n., **1957:** 210, 226, 244
  Euratom.
    See European Atomic Energy Community.
  European Defense Community Treaty, rejection, **1954:** 226, 297
  Faure, Edgar, **1955:** 170n.
  Four-power conference on Germany and Austria, proposed, **1953:** 238
  Gaillard, Felix, **1958:** 74
  Geneva conference on Indochina.
    See Geneva conferences.
  Granville, **1954:** 131
  Houghton, Ambassador Amory, **1959:** 203, 332n.
  Indochina, **1958:** 287
  Indochina war, **1953:** 143, 156, 255
    U.S. assistance, **1953:** 66
  Laniel, Joseph, **1953:** 254
    Joint statement with Western leaders, **1953:** 255
  Le Canadel, **1954:** 198n.
  London agreements.
    See main heading, London agreements.
  Mayer, Rene, **1953:** 37, 88
    Joint statement with, **1956:** 34
  Meeting (U.S., U.K.), proposed, **1956:** 298
  Mendes-France, Pierre, **1954:** 157, 200, 311, 341
  Middle East situation, **1956:** 26, 276
  Mollet, Guy, **1956:** 155

France — *continued*
  NATO
    Membership, **1954:** 3
  Position on, **1959:** 132
  Troops, **1956:** 78
  News conference remarks, **1953:** 15, 37, 88, 238; **1954:** 33, 39, 48, 57, 68, 115, 129, 157, 165, 168; **1956:** 32, 62, 78, 235, 298; **1957:** 22, 124, 210; **1958:** 42, 74, 83, 103; **1959:** 132, 154, 186, 191
  Orly Field, **1956:** 117
  Paris agreements.
    See Paris agreements.
  Paris summit conference.
    See Paris summit meeting.
  Pineau, Christian, **1956:** 229; **1957:** 38
  Policy on Berlin, **1960–61:** 38
  Ste. Mere Eglise, **1954:** 131
  Scientific contributions, **1957:** 230
  SEATO.
    See Southeast Asia Treaty Organization.
  SEATO membership, **1960–61:** 286
  Strasbourg, **1953:** 6
  Suez Canal problem.
    See Suez Canal
  Suez invasion (1956), **1960–61:,** 21
  Technical conference on nuclear detection.
    See Geneva conferences.
  Toulon, remarks on arrival, **1959:** 332
  Tours, **1959:** 204
  U. N. action on, **1957:** 34
  U.S.-French relations, **1960–61:** 121, 124
  U.S. nuclear bases, removal, **1960–61:** 24
  U.S. relations with, **1954:** 148n.; **1957:** 235, 298
  Vietnam, **1956:** 117
  Vimy Ridge, **1959:** 7
  Visits of the President, **1959:** 186, 191, 199, 201, 202, 205, 206, 207, 214, 277, 332, 334, 335, 336, 337; **1960–61:** 147, 154, 155, 156, 162, 163
  War in Indochina.
    See Dien Bien Phu, battle of; Indochina war.
  Wheat crop, statement, **1956:** 42
  Withdrawal of U.S. bombers, **1959:** 154
Francis, Clarence, **1954:** 263n.; **1957:** 26n.
  Chairman, Interagency Committee on Agricultural Surplus Disposal, letter, **1954:** 262
Francis, Dr. Thomas, Jr., **1955:** 112, 113
Franco, General, **1957:** 249; **1959:** 338, 341
  Joint statements with, **1959:** 340
  Letter, **1959:** 200
  Toast to, **1959:** 339
Franconia Notch, N.H., remarks at 150th anniversary of discovery of Old Man of the Mountain, **1955:** 136
Franklin, Benjamin, **1953:** 8, 240; **1954:** 47, 86, 88; **1955:** 121; **1956:** 107; **1957:** 60, 62, 87; **1959:** 107; **1960–61:** 171n., 240

Franklin, Benjamin A., **1959:** 223
Frantz, Harry W., **1953:** 31, 141; **1954:** 25, 161, 200; **1955:** 26; **1956:** 96, 121
Franz, Alwin F., **1959:** 211n.
Fraser, Colo., **1954:** 233n., 270
Frederick, Clarence, **1956:** 241
Fredericks, Marshall M., **1960–61:** 326n.
Frederik IX, **1960–61:** 209
   Exchange of toasts, **1960–61:** 321
   Message, **1960–61:** 41
   Welcoming remarks to, **1960–61:** 320
Frederika, Queen, **1953:** 230, 232, 233; **1959:** 327
Free enterprise.
   See Enterprise system.
Free market.
   See European Economic Community.
Free trade area, Europe, **1956:** 278; **1958:** 5 (p. 37)
   Joint statements with Prime Minister Macmillan, **1957:** 55, 226
   Joint statement with Premier Mollet, **1957:** 38
Free Trade Association.
   See European Free Trade Association.
Freedmen's Hospital, **1956:** 12 (p. 120); **1960–61:** 414 (p. 1009)
Freedom Celebration Day, Charlotte, N.C., address, **1954:** 114
Freedom monument, proposed
   Budget message, **1960–61:** 414 (p. 1023)
   Report, **1960–61:** 152
Freedoms Foundation, **1956:** 122
Freeman, Douglas S., death of, statement, **1953:** 106
Freeman, Mrs. Douglas S., **1953:** 106
Freeman, Orville L., **1954:** 347; **1960–61:** 330
Freitas, Paulin, **1960–61:** 324n.
Frelinghuysen, Repr. Peter, Jr., **1954:** 182
Freudenheim, Milton B., **1953:** 198; **1954:** 57, 157, 168; **1955:** 81, 119, 146, 185
Friedman, Milton, **1953:** 208, 225; **1954:** 9, 92; **1955:** 56; **1957:** 124; **1958:** 310
Fringe benefits, Government employees, **1956:** 2
Froessel, Charles W., **1960–61:** 166n.
Frolich, Stephen, **1956:** 241
Frondizi, Arturo, **1960–61:** 56, 57n., 58, 60, 61, 62, 67, 87, 228
   Exchange of toasts, **1959:** 16
   Toasts to, **1960–61:** 59, 63
   Joint declaration with, **1960–61:** 66
   Letter, **1958:** 164
   Message, **1955:** 13, 28
   News conference remarks on, **1959:** 17, 26
   Remarks of welcome, **1959:** 14
Frondizi, Senora, **1959:** 14, 16; **1960–61:** 56
Frontiers, American, **1956:** 107
Frontiers of Science Foundation, **1957:** 234 and n.
Fruits, **1958:** 60
   Surpluses, **1954:** 4

Fryingpan-Arkansas project, **1954:** 172; **1955:** 17 (p. 159); **1956:** 2; **1957:** 13; **1959:** 10 (p. 94); **1960–61:** 133
   Budget messages, **1956:** 12 (p. 135); **1960–61:** 13 (p. 83), 414 (p. 993)
FTC.
   See Federal Trade Commission.
Fuel, nuclear, **1958:** 145
Fuels, new, **1958:** 5 (p. 19)
Fuels, processing, **1953:** 153
Fuels Policy Committee, **1956:** 16
Fujiyama, Aiichiro, **1960–61:** 14, 16
Fulbright, Sen. J. W., **1957:** 145; **1958:** 23; **1960–61:** 103, 132
   Corporate tax proposal, **1957:** 132
   Development Loan Fund proposal, **1959:** 89
   Natural gas bill, Harris-Fulbright, **1957:** 13
   News conference remarks on, **1959:** 89, 123
   Student exchange program, **1960–61:** 80
Fulbright scholarships, **1957:** 222
Fulton, Repr. James G., **1956:** 234
Fundraising campaigns
   American-Korean Foundation, **1953:** 65
   Community Chest and United Defense Fund, **1953:** 115, 127, 179, 196
   Crusade for Freedom, **1955:** 79; **1956:** 66
   Hungarian relief, **1956:** 304
   March of Dimes, **1956:** 1
   National Foundation for Infantile Paralysis, **1956:** 1
   National health agencies. **1957:** 18
   Policy for Government campaigns, statement, **1956:** 132
   Radio Free Europe, **1955:** 32
   Red Cross, **1953:** 17; **1954:** 1, 46, 356; **1955:** 45; **1956:** 11; **1957:** 30, 39, 62; **1958:** 3, 38; **1959:** 20, 45; **1960–61:** 37, 65
   United Community Campaigns, **1954:** 183, 276; **1955:** 168, 218; **1956:** 221; **1958:** 270; **1959:** 238
   United Fund and Community Chest, **1956:** 185; **1957:** 154; **1958:** 184; **1959:** 159
   United Givers Fund, **1956:** 138; **1957:** 140; **1958:** 136; **1959:** 156; **1960–61:** 153, 210
   United Negro College Fund, **1953:** 81
   United Service Organizations, **1955:** 27
Furcolo, Foster, **1957:** 145; **1959:** 113
   Letter, **1959:** 12
Future Farmers of America, **1953:** 225; **1954:** 127; **1957:** 113; **1958:** 307; **1959:** 164, 169
   Address, **1953:** 216

Gabon, Republic of
   Independence, message to President M'ba, **1960–61:** 265
   N'Goua, Joseph, **1960–61:** 324n.

Gaillard, Felix, **1958:** 74
Gaither (H. Rowan, Jr.) panel report, withholding of, **1958:** 11
  Letter, **1958:** 19
Galard-Terraube, Genevieve de, Medal of Freedom, citation, **1954:** 176
Galbraith, William H., Jr., **1958:** 213
Galindez, Jesus, **1956:** 88, 96
Gallin-Douathe, Michel, **1960–61:** 324n.
Galloti, Luiz, **1960–61:** 50n.
Gama, Vasco da, **1960–61:** 160
Gandhi, Mrs. Indira, **1956:** 312
Gandhi, Mohandas K. (Mahatma), **1959:** 312, 316; **1960–61:** 93
Garcia, Carlos P., **1957:** 56, 69 and n.; **1960–61:** 182, 188, 190
  Exchange of toasts, **1958:** 140; **1960–61:** 185
  Joint statements with, **1958:** 143; **1960–61:** 189
  Messages, **1958:** 69; **1959:** 73; **1960–61:** 106, 112, 359
  News conference remarks on, **1958:** 141
  Welcoming remarks, **1958:** 139
Garcia, Madame Carlos P., **1958:** 139, 140; **1960–61:** 185
Garden City, N.Y., **1960–61:** 345
Garrett, George A., **1956:** 4
  Letter, **1955:** 55
Garrison Dam, closure ceremonies, **1953:** 100
Gary, Raymond, **1957:** 234 and n.
  Exchange of telegrams re Oklahoma semi-centennial, **1957:** 229 and n.
Gas, natural, **1957:** 13
  Alaskan gas leases, veto, **1959:** 182
  Budget message, **1959:** 10 (p. 96)
  Canadian, **1959:** 288
  News conference remarks, **1957:** 56, 72, 105, 115
Gas Act, amendment
  Approval, **1954:** 64
  News conference remarks, **1956:** 16, 32, 47
  Veto, **1956:** 41
Gas bill, **1955:** 146; **1958:** 37
Gas conservation, interstate compact, **1956:** 12 (p. 149)
Gas industry, report on, **1955:** 56
Gas and oil leases on public domain lands, **1960–61:** 13 (p. 86), 414 (pp. 941, 997)
Gas warfare, **1960–61:** 7
  World War I, **1955:** 118
Gasoline for farm use, tax refund, **1956:** 6, 83, 214, 250
  Approval of bill, **1956:** 72
  Budget message, **1956:** 12 (p. 127)
  News conference remarks, **1956:** 20
Gasoline filling stations, District of Columbia, improvements, **1953:** 149; **1956:** 153
Gasoline taxes, **1954:** 3, 14 (pp. 88, 99), 102, 273; **1955:** 41; **1958:** 324; **1960–61:** 133
  Aviation gasoline, **1958:** 5 (p. 45)

Gasoline taxes — *continued*
  Budget message, **1959:** 10 (pp. 41, 42, 79)
  Increase, **1959:** 104, 149, 187, 227, 252; **1960–61:** 13 (pp. 39, 43, 44, 69, 70), 414 (pp. 941, 975, 977), 423
    Aviation gasoline, **1959:** 10 (pp. 42, 79); **1960–61:** 13 (pp. 39, 43, 44, 69), 133, 222, 255, 414 (pp. 941, 975, 977)
  News conference remarks, **1954:** 33, 165; **1959:** 94, 102
  Tractors and machinery, repeal (1956), **1960–61:** 410
Gasperi, Alcide de, death of, **1954:** 205
Gasperi, Madame de, message, **1954:** 205
Gates, Thomas S., Jr., **1958:** 125
  See also Defense, Secretary of (Thomas S. Gates, Jr.).
  Letter, **1959:** 111
GATT.
  See General Agreement on Tariffs and Trade.
Gaulle, Charles de.
  See De Gaulle, Charles.
Gaulle, Madame de.
  See De Gaulle, Madame.
Gavin, Gen. James M., **1958:** 11
  War and Peace in the Space Age: A New Approach, **1958:** 222
Gaza Strip, **1957:** 34, 35
  Joint statement with Prime Minister Macmillan, **1957:** 55
  News conference remarks, **1957:** 50, 62
  U.N. emergency force in, **1958:** 8, 89, 148; **1960–61:** 330
GDR (German Democratic Republic).
  See Germany, East.
Geary County, Kansas, **1954:** 331
General Accounting Office, **1953:** 55; **1954:** 328; **1959:** 10 (p. 53)
  Availability of records and reports to, **1958:** 288, 310
  Budget message, **1958:** 5 (p. 32)
General Agreement on Tariffs and Trade, **1954:** 67; **1955:** 6, 72; **1956:** 2, 123, 310; **1957:** 32, 61; **1958:** 163; **1960–61:** 95
  See also Trade, international; Trade Agreements Act.
  Geneva negotiations, **1956:** 94 and ftn. (p. 452), 123
  Hat bodies, fur-felt, **1956:** 123
  Joint statement with Western leaders, **1959:** 335
  Lead and zinc tariffs, **1957:** 157, 160
  News conference remarks, **1956:** 94, 216
  Ninth Session, letter to Chairman of U.S. delegation, **1954:** 324
  Sixth Protocol Supplementary Concessions, **1956:** 123n.
  Sugar, liquid, **1956:** 123

General Agreement, Tariffs & Trade — *continued*
    Tariff concessions, **1958:** 25, 58
        See also Trade Agreements Act, extension.
    Seed wheat, **1958:** 217
    Textiles, **1955:** 149
    Woolen textiles, tariff increase, **1956:** 216
General Aniline and Film Corporation, **1957:** 72
General Armistice Agreement in Middle East,
    violation of, statement, **1955:** 234
General Eisenhower, use of term by press, **1958:**
    288
General Motors Research Center, remarks, **1956:**
    107
General Services Administration, **1954:** 14 (p. 187);
    1955: 17 (p. 179); **1960–61:** 5
    Budget messages, **1956:** 12 (p. 151); **1960–61:** 13
        (pp. 76, 102), 414 (p. 1019)
    Construction of fallout shelters in Government
        buildings, proposed, **1960–61:** 229
    Leasepurchase contracts, **1958:** 5 (p. 72), 70
    Paperwork reduction, **1956:** 110
    Redevelopment of Southwest Washington, **1956:**
        4n.
    RFC functions, **1957:** 78
    Surplus property management activities, **1957:**
        112n.
    Task force on procurement policies and pro-
        cedures, **1957:** 132
    Small business purchases, **1955:** 263
General Services Administrator (Franklin Floete),
    1957: 175; **1959:** 18n.
    Letters, **1960–61:** 118, 243
General Services Administrator (Edmund F.
    Mansure), **1956:** 20, 32, 113
    Chairman of Government Unit, Community
        Chest campaign, **1954:** 132
    Memorandum, **1953:** 273
Geneticists, on fallout, **1957:** 105
Geneva, **1955:** 37n., 168n., 169n.
Geneva, research reactor, **1955:** 100
    Remarks, **1955:** 165
Geneva Conference of 1954
    Foreign ministers, **1954:** 128, 225
        Indochina, **1954:** 92, 101, 165, 168
        Korea, **1954:** 92, 101, 143, 157, 178, 297
    French-Communist negotiations on Indochina
        (1954), **1954:** 63, 73, 90, 154; **1955:** 119
    General Agreement on Tariffs and Trade, Ninth
        Session, **1954:** 324
Geneva Conference of 1955, **1957:** 3, 100
    Atomic energy, **1955:** 100, 123, 149, 156, 176,
        177n., 228; **1956:** 2
    Message, **1955:** 191
    Foreign ministers, **1955:** 170, 185, 226; **1956:** 2,
        20, 23, 96, 266; **1958:** 7; **1959:** 7
    Statement re, **1955:** 227

Geneva Conference of 1955 — *continued*
    Heads of governments, **1955:** 99, 118, 126, 146,
        149, 162, 176, 190, 210, 227; **1956:** 2, 16,
        23, 52, 143, 166, 198, 251, 262, 266, 283;
        1958: 7, 74, 165, 318; **1959:** 42, 48;
        1960–61: 209
    Bipartisan meeting on, **1955:** 174
    Broadcast prior to departure, **1955:** 161
    Broadcast report on, **1955:** 175
    Closing statement, **1955:** 170
    Delegation, U.S., **1955:** 146 ftn. (p. 644)
    East-West contacts, statement, **1955:** 167
    Opening statement, **1955:** 164
    Remarks on arrival at Geneva airport, **1955:**
        163
    Remarks on departure, **1955:** 171
    Remarks on return from Geneva, **1955:** 173
    International Labor Organization, **1955:** 107, 119
    International technical conference, **1956:** 143
    U.S.-Communist China ambassadorial talks,
        1955: 176
Geneva Conference of 1956
    International Labor Organization, **1956:** 94, 121
    Trade agreement negotiations, **1956:** 94 and ftn.
        (p. 452), 123
Geneva Conference of 1958
    Controlled suspension of nuclear tests, **1958:** 311
    Peaceful uses of atomic energy, **1959:** 10 (p. 67)
        Remarks on opening U.S. exhibit, **1959:** 240
        Statement, **1958:** 188
    Prevention of surprise attack, **1958:** 310
    Technical experts on nuclear tests detection,
        1958: 67, 70, 74, 86, 103, 131, 149, 153,
        222, 288
        Agreement, **1958:** 213
        Statement on, **1958:** 219
        Letter to Premier Khrushchev, **1958:** 112
Geneva Conference of 1959
    Foreign ministers, **1959:** 29, 36, 42, 48, 57, 67 and
        ftn. (p. 292), 78, 89, 94, 102, 123 and ftn.
        (p. 425), 132, 148, 154, 161, 167, 172, 173,
        179, 192
    Nuclear test suspension, **1959:** 42, 48, 81, 89, 102,
        110, 123, 132 ftn. (p. 463), 191, 288
    Technical experts on nuclear tests detection,
        1959: 110, 132 ftn. (p. 463), 348
Geneva Conference of 1960
    Nuclear test suspension, **1960–61:** 4, 13 (p. 64),
        24, 34, 38, 101, 103, 127
        Joint declaration with Prime Minister
        Macmillan, **1960–61:** 102
    Seismic research activities, **1960–61:** 143 ftn. (p.
        410)
    Ten-Nation Disarmament Conference, **1960–61:**
        13 (p. 64), 34, 90, 92, 209, 229, 238, 255,
        302, 313

Geneva Conferences
International Labor Conferences, **1954:** 125, 126
News conference remarks, **1955:** 100, 119, 146,
149, 176, 185; **1956:** 16, 20, 94, 96, 121,
198; **1957:** 17, 80, 134; **1958:** 56, 74, 153,
213, 222, 288, 310
Genghis Khan, **1954:** 111; **1960–61:** 58
Geological Survey, **1960–61:** 414 (p. 999)
Geophysical Year.
See International Geophysical Year.
George, John M., **1959:** 30n.
George, Sen. Walter F., **1955:** 26, 59, 62, 112, 185
Bipartisan meeting on Suez Canal, **1956:** 184
Constitutional amendments on treatymaking
powers, **1954:** 25
Death of. statement, **1957:** 148
News conference remarks on, **1954:** 25, 57; **1956:**
20, 96
President's representative to North Atlantic
Community, **1956:** 97, 114
George, Mrs. Walter F., **1957:** 148
George II of England, **1954:** 39
George III of England, **1959:** 196
George Washington, U.S., **1960–61:** 255
Entrance into sea duty, statement, **1960–61:** 360
Georgescu (Valeriu C.) case, **1953:** 88
Georgetown University, **1957:** 109
Dedication of Edmund A. Walsh School of
Foreign Service, remarks, **1958:** 286
Georgia
Atlanta, **1958:** 285, 288
Augusta, **1953:** 249, 253; **1955:** 1n., 26 ftn. (p.
231), 71n. 72n., 73n., 74n.; **1956:** 80n.,
304n., 305n., 306n., 307n., 308n., 309n.,
310n.; **1957:** 17, 72, 76, 77, 80, 236, 237;
1958: 27n., 85n., 316n., 317n.; **1959:** 73n.,
74n., 76, 78, 80n., 81n., 89, 266n., 267,
268n., 271, 277, 279n., 281n., 282n., 283n.,
348n., 349n., 350n., 351n.; **1960–61:** 365,
396
Releases from **1954:** 82, 83, 185, 186, 342;
1960–61: 2, 116, 118, 119, 358–361, 363
Fort Benning, **1960–61:** 135
George, Sen. Walter F.
See main heading, George, Sen. Walter F.
Landrum, Phil M., **1959:** 172, 176, 180
Russell, Sen. Richard B., **1956:** 184; **1957:** 124,
145, 200 and n.; **1958:** 178
Thomasville, **1955:** 33; **1956:** 42n., 53; **1957:**
32n., 34; **1958:** 30n., 33n.; **1959:** 28n., 29
ftn. (p. 173)
Thomson, **1957:** 182
Vinson, Repr. Carl, **1955:** 149; **1958:** 108, 178
Georgia Institute of Technology, **1957:** 207
Gerhart, Maj. Gen. John K., **1953:** 33
Germ warfare, **1960–61:** 7
German scientists in U.S.S.R., **1957:** 210

Germantown, Md., dedication of AEC Building,
1957: 231 and n.
Germany, **1953:** 6, 50, 113, 185, 256, 265 ftn. (p.
843); **1954:** 84, 128, 154, 226, 282; **1955:**
210; **1956:** 2; **1957:** 15; **1959:** 70, 214,
243n.; **1960–61:** 23
See also Berlin; Bonn.
Adenauer, Konrad.
See main heading, Adenauer, Konrad.
Agreements on settlement of debts and claims,
1953: 46
Air safety over, Soviet-U.K. talks, **1953:** 41
Anderson-Dillon mission, **1960–61:** 362 ftn. (p.
864)
Statement, **1960–61:** 365
Assistance, **1955:** 17 (p. 124), 76
Assistance to less developed countries, **1959:**
191; **1960–61:** 362 ftn. (p. 864), 365
Atomic energy for mutual defense, U.S.-
Germany agreement
Memorandum, **1959:** 119
Message, **1959:** 120
Berlin.
See main heading, Berlin.
Bluecher, Franz, **1955:** 208n.
Bonn Conventions.
See under Bonn, Germany.
Bundestag
Action on food shortage in Soviet Zone, **1953:**
135n.
Resolution on political strikes, **1953:** 146
C-47 missing in, **1960–61:** 162
Camp David discussion with Premier
Khrushchev re, **1959:** 271
Campaign remarks, **1956:** 206, 210, 224; **1958:**
287, 290
Contractual agreement with (1952), **1954:** 172
Curtailment of State Department civilian oc-
cupation activities in, **1954:** 14 (p. 138)
Economy, **1954:** 189
Edelweiler, **1955:** 204n.
Erhard, Ludwig, **1958:** 70
Escapees and refugees from Soviet Zone, **1953:**
53, 146
Euratom.
See European Atomic Energy Community.
European Defense Community Treaty, ratifica-
tion, statement, **1954:** 66
Flood relief, **1954:** 175, 182, 195
Former German territories beyond Oder-Neisse
line, **1959:** 191
Four-power conference on, proposed, **1953:** 238,
254
Free all-German elections, question of, **1953:**
130n.
U.S. position, **1953:** 146
French-German agreement on Saar, **1954:** 307
General Aniline and Film Corporation, **1957:** 72

Germany — *continued*
  Geneva agreement on free elections (1955), **1958:** 318
  Gift to the President, **1955:** 22
  Heuss, Theodor, **1955:** 22; **1956:** 125; **1957:** 98 and n.; **1958:** 126, 127, 138; **1959:** 192, 214
  Hockey team, **1960–61:** 319n.
  Imports of agricultural products from U.S., **1960–61:** 365
  Israeli-German agreement, **1954:** 189n.
  Joint statements
    Chancellor Adenauer, **1957:** 100
    Premier Khrushchev, **1959:** 242
    Prime Minister Eden on, **1956:** 26
  Krekeler, Heinz L., **1955:** 22
  Letters to Premier Bulganin re, **1956:** 23, 166; **1958:** 7, 31
  London agreements.
  See main heading, London agreements.
  Luebke, Heinrich, **1960–61:** 91
  Military and economic growth, question re, **1959:** 167
  Military procurement, **1960–61:** 365
  NATO
    Accession to, **1954:** 332; **1956:** 2; **1958:** 287
    Membership in, **1954:** 3, 337, 351, 357; **1955:** 4, 99
    Troops, **1956:** 78
  Nazi affiliation of certain officials, question of, **1960–61:** 7
  Neutralized zone, **1957:** 80
  News conference remarks, **1953:** 41, 128, 225, 238, 243, 254; **1954:** 50, 68, 92, 101, 172, 182, 200; **1955:** 33, 41, 59, 62, 90, 112, 119; **1956:** 32, 78, 113, 121, 229; **1957:** 72, 80, 92, 105, 119, 145, 210; **1958:** 28, 318; **1959:** 7, 48, 161, 167, 173, 179, 186, 191, 271, 277; **1960–61:** 7, 24, 38, 93, 127, 143, 222
  Occupation agreements, comment on, **1959:** 57
  Paris agreements.
  See main heading, Paris agreements.
  Peace treaty with, U.S. proposal for conference on, **1959:** 67 ftn. (p. 292)
  Prisoners of war and civilian deportees held in Iron Curtain countries, question of release, **1954:** 314
  Rearming of, comment on, **1959:** 48
  Relations with Poland, **1959:** 191
  Restitution of Italian works of art, **1956:** 45n.
  Reunification, question of, **1953:** 121, 128, 130n., 146, 159, 255; **1954:** 225, 314; **1955:** 59, 112, 122, 164, 175, 190, 227; **1956:** 2, 23, 26, 87, 125, 166; **1957:** 38, 55, 100, 105, 226; **1958:** 7, 318; **1959:** 48, 191, 192, 195, 214; **1960–61:** 92, 222
    International commission on, question of, **1959:** 161

Germany — *continued*
  Scientific contributions, **1957:** 230
  Sovereignty, restoration of, question of, **1954:** 172, 307, 337, 351, 357
  Soviet treaty with, comment on, **1959:** 242
  Summit conference discussion re, question of, **1959:** 271
  Termination of occupation, protocol on, message, **1954:** 332
  Textbooks (1945), comment on, **1953:** 15
  Trade union recommendations on, **1953:** 128, 130
  U.S. Air Force transport accident, **1955:** 204
  U.S. armed forces in, **1955:** 119; **1956:** 229; **1957:** 100; **1960–61:** 362 ftn. (p. 864), 365
  Visit of President Eisenhower, **1959:** 173, 179, 186, 190, 191, 214
  Von Brentano, Heinrich, **1956:** 20; **1957:** 100; **1960–61:** 92
  War assets in United States, **1953:** 168; **1954:** 50, 251, 314; **1959:** 191
    Letter, **1954:** 189
  Weisbaden, **1960–61:** 91n.
  World War II, **1955:** 22; **1956:** 32, 113, 206
Germany, East, **1953:** 256; **1957:** 118; **1959:** 57; **1960–61:** 162
  Anti-Communist uprising, **1953:** 109, 128, 146, 159, 160
    Message to Chancellor Adenauer, **1953:** 121
  Armed forces, **1959:** 48
  Clothing, need for, U.S. assistance, **1953:** 188
  Flood relief, **1954:** 175, 182 ftn. (p. 678), 195
  Food shortage, assistance
    Letter to Mayor Ernst Reuter, **1953:** 185
    Messages to Chancellor Adenauer, **1953:** 135, 138, 188
    Refused by Soviet Union, **1953:** 134n., 138, 141
    Statement, **1953:** 134
    U.S. shipment of food to West Berlin for distribution, **1953:** 141, 159, 185, 188
  Freedom demonstration anniversary, **1956:** 125
  Letter to Premier Bulganin on, **1958:** 31
  News conference remarks, **1959:** 29, 36, 48, 53, 67, 102, 161; **1960–61:** 24, 256
  Representation at foreign ministers conference, question of, **1959:** 102
  Soviet armed forces in, **1953:** 88, 121n.
  Soviet treaty with, question of, **1959:** 67; **1960–61:** 24, 256
  Soviet troops in, **1959:** 53
  Trade union recommendations on, **1953:** 128, 130
Germany, Federal Republic of.
  See Germany.
Gettysburg, Pa., **1955:** 239n., 240n., 241n., 242n., 243n., 244n., 245n.; **1956:** 20, 136, 137, 138, 139, 140, 151, 207n., 208n., 314;

Gettysburg, Pa. — *continued*
    1957: 62, 157, 235, 250n.; **1958:** 1n., 123,
    283n.; **1959:** 1n., 65n., 68n., 117n., 179,
    180n., 182n., 225n., 241n., 242n.
    Battle (1863), **1954:** 31, 32; **1957:** 87; **1960–61:**
        370
    Campaign remarks, **1954:** 304
    Editor's note, **1955:** p. 822
    News conference and campaign remarks, **1956:**
        155, 206
    President's farm, **1955:** 127; **1956:** 314; **1957:**
        150, 157
    Primary election, President's plan to vote, **1958:**
        103
    Remarks in Lincoln Square, **1955:** 237
    Remarks at National Military Park, **1954:** 303
Gettysburg Address, anniversary, **1957:** 237
Gettysburg College, **1955:** 242n., 250n.
    Convocation address, **1959:** 71
    Presidency, rumor re, **1959:** 172
Ghana
    Accra, **1960–61:** 248
    Accra conference, **1958:** 180
    Ambassador Wilson C. Flake, **1958:** 44
    Apaloo, Lawrence K., **1958:** 23
    Forces, airlift to Congo by U.N., **1960–61:** 248
    Message to people, **1957:** 42 and n.
    Nkrumah, Kwame.
        Exchange of messages with, **1957:** 43 and n.
        Joint statement, **1958:** 180
        Letters, **1958:** 44; **1960–61:** 313
        Messages, **1960–61:** 220, 248
    U.N. membership, **1958:** 8, 148
Giardina, Susie, **1953:** 17
Gibbs, Josiah Willard, **1959:** 107
Gibraltar, **1953:** 267
Gibson, Daniel Z., **1954:** 136
Gibson, John R., **1957:** 119, 150, 169; **1958:** 56, 70,
    153, 222, 310; **1959:** 29, 67, 161, 223;
    1960–61: 34, 93, 103, 256
Gift to 4-H member by President, **1958:** 142
Gifts, acceptance by officials, **1957:** 150, 157, 228;
    1958: 74, 141
Gifts to the President, "rule of reason," **1958:** 141
Gillilland, Whitney.
    See Civil Aeronautics Board, Chairman.
Giralt, Hernan M., **1960–61:** 57n.
Girard (William S.) case, **1957:** 92, 105, 115, 134,
    150
Girl Scouts, **1957:** 203; **1959:** 156; **1960–61:** 153,
    210
Girls Nation, remarks to delegates, **1957:** 146
"Giveaway" foreign assistance programs, **1954:**
    149; **1959:** 29, 55
Glacier National Park, Mont., **1960–61:** 208
    Governors' Conference (1960), **1960–61:** 229
Gladstone, William E., **1960–61:** 276
Glaser, Kurt, immigration status, **1955:** 116

Glass, Carter, **1954:** 274, 327; **1956:** 255
Gleason, S. Everett, **1953:** 33
Glen Canyon Dam, Ariz., **1954:** 62; **1956:** 245;
    1960–61: 414 (p. 993)
    News conference and campaign remarks, **1956:**
        235, 256
Glennan, T. Keith, **1958:** 288
    See also National Aeronautics and Space Ad-
        ministrator (T. Keith Glennan).
    Letter, **1954:** 281
Glubb, Lt. Gen. John B., **1956:** 53
Gluck, Maxwell H., **1957:** 145
GNP (gross national product).
    See National product.
Golan, Samuel L., **1953:** 41
Gold, market price, **1960–61:** 341
Gold outflow, **1960–61:** 362
Gold reserves, **1959:** 271
Golden Insignia of the Pan American Society,
    remarks on acceptance, **1957:** 64 and n.
Goldfine, Bernard, **1958:** 141, 153, 198
Goldstone, Calif., **1960–61:** 258n.
Goldwater, Senator Barry, **1957:** 70; **1959:** 127
    Amendment to Taft-Hartley Act, proposed,
        1954: 101
    News conference remarks, **1956:** 235
Golf, **1956:** 155, 193; **1958:** 140n.
    British Open, **1953:** 140n.
    News conference remarks, **1958:** 11, 198, 288
    World amateur golf team championship confer-
        ence, remarks, **1958:** 91
Gomez, Carmen Vda de, **1960–61:** 224
Gomez, Soledad, **1960–61:** 224
Gompers, Samuel, **1956:** 283
    Pledge to Woodrow Wilson, **1955:** 84
Gomulka, Wladyslaw, **1957:** 62
Gonzales, Donald J., **1955:** 90, 176; **1957:** 45, 50,
    62, 115, 210, 228; **1958:** 63
Good Friday, observance, letters, **1956:** 68; **1957:**
    70
Goodpaster, Brig. Gen. Andrew J., **1959:** 145;
    1960–61: 425, 426, 427, 428, 429
    Medal of Freedom, citation, **1960–61:** 430
Goodrich, Lloyd, **1959:** 148 ftn. (p. 490)
Goonetilleke, Oliver E., message, **1959:** 241
Gore, Sen. Albert, letter, **1959:** 252
Gossett, John H., mining claim, disapproval, **1956:**
    179
Goulart, Joao, **1960–61:** 49n.
Government, U.S., **1959:** 21
    Comment on, **1960–61:** 174
    Improvement in operations and management,
        1956: 22, 226
        See also Hoover Commission, recommenda-
            tions.
    Military control of, **1959:** 29
Government Activities Affecting Prices and Costs,
    Committee on, establishment, statement,
    1959: 18

Government buildings, **1956:** 12 (pp. 150, 151, 152)
Government capital
  Cooperative banks, retirement, **1956:** 12 (p. 131)
  Federal intermediate credit banks, retirement, **1956:** 147
Government Contract Compliance, Committee on, **1953:** 41, 54, 88
Government Contracts, President's Committee on, **1960–61:** 410
  Budget message, **1960–61:** 414 (p. 1023)
  Report, statement, **1960–61:** 407
Government Corporations Control Act, proposed amendment, **1957:** 13; **1958:** 5 (p. 44)
Government employees, **1953:** 187; **1956:** 238; **1960–61:** 410
  Accident compensation, **1958:** 5 (p. 72)
  Administrative posts, filling of, **1956:** 94; **1957:** 145; **1959:** 36
  Awards for distinguished Federal civilian service, **1958:** 13; **1959:** 9; **1960–61:** 68, 389
  Benefits (pay, insurance, awards), **1956:** 2
  Bill for salary increase, **1957:** 185
  Budget messages, **1960–61:** 13 (pp. 101–104), 414 (pp. 938, 1019, 1020)
  Career executive development program, **1960–61:** 26, 27, 28
  Civil service standards, improvement, **1954:** 14 (p. 188)
  Civil service status, **1954:** 313
  Classification Act amendments, approval, **1954:** 234
  Conduct of, investigations, **1954:** 92, 311
    Federal Housing Administration, **1954:** 302
    Treasury Department, **1954:** 353
  Disability compensation, **1955:** 4, 17 (p. 106)
  Employment by defense contractors, **1959:** 132
  Equality of job opportunity, **1960–61:** 410
  Group life insurance, **1954:** 43, 116, 182, 273, 313; **1955:** 8
    Approval of bill, **1954:** 202
  Health insurance, **1954:** 137, 234; **1955:** 4; **1958:** 5 (p. 71); **1960–61:** 13 (p. 103), 410, 414 (p. 1019)
  Honorable discharges, question of, **1954:** 18, 25, 107
  Hoover Commission recommendations, letter, **1956:** 22
  Incentive awards, **1954:** 14 (p. 188); **1955:** 1
  Income taxes, exemptions, **1954:** 313
  Leave accumulated by officials of preceding administration, **1953:** 37
  Loyalty, **1953:** 69
  Merit system, **1953:** 32; **1954:** 107
  Motor vehicle operators, defense of suits against, **1960–61:** 180
  News conference remarks on, **1953:** 31, 37, 249, 254, 265; **1954:** 9, 18, 25, 39, 48, 92, 107, 182, 311, 341, 347, 353; **1957:** 62, 145; **1960–61:** 284, 362

Government employees — *continued*
  Occupational safety, memorandum, **1954:** 288
  Old-age and survivors insurance, **1955:** 4
  Overseas personnel, **1953:** 89, 92; **1955:** 8
  Partisan political activities, **1954:** 206
  Pay, **1954:** 43, 313, 349; **1955:** 4, 8, 59; **1958:** 5 (pp. 25, 71), 120, 169; **1960–61:** 13 (pp. 103, 104), 255, 414 (pp. 938, 1020)
    Disapproval of bill, **1954:** 208
    Proposed commission on, **1959:** 10 (pp. 108, 109)
    Scientists and technicians, **1958:** 64
    Veto of bill, **1960–61:** 217
  Payroll savings plan, **1955:** 186, 187
  Personnel program, statement, **1954:** 43
  Postal employees.
    See main heading, Postal employees.
  Privileged information re, **1960–61:** 380
  Recruitment, **1954:** 311
  Reduction, **1953:** 12 ftn. (p. 53), 101, 159; **1954:** 273, 286, 291, 316; **1960–61:** 410
    Overseas, **1960–61:** 362, 434
  Retirement, **1954:** 14 (p. 189), 43; **1955:** 4, 17 (pp. 96, 106, 145, 181, 182); **1956:** 12 (pp. 150, 152); **1958:** 5 (pp. 51, 52); **1960–61:** 13 (pp. 101–103), 410, 414 (p. 1020)
  Security program, **1953:** 6, 95, 101, 249, 254, 265; **1954:** 3, 9, 18, 25, 209, 273, 311, 341, 347; **1955:** 10; **1956:** 12 (p. 153), 96, 113; **1960–61:** 284
    Hatkin case, **1956:** 96
  Testimony in Congressional investigations, **1956:** 216
  Training, **1955:** 8; **1957:** 112; **1958:** 5 (p. 71); **1960–61:** 149
  Travel allowances, **1955:** 8
  Unemployment insurance, **1954:** 14 (pp. 182, 188), 313; **1955:** 17 (p. 182); **1956:** 12 (p. 152); **1960–61:** 414 (p. 1019)
  Uniforms, allowances for, **1954:** 313
  Wage rates, **1960–61:** 230
  Working conditions, **1956:** 12 (pp. 151, 152)
Government Employees Training Act, **1960–61:** 149
Government employment, **1956:** 2, 94, 226; **1957:** 13, 62; **1958:** 96
  Campaign remarks, **1958:** 292, 296, 308
  Security program, **1955:** 18, 41, 81, 146
Government Employment Policy, President's Committee on, **1960–61:** 410
  Report, **1960–61:** 217 ftn. (p. 545), 394
Government expenditures, reduction, **1954:** 316, 318; **1956:** 12 (pp. 154, 155)
Government officials
  Code of ethics, **1956:** 117
  Conduct of, **1955:** 176; **1958:** 49
    CAB code of ethics, **1958:** 74
    News conference remarks, **1958:** 141, 198
    President quoted, **1958:** 198

Government officials — *continued*
  Contacting of, **1956:** 94
  Violations of law, **1956:** 32
Government operations, reports, **1960–61:** 435
Government Operations, Advisory Committee on, **1955:** 74
Government Organization, President's Advisory Committee on, **1953:** 6; **1954:** 163, 348; **1960–61:** 349
  News conference remarks on, **1953:** 37, 62
  Report, letter, **1960–61:** 433
Government property, management, **1954:** 14 (pp. 187, 188)
Government reorganization, proposed, **1960–61:** 143
Government Reorganization Act, extension proposed, **1953:** 6
Governmental responsibility, division of, **1955:** 4
Governors
  Committee on refugees, proposed, **1954:** 187, 188
  Conference on dust storms, **1954:** 85, 92, 99
  Conference on Federal-State relations, **1953:** 15, 16n.
  Conference on highway safety, **1953:** 261
  Letters, **1953:** 47, 261; **1954:** 55, 187, 268; **1955:** 29; **1960–61:** 116
  Meeting on drought relief, **1953:** 216, 225
  Power Policy Committee, **1954:** 271
  Telegram, **1954:** 85
  United Defense Fund, **1954:** 55
  Visit to Korea, **1954:** 35, 164
  Wartime power to appoint Representatives, proposed, **1960–61:** 24
  White House conference, **1953:** 47
    Remarks, **1953:** 64, 67
  White House meeting on civil defense, **1960–61:** 229
Governors' Committee, Southern, **1957:** 205, 207
Governors Conference, Chairman, Gov. Arthur B. Langlie, letter, **1956:** 31
Governors' conferences
  1953, Seattle, Wash., **1953:** 77
    Remarks, **1953:** 156
  1954, Lake George, N. Y., **1954:** 35, 143; **1955:** 4, 39, 90; **1960–61:** 330
    Message, **1954:** 164
  1955, New England, **1955:** 222, 223
  1955, Washington, D. C., **1955:** 90
    Remarks, **1955:** 88
  1956, Atlantic City, N. J., Committee on Highway Safety, report of, **1957:** 14 and n.
  1957, Williamsburg, Va., **1957:** 115, 119, 124; **1958:** 5 (p. 42), 106; **1960–61:** 115n.
    Address, **1957:** 118 and n.
    Joint Federal-State Action Committee, **1957:** 138
  1958, Miami, **1958:** 120

Governors' conferences — *continued*
  1959, San Juan, P.R., **1960–61:** 229
    Committee on civil defense, **1959:** 277
    Message, **1959:** 174
  1960, Glacier National Park, Mont., **1960–61:** 229
    Remarks recorded for, **1960–61:** 208
Grady, Paul, **1954:** 12n.
Graham, John S., **1957:** 145
Graham, Rev. William F. (Billy), **1956:** 62; **1960–61:** 268, 354
Grainger, Jacqueline, **1960–61:** 178n.
Grains, price supports, **1953:** 225
Grand Canyon, aircraft collision, **1958:** 135
Grand Coulee Dam, **1960–61:** 419
Grand Junction, Colo., remarks at airport, **1954:** 256
Grand Lodge of North Dakota, relief of, veto, **1960–61:** 181
Grand Teton National Park, taxation of certain property, disapproval, **1954:** 222
Grandchildren, the President's, **1953:** 253; **1954:** 151, 305; **1958:** 295, 302, 320; **1959:** 243, 259, 292, 334; **1960–61:** 199, 213, 239, 355, 422
  Letter to grandson on national debt, **1959:** 274
  Vaccination against polio, **1955:** 113
Grant, Maj. Gen. U.S., 3d, letter to, **1958:** 14
Granville, France, **1954:** 131
Graphic Arts Corp. of Ohio, relief of, disapproval, **1954:** 232
Graves, William, **1955:** 119
Gray, Gordon, **1953:** 2n.; **1959:** 76; **1960–61:** 9, 94
  See also Defense Mobilization, Director, Office of.
  Bipartisan meeting on Suez Canal, **1956:** 184
  Designation as Chairman, Operations Coordinating Board, letter, **1960–61:** 8
  Medal of Freedom, citation, **1960–61:** 427
  Resignation, letter, **1960–61:** 412
  Special Assistant for National Security Affairs, letter, **1958:** 147
Gray, Ralph L., **1959:** 211n.
Graybiel, Lloyd E., **1960–61:** 332
Grazing of cattle in drought areas, **1957:** 50
Grazing on soil bank reserves, **1956:** 236
Great Books program, St. John's College, **1959:** 116
Great Britain.
  See United Kingdom.
Great Lakes, **1954:** 14 (p. 176), 253; **1956:** 224; **1959:** 141
  Water diversion, disapproval, **1956:** 177
Great Lakes Steel Corporation, **1959:** 211n.
  Agricultural Council, **1956:** 6, 7, 169; **1957:** 11, 12
  Conservation program, **1960–61:** 13 (p. 82), 414 (p. 992)
  Drought disaster in, **1957:** 11, 12, 41

Great Plains Program, **1956:** 2, 6, 7
  Agricultural Act of 1956, **1956:** 115
  Campaign remarks, **1956:** 190, 211, 214, 256
  Conservation program, approval, **1956:** 169
Greece, **1953:** 234; **1955:** 4; **1958:** 173, 207, 295;
    1960–61: 302
  See also Athens.
  Ambassador Ellis O. Briggs, **1959:** 324n., 327
  American Mission for Aid to, **1954:** 80
  Ancient civilization, **1960–61:** 328
  Armed forces in Korea, **1960–61:** 202
  Assistance, **1953:** 66, 233n.; **1955:** 76; **1957:** 6,
    90, 91, 152, 169; **1958:** 36; **1959:** 55;
    1960–61: 132, 133
  Atomic energy for mutual defense, U.S.-Greece
    agreement, **1959:** 119n., 120n.
  Averoff-Tossizza, Evanghelos, **1959:** 40
  Communist aggression in, **1953:** 66, 233n.
  Cyprus agreement, **1959:** 39, 40, 41
  Earthquake disaster, **1953:** 172
    Message, **1956:** 140
    Red Cross services, statement, **1953:** 173
  Immigration quota, **1956:** 2, 33
  Kanellopoulos, Panayiotis, **1959:** 327
  Karamanlis, Constantine, **1959:** 40, 324n., 325
    Joint statement with, **1959:** 327
  News conference remarks, **1956:** 78
  Participation in Korean War, **1959:** 325
  Paul I, **1953:** 230, 232, 233; **1956:** 140; **1959:** 324,
    326, 327
    Messages, **1953:** 172; **1957:** 48
  Prince Constantine, **1959:** 324n.
  Queen Frederika, **1953:** 230, 232, 233; **1959:** 327
  Rodopoulos, Constantine, **1959:** 325
  Theoklitos, Archbishop, **1959:** 325
  Tsatsos, Constantine, **1959:** 327
  Visit to, **1959:** 277, 324, 325, 326, 327
Greek shipowners, discussions with congressional
    committee on trade embargo with Com-
    munist bloc, **1953:** 41
Green, Glenn M., Jr., **1953:** 141
Green, Sterling F., **1953:** 62; **1959:** 26, 172, 173;
    1960–61: 422
Green, Senator Theodore F., **1957:** 176 and n.
  Bipartisan meeting on Suez Canal, **1956:** 184
  Letter, **1958:** 277
Green Peter-White Bridge project, Oreg., **1955:** 17
    (p. 158); **1956:** 12 (p. 136)
Greene, Charles J., Jr., **1954:** 63
Greene, Richard L. and Rose, mining claim, dis-
    approval, **1956:** 179
Greene, William A., letter, **1956:** 66
Greenewalt, Crawford, **1960–61:** 30n.
Greenland, U.S.-Denmark defense alliance, **1960–**
    61: 321n.
Greenland Sea, **1958:** 201
Greenwich, Conn., **1956:** 289
Gregg, Mrs. Frank C., estate, tax relief, **1958:** 237

Gregg, Gov. Hugh, **1953:** 187
Gregory, Nicolas P., **1954:** 165, 168
Greiner-Mattern, Associates, **1958:** 9n.
Grenada Reservoir project, Miss., mineral interests,
    1956: 154
Griffin, Charles, **1955:** 133n.
Griffin, Maj. Gen. Martin E., **1955:** 235
Griffin, Repr. Robert P., labor bill, **1959:** 172, 176,
    180
Griffin-Landrum Act, **1960–61:** 316
Griswold, Sen. Dwight P., death of, statement,
    1954: 80
Groat, Richard, **1960–61:** 353
Gromyko, Andrei A., **1957:** 92; **1958:** 152; **1959:**
    123 ftn. (p. 425), 148, 218, 242; **1960–61:**
    143
  News conference remarks on, **1958:** 28, 63, 83, 88
Gronchi, Giovanni, **1955:** 208n.; **1956:** 47; **1959:**
    291, 294; **1960–61:** 34
  Joint statements with, **1956:** 46, 49; **1959:** 293
  Messages to, **1956:** 39, 264
  Presentation of gift, **1956:** 45
Gross national product.
  See National product.
Gross, Robert E., **1956:** 257
Grosvenor, Melville B., **1957:** 221n.
Ground-to-air missiles, **1957:** 230
Ground-to-ground missiles, **1957:** 210
Ground inspection of key points.
  See Disarmament.
Ground Observer Corps, **1954:** 161; **1955:** 154
Group Life Insurance Act, **1955:** 4
Gruber, Dr. Karl, **1957:** 204n.
Gruening, Sen. Ernest, **1959:** 3n.
Gruenther, Gen. Alfred M., **1957:** 89 and n.; **1958:**
    144; **1960–61:** 30n., 175, 405
  Distinguished Service Medal, citation, **1956:** 317
  Lafayette Gold Medal Award, **1958:** 118
  Letter, **1960–61:** 214
  News conference remarks on, **1956:** 94, 171
  Nomination as Supreme Allied Commander,
    Europe, **1953:** 71, 74
    Letter, **1953:** 75
Gruhl, Helen M., **1953:** 108
Gruhl, Helmuth W., relief of, veto, **1953:** 108
Gruhl, Werner, **1953:** 108
Guam, **1954:** 125, 126; **1960–61:** 13 (p. 104), 414 (p.
    1021)
  Congressional representation, proposed, **1960–**
    61: 133
Guantanamo naval base, Cuba, **1960–61:** 228,
    388n.
  Statement, **1960–61:** 342
Guaranteed wage, **1955:** 119
Guatemala, **1955:** 18; **1957:** 91; **1958:** 80; **1960–61:**
    410
  Assistance, **1955:** 17 (p. 129), 76; **1957:** 90
  Castillo Armas, Carlos, **1955:** 230
    Death of, **1957:** 143, 145

Guatemala — *continued*
  Communist intervention in, **1954:** 115, 143, 157,
    203, 209, 225, 226, 273, 286, 297, 304, 316,
    317, 319, 320, 325
  News conference remarks, **1954:** 115, 143, 157,
    192; **1956:** 198, 210, 224, 283
  U.S. Ambassador John E. Peurifoy, **1954:** 192
  U.S. naval assistance, message to President
    Ydigoras Fuentes, **1960–61:** 368
  U.S. position in U.N. Security Council, **1955:**
    156
Gubser, Charles S., **1954:** 161; **1958:** 294
Guided missiles.
  See Missiles.
Guido, Jose Maria, **1960–61:** 58n.
Guinea, Republic of, Sekou Toure, **1959:** 269, 272
  Messages, **1958:** 309; **1960–61:** 364
Guirma, Frederic, **1960–61:** 324n.
Guizado, Jose Ramon, **1955:** 2
Gulf of Aqaba, **1957:** 34, 35
  Joint statement with Prime Minister Macmillan,
    1957: 55
  News conference remarks, **1957:** 45, 56, 62, 72,
    87
  U.S. shipping in, **1957:** 72
Gulf of Mexico, **1956:** 245
Gundersen, Dr. Gunnar, **1959:** 129
Gurney, Chan, letter, **1953:** 30
Gursel, Gen. Cemal, message, **1960–61:** 399
Guyer, Stanley H., **1958:** 296n.

H-bomb.
  See Hydrogen bomb.
Haakon VII
  50th anniversary of reign, letter, **1955:** 241
  Message on death of, **1957:** 192
Habomai Islands, **1954:** 328, 345
Hadley, Arthur T., **1953:** 37, 54, 109
Hadnot, Mr. and Mrs. John R., relief of, **1958:** 238
Hagerty, James C., **1953:** 12, 15, 22, 31, 36, 37, 41,
    54, 62, 77, 88, 109, 126, 128, 141, 198, 208,
    225, 230, 238, 243, 249, 254 and ftn. (p.
    800), 265; **1954:** 9, 18, 25, 33, 39, 48, 50,
    57, 63, 68, 73, 92, 101, 107, 115, 129, 138,
    143, 157, 161, 165, 168, 172, 182, 192, 200,
    311, 322, 328, 341, 345, 347, 353; **1955:** 10,
    18, 26, 33, 41, 47, 56, 59, 62, 81, 90, 95,
    100, 112, 119, 146 and ftn. (p. 644), 149,
    176, 185; **1956:** 5, 16, 20, 32, 47, 53, 56, 62,
    78, 88, 94, 96, 121, 155, 171, 189, 193, 198,
    205, 216, 229, 235, 241, 298; **1957:** 17, 22,
    28, 45, 50, 56, 62, 63, 70, 72n., 80, 87, 105,
    115, 119, 124, 134, 145, 150, 152, 157, 169,
    207, 210, 228; **1958:** 11, 28, 37, 42, 56, 63,
    70, 74, 83, 88, 103, 120, 141, 153, 198, 213,
    222, 274, 288, 310, 318; **1959:** 7, 17, 21, 26,

Hagerty, James C. — *continued*
    29, 36, 42, 48, 53, 67, 78, 89, 94, 102, 123,
    132, 148, 154, 161, 167, 171n., 172, 173,
    179, 186, 191, 223, 243, 267, 271, 277, 288;
    1960–61: 7, 21, 24, 34, 38, 93, 103, 127,
    143, 155n., 163n., 217n., 222, 228 and ftn.
    (p. 569), 231n., 256, 263, 268 and ftn. (p.
    648), 284 and ftn. (p. 682), 360n., 362,
    388n., 422
  Editor's note, **1955:** p. 822
  Role of, **1956:** 198
Hague Peace Conference, second, **1957:** 111
Haile Selassie I, **1954:** 129; **1957:** 50
  Exchange of toasts, **1954:** 124
  25th anniversary of reign, message, **1955:** 231
Haiti
  Hurricane, **1954:** 289
  Magloire, Paul E., message, **1954:** 289; **1955:** 23
  U.S. Ambassador Roy T. Davis, **1954:** 289
Hall, Rear Adm. G. B. H., **1954:** 289n.
Hall, George H., **1953:** 37; **1955:** 33, 100
Hall, Adm. John L., Jr., **1956:** 57n.
Hall, Leonard W., **1953:** 41; **1955:** 47, 247; **1956:**
    18, 206n., 209n., 290, 294n.; **1958:** 153
  See also Republican National Committee, Chair-
    man (Leonard W. Hall).
  News conference remarks on, **1956:** 62, 121;
    1957: 17, 45, 50, 56
  President's representative to Brussels Exhibition,
    1958: 79
  Resignation as chairman of Republican National
    Committee, **1957:** 9
Hall, Robert, **1955:** 47
Hall, Mr. and Mrs. Robert B., tax refund claim,
    disapproval, **1958:** 253
Halleck, Repr. Charles A., **1954:** 274; **1959:** 148,
    151n.; **1960–61:** 88, 263
  Bipartisan meeting on Suez Canal, **1956:** 184
  Election as House minority leader, statement,
    1959: 4
  Letters, **1959:** 34; **1960–61:** 272
Halloween, comment re, **1954:** 305
Halvorson, Alf, **1955:** 139
Hamil, David A.
  See Rural Electrification Administrator.
Hamilton, Alexander, **1960–61:** 34, 309
Hamilton, Eleanor, **1953:** 54
Hamilton, Wilbur H., **1956:** 283n.
Hamlet, Castle of, **1960–61:** 321
Hammarskjold, Dag.
  See United Nations, Secretary General (Dag
    Hammarskjold).
Hammett, Dashiell, **1953:** 126
Hancock, John, **1960–61:** 171n.
Hand, Learned, **1960–61:** 30n.
Handicapped persons, **1953:** 268; **1956:** 21, 226;
    1958: 99
  Deaf and blind, education, **1954:** 14 (p. 153)

Handicapped persons — *continued*
　Lake, Mrs. Louise, award, **1958:** 99
　President's Committee on Employment of the
　　Physically Handicapped, remarks, **1955:**
　　103; **1958:** 99
　Rehabilitation, **1954:** 3, 14 (p. 142), 139, 301
Hanford (Calif.) atomic energy facility, **1954:** 14 (p.
　128)
Hanley, Edward J., **1959:** 211n.
Hanna, Mrs. Frank S., **1958:** 94n.
Hannah, John A., **1959:** 128n.
Hannibal, **1958:** 93; **1959:** 124; **1960–61:** 304
Hanoi, North Vietnam, **1960–61:** 338
Hanover, N.H., **1953:** 104; **1958:** 138n.
Hansen, H.C., death of, **1960–61:** 41
Hanzal, Alfred, tax refund claim, veto, **1958:** 34
Harbor workers, safety code, **1959:** 10 (p. 101)
Hard work, news conference remarks, **1956:** 5
Harding, Warren G., **1953:** 28; **1954:** 115; **1955:** 18
Harding, William Barclay, **1956:** 38n.
Hardy, Royce A., **1959:** 18n.
Harger, Charles M., **1954:** 331
Harkness, Richard, **1953:** 12, 54, 62; **1954:** 39, 48,
　57, 63; **1955:** 146; **1956:** 78; **1958:** 120;
　1959: 161
Harlan, John M., nomination to U.S. Supreme
　　Court, **1954:** 341
　Comment on, **1955:** 26
Harlow, James G., **1957:** 234 and n.
Harmon, Lt. Gen. Hubert R., **1959:** 109
Harper, James Thomas, **1957:** 123
Harper, Mrs. Samuel, **1956:** 241
Harr, Karl G., Jr., letter, **1960–61:** 9
Harriman, E. Roland, **1953:** 117; **1955:** 208, 209;
　　1956: 47, 304n.; **1957:** 89 and n.
　Letter, **1953:** 3
Harriman, W. Averell, **1954:** 322, 347; **1955:** 90;
　　1960–61: 86
　Interview with Premier Khrushchev, **1959:** 154
　News conference remarks on, **1959:** 154, 161
　Recognition of East Germany, **1959:** 161
　Telegram to, **1958:** 33
Harris, Maj. Gen. Hugh P., **1960–61:** 135
Harris, John P., **1960–61:** 118n.
Harris, Lou, **1959:** 267
Harris, Repr. Oren, **1957:** 72, 115; **1959:** 37
Harris-Fulbright natural gas bill, **1957:** 13
Harry, Ralston E., medical care claim, veto, **1954:**
　159
Harsch, Joseph G., **1953:** 254; **1954:** 63, 73, 92, 138,
　　311, 345, 353; **1955:** 10, 33, 47, 59, 62
Hart, Howard, **1954:** 229
Hartford, Conn., **1954:** 295, 296; **1956:** 293
　Remarks on flood disaster, **1955:** 209
Hartmann, Robert T., **1957:** 17
Hartwell, John, **1956:** 250
Harvard University, **1954:** 129; **1956:** 201n.; **1958:**
　194n.

Hassan, Prince Moulay, **1959:** 343n.
Hassett, Thomas E., **1960–61:** 340n.
Hat bodies, trade concession, **1956:** 123
Hatch Act, **1954:** 206
Hatcher, Robert V., **1956:** 280
Hate mongering, **1958:** 288
Hatkin, Sidney, **1956:** 96
Hatoyama, Ichiro, message to, **1956:** 313
Hauck, Arthur A., **1959:** 222
Hauge, Gabriel, **1957:** 134; **1960–61:** 336
Haun, Cale P. and Julia Fay, tax relief, veto, **1958:**
　48
Havana, Cuba, **1953:** 260; **1960–61:** 388
Havens, Shirley Jean, **1960–61:** 23
Hawaii, **1954:** 125, 126; **1960–61:** 42, 80, 261n.
　Air carriers, West Coast-Hawaii Case, **1955:** 30,
　　33
　Aliens from, **1956:** 33; **1957:** 25
　East-West Cultural Center, **1960–61:** 205, 206,
　　414 (p. 969)
　Election in, comment on, **1959:** 172
　Fong, Sen. Hiram, **1959:** 184n.
　Honolulu, **1954:** 130; **1960–61:** 205, 206
　Inouye, Repr. Daniel K., **1959:** 184n.
　Long, Sen. Oren E., **1959:** 184n.
　News conference remarks, **1955:** 33, 56, 95
　Quinn, Gov. William F., **1959:** 184n.; **1960–61:**
　　205, 206
　Statehood, **1953:** 6, 15, 77, 268; **1954:** 3, 33, 50,
　　73, 161, 349; **1955:** 4, 56, 95, 247; **1956:** 2,
　　205; **1957:** 13; **1958:** 159; **1959:** 10 (p.
　　109), 53, 174, 225, 311; **1960–61:** 4, 13 (p.
　　104), 205, 206, 402, 410
　　Approval of act, **1959:** 60
　　Budget message, **1958:** 5 (p. 73)
　　Ceremony on admission, remarks, **1959:** 184
　　Letter to Gov. Quinn, **1959:** 61
　　Letter to Maurice H. Stans, **1959:** 62
　　News conference remarks, **1958:** 28, 42
　Sugar quotas, **1960–61:** 167n.
　Visit to, **1960–61:** 177, 205, 206
Hawaii Statehood Commission, **1959:** 184n.
Hawesville, Ky., **1956:** 182
Hawley, Paul R., **1955:** 51n.
Hay for drought disaster areas, **1956:** 236, 237
Hayden, Jay G., **1953:** 198; **1954:** 192; **1955:** 47, 90
Hayden, Martin S., **1953:** 54, 88, 208, 238; **1954:** 57,
　　341, 347; **1955:** 18, 90, 100, 112, 146;
　　1956: 20, 32, 198, 205, 216; **1957:** 28, 45,
　　62, 124, 150
Hayes, Albert J., **1957:** 57n.
Hays, Repr. Brooks, **1957:** 210
Hazza al-Majali, death of, **1960–61:** 277
Heads of state and governments, joint statements
　　with.
　See Joint statements with heads of state and
　　governments.

Heads of state and governments, meetings.
  See also Messages to heads of state and governments.
  American Republics, question of, **1960–61:** 268
  Bermuda meeting
    See main heading Bermuda Meeting of Western leaders.
  Congressional delegation, question of, comments on, **1955:** 59, 95, 112
  East-West summit, question of, **1953:** 54, 77, 88, 208, 230; **1954:** 50, 311, 341; **1959:** 29, 42, 48, 57, 67, 89, 94, 102, 123, 132, 148, 161, 167, 179, 191, 196, 214, 243, 267, 271, 277
    Joint statement with President de Gaulle, **1959:** 202
    Joint statement with King Mohammad Zahir, **1959:** 308
    Joint statement with Western leaders, **1959:** 336
    Letters to Premier Khrushchev on, **1959:** 337, 349
    United States, comment on, **1959:** 67, 102
  Geneva (1955), **1956:** 2, 16, 23, 52, 143, 166, 198, 251, 262, 266, 283; **1958:** 7, 74, 165, 318; **1959:** 42, 48; **1960–61:** 209
    See also Geneva conferences.
  Joint statement with Chancellor Adenauer on, **1955:** 122
  Joint statement with Prime Minister Fanfani, **1958:** 186
  Letters to
    Premier Bulganin, **1958:** 7, 31
    Premier Khrushchev, **1958:** 152, 177
    President Kubitschek, **1958:** 181
  News conference remarks, **1955:** 59, 62, 81, 95, 100, 112, 119, 146, 149; **1956:** 298; **1958:** 11, 28, 42, 56, 63, 70, 74, 83, 141, 198, 213
  Panama meeting of American Presidents, **1956:** 96, 121, 145, 146, 155, 272, 278
  Paris (1951), **1955:** 59
  Paris (1952), **1955:** 62
  Paris meeting of Western leaders (1959), **1959:** 332n., 335, 336, 337
    Comment on, **1959:** 267, 271, 277
  Paris (1960).
    See Paris summit meeting.
  Preparatory discussions for, **1958:** 28, 36, 42
  United Nations, on Near East situation, **1958:** 196, 198
  United States, United Kingdom, France, proposed, **1956:** 298
  Usefulness, comment on, **1960–61:** 209
  Washington, comment on, **1958:** 42
  Yalta (1945), **1954:** 345
Heads of state and governments, messages to.
  See Messages to heads of state and governments.
Heads of state and governments, visits.
  See Visitors, foreign.

Health, Education, and Welfare, Department of, **1953:** 101, 159; **1954:** 11, 127, 301; **1955:** 4, 25, 81; **1956:** 6, 13; **1958:** 2, 109; **1959:** 55; **1960–61:** 23, 235, 349, 358, 410, 433
  Advisory committee on education, proposed, **1954:** 14, (p. 154)
  Appropriation, **1959:** 181
  Assistance to States on desegregation programs, **1959:** 27
  Budget messages, **1954:** 14 (pp. 143, 154); **1958:** 5 (pp. 46–49); **1959:** 10 (pp. 86, 99, 101); **1960–61:** 13 (pp. 75, 87, 93, 94, 109), 414 (pp. 944, 982, 992, 996, 1011, 1017)
  Campaign remarks, **1956:** 224, 256; **1958:** 292, 296, 308
  Committee on education, proposed, **1953:** 28
  Education programs, proposed, **1958:** 24
  Establishment under Reorganization Plan 1, **1953:** 28
  Expenditures, **1957:** 13
  Medical care program for older persons, **1960–61:** 133
  News conference remarks, **1956:** 229
  Rural development program, **1957:** 156
  Social security, extension of coverage, study, **1953:** 155
Health, Education, and Welfare, Secretary of (Arthur S. Flemming), **1958:** 97, 195; **1959:** 68n.; **1960–61:** 44, 398
  Federal Radiation Council, Chairman, **1960–61:** 268 ftn. (p. 654)
  Letters, **1959:** 49, 280
  Reports, **1960–61:** 413, 433
  Resignation, letter, **1960–61:** 413
  Study on medical research and training, **1959:** 10 (p. 102)
  Study of public assistance programs, **1959:** 10 (p. 103)
Health, Education, and Welfare, Secretary of (Marion B. Folsom), **1956:** 6; **1957:** 68, 138
  Federal Council on Aging, **1956:** 74
  Health insurance plans, **1956:** 12 (p. 120)
  Letter on White House conference, **1959:** 119
  Meeting on legislation, **1956:** 318
  Military dependents medical care regulations, joint, **1956:** 244
  News conference remarks on, **1956:** 121, 155
  Older persons problems, **1956:** 63
  Report on Salk vaccine, **1956:** 303n.
  Resignation, **1958:** 97
  Sewage treatment, criteria for grants, **1956:** 137
  United Community Campaigns, chairman, **1957:** 154
  "Your Government and You" broadcast, **1956:** 246

Health, Education, and Welfare, Secretary of
(Oveta Culp Hobby), **1953:** 57, 265, 266,
268; **1954:** 127, 268, 307, 349; **1955:** 77n.,
78, 79, 96
See also Federal Security Administrator.
Appraisal by the President, **1955:** 100
Broadcast with the President, **1953:** 95
Budget message, **1955:** 17 (pp. 141, 144, 145)
Indian health services, **1955:** 17 (pp. 144, 145)
Letter, **1954:** 343
News conference remarks on, **1954:** 73, 182;
1955: 18, 100, 112, 119
Poliomyelitis vaccine program, **1955:** 113
Resignation
Comment on rumor of, **1955:** 100, 112
Letter, **1955:** 152
Remarks, **1955:** 153
Social security, extension of coverage, recom-
mendations, **1953:** 155
Health, Education, and Welfare, Under Secretary
of (Herold C. Hunt), rural development
committee, **1956:** 217n.
Health, Education, and Welfare, Under Secretary
of (Nelson A. Rockefeller), **1953:** 269
Health, National Institutes of, **1954:** 301; **1955:** 17
(p. 143)
Funds for, **1956:** 21
Health, welfare, and pension funds.
See Welfare and pension plans and funds.
Health agencies, fund-raising campaign, **1957:** 18
Health hazards from radioactive fallout.
See also Radioactive fallout.
Exchange of messages with Prime Minister
Kishi, **1957:** 208
Joint statement with Prime Minister Macmillan,
1957: 55
News conference remarks, **1957:** 105, 124
Health insurance, **1954:** 11, 209, 301; **1955:** 4;
1956: 2, 3, 19
Budget messages, **1954:** 14 (p. 143); **1955:** 17 (p.
143); **1956:** 12 (p. 119); **1960–61:** 13 (pp.
93, 103), 414 (p. 1019)
Extension of coverage, **1956:** 21
Government employees.
See under main heading, Government employ-
ees.
News conference remarks, **1954:** 25, 165; **1960–
61:** 103, 127
Plans, voluntary, **1957:** 13, 16
Re-insurance program, proposal, **1954:** 25; **1955:**
25
Health Organization, World, **1958:** 207; **1959:** 188;
1960–61: 279
Health problems, cooperation with Mexico, **1959:**
257
Health program, **1954:** 3, 180, 209, 349; **1955:** 25,
247; **1956:** 2; **1959:** 6, 181; **1960–61:** 410

Health program — *continued*
Budget messages, **1955:** 17 (pp. 94, 140–148);
1960–61: 13 (pp. 87, 93, 94), 414 (pp. 938,
939, 1006–1009)
Table, **1955:** 17 (p. 142)
Campaign remarks, **1956:** 234
Indians, **1955:** 17 (pp. 144, 145)
International, **1959:** 55
Message to Congress, **1954:** 11
New York State, **1954:** 301
Health research and facilities, **1956:** 151; **1957:** 13,
16, 22; **1959:** 10 (pp. 45, 46)
Health Resources Advisory Committee, **1953:** 15
ftn. (p. 59)
Health services, public, **1956:** 21, 161, 256
Budget messages, **1954:** 14 (pp. 140, 143–145);
1956: 12 (pp. 119–121)
Health of the President, **1953:** 230; **1956:** 15, 48,
117, 130; **1959:** 29, 243, 267, 288; **1960–
61:** 284
Campaign remarks, **1956:** 210, 268
Editor's note on illness, **1955:** p. 822
News conference remarks, **1956:** 5, 16, 20, 32, 47,
53, 56, 94, 96, 113, 155, 171, 189, 193, 216,
229, 235; **1957:** 45, 50, 56, 80, 228; **1958:**
11, 28, 37, 88, 198, 274
Recovery from heart attack, **1956:** 32
Recovery from ileitis operation, **1956:** 155
Remarks on return from Denver, **1955:** 236
Healy, Paul F., **1959:** 267
Hearing aid anecdote, **1959:** 107
Hearst, William Randolph, Jr.
Interview of Molotov, comment on, **1955:** 26
Letter, **1955:** 124
Heart disease, **1958:** 2
Conference on, message, **1955:** 34
Heat resistant materials, **1958:** 5 (p. 19)
Heaton, Maj. Gen. Leonard D., **1956:** 155
Hébert, Repr. F. Edward, **1959:** 167
Heeney, A.D.P., **1954:** 110n.
Heidenberger, Beter, **1953:** 225
Heintzleman, Gov. B. Frank, **1954:** 73
Hekmat, Reza, **1959:** 320
Helicopter, purchase by Premier Khrushchev,
1959: 243
Helicopter, use of by the President, **1957:** 56
Helicopter Society, American, remarks, **1960–61:**
145
Helium conservation, **1959:** 10 (p. 96); **1960–61:** 13
(p. 85), 414 (p. 998)
Heller, Robert, and Associates, report on White
House office space, **1957:** 45
Hell's Canyon project, **1953:** 77
Helmand Valley, Afghanistan, development, **1958:**
150
"Help Korea" trains ceremony, remarks, **1954:** 78
Henderson, Horace, **1953:** 98

Henderson, Loy W., **1953:** 129; **1954:** 184n.; **1959:** 19, 91
  See also State, Deputy Under Secretary.
  Award for Distinguished Federal Civilian Service, **1958:** 13
  Letter, **1954:** 186
Hendricks, Sterling B., Award for Distinguished Federal Civilian Service, **1958:** 13
Hendrickson, Waino, **1959:** 3n.
Hennepin, Louis, **1960–61:** 330
Hennings, Sen. Thomas C., Jr., **1953:** 109
Henry, Barklie McK., **1953:** 2n.
Henry, David Dodds, **1956:** 85n.
Henry, Patrick, **1953:** 83, 100; **1954:** 111, 118, 171n.; **1956:** 107; **1957:** 22; **1958:** 123; **1959:** 186
Henry the Navigator, **1960–61:** 157, 160
Hensel, H. Struve, **1954:** 351
Hensley, Stewart, **1957:** 92; **1958:** 153, 198, 274; **1959:** 148, 179, 277; **1960–61:** 34, 38, 228, 284
Henty, G. A., **1954:** 293
Hereford Association, American, dedication of building, remarks, **1953:** 218
Herling, John, **1953:** 77, 109; **1954:** 9, 25, 39, 50, 63, 101, 107, 129, 143, 168, 182, 311, 322, 328, 353; **1955:** 18, 47, 56, 81, 95, 112, 119, 149, 176; **1956:** 113, 121, 155, 198, 216, 229, 235, 298; **1957:** 17, 45, 50, 56, 62, 72, 80, 87, 134, 207, 228; **1958:** 11, 28, 37, 56, 83, 103, 120, 198, 274, 288; **1959:** 21, 67, 123, 132, 161, 167; **1960–61:** 38, 127, 143
Herman, Fred, telegram on small business, **1956:** 263
Herman, George E., **1954:** 25, 63, 68, 107, 143, 157, 161, 165, 192, 311, 322, 328
Hernandez, Jaime, **1960–61:** 224
Herrera, Felipe, **1960–61:** 72, 73
Hershey, Pa.
  Birthday greetings to the President, remarks, **1953:** 211
  Pennsylvania Republican Rally, remarks, **1953:** 212
Herter, Gov. Christian A., **1953:** 117, 187; **1954:** 325; **1956:** 292; **1959:** 44, 54, 76, 78
  See also State, Secretary of (Christian A. Herter); State, under Secretary of.
  News conference remarks on, **1956:** 155, 171, 189
Hesburgh, Rev. Theodore M., **1959:** 26; **1960–61:** 174
Hester, Adin, **1959:** 169
Heuss, Theodor, **1955:** 22; **1957:** 98 and n.; **1959:** 192
  Exchange of toasts, **1958:** 127
  Letter, **1958:** 138
  Meeting with, **1959:** 214
  Message, **1956:** 125
  Welcoming remarks, **1958:** 126

HEW.
  See Health, Education, and Welfare, Department of.
Hewlett, Frank, **1956:** 205
Hiawatha, Indian Chief, **1960–61:** 330
Hiawatha Bridge, Red Wing, Minn., dedication, remarks, **1960–61:** 330
Hickenlooper, Sen. Bourke B., **1953:** 268; **1956:** 212; **1958:** 290
Hickerson, John D., **1960–61:** 182n., 189
Hickok, James B. (Wild Bill), **1953:** 252
Higgins, Marguerite, **1956:** 20, 62, 96
High school
  Aptitude testing, **1957:** 234
  Conference at Defiance, Ohio, on teaching of science and mathematics, **1957:** 251n.
  Education beyond, **1956:** 8, 85, 222, 277; **1957:** 19
Hightower, John M., **1953:** 41; **1954:** 328, 345, 347; **1955:** 81, 90; **1957:** 72, 115, 119, 134, 150, 157; **1958:** 11, 28, 42, 103, 141, 274, 310; **1959:** 29, 179, 288; **1960–61:** 93, 103, 127, 222, 256, 263, 268
Highway, Inter-American, **1955:** 59, 64; **1958:** 5 (pp. 36, 37)
Highway Administrator, Federal (Bertram D. Tallamy), report, **1959:** 138
Highway bill, **1959:** 161, 167, 179
  Approval, **1959:** 227
  News conference remarks, **1956:** 88
Highway commissioners, State, **1959:** 138
Highway Construction Co. of Ohio, Inc., relief of, **1955:** 159
Highway safety.
  See also Traffic safety.
  Governors' conference on, **1953:** 261; **1957:** 14 and n.
  Letter to Secretary Weeks, **1958:** 299
  Regional conference, message, **1958:** 45
  Safe Driving Day, **1954:** 347, 352, 353; **1955:** 243
  White House conference on, **1954:** 37; **1956:** 36, 37
Highway system, interstate, **1954:** 3, 139, 164n., 273, 308, 318, 349; **1955:** 4, 19, 39; **1956:** 19, 186, 305; **1957:** 13; **1958:** 26, 29, 33, 110; **1959:** 104, 187, 225; **1960–61:** 208, 341, 387, 410
  Administration by authority or corporation, **1955:** 185
  Budget messages, **1954:** 14 (p. 176); **1955:** 17 (p. 92); **1956:** 12 (pp. 138, 139, 140); **1958:** 5 (pp. 23, 53); **1960–61:** 14 (pp. 70, 71), 414 (pp. 941, 976, 977)
  Campaign remarks, **1956:** 226, 272; **1958:** 292, 294, 296, 302, 303, 308
  Committee on a National Highway Program, **1954:** 346n., 349

Highway system, interstate — *continued*
 Federal aid for, **1954:** 33, 102; **1959:** 6, 10 (p. 50),
  227; **1960–61:** 13 (pp. 70, 71), 255, 330,
  414 (p. 977)
 Federal-Aid Highway Act, approval, **1954:** 102
 Federal Aid Highway Act of 1958, **1958:** 74
  Amendment, **1958:** 49
  Approval, **1959:** 227
  Statement, **1958:** 77
 Financing of, **1954:** 165; **1959:** 138
 Legislative recommendations, **1956:** 2
 Letters to
  Sen. Gore, **1959:** 252
  Minority leaders, re, **1958:** 43
  T. D. Sherard, **1959:** 149
  Secretary Weeks, **1958:** 299
 News conference remarks, **1954:** 33, 165; **1959:**
  94, 102, 186
 Report on, statement, **1956:** 186
 Study by Gen. Bragdon, **1959:** 227; **1960–61:** 93
Highway trust fund, **1958:** 5 (p. 45); **1959:** 104, 138,
 149, 187, 226n., 252
 Budget message, **1959:** 10 (pp. 80, 81)
Highways, **1955:** 39, 247; **1958:** 70; **1960–61:** 133,
 330
 See also Highway system, interstate.
 Accidents on, **1954:** 37, 255, 336, 351; **1959:** 129,
  185
 Advertising along Federal, **1957:** 72, 169; **1958:** 5
  (p. 53), 14, 77
 Budget messages, **1954:** 14 (pp. 170, 176); **1955:**
  17 (p. 167); **1958:** 5 (p. 54); **1959:** 10 (pp.
  45, 50, 80, 81); **1960–61:** 13 (pp. 44, 65,
  69–71), 414 (pp. 941, 977)
 Bureau of Indian Affairs activities, **1958:** 43
 Construction program, **1954:** 318
 Federal aid, **1954:** 3, 14 (p. 176), 33, 102, 165
 Federal Aid Highway Act, **1954:** 102; **1958:** 77;
  1959: 227
 Forest, **1956:** 12 (p. 140)
 Forest and access roads, **1954:** 14 (pp. 170, 176)
 Forest and public land, **1958:** 5 (p. 45)
 Improvement, **1953:** 268
 Letter to minority leaders re, **1958:** 43
 National park roads, **1958:** 43
 News conference remarks, **1955:** 26, 33, 62, 90,
  146, 185
 Trust funds, **1960–61:** 13 (pp. 44, 69–71), 133,
  414 (pp. 941, 977), 423
Higley, H.V. (Administrator of Veterans Affairs),
 1953: 269
 See also Veterans Affairs, Administrator of.
 Chairman, Community Chest campaign, **1955:**
  130
 Federal Council on Aging, **1956:** 74
Hildreth, Horace A., **1956:** 65
Hill, Sen. Lister, **1955:** 33

Hill, Raleigh, insurance claim, disapproval, **1954:**
 240
Hill, Robert C., **1959:** 275
Hillings, Repr. Patrick J., **1958:** 292, 294
Hilton, Conrad, **1956:** 28
Hiner, Louis C., **1955:** 41
Hines, Fred P., disability claim, **1955:** 200
 Relief of, veto, **1953:** 139
Hines, William M., Jr., **1957:** 115
Hinman, Wilbur S., Jr., President's Award for
  Distinguished Federal Civilian Service,
  1960–61: 389n.
Hirohito, Emperor, **1960–61:** 14, 188n., 308
Hiser, Leland, **1956:** 278
Historic sites and monuments, national, **1954:** 3, 14
 (p. 170)
History, President's place in, comment on, **1960–
 61:** 222
Hitchcock, Ethan A., **1958:** 100
Hitler, Adolf, **1953:** 187; **1954:** 72, 87, 111, 192;
  1955: 57; **1956:** 257; **1957:** 68; **1958:** 70,
  261, 274; **1959:** 7, 212, 344; **1960–61:** 58,
  355
 Mein Kampf, **1953:** 109
 News conference remarks on, **1953:** 15, 128;
  1960–61: 24, 34
 Storm troopers, **1957:** 200
Hjerpe, Eric and Ida Mae, relief of, disapproval,
 1960–61: 291
Hobby, Oveta Culp, **1956:** 94; **1957:** 145; **1960–61:**
 336
 See also Federal Security Administrator; Health,
  Education, and Welfare, Secretary of.
Hobby, William P., **1955:** 152
Hoblitzell, Sen. John D., Jr., **1958:** 302
Hobson, Brig. Gen. Howard M., **1960–61:** 396
Hockey international festival, remarks to partic-
  ipants, **1960–61:** 319
Hodgenville, Ky., **1954:** 88
Hodges, Governor Luther, **1957:** 205n.
Hoegh, Gov. Leo A., **1956:** 212; **1958:** 146
 See also Civil and Defense Mobilization, Office
  of, Director (Leo A. Hoegh).
Hoey, Sen. Clyde R., **1954:** 92, 109
Hoff, Neil, **1956:** 253
Hoffa, James, **1957:** 150; **1959:** 123
Hoffman, Repr. Clare, **1953:** 269
Hoffman, Paul, **1954:** 172, 274; **1956:** 235; **1959:**
 154
Hogan, Ben, **1954:** 77
 Telegram, **1953:** 140
Hogan, Mrs. Ben, **1953:** 140
Hogan, Frank S., **1960–61:** 34
Hogs, **1958:** 59, 60
 See also Livestock; Pork.
 Price supports, **1956:** 16
Hokkaido Island, **1954:** 328, 345

Holaday, William M.
　See Defense, Guided Missiles Director for Secretary of.
Holcomb, George B., **1956:** 121, 155, 229
Holeman, Frank, **1958:** 103; **1959:** 29, 179
Holiday accidents, **1954:** 157, 161, 255
Holifield, Repr. Chet, **1954:** 12n.
Holland.
　See Netherlands.
Holland, G. Kenneth, **1959:** 24, 287n.
Hollar, Philip A., **1954:** 78n.
Hollister, John B., **1954:** 12n.; **1955:** 74n.; **1959:** 154
　See also International Cooperation Administration, Director.
　Comment on, **1955:** 90
Hollister, Solomon C., **1954:** 12n.
Hollmer, Anita, **1959:** 131
Hollomon, Mr. and Mrs. W. G., claim, **1958:** 254
Hollyday, Guy T., **1954:** 92
Hollywood, Calif., **1956:** 242n.
Holman, Eugene, **1953:** 33n.
Holmdel, N.J., **1960–61:** 258n.
Holmes, Repr. Hal, **1954:** 271
Holmes, Oliver Wendell, **1956:** 87
Holstrom, Andrew, **1953:** 117
Holyoake, Keith, message, **1960–61:** 373
Home, Lord, **1960–61:** 307
Home improvements, **1956:** 2; **1958:** 12
Home life, value of, **1956:** 241
Home Loan Bank Board, Federal
　Home mortgage funds, **1958:** 49
　Independent agency, **1955:** 194
Home Mortgage Credit Program, Voluntary, **1956:** 12 (p. 147)
　Proposed extension, **1957:** 16
Home rule for District of Columbia, **1959:** 36
Homer, **1959:** 116, 129
Homer, Arthur B., **1959:** 211n.
Homlar, Harvey, tax refund claim, **1958:** 249
　Honduras Izaguirre, Gen. Carlos, **1956:** 144
　Lozano Diaz, Julio, **1956:** 144
Honest John missile, **1957:** 230
Honey, price supports, **1954:** 4
Honeycutt, Leslie R., **1953:** 12, 22
Hong Kong, arrival of four airmen from Communist China, **1955:** 112
Honolulu, **1954:** 130
　Remarks on arrival, **1960–61:** 205
　Remarks on departure, **1960–61:** 206
Honorary degree of Doctor of Laws, American University, **1957:** 109n.
Hook, Charles R., **1954:** 12n.; **1956:** 64; **1958:** 134n.
Hoover, Herbert, Jr., **1954:** 226, 345; **1955:** 94
　Discussion on Hungary, **1956:** 287
　Letters, **1954:** 185; **1957:** 20
　Term of service, **1957:** 20n.

Hoover, Mrs. Herbert, Jr., **1957:** 20
Hoover, Herbert, President, **1953:** 28, 105; **1954:** 27, 28, 29, 87, 122, 226, 322; **1955:** 4, 236; **1956:** 64, 89, 100; **1957:** 223; **1958:** 134; **1959:** 77, 100, 102, 141; **1960–61:** 405
　Citation for Distinguished Civilian Service, **1957:** Item 26 and n.
　Committee on Recent Social Trends, **1959:** 6
　80th birthday, **1954:** 190
　Letters, **1954:** 12, 190; **1956:** 261
　News conference remarks re, **1955:** 33; **1956:** 16, 189
　Second Hoover Commission, **1953:** 145
　Testimony on defense reorganization quoted, **1958:** 134n.
Hoover, J. Edgar.
　See Federal Bureau of Investigation, Director of.
Hoover Commission, **1953:** 6, 225; **1954:** 120, 122, 273; **1956:** 2; **1960–61:** 372
　Appointment of members, statement, **1953:** 145
　Budget messages, **1960–61:** 13 (p. 109), 414 (p. 1026)
　Letter to President Hoover, **1954:** 12
　Recommendations, **1954:** 163; **1955:** 4; **1956:** 9, 105, 108, 241; **1957:** 13, 58, 75, 86, 112; **1958:** 134n.
　　Budget messages, **1956:** 12 (pp. 76, 98); **1958:** 5 (p. 71); **1959:** 10 (p. 53)
　　Civil service, **1958:** 5 (p. 71)
　　Defense Department, **1956:** 62, 64
　　Federal budget and accounting, **1956:** 89, 100, 156
　　Government reporting requirements, **1956:** 110
　　Grouping of Government functions, **1959:** 221
　　Intelligence activities, **1956:** 9
　　Kestnbaum report, **1956:** 261
　　Letter to President Hoover, **1956:** 261
　　Line of authority, **1959:** 86
　　News conference remarks, **1955:** 41, 90, 100; **1956:** 16, 62; **1957:** 150
　　Paperwork reduction, **1955:** 41
　　Personnel and civil service, **1956:** 22
　　Water resources survey, **1954:** 271
Hoover Medal Award, acceptance, remarks, **1960–61:** 405
Hoover Report, Citizens Committee for the, **1957:** 26n.
Hope, Repr. Clifford R., **1953:** 268
　Letter, **1954:** 196
　News conference remarks on, **1954:** 9, 129
Hope, Henry Radford, **1959:** 148 ftn. (p. 490)
Hopkins, Harry, **1958:** 28
Hopkins, William J., President's Award for Distinguished Federal Civilian Service, **1960–61:** 68n.

Horner, Garnett D., **1954:** 50, 68, 107, 353; **1955:**
   33, 41, 47, 56, 90, 100, 176; **1956:** 96, 113,
   121, 171, 298; **1957:** 28, 157; **1958:** 28,
   103, 153, 198, 222; **1959:** 17, 21, 26, 36, 42,
   48, 53, 102, 132, 179, 243, 277; **1960–61:**
   24
Horner, John V., **1959:** 7; **1960–61:** 222, 263
Horton, Mildred McA., **1953:** 88
Horvath, Louis, **1954:** 203, 274
Hoskins, Harold B., **1959:** 130
Hospital, Sibley Memorial, site for, approval of
   bill, **1957:** 175
Hospital ship, mercy mission, **1959:** 29, 167
Hospital Survey and Construction Act amendment,
   proposed, **1954:** 3
Hospitalization insurance for Government em-
   ployees, **1958:** 5 (p. 71)
Hospitals and medical care facilities, **1954:** 11, 139,
   165, 180, 209, 301, 318; **1955:** 17 (pp. 94,
   138, 139), 25; **1956:** 19, 21; **1958:** 49, 110;
   1959: 129, 181; **1960–61:** 235, 410
   See also Medical care.
   Budget messages, **1956:** 12 (pp. 114, 120, 121);
      1958: 5 (pp. 46, 47, 51, 62, 63); **1959:** 10
      (pp. 45, 102, 107); **1960–61:** 13 (pp. 87, 93,
      94, 97, 100), 414 (pp. 1001, 1007, 1008,
      1015, 1016)
   Construction grants, **1956:** 161
   Health Amendments Act, approval, **1956:** 161
   Manhattan State Hospital, **1954:** 299
   Medical Center, State University of New York,
      1954: 300
   Veterans, **1956:** 12 (p. 114), 21, 224, 267; **1960–**
      61: 13 (pp. 97, 100), 414 (pp. 1015, 1016)
   Veterans hospitals, construction, **1954:** 14 (p.
      134)
Houghton, Amory, **1959:** 203, 332n.
Hound Dog missile (air-to-ground).
   See Missiles.
Houphouet-Boigny, Felix, message, **1960–61:** 254
Hours of work on Federal construction projects,
   1958: 5 (p. 51); **1959:** 10 (p. 101)
House, Col. Edward M., **1958:** 28
House Office Building, **1956:** 12 (p. 150)
Housing, **1954:** 21, 100, 139, 209, 308; **1955:** 4, 247;
   1957: 13, 16, 19; **1958:** 12, 16, 29, 33, 35,
   49, 96, 110; **1959:** 15; **1960–61:** 341, 410
   See also Urban renewal.
   Budget messages, **1954:** 14 (pp. 87, 146–151);
      1955: 17 (pp. 118, 136, 171–175); **1956:** 12
      (pp. 130, 138, 139, 145–147); **1958:** 5 (pp.
      24, 43, 44, 53, 56–59); **1959:** 10 (pp. 46, 63,
      82–86); **1960–61:** 13 (pp. 65, 71–75), 414
      (pp. 957, 978–983, 1014)
     Tables, **1954:** 14 (p. 147); **1958:** 5 (p. 54);
      1960–61: 13 (p. 67), 414 (p. 971)
   Budget (1960), statement, **1958:** 324

Housing — *continued*
   Campaign remarks, **1954:** 273, 316, 317, 318;
      1956: 224, 226, 256; **1958:** 292, 296, 303, 308
   College, **1954:** 14 (pp. 87, 151); **1955:** 17 (pp. 174,
      175); **1956:** 2, 12 (p. 147), 85n.; **1957:** 19,
      56, 75, 129; **1958:** 5 (pp. 53, 54, 59), 50, 96,
      110, 224; **1959:** 10 (pp. 82, 86), 26, 94, 153,
      208; **1960–61:** 13 (p. 75), 414 (pp. 982,
      983)
   Displaced families, **1958:** 5 (p. 58)
   Farm, **1956:** 12 (p. 130)
   Home improvements, **1956:** 2
   Letter to Administrator, HHFA, **1958:** 50
   Letter to minority leaders, **1958:** 43
   Loans, **1954:** 3, 14 (p. 150), 302
   Low-income groups, **1958:** 5 (p. 58)
   Meeting on, **1956:** 318
   Message to Congress, **1954:** 17
   Military personnel, **1954:** 3, 349, 351; **1955:** 4, 13,
      17 (p. 118); **1956:** 2, 12 (p. 146), 141;
      1958: 49, 62; **1959:** 10 (p. 63), 153;
      1960–61: 414 (p. 957)
     Approval of bill, **1954:** 237
     Overseas, **1956:** 241
     Substandard housing, **1956:** 81n.
   Minority groups, **1956:** 12 (p. 147)
   Mortgage insurance, **1954:** 3; **1958:** 5 (pp. 43,
      59), 43, 62, 224
   Mortgage purchases, **1958:** 5 (pp. 43, 53, 58)
   News conference remarks, **1954:** 68, 73, 101, 115,
      168, 182; **1955:** 18, 176; **1958:** 42, 63, 70;
      1960–61: 143, 256, 263
   Older persons, **1956:** 2, 12 (pp. 139, 145, 146), 19,
      63, 252, 256; **1958:** 5 (p. 59); **1959:** 153,
      208; **1960–61:** 410
   Private financing, **1958:** 5 (pp. 43, 59)
   Public, **1953:** 54, 266; **1954:** 3, 14 (pp. 150, 151),
      17, 68, 168, 179, 182, 349; **1955:** 4, 17 (p.
      174), 176, 194; **1956:** 2, 3, 12 (p. 145);
      1958: 5 (p. 54), 50, 96; **1959:** 10 (pp. 46,
      84), 153, 208; **1960–61:** 13 (pp. 72, 73),
      414 (p. 980)
     Racial discrimination, **1954:** 101, 182; **1959:** 26
   Veterans, **1953:** 62; **1955:** 17 (pp. 136, 173, 174);
      1956: 12 (pp. 112, 146, 147), 318; **1957:**
      16, 129, 172; **1958:** 5 (pp. 53, 54, 59), 43,
      49, 62, 63; **1959:** 10 (p. 85), 26, 146;
      1960–61: 13 (p. 74), 414 (pp. 981, 982,
      1014)
Housing Act amendment, proposed, **1956:** 2
Housing Act of 1957, approval, **1957:** 129 and n.
Housing bill, **1954:** 168, 302; **1955:** 185; **1960–61:**
   143
   Amendments of 1955, approval, **1955:** 194
   Approval, **1954:** 179
   News conference remarks, **1958:** 56, 63; **1959:**
      26, 29, 94, 102, 179
   Residential construction act, message, **1958:** 62

Housing bill — *continued*
  Statement on failure to enact, **1958:** 224
  Vetoes, **1959:** 153, 208
Housing and Home Finance Agency, **1954:** 95;
    1955: 222; **1956:** 4n.; **1958:** 43, 224;
    1960–61: 5, 358
  Area assistance, veto, **1958:** 258
  Bill extending direct loans for veterans housing,
    veto, **1957:** 172
  Budget messages, **1955:** 17 (p. 174); **1956:** 12 (p.
    149); **1958:** 5 (p. 53); **1959:** 10 (pp. 51,
    85); **1960–61:** 13 (p. 72), 414 (p. 979)
  Construction projects, **1958:** 50
  Home Loan Bank Board, made independent
    agency, **1955:** 194
  Loans for college and university housing, **1957:**
    19
  Public facility loans, **1960–61:** 13 (p. 72), 146
  Reorganization proposed, **1954:** 17
  RFC functions, **1957:** 78
  Southwest Washington redevelopment, **1956:** 4
  Talle, Henry O., **1959:** 18n.
Housing and Home Finance Agency, Administra-
    tor (Albert M. Cole), **1953:** 266; **1954:**
    182, 349
  Committee on Small Business, **1956:** 118
  Federal Council on Aging, **1956:** 74
  Flood insurance, **1956:** 167
  Housing for older persons, mortgages, letter,
    1956: 252
  Investigation of FHA, **1954:** 302
  Letter, **1958:** 50
  Memorandum, **1954:** 81
  News conference remarks on, **1953:** 37, 265
Housing inventory, **1956:** 12 (p. 123)
Houston, Samuel, **1960–61:** 336
Houston, Tex., **1956:** 216
  Address at Rice University, **1960–61:** 336
  Mayor Lewis Cutrer, **1960–61:** 336n.
Hovde, Frederick V., **1954:** 335
Howard, Katherine G., **1954:** 310
Howard, Richard, **1956:** 45n.
Howard University
  Budget messages, **1954:** 14 (pp. 153, 154); **1960–**
    61: 414 (p. 1009)
  Choir, **1954:** 33; **1960–61:** 23
  Hospital, **1956:** 12 (p. 120)
Howe, Walter, **1960–61:** 69n., 72n., 75n.
Howley, Gen. Frank, **1955:** 62
Howrey, Edward F.
  See Federal Trade Commission, Chairman.
Hughes, John C., **1953:** 2n.
Hughes, Rowland R.
  See Budget, Bureau of the, Director.
Huh Chung, **1960–61:** 198, 202, 204
  Joint statement with, **1960–61:** 203
  Toast to, **1960–61:** 200
Huh Chung, Madame, **1960–61:** 198n.

Hull, Cordell, **1958:** 58; **1959:** 42
Hull, Gen. John E., **1956:** 10n.
Human Rights, Universal Declaration of, **1956:**
    308
Human Rights Day, statement, **1956:** 308
Humphrey, George M.
  See Treasury, Secretary of the.
Humphrey, Mrs. George M., **1957:** 102 and n.
Humphrey, Sen. Hubert H., **1953:** 198; **1960–61:**
    93, 330
  Comment on, **1955:** 26
  Meeting with Khrushchev, **1958:** 318
Hungarian refugees, **1957:** 8, 25; **1960–61:** 410, 431
  See also Refugees.
  Admission to U.S., **1956:** 296, 306, 307; **1957:** 1,
    187, 250
  Bipartisan meeting, **1956:** 318
  International Red Cross aid, **1957:** 39
  News conference remarks, **1957:** 17, 70, 150
  President's Committee for relief of, report, **1957:**
    85 and n., 250
  President's representative for relief of (Tracy S.
    Voorhees), **1956:** 307
  Red Cross aid, **1956:** 304; **1957:** 39, 89
  Remarks to, **1956:** 301
  Termination of emergency program, **1957:** 250
  Transportation, **1956:** 306n.
  Vice President's report on, **1957:** 2, 25
Hungary, **1956:** 282, 315; **1957:** 17; **1958:** 2, 7, 222
  Addresses and messages, **1957:** 6, 15, 25, 35, 37,
    118, 230
  Boldocsky, Janos, **1954:** 182 ftn. (p. 678)
  Campaign remarks, **1956:** 272, 279, 283, 292;
    1958: 293
  Communism in, **1954:** 30
  Compensation claims of U.S. nationals, **1954:** 94
  Execution of Nagy and Maleter, **1958:** 141
  Flood relief, **1954:** 175, 182 ftn. (p. 678)
  Funds for relief of, statement, **1956:** 284
  Joint statement with Chancellor Adenauer, **1957:**
    100
  Joint statement with Prime Minister Macmillan,
    1957: 55
  Kadar regime, **1958:** 8
  Letters to Premier Bulganin, **1956:** 291; **1957:** 3;
    1958: 31
  Message, **1956:** 302
  Mindszenty, Cardinal Joseph, **1956:** 292
  National holiday, statement, **1957:** 51
  News conference remarks, **1956:** 298
  Red Cross aid, **1956:** 304
  Soviet troops in, **1956:** 270, 282, 283, 287, 291
  Soviet repression, **1960–61:** 410
  Statements on, **1956:** 270, 287, 291n., 296, 308
  Treaty of Peace, **1956:** 270
  U.N. action on, **1957:** 3, 6
    Report, **1958:** 8, 148

Hunt, Herold C., Under Secretary of Health, Education, and Welfare, **1956:** 217n.
Hunting, **1958:** 288
Hunting dog anecdote, **1959:** 107
Huntsville, Ala.
   George C. Marshall Space Flight Center, dedication, remarks, **1960–61:** 287
   Mayor R. B. Searcv, **1960–61:** 287
Hurley, Maj. Gen. Patrick J., **1953:** 22
Hurricane "Audrey," statement, **1957:** 121
Hurricane "Carol," message, **1954:** 264
Hurricane flood protection and prevention, **1958:** 73, 85, 155
Hurricane in Haiti, **1954:** 289
Hussein, King of Jordan, **1957:** 72, 91
   Exchange of toasts, **1959:** 66
   Message, **1960–61:** 277
Hussey, Barbara, **1953:** 17
Hutcheson, Maurice A., **1956:** 86n., 265
Hutcheson, Mrs. Maurice A., **1956:** 265
Hutcheson, William L., **1953:** 224; **1956:** 86
Hutchinson, Everett, **1954:** 161
Huttlinger, Joseph B., **1959:** 288
Hyde, Arthur W., mining claim, disapproval, **1956:** 179
Hyde, Repr. DeWitt S., **1958:** 308
   Letter, **1954:** 313
Hydroelectric Power Commission of the Province of Ontario, **1959:** 141n.
Hydroelectric power projects, **1953:** 77; **1954:** 14 (pp. 167–169), 271; **1955:** 17 (pp. 158–161); **1959:** 10 (p. 95); **1960–61:** 402, 410
   Middle East, **1953:** 217
Hydrogen bomb, **1953:** 256; **1954:** 72, 89; **1955:** 41, 47, 56; **1956:** 268; **1958:** 21, 88, 296, 300
   See also Nuclear tests; Nuclear weapons.
   Civil defense, **1956:** 142
   Clean bombs, **1956:** 229
   Delegation of authority re use, **1959:** 102
   Delivery range, **1954:** 57
   Dropped from B–52, **1956:** 113
   News conference remarks, **1954:** 57, 63, 73, 157, 165, 192, 341; **1956:** 5, 113, 229, 235; **1959:** 102, 132
   Sabotage in production, question of, **1954:** 73
   Soviet possession of, **1953:** 198, 208; **1954:** 73; **1960–61:** 422
   Test ban, **1956:** 88, 230, 235, 266
   Tests, **1957:** 17, 92, 105
Hynes, John B., **1954:** 325; **1957:** 80

IAEA.
   See International Atomic Energy Agency.
Ibanez del Campo, Carlos, cablegram to, **1958:** 81
Ibanez del Campo, Senora de, **1958:** 81
Ibrahim, Moulay Abdallah, **1959:** 343n.

Ibsen, Henrik, quoted, **1956:** 190
ICA.
   See International Cooperation Administration.
ICBM.
   See Missiles.
ICC.
   See Interstate Commerce Commission.
Ice breaker, nuclear-powered, veto, **1958:** 204
Icebreaker, U.S.S. *Atka*, **1955:** 47
Iceland, **1956:** 78
   Asgeir Asgeirsson, **1955:** 162
   Sen. Henry Dworshak, **1959:** 154
   Reactor testing station, **1956:** 12 (p. 101)
   Governor Robert E. Smylie, **1957:** 138
   Letter, **1960–61:** 115
Idaho Power Co., **1953:** 77
   Tax write-off allowances, **1957:** 80, 124
IGY.
   See International Geophysical Year.
Ikeda, Hayato
   Election as Prime Minister, message, **1960–61:** 252
   Letter, **1960–61:** 294
   Messages, **1960–61:** 252, 366
Ileitis attack, news conference remarks, **1956:** 155
Iliff, W.A.B., **1960–61:** 284, 297
Illery, Dr. Alma, **1957:** 4
Illinois, **1954:** 200
   Allen, Repr. Leo E., **1956:** 184, 214
   Arends, Repr. Leslie C., **1955:** 41; **1956:** 184, 214
   Candidates for public office, **1954:** 177; **1956:** 205, 214; **1960–61:** 246
   Chicago, **1954:** 119; **1955:** 47; **1958:** 11, 18, 45n., 223, 288, 295, 296, 297, 305; **1959:** 7, 36; **1960–61:** 23n., 245, 246, 310, 320n.
   Chiperfield, Repr. Robert B., **1953:** 111, 268; **1956:** 184
   Church, Rep. Marguerite Stitt, **1956:** 214
   Dirksen, Sen. Everett McK., **1956:** 78, 94, 214, 216, 229; **1958:** 83, 103, 296; **1959:** 127, 151n.; **1960–61:** 132, 143, 263, 271, 272
   Douglas, Sen. Paul H., **1957:** 92; **1958:** 120, 141; **1959:** 36
   Drury, **1956:** 148, 182
   Evanston, **1954:** 204
   Lake Michigan water diversion, disapproval, **1956:** 177
   Lemont, **1955:** 53n.
   Libertyville, **1956:** 197
   Mason, Repr. Noah M., **1954:** 92
   Northern Illinois District Court, **1954:** 228
   Peoria, **1955:** 18; **1956:** 214, 216
   Reed, Repr. Chauncey W., **1953:** 269
   Simpson, Repr. Sid., **1953:** 269
   Springheld, **1954:** 22, 203, 205n.; **1959:** 31
   State Fair, **1954:** 192
     Address, **1954:** 203

Illinois — *continued*
   Stratton, Gov. William G., **1954:** 192, 203; **1956:**
      198, 214, 216; **1957:** 124, 138; **1958:** 296;
      1960–61: 246
   Velde, Repr. Harold H., **1953:** 269
Illinois University, **1956:** 85n.
ILO.
   See International Labor Organization.
Immigration, **1953:** 6; **1960–61:** 410
   Admission of refugees, **1953:** 52, 187; **1960–61:**
      96, 133
      Approval of bill, **1960–61:** 233
   Budget messages, **1960–61:** 13 (p. 105), 414 (p.
      1022)
   Laws, **1955:** 4, 247; **1956:** 2, 33, 272; **1957:** 8, 25,
      250; **1959:** 10 (p. 110)
   Affecting refugees.
      See Refugees.
   Amendment, **1958:** 5 (p. 73)
   Meeting on, **1956:** 318
   News conference remarks, **1956:** 121; **1957:**
      70, 150
   Revision proposed, **1960–61:** 96, 133, 255
   Matters, message, **1956:** 33
   McCarran-Walter Immigration Act, **1953:** 54,
      208; **1954:** 9, 57, 92
   Message to Congress, **1960–61:** 96
   Quotas, **1960–61:** 310
   Sheepherders, nonquota visas for, **1954:** 250
Immigration and Nationality Act, **1957:** 25, 250
   Amendment, approval, **1957:** 187
   Quota system, **1957:** 25
Immigration and Naturalization Service, **1955:** 4;
      1956: 12 (p. 153); **1957:** 250; **1958:** 61;
      1960–61: 310
   Action on subversives, record of, **1954:** 130
   Budget message, **1955:** 17 (p. 182)
   Hungarian refugees, **1957:** 250
Immigration and Naturalization, Commissioner of
      (J.M.Swing), **1957:** 70; **1959:** 161
   Immigration study, **1956:** 33
   Mexican trips, **1956:** 235
   News conference remarks on, **1956:** 229, 235
Imports, **1954:** 67, 226; **1955:** 72; **1958:** 25, 95, 96;
      1960–61: 132
   See also General Agreement on Tariffs and
      Trade.
   Alloys, **1953:** 69
   Automobiles and parts for show purposes, **1958:**
      76
   From Canada, **1958:** 163
   Coffee, **1960–61:** 54
   Conference on trade policy, address, **1958:** 58
   Cotton, restrictions on, **1956:** 115
   Country of origin of repackaged articles and
      containers, marking of, disapproval,
      1960–61: 285
   Duties, revised valuation procedures, **1956:** 162

Imports — *continued*
   Hat bodies, fur-felt, **1956:** 123
   Iron ore, **1959:** 55
   Joint statement with Prime Minister Kishi, **1957:**
      117
   Lead and zinc, **1953:** 228; **1954:** 143; **1960–61:**
      280
   From less developed countries, **1958:** 32
   Letter to Repr. Mills, **1958:** 132
   Manganese, **1953:** 69
   Minerals and rubber, **1959:** 55
   Oil, **1953:** 62, 77, 141; **1956:** 239; **1957:** 28, 145
      and ftn. (p. 581); **1958:** 163; **1959:** 67;
      1960–61: 383, 432
      Comment on, **1955:** 33, 81
      Recommendations of special committee on,
         1958: 54 and n.
      Statement on control, **1959:** 51
   Quotas, **1956:** 32; **1958:** 96, 163, 217
   Spun silk yarn, restrictions, **1955:** 155
   Sugar, liquid, **1956:** 123
   Sugar quotas
      Cuba, **1960–61:** 21, 38, 93, 167n., 222, 223, 267,
         374
      Dominican Republic, **1960–61:** 267, 374, 418
      Letter to Senator Bennett, **1960–61:** 167
      Philippines, **1960–61:** 106
   Textiles, **1956:** 32, 198, 216; **1959:** 267
   Tin, **1953:** 156, 213
   Trade agreements program, **1957:** 32, 61, 157,
      160
   Treated seed wheat, **1958:** 217
   Tungsten, **1953:** 156; **1956:** 123
   U.S.-U.K. discussions on, **1959:** 67
   Violins and violas, **1956:** 123
   Wool, **1953:** 131; **1954:** 4, 48, 49; **1959:** 67, 161
   Woolen fabrics, tariff increase, **1956:** 216
   Zinc and lead, **1957:** 157, 160
Inaugural address, **1953:** 1; **1957:** 15
Inaugural Ball (1948), **1960–61:** 143
Inauguration, **1957:** 17
   Ceremonies commemorating second anniversa-
      ry, **1955:** 20
Incandescent lamp, 75th anniversary, remarks,
      1954: 305
Incentive awards, Government employees, **1954:**
      14 (p. 188); **1955:** 1; **1956:** 2
Incentives, career, for military personnel, **1955:** 17
      (pp. 91, 109); **1956:** 2, 81, 91
Incentives in Soviet economy, **1959:** 271
Inches, John S., **1956:** 160
Income, disclosure by congressmen and officials,
      1958: 74
Income, personal, **1960–61:** 256, 423
Income of the President, comment on, **1953:** 77
Income taxes, **1953:** 31, 82, 84, 95, 268; **1954:** 3, 14
      (pp. 91–94); **1955:** 41; **1958:** 103; **1959:** 7
   Budget message, **1960–61:** 13 (pp. 39, 64)

Income taxes — *continued*
  Deductions for certain charitable contributions, veto, **1960–61:** 169
  Exemptions, **1954:** 301, 313
  News conference remarks, **1954:** 68, 165, 192
  Reporting for payroll tax purposes, **1958:** 5 (p. 52)
Independent Offices Appropriation Act
  Approval, statement, **1960–61:** 229
  Veto, **1958:** 192
Independent Television Committee for Nixon and Lodge, **1960–61:** 344
India, **1953:** 249; **1957:** 91; **1958:** 123; **1959:** 282n.
  See also New Delhi.
  Agra, **1959:** 317
  Ambassador George V. Allen, **1954:** 44
  Ambassador Ellsworth Bunker, **1959:** 310n., 312, 313
  Ambassador John S. Cooper, **1956:** 155
  Assistance, **1953:** 143; **1954:** 14 (p. 139), 44; **1955:** 17 (p. 129); **1959:** 94; **1960–61:** 36, 136, 410
  Ayyangar, M.A., **1959:** 311n.
  Border dispute with Communist China, **1959:** 288
  Chagla, M. C., **1960–61:** 136n.
  Chairmanship, Neutral Nations Commission in Korea, **1953:** 210
  Communist aggression in, **1959:** 94
  Custodial forces in Korea, **1954:** 40
  Dispute with Pakistan, **1959:** 288
  Engineers from, steel training and education program for, **1960–61:** 315
  Food-for-peace program, **1960–61:** 410
    Agreement with U.S., **1960–61:** 136
  Freedom from Communist domination, **1953:** 156
  Gandhi, Mrs. Indira, **1956:** 312
  Indus River Basin development, **1960–61:** 36, 284
    Pakistan-India Pact, statement, **1960–61:** 297
  Kashmir dispute with Pakistan, **1960–61:** 284
  Nehru, Jawaharlal.
    See main heading, Nehru Jawaharlal.
  New Delhi.
    See main heading, New Delhi.
  News conference remarks, **1960–61:** 7, 284
  Patil, S.K., **1960–61:** 136
  Prasad, Rajendra, **1959:** 310, 312, 315, 316, 317, 318
    Message, **1959:** 281
  President's desire to visit, **1956:** 62
  Radhakrishman, Sarvepalli, **1959:** 311n., 314n., 315n.
  Visit of President Eisenhower, **1959:** 277, 281, 310, 311, 312, 313, 314, 315, 316, 317, 318; **1960–61:** 7

India and United States, 1959, Washington conference on, **1959:** 94
Indian Affairs, Bureau of, **1953:** 153; **1956:** 12 (p. 138)
  Roadbuilding, **1958:** 43
Indian Affairs, Commissioner of, vacancy in office, **1953:** 128
Indian Affairs, Commissioner of (Glenn L. Emmons), letter, **1953:** 180
Indian lands, **1953:** 153; **1954:** 14 (p. 170); **1956:** 12 (pp. 133, 137, 138); **1958:** 5 (p. 69); **1959:** 10 (p. 95)
Indiana
  Cannelton Bridge Commission, disapproval, **1956:** 182
  Capehart, Sen. Homer E., **1953:** 266; **1954:** 138, 165; **1959:** 42
  Craig, Gov. George N., **1954:** 203, 290
  Halleck, Repr. Charles A., **1954:** 274; **1956:** 184; **1959:** 4, 34, 148, 151n.; **1960–61:** 88, 263, 272
  Indianapolis, **1954:** 290, 291
  Address to National Institute of Animal Agriculture, **1954:** 291
  Campaign remarks, **1954:** 290
  Jackson, School Township, relief of, **1957:** 174
  Jenner, Sen. William E., **1953:** 238; **1955:** 10; **1956:** 235; **1957:** 50, 72; **1958:** 83, 318
  Lawrenceburg Bridge Commission, disapproval, **1956:** 182
  Madden, Repr. Ray J., **1957:** 124
  Primary election, **1956:** 96
  Purdue University, **1957:** 156
  Rensselaer, **1959:** 4n.
  White County Bridge Commission, **1956:** 182
Indiana State Society, remarks, **1960–61:** 88
Indiana University
  Fine Arts Department, **1959:** 148 ftn. (p. 490)
  Tablet honoring Ernie Pyle, dedication, **1953:** 204
Indians, **1956:** 120n., 190; **1958:** 142; **1960–61:** 330
  Alaska, **1956:** 12 (p. 120)
  Citizenship, **1955:** 100
  Crow Indian Tribe claim, veto, **1956:** 124
  Health, education, and welfare programs, **1955:** 4, 17 (pp. 144, 145), 100; **1956:** 2, 12 (p. 122), 21; **1960–61:** 402, 410
  Heirship, **1960–61:** 133
  Hospitalization, Bernalillo County, N. Mex., **1960–61:** 235
  Integration into community life, **1956:** 2
  Lands and resources, **1955:** 17 (p. 162); **1960–61:** 13 (p. 85), 414 (p. 997)
  Letter to Glenn L. Emmons on meetings with tribal groups, **1953:** 180
  State jurisdiction over cases arising on reservations, approval, **1953:** 166
  Termination of Federal supervision, Menominee Tribe, **1954:** 147

Indochina, **1953:** 6, 50; **1954:** 129, 148; **1955:** 12, 105; **1956:** 198; **1958:** 173, 261, 287; **1960–61:** 7

See also Cambodia; Laos; Viet Nam.

Assistance, **1953:** 66, 156; **1954:** 3, 14 (pp. 127, 139), 92

Communist aggression, **1954:** 3, 33, 203

Evacuees, resettlement of, **1954:** 273

Joint statement with Prime Minister Churchill re, **1954:** 154

Membership in defense alliance, question of, **1954:** 107

Military mission in, **1954:** 25, 33, 50

News conference remarks, **1953:** 37, 54; **1954:** 25, 33, 50, 73, 92, 107, 115, 157, 161, 165, 341; **1955:** 18, 41, 47, 119

Partition, comment on, **1954:** 92

Strategic importance of, **1954:** 73

U.S.-French conversations on, **1954:** 115

Indochina war, **1953:** 66, 143, 156; **1954:** 90, 209, 225, 286, 297, 325; **1956:** 16

See also Dien Bien Phu, battle of.

Armistice, statement, **1954:** 168

Campaign remarks, **1954:** 286, 317, 318, 319, 320

Congressional action on, question of, **1954:** 73

Joint statement with Western leaders, **1953:** 255

Negotiations.

See Geneva conferences.

News conference remarks, **1954:** 33, 39, 50, 57, 63, 73, 92, 101, 138, 165, 168, 192

Statement, **1954:** 101

U.S. involvement, question of, **1954:** 33, 50, 57, 73, 92, 165

Indonesia, **1956:** 171; **1958:** 120

Bandung conference, **1955:** 26

Letter to President Sukarno, **1960–61:** 313

North, **1958:** 80

Sukarno, Achmed, **1956:** 87, 106, 107, 120

U.S. neutrality with regard to civil strife, **1958:** 88

Indus River, **1959:** 288

Indus River Basin development, **1960–61:** 36, 284

India-Pakistan Pact, statement, **1960–61:** 297

Industrial accidents, **1954:** 100

Industrial capacity, U.S., **1955:** 3

Industrial College of the Armed Forces, dedication of new building, remarks, **1960–61:** 283

Industrial Conference Board, National, message, **1955:** 228

Industrial development projects, **1960–61:** 146

Industrial expansion, **1953:** 153

Industrial installations, Federal, **1960–61:** 410

Industrial and municipal water supply, **1956:** 12 (p. 135)

Industrial revolution, **1959:** 55

Industrial safety, **1955:** 17 (p. 177)

Technical and financial aid to, **1957:** 16

Industrial Use of Agricultural Products, President's Commission on, **1958:** 12

Budget message, **1958:** 5 (p. 67)

Industries, rural, **1960–61:** 12

Rural development program, **1958:** 313

Industry, dispersal of, comment on, **1955:** 90, 119

Support of higher education, **1957:** 223

Infant mortality, **1959:** 129

Infantile paralysis, National Foundation for, **1956:** 1; **1958:** 109

Citation, **1955:** 78

Vaccination program, **1955:** 112, 113; **1956:** 12 (p. 120), 303

Inflation, **1953:** 6, 57, 95, 216; **1954:** 21, 169, 209, 308; **1956:** 19, 263; **1958:** 18, 324; **1959:** 6, 11, 15, 43, 63, 76, 83, 124, 129, 144, 177, 188, 208, 244, 274; **1960–61:** 4, 17, 19, 117, 245, 410

Budget messages, **1960–61:** 13 (p. 105), 414 (pp. 935, 936)

Campaign remarks, **1954:** 273, 286, 291; **1956:** 224, 234, 251, 268, 272, 279; **1958:** 293, 295, 296, 303, 308; **1960–61:** 346, 350, 351, 352, 354, 355

Comment on, **1955:** 41, 47, 185

Definition of, **1959:** 102

Letter to Mrs. Rose Richards, **1956:** 289

News conference remarks, **1953:** 12, 31, 109, 208, 225, 230; **1954:** 172, 347; **1956:** 171, 298; **1958:** 70, 198, 213, 222, 310; **1959:** 17, 21, 42, 102, 148, 161, 186, 223; **1960–61:** 38, 362

Influence of Sea Power, **1957:** 215

Information

Approval of bill on mutual security program disclosures, **1959:** 171

Atomic exchange, question of, **1953:** 128, 265; **1954:** 38, 39, 73, 138, 154, 168, 223; **1958:** 83; **1960–61:** 24

Restricted data, proposals on, **1954:** 38

Availability of personal files for Congressional investigations, **1953:** 265; **1954:** 113; **1959:** 172

Availability of records and reports to General Accounting Office, **1958:** 288, 310

Ban on U.S. newsmen in Communist China, **1957:** 17, 45, 80, 134

Berlin, withholding by U.S. officials, **1960–61:** 7

Bill on withholding by Federal officers and agencies, approval, **1958:** 202

Books in U.S. overseas libraries, directive re, **1953:** 109, 126, 128

Classified and security, **1953:** 41

New procedures, **1953:** 109, 110

Statement, **1953:** 110

Truman order, **1953:** 54, 109

Communications between heads of governments, disclosure, **1958:** 74

[References are to items except as otherwise indicated]

Information — *continued*
  Directed to Iron Curtain countries, **1955:** 17 (p. 131)
  Disclosure of secret Government information by private citizen, **1957:** 119
  East-West exchange, **1955:** 167
  E.O. 10501, restrictions under, **1957:** 17
  FBI reports, availability, **1953:** 243; **1957:** 134, 169
  Intelligence-gathering activities, **1960–61:** 143, 154, 163
  International news in U.S. and foreign press, **1954:** 87
  Loyalty files, **1953:** 22; **1954:** 63, 107, 115, 138
  Military services, publicity activities, **1958:** 80, 96
  Mutual security evaluation reports, **1959:** 148, 172
    Iran and Thailand, **1959:** 342
    Vietnam, **1959:** 278
  News conference remarks, **1955:** 10, 59, 62, 81, 146; **1957:** 17, 22, 115, 119, 228
  Non-security, **1954:** 311
  Outer space development, **1957:** 228
  President's Committee on International Information Activities, **1953:** 2, 126, 128 and ftn. (p. 472), 230n.
  Privileged documents, **1956:** 16; **1957:** 22, 115; **1959:** 36, 148, 161, 277; **1960–61:** 380, 422
    Withholding of, Directive to Secretary of Defense, **1954:** 113, 115
    Memorandum of Attorney General, **1954:** 113n.
  Reports of Killian and Gaither panels, withholding of, letter, **1958:** 19
  Scientific and technical, **1958:** 326n.
    Exchange of **1957:** 230; **1958:** 2, 22, 83, 145, 236
  Sigma Delta Chireports, **1959:** 288
  Thermonuclear and atomic development, **1956:** 94
  Unclassified, proposed exchange with IAEA, **1958:** 145
  Yalta documents, **1955:** 59
Information activities, foreign, **1956:** 12 (pp. 80, 81, 108, 109)
Information Activities Abroad, President's Committee on, **1960–61:** 332 ftn. (p. 789)
Information Administration, International, **1953:** 89, 128 ftn. (p. 477)
Information Agency.
  See United States Information Agency.
Information and cultural exchange programs, **1954:** 14 (p. 86); **1958:** 23; **1959:** 10 (p. 75); **1960–61:** 98
  Budget message, **1958:** 5 (pp. 37, 40, 41)
    Table, **1958:** 5 (p. 37)
Information on foreign aspects of national security, conference on, **1958:** 42

Information — *continued*
  Letter to Eric Johnston, **1958:** 4
  Remarks, **1958:** 36
Information program, **1955:** 4
Ingrid, Queen, **1960–61:** 209, 321
  Welcoming remarks to, **1960–61:** 320
Injunctions
  Civil rights cases, **1957:** 8, 157, 178n.
  Merger cases, **1957:** 132
Inland Steel Company, **1959:** 211n.
Inland Waterways Corporation, **1954:** 14 (p. 175)
  Sale of, **1955:** 17 (p. 92)
Inouye, Repr. Daniel K., **1959:** 184n.
Inspection and control of nuclear weapons, **1957:** 2, 8, 80, 245
  See also Aerial inspection; Disarmament.
  Exchange of messages with Prime Minister Kishi, **1957:** 208
  Joint statement with Prime Minister Macmillan, **1957:** 226
  News conference remarks, **1957:** 80, 87, 105, 115, 119, 124, 150, 210
Installment credit, **1956:** 19, 32, 205
  Consumer, **1957:** 95
Institute of Inter-American Affairs, **1953:** 89; **1955:** 76
Institute of International Education, **1959:** 24
Insurance
  Crop, **1960–61:** 414 (p. 989)
  Disability, **1954:** 10; **1955:** 4, 17 (p. 106); **1958:** 5 (pp. 51, 52), 232, 234; **1959:** 10 (pp. 102, 104, 105), 234
    Longshoremen's, **1958:** 5 (p. 45)
  Disaster, **1955:** 222; **1956:** 12 (p. 149); **1957:** 62; **1958:** 5 (p. 54), 37
  Flood, **1956:** 2, 3, 12 (p. 149)
    Approval of bill, **1956:** 167
  Government employees, **1960–61:** 13 (p. 103), 410, 414 (p. 1019)
  Group health insurance, Federal employees, **1956:** 2, 21
  Group Life Insurance Act, **1955:** 4
  Group life insurance for Federal employees, **1954:** 43, 116, 182, 273, 313
    Approval of bill, **1954:** 202
  Health, **1954:** 11, 14 (p. 143), 25, 139, 165, 209, 301; **1955:** 4, 8, 17 (p. 143), 25; **1956:** 2, 3, 12 (p. 119), 19; **1960–61:** 13 (pp. 93, 103), 103, 127, 410, 414 (p. 1019)
    Extension of coverage, **1956:** 21
    Government employees, **1954:** 43, 137; **1958:** 5 (p. 71)
  Military personnel, **1955:** 17 (p. 145)
  Mortgage, **1954:** 3, 14 (pp. 148, 149), 17, 21, 179; **1955:** 17 (p. 172), 19; **1958:** 5 (pp. 43, 59), 43, 62, 224; **1959:** 10 (pp. 46, 47, 82, 84, 85), 102, 104, 153, 187, 208; **1960–61:** 13 (pp. 73, 74), 410, 414 (pp. 980, 981)

Insurance — *continued*
  Non-occupational disability, District of
      Columbia, **1956:** 2
  Old-age and survivors.
      See also main heading, Old-age and survivors'
      insurance.
  Property improvement loans, **1959:** 153, 208
  Railroad retirement, **1959:** 10 (pp. 104, 105)
  Savings accounts, **1960–61:** 13 (p. 73)
  Unemployment, **1954:** 3, 14 (pp. 132, 133, 182–
      185, 188), 21, 43, 73, 139, 143, 227, 236,
      273, 286, 308, 313, 316, 317, 318; **1955:** 17
      (pp. 136, 176, 177, 182), 19, 56, 112, 119;
      1956: 2, 12 (p. 117), 234, 235; **1957:** 13;
      1958: 5 (pp. 50, 51, 62), 18, 26, 49, 53, 56,
      72, 83, 96, 103, 110, 292, 303, 308, 324;
      1959: 10 (pp. 46, 48, 49, 96, 100, 101), 15,
      36, 53, 123; **1960–61:** 13 (pp. 87, 92, 93,
      97–99), 170, 410, 414 (pp. 1005, 1006,
      1009, 1019), 422
  U.S. Government life, **1957:** 73
  Veterans, **1954:** 14 (pp. 132–135); **1955:** 17 (pp.
      136–138); **1956:** 12 (p. 114), 267; **1958:** 5
      (pp. 62, 63)
      Claim of Elba H. Cash, **1959:** 236
      Claim of estate of Carlos M. Cochran, **1954:**
          230
      Claim of estate of Mary B. Denniger, **1954:**
          216
      Claim of Mary D'Agostino, **1959:** 235
      Claim of Raleigh Hill, **1954:** 240
      Claim of Anna Holder, **1954:** 42
      Claim of Mrs. Rose Kaczmarczyk, **1954:** 141
      Claim of Anna K. McQuilkin, **1954:** 228
      Claim of Ethel H. Morrison, **1953:** 162
      Claim of Rosaline Spagnola, **1954:** 239
      Table, **1955:** 17 (p. 140)
  Voluntary health, **1957:** 13, 16
      Extension of coverage, **1956:** 2, 3, 21
Insurance companies, taxes, **1960–61:** 414 (pp. 943,
      944)
      See also Civil rights.
  Armed forces, **1953:** 6; **1954:** 3, 51; **1956:** 190;
      1958: 102; **1959:** 27; **1960–61:** 410
      Campaign remarks, **1956:** 210, 224, 226, 241
  District of Columbia, **1954:** 3, 51, 347
  Federal aid in transition period, **1959:** 27
  Indian citizens, **1956:** 2
  Naval civilian facilities, report, **1953:** 243
      Statement, **1953:** 244
  News conference remarks, **1956:** 229; **1959:** 7,
      17, 21, 26, 102
  Public schools, **1954:** 115, 192, 341; **1956:** 69,
      241; **1957:** 8; **1958:** 98, 103, 295; **1959:** 6;
      1960–61: 137, 414 (p. 1022)
      See also Civil rights.
  Army posts, **1956:** 229
  Comment on, **1955:** 119, 149
  Court decisions on.
      See Courts, Federal.

Insurance companies, taxes — *continued*
  Interposition resolutions on Supreme Court
      decision, **1956:** 47
  Justice Department recommendations re,
      1953: 249
  Letter to J. Albert Rolston, **1958:** 267
  Little Rock situation.
      See Little Rock, Ark.
  Louisville, Ky., **1956:** 205
  Manifesto of members of Congress, **1956:** 56
  News conference remarks, **1956:** 20, 32, 47, 56,
      62, 113, 171, 193, 198, 205, 229, 235; **1957:**
      124, 134; **1958:** 198, 222, 274
  President's attitude on, **1958:** 213, 222
  Texas (Texarkana), **1956:** 198, 205
  Virginia, **1958:** 103, 213, 222, 274
  President's attitude on, **1959:** 17, 21
  Schools on military posts, **1953:** 36, 101, 198
  VA facilities, **1954:** 309; **1960–61:** 410
  Virginia, **1959:** 17, 26
Integration.
  See also Civil Rights.
  Armed forces, **1953:** 6; **1954:** 3, 51; **1956:** 190;
      1958: 102; **1959:** 27; **1960–61:** 410
  Campaign remarks, **1956:** 210, 224, 226, 241
  District of Columbia, **1954:** 3, 51, 347
  Federal aid in transition period, **1959:** 27
  Indian citizens, **1956:** 2
  Naval civilian facilities, report, **1953:** 243
      -Statement, **1953:** 244
  News conference remarks, **1956:** 229; **1959:** 7,
      17, 21, 26, 102
  VA facilities, **1954:** 309; **1960–61:** 410
Integration, public schools, **1954:** 115, 192, 341;
      1956: 69, 241; **1957:** 8; **1958:** 98, 103, 295;
      1959: 6; **1960–61:** 137, 414 (p. 1022)
  See also Civil rights.
  Army posts, **1953:** 36, 101, 198; **1956:** 229
  Comment on, **1955:** 119, 149
  Court decisions on.
      See Courts, federal.
  Interposition resolutions on Supreme Court de-
      cision, **1956:** 47
  Justice Department recommendations re, **1953:**
      249
  Letter to J. Albert Rolston, **1958:** 267
  Little Rock situation.
      See Little Rock, Ark.
  Louisville, Ky., **1956:** 205
  Manifesto of members of Congress, **1956:** 56
  News conference remarks, **1956:** 20, 32, 47, 56,
      62, 113, 171, 193, 205, 229, 235; **1957:** 124,
      134; **1958:** 198, 222, 274
  President's attitude on, **1958:** 213, 222; **1959:** 17,
      21
  Texas (Texarkana), **1956:** 198, 205
  Virginia, **1958:** 103, 213, 222, 274; **1959:** 17, 26
Intelligence, military, **1959:** 29
Intelligence activities of Government, Board of
      Consultants on, **1956:** 9, 10

Intelligence board, U.S., **1960–61:** 21

Intelligence briefings for Presidential nominees, **1960–61:** 103

Intelligence-gathering activities, **1960–61:** 143, 154, 163

Intelligence reports on foreign attairs (1952), **1956:** 198

Intelligence service, foreign, **1956:** 9, 10, 58

Intelligence services, U.S., **1959:** 48

Inter-agency ad hoc committee on textile industry
    Letter to New England Governors, **1959:** 112
    Letter to Secretary Strauss, **1959:** 113

Inter-agency Committee on Agricultural Disposal
    Letter to Chairman, **1954:** 262
    Letter to members, **1954:** 263

Inter-American Affairs, Institute of, **1953:** 89; **1955:** 76

Inter-American Affairs, National Advisory Committee on, **1960–61:** 42 and ftn. (p. 205), 51, 69, 228, 349
    Message to President Kubitschek, **1959:** 287

Inter-American bank, **1958:** 222

Inter-American Committee of Presidential Representatives, report, **1957:** 96 and n.

Inter-American Conference (1826), **1956:** 145n., 146

Inter-American Conference, 10th, at Caracas, **1954:** 25, 209, 225, 273, 286, 297; **1955:** 4; **1958:** 133
    Position on international communism, **1954:** 115, 143, 203, 209, 225, 273, 297, 304

Inter-American Congress of Municipalities, remarks, **1960–61:** 333

Inter-American Cultural and Trade Center, Miami, Fla., **1956:** 278

Inter-American Development Bank, **1959:** 6; **1960–61:** 36, 39, 42, 72, 73, 87, 245, 410, 415n.
    Budget messages, **1959:** 10 (pp. 44, 73, 74); **1960–61:** 13 (p. 63), 414 (pp. 961, 962, 965)
    Cutler, Robert, appointment as U.S. member, Board of Executive Directors, **1959:** 261
    Joint statement with President Lemus, **1959:** 54
    Message to Congress, **1959:** 98
    President (Felipe Herrera), **1960–61:** 72, 73

Inter-American Economic and Social Council, **1959:** 98

Inter-American Highway, **1954:** 102; **1955:** 59; **1958:** 5 (pp. 36, 37)
    Letter to Vice President and Speaker, **1955:** 64

Inter-American Institute of Agricultural Sciences, activities, **1957:** 96

Inter-American Investment Conference, message, **1955:** 44

Inter-American Medical Cruise Congress, **1953:** 260

Inter-American Nuclear Energy Commission, proposed establishment, **1957:** 96

Inter-American Peace Committee, **1960–61:** 73

Inter-American Press Association, remarks at meeting of, **1957:** 217 and n.

Inter-American Social and Economic Cooperation Program, **1960–61:** 414 (pp. 962, 966)

Inter-American system of collective security, **1956:** 2

Inter-American Treaty of Reciprocal Assistance (1947), **1956:** 146; **1958:** 96; **1960–61:** 42, 48, 73, 85, 87, 227, 268
    Joint statement with President Kubitschek, **1960–61:** 46

Interchurch Center, New York City, cornerstone laying, remarks, **1958:** 285

Intercontinental ballistic missiles (ICBM). *See* Missiles.

Interdepartmental Committee on Children and Youth, **1958:** 119

Interdepartmental Committee on Civilian Compensation and Pay Systems, **1958:** 169

Interdepartmental Committee to Coordinate Federal Area Assistance Programs, **1960–61:** 5, 176n.

Interdepartmental Committee on Migratory Labor, **1953:** 214

Interdepartmental Committee on Narcotics, **1954:** 343; **1956:** 31

Interdepartmental Committee for the Voluntary Payroll Savings Plan for the Purchase of United States Savings Bonds
    Letter to Chairman, **1955:** 186
    Memorandums, **1954:** 15; **1955:** 187

Interdepartmental Working Group on Aging, **1956:** 74

Interest expenditures, **1955:** 17 (pp. 95, 101, 183, 184); **1958:** 5 (p. 70)
    Table, **1955:** 17 (p. 184)

Interest on national debt, **1959:** 43, 124, 290; **1960–61:** 4
    Budget messages, **1954:** 14 (pp. 190, 191); **1959:** 10 (pp. 107, 108); **1960–61:** 13 (pp. 41, 42, 100), 414 (pp. 938, 1016)
    Tables, **1954:** 14 (p. 191); **1959:** 10 (p. 108)
    News conference remarks, **1959:** 102, 288

Interest rates, **1955:** 17 (pp. 96, 106)
    College housing loans, **1959:** 208
    Farm ownership loans, **1959:** 10 (p. 91)
    Federal bonds, **1959:** 36, 123, 124, 126, 144n., 161, 167, 179, 186, 188, 223, 230, 231; **1960–61:** 6, 13 (pp. 41, 42, 100, 101), 17, 133, 255, 414 (p. 942), 423
    Federal lending programs, **1958:** 5 (p. 44); **1959:** 10 (pp. 50, 51)
    Federal Reserve, **1956:** 88, 94, 171, 229, 235
    FHA insured mortgages, **1959:** 153, 208
    Government loans, **1957:** 3, 16, 75, 129
        News conference remarks, **1957:** 80, 169
        Savings bonds, **1957:** 76

Interest rates — *continued*
  Government loans — *continued*
    Veterans' loans, **1957:** 16, 129; **1958:** 5 (p. 59),
      62
    Letter to minority leaders, **1958:** 43
    Loans from Federal Treasury, **1959:** 30
    Loans to veterans, **1959:** 146
    Mortgages, **1958:** 62, 63; **1960–61:** 13 (p. 74), 414
      (p. 981)
    News conference remarks, **1953:** 63, 74, 120
    REA loans, **1954:** 33
    Ship mortgage loans, **1960–61:** 13 (p. 69), 414 (p.
      976)
    World Bank loans, **1959:** 32
Interference in internal affairs of foreign countries,
    1958: 222
Intergovernmental Committee for European Mi-
    gration, **1953:** 53, 89; **1956:** 12 (p. 107),
    58, 213n., 306; **1957:** 250
  Budget message, **1955:** 17 (p. 131)
  U.S. support of, **1955:** 76
Intergovernmental Relations, Advisory Commis-
    sion on, **1960–61:** 115, 208, 415n.
  Budget messages, **1960–61:** 13 (p. 105), 414 (p.
    1022)
Intergovernmental Relations, Commission on,
    1953: 159, 169; **1954:** 3, 14 (p. 190), 102,
    222, 273, 346; **1955:** 4; **1956:** 2; **1957:** 118;
    1960–61: 208
  Civil defense recommendations, **1955:** 149
  News conference remarks, **1953:** 37, 54, 198, 225;
    1955: 47, 146, 149
  Proposed, **1953:** 6, 16, 37, 54, 67, 156
    Message to Congress, **1953:** 39
  Reports, **1955:** 145; **1958:** 106
  Statements, **1953:** 16, 186
Inter-Parliamentary Union, Conference of the,
    greetings to delegates, **1953:** 209
Interior, Department of the, **1953:** 6, 40; **1956:** 67;
    1958: 43; **1959:** 62; **1960–61:** 358
  Appropriations for civil functions approved,
    1957: 161
  Budget messages, **1954:** 14 (p. 168); **1956:** 12 (p.
    140); **1958:** 5 (p. 69); **1959:** 10 (pp. 53,
    95); **1960–61:** 13 (pp. 84–86, 91, 108), 414
    (pp. 947, 956, 992, 995, 998, 999, 1025)
  Bureau of Commercial Fisheries, **1959:** 10 (p. 95)
  Central Valley Project, San Luis Unit, Calif.,
    1960–61: 168
  Civil water resources functions, **1960–61:** 414 (p.
    947)
  Coal research and conservation programs, **1959:**
    221; **1960–61:** 13 (p. 85), 402, 414 (p. 998)
  Federal property in Virgin Islands, **1955:** 14
  Hardy, Royce A., **1959:** 18n.
  Indian health services, **1955:** 17 (p. 144)
  Menominee Indian Tribe supervision, **1954:** 147
  Oil import program, **1960–61:** 383, 432
  Power transmission facilities, **1954:** 14 (p. 168)

Interior, Department of the — *continued*
  Projects starts, comment on, **1959:** 42
  Public lands, **1954:** 152
  Public works, appropriations, **1956:** 136
  Vetoes, **1959:** 194, 213
  Reorganization Plan 1 of 1959, **1959:** 101
  Report, **1960–61:** 402
  Rural development program, **1957:** 156
  Small business purchases, **1956:** 263
Interior, Secretary of the, **1955:** 14
  Authority to contract for coal research, pro-
    posed, **1959:** 221
  Filling of office of, **1956:** 96, 113
Interior, Secretary of the (Douglas McKay), **1953:**
    25; **1954:** 125, 126, 256, 270, 271, 347, 355
  Chairman, Community Chest and United De-
    fense Fund campaigns, National Capital
    area, **1953:** 127
  Colorado River development project, **1954:** 62
  Electric power, policy on, **1953:** 171
  Federal Council on Aging, representation on,
    1956: 74
  Letter to, **1956:** 54
  Minerals policy, letter, **1953:** 228
  Mission 66, plan for National Park Service,
    1956: 29
  News conference remarks on, **1953:** 15, 77, 126,
    128
  Red Cross campaign, Chairman, **1956:** 11
  Resignation, **1956:** 67
  Water resources, **1956:** 13
    Development, **1954:** 122
Interior, Secretary of the (Fred A. Seaton), **1956:**
    121, 165; **1957:** 12, 115; **1959:** 51n., 184n.;
    1960–61: 152
  Chairman, United Givers Fund campaign, **1957:**
    140
  Oil import program, **1958:** 54
  Oil supply study, **1956:** 239
  Pageant of Peace ceremonies, **1956:** 315
  Resignation, letter, **1960–61:** 402
  Theodore Roosevelt centennial ceremony, **1958:**
    100
Interior, Under Secretary of (Clarence A. Davis),
    1956: 121, 217
Intermediate range ballistic missiles (IRBM).
    See Missiles.
Internal Revenue, Bureau of, taxes on U. S.
    companies abroad, **1957:** 80
Internal Revenue Code
  Disapproval of amendment, **1955:** 198; **1956:**
    181, 183
  Revision, **1954:** 14 (p. 99), 199
Internal Revenue Service, **1954:** 14 (pp. 98, 187),
    353; **1955:** 17 (p. 179); **1956:** 12 (p. 150);
    1960–61: 151
  Rule on taxation of disability payments, **1960–**
    61: 291

[References are to items except as otherwise indicated]

Internal Revenue Service — *continued*
  Tax enforcement programs, **1960–61:** 13 (p. 101),
    414 (p. 1017)
  Tax refund claims
    Baurkot, Raymond, **1960–61:** 288
    Hjerpe, Eric and Ida Mae, **1960–61:** 291
Internal Revenue Service, Commissioner (T.
    Coleman Andrews), **1954:** 107
International agreements, bipartisanship, **1960–61:**
    7
International agreements, Communist attitude on,
    1959: 6
International agreements, World War II, **1953:** 12,
    14, 15
International agreements (1953)
  German settlement of debts and claims, **1953:** 46
  International Wheat Agreement, **1953:** 101
  U.S.-Spain, defense agreement, **1953:** 198
International agreements (1954)
  U.S.-Korea, Mutual Defense Treaty, **1954:** 3, 6,
    139, 168
  U.S.-Mexico, Migrant Labor Agreement, **1954:**
    56
International agreements (1955)
  Anglo-American Financial Agreement, amend-
    ment, **1957:** 44
  Austrian State Treaty, **1955:** 59, 81, 95, 98, 99,
    100, 114
  Civil uses of atomic energy, **1955:** 228
    U.S.-Belgium, Canada, United Kingdom,
      1955: 123
    U.S.-NATO, **1955:** 71
    U.S.-Turkey, **1955:** 89, 112
  Manila Pact (Southeast Asia Defense Treaty),
    1955: 4, 5, 35
  News conference remarks, **1955:** 41, 59, 81, 112
  Paris agreements, **1955:** 41, 54, 59, 62, 164
    U.S.-China, Mutual Defense Treaty, **1955:** 5,
      21, 35
  Statute of the International Atomic Energy
    Agency, **1957:** 54
International agreements (1958)
  Afghanistan, cultural agreement, **1958:** 150
  U.S.-Canada, air defense agreement, **1958:** 163
  U.S.-Euratom, **1958:** 145, 236
  U.S.-Soviet agreement on cultural and technical
    exchanges, letter, **1958:** 31
  U.S.-U.K. agreement on atomic energy for mu-
    tual defense
    Memorandum, **1958:** 156
    Message, **1958:** 157
International agreements (1959)
  Antarctic Treaty, **1959:** 284
  International coffee agreement, **1959:** 257
  U.S. agreements with Canada, France, Greece,
    U.K. on atomic energy for mutual de-
    fense, **1959:** 119n., 120n.

International agreements (1959) — *continued*
  U.S. agreements with Germany, Netherlands,
    and Turkey on atomic energy for mutual
    defense, **1959:** 119 and n., 120
  U.S.-Guinea, cultural agreement, **1959:** 272
International agreements (1960–61)
  U.S.-Canada, Columbia River Basin Treaty,
    1960–61: 416, 419
  U.S.-India, food-for-peace agreement, **1960–61:**
    136
  U.S.-Italy, atomic energy for mutual defense,
    1960–61: 420
  U.S.-Japan, Treaty of Mutual Cooperation and
    Security, **1960–61:** 14, 15, 16, 209, 245,
    410, 422
International agreements contravening the Consti-
    tution, statement, **1953:** 142; **1954:** 9, 25,
    50
International air cadet exchange group, remarks,
    1958: 200
International Association of Chiefs of Police, re-
    marks, **1960–61:** 314
International Atomic Energy Agency, **1956:** 2, 43,
    143, 299; **1957:** 8, 13, 16, 245; **1958:** 8,
    113, 145, 188; **1960–61:** 410
  See also Atomic energy for peaceful uses; Power
    projects.
  Budget message, **1959:** 10 (p. 68)
  Director General (W. Sterling Cole), **1958:** 148
  Joint statement with Prime Minister Eden, **1956:**
    26
  News conference remarks, **1957:** 150, 169
  Ratification of Statute, **1957:** 54, 144 and n.;
    1956: 143, 266; **1957:** 54, 144
    Conference on, **1956:** 273, 274
  U.S. participation, report, **1958:** 148; **1959:** 189
  U.S. Representative (Paul F. Foster), **1959:** 121
  Uranium 235 for, **1956:** 52, 274
  Vienna Conference, **1957:** 204
    Message, **1960–61:** 301
International Atomic Energy Agency, proposed,
    1954: 223, 260, 322; **1955:** 17 (p. 119), 59,
    79, 121, 156, 228
International Atomic Energy Commission, pro-
    posed, **1953:** 256
International Bank for Reconstruction and De-
    velopment, **1954:** 67, 150, 351; **1955:** 6,
    72, 156; **1957:** 50, 90, 157, 195 and n.;
    1958: 207; **1959:** 98; **1960–61:** 4, 36, 39,
    73, 86, 302, 410, 415n.
  See also International Development Association.
  Assistance in Indus River project, **1960–61:** 297
  Aswan Dam, **1957:** 70
  Budget messages, **1955:** 17 (p. 128); **1958:** 5 (p.
    39); **1959:** 10 (pp. 44, 71–74); **1960–61:** 13
    (p. 63), 414 (p. 964)
  Cuaderno, McGill, **1957:** 195n.
  Iliff, W. A. B., **1960–61:** 284, 297
  Increase in funds, **1959:** 32

International Bank — *continued*
Loans to Latin American countries, **1955:** 76
Meeting, remarks, **1956:** 218
Memorandum on International Finance Corporation, **1955:** 86
Mutual security loans, **1956:** 58
New Delhi meeting, **1958:** 312
Message, **1958:** 278
News conference remarks, **1956:** 20; **1959:** 94, 223, 288; **1960–61:** 7, 284
President (Eugene R. Black), **1960–61:** 284, 297
Remarks, **1959:** 244
U.S. contributions to, **1959:** 6
Wenzell, Adolphe H., **1955:** 146 and ftn. (pp. 657, 658)
International Boundary Commission, United States, Alaska, and Canada, Commissioner (Samuel L. Golan), **1953:** 41
International Boundary and Water Commission, **1959:** 38; **1960–61:** 335
Budget messages, **1960–61:** 13 (p. 83), 414 (p. 996)
United States and Mexico, **1953:** 222
International Brotherhood of Teamsters, **1955:** 232
International Chamber of Commerce
40th anniversary, remarks, **1959:** 84
United States Council, **1956:** 310
International Children's Emergency Fund, United Nations, U.S. contribution, **1953:** 143
International Christian Leadership, remarks, **1953:** 8
International Claims Commission of the United States, termination, **1954:** 94
International Coffee Study Group, **1959:** 38
International Confederation of Free Trade Unions, Third World Congress, **1953:** 130
International conferences, comment on, **1953:** 198
International Congress of Actuaries, remarks to, **1957:** 222
International Congress on Nutrition, remarks, **1960–61:** 279
International cooperation, **1960–61:** 248n.
International Cooperation Administration, **1957:** 36, 90; **1958:** 312; **1959:** 55; **1960–61:** 247, 315n., 349
Budget message, **1956:** 12 (p. 109)
Congressional attitude toward, **1959:** 26
Director, filling of vacancy, **1959:** 29
Hungarian refugees, funds for, **1956:** 307
Letter to Secretary of State re, **1955:** 74
Mutual security reports, **1959:** 148, 172
Iran and Thailand, **1959:** 342
Vietnam, **1959:** 278
News conference remarks, **1959:** 26, 29, 148, 172
Overseas personnel, reduction, **1960–61:** 362
Philippines, economic discussions, **1958:** 143
Report on Formosa aid, access to, **1958:** 288
U.S. aid to South America, documents re, **1960–61:** 380

International Cooperation Administration, Director (John B. Hollister), **1955:** 90; **1957:** 145, 150
Bipartisan conference, **1957:** 2
International Cooperation Administration, Director (James W. Riddleberger), **1959:** 154; **1960–61:** 315
International Cooperation Administration, Director (James H. Smith, Jr.), **1958:** 316; **1959:** 26
International Council of Christian Leadership, remarks, **1956:** 28
International Council of Scientific Unions, **1957:** 122, 211
International Court of Justice, **1953:** 129n.; **1957:** 45, 72, 87; **1958:** 89; **1959:** 6, 314; **1960–61:** 73
U.S. acceptance of jurisdiction, **1960–61:** 4, 13 (p. 65), 276 and ftn. (p. 665), 414 (p. 968)
International Development Advisory Board, **1958:** 4
International development association, **1958:** 222, 312; **1959:** 223, 244; **1960–61:** 36, 132, 410
Budget messages, **1960–61:** 13 (pp. 63, 64), 414 (pp. 964, 965)
U.S. participation, message to Congress, **1960–61:** 39
International Economic Growth, Committee for, address, **1960–61:** 132
International Educational Exchange Service, **1959:** 222n.
International field hockey festival, remarks to participants, **1960–61:** 319
International finance, **1960–61:** 13 (pp. 59–64), 414 (pp. 961–968)
Budget messages, **1954:** 14; **1959:** 10 (pp. 71–75)
Tables, **1954:** 14 (p. 137); **1959:** 10 (p. 72); **1960–61:** 13 (p. 61), 414 (p. 963)
International Finance Corporation, **1954:** 351; **1955:** 6, 44, 156; **1957:** 195
Budget message, **1955:** 17 (p. 128)
Remarks, **1959:** 244
U.S. participation in, message, **1955:** 86
International financial institutions, remarks to Governors of, **1957:** 195 and n.
International friendship, **1953:** 223
International Geophysical Year, **1955:** 47 ftn. (p. 308); **1956:** 12 (p. 123); **1958:** 27, 47, 274; **1959:** 115, 267, 284; **1960–61:** 11, 393
Argus project, **1959:** 67 and ftn. (p. 294)
Budget message, **1955:** 17 (p. 148)
News conference remarks, **1957:** 70, 210
Opening of, remarks, **1957:** 122
Satellite development, **1957:** 70, 211
Scientific activities in Antarctica, **1958:** 92
U.S. Committee, **1957:** 210
U.S. participation, **1954:** 152

International Information Activities, President's
    Committee on, **1953:** 230n.
    Establishment, statement, **1953:** 2
    Report, **1953:** 126, 128 and ftn. (p. 472)
International Information Administration, **1953:**
    89, 128 ftn. (p. 477)
International investments, **1957:** 80
    Joint statement with Prime Minister Suhra-
        wardy, **1957:** 131
International Joint Commission-United States and
    Canada, **1954:** 165, 271; **1956:** 177
International Labor Conferences, **1954:** 125, 126
International Labor Organization, **1953:** 249; **1954:**
    67; **1955:** 156; **1957:** 50, 72; **1959:** 189
    Action on forced labor, **1956:** 96
    Convention on social security standards, **1954:**
        126
    Conventions and recommendations, message,
        1955: 107
    Geneva conference, **1955:** 119; **1956:** 94, 121
    Recommendations on collective agreements and
        voluntary conciliation and arbitration,
        1954: 125
International law, **1960–61:** 7
    Remarks on, **1959:** 314
International Longshoremen's Association, **1953:**
    203; **1959:** 250
    Labor dispute, **1956:** 300
International Monetary and Financial Problems,
    National Advisory Council on, **1953:** 60,
    93; **1954:** 348; **1956:** 139; **1960–61:** 39
    Reports, **1959:** 32, 98
International Monetary Fund, **1954:** 67; **1955:** 72;
    1957: 13, 195; **1958:** 163; **1959:** 6; **1960–
    61:** 36, 95, 302, 410, 415n.
    Budget messages, **1959:** 10 (pp. 44, 71, 73);
        1960–61: 13 (p. 63)
    Increase in funds, **1959:** 32
    Meeting, remarks, **1956:** 218
    New Delhi meeting, **1958:** 312
        Message, **1958:** 278
    News conference remarks, **1959:** 94, 223
    Remarks at annual meeting, **1959:** 244
International news in U.S. and foreign press, **1954:**
    87
International observation of nuclear tests, **1957:** 55,
    124
International Olympic Committee, **1959:** 132
International Peasant Union Forum, **1953:** 264
International police force, proposed, **1960–61:** 330
International Press Institute, address, **1958:** 80
International Rules of Judicial Procedure, Com-
    mission on, **1960–61:** 13 (p. 105)
International School of Nuclear Science and En-
    gineering, foreign students, remarks,
    1955: 53
International Service, School of, American Uni-
    versity, remarks at ground breaking,
    1957: 109 and n.

International Tchaikovsky Piano Contest, **1958:** 78
International teacher development program, **1959:**
    222n.
International trade, **1957:** 8, 13, 32
    See also Trade, international.
    Communist countries, **1957:** 70, 105
    Joint statements
        Prime Minister Kishi, **1957:** 117
        Prime Minister Macmillan, **1957:** 55, 226
        Prime Minister Suhrawardy, **1957:** 131
International travel, **1954:** 67, 323
International Wheat Agreement, **1953:** 101; **1954:**
    14 (p. 160); **1960–61:** 13 (p. 77)
    Budget message, **1956:** 12 (p. 129)
    Renewal, **1956:** 6
Interposition resolutions on school integration de-
    cisions, news conference remarks, **1956:**
    47
Interstate Commerce Act, **1960–61:** 225
Interstate Commerce Commission, **1956:** 12 (p.
    149); **1960–61:** 225
    Budget messages, **1954:** 14 (p. 178); **1960–61:** 414
        (pp. 946, 984)
    Contracts with common carriers, authority re,
        1954: 246
    Knudson, James K., **1954:** 48
    Recommended action on railroads and trans-
        portation industry, **1958:** 82 and n.
Interstate Commerce Commission, Chairman (J.
    Monroe Johnson), **1954:** 57, 68, 161
Interstate highway system.
    See Highway system, interstate.
Interstate travel, racial discrimination, **1954:** 63,
    143, 161
Introduction to Outer Space, **1958:** 56, 74
    Statement, **1958:** 57
Investment Bankers Association of America,
    1960–61: 222
Investments abroad, **1953:** 6; **1954:** 14 (p. 97), 67,
    323, 324; **1955:** 4, 6, 76; **1956:** 2, 12 (p.
    107), 19, 58, 87; **1958:** 32; **1959:** 6, 55, 87,
    244, 258, 316; **1960–61:** 228
    Address to Canadian Parliament, **1958:** 163
    Budget messages, **1955:** 17 (pp. 128, 132); **1958:** 5
        (p. 36); **1959:** 10 (pp. 71, 73); **1960–61:** 13
        (p. 64), 414 (pp. 964, 965)
    Colombo Plan meeting, remarks, **1958:** 312
    Ghana, joint statement, **1958:** 180
    Joint statement with President Gronchi, **1956:** 49
    Less developed areas, **1955:** 17 (p. 128)
Iowa, **1958:** 288; **1959:** 75
    Ames, **1959:** 186
    Beardsley, Gov. William S., **1954:** 226
        Death of, statement, **1954:** 339
    Boone, **1956:** 212
    Candidates for public office, **1956:** 212
    Cedar Rapids, **1958:** 290, 305
    Colfax, **1956:** 211

Iowa — *continued*
  Des Moines, **1954:** 226; **1956:** 212, 216; **1959:** 21, 69, 186
  Hickenlooper, Sen. Bourke B., **1953:** 268; **1956:** 212; **1958:** 290
  Hoegh, Gov. Leo A., **1956:** 212
  Martin, Sen. Thomas E., **1956:** 212; **1958:** 290
  Muscatine Bridge Commission, **1956:** 148, 182
  Newton, **1956:** 198, 205
  Schwengel, Repr. Fred, **1959:** 31n.
  Soil bank payments, **1956:** 216
  State Fair, visit to, **1954:** 200, 226
Iran, **1953:** 156; **1954:** 297, 304, 320, 325; **1955:** 4, 18, 35, 76; **1956:** 117; **1957:** 6, 90, 91, 152; **1958:** 80, 207; **1960–61:** 23, 302, 341, 410
  See also Tehran.
  Ambassador Edward T. Wailes, **1959:** 319n., 322
  Aram, Abbas, **1959:** 322
  Assistance, **1953:** 129, 178; **1954:** 14 (p. 139); **1955:** 17 (p. 130); **1958:** 36; **1959:** 55
    Evaluation of, report on, **1959:** 342
  Azerbaijan, **1959:** 320
  Baghdad Pact, **1956:** 2
  Bilateral Agreement of Cooperation, **1959:** 251
  Campaign remarks, **1956:** 210; **1958:** 287, 290, 293, 302
  Communism in, **1953:** 22; **1954:** 192, 203, 209, 273, 286, 316, 318, 319, 320, 317, 353
  Earthquake disaster at Lar, **1960–61:** 126
  Eqbal, Manuchehr, **1959:** 251, 320, 322
  Hekmat, Reza, **1959:** 320
  Mossadegh, Mohammed, **1953:** 22, 156; **1954:** 192, 209; **1956:** 87; **1958:** 36, 287
    Message, **1953:** 129
  News conference remarks, **1956:** 16, 198
  Oil situation, **1953:** 129; **1954:** 209, 278, 286; **1958:** 36
    Settlement of dispute with foreign oil companies, letter, **1954:** 184, 185, 186, 226
  Pahlavi, Mohammad Reza, **1953:** 22; **1954:** 353; **1955:** 42; **1958:** 174; **1959:** 319, 320, 321, 323
    Joint statement with, **1959:** 322
    Letter, **1954:** 184
    Messages, **1954:** 264; **1960–61:** 126
  Relations with United Kingdom, **1953:** 129
  Sadr, Mohsed, **1959:** 320
  Tudeh (Communist Party), **1953:** 156
  U.S. Ambassador Loy W. Henderson, **1953:** 129; **1954:** 184n., 186
  Visit to, **1959:** 277, 319, 320, 321, 322, 323
  Zahedi, Fazollah, message, **1953:** 178
Iraq, **1957:** 6, 207
  Assistance, **1954:** 92
  Baghdad Pact, **1956:** 2
  Communism in, **1959:** 36, 89
  Crown Prince Abdul Ilah, **1957:** 28
  Letter to Premier Khrushchev on, **1958:** 177

Iraq — *continued*
  News conference remarks, **1959:** 36, 89, 94
  Outbreak in, **1958:** 171, 172, 173, 198
  U.S. foreign policy, comment on, **1959:** 89
IRBM (Intermediate Range Ballistic Missiles).
  See Missiles.
Ireland
  Frederick H. Boland, **1960–61:** 302n.
  Sean T. O'Kelly, **1956:** 208; **1959:** 58, 59, 64
Ireland, Northern, John A. Costello, **1956:** 56
Iron Curtain countries, **1955:** 81; **1958:** 80
  Exchange of students, **1958:** 23
Iron ore, imports, **1958:** 58, 96; **1959:** 55; **1960–61:** 132
Iron and Steel Institute, **1960–61:** 315
Iroquois, League of, **1960–61:** 330
Irrigation projects, **1954:** 3, 53, 201; **1955:** 17 (pp. 156–159); **1956:** 12 (pp. 134, 135); **1958:** 5 (p. 68); **1959:** 10 (p. 94)
  Budget message, **1954:** 14 (pp. 164, 167, 168)
Irvine Ranch (Calif.), **1953:** 137
Irving, Maj. Gen. F. A., **1954:** 333
Irwin, Donald, **1954:** 341; **1955:** 26
Isaac, **1955:** 325
Isabella, Queen, **1959:** 338
Isaiah, prophecy of, reference to, **1954:** 297
Islamic Center, remarks at opening ceremonies, **1957:** 120
Ismay, Lord, **1953:** 71, 255
  Letter, **1953:** 72
  Message, **1953:** 74
Isolationism, **1959:** 6; **1960–61:** 328
  United States, question of, **1953:** 88
Isotopes, radioactive, **1955:** 121
Israel, **1956:** 2, 282; **1957:** 6; **1958:** 293
  Arab boycott of, **1960–61:** 38
  Arms for, **1956:** 53, 56
  Assistance, **1953:** 225, 230; **1954:** 14 (p. 139), 92; **1955:** 17 (p. 130)
  Atomic research agreement, **1955:** 121
  Ben-Gurion, David, **1956:** 276, 295; **1957:** 34, 40
  Bombing incident, **1957:** 228
  Defense pact with U.S., comment on proposal, **1960–61:** 38
  Denial of access to Suez Canal, **1960–61:** 127
  Diplomatic break with Soviet Union, **1953:** 15
  Dispute with Arab States, **1953:** 230
  Eban, Abba, **1960–61:** 21, 24
  Egypt, invasion of territory, **1956:** 276, 282, 295, 298; **1957:** 34
    U.N. action, **1958:** 8, 148
  German-Israeli agreement, **1954:** 189n.
  Joint statement with Prime Minister Eden, **1956:** 26
  Jordan River development, **1953:** 217, 230
    Johnston plan, **1956:** 198, 298; **1958:** 198
  News conference remarks, **1956:** 53, 56, 113, 198, 216, 298; **1957:** 28, 45, 50, 56, 62, 207, 228; **1960–61:** 21, 38, 127

Israel — *continued*
Refugee problem, **1956:** 26
Shapiro, Moshe, **1957:** 228
Suez Canal, **1958:** 293
Blockade, **1956:** 216
Invasion (1956), **1960–61:** 21
Withdrawal of forces behind armistice lines, **1957:** 35 and n., 40
Israeli-Arab dispute, **1954:** 297; **1955:** 76, 239; **1956:** 143, 268, 282; **1958:** 293
Joint statement with Prime Minister Eden, **1956:** 26
News conference remarks, **1954:** 68, 157, 172; **1956:** 20, 198, 298
Statement, **1955:** 234
Issa, Abdullahi, **1960–61:** 324n.
Italian Red Cross, **1954:** 315n.
Italian Restitution Mission, **1956:** 45n.
Italy, **1953:** 234; **1954:** 84n., 319; **1955:** 4, 18, 54n.; **1956:** 2, 210; **1958:** 28, 32, 287; **1959:** 89, 124; **1960–61:** 355
See also Rome.
Aerial photography, message, **1956:** 264
Agreement with Yugoslavia on Trieste, **1954:** 283, 284, 286, 297, 316
Ambassador Clare Boothe Luce, **1954:** 283n.; **1955:** 61
Ambassador James D. Zellerbach, **1959:** 291n., 292, 294n.
Anzio, **1954:** 63; **1959:** 7
Atomic energy for mutual defense, agreement with U.S., **1960–61:** 420
Atomic research agreement, **1955:** 121
Brosio, Manlio, **1955:** 61; **1959:** 294n.
Christian Democratic Party, **1956:** 207
Communist infiltration into aircraft plants, question of, **1954:** 39
Compensation claims of U.S. nationals, **1954:** 94
Courts in, decision on Iranian oil, **1953:** 129n.
Einaudi, Luigi, message, **1954:** 283
Euratom.
See European Atomic Energy Community.
Fanfani, Amintore, **1956:** 207; **1958:** 211
Joint statement, **1958:** 186
Floods and landslides, statement on, **1954:** 315
Gift to the President, **1956:** 45
Gronchi, Giovanni, **1955:** 208n.; **1956:** 39, 45, 46, 47, 49, 264; **1959:** 291, 294; **1960–61:** 34
Joint statements with, **1956:** 49; **1959:** 293
Martino, Gaetano, **1955:** 61
Nettuno (Anzio), **1956:** 102, 113
Paris agreements.
See main heading, Paris agreements.
Pella, Giuseppe, **1959:** 203, 248, 291, 293, 294n.
Rome.
See main heading, Rome.
Scelba, Mario, joint statement, **1955:** 61
Scientific contributions, **1957:** 230

Italy — *continued*
Segni, Antonio, **1955:** 208n.; **1959:** 186, 214, 243, 247, 291, 293, 294
Joint statements with, **1959:** 203, 248
Trieste, **1956:** 16, 87, 117, 198, 210, 224; **1958:** 80, 287, 290, 302
Visit to, **1959:** 277, 291, 292, 293, 294
Works of art, restitution of, **1956:** 45n.
World War II military operations, **1956:** 113
Item veto, proposed, **1959:** 6, 10 (p. 52), 300n.; **1960–61:** 24
Budget messages, **1960–61:** 13 (p. 107), 414 (p. 1026)
Question of, **1954:** 9, 57
Ives, Sen. Irving M., **1953:** 68, 69; **1954:** 298, 300; **1958:** 306
Labor bill, **1958:** 216
News conference remarks on, **1954:** 48, 322
Ivory Coast, Republic of
Ekra, Mathieu, **1960–61:** 324n.
Independence, message to Prime Minister Houphouet-Boigny, **1960–61:**, 254
Iwo Jima Statue, inscription, **1954:** 294
Izaguirre, Gen. Carlos, death of, **1956:** 144

Jackson, Andrew, **1954:** 106; **1957:** 198; **1960–61:** 284
Jackson, Mrs. B. B., and son, **1956:** 241
Jackson, Charles D., **1953:** 2n., 33, 81, 126, 254 ftn. (p. 800); **1954:** 68; **1957:** 50
Jackson, Harry E.
News conference remarks on, **1956:** 16
Telegram to, **1956:** 15
Jackson, Thomas J. (Stonewall), **1953:** 240; **1959:** 133
Jackson, William H., **1953:** 2n., 128 ftn. (p. 472); **1956:** 96
News conference remarks on, **1953:** 22, 126
Jackson (William H.) Committee.
See President's Committee on International Information Activities.
Jackson School Township, Indiana, bill for relief of, approval, **1957:** 174 and n.
Jacksonville, Fla., **1956:** 279
Jacobs, Albert C., **1954:** 295
Jacobsen, Carlyle, **1954:** 300n.
Jacquinot, Louis, **1959:** 332
Jamestown, Va., **1957:** 118; **1959:** 259
Jamieson, Edward, **1954:** 168
Japan, **1954:** 35n., 67, 320; **1956:** 87; **1958:** 124
Anti-U.S. demonstrations, **1960–61:** 209, 245
Assistance to newly emerging countries, **1960–61:** 4, 36
China trade, **1957:** 70
Criminal cases involving U. S. military personnel, **1955:** 105

Japan — *continued*
  Crown Prince Akihito, **1960–61:** 140, 209, 294n., 308
  Crown Princess Michiko, **1960–61:** 140, 209, 294n., 308
  Diplomatic mission to U.S. (1860), **1960–61:** 14, 15, 16
    Centennial, statement, **1960–61:** 134
  Elections, **1960–61:** 366, 422
  Emperor Hirohito, **1960–61:** 14, 188n., 308
  Fishermen, injury by radioactive fallout, **1954:** 330
  Fujiyama, Aiichiro, **1960–61:** 14, 16
  Girard (William S.) case, **1957:** 92, 105, 115, 134, 150
  Hatoyama, Ichiro, **1956:** 313
  Ikeda, Hayato
    Letter, **1960–61:** 294
    Messages, **1960–61:** 252, 366
  Kishi, Nobusuke, **1957:** 115; **1959:** 288, 289; **1960–61:** 14, 15, 140, 209
    Exchange of messages, **1957:** 208 and n.
    Joint statements with, **1957:** 117; **1960–61:** 16
  Kosaka, Zentaro, **1960–61:** 294
  Lebanon, U.N. proposal on, **1958:** 198, 207
  Military alliance, **1958:** 96
  News conference remarks, **1954:** 25, 73, 157, 165, 182, 328; **1956:** 121, 198, 216; **1957:** 56, 70, 92, 105, 115, 119, 145, 150; **1958:** 37, 70, 261, 274; **1960–61:** 21 and ftn. (p. 131), 422
  Newsmen, visit to United States, **1954:** 157, 328
  Nuclear tests, exchange of messages, **1957:** 208 and n.
  Relations with U.S., **1960–61:** 14, 15, 16, 209, 294n.
  Research reactor, **1959:** 189
  Scientific contributions, **1957:** 230
  Textile exports to U.S., **1956:** 198, 216
  Tokyo, **1954:** 25; **1959:** 31
  Trade, **1954:** 73, 90, 149; **1956:** 87; **1957:** 105; **1958:** 37, 70; **1959:** 71; **1960–61:** 16
  Treaty of Amity and Commerce (1860), **1960–61:** 15, 134
  Treaty of Mutual Cooperation and Security, **1960–61:** 14, 15, 16, 209, 245, 410, 422
  United Nations membership, **1956:** 2, 143, 313; **1958:** 8
  U.S. treaty negotiations, **1959:** 288
    Statement, **1959:** 289
  Visit, proposed, **1960–61:** 15n., 21 and ftn. (p. 131), 177
    Cancellation, **1960–61:** 188n., 209, 294
  Visit after retirement, proposed, **1960–61:** 422
  War assets, **1957:** 145
  War assets in United States, **1954:** 330
  War criminals, **1954:** 330
  Withdrawal of U. S. forces, **1957:** 119

Japan — *continued*
  Yoshida, Shigeru, **1954:** 311, 322, 328
    Joint statement with, **1954:** 330
Japanese-American unit (World War II), **1960–61:** 205
Japanese-Americans, claims for evacuation during World War II, **1959:** 155
Japanese courts, decision on Iranian oil, **1953:** 129n.
Javits, Sen. Jacob K., **1956:** 198, 272; **1957:** 87
  Mutual defense pact with Israel proposed, **1960–61:** 38
Jay Treaty (1794), **1954:** 113n.
Jefferson, Thomas, **1953:** 78, 215, 219; **1954:** 86, 128, 136; **1955:** 94, 105; **1956:** 107, 235, 280, 308; **1957:** 118; **1958:** 138n.; **1959:** 107, 212; **1960–61:** 34, 45, 53
Jefferson, N.H., remarks to postmasters, **1955:** 138
Jefferson City, Mo., **1953:** 225
Jenkins, Herbert, Chief of Police, Atlanta, Ga., **1958:** 288
Jenkins, Martin D., **1955:** 51n.
Jenkins, Repr. Thomas A., **1953:** 164; **1954:** 106n.
Jenner, Sen. William E., **1953:** 238; **1955:** 10; **1956:** 235; **1957:** 50, 72; **1958:** 83, 318
Jet Propulsion Laboratory, Goldstone, Calif., **1960–61:** 258
Jewell, Ingrid M., **1955:** 59
Jewish New Year, statement, **1953:** 183; **1954:** 277; **1955:** 215
Jewish High Holy Days, statement, **1957:** 199; **1958:** 264; **1959:** 249; **1960–61:** 300
Jewish tercentenary dinner, address, **1954:** 297
Jews and Christians, National Conference of, message, **1953:** 132
Job, Biblical, reference to, **1960–61:** 245
Job Safety Week, statement, **1956:** 55
John XXIII
  Meeting with, **1959:** 277, 294
  Message, **1958:** 304
John Day Reservoir, Wash. and Oreg., **1956:** 12 (p. 136)
Johns Hopkins University, **1959:** 129; **1960–61:** 349
  Commencement exercises, remarks, **1958:** 130
Johnson, Alice F., **1953:** 77; **1954:** 9, 73, 200, 311; **1955:** 56; **1956:** 56
Johnson, Andrew, **1959:** 16, 255
Johnson, Edward, **1959:** 184n.
Johnson, Edwin C., **1953:** 77; **1956:** 259
Johnson, J. Monroe.
  See Interstate Commerce Commission, Chairman (J. Monroe Johnson).
Johnson, Joseph B., **1953:** 187; **1955:** 131
Johnson, Repr. Lester R., **1960–61:** 330
Johnson, Sen. Lyndon B., **1955:** 81, 90 ftn. (p. 471), 146; **1957:** 50, 105; **1958:** 36; **1959:** 42, 67, 148, 161, 186; **1960–61:** 222, 256, 272
  Bipartisan meeting on Suez Canal, **1956:** 184

Johnson, Sen. Lyndon B. — *continued*
  Candidacy for Vice President
    Briefings by CIA, telegram, **1960–61:** 236
    Election victory, telegram, **1960–61:** 356
  Farm program, **1956:** 20
  Killian and Gaither panel reports, letter, **1958:**
    19
  Mutual security appropriations, letter, **1960–61:**
    271
  News conference remarks on, **1954:** 63, 92, 353;
    1956: 20, 88; **1958:** 70, 88
  Recession, **1958:** 83
  Vice President-elect, **1960–61:** 356
Johnson, Roy W., **1959:** 277
Johnson, U. Alexis, **1955:** 176
Johnson, Vance, **1953:** 37
Johnson, Vernon A., **1953:** 267
Johnston, Clement D., **1955:** 85n.
Johnston, Don P., **1953:** 234n.
Johnston, Eric, **1957:** 50; **1960–61:** 132
  Conference on foreign aspects of national secu-
    rity, **1958:** 36n.
    Letter, **1958:** 4
  Conference on India and United States, Wash-
    ington, D.C., **1959:** 94
  Mission to Middle East
    Report, **1953:** 217n.
    Statement, **1953:** 217
Johnston Plan
  Jordan River development, **1958:** 198
  Middle East, **1956:** 198, 298
Joint Chiefs of Staff, **1954:** 3; **1955:** 3; **1957:** 87;
    1958: 65, 80, 90, 95; **1959:** 55, 148;
    1960–61: 36, 132, 162, 350
  Budget messages, **1954:** 14 (pp. 119, 123); **1959:**
    10 (p. 58); **1960–61:** 414 (pp. 950, 952)
  Defense reorganization.
    See main heading, Defense reorganization.
  News conference remarks on, **1953:** 62, 77, 88;
    1954: 50, 129; **1956:** 16, 53; **1958:** 63, 74,
    83; **1960–61:** 24, 93
  Puerto Rico meeting, **1956:** 53
  Reorganization Plan 6, message, **1953:** 61
  Review of National Guard programs, **1955:** 192
  Ridgway, Gen. Matthew B.
    See main heading, Ridgway, Gen. Matthew B.
  Taylor, Gen. Maxwell D.
    See main heading, Taylor, Gen. Maxwell D.
  Weapons responsibility, **1956:** 230
Joint Chiefs of Staff, Chairman (Gen. Omar N.
    Bradley), **1953:** 109 ftn. (p. 439)
Joint Chiefs of Staff, Chairman (Adm. Arthur W.
    Radford), **1953:** 225, 268; **1955:** 56, 81
  Bipartisan conference, **1957:** 2
  Bipartisan meeting on Suez Canal, **1956:** 184
  Discussions with Prime Minister Kishi, **1957:** 117
  Distinguished Service Medal, citation, **1957:** 151
  News conference remarks on, **1956:** 16, 155
  North Korea, **1957:** 62

Joint Chiefs of Staff, Chairman (Gen. Nathan F.
    Twining), **1958:** 213; **1960–61:** 24
Joint Commission on the Civilian Employee Com-
    pensation Policy of the Federal Govern-
    ment, establishment proposed, **1958:** 169;
    1959: 10 (p. 109)
Joint Committee on Atomic Energy, **1957:** 72,
    231n.
  U.S.-Australia agreement on atomic informa-
    tion, **1957:** 130
Joint Disarmament Study Group, Department of
    State, **1959:** 191 and ftn. (p. 611), 243
Joint Federal-State Action Committee, **1957:**
    118n.; **1959:** 10 (pp. 68, 98); **1960–61:** 116
  Appointment, **1957:** 138
  Budget message, **1958:** 5 (pp. 43, 46)
  Recommendations, **1957:** 138n.; **1958:** 106
  Report, letter, **1960–61:** 115
Joint regulations under Dependent's Medical Care
    Act, approval, **1956:** 244
Joint statements with heads of state and govern-
    ments
  Afghanistan
    King Mohammad Zahir, **1959:** 308
    Prime Minister Daud, **1958:** 150
  Argentina, President Frondizi, **1960–61:** 66
  Australia, Prime Minister Menzies, **1960–61:** 312
  Brazil, President Kubitschek,
  Burma, Prime Minister Nu, **1955:** 148
  Canada
    Prime Minister Diefenbaker, **1960–61:** 172
    Prime Minister St. Laurent, **1953:** 70, 247
  Chile, President Alessandri, **1960–61:** 76
  China, Republic of, President Chiang Kai-shek,
    1960–61: 195
  El Salvador. President Lemus, **1959:** 54
  France
    Premier Laniel, **1953:** 255
    Premier Mollet, France, **1957:** 38
    President de Gaulle, **1959:** 202; **1960–61:** 125,
      155
  Germany, Chancellor Adenauer, **1954:** 314;
    1955: 122; **1957:** 100; **1959:** 192; **1960–61:**
    92
  Ghana, Prime Minister Nkrumah, **1958:** 180
  Greece, Prime Minister Karamanlis, **1959:** 327
  Guinea, President Toure, **1959:** 272
  India, Prime Minister Nehru, **1956:** 314; **1959:**
    317
  Iran, Shah Mohammad Reza Pahlavi, **1959:** 322
  Italy,
    President Gronchi, **1956:** 46; **1959:** 293
    Prime Minister Fanfani, **1958:** 186
    Prime Minister Scelba, **1955:** 61
    Prime Minister Segni, **1959:** 203, 248
  Japan
    Prime Minister Kishi, **1957:** 117; **1960–61:** 16
    Prime Minister Yoshida. **1954:** 330

Joint statements with heads of state — *continued*
Korea
President Rhee, **1954:** 178
Prime Minister Huh Chung, **1960–61:** 203
Mexico, President López Mateos, **1959:** 38, 257; **1960–61:** 335
Morocco
King Mohammed V, **1957:** 240; **1959:** 345
Nepal, King Mahendra, **1960–61:** 130
Pakistan
President Ayub Khan, **1959:** 303
Prime Minister Suhrawardy, **1957:** 131
Panama, President Remon Cantera, **1953:** 200
Philippines, President Garcia, **1958:** 143; **1960–61:** 189
Saudi Arabia, King Saud, **1957:** 31
Spain, General Franco, **1959:** 340
Thailand, King Bhumibol Adulyadej, **1960–61:** 218
Tunisia, President Bourguiba, **1959:** 329
Turkey, President Bayar, **1959:** 297
United Kingdom
Prime Minister Churchill, **1953:** 255; **1954:** 154, 155
Prime Minister Eden, **1956:** 26, 27
Prime Minister Macmillan, **1957:** 55, 226; **1960–61:** 101, 102, 155, 307, 312
Uruguay, National Council of Government, **1960–61:** 84
U.S.S.R., Premier Khrushchev, **1959:** 218, 242
Vietnam, President Diem, **1957:** 83
Western leaders, **1953:** 255; **1959:** 335, 336; **1960–61:** 155
Joint statements with European Community for Coal and Steel, Rene Mayer, **1956:** 34
Jonas, Repr. Charles R., **1954:** 92, 345
Jones, Arnold R., **1957:** 124
Jones, C. Robert, **1958:** 290n.
Jones, Charles, **1958:** 292n.
Jones, Edmund L., **1953:** 59
Jones, Maj. Gen. Herbert M., **1956:** 317
Jones, John Paul, **1958:** 125
Jones, Robert T. (Bob), **1954:** 200; **1957:** 236n.
Jones, Roger W. (Chairman, Civil Service Commission)
Award for Distinguished Federal Civilian Service, **1958:** 13
Memorandum, **1960–61:** 28
Jones, Rowland, Jr., **1953:** 23n.
Jones, Russell, **1959:** 267
Jones, Wallace ("Wa-Wa"), **1956:** 226
Jones and Laughlin Steel Corporation, **1959:** 211n.
Jordan, **1956:** 53; **1957:** 91; **1958:** 207, 213; **1960–61:** 23
Assistance, **1955:** 17 (p. 130); **1959:** 55
Crisis in, statement, **1958:** 173
Hazza al-Majali, death of, **1960–61:** 277
King Hussein, **1957:** 72, 91; **1959:** 66

Jordan — *continued*
Message, **1960–61:** 277
Letters to Premier Khrushchev on, **1958:** 177, 179
News conference remarks, **1957:** 72, 207
Jordan, David Herrera, **1953:** 222n.
Jordan, Gov. Len, **1954:** 165, 271
Jordan River development, **1953:** 217, 230
Johnston plan, **1956:** 198; **1958:** 198
Josephs, Devereaux Colt, **1956:** 85n.
Journey to America (de Tocqueville), **1959:** 107
Joyce, J. Wallace, **1958:** 27
Juarez. Benito, **1959:** 255
Judd, Repr. Walter H., **1953:** 98; **1955:** 33; **1956:** 250; **1960–61:** 329, 330, 354
Judges, pay raise, **1955:** 47
Judgeships
Additional, proposed, **1960–61:** 133, 255, 268
Budget messages, **1960–61:** 13 (p. 105), 414 (p. 1023)
Creation of, **1959:** 10 (p. 111)
Judicial Conference of the District of Columbia, **1960–61:** 275
Judicial Conference of the United States, **1953:** 59; **1957:** 13; **1960–61:** 133
Judicial and Congressional Salaries, Commission on, **1958:** 169
Judicial Procedure, Commission on International Rules of, **1960–61:** 13 (p. 105)
Judiciary, Federal, **1955:** 112
See also Courts, Federal; Supreme Court.
Additional judges, **1957:** 13; **1958:** 70
Appointments, news conference remarks, **1956:** 56
Civil rights cases, **1957:** 145
District or circuit court judges, 70 years of age, **1957:** 13
News conference remarks, **1957:** 119, 145
Pay adjustments, **1958:** 169
Separation from politics, **1956:** 32
Juin, Marshal Alphonse, **1954:** 133
Juliana, Queen
Letter, **1953:** 53
Messages, **1953:** 7; **1960–61:** 138
Juliet, Raul, **1960–61:** 73n.
Julius Caesar, **1959:** 100
Junior Chamber of Commerce, National, address, **1953:** 98
Junior colleges, **1958:** 320
Junior Leagues of America, Association of, remarks, **1958:** 94
Jupiter (IRBM).
See Missiles.
Jurors, Federal, qualifications, **1957:** 147n.
Jury trial, civil rights cases, **1957:** 133, 147
News conference remarks, **1957:** 45, 87, 105, 145, 150, 157

Justice, Department of, **1953:** 95, 101; **1954:** 139, 273, 275, 286, 291; **1955:** 112; **1957:** 72, 207; **1958:** 288; **1959:** 155

See also Attorney General; Federal Bureau of Investigation.

Action on subversives, record of, **1954:** 129, 130, 209

Antitrust cases, **1956:** 234, 241, 268; **1958:** 293; **1960–61:** 411

Antitrust laws, enforcement, **1956:** 118, 263

Antitrust laws, study of, **1954:** 67; **1955:** 56

Assistant Attorney General
 Antitrust Division, **1956:** 56
 Civil rights, **1957:** 119, 133
 Nomination, **1958:** 103

Barnes, Stanley N., **1955:** 56

Bennett, James V., **1959:** 9n.

Budget messages, **1956:** 12 (p. 149); **1960–61:** 13 (p. 92), 414 (p. 1022)

Bureau of Prisons, overtime compensation claim, veto, **1954:** 41

Civil rights cases, **1957:** 134

Civil rights division, **1957:** 8; **1960–61:** 410, 411

Cuban nickel plant case, **1956:** 96, 113

Eligibility of President for office of Vice President, report, **1960–61:** 21

Immigration laws, **1955:** 4

Internal Security Division, **1955:** 4

Labor-management investigation, **1957:** 207

Little Rock case, **1957:** 178 and n.
 See also main heading, Little Rock.

Mergers, **1956:** 263

Montgomery, Ala., study of situation in, **1957:** 17

News conference remarks on, **1953:** 54, 243, 249, 254; **1954:** 9, 48, 192, 200; **1955:** 10, 18, 56, 112

Record of accomplishment, report, **1960–61:** 411

Rogers, William P., **1954:** 161

Reorganization Plan 4, **1953:** 51

School integration cases, **1956:** 32, 205; **1958:** 222

Security cases, **1955:** 18

Security program, **1953:** 95

Segregation in public schools, position on, **1953:** 249

Swing, Joseph M., trip to Mexico, **1956:** 235

Tompkins, William F., **1955:** 10

TV quiz investigation, **1959:** 277

Violations of law by public officials, investigation, **1956:** 32

Voting rights case, Alabama, **1958:** 318

Water resources, report, **1956:** 13

White (Harry Dexter) case, **1953:** 243

Juvenile court records, **1954:** 207

Juvenile Crime, Committee on, **1954:** 207

Juvenile delinquency, **1954:** 127; **1955:** 4, 25; **1956:** 2; **1957:** 13; **1960–61:** 100
 Budget message, **1956:** 12 (p. 125)
 Comment on, **1953:** 265
 News conference remarks, **1956:** 96
 Prevention, **1958:** 123

Kabul, Afghanistan.
 See also Afghanistan.
 Arrival, remarks, **1959:** 306
 Dinner given by King Zahir, toast, **1959:** 307
 Joint statement with King Zahir, **1959:** 308
 Remarks to American community, **1959:** 309

Kaczmarczyk, Rose, insurance claim, veto, **1954:** 141

Kaczmarczyk, William Paul, **1954:** 141

Kaiser, William J., relief of, veto, **1960–61:** 113

Kaiser Steel Corporation, **1959:** 211n., 271

Kamp, Joseph R., political attacks by, **1958:** 288

Kanellopoulos, Panayiotis, **1959:** 327

Kansas, **1954:** 317; **1956:** 211, 285; **1957:** 234, 235; **1958:** 288; **1959:** 75, 338
 See also Eisenhower, Dwight D.
 Abilene, **1953:** 225, 252; **1954:** 149, 167n., 331; **1956:** 242n., 268; **1957:** 68, 134; **1959:** 177, 179, 186, 258, 259; **1960–61:** 45, 290
 Eisenhower Library, **1960–61:** 21, 118
 Arn, Gov. Edward F., **1954:** 85n., 99, 143, 331
 Carlson, Sen. Frank, **1953:** 8, 269; **1954:** 39; **1955:** 62; **1956:** 28n.
 Dickinson County, **1954:** 331
 Docking, Gov. George, **1957:** 138; **1959:** 258, 259; **1960–61:** 118n.
 Eisenhower Presidential Library Commission, **1960–61:** 118
 Geary County, **1954:** 331
 Governor's National Committee for the Eisenhower Presidential Library, **1960–61:** 118n.
 Hope, Repr. Clifford R., **1953:** 268; **1954:** 9, 129, 196
 Rees, Repr. Edward H., **1953:** 269
 Schoeppel, Sen. Andrew F., **1956:** 235; **1957:** 108 and n.; **1958:** 42
 Sedgwick County Board of Commissioners, tax claim, **1956:** 112
 Topeka, **1954:** 14 (p. 134)
 Wichita, **1957:** 11 and n., 12 and n., 17, 41 and n.

Kansas City, Mo., **1953:** 216, 218, 225

Karachi, Pakistan, **1960–61:** 297
 Arrival, remarks, **1959:** 299
 Dinner honoring President Ayub, toast, **1959:** 304
 Joint statement with President Ayub, **1959:** 303
 Meeting of Baghdad Pact Ministerial Council, message, **1959:** 19

Karachi, Pakistan — *continued*
  Remarks
    Departure, **1959:** 305
    Polo field, **1959:** 302
    U.S. embassy, **1959:** 301
Karamanlis, Constantine, **1959:** 324n., 325
  Joint statement with, **1959:** 327
  Message, **1959:** 40
Karasik, Daniel, **1960–61:** 228, 362
Kasavubu, Joseph, **1960–61:** 364
  Message, **1960–61:** 216
Kashmir dispute between India and Pakistan, **1960–61:** 284
Kasserine Pass, battle of, **1954:** 290; **1956:** 206; **1958:** 310
Kasson, Minn., **1954:** 291
  1952 campaign, **1956:** 214
Kastenmeier, Repr. Robert W., **1960–61:** 7
Katmandu (Kathmandu), Nepal, **1958:** 123
Kawar, Irfan, relief of, **1956:** 59
Kean, Repr. Robert W., **1958:** 58
Kearney, Repr. Bernard W., **1953:** 22
Kearns, Carol, **1954:** 273
Kearsarge, U.S.S., **1960–61:** 97
Keating, Repr. Kenneth B., **1958:** 222, 305, 306; **1960–61:** 173
  Refugee mission, letter, **1956:** 213
Kee Young Chang, **1960–61:** 198n.
Kefauver, Sen. Estes, **1953:** 15; **1955:** 146, 149; **1957:** 124; **1959:** 42
  News conference remarks on, **1956:** 62, 78, 198, 205
Keflavik, Iceland, remarks at airport, **1955:** 162
Keith, Elden F. et al., mining claim, disapproval, **1956:** 179
Kekkonen, Urho K., telegram, **1956:** 311
Keller, Helen, letter, **1955:** 140
Keller, Ralph W., **1954:** 149n.
Kelley, Repr. Augustine B., **1956:** 94
Kelly, John B., **1956:** 96; **1960–61:** 103
Kelly, Thomas V., **1957:** 45, 210; **1958:** 222
Kelso, John H., **1954:** 9
Kemal, Mustafa.
  See Ataturk, Kemal.
Kempner Trust Association, relief of, disapproval, **1954:** 251
Kenesaw Mountain, battle, **1960–61:** 370
Kenison, Frank B., **1956:** 216
Kennan, George F., **1953:** 109
Kennedy, Sen. John F., **1954:** 73, 325; **1957:** 124; **1959:** 42
  Candidacy for President, **1960–61:** 93, 263
    Briefings by CIA, telegram, **1960–61:** 236
    Election victory, telegram, **1960–61:** 356
    Television debates, **1960–61:** 268
  News conference remarks on **1960–61:** 93, 263, 268, 284, 422
  President-elect, **1960–61:** 356, 422
    Joint statement with, **1960–61:** 369

Kennedy, Joseph P., **1954:** 12n.; **1956:** 10n.
Kennedy, Stephen P., **1960–61:** 314
Kennedy-Ives bill, **1958:** 216
Kennon, Gov. Robert F., **1953:** 219; **1955:** 88
Kent, Carleton, **1953:** 88, 198; **1954:** 157; **1956:** 53, 88, 94, 96, 193, 198; **1957:** 28, 50, 70; **1958:** 28, 37, 42, 70, 74, 103, 213, 288, 310; **1959:** 17, 29, 48, 94, 123, 223, 267, 277; **1960–61:** 24, 103, 127, 256, 268
Kenton, John E., **1954:** 92; **1955:** 81, 146, 176
Kentucky, **1956:** 216; **1958:** 26
  Barkley, Sen. Alben W., **1956:** 92
  Boone County, **1956:** 182
  Candidates for public office, **1954:** 319; **1956:** 155, 171, 226
  Chandler, Gov. Albert B., **1956:** 225
  Clements, Sen. Earle C., **1955:** 33; **1956:** 184
  Cooper, Sen. John Sherman, **1954:** 88, 89, 168, 172, 182, 319, 328; **1957:** 87, 124; **1959:** 29; **1960–61:** 5, 176
  Depressed areas, **1960–61:** 176n.
  Distribution of surplus farm products, **1959:** 67 and ftn. (p. 297)
  Hawesville, **1956:** 182
  Hodgenville, **1954:** 88
  Lexington, **1954:** 89; **1956:** 225, 226, 229
  Louisville, **1954:** 319, 320; **1956:** 90, 205; **1957:** 87
  Morton, Sen. Thruston B., **1959:** 75, 132; **1960–61:** 23, 245n., 309n., 395
  Paducah, **1954:** 14 (p. 128), 161 and ftn. (p. 622), 192, 193, 281
  Robsion, Repr. John M., Jr., **1956:** 226
  Siler, Repr. Eugene, **1956:** 226
Kenworthy, Carroll H., **1953:** 198; **1954:** 63, 345; **1956:** 96
Kenworthy, E. W., **1959:** 123, 172, 186, 223, 243, 271, 288; **1960–61:** 103, 127, 263, 268
Keough, Archbishop Francis P., **1958:** 123
Kern, William C., **1955:** 95
Kerr, Clark, **1960–61:** 30n.
Kerr, Walter, **1955:** 90, 95, 100, 112, 119; **1956:** 32, 47
Kestnbaum, Meyer, **1954:** 18, 346; **1957:** 26, 138; **1960–61:** 208
  Death of, statement, **1960–61:** 372
  Report on status of Hoover Commission recommendations, **1956:** 261n.; **1957:** 112 and n.
Kettering, Charles F., **1956:** 107
Key, Francis Scott, **1955:** 116
Key (Francis Scott) Memorial Auditorium, St. John's College, dedication, **1959:** 116
Key West, Fla., **1956:** 1, 3, 5, 16, 32
Key West Agreement, **1953:** 61, 62
Keyserling, Leon H., **1955:** 47

Khrushchev, Nikita S., **1955:** 95, 146; **1957:** 210,
        226; **1958:** 1, 181, 196, 257n., 261; **1959:**
        1n., 271 ftn. (p. 748), 290; **1960–61:** 21 ftn.
        (p. 131), 36, 147, 173, 231n., 328
    Address before Congress, question of, **1959:** 186
    Announcement of support for Castro regime in
        Cuba, statement, **1960–61:** 227
    Authority in negotiations, **1959:** 67
    Communist doctrine, **1959:** 243
    Conference on nuclear test detection, letter,
        1958: 131
    Defense spending, **1959:** 243
    Disarmament proposals, **1960–61:** 93
        U.N., **1959:** 223, 243
    Disarmament talk with Stassen, **1956:** 88
    East-West summit, letters, **1959:** 337, 349
    Helicopter, purchase of, **1959:** 243
    Interviews
        Catledge, Turner, **1958:** 11
        Harriman, W. Averell, in Moscow, **1959:** 154
        Thompson, Ambassador, re U.S. airmen,
            1959: 94 and ftn. (p. 361)
        TV interview, **1957:** 105
        U.S. Governors in Moscow, **1959:** 154
    Invitation to the President, **1959:** 29 and ftn. (p.
        173)
    Letters to, **1958:** 67, 86, 112, 131, 152, 165, 177,
        179, 189, 263; **1959:** 81, 110, 337, 349
    Meeting with members of Congress, **1959:** 223
    Meeting with President, proposed, letter on,
        1960–61: 313
    Messages, **1960–61:** 2, 97
    Minsk address, **1958:** 31
    Moscow address, **1959:** 26
    News conference remarks on, **1956:** 20, 53, 78,
        88, 96; **1958:** 11, 37, 56, 70, 83, 103, 141,
        198, 222, 274, 318; **1959:** 21, 26, 29, 36, 42,
        48, 53, 67, 94, 102, 123, 132, 154, 161, 167,
        172, 173, 179, 186, 267, 271, 277; **1960–61:**
        7, 24, 34, 38, 93, 127, 143, 222, 228, 256,
        268, 284, 422
    Nuclear test suspension, letters, **1959:** 81, 110
    Position taken at summit conference, **1960–61:**
        154, 155, 163, 313
    Reaction of Americans to, **1959:** 223, 243
    Soviet vs. U.S. system, **1959:** 271
    Summit conference, **1955:** 149
    U.N. General Assembly meeting, **1960–61:** 256,
        284
    Vice President Nixon's visit, **1959:** 167
    Visit to United States, **1959:** 21, 102, 154, 161,
        172, 179, 186, 191, 196, 198n., 200, 202,
        203, 214, 217, 218, 219, 223, 242, 248;
        1960–61: 38
        Announcement, **1959:** 173
        Evaluation of talks with, **1959:** 243
        Exchange of toasts, **1959:** 219

Khrushchev, Nikita S. — *continued*
    Visit to United States — *continued*
        Joint statements with, **1959:** 218, 242
        News conference remarks, **1958:** 56, 83
        Remarks of welcome, **1959:** 217
        Rumor of, **1956:** 88
Khrushchev, Madame, **1959:** 214, 217, 219
Kilday, Repr. Paul J., **1958:** 83
Kilian, James R., Jr., **1957:** 225n.; **1958:** 57, 64;
        1959: 107, 267; **1960–61:** 30n.
    Appointment as Chairman, Board of Consult-
        ants on Foreign Intelligence Activities,
        1956: 10
    Appointment as Special Assistant to President,
        for Science and Technology, **1957:** 230
    Geneva conference of technical experts, **1958:** 74
    News conference remarks on, **1958:** 28, 56, 70,
        141
    Panel report, withholding of, letter, **1958:** 19
Kilpatrick, H. Cecil, **1953:** 59
Kilpatrick, Gen. John Reed, **1956:** 272
Kilpatrick, Shirley Leeke, relief of, veto, **1958:** 61
Kim, Daeyung, **1960–61:** 250n.
Kimpton, Lawrence A., **1959:** 36
Kincheloe, Capt. Iven C., Jr., death of, **1958:** 314
Kincheloe, Mrs. Iven C., Jr., **1958:** 314n.
King, Dr. Charles Glen, **1960–61:** 279
Kinkaid, Adm. Thomas C., **1953:** 144; **1957:** 57n.
Kinnear, George C., **1956:** 251n.
Kirk, Grayson, **1954:** 128
Kishi, Nobusuke, **1957:** 115; **1959:** 288, 289; **1960–
        61:** 15, 140, 209
    Exchange of messages on nuclear testing, **1957:**
        208 and n.
    Exchange of toasts, **1960–61:** 14
    Joint statements with, **1957:** 117; **1960–61:** 16
Kistiakowsky, George B., **1958:** 310; **1959:** 132 ftn.
        (p. 463); **1960–61:** 143, 363n.
    Medal of Freedom, citation, **1960–61:** 429
    Resignation, letter, **1960–61:** 400
Kitty Hawk, N.C., **1953:** 267
Kiwanis Clubs, **1956:** 220
Kiwanis International, **1958:** 220
Klutznick, Philip M., **1953:** 252n.
Klyce Motors, Inc., indemnity claim, veto, **1954:**
        181
Knebel, Fletcher, **1953:** 15, 230, 249; **1954:** 25, 101,
        165; **1955:** 47, 176; **1956:** 155, 189, 193;
        1957: 50; **1959:** 173
Knight, Gov. Goodwin J., **1954:** 274; **1956:** 188,
        189, 258; **1958:** 288, 292, 294
Knight, O. A., **1959:** 287n.
Knighton, William H., Jr., **1958:** 42, 83, 88, 198,
        288; **1959:** 21, 29, 123, 179, 186, 267;
        1960–61: 7, 21, 24, 93, 268, 284, 422
Knipp, Howard F., tax claim, disapproval, **1959:**
        240
Know Your America Week, **1959:** 243, 245

Knowland, Sen. William F., **1954:** 273, 274; **1955:** 26, 41, 59; **1957:** 28, 87, 92, 157; **1958:** 36, 292, 294
  Admission of Communist China to United Nations, **1954:** 161
  Bipartisan meeting on Suez Canal, **1956:** 184
  Constitutional amendment on treatymaking powers, **1953:** 142; **1954:** 9, 33
  Letters to, **1958:** 43, 85, 221
  Measures to aid economic growth, letter, **1958:** 43
  News conference remarks on, **1953:** 31, 126, 230; **1954:** 9, 33, 48, 129, 157, 161, 168, 172, 341, 345; **1956:** 16, 20, 56, 78, 189; **1958:** 42, 83, 288
  Peaceful coexistence, **1954:** 341
  U.S. handling of Korean war, **1953:** 31
Knowland, Mrs. William F., **1954:** 273; **1958:** 221
Knowles, Clayton, **1954:** 33
Knox Corporation, bill for relief of, **1957:** 182
Knudsen, Mrs. Valley, **1958:** 94
Knudson, James K., **1954:** 48
Koerner, Theodor, **1957:** 5
  Message, **1955:** 98
Kohler, Foy D., **1959:** 218
Kohler, Gov. Walter J., **1953:** 15; **1954:** 165; **1957:** 150
Kootenai River, Libby Dam, **1960–61:** 419
  Budget message, **1960–61:** 414 (p. 994)
Korea, **1953:** 19, 26, 50, 256
Korea, **1954:** 128; **1955:** 12, 18, 21; **1956:** 2, 87, 117; **1957:** 25, 90, 91, 157, 230; **1958:** 80, 173, 207, 257n., 261, 274; **1959:** 89, 94; **1960–61:** 23, 133, 245, 302
  Allied prisoners unaccounted for, **1959:** 89
  American-Korean Foundation, **1953:** 65, 159, 258
  American Relief for, **1953:** 258
  Armed forces, **1953:** 6, 147; **1960–61:** 202
  Assistance, **1953:** 96, 148, 159; **1954:** 3, 14 (p. 139), 35, 150, 171n.; **1955:** 17 (pp. 104, 124, 129); **1956:** 12 (p. 104), 20; **1957:** 90, 91, 136, 152; **1958:** 32; **1959:** 10 (p. 69), 55; **1960–61:** 36, 203
  Campaign remarks, **1956:** 210, 224, 226, 234, 283; **1958:** 302, 308; **1960–61:** 348, 351, 352
  Chang Myon, message, **1960–61:** 274
  Communist aggression, **1953:** 96; **1954:** 3, 171n.
  Conference on, question of, **1953:** 238, 255
  Conference on collective security against Communism, **1954:** 157
  Economy, **1960–61:** 203
  Effects of war on, **1953:** 148
  Election, **1960–61:** 93, 127
  Geneva conference on.
    See Geneva conferences.
  "Help Korea" trains, **1954:** 78

Korea — *continued*
  Huh Chung, **1960–61:** 198, 200, 202, 204
    Joint statement with, **1960–61:** 203
  Indian custodial forces in, **1954:** 40
  Letter to Premier Khrushchev re, **1958:** 263
  Membership in Asian security pact, question of, **1954:** 168
  Membership in United Nations, question of, **1960–61:** 203
  Military alliance, **1958:** 96
  Mutual defense treaty, **1953:** 96; **1954:** 3, 6, 139, 168; **1960–61:** 201
  Neutral Nations Commission, **1953:** 210, 225
  News conference remarks, **1953:** 12, 22, 88, 128, 141, 225, 238; **1954:** 9, 33, 48, 101, 143, 157, 168, 347; **1956:** 198, 205; **1960–61:** 93, 127, 143
  Orphans and adopted children, **1957:** 25
  Panmunjom, **1953:** 87, 102
  Po Sun Yun, message, **1960–61:** 273
  Political changes, **1960–61:** 127
  Pusan, **1953:** 258
  Red Cross services in, **1953:** 17; **1954:** 48
  Relations with U.S., **1960–61:** 201, 203
  Reunification, question of, **1953:** 96, 128, 147, 238; **1954:** 101, 168, 178, 225; **1957:** 119; **1958:** 148; **1960–61:** 203
  Rhee, Syngman, **1953:** 109, 128, 141, 147, 159, 225; **1954:** 6, 165, 168, 171, 172, 174; **1957:** 80; **1960–61:** 127, 143
    Joint statement with, **1954:** 178
    Letters, **1953:** 96; **1960–61:** 141
  Seoul.
    See main heading, Seoul.
  Students of, message, **1960–61:** 250
  Treaty on, question of, **1960–61:** 143
  U.N. force in, **1958:** 89
  U. N. membership
    Proposed, **1956:** 143
    Soviet veto, **1958:** 8, 148
  United Nations Command, **1960–61:** 202, 203, 212
  U.S. Ambassador Ellis O. Briggs, **1953:** 141
  U.S. Ambassador Walter P. McConaughy, **1960–61:** 198n.
  U.S. troops in, **1953:** 12, 272; **1954:** 14 (pp. 122, 123), 33, 48
  Visit of the President (1952), **1954:** 174n.; **1956:** 205
  Visit of the President (1960), **1960–61:** 21 ftn. (p. 131), 177, 198, 199, 200, 201, 202, 203, 204, 209, 250, 274
    News conference remarks on, **1960–61:** 93, 127, 143
  Visit of U.S. Governors, **1954:** 164
    Letter, **1954:** 35
  Withdrawal of foreign troops, **1957:** 119
  Yalu River, **1956:** 16

[*References are to items except as otherwise indicated*]

Korea, North, **1953:** 141; **1955:** 185; **1957:** 62, 92;
  1958: 198; **1960–61:** 204
  Embargo on trade with, **1954:** 67
  Evacuation by Communist China, **1958:** 302, 303
  News conference remarks, **1954:** 9, 161
Korea, South, **1957:** 86, 92
Korean Reconstruction Agency, United Nations,
  U.S. contribution, **1953:** 148
Korean war, **1953:** 6, 12, 19, 30, 45, 57, 61, 70, 147,
  216, 246, 253; **1954:** 61, 79, 174n., 203,
  209, 275, 291, 297, 325; **1955:** 12, 13, 35,
  57, 118; **1956:** 232; **1958:** 18, 83, 173;
  1959: 311; **1960–61:** 80, 107, 141, 183,
  198, 201, 202, 209, 410, 422
  Armistice, **1953:** 54, 109, 126, 128, 141, 148, 159,
  187, 210, 272; **1954:** 9, 178, 225, 347;
  1955: 16
    Broadcast, **1953:** 147
    Letter to President Rhee, **1953:** 96
    Negotiations, **1953:** 50, 87, 88, 128, 141
    Report of Unified Command, **1953:** 272n.
  Budget for, **1953:** 37, 82
  Budget message, **1956:** 12 (pp. 112–114)
  Burial of Unknown American killed in, **1958:**
  122n.
  Campaign remarks, **1954:** 286, 317, 318, 319,
  320; **1956:** 214, 228, 279, 280; **1958:** 287,
  290, 293, 296; **1960–61:** 346, 348, 351, 352
  Colombian participation, **1960–61:** 108, 109
  Effect on peacetime defense, **1957:** 230
  Greek participation, **1953:** 233n.; **1959:** 325
  Joint statement with Prime Minister Huh Chung,
  1960–61: 203
  News conference remarks, **1953:** 12, 15, 31, 37,
  41, 54, 62, 77, 88, 109, 126, 128, 141, 225,
  254, 265; **1954:** 9, 57, 168, 192, 345, 347;
  1955: 10, 18, 26, 59; **1956:** 16, 20
  Prisoners of war, **1953:** 87, 96, 128, 210; **1954:**
  40; **1955:** 18
    Agreement on, **1953:** 102
    Dean, Maj. Gen. William F., **1953:** 225, 265
    Exchange of sick and wounded, **1953:** 41, 54
    Forced repatriation, question of, **1953:** 88
    U.S., disaffection under Communist indoctri-
    nation, **1953:** 225
    U.S., indemnity claims, **1954:** 94
    U.S., treatment of, **1953:** 54
  Turkish participation, **1954:** 23; **1959:** 297
  U.S. ammunition shortage, question of, **1953:** 37
  Veterans, U.S., **1953:** 144
    Medal of Honor awards, **1953:** 27, 122, 170,
    174, 175, 226, 229; **1954:** 8
Korteweg, Peter G., **1956:** 171; **1957:** 56
Kosaka, Zentaro, **1960–61:** 294n.
Kosciuszko, Thaddeus, **1956:** 265; **1960–61:** 310
Kossuth, Louis, **1957:** 51
Koterba, Edward V., **1957:** 105; **1959:** 172, 179,
  223; **1960–61:** 34, 103, 268, 284, 422

Kowalski, Repr. Frank, **1959:** 102
Kozlov, Frol R.
  Meeting with the President, **1959:** 148, 154
  Message, **1959:** 162
  Visit to United States, **1959:** 132, 148, 154, 161,
  167
Kra Peninsula, **1956:** 198
Kramer, Lawrence F., relief of, disapproval, **1954:**
  231
Kramer, Philip, **1954:** 231
Kramer, William C., **1956:** 278
Kraslow, David, **1958:** 288; **1959:** 94, 154, 161, 172,
  223, 277; **1960–61:** 7, 24, 38, 93, 222, 256,
  263, 284
Kreidler, Shirley, **1954:** 96
Krekeler, Heinz L., **1955:** 22
Kubiske, Edward, **1956:** 241
Kubitschek de Oliveira, Juscelino, **1960–61:** 45, 48,
  49n., 50, 53, 54, 55, 87, 228
  Joint statement with, **1960–61:** 46
  Letters, **1958:** 133, 181, 197, 319
  Messages, **1959:** 287; **1960–61:** 64, 119, 379
  Toast to, **1960–61:** 51
Kubitschek, Madame, **1960–61:** 51
Kuchel, Sen. Thomas H., **1954:** 273; **1956:** 258;
  1960–61: 333
  News conference remarks on, **1956:** 189
Kuh, Frederick, **1953:** 54, 249, 265; **1954:** 129, 165,
  345; **1955:** 41, 59; **1956:** 20
Kumpa, Peter J., **1956:** 189; **1957:** 72, 80, 87, 92,
  105, 115, 119, 124, 145, 150; **1958:** 310;
  1959: 36
Kurile Islands, **1954:** 328, 345; **1957:** 150; **1960–61:**
  97n.
Kutchuck, Fazil, **1960–61:** 262
Kyes, Roger M., 2n., **1953:** 266; **1954:** 68

Labor, **1953:** 6, 187; **1956:** 265
  American Samoa, labor standards, **1956:** 172
  Budget message, **1954:** 14 (pp. 182–185)
    Table, **1954:** 14 (p. 183)
  Campaign remarks, **1956:** 190, 210, 224, 226, 234,
  241, 251, 272
  Conferences with legislative leaders, **1954:** 9
  Forced, **1956:** 96
  Guaranteed annual wage, **1953:** 77
  International meeting in Stockholm, **1953:** 128,
  130
  Job placement services, **1954:** 14 (pp. 182–184)
  Legislation, **1953:** 159
  Message (1954), excerpt from, **1958:** 274
  Stamp in honor of, remarks, **1956:** 194
  State of the Union message, **1954:** 3
  Welfare of, report, **1956:** 196

Labor, Department of, **1953:** 6; **1958:** 29, 68; **1959:** 22; **1960–61:** 358
Appropriation, **1959:** 181
Budget messages, **1954:** 14 (p. 184); **1955:** 17 (p. 177); **1956:** 12 (pp. 117, 149, 152); **1958:** 5 (p. 50); **1959:** 10 (p. 100); **1960–61:** 13 (p. 92), 414 (pp. 992, 1005, 1006, 1019, 1020)
Clague, Ewan, **1955:** 18
Commission of Labor Reports, proposed, **1958:** 20
Consumer Price Index, **1959:** 10 (p. 100)
Filling of vacancies, comment on, **1953:** 77
International Labor Organization, **1957:** 72
Mashburn, Lloyd A., **1953:** 208, 230
McCauley, William R., **1960–61:** 389n.
Migratory labor program, **1954:** 14 (p. 184), 214
Minimum wage, increase, proposed, **1960–61:** 133
National salary survey, **1960–61:** 217 and ftn. (p. 545)
Record of accomplishment, report, **1960–61:** 401
Report on economy, **1958:** 283
Report on employment, **1954:** 107
Report on unemployment, **1954:** 308
Rural development program, **1956:** 6; **1957:** 156
Unemployment statistics, **1959:** 10 (p. 100)
Wilkins, J. Ernest, rumor of resignation, **1958:** 213
Labor, Secretary of, **1958:** 43, 235
Vacancy in office, **1953:** 198
Labor, Secretary of (Martin P. Durkin)
See also Durkin, Martin P.
Resignation, Statement, **1953:** 184
Labor, Secretary of (James P. Mitchell), **1953:** 208, 248, 266; **1954:** 100, 349; **1955:** 107; **1956:** 194; **1957:** 45, 50, 62, 138, 150; **1958:** 55n., 315n.
Accident prevention program, **1954:** 288
Address to CIO convention, **1954:** 347
AFL-CIO testimonial dinner, remarks, **1960–61:** 215
Appraisal by the President, **1958:** 293
Campaign remarks on, **1956:** 241
Chairman, Presidential Railroad Commission, **1960–61:** 378
Chairman, U.G.F. campaign, **1956:** 138
Committee on Small Business, **1956:** 118
Consultation in steel strike, **1956:** 150
Economic reports, statement, **1956:** 269
Factfinding on steel strike, **1959:** 167, 172
Federal Council on Aging, **1956:** 74
ILO conference, **1955:** 119
Labor-management practices, **1957:** 207
Labor racketeering, **1957:** 72, 77, 87
Letters, **1960–61:** 316, 401
Migratory labor program, letter, **1954:** 214
Minimum wage and "right to work" laws, **1954:** 353

Labor, Secretary of (Mitchell) — *continued*
News conference remarks on, **1954:** 48, 311, 347, 353; **1955:** 18, 90, 119, 176; **1956:** 94, 121; **1958:** 37, 198, 274; **1959:** 123, 107, 172, 223; **1960–61:** 7, 21
President's Committee on Employment of Physically Handicapped, **1957:** 94 and n.
President's Conference on Occupational Safety, **1956:** 104
Report on steel wage negotiations, **1959:** 211
Report on welfare of workers, **1956:** 196
Resignation, letter, **1960–61:** 401
Small business, **1957:** 196
"Your Government and You" broadcasts, **1956:** 246
Labor, Under Secretary of (Arthur Larson).
See also Larson, Arthur; United States Information Agency, Director.
News conference remarks on, **1956:** 171
Rural development committee, **1956:** 217n.
Labor Day, **1956:** 196
Stamp commemoration ceremonies, remarks, **1956:** 194
Statements, **1953:** 181; **1954:** 259; **1955:** 212; **1956:** 195; **1957:** 168; **1958:** 241; **1959:** 209; **1960–61:** 282
Weekend, safe driving, statement, **1954:** 255
Labor disputes, **1953:** 6; **1958:** 26, 303; **1960–61:** 343, 410
Atomic energy facilities, **1954:** 161 and ftn. (p. 622), 192, 193, 281; **1956:** 95; **1957:** 88
Automobile industry, comment on, **1955:** 112
Copper industry, **1955:** 176
Injunctions, use of, **1954:** 5
Jurisdiction of States, **1954:** 5, 39, 101
Louisville and Nashville Railroad strike, **1955:** 90, 95
Maritime industry, **1956:** 300
Strike, **1953:** 198, 203; **1954:** 68; **1959:** 250
Railroads, **1954:** 39
Role of Government, **1955:** 90, 112, 119, 149, 176; **1959:** 67, 94, 161, 179, 186
Secret ballots, **1954:** 9
Southern Bell Telephone Co., and employees, **1955:** 90, 95
Steel strike, **1956:** 150; **1959:** 142, 161, 167, 211, 243, 253, 264, 265; **1960–61:** 4, 7, 21
Transit strike, Washington, D.C., **1955:** 149, 176, 206
Labor legislation (1956), **1955:** 247
Labor-management bills, **1959:** 176
Landrum-Griffin bill, **1959:** 172, 176
Statement, **1959:** 180
News conference remarks, **1959:** 21, 36, 89, 123, 172, 179, 186
Labor-management practices, news conference remarks, **1957:** 207

Labor-management relations, **1953:** 6, 248; **1955:** 4,
    245; **1956:** 190, 234; **1958:** 16; **1959:** 6, 15,
    176; **1960–61:** 4, 328, 343, 378, 401
  Budget messages, **1954:** 14 (p. 185); **1959:** 10 (pp.
    46, 101)
  Conference, proposed, **1960–61:** 127 and ftn. (p.
    368)
  Message to Congress, **1954:** 5; **1958:** 20; **1959:** 22
  News conference remarks, **1954:** 39, 50; **1958:**
    198, 222, 274; **1959:** 21, 167
  Power of States to handle, **1954:** 39
  Principles and guarantees, statement, **1958:** 242
  "Right to work" law, **1958:** 274, 293
  Statement, **1958:** 216
Labor-Management Relations Act.
  See also Taft-Hartley Act.
  News conference remarks, **1960–61:** 7, 21
  Proposed amendments, **1956:** 2
  Revision, question of, **1960–61:** 21
Labor-Management Relations Panel, Atomic En-
    ergy, transfer to AEC, memorandum,
    1956: 95
Labor-Management Reporting and Disclosure Act
    (1959), **1960–61:** 341, 401, 410
  Effectiveness, report, **1960–61:** 316
Labor organizations, **1953:** 6; **1954:** 353; **1958:** 20;
    1960–61: 316n., 410
  Affidavits by officials disclaiming Communist
    membership, **1953:** 109; **1954:** 5, 275
  AFL-CIO, **1955:** 47, 245; **1956:** 193, 198, 229,
    265n.; **1958:** 70, 288; **1959:** 163, 186;
    1960–61: 139, 215
    See also main heading, AFL-CIO.
  Code of ethical conduct, **1957:** 45, 56, 87
  Dedication of building, remarks, **1956:** 119
  American Federation of Labor, **1953:** 130, 193;
    1954: 107, 274n.
    See also main heading, American Federation of
    Labor.
  Cornerstone-laying ceremony, **1955:** 84
  Brotherhood of Railway and Steamship Clerks,
    1954: 39
  Budget message, **1956:** 12 (pp. 115–118)
  Campaign remarks, **1956:** 224, 234, 241, 258;
    1958: 293, 294, 296, 303, 308
  Civil rights action, **1956:** 113
  Communist Control Act, provisions re, **1954:** 210
  Congress of Industrial Organizations, **1953:** 130,
    248; **1954:** 107, 347
    See also main heading, Congress of Industrial
    Organizations.
  Federated Iron Workers Association of Austra-
    lia, **1954:** 77
  International Brotherhood of Teamsters, **1955:**
    232; **1957:** 50, 87, 150, 207; **1958:** 56
  International Confederation of Free Trade Un-
    ions, **1953:** 128, 130

Labor organizations — *continued*
  International Labor Organization, **1953:** 249;
    1954: 67, 125, 126
  International Longshoremen's Association,
    1953: 203; **1956:** 300; **1959:** 250
  Land, sea and air workers, **1957:** 150
  News conference remarks, **1956:** 113, 150, 193,
    198, 229, 298; **1959:** 17, 21, 67, 94, 123,
    161, 223
  Racketeering and abuses of trust and power,
    1957: 17, 72, 77, 87; **1958:** 20, 216, 222,
    292, 294, 296, 303, 308; **1959:** 6, 10 (p.
    101), 21, 123, 176, 223; **1960–61:** 13 (p. 92)
  Responsibility for wage-price stability, **1956:**
    298; **1957:** 8, 16, 119, 124; **1958:** 16, 63,
    103, 110, 120, 198, 213, 303, 308; **1959:** 15,
    17, 67, 123
  Rumor of merger of Teamsters and Longshore-
    men, comment on, **1959:** 161
  Point program for, **1959:** 22
  United Automobile Workers of America, **1954:**
    26; **1956:** 198
    Studebaker Local No. 5, **1954:** 203n., 274n.
  United Brotherhood of Carpenters and Joiners
    of America, **1953:** 224; **1956:** 86, 265
  United Gas, Coke and Chemical Workers, **1954:**
    193
  United Mineworkers, **1957:** 215
  United Steelworkers of America, **1953:** 77; **1956:**
    150, 229; **1958:** 120; **1959:** 94, 142, 160,
    211, 246, 265
    See also Labor disputes; Steel strike.
  United Textile Workers of America, **1956:** 198,
    216
  Welfare and Pension Plans Disclosure Act, **1958:**
    235
  Welfare and pension plans and funds, **1954:** 5, 9;
    1957: 56, 77; **1958:** 20, 83, 216, 242, 294;
    1959: 10 (pp. 46, 96–105)
Labor programs, budget messages, **1960–61:** 13 (pp
    87, 92, 93), 414 (pp. 999, 1005, 1006)
  Tables, **1960–61:** 13 (p. 88), 414 (pp. 1000, 1001)
Labor reform, **1959:** 225
Labor Relations Board, National, **1960–61:** 13 (p.
    92), 414 (p. 946)
  Acting General Counsel, proposal, **1958:** 20
Labor Statistics, Bureau of, **1957:** 45, 119; **1960–61:**
    217 ftn. (p. 545)
  Budget message, **1960–61:** 414 (p. 1006)
  Consumer price index, **1956:** 193
  Employment reports, **1958:** 283
Labor surplus areas.
  See also Depressed areas; Unemployment.
  Budget message, **1956:** 12 (pp. 145, 148)
  Industries for, **1956:** 12 (p. 145)
  Letter to minority leaders, **1958:** 43
Labor unions.
  See Labor organizations.

Laboratories, Government and non-Government, research in, **1958:** 326n.

Laboratories, medical, **1956:** 21, 151

Labouisse, Henry, **1959:** 29

Lackland Air Force Base, Texas, **1957:** 124

Laconia, N.H., remarks, **1955:** 134

Ladejinsky, Wolf, comment on, **1955:** 10, 18, 56

Lafayette, Marquis, **1958:** 123; **1959:** 201; **1960–61:** 317

Lafayette Fellowship Foundation, **1958:** 118

Lafayette Gold Medal Award, presentation to General Gruenther, **1958:** 118

Lafayette Square, building construction proposed, **1960–61:** 243

Lafer, Horacio, **1960–61:** 46n.

La Guardia Airport, N.Y., plane crash, **1959:** 26

Lahey, Edwin A., **1957:** 62; **1959:** 277

Lahey, Mrs. Frank H., **1954:** 334

Lahey Memorial Award
  Acceptance, remarks, **1954:** 334
  Sloan, Alfred P., **1957:** 223

Lahr, Raymond M., **1959:** 179

Lake, Mrs. Louise, **1958:** 99

Lake Alice National Wildlife Refuge, North Dakota, **1956:** 79

Lake George, N.Y., **1954:** 164

Lake Michigan, increased water diversion, disapproval, **1954:** 253; **1956:** 177

Lake Ontario Engineering Board, Joint, **1956:** 177

Lamb, Edward O., **1955:** 41

Lambert, H. P., Co., Inc., and Southeastern Drilling Corp., relief of, disapproval, **1960–61:** 292

"Lame duck" President, **1957:** 150

Lamp of Freedom, gift to the President, **1955:** 115

Lancaster, N.H., remarks, **1955:** 137

Land, Federal surplus, restoration to States, **1957:** 75

Land, Frank S., **1955:** 43n.

Land conservation and development, **1953:** 153

Land in drought-stricken areas, **1957:** 11, 16

Land Grant Act, **1957:** 68, 108

Land-Grant Colleges and Universities, Association of, remarks, **1954:** 335

Land Management, Bureau of, **1953:** 153; **1954:** 14 (p. 170); **1960–61:** 414 (p. 997)

Land resources, **1956:** 12 (p. 133 ff.); **1958:** 12
  Budget message, **1955:** 17 (pp. 158–163)
  Conservation and development, **1954:** 14 (pp. 162, 163, 166–169)
  Indian lands, **1955:** 17 (p. 162)

Land and timber exchanges, **1960–61:** 13 (p. 86), 414 (pp. 997, 998)

Landrum, Repr. Phil M., labor bill, **1959:** 172, 176, 180

Landrum-Griffin Act.
  See Labor-Management Reporting and Disclosure Act (1959).

Laney, D. S. and Elizabeth, tax refund claim, veto, **1958:** 205

Langelle, Russell A., **1959:** 271

Langer, Sen. William, **1959:** 123

Langlie, Gov. Arthur B., **1953:** 156; **1954:** 271; **1956:** 253
  Campaign and news conference remarks on, **1956:** 189, 251
  Letter on narcotics problem, **1956:** 31

Language training programs, **1960–61:** 13 (p. 64)

Languages, foreign, **1958:** 5 (p. 49), 24, 32, 120, 125, 144
  Teaching, **1957:** 234n.

Laniel, Joseph, **1953:** 254
  Cabinet, fall of, letter to President Coty, **1954:** 148
  Joint statement with Western leaders, **1953:** 255

Lanuti, Mrs. Mary, **1956:** 268

Laos, **1953:** 54; **1960–61:** 183, 410
  Assistance, **1955:** 17 (p. 129); **1959:** 55, 186; **1960–61:** 256
  Communist aggression, **1953:** 70; **1959:** 179, 186, 214
  Indochina war, U.S. assistance, **1953:** 66
  International Control Commission, **1960–61:** 422
  Joint statement with President Diem, **1957:** 83
  Joint statement with Western leaders, **1953:** 255
  Medico organization, **1960–61:** 174n.
  Membership in defense alliance, question of, **1954:** 107
  News conference remarks, **1954:** 101, 107, 168; **1959:** 179, 186, 223; **1960–61:** 256, 263, 422
  Phoumi Nosavan, **1960–61:** 422
  Rebellion, **1960–61:** 256, 263, 422
  Sisavang Vong, messages, **1954:** 82, 117
  United Nations observers in, **1959:** 214

Lapp, Ralph, **1956:** 62

La Quinta, Calif., **1959:** 249n., 250n.

Lar, Iran, earthquake, **1960–61:** 126

Lard, exports, **1958:** 58

Larkin, Thomas A., **1956:** 279n.

Larmon, Sigurd, **1953:** 2n.

LaRoche, Chester J., **1958:** 307n.

Larrabee, Donald R., **1954:** 63

Larsen, Roy E., **1955:** 96

Larson, Arthur, *A Republican Looks at His Party*, **1956:** 193
  See also United States Information Agency, Director; Labor, Under Secretary of.

Larson, Charles R., **1959:** 177n.

Larson, Jay G., **1958:** 312n.

La Salle, Robert de, **1959:** 141n.

Latin America, **1955:** 18, 35, 43; **1956:** 2, 164; **1957:** 217; **1959:** 6, 50n., 98, 287; **1960–61:** 49, 51, 349, 368n.
  See also American Republics; Inter-American; Organization of American States; *specific countries.*

Latin America — *continued*
  Anti-American demonstrations, **1958:** 101, 103, 107
  Assistance, **1953:** 66, 143; **1954:** 14 (p. 139), 150; **1955:** 17 (pp. 129, 130), 76; **1956:** 12 (p. 104), 58; **1959:** 55, 94; **1960–61:** 36, 42, 49, 72, 80, 86, 87, 228, 242, 247, 255, 256, 263, 302, 380, 414 (pp. 961, 966, 968)
    Documents re, President's certification forbidding disclosure to Congress, **1960–61:** 380
  Budget message, **1959:** 10 (pp. 44, 73)
  Campaign remarks, **1956:** 278
  Common market, proposed, **1960–61:** 73, 75, 80
  Delegates to U.N. General Assembly, luncheon honoring, remarks, **1960–61:** 303
  Economic development, **1960–61:** 72, 76, 87, 111n., 247
  Economic integration of Central America, joint statement on, **1959:** 54
  Escapees settling in, **1953:** 257n.
  Industrial revolution, **1959:** 55
  Milton S. Eisenhower report on U.S.-Latin American relations, **1959:** 261n., 287n.
  News conference remarks, **1954:** 18, 39, 143, 192; **1956:** 216; **1958:** 103, 222, 288; **1959:** 94, 148; **1960–61:** 38, 228, 256, 263
  Newsmen, visit to U.S., **1956:** 155
  Panama meeting of Presidents.
    See Panama.
  "People's Capitalism" exhibit, **1956:** 75n.
  Point 4 program, **1960–61:** 53
  Raw commodity prices, **1960–61:** 80
  Relations with United States, **1954:** 39
  Representatives of the American Presidents, meeting of, **1957:** 64
  Statement, **1960–61:** 228
  Trade with U.S., **1960–61:** 80
  U.S. information centers, **1960–61:** 414 (p. 968)
  U.S. loan policy toward, **1954:** 18
  Visit of Milton S. Eisenhower, **1953:** 48, 101, 141, 213, 265; **1958:** 197
    Report, **1953:** 48n., 198 and ftn. (p. 624)
  Visit of President Eisenhower, question of, **1953:** 31
    See also Visits, foreign.
  Visit of Vice President Nixon, **1958:** 101, 103, 107, 133n., 197; **1960–61:** 38
Latvia, immigration quota, **1956:** 33
Lau, Lawrence, **1959:** 184n.
Laurianti, Mrs. Margarite, **1956:** 268
Lausanne, Switzerland, question of summit conference in, **1955:** 112, 119
Lausche, Gov. Frank J., **1953:** 215
Lautier, Louis R., **1953:** 54; **1954:** 39, 92, 129; **1956:** 205; **1957:** 87, 92, 105, 134
Law, international, **1958:** 89; **1960–61:** 7
Law, Vernon, **1960–61:** 353

Law Day, statement, **1958:** 89
Law enforcement, cooperation of Federal, State, and local governments, **1957:** 232
Lawrence, Ernest O., **1957:** 119, 124, 210
  Award in memory of, proposed, **1958:** 239
  Death of, statement, **1958:** 233
  Sylvanus Thayer Award, citation, **1958:** 52
  Telegram, **1958:** 149n.
Lawrence, Joseph C., **1956:** 251n.
Lawrence, William H., **1953:** 88, 198, 208, 230, 238; **1954:** 341; **1955:** 10, 47, 59, 90, 95, 100, 119, 146, 149; **1956:** 5, 16, 53, 62, 88, 189, 198, 298; **1957:** 22, 28, 45, 50, 56, 62, 70, 72, 87, 92, 115, 119, 134, 145, 150, 152, 157, 207, 210, 228; **1958:** 74, 120, 141, 153; **1959:** 7n., 21, 26, 36, 42, 102, 154, 161, 179
Lawrence, Mass., **1954:** 9
Lawson, Lawrence M., **1953:** 222n.
Lawson, Marjorie, mining claim, disapproval, **1956:** 179
Lawson, Wallace (Wally), mining claim, disapproval, **1956:** 179
Lawton, Frederick J., President's Award for Distinguished Federal Civilian Service, **1960–61:** 389n.
Lawyers, social security coverage, **1956:** 158
Lay, James S., Jr., **1953:** 33
Laycook, L. G., **1953:** 225; **1954:** 39; **1955:** 26
Lazzio, Thomas, **1960–61:** 344n.
Leach, Paul R., **1953:** 41, 62, 77, 265; **1954:** 9, 25, 50, 107, 157; **1955:** 59
Lead, **1958:** 28
  U.S.-Canadian discussions on, **1958:** 153
Lead and zinc
  Producers, payment of subsidies to, disapproval, **1960–61:** 280
  Production, consumption, and importation, **1953:** 228
  Joint statements with President López Mateos on, **1959:** 38, 257
  Tariffs, **1954:** 143, 200; **1957:** 157
    Letter to Chairman, House Ways and Means Committee, **1957:** 160
Leader, Governor George M., **1957:** 138
Leadership of the President
  Churchill on, **1956:** 216
  Foreign and domestic affairs, **1959:** 179
  Government, **1959:** 132
Leadership of the United States **1954:** 182; **1956:** 88
League of Nations, **1958:** 173; **1959:** 116; **1960–61:** 330, 340
League of Red Cross Societies, **1954:** 175, 182 ftn. (p. 678); **1955:** 37, 49
League of Women Voters
  Recorded interview for, **1954:** 91
  Remarks to National Council, **1957:** 79 and n.

Leahy, Adm. William D., death of, statement,
    1959: 166
Lease-purchase contracts for Federal building,
    1958: 70
  Budget message, **1958:** 5 (p. 72)
Leasing of Government farm lands, memorandum,
    1956: 111
Leave for Presidential appointees, payment for,
    memorandum, **1953:** 55
Leavenworth Staff College, **1957:** 235
Lebanon, **1957:** 207; **1958:** 172, 261, 296; **1959:** 6;
    1960–61: 23, 302, 330, 410
  Assistance, **1955:** 17 (p. 130); **1959:** 55
  Atomic research agreement, **1955:** 121
  Beirut, **1958:** 173, 174n.
  Chamoun, Camille, **1958:** 171, 172, 173, 174n.,
    176, 177
    Letter, **1958:** 182
    Message, **1956:** 61
  Joint statement with Prime Minister of Ghana re
    withdrawal of U. S. troops, **1958:** 180
  Letters to Premier Khrushchev on, **1958:** 177,
    179, 189
  Malik, Charles, **1957:** 28
  Message to Vice President Nixon re, **1958:** 289
  News conference remarks, **1958:** 103, 120, 141,
    198
  Request for U.S. armed forces, **1958:** 171, 173,
    174, 177, 207
  Soviet veto of U.N. resolutions, **1958:** 207
  U.N. address, **1958:** 207
  U.N. observers, **1958:** 171
  U.S. armed forces in, **1958:** 172, 174n., 177,
    182n., 198, 207, 213
    Messages to, **1958:** 176, 291
    Statement, **1958:** 173
    Withdrawal, **1958:** 291
Le Canadel, France, **1954:** 198n.
Leclerc, Marshal Jacques Philippe, **1954:** 133
Lecture, Max W. Salvadori, **1956:** 62
Lederer, William J., *The Ugly American*, **1960–61:**
    184
Lee, Mrs. John G., **1954:** 91
Lee, Richard Henry, **1956:** 283
Lee, Robert E., **1953:** 240; **1954:** 88, 127; **1956:**
    280; **1957:** 87; **1958:** 93; **1960–61:** 246
  Memorial Foundation, **1958:** 93n.
  News conference remarks on, **1954:** 50, 345
  Quoted, **1957:** 27, 108
Lee, Thomas, **1958:** 93
Legion of Merit, presentations
  Anderson, Comdr. W. R., **1958:** 201
  Bayar, President Celal (Turkey), **1954:** 20
  Beach, Capt. Edward L., **1960–61:** 142
  Bhumibol Adulyadej, **1960–61:** 212
  King Paul of Greece, **1953:** 233
  Pibulsonggram, Field Marshall **1955:** 87
  Walsh, Lt. Don., **1960–61:** 25

Legislation
  Domestic, meeting of Republican Congressional
    leaders on, **1955:** 247
  Extraneous amendments, comment on, **1955:**
    149
  Item veto, **1958:** 5 (p. 73)
  Presidential function, **1959:** 154
  Priority list, **1955:** 146; **1959:** 102, 132, 179, 186
Legislation, statements upon approval
  Agricultural Act, **1954:** 221; **1956:** 115
  Agricultural Adjustment Act, amendment, **1954:**
    24
  Agricultural Trade Development and Assistance
    Act, **1954:** 162
    Amendment, **1955:** 202
    Extension, **1959:** 226
  Aid to schools in federally affected areas, **1958:**
    203
  Alaska statehood, **1958:** 159
  American Samoa labor standards, **1956:** 172
  Appropriation Act, Treasury-Post Office (1958),
    1957: 99
  Appropriations, Atomic Energy Commission,
    1957: 159; **1958:** 193
  Appropriations, civil functions, Army and Inte-
    rior Departments, **1957:** 161
  Atomic Energy Act, **1954:** 223
  Authorizing conveyance of property to Panama,
    1957: 167
  Authorizing permanent certification, certain air
    carriers, **1957:** 162
  Authorizing sale of long staple cotton, **1957:** 128
  Automobile dealers, suits by, **1956:** 174
  Automobile imports, **1958:** 76
  Bank Holding Company Act of 1956, **1956:** 99
  Bataan Day observance, **1954:** 75
  Brucellosis eradication program, **1956:** 72
  Budget and accounting methods and procedures,
    1956: 156
  Career incentives, medical and dental officers,
    1956: 91
  Civil Rights Act, **1960–61:** 137
  Communications Act, amendment, **1959:** 216
  Communist Control Act, **1954:** 210
  Construction of superliner passenger vessels,
    1958: 170
  Cuban sugar quota, **1960–61:** 223
  Customs Simplification Act, **1953:** 164; **1956:**
    162
  Debt limit, increase, **1954:** 219
  Denmark, payment, **1958:** 129
  Department of Defense Appropriation Act,
    1955: 155; **1958:** 218
  Department of Defense Reorganization Act of
    1958, **1958:** 199
  Departments of Labor, and Health, Education,
    and Welfare Appropriation Act, 1960,
    1959: 181

[References are to items except as otherwise indicated]

Legislation, statements upon approval — *continued*
    District of Columbia
        Inspection of police arrest books, **1954:** 207
        Public transportation, **1955:** 206
        Treatment for narcotics users, **1953:** 116
        Unemployment insurance, **1954:** 227
    Durum wheat, additional acreage allotments,
        1957: 59
    Euratom Cooperation Act of 1958, **1958:** 236
    Farm Credit Act, **1953:** 158; **1956:** 147
    Federal-Aid Highway Act, **1954:** 102; **1958:** 77;
        1959: 227
    Federal Airport Act, amendment, **1959:** 143
    Federal employees fringe benefits, **1954:** 234
    Federal Employees' Group Life Insurance Act,
        1954: 202
    Federal Flood Insurance Act of 1956, **1956:** 167
    Fish and Wildlife Act of 1956, **1956:** 173
    Flag, display of, **1953:** 133
    Flood Control Act, **1954:** 249; **1958:** 155
    Gasoline for farm use, tax relief, **1956:** 72
    Great Plains conservation program, **1956:** 169
    Hawaii statehood, **1959:** 60
    Health Amendments Act of 1956, **1956:** 161
    Health Research Facilities Act of 1956, **1956:**
        151
    Highway bridge across Lake Texoma, **1955:** 158
    Highway Construction Co. of Ohio, Inc., relief
        of, **1955:** 159
    Housing Act, **1954:** 179; **1957:** 129 and n.
        Amendments, **1955:** 194
    Housing for military personnel, **1954:** 237
    Immigration and Nationality Act, amendment,
        1957: 187
    Increase in interest rates, Series E and H savings
        bonds, **1957:** 76
    Increases in service-connected disability com-
        pensation and dependency allowances,
        1957: 163
    Independent Offices Appropriation Act, **1960–**
        61: 229
    Indian reservations, State jurisdiction over cases
        arising on, **1953:** 166
    Information, withholding of, **1958:** 202
    Internal Revenue Code revision, **1954:** 199
    Joint Resolution on Formosa, **1955:** 24
    Joint resolution on Middle East, **1957:** 46
    Library services, **1956:** 127
    Madeira Beach, Fla., relief of, **1959:** 232
    Marr, Pearl O., mineral rights, **1954:** 238
    Materials Act of 1947, amendments, **1955:** 172
    Menominee Indian Tribe, termination of Fed-
        eral supervision, **1954:** 147
    Merchant Marine Act, amendment, **1954:** 213
    Mexican migrant labor, **1954:** 56
    Muscatine Bridge Commission, creation of,
        1956: 148

Legislation, statements upon approval — *continued*
    Mutual Security Act of 1959, **1959:** 171; **1960–**
        61: 148
    Mutual Security Appropriation Act, **1955:** 182;
        1956: 152; **1957:** 173
    National Aeronautics and Space Act of 1958,
        1958: 185
    National Defense Education Act, **1958:** 243
    National Music Council, incorporation, **1956:**
        159
    Natural Gas Act, amendment, **1954:** 64
    Naval officers, promotion and retirement of,
        1959: 178
    Oregon lands, administrative jurisdiction over,
        1954: 152
    Pakistan, wheat for drought relief, **1953:** 119
    Pledge of allegiance to the flag, amendment,
        1954: 140
    Postal Field Service Compensation Act, **1955:**
        120
    Postal Policy Act of 1958, **1958:** 117
    Postal Rate Increase Act, 1958, **1958:** 117
    Potomac River bridges, **1954:** 224
    Price supports on butterfat and manufacturing
        milk, **1960–61:** 295
    Public Works Appropriation Act, 1957, **1955:**
        157; **1956:** 136; **1958:** 244
    Railroad Retirement Act, amendment, **1954:**
        145; **1956:** 168
    Reclamation projects, **1955:** 180
    Red River flood control project, **1955:** 184
    Reenlistment bonuses for military personnel,
        1954: 166
    Refugee Relief Act, **1953:** 160
    Refugees, admission to U.S., **1960–61:** 233
    Relief of
        Jackson School Township, Indiana, **1957:** 174
        Kawar, Irfan, **1956:** 59
        Ovens, Michael D., **1957:** 181
        Wright, Mr. and Mrs. Derfery William, **1956:**
            24
    Reserve Forces Act, **1955:** 192
    Residential construction, message, **1958:** 62
    River and Harbor Act, **1954:** 249; **1958:** 155
    Salary payment to interim appointee, AEC,
        1955: 193
    San Luis Unit, Central Valley Project, **1960–61:**
        168
    Santa Margarita River water storage facilities,
        1954: 173
    School construction aid, Federally-affected,
        1957: 170
    School milk program, **1956:** 72
    Second Supplemental Appropriation Act, 1956,
        1956: 109
    Servicemen's and Veterans' Survivor Benefits
        Act, **1956:** 157

Legislation, statements upon approval — *continued*
  Sheepherders, nonquota immigrant visas for, **1954:** 250
  Sibley Memorial Hospital, **1957:** 175
  Small reclamation projects, Federal aid, **1956:** 165
  Social Security Amendments, **1954:** 235; **1956:** 158; **1958:** 234
  Submerged Lands Act, **1953:** 86
  Sugar Act of 1948, amendment and extension, **1956:** 116
  Supplemental Appropriation Act, **1959:** 197
  Tanker fleet modernization, **1954:** 191
  Tennessee Valley Authority Act, **1959:** 175
  Trade Agreements Extension Act, **1953:** 161; **1955:** 129; **1958:** 215
  Unemployment insurance, extension of coverage, **1954:** 236
  Veterans benefits, **1954:** 220
  Veterans' loans, **1959:** 146
  Vocational Rehabilitation Amendments, **1954:** 180
  Washita River Basin reclamation project, Oklahoma, **1956:** 44
  Water Facilities Act, amendment, **1954:** 201
  Water Pollution Control Act Amendments of 1956, **1956:** 137
  Water Supply Act, **1958:** 155
  Watershed Protection and Flood Prevention Act amendment, **1956:** 170
  Welfare and Pension Plans Disclosure Act, **1958:** 235
  Wheat acreage allotments and marketing quotas (1960), extension of announcement date, **1959:** 108
Legislation, Vetoes and Memorandums of Disapproval.
  See also Memorandums of Disapproval; Veto Messages.
  Airports, Federal aid, **1958:** 246
  Apple price predictions, prohibition of Government publication, **1955:** 147
  Area redevelopment bill, **1958:** 258
  Challenges in civil cases, **1958:** 250
  Chamberlain Water Co., relocation costs, **1958:** 225
  Civil Service Retirement Act, amendment, **1955:** 201
  Crow Indian Tribe, payment to, **1956:** 124
  Date of meeting, 85th Congress, **1956:** 175
  Declaration of Taking Act, amendment, **1958:** 250
  District of Columbia, certain gasoline filling stations, **1956:** 153
  Extension of direct loan program for veterans' housing, **1957:** 172
  Farm bill, **1956:** 82
  Farm "freeze" bill, **1958:** 59

Legislation, Vetoes and Disapproval — *continued*
  Importation of seed wheat, **1958:** 217
  Independent Offices Appropriation Act, **1958:** 192
  Internal Revenue Code of 1954, amendment, **1955:** 198
  Military installations, housing, **1956:** 141
  Mineral interests, lands acquired by U. S. for reservoir projects, **1956:** 154
  Minerals programs, **1955:** 205; **1958:** 206
  Mining claims, specified persons, **1956:** 179
  Natural Gas Act, amendment, **1956:** 41
  Nuclear-powered ice breaker, **1958:** 204
  Ogletree, Stephen Swan, change of military record, **1955:** 197
  Ohio River bridge commissions, **1956:** 182
  Postal field service compensation bill, **1955:** 102
  Reconveyance to former owners of certain reservoir project lands in Texas, **1955:** 199
Relief of
  Albrecht, E. J., Co., **1955:** 196
  Axelroad, Colonel Benjamin, **1957:** 123
  Berry, Walter H., **1957:** 155
  Board of Commissioners, Sedgwick County, Kans., **1956:** 112
  Boutwell, William A., **1958:** 228
  Brennan, Mrs. John William, **1957:** 73
  Browne, Mary M., **1958:** 230
  Caesar, George P. E., Jr., **1958:** 245
  Compton, Mr. and Mrs. Thomas V., **1956:** 126
  Cooper Tire and Rubber Co., **1958:** 252
  Cooperman, Philip, **1957:** 184
  Continental Hosiery Mills, Inc., **1958:** 187
  Cowan, Roy, and others, **1956:** 79
  Dew Hong-to, **1958:** 124
  Duff, Harry N., **1958:** 248
  Elkins, W. Va., **1956:** 163
  Glaser, Kurt, **1955:** 116
  Gregg, Mrs. Frank C., estate, **1958:** 237
  Hadnot, Mr. and Mrs. John R., **1958:** 238
  Hall, Mr. and Mrs. Robert B., **1958:** 253
  Hanzal, Alfred, **1958:** 34
  Haun, Cale P. and Julia Fay, **1958:** 48
  Hines, Fred P., **1955:** 200
  Hollomon, Mr. and Mrs. W. G., **1958:** 254
  Kilpatrick, Shirley Leeke, **1958:** 61
  Knox Corporation, **1957:** 182
  Laney, D. S. and Elizabeth, **1958:** 205
  Malowney Real Estate Co., Inc., **1958:** 227
  Mnatzakanian, Ashot and Ophelia, **1956:** 73
  Moore, Duncan and Marjorie, **1958:** 256
  North Counties Hydro-Electric Co., **1958:** 229
  O'Brien, Peter J., **1958:** 251
  Pacific Customs Brokerage Company, **1957:** 183
  Page, Mr. and Mrs. Charles H., **1957:** 180
  Pfeifer, Jean, **1956:** 160
  Powell, Mrs. Hannah Mae, **1957:** 179

Legislation, Vetoes and Disapproval — *continued*
  Relief of — *continued*
    Roach, Lucian, **1958:** 212
    Ryan, Mary K., **1958:** 228
    Santos, Bonifacio, **1958:** 231
    Shriro, Aron, **1957:** 184
    Southwest Research Institute, **1958:** 247
    Spencer, Susie Lee, estate, **1956:** 134
    Stackman, Samuel, **1957:** 184
    Symms, Marion S., **1958:** 232
    Thomson Contracting Co., Inc., **1958:** 208
    Toley's Charter Boats, Inc., and others, **1958:** 249
    Whitaker, D A., and others, **1958:** 255
  River and harbor and flood control, certain projects, **1956:** 180
  Rivers and harbors bill, **1958:** 73
  Salary increases for Postal and other Federal employees, **1957:** 185
  Settlement of certain damage claims by Department of Defense, **1958:** 259
  Southwestern Power Administration rates, **1956:** 178
  Stone, William E., claim of, **1956:** 135
  Subversive Activities Control Board, term of office, **1955:** 189
  Tax credit for certain taxes of United Kingdom, **1956:** 181
  Taxation of real estate investment trusts, **1956:** 183
  Vicksburg National Military Park, facility, **1958:** 226
  Wage rates, Portsmouth naval shipyard, **1958:** 191
  Water diversion from Lake Michigan, **1956:** 177
Legislative program, **1954:** 72, 139, 197, 203, 209, 273, 286, 308
  Conference on, with Republican congressional leaders and chairmen of standing committees, **1953:** 266, 268, 269
  Meetings with Republican leaders, **1954:** 349
  Message to Congress, **1960–61:** 133
  News conference remarks, **1953:** 126, 230, 238, 249, 254, 265; **1954:** 9, 33, 63, 92, 129, 138, 143, 157, 161, 168, 172, 182, 200, 322, 347, 353; **1960–61:** 256, 263, 284
Legislative recommendations, messages and letters, **1957:** 157
  See also Congress, messages to; Congress, letters to Members of.
  Agriculture, **1956:** 6; **1958:** 12
  Airways Modernization Board, **1957:** 71
  Budget and accounting practices, appropriation for, **1956:** 100
  Budget messages, **1956:** 12 (pp. 84, 87, 93 ff.); **1957:** 13, 75; **1958:** 5 (pp. 32 ff.)
    Table, **1956:** 12 (p. 88)
  Child Health Day, **1958:** 175
  Defense mobilization bill, transmittal letter, **1958:** 75

Legislative recommendations — *continued*
  Defense reorganization
    Draft of bill, letter, **1958:** 75
    Message, **1958:** 65
  Drought and other natural disasters, **1957:** 41
  Economic report, **1957:** 16; **1958:** 16
  Education, **1958:** 195
  Establishment of Joint Commission on the Civilian Employee Compensation Policy of the Federal Government, **1958:** 169
  Farm "freeze" bill, veto message, **1958:** 59
  Federal aid to education, **1956:** 8; **1957:** 19
  Federal Aviation Agency, **1958:** 135
  Federal intermediate credit banks, **1956:** 147
  Federal-State Action Committee recommendations, **1958:** 106
  Health, **1956:** 21
  Hoover Commission recommendations, **1957:** 112 and n.
  Hurricane flood prevention, letter, **1958:** 85
  Immigration matters, **1957:** 25
  Immigration policies, **1956:** 33
  Labor-management relations, **1958:** 20
  Measures to aid economy, letter, **1958:** 43
  Middle East, **1957:** 6
  Military career incentives, **1956:** 81
  Military installations, construction at, **1956:** 141
  Mutual security program, **1956:** 58; **1957:** 90; **1958:** 32
  National Aeronautics and Space Agency, **1958:** 64
  Organization for Trade Cooperation, **1957:** 61
  Passport control, **1958:** 161
  Quesada, E. R., restoration of status in Air Force, **1958:** 272
  Reorganization plans of 1956, **1956:** 105, 108
  Space science and exploration, **1958:** 105
  State of the Union message, **1956:** 2; **1957:** 8
  Status of Forces overseas, **1957:** 139
  Unemployment compensation, **1958:** 53
  VA housing, interest rates and mortgage purchases, **1958:** 62
  Water resources development projects, letter, **1958:** 85
Lehman, Sen. Herbert H., **1953:** 37; **1954:** 168; **1956:** 189
Leichter, Otto, **1954:** 68
Leigh-Pemberton, John, **1955:** 167n.
Leisure, use of, **1955:** 121; **1958:** 63
LeMay, Gen. Curtis E., **1957:** 72, 233 and n.
Lemnitzer, Gen. Lyman L., **1960–61:** 135, 283
Lemont, Ill., **1955:** 53n.
Lemus, José Mariá
  Exchange of toasts, **1959:** 52
  Joint statement with, **1959:** 54
  Remarks of welcome, **1959:** 50
Lemus, Senora, **1959:** 50, 52
Lending institutions, taxes on, **1960–61:** 414 (pp. 943, 944)

[References are to items except as otherwise indicated]

Lenin, Nikolai, **1953:** 109; **1956:** 78, 87; **1959:** 17; **1960–61:** 222, 328

Lennox-Boyd, Alan, **1959:** 39

Leonard, Lt. Gen. John W., **1955:** 52

Leopold, King, **1957:** 153 and n.

Leopoldville, Congo, **1960–61:** 248

Lepervanche Parparcen, Rene, **1953:** 48n.

Lester, Wilbur R., **1953:** 59

Leviero, Anthony H., **1953:** 22, 31, 41, 62, 77, 88, 109, 126, 238, 243, 249, 254, 265; **1954:** 9, 25, 33, 48, 50, 92, 107, 115; **1955:** 149; **1956:** 53, 56, 78, 94

   Death of, remarks, **1956:** 198

Levittown, Pa, **1954:** 101; **1959:** 179

Levy, Asher, **1954:** 297

Levy, Harold R., **1957:** 105; **1959:** 29, 94, 167; **1960–61:** 21

Levy, Lillian, **1957:** 28, 62, 124, 134, 150, 228; **1958:** 153; **1959:** 167; **1960–61:** 7, 21, 38, 127, 143, 222, 263, 268, 422

Lewis, J. Anthony, **1956:** 32, 56, 62, 113, 171, 193; **1957:** 169, 210; **1958:** 198, 213, 274; **1959:** 123; **1960–61:** 21

Lewis, John L., **1959:** 123

Lewis, Joseph, **1960–61:** 139

Lewis, Meriwether, **1956:** 107

Lewis and Clark expedition, **1954:** 271

Lexington, Ky., **1954:** 89; **1956:** 225, 226, 229

Libby, Willard F., **1955:** 89n., 191n.; **1958:** 157

   Memorandum, **1956:** 156

Libby Dam, **1954:** 271; **1960–61:** 419

   Budget message, **1960–61:** 414 (p. 994)

Liberia

   W. V. S. Tubman, **1954:** 292; **1959:** 224

      Exchange of toasts, **1954:** 293

Libertyville, Ill., **1956:** 197

Libraries, AEC technical, in United States and abroad, **1955:** 228

Libraries, overseas, **1956:** 12 (p. 108)

   Selection of books for, **1953:** 109, 126, 128

Library of American Study, Anthony Wayne (Defiance College), **1953:** 215

Library Association, American, **1953:** 120

Library of Congress, **1956:** 198

Library (Eisenhower), Abilene, Kans., for Eisenhower papers, **1957:** 134; **1959:** 179; **1960–61:** 21, 118

   Ground-breaking ceremony, **1959:** 258, 259

Library services, statement, **1956:** 127

Libya, **1958:** 32

   Assistance, **1955:** 17 (p. 130); **1959:** 55

   Tobruk, **1959:** 96

Life expectancy of man, **1955:** 121

Life insurance for Federal employees, **1954:** 43, 116, 182, 273, 313

   Approval of bill, **1954:** 202

Lighthouse Service, employees benefits, **1954:** 137

Lightner, Milton C., **1959:** 83n.

Ligonier, Pa., **1958:** 269

Lilly, Eli, & Co., **1955:** 100

Lincoln, Abraham, **1953:** 11, 100, 147, 187, 240; **1954:** 22, 31, 32, 51, 54, 72, 89, 106, 144, 203, 258, 270, 271, 273, 275, 286; **1955:** 35, 121, 126, 181, 213; **1956:** 75, 84, 107, 190, 206, 211, 214, 224, 235, 258, 315; **1957:** 22, 50, 60, 68, 87, 198; **1958:** 26, 127n., 303; **1959:** 7, 21, 31, 58n., 151, 176, 255n., 269n., 270, 318; **1960–61:** 23, 34, 58, 107, 131, 171n., 173, 174, 187, 246, 318, 347

   Birthplace, visit, remarks, **1954:** 88

   Quoted, **1957:** 68, 86, 108, 237

Lincoln, G. Gould, **1953:** 12, 41, 198, 265; **1954:** 57, 115; **1955:** 146; **1956:** 32; **1957:** 17

Lincoln, N.H., remarks, **1955:** 135

Lincoln Center for the Performing Arts, ground-breaking ceremonies, remarks, **1959:** 106

Lincoln Day Box Supper

   Incident at, comment on, **1954:** 33

   Remarks, **1954:** 31

Lincoln Day Dinners, address, **1954:** 22

Lincoln Group of the District of Columbia, **1959:** 31n.

Lincoln Memorial, **1959:** 31

Lincoln Sesquicentennial Commission, **1958:** 74; **1959:** 21, 31n.

Lincoln Sesquicentennial Dinner, National, remarks, **1959:** 31

Lindquist, Leonard L., **1960–61:** 329n.

Linseed oil and seeds, surplus disposal, **1956:** 6

Lippmann, Walter, **1959:** 48

Liquor, excise tax on, **1954:** 3, 14 (pp. 88, 99); **1955:** 41; **1957:** 13

Lisagor, Peter, **1956:** 47, 56, 78, 94, 121, 155, 171, 193, 198, 205; **1957:** 28, 72, 80, 115, 124, 134, 228; **1958:** 28, 42, 56, 83, 103, 198, 274, 318; **1959:** 21, 26, 29, 36, 42, 48, 53, 67, 132, 154, 161, 186; **1960–61:** 93, 103, 127, 256, 263

Lisbon, **1958:** 144

   Remarks on arrival, **1960–61:** 157

   Remarks on departure, **1960–61:** 161

   Remarks at U.S. embassy, **1960–61:** 158

   Toasts to President Thomaz, **1960–61:** 159, 160

Lithuania, immigration quota, **1956:** 33

Little, Lou (Luigi Piccolo), **1958:** 286

Little league baseball, **1960–61:** 199

Little Rock, Ark.

   Broadcast on situation in, **1957:** 198

   Brown, Bishop Robert B., **1957:** 207, 228

   Closed schools, **1958:** 274

   Executive Order 10730, **1957:** 198n.

   News conference remarks, **1957:** 115, 134, 169, 207, 210, 228; **1958:** 11, 42, 56, 103, 222, 274

   Proclamation 3204, **1957:** 198n.

   School Board, **1957:** 169, 178, 198

Little Rock, Ark. — *continued*
  Statements
    Continued Federal surveillance, **1957:** 205
    Decision of Eighth Circuit Court, **1958:** 214
    Developments, **1957:** 193
    Governor Faubus, **1957:** 205n., 207
    Meeting with Governor Faubus, **1957:** 18
    Meeting with Southern Governors, **1957:** 205n.
    Occurrences at Central High School, **1957:** 197
    Supreme Court decision of Sept. 12, 1958, **1956:** 262, 275
    Troop removal, **1958:** 98
    Telegram to Governor Faubus, **1957:** 188
    Telegram to Senator Russell on use of Federal troops, **1957:** 200
    Troops in, **1958:** 42
    U. S. District Court, **1957:** 134, 169, 178, 197, 198, 205, 207; **1958:** 98, 274
Livestock, **1953:** 218; **1956:** 6
  Brucellosis control, **1958:** 59
  Brucellosis eradication bill, **1956:** 72, 83
  Disaster relief, **1956:** 235, 236, 237
  Effect of agricultural surpluses, **1956:** 6
  Humane methods of slaughter bill, **1958:** 222
  Mexican purchase, **1956:** 235, 236
  Prices, **1953:** 101, 216, 225, 227, 230, 249 and ftn. (p. 780); **1956:** 83, 236
  Purchase programs, **1956:** 83
  Screw worm problem, **1959:** 38
Livestock and Horse Show, American Royal, **1953:** 218n.
Livingston, J. A., **1953:** 249
Livingston, Robert R., **1953:** 219
Lleras Camargo, Alberto
  Discussions with, statement, **1960–61:** 111
  Exchange of toasts, **1960–61:** 109, 110
  Letter, **1958:** 137
  Remarks of welcome, **1960–61:** 108
Lleras, Senora, **1960–61:** 109, 110
Lloyd, Selwyn, **1956:** 78, 229; **1957:** 55, 226n.; **1958:** 293; **1959:** 39, 123 and ftn. (p. 425)
Loans
  Federal, assistance to depressed areas, **1960–61:** 146
  Housing, college and university, **1957:** 19, 56
  Long-term development assistance, **1957:** 90, 91, 152n.
  VA-guaranteed home loans, interest rates, **1957:** 16
Lobbying, **1957:** 87; **1958:** 70
Lockheed Aircraft Corp., **1956:** 257n.
Lockley, Sidney L., **1956:** 234
Lodge, George, **1958:** 213
Lodge, Henry Cabot, Jr.
  Candidacy for Vice President, **1960–61:** 256, 263, 290, 309, 341

Lodge, Henry Cabot, Jr. — *continued*
  Candidacy for Vice President — *continued*
    Campaign remarks on, **1960–61:** 344, 345, 346, 347, 348, 350, 353, 354, 355
    Post election telegram, **1960–61:** 357
  News conference remarks on, **1960–61:** 256, 263, 268, 284
  President's representative at Pulaski Day Parade, letter, **1956:** 227
  U. S. Representative to U.N., **1953:** 187; **1954:** 73, 322; **1955:** 156; **1958:** 148, 172, 179, 189, 196; **1959:** 218; **1960–61:** 238, 302
    Economic humanism, **1959:** 21
    Resignation, letter, **1960–61:** 266
Lodge, Mrs. Henry Cabot, **1960–61:** 357
Lodge, John, **1959:** 338n.
Lodge, Gov. John D., **1953:** 187
  Birthday celebration, remarks, **1954:** 296
Lodge-Nixon, American Nationalities for, remarks, **1960–61:** 298
Loftus, Joseph A., **1953:** 198; **1954:** 161, 168, 172, 192, 311, 322, 345; **1955:** 10, 18; **1959:** 89, 223
London, Jack, **1960–61:** 178
London, **1953:** 128; **1958:** 158; **1959:** 192n.; **1960–61:** 121, 124, 279
  Agreements, **1954:** 189n., 282, 286, 314, 351
  Anderson-Dillon discussions with officials, **1960–61:** 365
  Broadcast with Prime Minister Macmillan, **1959:** 196
  Conference, **1954:** 332, 337
    Statement, **1954:** 282
  Meeting with Fernando Maria Castiella, **1959:** 200
  Meeting of foreign ministers, **1953:** 225
  Remarks on arrival, **1959:** 193
  Remarks on departure, **1959:** 198
London disarmament conference.
  See Disarmament conference, London; Disarmament Subcommittee, U.N.
London Suez conferences
  18-nation proposal, **1956:** 184, 192, 198, 205, 216, 235
    Dulles report, statement, **1956:** 192
  3-power (U. S., U. K., France), Dulles report, TV remarks, **1956:** 164
Long, Mrs. Glenn, **1953:** 240
Long, Huey, **1953:** 37
Long, Sen. Oren E., **1959:** 184n.
Long Beach (nuclear-powered cruiser), **1960–61:** 13 (p. 55), 414 (p. 954)
Longfellow, Henry Wadsworth, **1960–61:** 330
Longshoremen
  Disability compensation, **1958:** 5 (p. 45)
  Labor dispute, **1959:** 250
  Safety codes, **1959:** 10 (p. 101)

Longshoremen's and Harbor Workers Compensation Act, **1956:** 2
Budget message, **1956:** 12 (p. 117)
López Mateos, Adolfo, **1959:** 37; **1960–61:** 303, 333, 334n.
Exchange of toasts, **1959:** 255, 256
Joint statements with, **1959:** 38, 257; **1960–61:** 335
Letter, **1958:** 317
Message, **1959:** 275
News conference remarks on **1959:** 21, 36, 42, 243
Remarks of welcome, **1959:** 254
López Mateos, Senora, **1959:** 254, 255, 256
Lorant, Stefan, *The Presidency,* **1958:** 288
Lord, Mrs. Oswald B., **1953:** 43; **1955:** 156
Los Angeles, Calif., **1958:** 71, 288, 292, 305; **1960–61:** 23, 320n.
Campaign remarks, **1954:** 273, 274
Remarks to AFL convention, **1954:** 275
Louis XV, **1960–61:** 328
Louisiana
Brooks, Repr. Overton, **1954:** 120n.; **1955:** 100
Ellender, Sen. Allen J., Sr., **1954:** 143
Hébert, Repr. F. Edward, **1959:** 167
Hurricane Audrey, statement, **1957:** 121
Kennon, Gov. Robert F., **1953:** 219; **1955:** 88
New Orleans, **1953:** 219, 220; **1955:** 44
Louisiana Purchase, coinage of 50-cent pieces to commemorate sesquicentennial, veto, **1954:** 29
150th anniversary, address, **1953:** 219
Louisiana Sesquicentennial Commission, **1953:** 219n.
Louisville, Ky., **1954:** 320; **1956:** 205; **1957:** 87
Alcohol butadiene plant, **1956:** 90
Campaign remarks, **1954:** 319
Louisville and Nashville Railroad strike, **1955:** 90, 95
Lovett, Robert A., **1954:** 107; **1956:** 10n.
Lovre, Repr. Harold O., **1953:** 101
Lowe, Herman A., **1955:** 112; **1956:** 155, 235; **1957:** 70, 150
Lowell, James Russell, **1960–61:** 306
Low-income housing, **1953:** 266; **1955:** 4
Lowry, Rev. Charles W., **1954:** 327
Message, **1956:** 201
Loyalty affidavit, loan requirement under National Defense Education Act, **1960–61:** 13 (p. 89), 414 (p. 1003)
Loyalty Board records, comment on release to Congress, **1954:** 115
Loyalty of clergymen, attacks on, **1953:** 132
Loyalty Day, statement, **1958:** 175
Loyalty files, availability, **1953:** 22
Loyalty oath requirement in Federal student loan program, comment on, **1959:** 288

Loyalty program, **1953:** 15
See also Security program for Government employment.
Lozano Diaz, Julio, message, **1956:** 144
Lucas families, **1956:** 251
Luce, Clare Boothe, **1954:** 283n.; **1959:** 94
Congressional action on appointment, **1959:** 89, 102
Meeting with Prime Minister Scelba, **1955:** 61
Lucey, Charles T., **1953:** 128, 238; **1954:** 25, 92; **1956:** 47, 155
Luebke, Heinrich, **1960–61:** 91
Lumumba, Patrice, **1960–61:** 263, 284
Lunar probes.
See Moon probes.
Lund, Arnold, **1956:** 278
Luns, Joseph M. A. H., **1959:** 70, 186, 214
Luxembourg, **1954:** 84n.; **1955:** 54n.
Euratom.
See European Atomic Energy Community.
European Defense Community Treaty, ratification, statement, **1954:** 74
Lyons, Eugene L. (Special Assistant to the President for Personnel Management), **1960–61:** 26, 28
Memorandum, **1960–61:** 27

MAAG.
See Military Assistance Advisory Group.
Maas, Gen. Melvin J., **1954:** 96; **1955:** 103; **1957:** 94 and n.; **1958:** 99
Citation, **1960–61:** 417
MacArthur, Gen. Douglas, **1953:** 254 ftn. (p. 800); **1954:** 63; **1955:** 146 ftn. (p. 644); **1958:** 139, 307; **1960–61:** 182, 186
80th birthday, statement, **1960–61:** 20
Macaulay, Thomas Babington, **1957:** 105
MacDonald, Kenneth, **1956:** 87
MacDonald, Mrs. Kenneth, **1956:** 87
Machinery, British, rejection of bid re, **1953:** 54
Machine-tool industry, **1958:** 42
Exports, **1958:** 58
Mack, Richard A., **1958:** 37
Mackinac conference, Republican (1943), **1959:** 21
MacLeish, Rod, **1957:** 119, 124, 134, 145, 157, 207, 210, 228; **1958:** 37, 56, 63, 70, 83, 103, 141, 213, 222, 288; **1959:** 17, 26, 36, 42, 191
MacMahon, Lloyd, **1958:** 306n.
Macmillan, Harold, **1957:** 230; **1958:** 293; **1959:** 81, 110, 193, 198, 214, 349, 337n., 349; **1960–61:** 103, 147, 154, 162, 163, 313, 360n.
Bermuda conference, **1957:** 53, 55
Broadcast with, **1959:** 196
East-West summit conference, agreement with Western leaders on, **1959:** 337
Exchange of letters, **1957:** 10 and n.

Macmillan, Harold — *continued*
  Introduction at Johns Hopkins University, **1958:** 130
  Joint statements with, **1957:** 55, 226; **1960–61:** 101, 102, 155, 307, 312
  Joint statements with Western leaders, **1959:** 335, 336
  Meeting with, **1958:** 141
    Comment on, **1959:** 67
  Message, **1959:** 39
  News conference remarks, **1957:** 17, 28, 50, 119, 228; **1959:** 36, 42, 48, 67, 102, 123, 173, 179, 191, 271
  Visit to Soviet Union, **1959:** 36, 42, 48
  Visit to United States, **1957:** 219
MacRae, Gordon, **1960–61:** 23
Macy, R. H., and Co., **1953:** 208
Madden, Repr. Ray J., **1957:** 124
Madeira Beach, Fla., relief of, approval, **1959:** 232
Madigan, John, **1953:** 54, 128
Madison, James, **1954:** 86, 87
Madison, Wis., **1959:** 89
Madrid
  Joint statement with General Franco, **1959:** 340
  Remarks on arrival, **1959:** 338
  Remarks on departure, **1959:** 341
  Toast to General Franco, **1959:** 339
Maga, Hubert, message, **1960–61:** 249
Magistrati, Massimo, **1955:** 61
Magloire, Paul E.
  Exchange of toasts, **1955:** 23
  Message, **1954:** 289
Magloire, Mrs. Paul E., **1955:** 23
Magna Carta, **1953:** 109, 250
Magruder, Gen. Carter B., **1960–61:** 202
Magsaysay, Ramon, **1954:** 101; **1957:** 56, 166; **1960–61:** 359
  Champion of Liberty Stamp ceremony, remarks, **1957:** 166
  Death of, **1957:** 52
  Exchange of messages, **1956:** 80
Mahan, Adm. Alfred T., **1957:** 215
Mahendra Bir Bikram
  Exchange of toasts, **1960–61:** 129
  Joint statement, **1960–61:** 130
  Welcoming remarks to, **1960–61:** 128
Maher, Mayor James, **1960–61:** 239n.
Mahon, Repr. George H., **1953:** 62
Maia, José Joaquim da, **1960–61:** 45
Mail, the President's, on taxes and on defense reorganization, **1958:** 70
Mail service, **1957:** 56, 62, 72
Mailliard, Repr. William S., **1958:** 294
Maine, **1956:** 206
  Bangor, **1955:** 143
  Cross, Gov. Burton M., **1953:** 187
  Election, **1958:** 274
  Muskie, Gov. Edmund S., **1955:** 142, 143; **1959:** 92n.

Maine — *continued*
  Parmachenee Lake, **1955:** 140n.
  Payne, Sen. Frederick G., **1955:** 142; **1958:** 120
  Primary election, **1956:** 205
  Rangeley, **1955:** 141
  Searsport, **1959:** 250
  Skowhegan, **1955:** 142
  Smith, Sen. Margaret Chase, **1954:** 48; **1955:** 47, 95, 142
Maine, sinking of (1898), **1959:** 179
Maiwandwal, M. H., **1959:** 306n.
Makarios, Archbishop (President of Cyprus), message, **1960–61:** 262
Makeef (Berberova), Nina, relief of, disapproval, **1954:** 212
Malacanang, Philippines, **1958:** 140n.
Malagasy Republic
  Independence, message to President Tsiranana, **1960–61:** 207
  Rakotomalala, Louis, **1960–61:** 324n.
Malaria eradication programs, **1957:** 90, 96; **1958:** 2, 32; **1959:** 6, 55; **1960–61:** 13 (p. 63)
  Budget message, **1959:** 10 (p. 75)
  Mexico, joint statement on, **1959:** 257
Malaya, **1953:** 6, 50, 156; **1954:** 165
  Ambassador Kamil, **1960–61:** 339
  Prime Minister Rahman, exchange of toasts, **1960–61:** 339
  Supreme Ruler, Tuanka Syed Putra, **1960–61:** 339
    Message, **1960–61:** 390
  U.N. membership, **1958:** 8, 148
Malenkov, Georgi M., **1953:** 187; **1954:** 87; **1955:** 33, 95; **1956:** 56; **1957:** 228
  News conference remarks on, **1953:** 41, 208; **1954:** 157, 311
Maleter, Pal, execution of, **1958:** 141
Mali, Republic of, Ousmane Ba, **1960–61:** 324n.
Malik, Charles, **1957:** 28
Malinovsky, Rodion L., **1959:** 26
Mallott, Deane W., **1960–61:** 344n.
Malo France, Afranio de, **1960–61:** 51
Malone, Sen. George W., **1956:** 235; **1957:** 50; **1958:** 310
Malott, Deane W., **1953:** 33n.
Malowney Real Estate Company, Inc., tax refund claim, **1958:** 227
Man-in-space (Project Mercury), **1960–61:** 13 (p. 66), 414 (p. 972)
Management counseling for small business, **1956:** 263
Management improvement in Government, **1957:** 13
Manchuria, occupation by Japan, **1958:** 261, 274
Maneuvers, naval, **1957:** 107n.
Manganese imports, **1953:** 69; **1959:** 55
Manhattan State Hospital, remarks, **1954:** 299
Manifesto of Communist representatives (1957), **1958:** 31

Manifesto of members of Congress on school integration, **1956:** 56

Manila, **1955:** 4; **1958:** 140n.; **1960–61:** 286
Address to Congress of Philippines, **1960–61:** 183
Arrival, remarks, **1960–61:** 182
Chamber of Commerce, remarks, **1960–61:** 187
Civic reception, remarks, **1960–61:** 188
Departure, remarks, **1960–61:** 190
Joint statement with President Garcia, **1960–61:** 189
Toast to President Garcia, **1960–61:** 185
University of Philippines, remarks, **1960–61:** 186
U.S. embassy, remarks, **1960–61:** 184

Manila Pact.
See Southeast Asia Collective Defense Treaty.

Manion, Clarence E., **1953:** 225; **1954:** 50

Manion (Clarence E.) Commission.
See Commission on Intergovernmental Relations.

Mann, Thomas C., visit to Venezuela, **1958:** 323

Manpower, military, **1953:** 144; **1954:** 3, 14 (pp. 184, 185)

Mansfield, Sen. Mike, **1956:** 198; **1957:** 145; **1959:** 342; **1960–61:** 164
Amendment to Joint Resolution on Middle East, **1958:** 120
Letter, **1959:** 278
News conference remarks on, **1959:** 36, 42
Peace in Far East, **1958:** 83
Telegram, **1960–61:** 232

Mansure, Edmund F., **1954:** 132; **1956:** 20, 32, 113

Manufacture of fissionable materials for weapons purposes, cessation, **1957:** 80, 115, 119, 158, 165, 245
Exchange of messages with Prime Minister Kishi, **1957:** 208n.

Manufactured products, imports and exports, **1958:** 96

Manzanillo, Mexico, **1959:** 275

Mao Tse-tung, **1958:** 198, 213, 261

Mar del Plata, Argentina, **1960–61:** 42n., 60n.
Mayor Todoro Bronzini, **1960–61:** 61n.
Remarks on arrival, **1960–61:** 61

Marble Collegiate Reformed Church, New York City, **1957:** 232n.

Marcelino Gonzaga, Desembargador J., **1960–61:** 52n.

March of unemployed on District of Columbia, **1959:** 36

Marconi, Marquis Guglielmo, **1956:** 283

Marder, Murrey, **1953:** 41

Margaret, Princess, **1953:** 34

Mariana Islands, **1954:** 125

Marin, Mr. (International News Service), **1953:** 198

Marine Corps, **1954:** 225; **1957:** 17; **1958:** 65, 292; **1959:** 57; **1960–61:** 245, 410
Beirut, **1958:** 173
See also Armed forces, U.S., in Lebanon.

Marine Corps — *continued*
Budget messages, **1954:** 14 (p. 123); **1955:** 17 (pp. 112, 113, 117); **1959:** 10 (pp. 60, 61, 64); **1960–61:** 13 (pp. 48, 56, 57), 414 (pp. 949, 955)
Caribbean, **1958:** 103
Decline in reenlistment rate, **1955:** 13
Federal property in Virgin Islands, **1955:** 14
Medal of Honor citation to William R. Charette, **1954:** 8
Mediterranean, **1956:** 78
Promotion and retirement of officers, approval of bill, **1959:** 178
Singapore, **1958:** 213

Mariner project, **1960–61:** 414 (p. 972)

Maritime Administration, **1954:** 14 (pp. 174, 178); **1955:** 79; **1959:** 48; **1960–61:** 13 (p. 69), 414 (pp. 975, 976)
Budget message, **1959:** 10 (pp. 51, 80)
Nuclear-powered merchant ship, construction, **1956:** 243

Maritime Board, Federal, construction and sale of superliner passenger vessels, approval, **1958:** 171

Maritime industry
Employees, **1954:** 5
Labor disputes, **1956:** 300
Strike, **1953:** 198; **1954:** 68
Injunction, letter to Attorney General Brownell, **1953:** 203
Injunction, letter to Attorney General Rogers, **1959:** 250

Markel, Hazel, **1954:** 9, 33, 161, 311; **1955:** 146; **1956:** 47, 216; **1957:** 28, 45, 56, 210

Market research, **1958:** 110

Marketing quotas, **1959:** 23
Agricultural products, **1957:** 13
Wheat, **1960–61:** 32

Markham Ferry project, Okla., **1955:** 4, 17 (p. 158); **1956:** 12 (p. 134)

Marlborough, Duke of, **1959:** 100

Marques, Guillermo Martinez, **1957:** 217n.

Marr, John W., **1954:** 238

Marr, Pearl O., mineral rights claim, approval, **1954:** 238

Marriage, comment on, **1959:** 148

Mars, **1959:** 130; **1960–61:** 287

Marshall, Mrs. Catherine, **1956:** 268

Marshall, Gen. George C., **1953:** 109 ftn. (p. 439), 192, 238; **1955:** 135; **1956:** 280; **1957:** 106 and n.; **1958:** 318; **1959:** 133; **1960–61:** 91n., 287, 405
Death of, statement, **1959:** 262
News conference remarks on, **1954:** 165, 182; **1959:** 7, 36, 42
References to, in 1952 election campaign, **1954:** 165

Marshall, George C., Space Flight Center, dedi-
cation, remarks, **1960–61:** 287
Marshall, Mrs. George C., **1957:** 106n.; **1959:** 262;
1960–61: 91n., 287
Marshall, John, **1960–61:** 50
Bicentennial, **1955:** 210
Marshall, Brig. Gen. Samuel L. A., **1960–61:** 405
Marshall Islands, **1954:** 68n.
Marshall Plan, **1954:** 204; **1959:** 55, 167; **1960–61:**
91n., 287
Anniversary, **1957:** 106
News conference remarks, **1960–61:** 228, 263,
362
Martial law proclaimed during civil defense test
exercise, **1955:** 149
Martin, Sen. Edward, **1953:** 268; **1954:** 111; **1956:**
234; **1958:** 269, 303
Martin, I. Jack, **1955:** 181; **1958:** 28
Martin, Rep. Joseph W., Jr., **1956:** 190, 292; **1957:**
45, 139; **1958:** 11, 36; **1959:** 127
See also, Speaker of the House of Representa-
tives (Joseph W. Martin, Jr.).
Bipartisan meeting on Suez Canal, **1956:** 184
Letters to, **1958:** 43, 85
Statement re, **1959:** 4
Martin, Lillian I., **1954:** 320
Martin, Mrs. Louis, **1956:** 268
Martin, Paul, **1953:** 15, 208; **1955:** 10; **1957:** 50, 87;
1959: 277; **1960–61:** 263
Martin, Sen. Thomas E., **1956:** 212; **1958:** 290
Martin, Bishop William C., **1953:** 250n.
Martin, William H., defector to Soviet Union,
1960–61: 284
Martin, William McC., Jr., **1953:** 4; **1959:** 186
Martinez, Homero, **1960–61:** 78n.
Martino, Gaetano, **1955:** 61
Marx, Karl, **1953:** 109; **1954:** 87; **1956:** 265; **1959:**
152; **1960–61:** 328
Doctrines, **1955:** 146, 245; **1959:** 123
Mary, Queen Mother, death of, message, **1953:** 34
Mary Baldwin College, **1960–61:** 340
Maryland, **1956:** 206
Aircraft collision, **1958:** 135
Annapolis, **1953:** 80, 81; **1956:** 128n., 241; **1958:**
125; **1959:** 116
Baltimore, **1958:** 308
Beall, Sen.J. Glenn, **1957:** 231 and n.; **1958:** 123,
308
Butler, Sen. John M., **1957:** 210; **1958:** 83, 308
Candidates for public office, **1960–61:** 290n.
Chestertown, **1954:** 136
Devereux, Repr. James P.S., **1958:** 308
Emmitsburg, **1958:** 123
Germantown, **1957:** 231n.
Hyde, Repr. DeWitt S., **1954:** 313; **1958:** 308
McKeldin, Gov. Theodore R., **1954:** 136; **1957:**
138, 205n.; **1958:** 123, 125, 308
Miller, Repr. Edward T., **1958:** 308

Maryland — *continued*
Small, Repr. Frank J., **1954:** 313
Tawes, Gov. J. Millard, **1959:** 116
Maryland, University of, **1960–61:** 100
Mashburn, Lloyd A., **1953:** 208, 230
Mason, Repr. Noah M., **1954:** 92
Masonic breakfast, remarks, **1955:** 43
Masons, Grand Lodge of North Dakota, relief of,
veto, **1960–61:** 181
Massachusetts
Boston, **1953:** 187; **1954:** 325; **1956:** 292, 293;
1959: 191 ftn. (p. 611); **1960–61:** 230,
309n.
Candidates for public office, **1956:** 292
Concord, **1956:** 87
Curtis, Repr. Laurence, **1956:** 292
Disaster areas, **1957:** 145
Furcolo, Foster, **1957:** 145; **1959:** 112, 113
Herter, Gov. Christian A., **1953:** 117, 187; **1954:**
325; **1956:** 155, 171, 189, 292
Kennedy, Sen. John F., **1954:** 73, 325; **1957:** 124;
1958: 216; **1959:** 42; **1960–61:** 93, 236,
263, 268, 284, 356, 369, 422
Lawrence, **1954:** 9
Martin, Repr. Joseph W., Jr., **1953:** 6, 14, 15, 41,
52, 63, 136, 145n., 187, 190n.; **1954:** 12n.,
87, 106, 157, 274, 286; **1956:** 184, 190,
292; **1957:** 45, 139; **1958:** 11, 36, 43, 85;
1959: 4, 127
McCormack, Repr. John W., **1955:** 95, 146
North Attleboro, **1959:** 4n.
Northampton, **1954:** 27
Primary election, **1956:** 88
Rogers, Repr. Edith Nourse, **1953:** 269
Saltonstall, Leverett, **1953:** 187; **1954:** 33, 92,
100, 325; **1956:** 184, 292; **1959:** 113
Tornado disaster, **1953:** 117
Whittier, Lt. Gov. Sumner, **1956:** 292
Worcester, **1953:** 117
Massachusetts Institute of Technology, **1953:** 31
Lincoln Laboratory, **1959:** 125n.
President of, **1957:** 225n., 230
Massena, N.Y., **1959:** 36
Massey, Vincent, **1954:** 101
"Massive retaliation," **1954:** 57, 107
Matador missile, **1957:** 230
Materials Act of 1947, amendment, **1955:** 172
Materials Policy Commission, President's, **1953:**
228
Maternal and child health and welfare services,
1958: 234
Mathematics education, **1959:** 10 (pp. 46, 98, 99)
Teaching of, **1957:** 234 and n., 251; **1958:** 5 (p.
48), 24
Mathews, Kenneth, **1956:** 241
Matsu, **1955:** 26, 62, 90, 112; **1956:** 16; **1957:** 62;
1958: 261; **1960–61:** 143
Campaign remarks, **1958:** 293, 295, 296

Matsu — *continued*
  Letter to Sen. Green. **1958:** 277
  Letter to Premier Khrushchev re, **1958:** 263
  Message to Vice President re, **1958:** 289
  News conference remarks, **1958:** 222, 274, 288
  Statement by Secretary Dulles, **1958:** 257
Matthews, Irvin J., **1954:** 257n.
Mauthe, J. L., **1955:** 211n.
Mautz, Robert, **1956:** 255n., 256n.
May, Ronald W., **1957:** 72, 105, 145; **1958:** 74; **1959:** 89; **1960–61:** 7
Maybank, Sen. Burnet R., death of, statement, **1954:** 233
Mayer, Rene, **1953:** 37, 88
  Joint statement with the President, **1956:** 34
Mayflower, **1954:** 32
Mayors, conference in Washington, D.C., remarks, **1954:** 346
Mayors, White House Conference of, remarks, **1953:** 262
Mayport, Fla., **1957:** 107n.
Mazeroski, William, **1960–61:** 353
Mazo, Earl, **1956:** 5, 20, 78
M'ba, Leon, message, **1960–61:** 265
McAllister, Breck P., **1953:** 59
McAllister, Mayor Robert R., **1960–61:** 333
McArdle, Richard E., **1954:** 270
  President's Award for Distinguished Federal Civilian Service, **1960–61:** 389n.
McCabe, Thomas B., **1960–61:** 305
McCann, Kevin and Ruth, **1953:** 215
  Letter to, **1957:** 251
McCarran, Sen. Pat, **1953:** 37
McCarran-Walter Immigration Act, **1953:** 54, 208; **1954:** 9, 57, 92; **1955:** 56
McCarthy, Sen. Joseph R., **1953:** 269; **1957:** 50
  Army-McCarthy hearings, **1954:** 63, 92, 101, 107, 113, 115
  Censure proceeding, **1954:** 345, 347
  Congressional hearings, **1956:** 216
  Discussions with foreign shipowners on trade embargo with Communist bloc, **1953:** 41
  Investigation of Voice of America, **1953:** 15, 22
  News conference remarks on, **1953:** 15, 22, 31, 37, 41, 109, 141; **1954:** 33, 48, 50, 63, 73, 92, 101, 107, 115, 129, 182, 345, 347; **1956:** 216, 235
McCaskey, I. Willits, **1956:** 234
McCauley, William R., President's Award for Distinguished Federal Civilian Service, **1960–61:** 389n.
McClellan, George B., **1954:** 31, 88
McClellan, Harold C., **1955:** 80n.
McClellan, Sen. John L., **1954:** 12n., 120n.; **1957:** 150; **1958:** 56, 216, 292; **1959:** 6, 176, 180
  News conference remarks on, **1959:** 21, 89, 123, 167

McClendon, Sarah, **1953:** 12, 15, 22, 31, 37, 54, 62, 77, 88, 126, 128, 141, 225, 230, 249, 265; **1954:** 9, 18, 33, 39, 48, 50, 57, 63, 73, 92, 101, 107, 115, 129, 138, 143, 157, 161, 165, 168, 172, 192, 200, 311, 322, 328, 341, 345, 347; **1955:** 10, 18, 26, 33, 41, 47, 56, 59, 62, 81, 90, 95, 100, 112, 119, 146, 149, 176, 185; **1956:** 16, 20, 32, 47, 53, 56, 62, 78, 88, 94, 96, 121, 155, 171, 193, 198, 205, 216, 229, 235, 298; **1957:** 17, 22, 28, 45, 50, 56, 62, 70, 80, 87, 92, 105, 115, 124, 134, 145, 150, 157, 169, 207, 228; **1958:** 11, 28, 37, 42, 56, 63, 70, 74, 83, 103, 120, 141, 198, 213, 222, 274, 288, 310; **1959:** 17, 21, 26, 42, 48, 53, 67, 89, 94, 102, 123, 148, 154, 161, 167, 172, 186, 223, 271, 277, 288; **1960–61:** 7, 21, 34, 38, 93, 127, 143, 256, 263, 268, 422
McClintock, Robert M., **1954:** 280n.
McCloy, John J., **1954:** 107; **1959:** 89; **1960–61:** 91n.
McConaughy, Walter P., **1960–61:** 198n.
McConaughy, Mrs. Walter P., **1960–61:** 198n.
McCone, John A.
  See Atomic Energy Commission, Chairman (John A. McCone).
McConnell, Repr. Samuel K., Jr., **1953:** 266; **1954:** 9; **1956:** 94
McCook, Nebr., remarks at airport, **1954:** 258
McCormack, Repr. John W., **1955:** 95, 146
McCormick, Chauncey, **1954:** 12n.
McCormick, Jimmy, **1960–61:** 123n.
McCormick, Adm. Lynde D., **1953:** 77
McCormick, Robert R., death of, statement, **1955:** 63
McCormick, Stephen J., **1958:** 42, 88
McDonald, David J., **1953:** 77; **1958:** 120; **1959:** 223
  Letter, **1959:** 142, 211
McDonnell, William A., **1958:** 90; **1959:** 87
McElroy, Neil H., **1957:** 150, 206 and n.; **1960–61:** 350
  See also Defense, Secretary of (Neil H. McElroy).
  Chairman, White House Conference on Education, **1955:** 95, 96
  Letter, **1956:** 103
McEntegart, Most Rev. Bryan J., **1953:** 251
McGaffin, William, **1956:** 32, 78, 96, 113, 121, 155, 171, 205, 229, 298; **1957:** 22, 28, 45, 56, 62, 72, 80, 87, 105, 169, 207; **1958:** 11, 28, 70, 103, 141, 153, 213, 274; **1959:** 17, 36, 48, 53, 89, 94, 102, 148, 161, 167, 172, 223, 277, 288; **1960–61:** 21, 34, 103, 256, 284, 422
McGinley, Rev. Laurence J., **1959:** 106
McGonigle, Arthur, **1958:** 303
McGrath, Earl J., **1953:** 54
McGrath, J. Howard, **1954:** 115

McGrath, William L., **1955:** 119
McGregor, Repr. J. Harry, **1954:** 33
McGuire, Perkins, **1959:** 18n.
McGuire, Peter J., **1956:** 194n.
McGuire family, **1956:** 194
McIntire, Vice Adm. Ross T., **1953:** 192
McIntosh, Alan C., **1954:** 149
McKay, Douglas.
  See also Interior, Secretary of the.
  Candidacy for the Senate, **1956:** 54, 255, 256
  Death of, statement, **1959:** 168
  News conference remarks on, **1956:** 113, 121
McKay, Mrs. Douglas, **1959:** 168
McKeldin, Gov. Theodore R., **1954:** 136; **1957:**
      138, 205n.; **1958:** 123, 125, 308; **1959:** 116
McKeldin (Theodore R.) Planetarium, St. John's
      College, dedication, **1959:** 116n.
McKenzie River development program, statement,
      1954: 34
McKibbin, John M., **1959:** 18n.
McKinley, William, **1953:** 252; **1956:** 193, 198;
      1958: 2, 96; **1959:** 42, 177
  Quoted, **1957:** 108
McKinney, Robert, **1956:** 30
McLain, Lt. Gen. Raymond S., **1953:** 144
McLaughlin, Alford L., Medal of Honor award,
      1953: 174, 229n.
McLaughlin, Robert E., **1960–61:** 325
McLean, Robert, **1955:** 79
McLean, William B., Award for Distinguished
      Federal Civilian Service, **1958:** 13
McLeod, Scott, **1954:** 48; **1957:** 70, 72
  Administrator, Refugee Relief Act, **1956:** 296
McMahon line between India and China, **1959:** 288
McMillin, Alvin N. (Bo), **1958:** 307
McNary, Charles L., **1954:** 271
McNary, Mrs. Charles L., **1954:** 271
McNary Dam, Walla Walla, Wash., dedication,
      address, **1954:** 271
McNeil, Marshall, **1953:** 208; **1955:** 56
McNeil, W. J., **1954:** 351
McOsler, William, **1957:** 124
McQuilkin, Anna K., insurance claim, disapproval,
      1954: 228
MDAP.
  See Mutual Defense Assistance Program.
Mead, James M., **1955:** 95
Means, Marianne, **1959:** 288
Meany, George, **1954:** 274n., 275; **1955:** 84, 245;
      1956: 119, 194, 265; **1958:** 70; **1959:** 223;
      1960–61: 30n., 139, 215n.
  Letter, **1959:** 163
  Message, **1953:** 130
  News conference remarks on, **1953:** 109, 128;
      1960–61: 38, 127 and ftn. (p. 368)
Meat
  Grading, question of, **1959:** 161
  Price supports, **1954:** 4, 14 (p. 162)
  Surplus, comment on, **1958:** 56

Mechem, Gov. Edwin L., **1954:** 33, 85n., 99
Mecklenburg Convention, **1954:** 114
Medals, remarks on presentation or acceptance.
    See also Addresses or remarks at presentation
      ceremonies; Awards and citations.
  Distinguished Federal Civilian Service Awards,
      1960–61: 68n., 389n.
    Henderson, Loy W., **1958:** 13
    Jones, Roger W., **1958:** 13
    McLean, William B., **1958:** 13
    Murphy, Robert, **1959:** 9n.
    Overholser, Dr. Winfred, **1960–61:** 68n.
    Page, Robert M., **1960–61:** 68n.
    Rechnitzer, Andreas B., **1960–61:** 25
    Stiebeling, Hazel K., **1959:** 9n.
    Von Braun, Wernher, **1959:** 9n.
  Distinguished Service Medal
    Carney, Adm. Robert B., **1955:** 188
    Greunther, Gen. Alfred M., **1956:** 317
    Radford, Adm. Arthur W., **1957:** 151 and n.
    Ridgway, Gen. Matthew B., **1955:** 144
    Taylor, Gen. Maxwell D., **1959:** 145
    Van Flect, Gen. James A., **1953:** 19
  Football Hall of Fame Award, acceptance, **1958:**
      307
  Hoover Medal Award, acceptance, **1960–61:** 405
  Lafayette Gold Medal Award, General Gruen-
      ther, **1958:** 118
  Legion of Merit
    See main heading, Legion of Merit
  Medal of Freedom
    Anderson, Robert B., **1955:** 183
    De Galard-Terrau be, Genevieve, **1954:** 176
    Douglas, James H., **1960–61:** 425
    Dulles, John Foster, **1959:** 114
    Gates, Thomas S., Jr., **1960–61:** 426
    Goodpaster, Gen. Andrew J., **1960–61:** 430
    Gray, Gordon, **1960–61:** 427
    Herter, Christian A., **1960–61:** 428
    Kistiakowsky, George B., **1960–61:** 429
    McElroy, Neil H., **1959:** 286
    Strauss, Lewis L., **1958:** 166
    Von Neumann, Dr. John, **1956:** 40
    Wilson, Secy. Charles E., **1957:** 212
  Medal of Honor.
    Bleak, David B., **1953:** 122, 229n.
    Charette, William R., **1954:** 8
    Dewey, Duane E., **1953:** 27
    McLaughlin, Alford L., **1953:** 174, 229n.
    Miyamura, Hiroshi H., **1953:** 229n.
    Mize, Ola L., **1954:** 61
    Murphy, Lt. Raymond G., **1953:** 226, 229n.
    O'Brien, Lt. George H., Jr., **1953:** 170, 229n.
    Schowalter, Edward R., Jr., **1954:** 8
    Simanek, Robert E., **1953:** 175, 229n.
    Stone, Lt. James L., **1953:** 229n.
    West, Ernest E., **1954:** 8
    Wilson, Benjamin F., **1954:** 79

Medals, remarks — *continued*
Medal of Honor — *continued*
Medallion, Winston Churchill, **1955:** 244
Medals, acceptance, **1960–61:** 23, 74, 79, 81, 178n., 206
National Geographic Society Medal, Prince Philip, **1957:** 221 and n.
National Security Medal
Donovan. Maj. Gen. William J., **1957:** 66
Hoover, J. Edgar, **1955:** 110
Murphy, Robert, **1960–61:** 375
Pan American Society Golden Insignia, acceptance, **1957:** 64 and n.
Presidential Unit Citation, U.S.S. *Nautilus*, **1958:** 201
U.S. Mint medal, Prime Minister Kishi, **1960–61:** 15n.
Medaris, Maj. Gen. John B., **1959:** 267
Medaris, John E., **1956:** 241
Medical Association, American, **1958:** 109; **1960–61:** 263
Address, **1959:** 129
Remarks, **1953:** 29
Medical Association, Pan American
Letter to Executive Director (Dr. Joseph J. Eller), **1953:** 260
Remarks to officers, **1953:** 259
Medical Care
See also Hospitals and medical care facilities.
Budget messages, **1960–61:** 13 (pp. 93, 97, 100, 103), 414 (pp. 939, 1010, 1011, 1013, 1015, 1016)
Cost of, **1955:** 25; **1956:** 19, 21
Dependents of military personnel, **1954:** 3, 208, 349, 351; **1956:** 2, 21, 91n., 232, 244
Disabled persons, **1956:** 21, 158
Government employees, **1960–61:** 13 (p. 103), 414 (p. 1019)
Indians, **1960–61:** 235
Military dependents, **1955:** 4, 13
Older persons, **1959:** 167; **1960–61:** 103, 133, 255, 263, 410, 414 (pp. 939, 1010, 1011)
Public assistance recipients, **1956:** 12 (pp. 119, 158)
Veterans, **1954:** 14 (p. 134); **1956:** 12 (p. 114), 267; **1960–61:** 13 (pp. 97, 100), 414 (pp. 1013, 1015, 1016)
Medical Cruise Congress, Inter-American, **1953:** 260
Medical and dental facilities, **1957:** 13
Medical and dental officers
Military career incentives, **1956:** 2, 81n., 91
Service credits, **1956:** 91
Medical education
Federal aid, **1957:** 223; **1960–61:** 414 (p. 1008)
National Fund for, **1959:** 238
Acceptance of Frank H. Lahey Award from, remarks, **1954:** 334
Address, **1957:** 223

Medical insurance for Government employees, **1958:** 5 (p. 71)
Medical research, **1954:** 3, 11, 14 (p. 143), 301, 318; **1955:** 247; **1956:** 2, 12 (pp. 116, 120); **1959:** 55, 102, 181, 238; **1960–61:** 23, 286, 410, 413
Budget messages, **1959:** 10 (pp. 68, 102); **1960–61:** 13 (pp. 93, 94), 414 (p. 1007)
Facilities for, **1956:** 151
Federal aid, **1956:** 21
Use of atomic energy, **1957:** 13, 231; **1959:** 10 (p. 68)
Medical schools
Federal grants, **1956:** 21
Teaching and research facilities, **1958:** 5 (p. 51)
Medical supplies, stockpiling, **1954:** 14 (p. 121)
Medical supplies for civil defense purposes, **1956:** 142
Medical and Surgical Service, VA, **1958:** 169
Medical training, **1956:** 2
Medico (Medical International Cooperation), **1955:** 174n.
Mediterranean area, message to armed forces in, **1958:** 176
Mediterranean Sea, **1955:** 4
Joint statement on, **1959:** 327
Mediterranean theatre, World War II, **1956:** 113
Meek, Joseph T., letter, **1954:** 177
"Megalopolis," **1959:** 8
Mein Kampf (Hitler), **1953:** 109
Mellon, Paul, **1959:** 116
Mellon, Gen. Richard J., **1958:** 269
Mellon Laboratory, St. John's College, dedication, **1959:** 116n.
Melton, James, **1953:** 117
Memoirs of Field-Marshal Montgomery, **1958:** 288
Memorandums of Disapproval.
See also Veto Messages.
Airports, Federal aid, **1958:** 246
Alaska Railroad, economic regulation under Interstate Commerce Act, **1960–61:** 225
Bankruptcy Act, amendment, **1960–61:** 289
Bernalillo County, N. Mex., payments for hospitalization of Indians, **1960–61:** 235
Challenges in civil cases, **1958:** 250
Chamberlain Water Co., relocation costs, **1958:** 225
Civil Service Retirement Act, amendment, **1955:** 201
Coal Research and Development Commission, creation, **1959:** 221
Common carriers, finality of contracts with Federal Government, **1954:** 246
Cuban-American Sugar Co., tax refund. claim, **1954:** 244
Date of meeting, 85th Congress, **1956:** 175
Declaration of Taking Act, amendment, **1958:** 250

Memorandums of Disapproval — *continued*
  Denver, Federal payments for street improvements, **1953:** 169
  District of Columbia, certain gasoline filling stations, **1956:** 153
  District of Columbia public transportation commission, **1954:** 252
  Elephant Butte Dam construction, claims, **1954:** 243
  Federal Boating Act, amendment, **1959:** 228
  Federal employees pay bill, **1954:** 208
  Food, drugs, and cosmetics, revision of laws, **1954:** 254
  Grand Teton National Park, taxation of property, **1954:** 222
  Increase in benefits for retired C.C. policemen, firemen, and other specialized personnel, **1955:** 239
  Internal Revenue Code of 1954, amendment, **1955:** 198
  Lake Michigan, increased water diversion, **1954:** 253
  Labels on packages containing foreign-produced trout, **1954:** 243
  Mineral interests, lands acquired by U. S. for reservoir projects, **1956:** 154
  Minerals purchase programs, extension, **1955:** 205
  Mining claims, specified persons, **1956:** 179
  Motion picture performances, admissions tax repeal, **1953:** 157
  Ogletree, Stephen Swan, change of military record, **1955:** 197
  Ohio River bridge commissions, **1956:** 182
  Public Health Service quarantine inspection personnel, overtime pay, **1954:** 218
  Reconveyance to former owners of certain reservoir project lands in Texas, **1955:** 199
  Relief of
    Abbott, Harold W., and others, **1955:** 237
    Albrecht, E. J., Co., **1955:** 196
    Baurkot, Raymond, **1960–61:** 288
    Berney, E. S., **1954:** 242
    Boutwell, William A., **1958:** 228
    Browne, Mary M., **1958:** 230
    Buzzanca, Sam J., **1960–61:** 226
    Caesar, George P. E., Jr., **1958:** 245
    Cash, Elba H., **1955:** 236
    Cochran, Carlos M., estate, **1954:** 230
    Cooper Tire and Rubber Co., **1958:** 252
    Cooperman, Philip, **1957:** 184
    Copin, Margaret P., **1960–61:** 234
    Cunningham, Col. Harry F., **1953:** 168
    D'Agostino, Mary, **1955:** 235
    Davis, Harold J., **1953:** 167
    Denninger, Mary B., estate, **1954:** 216
    Duff, Harry N., **1958:** 248
    Elkins, W. Va., **1956:** 163

Memorandums of Disapproval — *continued*
  Relief of — *continued*
    Elliott, T. C., **1954:** 247
    Estes, Lourene O., **1959:** 234
    Graphic Arts Corp. of Ohio, **1954:** 232
    Gregg, Mrs. Frank C., estate, **1958:** 237
    Hadnot, Mr. and Mrs. John R., **1958:** 238
    Hall, Mr. and Mrs. Robert B., **1958:** 253
    Hill, Raleigh, **1954:** 240
    Hines, Fred P., **1955:** 200
    Hjerpe, Eric and Ida Mae, **1960–61:** 291
    Hollomon, Mr. and Mrs. W. G., **1958:** 254
    Kempner Trust Association, **1954:** 251
    Knipp, Howard F., **1959:** 240
    Knox Corporation, **1957:** 182
    Kramer, Lawrence F., **1954:** 231
    Lambert, H. P., Co., Inc., and Southeastern Drilling Corp., **1960–61:** 292
    Makeef (Berberova), Nina, **1954:** 212
    Malowney Real Estate Co., Inc., **1958:** 227
    McQuilkin, Anna K., **1954:** 228
    Mnatzakanian, Ashot and Ophelia, **1956:** 73
    Moore, Duncan and Marjorie, **1958:** 256
    Morrison, Ethel H., **1953:** 162
    North Counties Hydro-Electric Co., **1958:** 229
    O'Brien, Peter J., **1958:** 251
    Pacific Customs Brokerage Company, **1957:** 183
    Page, Mr. and Mrs. Charles H., **1957:** 180
    Pantelas, George, **1954:** 215
    Penman, Florence P., **1954:** 229
    Peony Park, Inc., and others, **1959:** 229
    Pfeifer, Jean, **1956:** 160
    Piowaty, Carl and W. J., **1954:** 245
    Powell, Mrs. Hannah Mae, **1957:** 179
    Prather, S. H. and S. H., Jr., **1954:** 229
    Quintos, Juan D., and others, **1960–61:** 224
    Ryan, Mary K., **1958:** 228
    Santos, Bonifacio, **1958:** 231
    Shriro, Aron, **1957:** 184
    Southwest Research Institute, **1958:** 247
    Spagnola, Rosaline, **1954:** 239
    Stackman, Samuel, **1957:** 184
    Symms, Marion S., **1958:** 232
    Toley's Charter Boats, Inc., and others, **1958:** 249
    Webb, Mary Thaila W., **1953:** 163
    Weyel, Merle C., **1954:** 241
    Whitaker, D. A., and others, **1958:** 255
    Woods, Nathaniel H., estate, **1959:** 233
  Repackaged imports, marking of country of origin, **1960–61:** 285
  River and harbor and flood control, certain projects, **1956:** 180
  Salary increases, Federal employees, **1957:** 185
  Settlement of certain damage claims by Department of Defense, **1958:** 259

Memorandums of Disapproval — *continued*
  Southwestern Power Administration rates, **1956:** 178
  Subsidies for lead and zinc producers, **1960–61:** 280
  Subversive Activities Control Board, term of office, **1955:** 189
  Tax credit for certain taxes of United Kingdom, **1956:** 181
  Taxation of real estate investment trusts, **1956:** 183
  Veterans housing, direct loan program, **1957:** 172
  Vicksburg National Military Park, facility, **1958:** 226
  Wage rates, Portsmouth (N.H.) naval shipyard, **1960–61:** 230
  Water diversion from Lake Michigan, **1956:** 177
Memorandums and letters to heads of Federal agencies
  Agricultural commodities for Bolivian relief, **1953:** 206
  Awards for Distinguished Federal Civilian Service, **1957:** 13
  Career Executive Development Program, **1960–61:** 26
  Civil defense exercise, **1953:** 195; **1954:** 98; **1955:** 101
  Community Chest and United Fund campaigns, **1953:** 115, 179; **1954:** 132, 183; **1955:** 130; **1956:** 185; **1957:** 154; **1958:** 184; **1959:** 159; **1960–61:** 210
    National Capital area, **1953:** 127
  Economies in Government, **1953:** 165
  Federal Council on Aging, **1956:** 74
  Flood relief in Central and Eastern Europe, **1954:** 195
  Foreign aid programs, administration, **1954:** 323
  Government Employees Incentive Awards Program, **1955:** 1
  Hungarian refugees, **1956:** 307
  Interdepartmental Savings Bond Committee, **1954:** 15
  Leasing of farm lands by Federal agencies, **1956:** 111
  National Health Agencies, fund raising campaign, **1957:** 18
  Occupational safety in Government, **1954:** 288
  Organization of executive branch for conduct of foreign affairs, **1953:** 92
  Payment to Presidential appointees for unused leave, **1953:** 55
  Payroll Savings Plan, **1955:** 187
  President's Conference on Administrative Procedure, **1953:** 59
  Red Cross campaigns, **1953:** 4; **1954:** 1, 356; **1956:** 11; **1957:** 30; **1958:** 3; **1959:** 20; **1960–61:** 37
  Report of Commission on Foreign Economic Policy, **1955:** 16

Memorandums and letters — *continued*
  United Community campaigns, **1954:** 183; **1955:** 168
  United Fund campaigns.
    See Community Chest and United Fund campaigns *above.*
  United Givers Fund, National Capital area, **1956:** 138; **1957:** 140; **1958:** 136; **1959:** 156; **1960–61:** 153
Memorial Press Center, New York City, dedication, remarks, **1954:** 350
Memphis, Tenn., **1954:** 39
  Conference on rural development program, statement, **1958:** 128
  Power projects in area, **1955:** 56, 146, 149
  See also Dixon-Yates contract.
Menderes, Adnan, **1954:** 129; **1959:** 36, 297, 298
  Messages, **1959:** 41, 283
Mendes-France, Pierre, **1954:** 341
  Amendments to EDC pact, **1954:** 200
  News conference remarks on, **1954:** 157, 200, 311
Menominee Indian Tribe, termination of Federal supervision, approval, **1954:** 147
Menshikov, Mikhail A., **1958:** 22, 37; **1959:** 218
Mental health, **1955:** 25; **1959:** 72
  Alaska, **1956:** 12 (p. 120)
  Budget message, **1956:** 12 (pp. 119, 120)
  Grants, **1956:** 21, 161
Mental Health Association, **1960–61:** 153
Mentally retarded children, **1956:** 2
Menzies, Robert G., **1956:** 205
  Joint statement, **1960–61:** 312
Merchant, Livingston T., **1953:** 254 ftn. (p. 800); **1955:** 61, 146 ftn. (p. 644)
Merchant fleet, **1956:** 12 (pp. 141, 142)
Merchant marine, **1954:** 67; **1955:** 17 (pp. 167, 168); **1959:** 10 (pp. 79, 80); **1960–61:** 13 (p. 69), 414 (p. 975)
  Budget message, **1954:** 14 (pp. 143, 174, 175)
Merchant Marine Act, amendment, approval, **1954:** 213
Merchant ships
  Budget message, **1956:** 12 (pp. 139, 142)
  Nuclear-powered, **1955:** 79, 121; **1956:** 12 (p. 142), 243
    News conference remarks, **1955:** 81, 112, 146
    World tour proposed, **1955:** 146
Mercury project (man-in-space), **1960–61:** 13 (p. 66), 414, (p. 972)
Mergers
  Affecting small business, **1956:** 263; **1957:** 13, 132
  Budget message, **1956:** 12 (p. 149)
  Campaign remarks, **1956:** 241
  Production credit corporations and Federal intermediate credit banks, **1956:** 147
Merit system of employment, Federal, anniversary, **1958:** 13

Merrow, Repr. Chester E., **1955:** 139
Messages to the American people, **1957:** 92, 157
    See also Election campaign addresses or
        remarks.
    Achievements of administration and Congress,
        1953: 159
    Administration's goals and accomplishments,
        1954: 2
    Americans overseas, **1959:** 152
    Announcement of candidacy for second term,
        1956: 48
    Budget (1960), **1959:** 11
    Congressional achievements, **1954:** 209
    Cost of Government, **1957:** 86
    Developments in Eastern Europe and Middle
        East, **1956:** 282
    Election eve remarks, **1954:** 321
    Election victory address, **1956:** 294
    Farewell address, **1960–61:** 421
    Farm bill veto, **1956:** 83
    Farm "freeze" bill, veto, **1958:** 60
    Formosa Strait situation, **1958:** 261
    Future security, **1957:** 234
    Geneva conference
        Broadcast prior to departure, **1955:** 161
        Broadcast report on, **1955:** 175
    Inaugural address, first, **1953:** 1
    Inaugural address, second, **1957:** 15
    Korean armistice, **1953:** 147
    Labor-management relations, **1959:** 176
    Little Rock situation, **1957:** 197
    Middle East situation, **1957:** 35
    Mutual security, **1957:** 91
    National security, **1953:** 82, 83, 95
    NATO conference, Paris, **1957:** 249
    Opening of campaign for reelection, **1956:** 210
    Paris summit conference, **1960–61:** 163
    Science in national security, **1957:** 230
    Security in the free world, **1959:** 57
    State of the Nation, **1954:** 72
    State of the Union message, remarks, **1956:** 3
    Suez Canal, **1956:** 164
    Tax program, **1954:** 54
    Visits to
        Asia, **1960–61:** 209
        Europe, Asia, and Africa, **1959:** 290
        Great Britain, France, and Germany, **1959:**
            214
        Latin America, **1960–61:** 42, 87
Messages to the Congress.
    See Congress, letters to Members of; Congress,
        messages to.
Messages to heads of state and governments
    Argentina
        President Aramburu, **1957:** 233
        President Frondizi, **1958:** 164; **1959:** 13, 28
    Austria
        Chancellor Raab, **1957:** 5, 186
        President Koerner, **1955:** 98

Messages to heads of state — *continued*
    Belgium
        King Baudouin, **1953:** 7; **1958:** 79
        Prime Minister Zan Acker, **1957:** 153
    Bolivia, President Paz Estenssoro, **1953:** 213
    Brazil, President Kubitschek, **1958:** 133, 181,
        197, 319; **1959:** 287; **1960–61:** 64, 119, 379
    Burma, Prime Minister Nu, **1955:** 169; **1956:** 60
    Cambodia, King Norodom Sihanouk, **1954:** 280
    Canada
        Prime Minister Diefenbaker, **1959:** 125
        Prime Minister St. Laurent, **1956:** 71
    Central African Republic, Prime Minister
        Dacko, **1960–61:** 259
    Chad, Republic of, Prime Minister Tombalbaye,
        1960–61: 257
    Chile
        President Alessandri, **1960–61:** 175
        President Ibanez del Campo, **1958:** 81
    China, Republic of, President Chiang Kai-shek,
        1955: 36; **1958:** 282
    Colombia, President-elect Lleras Camargo, **1958:**
        137
    Congo, Republic of
        President Kasavubu, **1960–61:** 216
        President Youlou, **1960–61:** 260
    Cyprus, President Makarios, **1960–61:** 262
    Dahomey, Prime Minister Maga, **1960–61:** 249
    Denmark, King Frederik, **1960–61:** 41
    Ethiopia, Emperor Haile Selassie I, **1955:** 231
    Finland, President Kekkonen, **1956:** 311
    France
        Premier de Gaulle, **1958:** 273
        President Coty, **1953:** 270; **1954:** 83, 104, 148,
            265; **1957:** 103
    Gabon, President M'ba, **1960–61:** 265
    Germany
        Chancellor Adenauer, **1953:** 121, 135, 138,
            146, 188; **1954:** 189; **1955:** 190, 204; **1956:**
            129; **1958:** 210; **1959:** 220
        President Heuss, **1956:** 125; **1958:** 138
    Ghana, Prime Minister Nkrumah, **1957:** 43;
        1958: 44; **1960–61:** 220, 248, 313
    Greece
        King Paul I, **1953:** 172; **1956:** 140; **1957:** 48
        Prime Minister Karamanlis, **1959:** 40
    Guatemala
        President Castillo Armas, **1955:** 230
        President Ydigoras Fuentes, **1960–61:** 368
    Guinea, Prime Minister Toure, **1958:** 309; **1960–
        61:** 364
    Haiti, President Magloire, **1954:** 289
    Honduras, Supreme Chief of State Lozano Diaz,
        1956: 144
    India
        President Prasad, **1959:** 281
        Prime Minister Nehru, **1953:** 102; **1954:** 40,
            44; **1956:** 130; **1957:** 244; **1959:** 279;
            1960–61: 313

Messages to heads of state — *continued*
Indonesia, President Sukarno, **1956:** 120; **1960–61:** 313
Iran
    Prime Minister Zahedi, **1953:** 178
    Shah Mohammad Reza Pahlavi, **1954:** 184, 264; **1955:** 42; **1958:** 174; **1960–61:** 126
Ireland, President O'Kelly, **1956:** 208
Israel, Prime Minister Ben-Gurion, **1956:** 295; **1957:** 40
Italy
    Premier Fanfani, **1958:** 211
    President Einaudi, **1954:** 283
    President Gronchi, **1956:** 264
Ivory Coast, Prime Minister Houphouet-Boigny, **1960–61:** 254
Japan
    Prime Minister Hatoyama, **1956:** 313
    Prime Minister Ikeda, **1960–61:** 252, 294, 366
    Prime Minister Kishi, **1957:** 208
Jordan, King Hussein I, **1960–61:** 277
Korea
    President Po Sun Yun, **1960–61:** 273
    President Rhee, **1953:** 96
    Prime Minister Chang Myon, **1960–61:** 274
Laos, King Sisavang Vong, **1954:** 82, 117
Lebanon, President Chamoun, **1958:** 182
Liberia, President Tubman, **1959:** 224
Malagasy, President Tsiranana, **1960–61:** 207
Malaya, Tuanku Syed Putra, **1960–61:** 390
Mexico
    President Ruiz Cortines, **1954:** 158; **1955:** 216, 229; **1956:** 70
    President Lopez Mateos, **1958:** 317; **1959:** 275
Morocco
    King Mohamed V, **1957:** 84; **1960–61:** 99
    Sultan Mohammed ben Youssef, **1955:** 240
Netherlands, Queen Juliana, **1953:** 7, 53; **1960–61:** 138
New Zealand
    Prime Minister Holyoake, **1960–61:** 373
    Prime Minister Nash, **1960–61:** 367
Niger, Republic of, Prime Minister Diori, **1960–61:** 251
Nigeria, Governor General Azikiwe, **1960–61:** 361
Norway
    King Haakon VII, **1955:** 241
    King Olav V, **1957:** 192
Pakistan
    President Mirza, **1956:** 65; **1958:** 174
    Prime Minister Mohammed Ali, **1953:** 124
Panama, President Arias Espinosa, **1956:** 101
Philippines
    President Garcia, **1957:** 69; **1958:** 69; **1959:** 73; **1960–61:** 106, 112, 358
    President Magsaysay, **1956:** 80

Messages to heads of state — *continued*
Saudi Arabia, King Saud ibn Abd al-Aziz al-Saud, **1953:** 245
Somali, President Osman, **1960–61:** 219
Spain, General Franco, **1959:** 200
Thailand, Prime Minister Pibulsonggram, **1956:** 302; **1957:** 36
Tunisia, King Mohamed Lamine, **1957:** 101
Turkey
    General Gursel, **1960–61:** 399
    President Bayar, **1957:** 49; **1958:** 174; **1959:** 282
    Prime Minister Menderes, **1959:** 41, 283
United Arab Republic, President Nasser, **1960–61:** 313
United Kingdom
    Prime Minister Churchill, **1953:** 123
    Prime Minister Macmillan, **1957:** 10; **1959:** 39
    Queen Elizabeth, **1953:** 7, 34; **1958:** 209
Upper Volta, Prime Minister Yameogo, **1960–61:** 253
Uruguay, President Echegoyen, **1959:** 95
U.S.S.R.
    Chairman Presidium of the Supreme Soviet, K. E. Voroshilov, **1959:** 1; **1960–61:** 2
    Premier Bulganin, **1955:** 220; **1956:** 23, 52, 166, 262, 291; **1957:** 3; **1958:** 7, 17, 31
    Premier Khrushchev, **1958:** 67, 86, 112, 131, 152, 165, 177, 179, 189, 263; **1959:** 81, 110, 337, 349; **1960–61:** 2, 97
Vatican City State
    Supreme Pontiff John XXIII, **1958:** 304
    Supreme Pontiff Pius XII, **1955:** 46; **1958:** 280
Venezuela, President Betancourt, **1958:** 323; **1960–61:** 122
Vietnam
    Chief of State Bao Dai, **1954:** 83, 105; **1955:** 48
    President Diem, **1954:** 306; **1956:** 271; **1957:** 97; **1959:** 158; **1960–61:** 338
Western European Union, Prime Ministers of member nations, **1955:** 54
Yugoslavia, President Tito, **1954:** 284; **1960–61:** 313
Metals, production and utilization, **1953:** 228
Metcalf, Repr. Lee, **1959:** 161
Meteorological Organization, World, **1959:** 188
Meteorological satellites.
    See Weather satellites.
Meteorology programs, **1959:** 10 (p. 76)
Methodist Church, **1957:** 109
Metropolitan areas, growth and development, **1957:** 118; **1960–61:** 4, 410
Metropolitan Opera Association, **1953:** 117
Metropolitan planning, **1958:** 5 (p. 57), 106
Mexican migratory labor, **1955:** 17 (p. 177)
    Approval of bill, **1954:** 56
    Budget message, **1954:** 14 (p. 184)
    News conference remarks, **1954:** 33, 39, 165, 168

Mexicans, deportation of, **1956:** 121
Mexico, **1957:** 157
　See also Acapulco.
　Ambassador Robert C. Hill, **1959:** 275
　Ambassador Francis White, **1955:** 229
　Amistad Dam construction, **1960–61:** 13 (p. 83),
　　　303, 334, 335, 414 (p. 995)
　Anniversary of independence, **1960–61:** 334
　Ciudad Acuna.
　　See main heading, Ciudad Acuna, Mexico.
　Flood, **1954:** 158
　Friendship with United States, **1953:** 222, 223
　Highways to, **1955:** 39
　International Boundary and Water Commission,
　　　1953: 222; **1960–61:** 13 (p. 83), 335, 414
　　　(p. 996)
　Livestock purchase loan, **1956:** 235, 236
　Lopez Mateos, Adolfo, **1958:** 317; **1959:** 21, 36,
　　　37, 42, 243, 254, 255, 256, 275; **1960–61:**
　　　303, 333, 334n.
　　Joint declaration, **1960–61:** 335
　　Joint statements with, **1959:** 38, 257
　　Letter to, **1959:** 275
　Manzanillo disaster, letter re, **1959:** 275
　Mexico City, **1956:** 70; **1959:** 21
　News conference remarks, **1958:** 153, 213
　Participation in Falcon Dam construction, **1953:**
　　　222
　Relations with U.S., **1960–61:** 131
　Ruiz Cortines, Adolfo, **1953:** 221, 222, 223, 225;
　　　1955: 216, 229; **1956:** 53, 70; **1958:** 153;
　　　1959: 21
　　Message, **1954:** 158
　Tampico flood relief, **1955:** 229
　Tello, Manuel, **1954:** 33
　Trade with Soviet Union, **1954:** 101
　U.S.-Mexico Migrant Labor Agreement, **1954:**
　　　56
　U.S.-Mexico water treaty, **1960–61:** 335
　Visit to, **1959:** 37, 38; **1960–61:** 333, 334, 335
　　Mention of, **1959:** 21, 36, 42, 254, 256n., 257
　Wetbacks, **1957:** 70
Meyer, Ben F., **1956:** 171
Meyer, Charles A., **1959:** 287n.
Meyer, Eugene, death of, statement, **1959:** 165
Meyer, Mrs. Eugene, **1959:** 165
　Letter to, **1957:** 21 and n.
Meyner, Governor Robert B., **1957:** 87; **1959:** 173
Miami, Fla., **1959:** 185
　Campaign remarks, **1956:** 278
　Governors' Conference, **1958:** 120
　Refugee Center, **1960–61:** 431
　Regional conference on traffic safetv, **1958:** 45n.
Mica imports, **1958:** 58, 96
Michael, Archbishop, death of, statement, **1958:**
　　　167
Michel, Robert, **1956:** 214
Michelson, Edward, **1954:** 92

Michener, Roland, **1958:** 163n.
Michigan
　Ann Arbor, **1958:** 138n.
　Candidates for public office, **1954:** 318; **1958:**
　　　213
　Detroit, **1954:** 33, 130, 318, 320; **1955:** 112; **1956:**
　　　107, 198; **1957:** 183; **1958:** 138n.; **1959:**
　　　154; **1960–61:** 326, 327, 328
　Disposition of farm surpluses, **1956:** 20
　Dondero, Repr. George A., **1953:** 128, 268; **1954:**
　　　110n.
　Ferguson, Sen. Homer, **1954:** 12n., 33, 110n., 318
　Griffin, Repr. Robert P., **1959:** 172, 176, 180
　Hoffman, Repr. Clare, **1953:** 269
　Monroe, **1956:** 198
　Potter, Sen. Charles E., **1954:** 157; **1958:** 213
　Saginaw, **1953:** 242n.
　Williams, Gov. G. Mennen, **1954:** 347; **1957:** 80;
　　　1960–61: 328
　Wolcott, Repr. Jesse P., **1953:** 266; **1954:** 68
　Unemployment compensation, **1957:** 80
Michiko, Crown Princess, **1960–61:** 140, 209, 294n.,
　　　308
Mickel, Ernest, **1954:** 92
Midas earth satellite, **1960–61:** 143
　Budget message, **1960–61:** 414 (p. 953)
Middle East Doctrine, **1957:** 6, 46, 111
　News conference remarks, **1957:** 17, 28, 45, 72,
　　　157, 228
Middle East Joint Resolution, **1958:** 41, 174n.;
　　　1959: 55
　Joint statement with Prime Minister Macmillan,
　　　1957: 55
　Mansfield amendment, **1958:** 120
　News conference remarks, **1957:** 45, 169
　Report to Congress on, **1957:** 149
　Statement on signing, **1957:** 146 and n.
　White House statement, **1957:** 157n.
Middle East and Near East, **1953:** 77; **1954:** 3, 44,
　　　45, 184n., 185, 186; **1955:** 4, 18, 248; **1956:**
　　　2, 87, 280, 281, 282; **1958:** 36, 80; **1960–**
　　　61: 330, 410
　See also specific countries.
　Arms control proposed, **1958:** 207
　Assistance, **1953:** 66, 143; **1954:** 14 (p. 139), 150;
　　　1955: 17 (pp. 125, 130); **1956:** 12 (pp. 104,
　　　105), 53, 58, 298; **1957:** 6, 17, 31, 90, 91,
　　　152; **1958:** 5 (p. 35), 198; **1959:** 55;
　　　1960–61: 7, 302
　Bases in Near East, **1958:** 32
　Bipartisan conference on, **1957:** 2
　Budget message, **1958:** 5 (pp. 35, 41)
　Campaign remarks, **1958:** 293
　Disease prevention in Near East, **1958:** 207
　Indirect aggression in, **1958:** 198
　Israeli-Arab dispute.
　　See Israeli-Arab hostilities.
　Johnston (Eric) mission, **1953:** 217

Middle East and Near East — *continued*
  Johnston plan for, **1956:** 198, 298
  Joint Resolution (1957), **1959:** 251
  Joint statements
    King Saud, **1957:** 31
    Premier Mollet, **1957:** 38
    President Bayar, **1959:** 297
    Prime Minister Eden, **1956:** 26
    Prime Minister Fanfani, **1958:** 186
    Prime Minister Macmillan, **1957:** 55
    Prime Minister Nkrumah on, **1958:** 180
    Shah Mohammed Reza Pahlavi, **1959:** 322
  Letters
    Premier Bulganin, **1958:** 7
    Premier Khrushchev, **1958:** 177, 179, 189
    President Kubitschek, **1958:** 181
  Meeting on, **1956:** 287
  Message to Rabbi Silver, **1955:** 239
  Messages, **1956:** 302; **1957:** 6, 8, 13, 37, 90, 149
  Military assistance by U.S. armed forces, **1957:** 17
  Mission to, **1957:** 6, 17, 46, 72
  Mutual security assistance, **1957:** 157n.
  Near East crisis, **1958:** 207
  Neutralization proposal, **1958:** 198
  News conference remarks, **1954:** 68, 157; **1956:** 16, 20, 32, 53, 56, 62, 78, 88, 96, 298; **1957:** 17, 45, 56, 80, 134, 157 and n., 207; **1958:** 120, 198, 222; **1960–61:** 7, 38
  Oil, **1956:** 62, 184, 239n.
  "People's Capitalism" exhibit, **1956:** 75n.
  Petroleum resources, **1957:** 6
  Power projects, **1953:** 217
  Report on, **1957:** 149; **1958:** 41
  Soviet arms for, **1956:** 26, 53, 298; **1960–61:** 38
  Statements, **1955:** 234; **1956:** 276
    Crisis in Near East, **1958:** 173
  Suez Canal problem.
    See Suez Canal.
  Tripartite Declaration (1950), **1955:** 234, 239; **1956:** 26, 53, 56, 62, 276
  U.N. action, report, **1958:** 8, 148
  U.N. address, **1958:** 207
  U.N. forces in, **1957:** 13
  U.S. companies in, **1957:** 80
  U.S.-Soviet action, comment on, **1958:** 198
  Visit to (1959).
    See Visits, foreign.
  Visit of Secretary Dulles, **1953:** 101, 217
  Water resources development, **1954:** 68; **1958:** 207
Middle-of-the-road policy, **1958:** 223, 274, 310; **1959:** 21, 179; **1960–61:** 246
  Campaign remarks, **1956:** 234
Middle South Utilities Co., **1955:** 149 ftn. (p. 669)
Middle West (U.S.), **1957:** 157
Middleton, Lt. Gen. Troy, reminiscence re, **1959:** 36

Midway, visit to Capetown, South Africa, **1955:** 18
Midway Island, **1960–61:** 97n.
Midwestern Gas Transmission Co., **1959:** 288
Midwestern Universities Research Association, **1959:** 89
Migrant Labor Agreement, U.S.-Mexico, **1954:** 56
Migrants, contribution to U. N. for, **1957:** 90
Migratory farm workers, **1956:** 190; **1959:** 223
  Children of workers, educational problem, **1954:** 14 (p. 153)
  Employment of, **1954:** 14 (p. 184)
  Letter to Secretary Mitchell, **1954:** 214
  Mexican, **1954:** 14 (p. 184), 33, 39, 56, 165, 168; **1955:** 17 (p. 177)
  Social and economic status, improvement of, **1954:** 14 (p. 184)
Migratory Labor, Interdepartmental Committee on, **1954:** 214
Mikan, George, **1956:** 250
Mikolajczyk, Stanislaw, message, **1953:** 264
Mikoyan, Anastas I.
  Appraisal of, **1959:** 17
  Berlin situation, **1959:** 17, 21
  Meeting with U.S. labor leaders, **1959:** 21
  Motives for visit, **1959:** 17
  News conference remarks on, **1959:** 7, 17, 21, 48
  U.S. visit, **1959:** 21
  Visit to Cuba, **1960–61:** 38
Military Air Transport Service, **1957:** 250
Military Assistance Advisory Group, Formosa, **1955:** 90
Military assistance and defense support, **1953:** 92, 143, 233n.; **1954:** 3, 44, 45, 92, 150, 337; **1955:** 76; **1956:** 53, 58, 87; **1958:** 35, 36, 96; **1959:** 6, 55, 90, 136, 137, 302; **1960–61:** 4, 36, 133, 148, 302, 410
  See also Foreign assistance; Mutual security program.
  Appropriation, budgeting of, comment on, **1959:** 288
  Budget messages, **1954:** 14 (pp. 85, 86, 107, 108, 118, 125–128, 135, 136); **1955:** 17 (pp. 123–125, 128–130); **1958:** 5 (pp. 20, 26, 34–36); **1959:** 10 (pp. 55, 58, 69, 70, 74); **1960–61:** 13 (pp. 46, 57, 58, 60, 62), 414 (pp. 938, 951, 958, 959, 962, 966, 967)
  Campaign remarks, **1958:** 294
  Committee on.
    See President's Committee to Study the U.S. Military Assistance Program.
  Funds for, **1958:** 32
  Joint statements
    General Franco, **1959:** 340
    King Saud, **1957:** 31
    President Garcia, **1958:** 143; **1960–61:** 189
    Prime Minister Suhrawardy, **1957:** 131
    Prime Minister Yoshida, **1954:** 330
  Letter to Secretary of State, **1955:** 74

Military assistance & defense support — *continued*
   Messages, **1957:** 6, 8, 90, 91
   NATO countries, new weapons, **1958:** 42
   News conference remarks, **1953:** 62, 198, 249,
      254, 265; **1955:** 10, 90, 119; **1959:** 94, 148,
      288
   Study by committee, letter to William H. Draper,
      Jr., **1958:** 316
   White House statements, **1957:** 152n., 157n.
Military Chaplains Association, remarks, **1954:**
   103; **1956:** 98
   Distinguished service award, presentation to Sec-
      retary of Navy, **1956:** 98n.
Military control of Government, comment on,
   1959: 29
Military decisions and internal domestic politics,
   news conference remarks, **1956:** 16
Military discipline, **1956:** 113
Military installations, **1954:** 14 (p. 124); **1958:** 5
   (pp. 21, 32)
   Construction projects, veto, **1956:** 141
   Fort Lewis, Wash., **1956:** 253
   School integration, **1956:** 229
Military intelligence, **1959:** 29
Military manpower policies, statement, **1953:** 144
Military personnel
   See also Armed forces, U.S.
   Budget messages, **1954:** 14 (pp. 123, 184, 185);
      1956: 12 (pp. 93 ff.); **1959:** 10 (pp. 59, 60,
      64, 65); **1960–61:** 13 (pp. 48, 49), 414 (pp.
      950, 956, 957, 1020)
   Career incentives, **1955:** 17 (pp. 91, 109); **1956:**
      81
      Medical and dental officers and nurses, **1956:**
         2, 81n., 91
   Children of, public school education, **1960–61:**
      137
   Classified information, responsibility re, **1954:**
      107, 138
   Commissary and post exchange privileges, **1955:**
      100
   Dependents
      Medical care, **1954:** 3, 208, 349, 351
      Overseas, **1954:** 341; **1960–61:** 362, 434
   Discussion of war plans, comment on, **1955:** 62
   Doctors and dentists, induction, **1955:** 12
   Housing, **1954:** 3, 349, 351; **1960–61:** 414 (p. 957)
      Approval of bill, **1954:** 237
   Indochina, **1954:** 25, 33, 50
   Insurance, **1955:** 17 (p. 145)
      Benefits, **1956:** 81n.
      Old-age and survivors, **1956:** 12 (p. 111)
   Integration in schools on military posts, **1953:**
      198
   Letter to Secretary Wilson, **1955:** 3
   Pay, **1954:** 349, 351; **1955:** 4, 13, 59; **1958:** 5 (pp.
      25, 30, 31, 71), 169; **1959:** 10 (p. 59);
      1960–61: 13 (p. 49), 255
   Retirement **1960–61:** 414 (p. 956)

Military personnel — *continued*
   Promotion and retirement of naval officers,
      1959: 178
   Promotions and assignments, **1958:** 80
   Public school education in Federally affected
      areas, **1959:** 17
   Reduction, **1958:** 5 (p. 20)
   Reenlistment bonuses, **1954:** 166
   Retirement, **1955:** 4, 17 (p. 145); **1956:** 81n.;
      1958: 5 (pp. 51–53)
   Social security coverage, **1956:** 232
   Survivorship benefits, **1954:** 208, 349, 351; **1955:**
      4, 13, 17 (p. 134); **1956:** 2, 157
   Training under land-grant colleges, **1954:** 335
   Travel expenses, **1960–61:** 414 (p. 950)
   Turnover, message, **1955:** 13
   Use for work other than military duty, **1959:** 102
Military procurement.
   See Defense procurement.
Military program.
   See Defense program.
Military property, **1959:** 10 (pp. 65, 66)
Military rank, the President's, restoration pro-
   posed, **1960–61:** 422
Military Reserve Week (1956), **1956:** 51
Military Sea Transport Service, **1957:** 250
Military service credits for retirement benefits,
   1958: 5 (pp. 52, 53); **1960–61:** 13 (pp. 95,
   96), 414 (p. 1011)
Military status of President, **1958:** 288
Military strength, Soviet, **1954:** 14 (p. 119); **1956:**
   58, 87; **1957:** 28; **1958:** 295; **1959:** 26, 55,
   120; **1960–61:** 21, 36
Military strength, U.S., **1953:** 1, 6, 61, 66, 82, 98,
   101; **1954:** 3, 14 (p. 118), 87, 273, 286, 291,
   297, 318, 325, 351; **1955:** 4, 10, 12; **1956:**
   58, 87; **1957:** 8, 28, 230; **1958:** 2, 35, 36,
   80, 90, 95; **1959:** 6, 55, 290; **1960–61:** 4,
   42, 163, 173, 209, 245, 255, 397, 410
   Budget message, **1958:** 5 (pp. 18, 19)
   Campaign remarks, **1956:** 190, 210, 251, 279;
      1958: 287, 292, 295, 296; **1960–61:** 341,
      354
   Far East, **1958:** 274
   Letter to Secretary Wilson, **1955:** 3
   News conference remarks, **1953:** 31, 37, 41, 62,
      77, 88, 208; **1954:** 341, 353; **1956:** 96, 113;
      1958: 213, 274; **1959:** 26, 48, 53
Milk, **1956:** 83
   Consumption of, **1954:** 115, 347; **1958:** 49
   Dried, surplus disposal, **1956:** 6
   Needy children, **1960–61:** 13 (p. 96), 414 (p.
      1012)
   Price supports, **1960–61:** 295
Milk programs
   Armed forces, **1955:** 17 (p. 152); **1958:** 59
   Schools, **1955:** 17 (p. 144); **1956:** 6, 72; **1958:** 5
      (p. 66), 12, 59

[References are to items except as otherwise indicated]

Miller, Repr. A. L., **1953:** 268; **1954:** 138
Miller, Repr. Edward T., **1958:** 308
Miller, J. Roscoe, **1954:** 204
Miller, Repr. William E., **1953:** 128
Millikin, Sen. Eugene D., **1955:** 81
  Bipartisan meeting on Suez Canal, **1956:** 184
  Constitutional amendment on treaty-making
      powers, **1954:** 33
Mills, Repr. Wilbur D., **1958:** 58
  Trade agreements bill, letter, **1958:** 132
Millsop, Thomas E., **1959:** 211n.
Millstone Hill Radar Observatory, **1959:** 125n.
Milne, Edward J., **1953:** 31, 37, 77, 126, 208, 225,
      243; **1954:** 25, 33, 101, 129, 347; **1955:** 18,
      100, 119, 149, 176; **1956:** 20, 53, 94, 229,
      235; **1958:** 213
Milton, John, **1954:** 327
Milwaukee, Wis., **1956:** 129
Mindanao, **1958:** 140
Mindszenty, Cardinal Joseph, **1954:** 30; **1956:** 292
Mineral interests in lands acquired for reservoir
      projects, reconveyance, disapproval,
      1956: 154
Mineral lands, approval of bill restricting multiple
      use, **1955:** 172
Mineral leases, **1956:** 12 (pp. 133, 138); **1958:** 5 (p.
      68)
Mineral resources, **1954:** 67; **1955:** 4; **1956:** 12 (p.
      138); **1958:** 5 (p. 69); **1960–61:** 13 (pp. 85,
      86), 414 (p. 998)
  Budget messages, **1954:** 14 (pp. 164, 170, 171);
      1955: 17 (p. 163)
  Development of, **1953:** 228
Mineral rights claim of Pearl O. Marr, approval,
      1954: 238
  Processing, **1953:** 153
  Research, **1954:** 14 (p. 171)
Minerals Mobilization, Office of, funds, **1956:** 12
      (p. 138)
Minerals Policy, Committee on, **1954:** 14 (p. 170);
      1955: 17 (p. 163); **1956:** 12 (p. 138)
  Establishment, **1953:** 228
Minerals programs, **1956:** 12 (p. 133); **1958:** 206
  Extension, disapproval, **1955:** 205
Mines, Bureau of, **1954:** 14 (p. 171); **1956:** 12 (p.
      138); **1960–61:** 383
  Budget messages, **1960–61:** 13 (p. 85), 414 (p.
      998)
Minimum wage, **1955:** 4, 19; **1959:** 17, 161; **1960–
      61:** 284
  American Samoa, **1956:** 172
  Budget messages, **1956:** 12 (p. 116); **1960–61:** 414
      (p. 1006)
  Campaign remarks, **1956:** 241
  Extension of coverage, **1953:** 230; **1955:** 81, 112;
      1956: 2, 3, 229; **1957:** 16; **1958:** 5 (p. 51);
      1959: 10 (p. 46)

Minimum wage — *continued*
  Increase, **1953:** 230, 265; **1954:** 25, 353; **1960–61:**
      133, 255
  News conference remarks, **1955:** 26, 81, 90, 119,
      149, 176; **1956:** 229
Mining equipment, exports, **1958:** 58
Mining industry, Mexican, joint statement with
      President Lopez Mateos on, **1959:** 257
Minneapolis, Minn., **1953:** 98, 99; **1956:** 229; **1958:**
      116n.; **1960–61:** 329
  Campaign remarks, **1956:** 247, 250
Minnesota
  Anderson, Gov. C. Elmer, **1953:** 98
  Andresen, Repr. August H., death of, **1958:** 10
  Candidates for public office, **1956:** 249, 250
  Freeman, Gov. Orville L., **1960–61:** 330
  Humphrey, Sen. Hubert H., **1953:** 198; **1955:** 26;
      1958: 318; **1960–61:** 93, 330
  Kasson, **1954:** 291; **1956:** 214
  Judd, Repr. Walter H., **1953:** 98; **1955:** 33; **1956:**
      250; **1960–61:** 329, 330, 354
  Nelsen, Ancher, **1956:** 249, 250
  O'Hara, Repr. Joseph P., **1957:** 72
  Primary election, **1956:** 62, 117
  Quie, Repr. Albert H., **1960–61:** 330
  Red Wing, Hiawatha Bridge dedication,
      remarks, **1960–61:** 330
  Rural development, pilot project, **1956:** 250
  St. Paul, **1956:** 229, 249
  Thye, Sen. Edward J., **1954:** 200; **1955:** 33; **1956:**
      249, 250
  Worthington, **1956:** 250
Minshall, Repr. William E., **1960–61:** 350
Minsk, U.S.S.R., **1958:** 31
Minton, Sherman, **1956:** 205
  Resignation as Supreme Court Justice, **1956:** 202
Minuteman missile.
  See Missiles.
Miriani, Louis C., **1960–61:** 326n., 328
  Refusal to meet with Kozlov, **1959:** 154
Mirza, Iskander, letters, **1956:** 65; **1958:** 174
Missile sites, **1958:** 5 (p. 19)
Missile Test Center, Cape Canaveral, inspection,
      1960–61: 34
  Remarks, **1960–61:** 33
Missiles, **1955:** 149; **1956:** 58, 232; **1957:** 8, 86, 230,
      234; **1958:** 2, 26, 36, 64, 65, 80, 96, 223;
      1959: 55, 57, 266; **1960–61:** 4, 42, 410
  See also Armistice Day; Weapons.
  Aerodynamic, **1957:** 210; **1958:** 274, 293
  Air-breathing, **1959:** 21
  Air-to-ground, Hound Dog, **1959:** 10 (p. 57);
      1960–61: 13 (p. 53)
  Anti-aircraft
    Bomarc missile, **1957:** 230; **1959:** 10 (p. 57),
      102, 123; **1960–61:** 13 (p. 54), 414 (p. 954)
    Nike-Ajax, **1959:** 10 (pp. 57, 60)

Missiles — *continued*
Anti-aircraft — *continued*
Nike-Hercules, **1959:** 10 (pp. 57, 60), 102, 123; **1960–61:** 13 (p. 54), 414 (p. 954)
Antimissile missiles, **1958:** 5 (p. 30)
Nike-Zeus, **1959:** 10 (p. 57); **1960–61:** 13 (pp. 54, 55), 414 (p. 953)
Ballistic Missile Early Warning System, **1960–61:** 414 (p. 953)
Budget messages, **1956:** 12 (pp. 97, 141); **1958:** 5 (pp. 18–20, 29, 30, 35, 60); **1959:** 10 (pp. 57, 58, 60, 63, 64); **1960–61:** 13 (pp. 51–56, 66, 68), 414 (pp. 938, 949–955, 957)
Campaign remarks, **1958:** 292, 293, 296, 303, 308
Communist China, **1959:** 154
Defensive, **1958:** 5 (p. 19)
Detection system, **1958:** 5 (p. 30)
Development of, comment on, **1959:** 267
Duplication in Department of Defense, **1959:** 102
Earth satellites.
See Satellites, earth.
Effect of steel strike on construction, **1959:** 268
German use, **1956:** 32
ICBM, **1956:** 88; **1957:** 169, 210, 230; **1958:** 2, 5 (pp. 29, 30), 141, 274, 293, 318; **1959:** 21; **1960–61:** 10, 13 (p. 66), 24, 245, 341
Atlas, **1959:** 6, 7, 10 (p. 57, 60), 26, 172, 267, 288; **1960–61:** 4, 13 (pp. 51–53, 66, 68), 42, 410, 414 (pp. 951, 952), 422
Minuteman, **1960–61:** 13 (pp. 52–54), 21, 410, 414 (pp. 938, 951, 952)
Soviet, **1956:** 32, 88
Titan, **1959:** 10 (p. 57); **1960–61:** 13 (pp. 52, 53), 410, 414 (pp. 951, 952), 422
IRBM, **1957:** 56, 80, 210, 230; **1958:** 2, 5 (pp. 29, 30), 32, 274, 293; **1959:** 6, 55, 94; **1960–61:** 10, 24, 245
Jupiter, **1959:** 10 (pp. 57, 58), 267; **1960–61:** 13 (pp. 51, 66), 287, 410, 414 (p. 951)
Polaris, **1959:** 10 (pp. 57, 60, 64); **1960–61:** 4, 7, 13 (pp. 51–55), 42, 244, 245, 255, 360, 410, 414 (pp. 938, 951, 952, 954)
Regulus, **1960–61:** 13 (p. 51)
Thor, **1959:** 10 (pp. 57, 58), 267; **1960–61:** 13 (pp. 51, 66), 410, 414 (p. 951)
Joint statement with Prime Minister Macmillan, **1957:** 55
Joint study with United Kingdom, **1957:** 226n.
Long-range, **1956:** 2
Man-carried, **1960–61:** 245, 414 (p. 955)
NATO countries, **1958:** 5 (p. 35)
News conference remarks, **1956:** 32, 53, 88; **1957:** 17, 28, 56, 72, 80, 87, 169, 210; **1958:** 74, 141, 222, 274, 310, 318; **1959:** 7, 21, 26, 94, 102, 154, 172, 267, 277, 288; **1960–61:** 7, 21, 24, 34, 422

Missiles — *continued*
Nike, **1955:** 17 (p. 116); **1958:** 74
Cost of, **1957:** 234
Nose cone, recovery, **1957:** 230
Operational units, **1959:** 6
Outerspace missiles, control and development of, **1957:** 8, 210, 228, 230, 234
Research, **1958:** 5 (pp. 19, 26, 29)
Short-range (Corporal, Sergeant, Red-stone), **1958:** 293; **1959:** 10 (p. 58), 267; **1960–61:** 13 (p. 56), 287, 414 (p. 955)
Corporal missile, **1957:** 230
Redstone missile, **1958:** 293
Soviet, **1957:** 86, 169, 210; **1958:** 2, 141, 177, 222, 296, 318; **1959:** 6, 7, 21, 26, 172; **1960–61:** 7, 24, 34, 245
Submarine based (Polaris), **1959:** 10 (pp. 57, 60, 64)
Tactical, **1958:** 296; **1959:** 10 (p. 63)
Types in operation or development, **1957:** 230
United Kingdom, **1957:** 56, 72, 226n.
Mission 66, National Park System plan, **1956:** 29, 256
Budget message, **1956:** 12 (p. 138)
Coleman, Gov. J. P., **1957:** 138; **1959:** 88
Eastland, Sen. James O., **1958:** 103
Fort Pemberton, **1958:** 226
Mineral rights, reservoir projects, **1956:** 154
Parker, Mack Charles, case of, **1959:** 88, 94, 123
Stennis, Sen. John C., **1954:** 33, 50
Mississippi River, **1956:** 148
Barge service, **1954:** 14 (p. 175)
Hiawatha Bridge, **1960–61:** 330
Mississippi Valley Generating Co., **1955:** 149 ftn. (p. 669)
Missouri
Carnahan, Repr. A. S. J., **1956:** 184
Donnelly, Gov. Phil M., **1953:** 216, 225
Drought relief, **1953:** 230
Hennings, Sen. Thomas C., Jr., **1953:** 109
Interstate highway system, **1956:** 186
Jefferson City, **1953:** 225
Kansas City, **1953:** 216, 218, 225
St. Joseph, **1959:** 270
St. Louis, **1953:** 57, 193; **1954:** 130
Short, Repr. Dewey, **1953:** 266; **1956:** 184
Symington, Sen. Stuart, **1953:** 31; **1954:** 39, 129; **1956:** 32, 113; **1959:** 7, 94
Tornado, **1959:** 29
Missouri River flood (1903), **1953:** 100
MIT.
See Massachusetts Institute of Technology.
Mitchell, Bernon F., defector to Soviet Union, **1960–61:** 284
Mitchell, James P.
See Labor, Secretary of (James P. Mitchell).
Mitchell, Sidney A., **1954:** 12n.
Mitchell, Stephen A., **1954:** 200

Miyamura, Hiroshi H., Medal of Honor, award and citation, **1953:** 229n.
Mize, Ola L., Medal of Honor, citation, **1954:** 61
Mnatzakanian, Ashot and Ophelia, relief of, **1956:** 73
Mobilization base, **1954:** 3
Mobilization of NATO forces, comment on, **1959:** 48
Modern Republicanism, **1958:** 310; **1959:** 7
  Election victory remarks, **1956:** 294
  News conference remarks, **1956:** 193, 298; **1957:** 17, 22, 50, 87
Mohamed V, **1959:** 343, 344
  Exchange of greetings, **1957:** 239 and n.
  Joint statements, **1957:** 240; **1959:** 345
  Letter, **1957:** 84 and n.
  Message on earthquake disaster at Agadir, **1960–61:** 99
Mohamed Lamine, King of Tunisia, exchange of messages, **1957:** 101 and n.
Mohammed Ali, **1953:** 249
Mohammed ben Youssef, message, **1955:** 240
Mohr, Charles H., **1958:** 288; **1959:** 67, 94, 132, 161, 191, 223, 243, 288; **1960–61:** 24, 38, 93, 143, 222, 268
Mollenhoff, Clark R., **1954:** 9, 57, 68, 115, 311, 322, 347, 353; **1955:** 5, 10, 18, 26, 33, 41, 59, 62, 81, 95, 146, 149, 176, 185; **1956:** 16, 20, 32, 171, 198, 216; **1958:** 37, 141, 310; **1959:** 161, 172; **1960–61:** 93
Mollet, Guy, **1956:** 155; **1957:** 62
  Joint statement with President, **1957:** 38 and n.
Mollohan, Repr. Robert H., **1956:** 229, 235
Molotov, Vyacheslav M., **1953:** 254, 265; **1954:** 18, 128, 314; **1955:** 26, 33, 146; **1957:** 228
  Quoted, **1957:** 6
Monberg, Helene C., **1954:** 39
Monetary and Financial Commission, National, proposed, **1957:** 8, 16
Monetary policies, **1957:** 13
  News conference remarks, **1957:** 80
Monnet, Jean, **1953:** 109, 111
Monopolistic practices, **1956:** 19
Monroe, James, **1953:** 219
Monroe, Marvin E., **1955:** 181n.
Monroe, Mich., **1956:** 198
Monroe Doctrine, **1960–61:** 268
Monroney, Sen. Mike, **1953:** 249
Montana, **1957:** 12
  Aronson, Gov. J. Hugo, **1954:** 270, 271; **1960–61:** 208
  D'Ewart, Repr. Wesley A., **1954:** 270
  Fort Peck dam power project, **1956:** 12 (p. 135)
  Glacier National Park, **1960–61:** 208, 229
  Mansfield, Sen. Mike, **1956:** 198; **1957:** 145; **1958:** 83, 120; **1959:** 36, 42, 278, 342; **1960–61:** 164, 232
  Metcalf, Repr. Lee, **1959:** 161
Missoula, **1954:** 270

Montcalm de Saint-Veran, Louis de, **1959:** 141n.
Monte Cassino, battle of, **1954:** 112
Montevideo, Uruguay, **1960–61:** 42n.
  Address to Congress of Uruguay, **1960–61:** 80
  Arrival, remarks, **1960–61:** 78
  Crespo, Mayor Daniel Fernandez, **1960–61:** 79n.
  Declaration of Montevideo, **1960–61:** 84
  Departure, remarks, **1960–61:** 85
  Remarks on receiving medals, **1960–61:** 79, 81
  Toast to President Nardone, **1960–61:** 82
  U.S. embassy staff, remarks, **1960–61:** 83
Montgomery, Field Marshal Bernard L., **1954:** 133
  Letter, **1958:** 265
  Memoirs, comment on, **1958:** 288
  News conference remarks on, **1959:** 7, 89, 94
  U.S. leadership, **1959:** 89
Montgomery, Ruth S., **1953:** 238; **1954:** 129, 138, 345; **1956:** 88, 121, 171, 205; **1957:** 28, 157, 207; **1958:** 141, 310; **1959:** 17, 89, 123, 148; **1960–61:** 93, 143
Montgomery, Ala., **1957:** 17, 28; **1959:** 31
  Boycott of buses by Negroes, **1956:** 62
Montini, Giovanni Cardinal, **1960–61:** 174n.
Montreal, Canada, **1959:** 36, 141n.
Monument, carillon, gift from Netherlands, **1960–61:** 138
Monument Commission, National, report on proposed Freedom Monument, **1960–61:** 152
Monuments, national, **1953:** 153; **1954:** 3, 14 (p. 170)
Moon probes, **1958:** 28
  Budget messages, **1959:** 10 (pp. 57, 58, 76); **1960–61:** 414 (p. 972)
  Exploratory rockets, **1958:** 295
  Pioneer, **1958:** 308
  Soviet, **1959:** 89, 217n., 223; **1960–61:** 24
  White House statement, **1958:** 57n.
Mooney, Cardinal Edward, death of, statement, **1958:** 301
Mooney, Richard E., **1960–61:** 127
Moore, Repr. Arch A., Jr., **1958:** 302
Moore, Duncan and Marjorie, tax refund claim, **1958:** 256
Moore, Edwin Dayton, **1953:** 62, 128, 208, 254; **1954:** 50, 115, 172; **1956:** 235; **1957:** 115, 119, 124; **1958:** 42, 56, 70, 74, 88, 120, 153, 198, 213, 222; **1959:** 26
Moore, George T., **1959:** 18n.
Moos, Malcolm, *Republicans; a History of their Party*, **1956:** 198
Morality, public, comment on, **1959:** 277
Morcell, Adm. Ben, **1954:** 12n.
Morgan, Edward P., **1955:** 41, 59, 81, 90, 95, 100, 112, 149, 176; **1956:** 16, 20, 47, 56, 62, 88, 94, 96, 113, 121, 155, 205, 216, 229, 298; **1957:** 17, 22, 28, 56, 70, 72, 80, 87, 92, 105, 115, 119, 124, 134, 150, 228; **1958:** 11, 28, 42, 56, 63, 83, 88, 103, 120, 141, 153, 198,

Morgan, Edward P. — *continued*
  274, 288, 310; **1959:** 17, 26, 29, 36, 48, 53,
  94, 102, 123, 132, 148, 154, 161, 271, 277;
  1960–61: 24, 34, 93, 103, 127, 143, 263,
  268, 422
Morgan, George A., **1953:** 33
Morgan, Gerald D., **1955:** 56, 181; **1959:** 115, 161;
  1960–61: 380n., 417
Morgan, Repr. Thomas E., bipartisan meeting on
  Suez Canal, **1956:** 184
Morhouse, L. Judson, **1956:** 272; **1958:** 305n.
Mormon, Church, **1956:** 241
Morocco
  See also Casablanca.
  Assistance, **1958:** 32; **1959:** 55
  Balafrej, Ahmed, **1957:** 84
  Bases in, **1958:** 32
  Economic and technical assistance, **1957:** 240
  Ibrahim, Moulay Abdallah, **1959:** 343n.
  Mohamed V.
    See main heading, Mohamed V.
  Mohammed ben Youssef, **1955:** 240
  Prince Moulay Hassan, **1959:** 343n.
  U.N. membership, **1958:** 8
  U.S. Ambassador, **1957:** 84
  Visit of President Eisenhower, **1959:** 277, 343,
    344, 345
  Withdrawal of U.S. forces, joint statement, **1959:**
    345
  Yost, Ambassador Charles W., **1959:** 343n.
Moros, **1958:** 140
Morrill, Justin Smith, **1954:** 335; **1957:** 108
Morrill Act, **1954:** 335
Morris, George M., **1953:** 59
Morris, John D., **1953:** 41; **1954:** 182; **1955:** 18
Morrison, De Lesseps S., **1953:** 219
Morrison, Ethel H., insurance claim, disapproval,
  1953: 162
Morrison, Herbert O., **1956:** 234
Morrison, William McK., Jr., **1953:** 162
Morrow, E. Frederic, quoted, **1958:** 102
Morse, True D., Under Secretary of Agriculture,
  1956: 217n.; **1957:** 12n.; **1959:** 18n., 67
  ftn. (p. 297); **1960–61:** 322
Morse, Sen. Wayne, **1953:** 15; **1955:** 100; **1957:** 150
Mortgage Association, Federal National.
  See Federal National Mortgage Association.
Mortgage Credit Committee, Voluntary Home,
  1960–61: 414 (p. 982)
  Continuance proposed, **1959:** 153
Mortgage insurance, **1954:** 3, 17, 21, 179; **1955:** 19;
  1958: 5 (pp. 43, 59), 43, 62, 224; **1959:**
  102, 104, 153, 187, 208; **1960–61:** 410
  Budget messages, **1954:** 14 (pp. 148, 149); **1955:**
    17 (p. 172); **1959:** 10 (pp. 46, 47, 82, 84,
    85); **1960–61:** 13 (pp. 73, 74), 414 (pp. 980,
    981)

Mortgage purchases and sales, Federal, **1954:** 14
  (pp. 149, 150); **1958:** 5 (pp. 43, 53, 58);
  1959: 10 (pp. 48, 49); **1960–61:** 13 (pp. 74,
  75), 414 (p. 982)
  Interest rates, **1960–61:** 13 (p. 74), 414 (p. 981)
  Ship mortgage loans, **1960–61:** 13 (p. 69), 414 (p.
    976)
Morton, Thruston, **1956:** 226; **1959:** 75, 132
  See also Republican National Committee, Chair-
    man
Moscow, Russia, **1956:** 291n.; **1957:** 62
  Conference on agenda for summit meeting,
    1958: 177
  Damage to U.S. Embassy, **1958:** 189
  U.S. cultural exhibit, **1959:** 102, 148, 161, 179;
    1960–61: 410
    Opening by Vice President Nixon, **1959:** 80
  U.S. Embassy, **1957:** 105
Moscow Declaration on Austria (1943), **1955:** 114
Moscow Manifesto (1957), letter to Premier
  Bulganin, **1958:** 31
Moses, Robert, **1959:** 106
Mossadegh, Mohammed, **1953:** 22, 156; **1954:** 192,
  209; **1956:** 87; **1958:** 36, 287
  Message, **1953:** 129
Motion picture performances, admissions tax re-
  peal, disapproval, **1953:** 157
Motor carriers
  Recommendations on, **1958:** 82n.
  Regulations, **1956:** 12 (p. 149)
Motor trucks and coaches, exports, **1958:** 58
Motor vehicle operators, Federal, defense of suits
  against, veto, **1960–61:** 180
Mount Eisenhower, dedication, **1958:** 220
Mount Rushmore National Monument, **1953:** 101
Mount Saint Mary's College, commencement ad-
  dress, **1958:** 123
Mount Vernon, **1958:** 127n.; **1959:** 105n.
Mountbatten, Vice Adm. Louis, **1955:** 119
MSA.
  See Mutual Security Agency.
Mudd, Roger, **1957:** 50
"Mudslinging," comment on, **1955:** 62
Mueller, Frederick H.
  See Commerce, Secretary of (Frederick H.
    Mueller).
Mullady, Bernard, **1953:** 230
Muller, Will, **1954:** 33
Mundt, Sen. Karl E., **1953:** 101; **1954:** 157; **1958:**
  23
Mundy, Lt. Gen. George W., **1960–61:** 283
"Munich," **1958:** 261
Municipalities, Inter-American Congress of,
  remarks, **1960–61:** 333
Munitions Board (Department of Defense), **1953:**
  61
Munitions lobby, **1959:** 123, 132

Muniz, Joao Carlos, **1956:** 274
  Letter, **1956:** 273
Munoz Marin, Gov. Luis, **1954:** 48; **1959:** 102;
  1960–61: 43, 86
Munro, Dana G., **1959:** 287n.
Munroe, Pat, **1953:** 22, 128, 265; **1954:** 33, 63, 101,
  143, 172; **1955:** 56, 100, 146; **1956:** 94,
  113, 198, 205, 216, 235; **1957:** 22, 145;
  1958: 11, 42, 88, 103, 120, 222, 310; **1959:**
  17, 102, 132, 271; **1960–61:** 34, 143
Murillo, Gerardo (Dr. Atl), **1959:** 256
Murphy, George, **1956:** 258n.; **1958:** 307n.
Murphy, Lt. Raymond G., Medal of Honor award,
  1953: 226, 229n.
Murphy, Robert, **1954:** 125, 126, 284n.; **1956:** 45n.;
  1959: 277 ftn. (p. 766), 293, 297, 308, 322,
  327; **1960–61:** 8, 9
  Award for Distinguished Federal Civilian Serv-
    ice, **1959:** 9n.
  National Security Medal, citation, **1960–61:** 375
Murray, Archbishop John Gregory, **1956:** 249
Murray, Gov. Johnston, **1954:** 85n., 99
Murray, Robert B., Jr., letter, **1953:** 194; **1954:** 123
Murray, Robert V., **1960–61:** 314
Murray, Thomas E., **1954:** 328; **1956:** 78; **1957:** 72
Murrow, Edward R., **1954:** 73
Muscatine, Iowa, **1956:** 148
Muscatine Bridge Commission, **1956:** 182
  Creation, approval, **1956:** 148
Museum (Eisenhower), Abilene, Kans.
  See under Abilene, Kans.
Museum of History and Technology, **1956:** 12 (p.
  124)
Music Council, National, incorporation, approval,
  1956: 159
Muskie, Gov. Edmund S., **1955:** 142, 143; **1959:**
  92n.
Mussolini, Benito, **1954:** 72, 111; **1958:** 70, 261;
  1960–61: 355
Mutual Cooperation and Security, Treaty of, U.S.-
  Japan, **1960–61:** 14, 16, 209, 245, 410, 422
  Remarks at signing, **1960–61:** 15
Mutual defense assistance program, **1954:** 45
Mutual Defense Treaty
  U.S.-Korea, **1954:** 3, 6, 139, 168; **1960–61:** 201
  U.S.-Philippines, **1960–61:** 188
    Joint statement with President Garcia, **1960–
      61:** 189
  U.S.-Republic of China, **1954:** 345, 351; **1960–
    61:** 194
    Joint statement with President Chiang Kai-
      shek, **1960–61:** 195
Mutual military program.
  See Military assistance and defense support.
Mutual Security, Director for (Harold E. Stassen),
  1953: 2n.; **1958:** 30n.
  See also Foreign Operations Administration,
    Director.

Mutual Security, Director for — *continued*
  European storm disaster relief, **1953:** 7n.
  Food for East Germans, **1953:** 134, 138
  Mutual security appropriations, **1953:** 143
  News conference remarks on, **1953:** 41, 62
  Pakistan drought relief, **1953:** 97
Mutual Security, Public Advisory Board for,
  report, **1953:** 22 and ftn. (p. 86)
Mutual Security Act, 1954, **1954:** 323
  Approval, **1960–61:** 148
Mutual Security Agency, **1953:** 141
  See also Foreign Operations Administration.
  Information programs, **1953:** 89
  Payment of ocean freight on relief shipments,
    1953: 92
  Rand, William M., **1953:** 111n.
  Roberts, Frank N., **1953:** 33
Mutual Security Agreement, U.S.-Pakistan, state-
  ment with Prime Minister Suhrawardy,
  1957: 131
Mutual Security Appropriation Act, **1955:** 182;
  1956: 152
  Federal Boating Act funds, **1959:** 228
Mutual Security Appropriation Bill, **1957:** 152
  Approval, **1957:** 173
Mutual Security Authorization Act, **1957:** 152, 157,
  164
Mutual Security Bill, **1959:** 154, 172
  Approval, **1959:** 171
  Statement re House action on, **1957:** 136
Mutual security program, **1953:** 6, 125; **1954:** 44,
  45, 67, 323, 347, 349; **1955:** 57, 76, 146;
  1956: 2, 58, 87; **1957:** 6, 8, 13, 86, 90, 91,
  234; **1958:** 2, 18, 26, 36, 96, 102, 110,
  316n.; **1959:** 6, 24, 57, 71, 87, 90, 170, 183,
  225, 278, 290, 342; **1960–61:** 23, 39, 42,
  131, 132, 133, 148, 163, 209, 255, 336, 380,
  409, 410
  See also Economic assistance; Foreign assis-
    tance; Military assistance and defense
    support; Technical assistance to less
    developed countries.
  Action of House Appropriations Committee,
    statement, **1959:** 154
  Appropriations, **1953:** 143
    Conference action on, letters re, **1960–61:** 271,
      272
    Statement, **1960–61:** 270
  Authorization and appropriation request, **1956:**
    58n.
  Bipartisan conference, **1954:** 351; **1956:** 318;
    1957: 2
  Budget messages, **1954:** 14 (pp. 135–137); **1955:**
    17 (pp. 91, 97, 104, 108, 122, 123, 128–
    130); **1956:** 12 (pp. 80, 81, 102–107, 155);
    1958: 5 (pp. 34–36, 38–40); **1959:** 10 (pp.
    44, 68–70, 75); **1960–61:** 13 (pp. 38, 46, 57,
    58, 60–63), 414 (pp. 938, 951, 958, 962–
    964, 967)

[References are to items except as otherwise indicated]

Mutual security program — *continued*
  Budget messages — *continued*
    Tables, **1954:** 14 (p. 136); **1955:** 17 (p. 123); **1958:** 5 (pp. 26, 28, 34, 37); **1959:** 10 (p. 70); **1960–61:** 13 (p. 62), 414 (p. 964)
  Commission study of, **1958:** 318
  Expenditures, **1957:** 13
  Funds for, statement, **1958:** 151
  International pool, proposed, **1960–61:** 38
  Joint statements
    King of Morocco, **1957:** 240
    King Saud, **1957:** 31
    President Diem, **1957:** 83
    Prime Minister Kishi, **1957:** 117
    Prime Minister Suhrawardy, **1957:** 131
  Letters
    Secretary of State, **1955:** 74
    Senator Bridges, **1953:** 143
    William H. Draper, Jr., **1958:** 316
  Long range commitment, **1959:** 89
  Messages to Congress, **1953:** 66; **1954:** 150; **1958:** 32; **1959:** 55; **1960–61:** 36
  News conference remarks, **1956:** 94, 121; **1957:** 45, 62, 87, 145, 152 and n., 157 and n., 169; **1958:** 37, 42, 70, 103, 198, 213, 222; **1959:** 29, 89, 94, 154, 186; **1960–61:** 21, 38
  Presidential powers re transfer of foreign assistance funds, **1954:** 3, 14 (p. 126)
  President's Citizen Advisers Committee on **1957:** 45
  Propaganda in support of (Dworshak amendment), **1959:** 154
  Spending authority, **1957:** 75
  Statement, **1955:** 69
  White House statement, **1956:** 121 ftn. (p. 556)
  Withholding of aid from countries discriminating against U.S. citizens, **1960–61:** 21
Mutual Security and Related Agencies Appropriation Act (1961), **1960–61:** 270n.
Muzzey, David S., **1960–61:** 19
Myers, William I., **1954:** 200
Mynatt, E. F., **1957:** 22

NAACP.
  See National Association for the Advancement of Colored People.
Nabuco, Joaquim, **1960–61:** 45, 51
NACA.
  See National Advisory Committee for Aeronautics.
Nadjakov, Gueorgui, **1960–61:** 301n.
Nagy, Imre, execution of, **1958:** 141
Nakamura, Harry H., relief of, veto, **1959:** 155
Nantucket Island, **1956:** 149n.

Napoleon Bonaparte, **1953:** 219; **1954:** 72, 93, 111; **1955:** 59, 118; **1957:** 124; **1959:** 100, 132, 212; **1960–61:** 58, 187
  Political constitutions, **1959:** 71
Napoleon III, **1959:** 255
Narcotics, international control, **1955:** 4
Narcotics problem, **1954:** 343; **1956:** 31
Narcotics users, treatment in District of Columbia, approval, **1953:** 116
Nardone, Benito, **1960–61:** 78, 79, 85, 87
  Toast to, **1960–61:** 82
Nardone, Senora de, **1960–61:** 82, 85
NASA.
  See National Aeronautics and Space (Agency) Administration.
Nash, Frank C., **1953:** 33, 254 ftn. (p. 800)
Nash, Philleo, **1960–61:** 330
Nash, Walter, message, **1960–61:** 367
Nashville, Tenn., **1960–61:** 143
Nasser, Gamal Abdel, **1956:** 164, 192, 205; **1957:** 62; **1960–61:** 127
  Letter, **1960–61:** 313
National Academy of Sciences, **1957:** 122, 225n.; **1958:** 64; **1959:** 68, 107; **1960–61:** 13 (p. 91)
  IGY Committee, **1959:** 67 ftn. (p. 294)
  Radiation study, **1956:** 266
  Radiation report, **1957:** 105
  Satellite development, statement, **1957:** 211
National Advisory Committee for Aeronautics, **1954:** 14 (p. 174); **1955:** 17 (p. 170); **1956:** 12 (p. 141); **1958:** 64, 105, 185
  Budget message, **1958:** 5 (pp. 20, 48, 60)
  Report, **1959:** 85
National Advisory Committee on Inter-American Affairs, **1960–61:** 42 and ftn. (p. 205), 51, 69, 228, 349
  Message to President Kubitschek, **1959:** 287
National Advisory Committee on Poliomyelitis Vaccine, **1955:** 81, 90, 113
National Advisory Council on International Monetary and Financial Problems, **1953:** 60, 93; **1954:** 348; **1956:** 139; **1959:** 32, 98; **1960–61:** 39
National Aeronautics and Space Act of 1958, **1960–61:** 47
  Amendments, proposed
    Budget messages, **1960–61:** 13 (p. 66), 414 (p. 970)
    Message to Congress, **1960–61:** 11
  Statement on signing, **1958:** 185
National Aeronautics and Space (Agency) Administration, **1958:** 64, 185, 288; **1959:** 25; **1960–61:** 11, 12n., 349, 358, 410, 433
  Army Ballistic Missile Agency, proposed transfer to, **1959:** 266, 267
  Budget messages, **1959:** 10 (pp. 58, 76); **1960–61:** 13 (pp. 38, 47, 65, 66, 109), 414 (pp. 944, 960, 970)

NASA — *continued*
  Campaign remarks, **1958:** 292, 308
  Civilian-Military Liaison Committee, **1960–61:** 11
  Communication satellites, utilization, **1960–61:** 386
  Dryden, Hugh L., **1960–61:** 68n., 287
  Effect of steel strike on programs, **1959:** 268
  News conference remarks, **1959:** 102, 267, 277; **1960–61:** 24, 263
  Research functions, **1958:** 64
  Space vehicle development operations, transfer from Army Ballistic Missile Agency, **1960–61:** 10
  Statement, **1958:** 105
National Aeronautics and Space Administrator (T. Keith Glennan), **1958:** 288; **1959:** 172, 267; **1960–61:** 104, 287, 350
  Letter, **1959:** 46
  Space vehicles development, letter, **1960–61:** 12
National Aeronautics and Space Board, **1958:** 64
National Aeronautics and Space Council, **1960–61:** 11
National Agricultural Advisory Commission, **1953:** 6, 153, 216; **1954:** 196
  News conference remarks **1953:** 12, 225, 230, 238
  Statement, **1953:** 227
National American Woman Suffrage Association, **1957:** 215
National Archives, **1958:** 314n.
National Archives Building, **1956:** 190
National Archives and Records Service, **1960–61:** 118
National Association for the Advancement of Colored People, **1954:** 51, 347; **1959:** 167
  Membership in, **1956:** 216
National Association of Manufacturers, **1957:** 45
  Remarks, **1959:** 83
National Association of Postmasters, remarks, **1959:** 270
National Association of Real Estate Boards, remarks, **1960–61:** 19
National Association of Retail Grocers Convention, remarks, **1954:** 144
National Association of Radio and Television Broadcasters, **1955:** 105; **1958:** 87
National Association of Radio and Television Farm Directors, remarks, **1955:** 127; **1957:** 114 and n.
National Automobile Show Dinner, address, **1960–61:** 328
National Blood Program, **1953:** 4
National Boy Scout Jamboree (1953), recorded message, **1953:** 137
National Broadcasting Company, dedication of radio-TV facilities, remarks, **1958:** 111

National Bureau of Standards, **1955:** 17 (p. 148); **1956:** 12 (pp. 123, 151); **1960–61:** 13 (p. 91), 414 (p. 1004)
  Boulder, Colo., laboratories, dedication, remarks, **1954:** 267
  Budget message, **1954:** 14 (p. 153)
National Bureau of Standards, Director (A. V. Astin), **1953:** 41
National Capital Housing Authority, **1956:** 4n.
National Capital Planning Commission, **1956:** 4n.; **1960–61:** 243
  Budget message, **1958:** 5 (p. 72)
  Report on transportation survey of Washington area, **1959:** 157
National Cartoonists Society, remarks, **1954:** 151
National Catholic Welfare Conference, **1960–61:** 371
National Churches of Christ in the United States, **1954:** 47n.
National Citizens Commission for the Public Schools, **1955:** 96
National Citizens for Eisenhower Congressional Committee
  Meeting of district chairmen, address, **1954:** 139
  News conference remarks on, **1954:** 138, 347
National Citizens for Eisenhower Executive Campaign Conference, remarks, **1956:** 117
National civic auditorium, report on, **1957:** 21 and n.
National Civil Defense Week, **1956:** 203; **1957:** 190
National Committee for a Free Europe, **1956:** 66
National Community Christmas Tree and Pageant of Peace, **1953:** 271; **1954:** 355; **1955:** 250; **1956:** 315; **1957:** 248 and n.; **1958:** 325; **1959:** 347
National Conference of Catholic Charities, Golden Jubilee Dinner, address, **1960–61:** 306
National Conference of Christians and Jews, letter, **1955:** 40
  Message, **1953:** 132
National Conference on Civil Rights, remarks, **1959:** 128
National Conference of Republican Women, remarks, **1954:** 77
National Corn Picking Contest, remarks, **1958:** 290
National Cotton Council of America, **1959:** 267
National Council of Catholic Women, address, **1954:** 325
National Council of Churches
  General Board meeting, **1953:** 250
  Remarks, **1959:** 212
  United Church Women, address, **1953:** 205
National Council of the League of Women Voters, remarks to, **1957:** 79 and n.
National Council of the United Service Organizations, remarks, **1956:** 57
National Cultural Center, **1958:** 190; **1960–61:** 414 (p. 1023)

National Day of Prayer, **1954:** 269; **1958:** 274
National debt.
   See Debt, national.
National defense bipartisan conference, **1957:** 2
National Defense Education Act, **1960–61:** 410,
   413
   Budget messages, **1960–61:** 13 (p. 89), 414 (pp.
    1002, 1003)
   Loyalty affidavit, repeal proposed, **1960–61:** 13
    (p. 89), 414 (p. 1003)
National defense education bill
   Approval, **1958:** 243
   Letter to Repr. Wainwright, **1958:** 162
National Defense Executive Reserve Conference,
   remarks, **1957:** 235 and n.
National Defense Week, letter to Col. C. M. Boyer,
   1953: 11
National economy.
   See Economy, national.
National Editorial Association, remarks, **1954:** 149
National Education Association, **1954:** 182
   Address, **1957:** 68
   Message, **1956:** 222
National Education Week, **1957:** 234
National Federation of Republican Women, **1954:**
   273
National field days and plowing matches, cam-
   paign remarks, **1956:** 211
National Food Conference, remarks, **1958:** 35
National Football Foundation, remarks, **1958:** 307
National forests.
   See Forests, national.
National Foundation for Infantile Paralysis, **1956:**
   303; **1958:** 109
   Citation, **1955:** 78
   Vaccination program, **1955:** 112, 113
National 4-H Club Center, dedication, remarks,
   1959: 131
National 4-H Conference, remarks, **1957:** 113;
   1958: 142; **1960–61:** 123
National Fund for Medical Education, **1959:** 238
   Acceptance of Frank H. Lahey Award from,
    remarks, **1954:** 334
   Address, **1957:** 223
National Geographic Society Medal, presentation
   to Prince Philip, **1957:** 221 and n.
National goals, committee on, **1959:** 6; **1960–61:** 21
   Letters to Chairman, **1960–61:** 29, 240
   Memorandum, **1960–61:** 30
   News conference remarks on, **1959:** 36, 89, 154,
    179, 271
   Selection of members, **1959:** 271
National Granges, **1956:** 20, 250
National groups, addresses or remarks to.
   See Addresses or remarks to national groups.
National Guard, **1954:** 33, 138; **1955:** 12, 119, 192;
   1957: 22, 28
   Civil defense, **1956:** 142
   Little Rock, Ark., **1957:** 198, 200, 207, 210

National Guard Armory, Washington, D.C., **1959:**
   30n.
National Housing Act, proposed amendments,
   1954: 17
National Ike Day Committee, **1956:** 242n.
National Industrial Conference Board, message,
   1955: 228
National Industrial Reserve Committee, abolish-
   ment recommended, **1957:** 112n.
National Institute of Animal Agriculture, address,
   1954: 291
National Institutes of Health, **1954:** 11, 301; **1955:**
   17 (p. 143); **1959:** 181; **1960–61:** 13 (pp.
   93, 94), 414 (p. 1007)
   Budget messages, **1956:** 12 (p. 121); **1958:** 5 (p.
    48); **1959:** 10 (p. 101)
   Expenditures for, **1956:** 21
National Junior Chamber of Commerce, address,
   1953: 98
National Labor Relations Act, **1954:** 5
   Amendment proposed, **1958:** 20
National Labor Relations Board, **1954:** 5; **1960–61:**
   13 (p. 92), 414 (p. 946)
   Acting General Counsel, proposed, **1958:** 20
   Areas outside jurisdiction, **1959:** 89
   Beeson, Albert C., nomination, **1954:** 25
   Budget message, **1954:** 14 (p. 185)
   General Counsel, designation by the President,
    1959: 22
National Lincoln Sesquicentennial Dinner,
   remarks, **1959:** 31
National Mediation Board, **1955:** 112
National Monetary and Financial Commission,
   establishment proposed, **1957:** 8, 16
National Monument Commission, report on pro-
   posed Freedom Monument, **1960–61:** 152
National Music Council, incorporation approved,
   1956: 159
National Newspaper Publishers Association,
   remarks, **1958:** 102
National Newspaper Week, **1953:** 204n.
   Statements, **1953:** 199; **1954:** 279; **1956:** 220;
    1957: 202; **1958:** 271; **1959:** 260; **1960–61:**
    323
National Park Service, **1953:** 153; **1954:** 14 (p. 170);
   1956: 285n.; **1960–61:** 13 (p. 86), 414 (pp.
   996, 998)
   Mission 66, **1956:** 12 (p. 138), 29, 256
National Park Service, Director (Conrad L. Wirth),
   1956: 29
National parks.
   See Parks, national.
National Petroleum Council, oil supply, **1956:** 239
National Press Club, **1954:** 143
   Golden anniversary celebration, remarks, **1959:**
   7
National Probation and Parole Association, **1954:**
   207

National product, **1954:** 194, 308, 320; **1955:** 4, 19, 39, 41, 79; **1957:** 16, 17, 62; **1958:** 95; **1959:** 7, 15, 29, 76; **1960–61:** 17, 107, 245, 283, 328, 341, 410, 423
  Budget messages, **1960–61:** 13 (p. 42), 414 (p. 935)
  Campaign remarks, **1958:** 295
  Economic report, **1958:** 16
  News conference remarks, **1958:** 103; **1960–61:** 7, 143, 222, 256
National purpose, comment on, **1960–61:** 284
National Radio Month, statement, **1958:** 87
National Republican Congressional Committee, **1960–61:** 278n.
National Rivers and Harbors Congress, remarks, **1954:** 120
National Rural Electric Cooperative Association, remarks, **1959:** 30
National Rural Letter Carriers Association, remarks, **1959:** 177
National Safety Council, **1958:** 45
  Remarks, **1958:** 297
National School Boards Association, **1955:** 96
National Science Board, **1958:** 24
  Chairman, letter, **1954:** 153
National Science Foundation, **1954:** 60, 153n.; **1955:** 17 (p. 148); **1956:** 21, 90; **1958:** 64; **1959:** 10 (pp. 98, 99); **1960–61:** 358
  Budget messages, **1954:** 14 (pp. 87, 153, 155); **1956:** 12 (p. 123); **1958:** 5 (pp. 20, 46–49); **1960–61:** 13 (pp. 87, 89, 91), 414 (pp. 1002, 1004)
  Commission for rubber research, **1956:** 90
  Coordination of scientific information activities, **1958:** 326n.
  Education programs, **1958:** 24
  Funds for, **1958:** 2
  International Geophysical Year Office, **1958:** 27
  News conference remarks, **1956:** 78
  Report, **1960–61:** 393
  Satellite development, **1957:** 210, 211
  Scientists and engineers, committee on development, **1956:** 76
  Transfer of certain research functions from Department of Defense, proposed, **1954:** 14 (p. 155)
National Science Foundation, Director (Alan T. Waterman), **1956:** 74; **1958:** 47; **1959:** 267
  Report, letter, **1960–61:** 393
National Science Youth Month, statement, **1960–61:** 299
National security, **1953:** 1, 6, 11, 33, 49, 61, 84, 89, 98, 101, 143, 156, 159, 187, 262; **1954:** 2, 3, 38, 54, 67, 169, 308; **1955:** 4, 12, 13, 67, 81; **1956:** 2, 3; **1958:** 18, 26, 35, 90; **1959:** 6, 11, 51, 57, 63, 71, 83, 87, 225, 276, 278, 290; **1960–61:** 4, 23, 36, 42, 107, 131, 135, 245, 283, 332, 410, 412

National security — *continued*
  Bipartisan meeting on, **1954:** 337, 351; **1955:** 248
  Broadcasts, **1953:** 82, 83, 95
  Budget messages, **1954:** 14 (pp. 85, 86, 107, 113, 117–130); **1955:** 17 (pp. 91, 97, 104, 107–126); **1956:** 12 (pp. 80, 81, 93–107); **1958:** 5 (pp. 18–21, 24–36); **1959:** 10 (pp. 55–71); **1960–61:** 13 (pp. 46–59), 414 (pp. 939, 947–961)
    Tables, **1954:** 14 (pp. 120, 121); **1955:** 17 (pp. 104, 110); **1956:** 12 (p. 81); **1958:** 5 (p. 28); **1959:** 10 (p. 56); **1960–61:** 13 (p. 47), 414 (p. 948)
  Conference on foreign aspect of, **1958:** 42
    Address, **1958:** 36
    Letter to Eric A. Johnston, **1958:** 4
  Discussions with President-elect Kennedy, **1960–61:** 369
  Information affecting, **1959:** 36
  Letter to Secretary Wilson, **1955:** 3
  News conference remarks, **1953:** 15, 54, 62, 77, 249, 254; **1954:** 50, 311; **1959:** 7, 36, 42, 53, 148, 186; **1960–61:** 7, 34, 38, 222, 362
  President's authority, **1959:** 53
  Statement, **1958:** 154
National Security Act, statement on anniversary, **1957:** 194
National Security Agency, **1960–61:** 284
National Security Committee, **1956:** 51
National Security Council, **1953:** 6, 89, 92, 246, 265 ftn. (p. 843); **1954:** 3, 7, 348, 354; **1955:** 24n., 57, 76, 119; **1956:** 16, 48, 139, 142; **1957:** 17, 92, 157, 194, 206; **1959:** 137, 286n.; **1960–61:** 8, 9, 309, 355, 380, 412
  Budget message, **1954:** 14 (p. 140)
  Editor's note, **1955:** p. 822
  Meeting in Denver, statement, **1954:** 266
  News conference remarks on, **1953:** 31, 54, 109, 198, 208; **1954:** 9, 18; **1958:** 63, 213; **1960–61:** 38, 362
  Operations Coordinating Board, **1953:** 128 ftn. (p. 472)
  Reorganization Plan 1 of 1958, **1958:** 84
  Reports of Killian and Gaither panels, **1958:** 19
  St. Lawrence Seaway project, recommendations re, **1953:** 56
  White House statement, **1953:** 33
National Security Industrial Association, Forrestal Memorial Award dinner, remarks, **1954:** 308
National Security Medal, presentations
  Donovan, Maj. Gen. William J., **1957:** 66 and n.
  Hoover, J. Edgar, **1955:** 110
  Murphy, Robert, **1960–61:** 375
National security policy statement, preamble quoted, **1956:** 114

National Security Resources Board, **1953:** 41, 49
  Abolishment under Reorganization Plan 3, **1953:** 40
National Security System, assistance for Korea, survey of, review, **1953:** 148
National Security Training Commission, **1954:** 3, 14 (p. 185)
  Expiration, **1957:** 57 and n.
  Reports, **1954:** 7; **1957:** 57n.
  Statement, **1953:** 144
National Security Training Mission, **1955:** 12
National Service Life Insurance, **1959:** 236
  Claim of
    D'Agostino, Mary, **1959:** 235
    Holder, Anna, **1954:** 42
    Morrison, Ethel H., **1953:** 162
National Society of the Daughters of the American Revolution, remarks, **1954:** 86
National Society of Editors, **1955:** 271
National Taxpayers Conference, **1959:** 63
National Tribune, **1956:** 267
National Urban League, message, **1958:** 315
National Vegetable Week, recorded message, **1953:** 150
National Wool Act, extension, **1958:** 5 (p. 66), 12; **1960–61:** 414 (p. 989)
National Wool Growers Association, **1959:** 161
National Young Republican Organization, address, **1953:** 101
National Zoological Park, **1955:** 141n.; **1959:** 214n.
Nationalism, **1956:** 114; **1958:** 198, 207; **1959:** 55
  Africa, **1956:** 62
  Arab states, **1958:** 198
  Comments on, **1960–61:** 38, 183
  Growth of, **1958:** 36
  News conference and campaign remarks, **1956:** 62, 210
Nationality groups for Nixon-Lodge, **1960–61:** 298
NATO.
  See North Atlantic Treaty Organization.
Natural gas, **1957:** 13; **1959:** 10 (p. 96)
  News conference remarks, **1957:** 56, 72, 105, 115
Natural Gas Act, amendment, **1954:** 64
  News conference remarks, **1956:** 16, 32, 47
  Veto, **1956:** 41
Natural gas bill, **1955:** 146; **1958:** 37
Natural resources, **1953:** 112, 171; **1954:** 9, 67, 139; **1956:** 235; **1960–61:** 133, 410
  See also specific resources, land, minerals, water, etc.
  Answer to charge of "giveaway," **1956:** 256
  Budget messages, **1954:** 14 (pp. 162–171); **1955:** 17 (pp. 93, 155–163); **1956:** 12 (pp. 125, 131–138); **1958:** 5 (pp. 24, 41, 45, 63, 64, 66, 68–70); **1959:** 10 (pp. 92–96); **1960–61:** 13 (pp. 82–86), 414 (pp. 939, 993–999)
    Tables, **1954:** 14 (p. 165); **1955:** 17 (p. 157); **1958:** 5 (pp. 64, 69); **1959:** 10 (p. 93); **1960–61:** 13 (p. 84), 414 (p. 994)

Natural resources — *continued*
  Campaign remarks, **1956:** 251, 256
  Conference on, **1953:** 25
  Conservation, **1953:** 6, 25, 153, 234; **1954:** 3, 4, 14 (pp. 162–171), 201; **1955:** 4, 17 (pp. 155–163), 172; **1956:** 2, 3, 169, 170, 180, 285, 318; **1958:** 5 (pp. 63, 64, 66, 68), 100
  Conservation-reserve program (soil bank), **1956:** 6
  Message to Congress, **1953:** 153; **1957:** 8, 13, 16, 75
  Sale of, **1958:** 5 (p. 45)
  Sea resources, joint statement on, **1959:** 257
Naumann, Oscar E., **1954:** 9
Nautilus, U.S.S., **1954:** 14 (p. 129), 38; **1955:** 81; **1958:** 15, 201, 210, 211
  Budget message, **1955:** 17 (p. 121)
Naval Academy, U. S.
  Commencement, address, **1958:** 125
  Oyster Bowl Game, **1957:** 207
Naval carriers, **1957:** 230
Naval chaplains, NATO, remarks to, **1955:** 213
Naval Gun Factory, **1953:** 118n.
Naval petroleum reserves, **1959:** 10 (p. 66), 17
Naval Research Laboratory
  Page, Robert, M., **1960–61:** 68n.
  Satellite development, **1957:** 210, 211, 234
Naval shipyard, Portsmouth, N. H., wage rates, **1958:** 191; **1960–61:** 230
Naval Vessels, Commission on, **1957:** 112n.
Navigation aids and facilities, **1955:** 17 (pp. 168, 169)
Navigation development
  Arkansas River Basin, **1956:** 136
  Budget message, **1956:** 12 (pp. 139, 142, 143)
Navigation projects, **1954:** 14 (pp. 167, 169, 175, 176); **1958:** 5 (p. 68), 155; **1959:** 10 (pp. 45, 94)
Navigation satellites, **1960–61:** 264, 424
Navy, **1953:** 118; **1954:** 225; **1955:** 17 (pp. 112, 113, 117); **1959:** 350; **1960–61:** 245
  Aid to Guatemala, **1960–61:** 368
  Air power, **1953:** 83, 98
  Budget messages, **1954:** 14 (pp. 123, 124); **1959:** 10 (pp. 60–62, 66); **1960–61:** 13 (pp. 48, 55, 56, 91), 414 (pp. 949, 951, 952, 954, 956)
  Civilian facilities, integration, report, **1953:** 243
    Statement, **1953:** 244
  Claim of E. S. Berney, **1954:** 242
  Claim of Merle C. Weyel, **1954:** 241
  News conference remarks, **1960–61:** 38, 284
  Petroleum reserves, **1959:** 10 (p. 66); **1960–61:** 414 (p. 956)
  Policy on ships trading with Israel, **1960–61:** 38
  Promotion and retirement of others, approval of bill, **1959:** 178
  Rescue of four Soviet soldiers, **1960–61:** 97
  Resettlement of Indochinese evacuees, **1954:** 273

Navy — *continued*
    Seventh Fleet, **1953:** 6; **1954:** 200; **1960–61:** 191
    Sixth Fleet, **1959:** 327n., 331
Navy, Department of the, **1955:** 3, 13; **1957:** 92,
       230; **1958:** 208; **1959:** 17, 132; **1960–61:**
       349
    See also Armed forces, U. S.; Military personnel.
    Assistant Secretary for Research and Devel-
       opment, reorganization plan, **1956:** 105
    Career incentives and service credits for medical
       and dental officers, **1956:** 91
    Death compensation claim by estate of Susie Lee
       Spencer, veto, **1956:** 134
    Defense reorganization message, **1958:** 65
    Federal property in Virgin Islands, **1955:** 14
    Housing at military installations, **1956:** 141
    McLean, William B., Award for Distinguished
       Federal Civilian Service, **1958:** 13
    Naval Research Laboratory, satellite develop-
       ment, **1957:** 210, 211, 234
    News conference remarks, **1956:** 56, 94
    Reorganization Plan 6, message to Congress,
       1953: 61
    Submerged lands, naval reserve, **1956:** 56
    Vanguard project.
       See main heading, Vanguard project.
Navy, Secretary of the (Robert B. Anderson),
       report on integration in civilian facilities,
       1953: 244
Navy, Secretary of the (Thomas S. Gates, Jr.),
       1958: 125
    Letter, **1959:** 111
Navy, Secretary of the (Charles S. Thomas), award
       by military chaplains, **1956:** 98
Navy Commendation Ribbon with Metal Pendant,
       presentation to Lt. Lawrence A.
       Shumaker, **1960–61:** 25
Navy patrol plane, attack over Sea of Japan, **1959:**
       132
    Nazism, **1953:** 233n.; **1954:** 189; **1955:** 115, 163;
       1959: 115; **1960–61:** 72, 355
Neal, Repr. Will E., **1958:** 302
Near East.
    See Middle East and Near East.
Nebraska
    Anderson, Gov. Victor E., **1957:** 138
    Butler, Sen. Hugh, **1953:** 268
    Crosby, Gov. Robert B., **1954:** 258
    Curtis, Repr. Carl T., **1953:** 268
    Griswold, Sen. Dwight P., death of, **1954:** 80
    McCook, **1954:** 258
    Miller, Repr. A. L., **1953:** 268; **1954:** 138
    Omaha, **1958:** 88
Neely, Sen. Matthew M., **1955:** 81, 185
Negro College Fund Luncheon, remarks, **1953:** 81
Nehru, Jawaharlal, **1955:** 119; **1959:** 31, 94, 288,
       310, 311, 312, 314, 315, 316, 318; **1960–61:**
       136, 297

Nehru, Jawaharlal — *continued*
    Cablegram on nuclear disarmament, **1957:** 244
       and n.
    Exchange of greetings, **1956:** 312
    Exchange of messages, **1956:** 130
    Joint statements with, **1956:** 314; **1959:** 317
    Letters, **1954:** 44; **1960–61:** 313
    Messages, **1953:** 102; **1954:** 40
    News conference remarks on, **1960–61:** 7, 284
    Proposed visit, **1956:** 62, 198, 216
    70th birthday, message, **1959:** 279
Neighborhoods, council on improvement, remarks,
       1954: 333
Nelsen, Ancher, **1956:** 249, 250
    Letter, **1954:** 278
Nelson, G. M., **1956:** 278
Nepal
    Katmandu, **1958:** 123
    Mahendra Bir Bikram, **1960–61:** 128, 129
       Joint statement, **1960–61:** 130
    Ratna Rajya Lekshmi, **1960–61:** 128, 129
Nepotism in Congress, **1959:** 67
Nerve gases, **1959:** 132
Netherlands, **1954:** 84n.; **1955:** 54n.; **1956:** 171;
       1959: 214
    Amsterdam, **1960–61:** 279
    Assistance, **1960–61:** 138n.
    Atomic energy for mutual defense, U.S.-
       Netherlands agreement, **1959:** 119n., 120
    Euratom.
       See European Atomic Energy Community.
    European Defense Community Treaty ratifica-
       tion, statement, **1954:** 13
    Floods in, **1953:** 53n.
    Hockey team, **1960–61:** 319n.
    Prime Minister Willem Drees, **1957:** 56
    Prince Bernhard, **1953:** 53
    Queen Juliana
       Letter, **1953:** 53
       Messages, **1953:** 7; **1960–61:** 138
    Storm disaster, **1953:** 7, 8
Nettuno (Anzio), Italy, **1956:** 102, 113
Neudoerfer, John L., **1959:** 211n.
Neutrality
    Afghanistan, joint statement on, **1958:** 150
    Austria, **1955:** 100
    Germany, joint statement with Chancellor Aden-
       auer on, **1955:** 122
    News conference remarks, **1956:** 121
    Satellite countries, comment on, **1955:** 119
    White House statement on, **1956:** 121 ftn. (pp.
       556, 557)
Nevada, **1957:** 92
    Atom bomb test, **1953:** 31
    Malone, Sen. George W., **1956:** 235; **1957:** 50;
       1958: 310
    McCarran, Sen. Pat, **1953:** 37
New Amsterdam, Dutch colony, **1954:** 297

New Bern, N.C., **1954:** 86n.
New Deal, **1954:** 18, 290; **1959:** 21
New Delhi, India, **1955:** 47
  Address to Indian Parliament, **1959:** 311
  Arrival, remarks, **1959:** 310
  Departure, broadcast, **1959:** 318
  Joint statement with Prime Minister Nehru,
    1959: 317
  Lincoln Society, **1959:** 31
  Mayor Trilok Chand Sharma, **1959:** 316n.
  Meeting of World Bank and International Mon-
    etary Fund, **1958:** 312
    Message, **1958:** 278
  Remarks at civic reception, **1959:** 316
  Remarks at Delhi University, **1959:** 314
  Remarks at U.S. embassy, **1959:** 313
  Toast to President Prasad, **1959:** 312
  Visit of Secretary of the Treasury, **1959:** 83
  World Agriculture Fair, **1959:** 277, 316, 317;
    1960–61: 136
    Remarks at opening, **1959:** 315
New England, depressed areas, **1954:** 9
New England "Forward to '54" Dinner, address,
  1953: 187
New Hampshire
  Bass, Repr. Perkins, **1955:** 139
  Berlin, **1955:** 139
  Bridges, Sen. Styles, **1953:** 37, 143, 187; **1954:** 39;
    1955: 134, 135, 139; **1956:** 78, 184, 216;
    1958: 63
  Concord, **1955:** 133
  Cotton, Sen. Norris, **1955:** 139
  Dwinell, Gov. Lane, **1955:** 133, 135, 136, 139;
    1957: 138
  Franconia Notch, **1955:** 136
  Gregg, Gov. Hugh, **1953:** 187
  Hanover, **1953:** 104; **1958:** 138n.
  Jackson, Harry E., Deputy Secretary of State,
    1956: 15, 16
  Jefferson, **1955:** 138
  Kenison, Chief Justice Frank B., **1956:** 216
  Laconia, **1955:** 134
  Lancaster, **1955:** 137
  Lincoln, **1955:** 135
  Merrow, Repr. Chester E., **1955:** 139
  Portsmouth, **1958:** 191; **1960–61:** 230
  Powell, Gov. Wesley, **1959:** 112, 113
  Primary election, **1956:** 15, 16, 47, 56, 117
New Jersey, **1958:** 287n.
  Atlantic City, **1953:** 205, 208; **1957:** 14; **1958:**
    45n.; **1959:** 129
  Auchincloss, Repr. James C., **1955:** 20
  Camden, **1958:** 11
  Camp Kilmer, **1956:** 301
  Candidates for public office, **1954:** 192; **1957:**
    228; **1958:** 28
  Case, Repr. Clifford, **1954:** 165, 192; **1957:** 87;
    1958: 70

New Jersey — *continued*
  Congressional election, **1953:** 238
  Driscoll, Gov. Alfred E., **1953:** 15, 205
  Frelinghuysen, Repr. Peter, Jr., **1954:** 182
  Gubernatorial election, **1953:** 198, 230, 238
  Holmdel, **1960–61:** 258n.
  Kean, Repr. Robert W., **1958:** 58
  Meyner, Gov. Robert B., **1957:** 87; **1959:** 173
  Pleasantville, **1956:** 288
  Smith, Sen. H. Alexander, **1953:** 266; **1954:** 9, 25;
    1956: 63, 184; **1958:** 23
"New look" in defense, comment on, **1954:** 50, 57
New Market, Battle of, **1959:** 133
New Mexico, **1958:** 56
  Anderson, Sen. Clinton P., **1953:** 58; **1954:** 33,
    50; **1955:** 10, 71; **1956:** 30, 230; **1957:** 134;
    1958: 88
  Atomic explosions (1945), **1956:** 266
  Bernalillo County, **1960–61:** 235
  Chavez, Sen. Dennis, **1953:** 22; **1954:** 63; **1956:**
    113; **1958:** 88
  Lead and zinc mines, **1958:** 28
  Mechem, Gov. Edwin L., **1954:** 33, 85n., 99
  Mining claims, disapproval, **1956:** 179
  Unemployed, **1958:** 28
  U.S. District Court, **1954:** 243
New obligational authority, **1957:** 13, 75
  Budget message, **1956:** 12 (pp. 86, 87, 153)
    Table, **1956:** 12 (p. 87)
  Housing Act of 1957, **1957:** 129
  News conference remarks, **1957:** 92 ftn. (p. 403),
    169
New Orleans, La., **1953:** 219, 220
  Inter-American Investment Conference, **1955:** 44
  Morrison, Mayor Delesseps S., **1953:** 219
New Year, Jewish, statement, **1957:** 199
New York, **1959:** 75
  Albany, **1958:** 306
  Barry, Repr. Robert R., **1960–61:** 346
  Bear Mountain State Park, **1960–61:** 173
  Buckley, Repr. Charles A., **1958:** 190
  Candidates for public office, **1954:** 200; **1956:** 94,
    272; **1957:** 56; **1958:** 153, 222, 305, 306;
    1960–61: 346
  Cole, Repr. W. Sterling, **1953:** 268; **1954:** 57, 129
  Committee on refugees, **1954:** 188
  Corsi, Commissioner Edward, **1954:** 188
  Dewey, Gov. Thomas E., **1953:** 68, 69, 105, 128,
    230, 265; **1954:** 18, 115, 143 and ftn. (p.
    568), 188, 298, 300, 301
  Disposition of farm surpluses, **1956:** 20
  Garden City, **1960–61:** 345
  Great Lakes water level discussion, **1956:** 177
  Harriman, Gov. W. Averell, **1958:** 33
  Health program, **1954:** 301
  Ives, Sen. Irving M., **1953:** 68, 69; **1954:** 48, 298,
    300, 322; **1958:** 216, 306
  Javits, Sen. Jacob K., **1957:** 87; **1960–61:** 38

New York — *continued*
Kearney, Repr. Bernard W., **1953:** 22
Keating, Kenneth B., **1956:** 213; **1958:** 222, 305, 306; **1960–61:** 173
Lake George, **1954:** 164
Lehman, Sen. Herbert H., **1953:** 37; **1954:** 168; **1956:** 189
Manhattan State Hospital, **1954:** 299
Maritime strike, **1954:** 68
Massena, **1959:** 36
Miller, Repr. William E., **1953:** 128
New York City.
See *main heading*, New York City.
Niagara Falls power project, **1953:** 31, 77, 88, 128, 208, 265; **1955:** 10
Oyster Bay, **1953:** 105
Powell, Repr. Adam C., Jr., **1956:** 32; **1957:** 191, 228; **1958:** 11
Power Authority, **1959:** 141n.
Reed, Repr. Daniel A., **1953:** 31, 41; **1954:** 48
Republican State Committee, addresses, **1953:** 68, 69
Rochester, **1956:** 263
Rockefeller, Gov. Nelson A., **1959:** 26, 48, 94, 148, 167, 277; **1960–61:** 7, 103, 222, 256, 306
St. George, Repr. Katharine, **1960–61:** 173
St. Lawrence power project, **1953:** 15, 22, 31, 54, 70, 77, 246, 247; **1954:** 14 (pp. 175, 176); **1956:** 96
Santangelo, Repr. Alfred E., **1959:** 167
Southern New York District Court, **1953:** 203n.; **1959:** 250n.
State University Medical Center, dedication, remarks, **1954:** 300
Syracuse, **1956:** 263
Taber, Repr. John, **1953:** 266
Tarrytown, **1960–61:** 346
Television quiz investigation (1959), **1960–61:** 34
Wainwright, Repr. Stuyvesant, **1958:** 162, 195
West Point, U. S. Military Academy, **1956:** 241
Westchester County, **1960–61:** 346
New York Bar Association, **1955:** 18
New York City, **1953:** 5n., 68, 69, 238; **1954:** 32n., 87, 128, 130, 194, 300, 301; **1955:** 27, 79, 219, 228n., 239n., 245; **1956:** 227, 229, 242n., 261, 285; **1957:** 223; **1958:** 110n., 118, 284, 285, 307, 315; **1959:** 26, 106, 107, 148 and ftn. (p. 490), 190n.; **1960–61:** 23n., 306, 307n.
Address before U.N. General Assembly, **1960–61:** 302
Addresses, **1954:** 297, 301
Campaign remarks, **1954:** 298, 320; **1958:** 305, 306; **1960–61:** 347, 348
Coinage of 50-cent pieces for tercentennial, veto, **1954:** 28
District Attorney Frank S. Hogan, **1960–61:** 34

New York City — *continued*
Fire Department, **1960–61:** 113
Kennedy, Stephen P., **1960–61:** 314
Memorial Press Center, dedication, remarks, **1954:** 350
Police, **1960–61:** 314
Remarks to Latin American delegates to U.N. General Assembly, **1960–61:** 303
Wagner, Mayor Robert F., **1954:** 301; **1960–61:** 306
World's Fair (1964–65), **1960–61:** 358, 376, 414 (p. 984)
New York Philharmonic Symphony Orchestra, **1959:** 106
New York Power Authority, **1953:** 246; **1954:** 138
New York Shipbuilding, **1959:** 48
New Zealand, **1954:** 115, 129; **1959:** 96n.; **1960–61:** 410
Armed forces in Korea, **1960–61:** 202
Defense treaty with United States, **1953:** 96
Holyoake, Keith, message, **1960–61:** 373
Nash, Walter, message, **1960–61:** 367
SEATO.
See Southeast Asia Treaty Organization.
Newcomb, Elliott, meeting with, statement, **1953:** 26
Newport, R. I., **1957:** 176, 177, 178n., 186n., 187n., 188n., 189n., 191n., 193n., 197, 200n., 201n., 228; **1958:** 239n., 240, 242n., 243n., 244n., 245n., 246n., 247n., 248n., 249n., 250n., 251n., 252n., 253n., 254n., 255n., 256n., 257n., 260n., 262n., 263n., 264n., 265n., 266n.; **1960–61:** 228
Eisenhower Park, dedication, remarks, **1960–61:** 239
Maher, Mayor James, **1960–61:** 239n.
News conference remarks, **1957:** 134, 207
Releases from, **1960–61:** 227, 229–238, 240–243, 248–254
Newport Harbor, Calif., **1953:** 137n.
News, international, in U.S. and foreign press, **1954:** 87
News conferences
Censorship, **1955:** 26
Comment on, **1953:** 198; **1954:** 25; **1958:** 88; **1959:** 7; **1960–61:** 222, 422
First TV and newsreel recording, editor's note, **1955:** 18 (p. 185)
Forty-third anniversary, **1956:** 56
News conferences, the President's
1953
February 17 (No. 1), **1953:** 12
February 25 (No. 2), **1953:** 15
March 5 (No. 3), **1953:** 22
March 19 (No. 4), **1953:** 31
March 26 (No. 5), **1953:** 37
April 2 (No. 6), **1953:** 41
April 23 (No. 7), **1953:** 54

News conferences, the President's — *continued*
  1953 — *continued*
    April 30 (No. 8), **1953:** 62
    May 14 (No. 9), **1953:** 77
    May 28 (No. 10), **1953:** 88
    June 17 (No. 11), **1953:** 109
    July 1 (No. 12), **1953:** 126
    July 8 (No. 13), **1953:** 128
    July 22 (No. 14), **1953:** 141
    September 30 (No. 15), **1953:** 198
    October 8 (No. 16), **1953:** 208
    October 21 (No. 17), **1953:** 225
    October 28 (No. 18), **1953:** 230
    November 4 (No. 19), **1953:** 238
    November 11 (No. 20), **1953:** 243
    November 18 (No. 21), **1953:** 249
    December 2 (No. 22), **1953:** 254
    December 16 (No. 23), **1953:** 265
  1954
    January 13 (No. 24), **1954:** 9
    January 27 (No. 25), **1954:** 18
    February 3 (No. 26), **1954:** 25
    February 10 (No. 27), **1954:** 33
    February 17 (No. 28), **1954:** 39
    March 3 (No. 29), **1954:** 48
    March 10 (No. 30), **1954:** 50
    March 17 (No. 31), **1954:** 57
    March 24 (No. 32), **1954:** 63
    March 31 (No. 33), **1954:** 68
    April 7 (No. 34), **1954:** 73
    April 29 (No. 35), **1954:** 92
    May 5 (No. 36), **1954:** 101
    May 12 (No. 37), **1954:** 107
    May 19 (No. 38), **1954:** 115
    June 2 (No. 39), **1954:** 129
    June 10 (No. 40), **1954:** 138
    June 16 (No. 41), **1954:** 143
    June 30 (No. 42), **1954:** 157
    July 7 (No. 43), **1954:** 161
    July 14 (No. 44), **1954:** 165
    July 21 (No. 45), **1954:** 168
    July 28 (No. 46), **1954:** 172
    August 4 (No. 47), **1954:** 182
    August 11 (No. 48), **1954:** 192
    August 17 (No. 49), **1954:** 200
    October 27 (No. 50), **1954:** 311
    November 3 (No. 51), **1954:** 322
    November 10 (No. 52), **1954:** 328
    November 23 (No. 53), **1954:** 341
    December 2 (No. 54), **1954:** 345
    December 8 (No. 55), **1954:** 347
    December 15 (No. 56), **1954:** 353
  1955
    January 12 (No. 57), **1955:** 10
    January 19 (No. 58), **1955:** 18
    February 2 (No. 59), **1955:** 26
    February 9 (No. 60), **1955:** 33
    February 23 (No. 61), **1955:** 41

News conferences, the President's — *continued*
  1955 — *continued*
    March 2 (No. 62), **1955:** 47
    March 16 (No. 63), **1955:** 56
    March 23 (No. 64), **1955:** 59
    March 30 (No. 65), **1955:** 62
    April 27 (No. 66), **1955:** 81
    May 4 (No. 67), **1955:** 90
    May 11 (No. 68), **1955:** 95
    May 18 (No. 69), **1955:** 100
    May 31 (No. 70), **1955:** 112
    June 8 (No. 71), **1955:** 119
    June 29 (No. 72), **1955:** 146
    July 6 (No. 73), **1955:** 149
    July 27 (No. 74), **1955:** 176
    August 4 (No. 75), **1955:** 185
  1956
    January 8 (No. 76), **1956:** 5
    January 19 (No. 77), **1956:** 16
    January 25 (No. 78), **1956:** 20
    February 8 (No. 79), **1956:** 32
    February 29 (No. 80), **1956:** 47
    March 7 (No. 81), **1956:** 53
    March 14 (No. 82), **1956:** 56
    March 21 (No. 83), **1956:** 62
    April 4 (No. 84), **1956:** 78
    April 25 (No. 85), **1956:** 88
    May 4 (No. 86), **1956:** 94
    May 9 (No. 87), **1956:** 96
    May 23 (No. 88), **1956:** 113
    June 6 (No. 89), **1956:** 121
    August 1 (No. 90), **1956:** 155
    August 8 (No. 91), **1956:** 171
    August 22 (No. 92), **1956:** 189
    August 31 (No. 93), **1956:** 193
    September 5 (No. 94), **1956:** 198
    September 11 (No. 95), **1956:** 205
    September 27 (No. 96), **1956:** 216
    October 5 (No. 97), **1956:** 229
    October 11 (No. 98), **1956:** 235
    November 14 (No. 99), **1956:** 298
  1957
    January 23 (No. 100), **1957:** 17
    January 30 (No. 101), **1957:** 22
    February 6 (No. 102), **1957:** 28
    March 7 (No. 103), **1957:** 45
    March 13 (No. 104), **1957:** 50
    March 27 (No. 105), **1957:** 56
    April 3 (No. 106), **1957:** 62
    April 10 (No. 107), **1957:** 70
    April 17 (No. 108), **1957:** 72
    May 8 (No. 109), **1957:** 80
    May 15 (No. 110), **1957:** 87
    May 22 (No. 111), **1957:** 92
    June 5 (No. 112), **1957:** 105
    June 19 (No. 113), **1957:** 115
    June 26 (No. 114), **1957:** 119
    July 3 (No. 115), **1957:** 124

[References are to items except as otherwise indicated]

News conferences, the President's — *continued*
  1957 — *continued*
    July 17 (No. 116), **1957:** 134
    July 31 (No. 117), **1957:** 145
    August 7 (No. 118), **1957:** 150
    August 14 (No. 119), **1957:** 152
    August 21 (No. 120), **1957:** 157
    September 3 (No. 121), **1957:** 169
    October 3 (No. 122), **1957:** 207
    October 9 (No. 123), **1957:** 210
    October 30 (No. 124), **1957:** 228
  1958
    January 15 (No. 125), **1958:** 11
    February 5 (No. 126), **1958:** 28
    February 26 (No. 127), **1958:** 37
    March 5 (No. 128), **1958:** 42
    March 26 (No. 129), **1958:** 56
    April 2 (No. 130), **1958:** 63
    April 9 (No. 131), **1958:** 70
    April 16 (No. 132), **1958:** 74
    April 23 (No. 133), **1958:** 83
    April 30 (No. 134), **1958:** 88
    May 14 (No. 135), **1958:** 103
    May 28 (No. 136), **1958:** 120
    June 18 (No. 137), **1958:** 141
    July 2 (No. 138), **1958:** 153
    August 6 (No. 139), **1958:** 198
    August 20 (No. 140), **1958:** 213
    August 27 (No. 141), **1958:** 222
    October 1 (No. 142), **1958:** 274
    October 15 (No. 143), **1958:** 288
    November 5 (No. 144), **1958:** 310
    December 10 (No. 145), **1958:** 318
  1959
    January 14 (No. 146), **1959:** 7
    January 21 (No. 147), **1959:** 17
    January 28 (No. 148), **1959:** 21
    February 4 (No. 149), **1959:** 26
    February 10 (No. 150), **1959:** 29
    February 18 (No. 151), **1959:** 36
    February 25 (No. 152), **1959:** 42
    March 4 (No. 153), **1959:** 48
    March 11 (No. 154), **1959:** 53
    March 25 (No. 155), **1959:** 67
    April 15 (No. 156), Augusta, Ga., **1959:** 78
    April 29 (No. 157), **1959:** 89
    May 5 (No. 158), **1959:** 94
    May 13 (No. 159), **1959:** 102
    June 3 (No. 160), **1959:** 123
    June 17 (No. 161), **1959:** 132
    July 1 (No. 162), **1959:** 148
    July 8 (No. 163), **1959:** 154
    July 15 (No. 164), **1959:** 161
    July 22 (No. 165), **1959:** 167
    July 29 (No. 166), **1959:** 172
    August 3 (No. 167), **1959:** 173
    August 12 (No. 168), Gettysburg, Pa., **1959:** 179

News conferences, the President's — *continued*
  1959 — *continued*
    August 25 (No. 169), **1959:** 186
    August 27 (No. 170), Bonn, Germany, **1959:** 191
    September 17 (No. 171), **1959:** 223
    September 28 (No. 172), **1959:** 243
    October 22 (No. 173), Augusta, Ga., **1959:** 267
    October 28 (No. 174), **1959:** 271
    November 4 (No. 175), **1959:** 277
    December 2 (No. 176), **1959:** 288
  1960–61
    January 13 (No. 177), **1960–61:** 7
    January 26 (No. 178), **1960–61:** 21
    February 3 (No. 179), **1960–61:** 24
    February 11 (No. 180), **1960–61:** 34
    February 17 (No. 181), **1960–61:** 38
    March 16 (No. 182), **1960–61:** 93
    March 30 (No. 183), **1960–61:** 103
    April 27 (No. 184), **1960–61:** 127
    May 11 (No. 185), **1960–61:** 143
    July 6 (No. 186), **1960–61:** 222
    July 11 (No. 187), Newport, R.I., **1960–61:** 228
    August 10 (No. 188), **1960–61:** 256
    August 17 (No. 189), **1960–61:** 263
    August 24 (No. 190), **1960–61:** 268
    September 7 (No. 191), **1960–61:** 284
    November 16 (No. 192), **1960–61:** 362
  1962
    January 18 (No. 193), **1960–61:** 422
Newsmen
  Asian, **1954:** 157, 328
  Communist China, **1957:** 17, 45, 80, 134
    U.S. ban, **1956:** 193
  Disclosure of sources of information at Congressional hearings, **1955:** 10
  Importance of, **1959:** 179
  Latin American, visit, **1956:** 155
  NATO countries, **1954:** 33, 328
  Nuclear test coverage, **1956:** 78; **1958:** 56
  Relationship with, **1953:** 12; **1960–61:** 422
  Visit to scene of Normandy invasion, **1954:** 131
  White House dinner, **1959:** 167
Newspaper Editors, American Society of, **1955:** 79, 99n.; **1960–61:** 80n.
  Addresses, **1953:** 50; **1956:** 87; **1958:** 80
  News conference remarks, **1956:** 88
Newspaper Publishers Association, American
  Address, **1954:** 87
  Remarks, **1958:** 102
Newspaper Week, National, **1953:** 204n.
  Statements, **1953:** 199; **1954:** 279; **1956:** 220; **1957:** 202; **1958:** 271; **1959:** 260; **1960–61:** 323
Newspaperboys, participation in Crusade for Freedom campaign, **1955:** 79
Newspaperboys of America, messages, **1956:** 231; **1957:** 209; **1958:** 276; **1959:** 263

[References are to items except as otherwise indicated]

Newspapers, leakage of information to, **1953:** 198
Newsprint, imports, **1958:** 58, 96
Newsweek, **1960–61:** 263
Newton, Virgil M., Jr., **1959:** 288
Newton, Iowa, **1956:** 198, 205
N'Goua, Joseph, **1960–61:** 324n.
Niagara Falls power project, **1953:** 31, 77, 88, 128,
    208, 265; **1955:** 10; **1956:** 96; **1957:** 13
  Private vs. public power, **1954:** 138
Nicaragua, **1960–61:** 368n.
  Anastasio Somoza, **1956:** 219
Nichols, Marvin C., **1953:** 126
Nichols, Walter H., Jr., **1954:** 240
Nicholson, Mayor W. F., **1956:** 259
Nickel, imports, **1958:** 58, 96
Nickel plant, Cuba, **1956:** 20, 96, 113
Nickerson, Col. John, **1957:** 80
Nickname of President, use by newsmen, comment
  on, **1953:** 265
Nicolas I, **1953:** 187
Nielsen, Aksel, **1959:** 133n.; **1960–61:** 320
Nieuw Amsterdam, S.S., **1953:** 260
Niger, Republic of
  Djermakoye, Issofou, **1960–61:** 324
  Independence, message to Prime Minister Diori,
    1960–61: 251
Nigeria, Federation of
  Azikiwe, Nnamdi, letter, **1960–61:** 361
  Independence, message to people, **1960–61:** 311
  Wachuku, Jaja, **1960–61:** 324n.
NIH.
  See National Institutes of Health.
Nike missiles.
  See Missiles.
Nimitz, Adm. Chester W., **1960–61:** 143
Niven, Paul, **1956:** 62
Nixon, Frank A.
  Announcement of illness, **1956:** 189
  Death of, statement, **1956:** 199
Nixon, Richard M.
  See Candidacy for second term; Vice President.
Nixon, Mrs. Richard M., **1953:** 265; **1954:** 171n.,
    312; **1956:** 293; **1957:** 116, 248; **1958:** 101,
    107; **1959:** 210, 214; **1960–61:** 107, 357,
    403
Nixon-Lodge, American Nationalities for, remarks,
    1960–61: 298
Nixon for President Committee of Pennsylvania
  Message, **1960–61:** 337
  Rally, address, **1960–61:** 341
Nkrumah, Kwame, **1957:** 43
  Joint statement with President, **1958:** 180
  Letters to, **1958:** 44; **1960–61:** 313
  Messages, **1960–61:** 220, 248
NLRB.
  See National Labor Relations Board.
Nobel Prize, **1959:** 107
  Peace, **1960–61:** 287
  Science recipient, Dr. Lawrence, **1958:** 52

Nomination of President, 1952, Democratic groups
  for, news conference remarks, **1956:** 171
Nomination of President, 1956, acceptance broad-
  cast, **1956:** 190
Nomination of Vice President, news conference
  remarks, **1956:** 189
Nomy, Adm. Henri, **1959:** 332n.
Nonaggression pacts, comment on, **1959:** 42
Norblad, Rep. Walter, **1956:** 256
Norfolk, Virginia, **1957:** 50
  Education of children of military personnel,
    1959: 17
Norman, E. H., **1957:** 70, 72
Norman, Jack, **1955:** 26; **1956:** 205
Normandy, battle of (1944), **1960–61:** 405
Normandy Beach, **1956:** 253; **1957:** 91
Normandy invasion, 10th anniversary, **1954:** 9
  Statement, **1954:** 133
  Visit to scene by newsmen, **1954:** 131
Norodom Sihanouk, message, **1954:** 280
Norstad, Gen. Lauris.
  See Supreme Allied Commander Europe.
North, Thomas, **1956:** 102
North America, inspection of, **1957:** 150
North American Defense Command, **1958:** 5 (p.
  30); **1959:** 10 (p. 61); **1960–61:** 13 (p. 54)
North American Ecclesiastical College, Vatican
  City, **1959:** 294n.
North Atlantic Alliance.
  See North Atlantic Treaty Organization.
North Atlantic Community
  Joint statement with President Gronchi on, **1956:**
    49
  Letter to Sen. Walter F. George, **1956:** 97
North Atlantic Council, **1954:** 353; **1955:** 54; **1956:**
    97; **1957:** 100, 226, 228, 243n.; **1959:** 350,
    351
  Chairman, Lord Ismay, **1953:** 71
  Declaration on Berlin (1958), **1959:** 336
  Foreign ministers meeting, remarks, **1959:** 70
  Joint statement with Prime Minister Eden on,
    1956: 26
  Joint statement with Western leaders on, **1959:**
    336
  Letter, **1953:** 72
  Message, **1953:** 74
  Ministerial meetings in Paris, **1953:** 54, 66, 70,
    265 ftn. (p. 843)
  News conference remarks, **1956:** 78
  Paris meeting, **1959:** 154
  Perkins, George W., U.S. Permanent Represen-
    tative, **1955:** 71
  President (Joseph M. A. H. Luns), **1959:** 70, 214
    Meeting with President Eisenhower, **1959:** 186
North Atlantic Treaty, **1953:** 42, 255; **1954:** 71, 84,
    155, 225; **1955:** 54; **1956:** 125; **1957:** 22,
    91
  Joint statement with Prime Minister Eden on,
    1956: 26

North Atlantic Treaty — *continued*
  Joint statement with Prime Minister Macmillan,
    1957: 226
  Protocol on accession of Germany, message,
    1955: 332
  Question re invoking, **1959:** 42
  Statement on anniversary, **1957:** 67
North Atlantic Treaty Council, **1958:** 316n., 318
North Atlantic Treaty Organization, **1953:** 50, 61,
    75, 143; **1954:** 3, 36, 84, 148n., 154, 209,
    273; **1955:** 3, 54, 72, 144, 162, 175; **1956:**
    2, 46, 58, 114, 218, 317; **1957:** 3, 148, 213,
    248; **1958:** 32, 96, 118, 163; **1959:** 40, 41,
    57, 100, 214, 291, 296, 326, 350, 351;
    1960–61: 36, 121, 157, 159, 162, 245, 320,
    321, 360n., 365, 410
  Advisory Group, Aeronautical Research and
    Development, letter to Chairman, **1957:**
    238
  Anniversary statements
    Fourth, **1953:** 42
    Fifth, **1954:** 71
    Seventh, **1956:** 78
    Tenth, **1959:** 70
  Assistance, **1959:** 55
    To members, **1956:** 12 (p. 104), 58
  Atlantic Treaty Association, message, **1959:** 204
  Atomic information exchange, **1954:** 138
    Agreement for cooperation regarding, **1956:**
    71
    Question of, **1953:** 265
  Broadcast in London re, **1959:** 196
  Budget messages, **1954:** 14 (pp. 126, 127); **1958:** 5
    (pp. 25, 35); **1960–61:** 13 (pp. 38, 57, 58,
    63), 414 (pp. 955, 958)
  Campaign remarks, **1956:** 210, 278; **1958:** 287
  Chaplains, Naval, remarks to, **1957:** 213
  Commander in Chief, South (Adm. Robert B.
    Carney), **1953:** 71, 72
    Letter, **1953:** 76
  Effect of atomic bomb, **1956:** 78
  Financial support of U.S. personnel, question of,
    1960–61: 362
  Forces, **1957:** 22, 28, 34, 72, 119, 226
  France, attitude of, **1959:** 132
  Germany
    Accession of, **1956:** 2; **1958:** 287
    Admission question of, **1954:** 297, 307, 314,
    332, 337, 351, 357
    Berlin, action on, comment, **1959:** 42
    Membership in, **1955:** 4, 99
  Joint statements
    Chancellor Adenauer, **1957:** 100; **1959:** 192
    President Bayar, **1959:** 297
    President de Gaulle, **1959:** 202
    President Gronchi, **1959:** 293
    Prime Minister Fanfani, **1958:** 186
    Prime Minister Karamanlis, **1959:** 327

North Atlantic Treaty Organization — *continued*
  Joint statements — *continued*
    Prime Minister Macmillan, **1957:** 55, 226
    Prime Minister St. Laurent, **1953:** 70, 247
    Prime Minister Scelba, **1955:** 61
    Prime Minister Segni, **1959:** 203, 248
    Western leaders, **1953:** 255; **1959:** 336
  Letter to Premier Bulganin re, **1958:** 7
  Meetings, **1956:** 88; **1958:** 2
  Ministerial Council meetings, **1953:** 54, 66, 70,
    265 ftn. (p. 843); **1959:** 277 ftn. (p. 766)
  Mobilization of forces, comment on, **1959:** 48
  Modernization of military forces proposed, **1959:**
    90
  News conference remarks on, **1953:** 37, 54, 128,
    230, 238, 249, 265; **1954:** 33, 57, 63, 138,
    328, 345; **1956:** 56, 78, 88, 298; **1957:** 22,
    28, 34, 70, 72, 119, 124, 134, 228; **1958:** 28,
    37; **1959:** 42, 48, 94, 132, 186, 191
  Nuclear weapons for, **1960–61:** 420
    Use of, **1959:** 120
  Paris meetings, **1957:** 243, 245, 246, 247, 249;
    1960–61: 163
  Permanent Council, remarks, **1959:** 205
  President's association with, **1956:** 78
  Remarks to young political leaders from NATO
    countries, **1960–61:** 165
  Report on, **1953:** 265 ftn., (p. 843)
  Role, **1956:** 78
  Science program, U.S. support, **1960–61:** 13 (p.
    63)
  Scientific committee on research, proposed,
    1957: 230
  Secretary General (Lord Ismay), **1953:** 71, 72, 74,
    255
  Secretary General (Paul-Henri Spaak), **1957:**
    228; **1959:** 70, 214
    Discussions with the President and Prime
    Minister Macmillan, **1957:** 226
    Meeting with President Eisenhower, **1959:** 186,
    214
    Paris meetings, **1957:** 243 and n.
  Spain, adherence of, question re, **1959:** 191
  Status of Forces agreement, **1957:** 139
  U.S. mission, **1953:** 89
North Attleboro, Mass., **1959:** 4n.
North Carolina
  Charlotte, **1954:** 92, 114, 115
  Cooley, Repr. Harold D., **1957:** 45
  Durham, Repr. Carl T., **1957:** 231 and n.
  Hodges, Gov. Luther, **1957:** 205n.
  Hoey, Sen. Clyde R., **1954:** 92, 109
  Jonas, Repr. Charles R., **1954:** 92, 345
  Kitty Hawk, **1953:** 267
  New Bern, **1954:** 86n.
  Umstead, Gov. William B., **1954:** 92, 114
North Counties Hydro-Electric Co., damages
    claim, **1958:** 229

North Dakota
    Brunsdale, Gov. Norman, **1953:** 100
    Election, **1960–61:** 222
    Lake Alice National Wildlife Refuge, **1956:** 79
    Langer, Sen. William, **1959:** 123
    Young, Sen. Milton R., **1953:** 225; **1954:** 18
North Korea, news conference remarks, **1957:** 119
North Polar Sea, submarine voyages under, **1959:** 6
North Pole, **1958:** 15, 163
    Underwater crossing, *Nautilus*, **1958:** 201
North Vietnam
    Joint statement with President Diem, **1957:** 83
    Vietnamese Communist military forces, **1957:** 83
Northampton, Mass., coinage of 50-cent pieces to
    commemorate tercentennial of founding,
    veto, **1954:** 27
Northeast, soil bank program, **1956:** 241
Northeastern States flood control, **1956:** 12 (p. 135)
Northrup, Doyle L., Award for Distinguished Fed-
    eral Civilian Service, **1959:** 9n.
Northwest Airlines, **1957:** 162
    Certification, **1955:** 30, 33
    Great Circle route operating certificate, **1956:**
      14n.
    Trans-Pacific operating certificate, **1956:** 56
Northwest Power Pool, **1954:** 271
Northwestern University, **1954:** 192, 204
Norwalk, Conn., Communist activities in, question
    of, **1954:** 18
Norway, **1957:** 56; **1960–61:** 321n.
    Haakon VII, **1955:** 241
      Message on death of, **1957:** 192
    Olav V, message to, **1957:** 192
Nose cone of missile, recovery, **1957:** 230
Notre Dame, University of, commencement exer-
    cises, address, **1960–61:** 174
Nover, Barnet, **1953:** 15, 128
NS *Savannah*, **1959:** 10 (p. 80)
    News conference remarks, **1959:** 48
Nu (U)
    Joint statement with President, **1955:** 148
    Letters, **1955:** 169; **1956:** 60
    News conference remarks on, **1955:** 146
Nuclear aircraft, **1955:** 17 (p. 121)
Nuclear Energy Commission, Inter-American, pro-
    posed establishment, **1957:** 96
Nuclear fuel for foreign power projects, statement,
    1956: 299
Nuclear power projects, **1956:** 43, 256, 263
    See also Power projects.
    Foreign, statement, **1956:** 299
    Monroe, Mich., **1956:** 198
    Shippingport, Pa., **1956:** 263
Nuclear-powered aircraft.
    See under Aircraft.
Nuclear-powered ships.
    See Ships, nuclear-powered.

Nuclear propulsion plant for submarines, transfer
    to United Kingdom, **1958:** 156
Nuclear reactors.
    See Reactors, nuclear.
Nuclear relationship and cooperation with United
    Kingdom, study of, **1957:** 226n.
Nuclear Science and Engineering, International
    School of, foreign students, remarks,
    1955: 53
Nuclear war, **1953:** 50, 95, 114, 208, 256; **1955:** 33,
    79, 175; **1958:** 32; **1959:** 55, 57, 70;
    1960–61: 4, 147, 163, 185, 193, 409
    Budget message, **1959:** 10 (p. 67)
    News conference remarks, **1959:** 53, 167, 223
    U.S. preparedness, **1958:** 222
Nuclear warheads, **1957:** 56, 230; **1956:** 32
    U.S.S.R., **1957:** 245
Nuclear weapons, **1953:** 50, 205, 256; **1954:** 38, 223,
    346; **1955:** 4, 166; **1956:** 2, 210, 232, 258,
    266; **1957:** 8, 165, 230, 234, 245; **1958:** 65,
    96, 148, 207; **1959:** 71; **1960–61:** 4, 42,
    185, 193, 209, 255
    See also Bombs; Disarmament; Missiles; Nu-
      clear weapons tests.
    Allies, question of, **1960–61:** 24
    Authority to use during President's absence,
      comment on, **1959:** 288
    Based abroad, **1960–61:** 24
    Budget messages, **1955:** 17 (p. 109); **1958:** 5 (p.
      18); **1959:** 10 (pp. 66, 67); **1960–61:** 13
      (pp. 46, 58), 414 (pp. 947, 950–952, 956,
      959)
    Cablegram to Prime Minister Nehru, **1957:** 244
      and n.
    Denuclearization of Central Europe, Soviet pro-
      posal, **1958:** 7, 28
    Deterrent to war, **1954:** 25
    Development and testing, statement, **1956:** 266
    Disarmament, **1960–61:** 302
    Exchange of messages with Prime Minister
      Kishi, **1957:** 208 and n.
    Exchange with NATO countries, question of,
      1953: 265
    Expenditures for, **1960–61:** 24
    Information exchange with allies, **1954:** 3, 39;
      1958: 83
    Joint statements
      Chancellor Adenauer, **1957:** 100
      Prime Minister Kishi, **1957:** 117
      Prime Minister Macmillan, **1957:** 55, 226
    Letter to Premier Khrushchev, **1958:** 67
    Letters to Premier Bulganin, **1956:** 52, 166; **1958:**
      7, 31
    News conference remarks, **1953:** 12, 109, 208,
      230, 265; **1954:** 25, 39, 57, 192, 353; **1955:**
      10, 33, 41, 47, 56, 59, 149; **1956:** 32, 62,
      113; **1957:** 17, 28, 56, 80, 105, 119, 134,
      145; **1958:** 56, 63, 83, 88, 222; **1959:** 53,
      154, 288; **1960–61:** 24, 34, 38, 103, 422

Nuclear weapons — *continued*
 Nunn, Rear Adm. Ira H., **1959:** 89
 Presidential power re use of, **1959:** 154
 Small, **1956:** 266; **1957:** 70, 80, 192
 Soviet, **1953:** 6, 12, 205, 208, 246, 256; **1955:** 33,
   47; **1960–61:** 103, 422
 Spread to smaller nations, question of, **1960–61:**
   24, 38, 103
 Strategic and tactical, **1955:** 10, 56; **1958:** 88, 222
 United Kingdom and Canada, **1953:** 256
 Use by NATO, **1959:** 120; **1960–61:** 420
Nuclear weapons tests, **1954:** 72
 See also Nuclear weapons.
 AEC report on effects of, **1955:** 41, 56
 Antarctica, **1959:** 284
 Atmospheric, **1959:** 81
 Atomic bomb, **1953:** 31, 256
 Ban or suspension, **1955:** 41; **1956:** 88, 229, 230,
   235; **1957:** 105, 115, 119, 145, 158, 165;
   1958: 31, 70, 86, 288; **1960–61:** 4, 16, 23,
   24, 103, 127, 163, 263
  Geneva conference.
  See Geneva conferences.
 International agreement, proposed, **1960–61:**
   102
 Joint declaration with Prime Minister
   Macmillan, **1960–61:** 102
 Letters to Premier Khrushchev, **1959:** 81, 110
 Soviet Union, **1958:** 56, 63
 Statement, **1958:** 300
 United States, **1958:** 219, 222, 311; **1959:** 10 (p.
   67), 186, 191 ftn. (p. 615), 277, 348;
   1960–61: 34 and ftn. (p. 167), 38, 103, 222,
   256, 284
 White House statement on Khrushchev letter,
   1959: 110n.
 Budget message, **1958:** 5 (p. 33)
 Cablegram to Prime Minister Nehru, **1957:** 244
   and n.
 Campaign remarks, **1956:** 234, 258
 Detection, **1958:** 56, 63, 67, 70, 86; **1959:** 81, 110;
   1960–61: 102, 127
  Project VELA, **1960–61:** 143 ftn. (p. 410)
  Technical conference on.
  See Geneva conferences.
 Underground tests, **1959:** 81, 132 and ftn. (p.
   463), 277, 288, 348
 Exchange of messages with Prime Minister
   Kishi, **1957:** 208 and n.
 Fallout.
  See Radioactive fallout.
 Foreign observers, **1956:** 78
 Inspection and control, **1959:** 243; **1960–61:** 34,
   103, 127
  News conference remarks, **1959:** 48, 89, 102,
   132, 186, 191, 243, 277, 288
  Soviet proposal, **1959:** 110, 348; **1960–61:** 38
  U.K. proposal, **1959:** 48, 89, 102, 110

Nuclear weapons tests — *continued*
 Inspection and control — *continued*
  U.S. proposal, **1959:** 81, 89, 110
 International observation, **1957:** 55, 124; **1958:**
   37, 56, 67
 Joint statements with Prime Minister Macmillan,
   1957: 55, 226
 Letters to Premier Bulganin, **1956:** 262; **1958:** 7
 Letters to Premier Khrushchev, **1958:** 67, 86
 Memorandum, **1956:** 266n.
 Nevada, **1953:** 31
 News conference remarks, **1953:** 31, 109, 208;
   1954: 63, 68, 311, 341; **1956:** 5, 78, 88,
   113, 193, 229, 235; **1957:** 17, 87, 92, 105,
   115, 119, 124, 145; **1958:** 37, 56, 63, 70, 88,
   222, 288; **1960–61:** 24, 34 and ftn. (p.
   167), 38, 103, 127, 143 and ftn. (p. 410),
   222, 256, 263, 284
 News coverage, **1956:** 78
 Newsmen in attendance, question of, **1954:** 63
 Pacific, **1954:** 63, 68; **1955:** 56
  Statement, **1958:** 56
 Peaceful purposes, **1958:** 219
 Policies and actions, statement, **1956:** 266
 President's decision not to attend, **1956:** 78
 Soviet, **1953:** 109, 208; **1954:** 68, 311; **1955:** 185;
   1956: 191, 193, 229; **1958:** 56, 63, 74, 311
 Stassen proposal, comment on, **1958:** 37
 Suspension, disarmament proposal, **1957:** 158
 Underground tests, **1960–61:** 34 and ftn. (p. 167),
   38, 102, 103, 127, 143 and ftn. (p. 410),
   222, 256, 414 (p. 959)
Nurses, **1959:** 129
 Military career incentives, **1956:** 2, 81
 Training grants and traineeships, **1956:** 21, 161
 Training programs, **1955:** 25
Nutrition, Fifth International Congress, remarks,
   1960–61: 279
Nutting, Charles B., **1953:** 59

Oak Ridge, Tenn.
 Atomic facility
  Expansion, **1954:** 14 (p. 128)
  Federal ownership and operation, termination
    proposed, **1954:** 14 (p. 30)
  Labor dispute, **1954:** 161 and ftn. (p. 622), 192,
    193, 281
  Self-government, **1955:** 17 (p. 121)
OAS.
 See Organization of American States.
Oath of office, President, **1958:** 285
 Second term, **1957:** 15n.
Oath of office, Vice President, **1958:** 42
Oberdorfer, Don, **1958:** 222, 310; **1959:** 67, 102,
   132; **1960–61:** 7

O'Boyle, Archbishop Patrick A., **1953:** 251n.; **1958:** 286; **1959:** 64

O'Brien, Edward W., **1956:** 47, 155; **1958:** 274; **1959:** 172, 179

O'Brien, Frank, Jr., **1953:** 62

O'Brien, Lt. George H., Jr., Medal of Honor award, **1953:** 170, 229n.

O'Brien, Msgr. John A., **1953:** 132

O'Brien, John C., **1953:** 265; **1955:** 18

O'Brien, Peter J., claim for death of son, **1958:** 251

OCB.
   See Operations Coordinating Board.

Occidental College, **1956:** 298

Occupational diseases, **1959:** 129

Occupational safety, **1955:** 4; **1956:** 2, 226
   Budget message, **1956:** 12 (p. 117)
   Conference on, **1956:** 55, 104
      Remarks, **1958:** 55

Occupational Safety, President's Conference on, remarks, **1954:** 100

Occupational safety in Government, memorandum, **1954:** 288

Ocean freight payment, relief supplies, **1956:** 58
   U.N. Child Welfare Program, **1956:** 88

Oceanography
   Awards for research, **1960–61:** 25
   Budget messages, **1960–61:** 13 (p. 91), 414 (p. 999)

O'Connor, Basil, **1955:** 78
   Message to, **1956:** 1

O'Daniel, Lt. Gen. John W., **1954:** 39

Oder-Neisse line between Germany and Poland, **1959:** 191

O'Donnell, John, **1953:** 62

OEEC.
   See Organization for European Economic Cooperation.

Office, government, indiscretion in use of, **1955:** 176

Office buildings, Federal, construction of, **1959:** 10 (p. 108)

Office of Business Economics.
   See Business Economics, Office of.

Office of Coordinator of Public Works Planning, proposed, **1955:** 19

Office of Education.
   See Education, Office of.

Office of Executive Management, proposed, **1960–61:** 414 (pp. 945, 946), 422

Office of Price Stabilization.
   See Price Stabilization, Office of.

Office space, Presidential, **1960–61:** 133, 243
   Advisory Commission on, **1957:** 45, 105; **1960–61:** 414 (p. 1017)
      Proposed, **1956:** 131
   Budget message, **1960–61:** 414 (pp. 1017–1019)
   Heller report, **1957:** 45
   Letter, **1957:** 135 and n.

Official entertaining, proposed commission on, **1957:** 105

Offshore procurement contracts, **1955:** 76

Ogdensburg Declaration, U.S.-Canada (1940), joint statements with Prime Minister St. Laurent, **1953:** 70, 247

O'Hara, Repr. Joseph P., **1957:** 72

O'Higgins, Bernardo, **1960–61:** 69

Ohio
   Akron, **1956:** 90
   Ayres, Repr. William H., **1957:** 145; **1959:** 92n.
   Bender, George H., **1954:** 317; **1956:** 224, 229
   Bolton, Repr. Frances P., **1960–61:** 350
   Bricker, Sen. John W., **1953:** 31, 126, 215, 269; **1955:** 59; **1956:** 78, 224; **1957:** 50; **1958:** 310
   Brown, Repr. Clarence J., **1953:** 238; **1954:** 12n.; **1959:** 77n.
   Candidates for public office, **1954:** 317; **1956:** 224; **1960–61:** 350
   Cincinnati, **1954:** 301
   Cleveland, **1954:** 130, 317, 320; **1956:** 223, 224; **1960–61:** 350, 351, 352
   Defiance, **1953:** 215
   Defiance College, **1957:** 251n.
   Great Lakes water level discussion, **1956:** 177
   Jenkins, Repr. Thomas A., **1953:** 164; **1954:** 106n.
   Lausche, Gov. Frank J., **1953:** 215
   McGregor, Repr. J. Harry, **1954:** 33
   Minshall, Repr. William E., **1960–61:** 350
   Portsmouth, **1954:** 14 (p. 128)
   Taft, Sen. Robert A., **1953:** 15, 22, 41, 88, 98, 154, 159, 215
   Vorys, Repr. John M., **1956:** 184
   Waverly, **1957:** 88
   Willard, **1953:** 214

Ohio River bridge commissions, disapproval, **1956:** 182

Ohio State University, **1956:** 77

Ohio Wesleyan University, **1957:** 29n.

Oil
   Address to Canadian Parliament, **1958:** 163
   Alaskan oil leases, veto, **1959:** 182
   Conservation, interstate compacts, **1956:** 12 (p. 149)
   Distribution, memorandum, **1956:** 239
   Imports, **1953:** 62, 77, 141; **1955:** 33, 81; **1957:** 145; **1958:** 58, 96; **1959:** 67
      Controls, statement, **1959:** 51
      Proclamations re, statements, **1960–61:** 383, 432
   Recommendations of special committee on, **1958:** 54 and n.
   Special committee to investigate, **1957:** 145 ftn. (p. 581)
   Voluntary restrictions on, **1958:** 163

Oil — *continued*
  Iran, **1953:** 129; **1954:** 209, 273, 286; **1955:** 76
    Settlement of dispute with foreign companies,
      1954: 184, 185, 186, 226
  Middle East, **1956:** 62, 239
  Messages, **1957:** 6, 8
  Naval petroleum reserves, **1959:** 10 (p. 66), 17;
      1960–61: 414 (p. 956)
  Overseas supply, **1959:** 17
  Public utility controls over wells and producers,
      1957: 105
  Reserves, **1958:** 28
  Tidelands dispute.
    See Tidelands.
  U.S.-Canadian discussions on, **1958:** 153
  U.S. deliveries to Europe, **1957:** 28
Oil companies, U.S., overseas, **1957:** 13, 72, 80
  Aramco, **1957:** 72, 80
Oil depletion allowances, **1957:** 92, 145; **1958:** 28
Oil and gas leases on public domain lands, **1960–**
      61: 13 (p. 86), 414 (pp. 941, 997)
Oil and gas reserves, development, **1954:** 14 (p.
      171)
Oil seeds, price supports, **1954:** 4
Oil tankers, memorandum, **1956:** 239
Okala, Charles, **1960–61:** 324n.
O'Kelly, Sean T.
  Exchange of toasts, **1959:** 59, 64
  Message, **1956:** 208
  Remarks of welcome, **1959:** 58
O'Kelly, Mrs. Sean T., **1959:** 58, 59, 64
Okinawa
  U.S. bases in, **1954:** 3
  Visit to, **1960–61:** 177, 197, 209
Oklahoma, **1956:** 293; **1957:** 62
  Albert, Repr. Carl, **1956:** 184
  Cancellation of meeting, telegram, **1956:** 281n.
  Gary, Gov. Raymond, exchange of telegrams,
      1957: 229 and n.
  Monroney, Sen. Mike, **1953:** 249
  Murray, Gov. Johnston, **1954:** 85n., 99
  Semi-centennial celebration, **1957:** 229 and n.
  Washita River Basin reclamation project, **1956:**
      44
Oklahoma City, Okla., **1957:** 234
  Deffner, Hugo, **1957:** 94 and n.
  New Frontiers Exposition, **1957:** 229n.
O'Konski, Repr. Alvin E., **1953:** 225
Olav V, message, **1957:** 192
Old-age assistance, **1956:** 12 (pp. 118, 119)
Old-age and survivors insurance, **1953:** 6, 82, 268;
      1954: 10, 21, 145, 317; **1955:** 4, 13; **1956:**
      2, 3, 19; **1959:** 10 (pp. 102, 104, 105)
  Budget messages, **1954:** 14 (pp. 133, 141–144);
      1955: 17 (pp. 94, 134, 140, 141, 143–146);
      1956: 12 (pp. 111, 113, 118, 119); **1958:** 5
      (pp. 23, 51–53); **1960–61:** 13 (pp. 95, 96),
      127, 414 (pp. 942, 943, 1009–1011)

Old-age and survivors insurance — *continued*
  Campaign remarks, **1954:** 286, 317
  Claim of Helmuth W. Gruhl, **1953:** 103
  Extension of coverage, **1954:** 221, 235, 286
  Proposed, **1953:** 95, 155, 159
  Military service credits, **1958:** 5 (p. 53)
  Servicemen and veterans, **1956:** 12 (pp. 111, 113),
      81n.
    Appropriation, **1956:** 157
  Social security amendments, **1956:** 158; **1958:**
      234
  Trust fund, **1953:** 82, 84; **1954:** 14 (p. 144);
      1960–61: 13 (p. 96), 414 (pp. 942, 943,
      1009, 1011)
Old-Age and Survivors Insurance, Bureau of,
      lump-sum death payment to Mrs. Jean
      Pfeifer, disapproval, **1956:** 160
Old Man of the Mountain, 150th anniversary of
      discovery, remarks, **1955:** 136
Old Rag Mountain, Va., **1960–61:** 340
Old River Control project, La., **1955:** 17 (p. 160)
Older persons.
  See also Aged persons.
  Budget messages, **1960–61:** 13 (pp. 95, 96), 414
      (pp. 939, 1010–1012)
  Campaign remarks, **1956:** 190, 226, 241
  Ebenezer Home for the Aged, remarks, **1953:** 99
  Effects of inflation, **1955:** 41; **1956:** 235, 263;
      1958: 120, 308
  Employment, **1956:** 12 (p. 117), 226
  Federal aid for needy, **1960–61:** 13 (p. 95), 127
      ftn. (p. 362), 410, 414 (p. 1010)
  Federal Council on Aging, **1956:** 63, 74; **1959:** 49
    Report, letter, **1959:** 280
  Financial security, **1959:** 124, 129
  Health, message, **1956:** 21
  Housing, **1956:** 2, 12 (pp. 139, 145, 146), 19, 63,
      252, 256; **1958:** 5 (p. 59); **1959:** 153, 208;
      1960–61: 410
  Letter to Sen. Smith re problems of, **1956:** 63
  Medical care, **1955:** 25; **1959:** 167; **1960–61:** 103,
      133, 255, 203, 410, 414 (pp. 939, 1010,
      1011)
  News conference remarks, **1955:** 41, 119; **1956:**
      235
  Public assistance, **1956:** 12 (p. 118)
  White House Conference on Aging (1961), **1959:**
      10 (p. 104), 49, 280; **1960–61:** 13 (p. 96),
      398, 414 (p. 1012)
O'Leary, Jerry A., **1954:** 18; **1959:** 102, 132, 172;
      1960–61: 34
Oleomargarine prices, **1953:** 41
Olin, Spencer, **1958:** 287
Olive Branch Petition (1775), **1960–61:** 171n.
Oliver, D. Harold, **1953:** 109, 128
Olofson, Darwin R., **1953:** 225
Olympic Committee, International, **1959:** 132
  Remarks, **1954:** 287

Olympic Day, **1954:** 287
Olympic games (1956), **1960–61:** 24
Olympic games (1960), **1958:** 5 (pp. 72–73)
Omaha, Nebr.
  See under Nebraska.
O'Mahoney, Sen. Joseph C., **1957:** 72, 124
O'Mara, Adelaide, **1956:** 241
O'Neill, Michael J., **1958:** 11; **1959:** 167, 191
O'Neill, Thomas, **1953:** 62
Ontario, Canada, **1959:** 141n.
  St. Lawrence power project, **1953:** 22, 31, 77
  St. Lawrence Seaway project, **1954:** 14 (pp. 175, 176)
"Open skies," **1957:** 8, 80, 245; **1960–61:** 143, 163, 209
  See also Disarmament; Inspection and control of nuclear weapons.
Operation Alert.
  See Civil defense.
Operation Overlord, **1960–61:** 405
Operation Pan America, **1959:** 287; **1960–61:** 49, 53, 87, 228
  Joint statement with President Alessandri, **1960–61:** 76
  Joint statement with President Kubitschek, **1960–61:** 46
Operation Skywatch, 3rd anniversary, letter to Secretary Wilson, **1955:** 154
Operational and executive personnel program, U.N., **1960–61:** 302
Operations Coordinating Board, **1954:** 354; **1957:** 194; **1958:** 63; **1960–61:** 9, 380, 412n.
  Letter to Chairman, **1960–61:** 8
Oppenheimer, J. Robert, **1953:** 128; **1958:** 11
  Case, comments on, **1954:** 92, 129, 143, 157
Order of Liberation, **1958:** 120
Order of Sikatuna, Rajah, presentation to the President, **1960–61:** 188
Oregon
  Candidates for public office, **1956:** 54, 255, 256
  Certain public lands in, administrative jurisdiction over, approval, **1954:** 152
  Coon, Repr. Sam, **1956:** 256
  Cordon, Sen. Guy, **1954:** 34, 152, 271, 272
  Ellsworth, Repr. Harris, **1954:** 34, 152; **1956:** 256
  Eugene, **1954:** 34; **1956:** 12 (p. 134)
  Forest areas, construction of access roads to, **1954:** 14 (p. 170)
  Morse, Sen. Wayne, **1953:** 15; **1955:** 100; **1957:** 150
  Norblad, Repr. Walter, **1956:** 256
  Patterson, Gov. Paul, **1954:** 271, 272
    Death of, statement, **1956:** 25
  Pendleton, **1954:** 272
  Portland.
    See main heading, Portland.
  Primary election, **1956:** 121
  Roth, Philip, **1956:** 256

Oregon — *continued*
  Smith, Gov. Elmo, **1956:** 256
  Umatilla, **1954:** 271
Oregon and California Railroad, **1954:** 152
Organization of American States, **1956:** 114, 146, 218; **1957:** 64, 91, 96, 177 and n., 226; **1958:** 207; **1959:** 98, 287; **1960–61:** 22, 36, 42, 49, 72, 73, 78, 80, 87, 109, 111, 267, 303, 374, 410
  See also American Republics.
  Address before Council, **1953:** 48
  Bogota economic conference, **1960–61:** 228 and ftn. (p. 569), 256
  Caribbean situation, **1959:** 148, 161
  Committee of Nine, **1960–61:** 49
  Costa Rican dispute, action on, **1955:** 10
  Council on economic cooperation, **1960–61:** 49n., 255, 267
  Cuba, action, on, **1960–61:** 263
  Dominican Republic, action on, **1960–61:** 263
  Foreign ministers meetings
    San Jose (1960), **1960–61:** 228, 263, 267, 268
    Santiago (1959), **1960–61:** 73, 76, 228
  Guatemalan situation, **1955:** 156
  Joint statements
    President Kubitschek, **1960–61:** 46
    President Lopez Mateos **1959:** 38
    Prime Minister Macmillan, **1957:** 226
  Letter to President Kubitschek, **1958:** 197
  News conference remarks, **1955:** 10, 26; **1959:** 94, 148, 161; **1960–61:** 222, 228, 268
  Technical assistance, **1956:** 12 (p. 106), 58
    Funds for, **1958:** 32
    U.S. contributions, **1955:** 76; **1959:** 55
Organization of American States, Council of, address, **1953:** 48
Organization for Economic Cooperation and Development, **1960–61:** 414 (p. 965)
Organization for European Economic Cooperation, **1956:** 114; **1959:** 200; **1960–61:** 4, 263
  Budget message, **1960–61:** 414 (p. 965)
  Joint Statements
    Chancellor Adenauer, **1960–61:** 92
    General Franco, **1959:** 340
    Prime Minister Eden, **1956:** 26
    Western leaders, **1959:** 335
Organization for Trade Cooperation, **1956:** 2, 19, 87, 310
  Budget messages, **1956:** 12 (p. 110); **1958:** 5 (p. 38)
  Messages and remarks, **1957:** 8, 13, 16, 32, 61, 110 and n.
  News conference remarks, **1956:** 94 and ftn. (p. 452)
  U.S. membership proposed, **1955:** 129, 160, 248
    Message, **1955:** 72
  White House statement, **1957:** 2

Organization of World Touring and Automobile Clubs, General Assembly, remarks, **1955:** 93

Orioles, baseball team, **1960–61:** 290

Orosa, José, **1960–61:** 187

Orphans, admission to U.S., **1957:** 25; **1959:** 10 (p. 110)

    Recommendations under Refugee Relief Act, **1955:** 109

Orr, Dr. Louis M., **1959:** 129

Orthopaedic Association of the English-Speaking World, remarks, **1958:** 104

O'Shaughnessy, Elim (U.S. Charge d'Affaires at Moscow), **1953:** 134, 135

Osler, William, **1959:** 129

Osman, Aden A., message, **1960–61:** 219

Ota, Seisaku, **1960–61:** 197

O.T.C.

    See Organization for Trade Cooperation.

Ottawa, Canada, **1953:** 208, 246; **1956:** 71n.; **1959:** 141

    Address to Canadian Parliament, **1958:** 163

Our Lady of the Lake Church, relief of, veto, **1960–61:** 179

Outdoor Recreation Resources Review Commission, **1959:** 10 (pp. 95, 96); **1960–61:** 414 (p. 998)

Outer Continental Shelf, **1960–61:** 13 (p. 86), 414 (p. 997)

    Oil and gas reserves, **1954:** 14 (p. 171)

Outer space.

    See Space, outer.

Ovens, Michael D., bill for relief of, **1957:** 181

Ovens, Verne E., **1957:** 181

Ovens, Mrs. Verne E., **1957:** 181

Overby, Andrew N., **1953:** 33, 213n.

Overholser, Dr. Winfred, President's Award for Distinguished Federal Civilian Service, **1960–61:** 68n.

Overlord operation, World War II, **1959:** 7; **1960–61:** 405

Overseas Americans, message, **1959:** 152

Overseas personnel, Federal, **1955:** 8

Overseas Press Club, **1954:** 350

Oxcart, **1958:** 93

Oxnam, Bishop G. Bromley, **1953:** 15

Oyster Bay, N.Y., **1953:** 105

Oyster Bowl Game, **1957:** 207

Paarlberg, Don, **1958:** 274; **1959:** 161; **1960–61:** 136n., 242n.

Paasikivi, Juho Kusti, death of, message, **1956:** 311

Pace, Frank, Jr., **1960–61:** 30n., 240n.

Pacific air routes, **1956:** 14, 56

Pacific area, western, **1958:** 261, 277

Pacific Charter, **1954:** 297, 329; **1955:** 4

Pacific Customs Brokerage Company, bill for relief of, **1957:** 183

Pacific Islands, Trust Territory of the, **1954:** 125, 126

    Budget message, **1954:** 14 (p. 190)

Pacific Northern Airlines

    Certification, **1955:** 106

    Permanent certification, **1957:** 162

Pacific Northwest, **1956:** 12 (p. 136), 256

Pacific Proving Ground, nuclear tests, **1955:** 56; **1956:** 5, 78, 266; **1957:** 92, 105; **1958:** 56

Paducah, Ky., atomic facility

    Expansion, **1954:** 14 (p. 128)

    Labor dispute, **1954:** 161 and ftn. (p. 622), 192, 193, 281

Page, Mr. and Mrs. Charles H., bill for relief of, **1957:** 180

Page, Charles H., Jr., **1957:** 180

Page, Robert M., President's Award for Distinguished Federal Civilian Service, **1960–61:** 68n.

Pageant of Peace, remarks, **1954:** 355; **1955:** 250; **1956:** 315; **1957:** 248 and n.; **1958:** 325; **1959:** 347; **1960–61:** 381

Pahlavi, Mohammad Reza, **1953:** 22; **1954:** 353; **1959:** 319, 320, 321, 323

    Joint statement with, **1959:** 322

    Letters, **1954:** 184; **1958:** 174

    Messages, **1954:** 264; **1955:** 42; **1960–61:** 126

Painting, avocation of President, **1956:** 20

Pakistan, **1954:** 273; **1955:** 4; **1956:** 2; **1957:** 6

    See also Karachi.

    Ambassador William Rountree, **1959:** 299n., 301n., 304n., 305n.

    Assistance, **1953:** 95, 97, 109, 119, 124, 143, 249; **1954:** 14 (p. 139); **1956:** 12 (p. 104); **1959:** 55, 94, 302, 303; **1960–61:** 36

        Letter to Prime Minister Nehru of India, **1954:** 44

        Statement, **1954:** 45

    Atomic energy for peaceful uses, **1959:** 302

    Ayub Khan, Mohammed, **1959:** 299, 302, 304, 305; **1960–61:** 284, 297

        Joint statement with, **1959:** 303

    Cultural exchange with United States, **1959:** 302

    Dispute with India, **1959:** 288

    Flood relief, **1954:** 195n.

    Freedom from Communist domination, **1953:** 156

    Indus River Basin development, **1960–61:** 36, 284

    India-Pakistan Pact, statement, **1960–61:** 297

    Kashmir dispute with India, **1960–61:** 284

    Military agreement with Turkey, **1954:** 44, 45

    Mirza, Iskander, **1958:** 174

        Letter, **1956:** 65

    Mohammed Ali, **1953:** 249

        Message, **1953:** 124

Pakistan — *continued*
  Mutual defense assistance, **1957:** 91, 131, 136,
    157
  News conference remarks, **1959:** 94, 277, 288
  SEATO.
    See Southeast Asia Treaty Organization.
  Suhrawardy, Huseyn Shaheed, Joint statement,
    1957: 131
  Visit to, **1959:** 299, 301, 302, 303, 304, 305
    Comment on, **1959:** 277
  Wheat for drought relief, **1953:** 95, 159
    Approval of bill, **1953:** 119
    Message to Congress, **1953:** 97
    Message to Prime Minister Mohammed Ali,
      1953: 124
"Palace guard," comment on, **1958:** 63
Palestine, **1957:** 6
  Development of water resources, **1955:** 76
  Refugees, **1953:** 89; **1956:** 58, 298; **1958:** 207
    Budget message, **1956:** 12 (p. 107)
    U.N. activities, report, **1958:** 8
Palestine Armistice Agreements, **1958:** 207
Palestinian mandated territory, **1956:** 282
Palm Springs, Calif, **1960–61:** 331n.
Palmer, H. Bruce, **1959:** 274
Pan American games, **1957:** 45
Pan American Highway, **1955:** 93
Pan American Medical Association
  Letter to Executive Director (Dr. Joseph J.
    Eller), **1953:** 260
  Remarks to officers, **1953:** 259
Pan American Society of the United States, award
  to the President, **1957:** 64 and n.
Pan American Union, **1953:** 48; **1957:** 96n.; **1959:**
  98
Pan American World Airways, **1957:** 162
  Certification, **1955:** 30, 33
  Use of Great Circle route, letter, **1956:** 14
Pan Americanism, **1958:** 133
Panama, **1956:** 130, 142; **1959:** 50
  Anti-U.S. demonstrations, comment on, **1959:**
    277
  Arias Espinosa, Ricardo M., **1956:** 101, 145
  Compensation claims of U.S. nationals, **1954:** 94
  Congress of Panama (1826), **1956:** 96
  Declaration of Principles, **1956:** 146
  Guizado, Jose Ramon, **1955:** 2
  Joint statement with President Remon Cantera,
    1953: 200
  Meeting of Presidents of American Republics,
    1956: 96, 121, 145, 146, 155, 272, 278;
    1957: 96n., 228
  News conference remarks, **1956:** 96, 121, 155,
    171, 189
  Reminiscence re service in, **1958:** 287
  Remon, Jose Antonio, **1955:** 2
  Transfer of property to, **1957:** 167
  U.S.-Panama treaties, **1956:** 12 (p. 153); **1959:**
    277, 288; **1960–61:** 24

Panama Canal, **1953:** 200; **1960–61:** 382
  Budget messages, **1960–61:** 13 (pp. 69, 70), 414
    (p. 976)
  Flag of Panama flown in Canal Zone, **1959:** 288;
    1960–61: 24 and ftn. (p. 150)
  Internationalization or construction of second
    canal, comment on, **1959:** 277
Panama Canal Company, **1954:** 14 (p. 178)
  Budget messages, **1960–61:** 13 (p. 70), 414 (p.
    976)
  Operation of Panama Steamship Line, **1960–61:**
    382, 414 (p. 976)
  Passenger lists, **1956:** 235
Panama Canal Zone, **1954:** 14 (p. 190); **1956:** 12 (p.
  153)
  Inter-American highway, **1955:** 64
Panama Steamship Line, **1960–61:** 382, 414 (p. 976)
Pandit, Mme. Vijaya, **1953:** 256
  Conference with, statement, **1953:** 210
Panel on Seismic Improvement, **1960–61:** 143 ftn.
  (p. 410)
  Report (Berkner report), **1959:** 132 and ftn. (p.
    463)
Panmunjom, Korea, **1953:** 87, 102
Pantelas, George, deportation case, disapproval,
  1954: 215
Pantelleria, **1960–61:** 355
  Capture of, **1955:** 59
Paola, Princess, **1960–61:** 317
Papers of the President, **1960–61:** 21
  Offer as gift to U.S., **1960–61:** 118
Paperwork management program, comment on
  proposal, **1955:** 41
Paperwork reduction, **1956:** 110, 263; **1958:** 5 (p.
  52)
  Hoover Commission recommendations, **1955:** 41
Pardons, Presidential, disclosure of, **1953:** 95
Parent Teachers Associations, **1957:** 234
Paris, **1953:** 71; **1957:** 243, 244, 245, 246, 247; **1959:**
  202n., 203n., 204n.; **1960–61:** 124, 279
  Anderson-Dillon discussions with officials,
    1960–61: 365
  Capture plans of allies (1944), **1959:** 7
  East-West summit (1960), proposed, **1959:** 336,
    337, 349
  Heads of government meeting (1951), **1955:** 59
  Meeting with President de Gaulle, **1959:** 202, 214
  Meeting of Prime Ministers of French Com-
    munity, **1959:** 214
  Meeting of Western leaders, **1959:** 271 ftn. (p.
    748), 277, 335, 336
  NATO Council meetings, **1953:** 54, 66, 70, 265
    ftn. (p. 843); **1959:** 277 ftn. (p. 766);
    1960–61: 163
  Pact of Paris, **1958:** 31
  Trade council, **1960–61:** 103

Paris — *continued*
  Visit to (1959), **1960–61:** 121, 260n.
    Remarks on arrival, **1959:** 199
    Remarks on departure, **1959:** 207
    Remarks at Hotel de Ville, **1959:** 201
    Remarks to Permanent Council, NATO, **1959:**
      205
    Remarks at SHAPE headquarters, **1959:** 206
    Remarks at U.S. embassy, **1959:** 334
  World War II, **1958:** 288
Paris agreements (1954), **1954:** 282n., 307, 314, 320,
    332, 351
  News conference remarks, **1954:** 311, 341
  Ratification by France, statement, **1954:** 357
Paris agreements (1955), **1955:** 54, 164
  News conference remarks, **1955:** 41, 59, 62
  Ratification by France and Italy, comment on,
    1955: 62
Paris 9-power conference, **1954:** 297, 332, 337
Paris summit meeting (1960), **1960–61:** 16, 71, 73,
    129n., 158, 160, 162, 209, 245, 313, 410
  Joint statement with President de Gaulle and
      Prime Minister Macmillan, **1960–61:** 155
  Joint statement with Prime Minister Kishi,
      1960–61: 16
  News conference remarks, **1960–61:** 7, 34, 38, 93,
      103, 127, 143
  Remarks on arrival, **1960–61:** 147
  Remarks on departure, **1960–61:** 156
  Statement on position taken by Premier
      Khrushchev, **1960–61:** 154
Paris Treaty, **1954:** 154, 189n.
Parity index, campaign remarks, **1954:** 317, 318
Parity prices, **1956:** 82, 83, 214; **1957:** 45; **1958:** 12,
    37
  News conference remarks, **1956:** 62, 78
Park, Air Vice Marshal, **1960–61:** 405
Park police, U.S., increase in benefits, disapproval,
    1959: 239
Park Service, National.
  See National Park Service.
Parke, Davis & Co., **1955:** 100
Parker, John, **1956:** 205
Parker (Mack Charles) case
  News conference remarks, **1959:** 94, 123
  Telegram to Gov. Coleman, **1959:** 88
Parks, monuments, and historic sites, national,
    1955: 4, 17 (p. 163)
Parks, national, **1953:** 153; **1954:** 3; **1955:** 4, 17 (p.
    163); **1956:** 2; **1960–61:** 341, 410
  Budget messages, **1954:** 14 (pp. 164, 170); **1956:**
    12 (pp. 133, 137, 138); **1960–61:** 13 (p. 86),
    414 (p. 998)
  Campaign remarks, **1956:** 256
  Conservation, **1959:** 10 (p. 95)
  Gettysburg National Military Park, **1954:** 303
  Grand Teton National Park, **1954:** 222
  Improvement of roads and facilities, **1958:** 43

Parks, national — *continued*
  Mission 66, **1956:** 12 (p. 138), 29, 256; **1960–61:**
    402, 410
  Vicksburg National Military Park facility, **1958:**
    226
Parliamentary system of government, comment on,
    1959: 123
Parmachenee lake, Maine, **1955:** 140n.
Partisan politics, comment on, **1954:** 33, 39
Party alignments, **1956:** 171
Party responsibility, **1956:** 47, 268, 298
  Comment on, **1959:** 223
Party responsibility of President, **1954:** 128
Party system, news conference remarks, **1957:** 105
Passamaquoddy Bay hydroelectric power survey,
    1955: 17 (p. 161); **1956:** 12 (p. 136)
Passchendaele, Belgium, **1959:** 7
Passport control
  Authority of Secretary of State, **1959:** 10 (p. 75)
  Message, **1958:** 161
Passports, letters included with, **1957:** 141
Pasternak, Boris, **1958:** 310
Pasteur, Louis, **1959:** 107
Pastore, Sen. John O., **1959:** 113
Patagonia, Argentina, **1960–61:** 62
Patent fees, **1958:** 5 (p. 45)
Patent Office, **1956:** 12 (p. 148)
Patents in atomic energy, **1954:** 38
Paterson (N. J.) *Evening News*, editorial on reces-
    sion, **1958:** 37
Patil, S. K., **1960–61:** 136
Patrick Henry, U.S.S., **1960–61:** 360
  Firing of Polaris missile, statement, **1960–61:** 244
Patterson, F. D., **1953:** 81
Patterson, Garnet L., **1953:** 59
Patterson, James J., **1954:** 50
Patterson, Gov. John, **1960–61:** 287
Patterson, John S., **1959:** 18n.
Patterson, Morehead, **1954:** 322
Patterson, Gov. Paul, **1954:** 271, 272
  Death of, statement, **1956:** 25
Patterson, Mrs. Paul, **1956:** 25
Patton, Gen. George S., **1955:** 81; **1956:** 229; **1957:**
    246
Paul I, **1953:** 230; **1959:** 324, 326, 327
  Exchange of toasts, **1953:** 233
  Legion of Merit, citation, **1953:** 233
  Messages, **1953:** 172; **1956:** 140; **1957:** 48
  Welcoming remarks to, **1953:** 232
Paul, Willard S., **1959:** 71
Pavilion at Brussels Exhibition, U.S., **1958:** 79
Pay, **1958:** 2, 20
  Advisory Committee on Professional and Tech-
      nical Compensation (Defense Depart-
      ment), **1957:** 13
  Armed forces, **1958:** 2
  Bill for relief of Walter H. Berry, **1957:** 155

Pay — *continued*
Bills providing increases for Federal employees,
1957: 185
Campaign remarks, **1958:** 296, 303, 308
Claims of D. A. Whitaker and others, **1958:** 255
Commission on Judicial and Congressional,
1958: 169
Congress, **1953:** 77; **1955:** 47
Equal pay for equal work, **1956:** 2, 190, 253, 272;
1958: 5 (p. 50); **1959:** 10 (p. 101)
Legislation proposed, **1957:** 13
Government employees, **1954:** 43, 313, 349;
1955: 4, 8, 59; **1956:** 2; **1958:** 5 (pp. 25,
71), 120, 169; **1960–61:** 13 (pp. 103, 104),
255, 414 (pp. 938, 1020)
Disapproval of bill, **1954:** 208
Proposed commission on, **1959:** 10 (pp. 108,
109)
Scientists and technicians, **1958:** 64
Veto of bill, **1960–61:** 217
Judges, **1955:** 47
Military personnel, **1954:** 349, 351; **1955:** 4, 13,
59; **1958:** 2, 5 (pp. 25, 30, 31, 71), 120;
1959: 10 (p. 59); **1960–61:** 13 (p. 49), 255
Retirement pay, **1960–61:** 414 (p. 956)
Postal employees, **1955:** 4, 9, 59, 90, 100; **1958:** 5
(pp. 25, 55, 71), 117, 120; **1959:** 10 (pp. 50,
81); **1960–61:** 13 (p. 104), 217
Approval of Postal Field Service Compensa-
tion Act, **1955:** 120
Veto of bill, **1955:** 102
Wage and incentive plan, **1956:** 2
Quarantine inspection personnel, overtime pay,
1954: 218
Teachers, **1959:** 6, 7, 118
Payne, Ethel, **1954:** 33, 57, 63, 73, 101, 143, 161,
182; **1955:** 26
Payne, Sen. Frederick G., **1955:** 142
Bill for relief of depressed areas, **1958:** 120
Payroll Savings Plan, **1954:** 15
Letter to Mrs. Priest, Chairman of Committee,
1955: 186
Memorandum on, **1955:** 187
Paz Estenssoro, Victor, letter, **1953:** 213
Peace, address on, **1953:** 50; **1960–61:** 164
Peace commission, comment on, **1958:** 141
Peace Corps, comment on, **1960–61:** 350
Peace force, United Nations, **1958:** 207
Peace pipe, presentation to President, **1958:** 142
Peaceful coexistence with Soviet Union, **1957:** 100
Peaceful use of Antarctica, statement, **1958:** 92
Peaceful uses of atomic energy.
See Atomic energy for peaceful uses; Atoms-
for-Peace Program.
Peaceful uses of outer space.
See Space, outer.
Peale, Norman Vincent, **1957:** 232 and n.

Peanuts
Acreage allotment, **1956:** 6; **1958:** 12
Price supports, **1954:** 4; **1956:** 83; **1959:** 23
Pearl Harbor, attack on, **1954:** 9, 57; **1958:** 65, 90,
124, 159, 222; **1960–61:** 163, 336
Pearson, Drew, *U.S.A.: Second-Class Power?*, **1959:**
167
Pearson, Lester B., **1953:** 70, 104
Peasant Union Forum, International, **1953:** 264
Peaslee, Amos J., **1956:** 155
Peenemünde, Germany, **1957:** 210
Peiping, China, **1955:** 16; **1957:** 28; **1958:** 261, 263
Pelka, Fred, **1956:** 241
Pella, Giuseppe, **1959:** 203, 248, 291, 293, 294n.
Pendleton, Oreg., remarks at airport, **1954:** 272
Penghu (Pescadores) Islands, **1955:** 18, 21, 24n., 33;
1958: 261, 277; **1960–61:** 143
Letter to Premier Khrushchev re, **1958:** 263
News conference remarks, **1958:** 222, 274
Penman, Florence P., relief of, disapproval, **1954:**
229
Penn, William, **1956:** 120n.
Pennsylvania, **1958:** 28; **1959:** 67, 75
Bonin, Repr. Edward J., **1954:** 341
Candidates for public office, **1954:** 304; **1956:**
234; **1957:** 56; **1958:** 56, 303; **1960–61:**
354
Corbett, Repr. Robert J., **1956:** 234
Depressed areas, **1960–61:** 176n.
Duff, Sen. James H., **1953:** 128; **1954:** 341; **1956:**
234, 283
Easton, **1960–61:** 288
Fine, Gov. John S., **1954:** 35n., 304
Fulton, Repr. James G., **1956:** 234
Gettysburg, **1954:** 31, 32, 303, 304; **1955:** 237,
239n., 240n., 241n., 242n., 243n., 244n.,
245n.; **1956:** 20, 136, 137, 138, 139, 140,
151, 155, 206, 207n., 208n., 314; **1957:** 62,
87, 150, 157, 235, 250n.; **1958:** 1n., 103,
123, 283n.; **1959:** 1n., 65n., 68n., 117n.,
179, 180n., 182n., 225n., 241n., 242n.
Editor's note, **1955:** p. 822
Gubernatorial election, **1953:** 128
Hershey, **1953:** 211, 212
Kelley, Repr. Augustine B., **1956:** 94
Leader, Gov. George M., **1957:** 38
Levittown, **1954:** 101; **1959:** 179
Ligonier, **1958:** 269
Martin, Sen. Edward, **1953:** 268; **1954:** 111;
1956: 234; **1958:** 269, 303
McConnell, Repr. Samuel K., Jr., **1953:** 266;
1954: 9; **1956:** 94
Morgan, Repr. Thomas E., **1956:** 184
Nixon for President Committee
Message, **1960–61:** 337
Rally, address, **1960–61:** 341
Philadelphia.
See main heading, Philadelphia.

Pennsylvania — *continued*
Pittsburgh.
See main heading, Pittsburgh.
Primary elections, **1956:** 88; **1958:** 30, 103
Reading, **1958:** 303
Rehabilitation of hard coal region, commission on, **1954:** 168
Republican Rally, remarks, **1953:** 212
Saylor, Repr. John P., **1956:** 234
Scott, Repr. Hugh, **1958:** 303; **1959:** 150; **1960–61:** 176, 354
Shippingport, **1954:** 260; **1956:** 263; **1958:** 113; **1959:** 10 (p. 67)
Simpson, Repr. Richard M., **1953:** 41, 54, 141; **1954:** 157; **1956:** 234; **1957:** 108, 169; **1959:** 127n.
Death of, **1960–61:** 3
Stassen campaign badge, **1958:** 56
Valley Forge, **1953:** 137, 271; **1954:** 32; **1956:** 122
Van Zandt, Repr. James E., **1960–61:** 31n.
Walter, Repr. Francis E., **1955:** 59, 62
Water drainage in anthracite coal region, **1955:** 17 (p. 163)
Western Pennsylvania District Court, **1959:** 265n.
Wood, Lt. Gov. Lloyd H., **1954:** 304
Pennsylvania Academy of Fine Arts, **1959:** 148 ftn. (p. 490)
Pennsylvania Monument, Gettysburg National Park, **1954:** 303, 304
Pennsylvania State College, **1953:** 48, 101
Pennsylvania State University, **1957:** 196n.
Atomic reactor, **1955:** 121
Commencement address, **1955:** 121
News conference remarks on, **1955:** 149
Pension plans and funds.
See Welfare and pension plans and funds.
Pensions, veterans, **1954:** 14 (p. 133), 220
Budget message, **1956:** 12 (p. 111)
Commission on, **1956:** 2, 267n.
Pentagon reprograming, **1957:** 169
Peony Park, Inc., and others, tax refund claim, disapproval, **1959:** 229
"People Ask the President," **1956:** 241
People-to-people conference, remarks, **1956:** 204
People-to-people program, **1956:** 114, 121; **1958:** 36, 91, 104, 125, 142; **1960–61:** 72, 209, 315, 319
See also Cultural exchange; East-West contacts; Exchange of persons; Exchange of students; Exchange of teachers.
American Field Service, **1958:** 168; **1959:** 164
Budget message, **1958:** 5 (p. 40)
Latin America, **1958:** 288
"People's Capitalism," exhibit, **1956:** 75
Peoria, Ill., **1956:** 216
Campaign address, **1956:** 214
Campaign remarks (1952), **1955:** 18

Pepin, Lake, **1960–61:** 330
Pepper, Claude, **1955:** 210
Percy, Charles H., **1954:** 119; **1956:** 242
Peress, Irving, **1954:** 48
Pericles, Age of, **1955:** 121; **1957:** 235; **1958:** 93
Perishable agricultural commodities, **1956:** 12 (pp. 126, 130), 83, 214, 216
Perkins, Fred W., **1953:** 41, 208; **1956:** 171
Perkins, George W., **1955:** 71
Permanent Joint Board on Defense, United States and Canada, **1953:** 246
Joint statements with Prime Minister St. Laurent, **1953:** 70, 247
Peron, Juan D., **1956:** 216
Campaign remarks on, **1956:** 251, 272, 278
Pershing missile (short-range).
See Missiles.
Persian Gulf, **1956:** 26
Personnel Administration, Conference of the Society for, remarks, **1954:** 108
Personnel management, Federal, **1954:** 311; **1955:** 8; **1959:** 10 (pp. 108, 109)
Personnel Management, President's Adviser on (Philip Young).
Fund-raising campaigns, policy, **1956:** 132n.
Report on personnel and civil service, letter, **1956:** 22
Resignation, **1957:** 33 and n.
Personnel Management, Special Assistant to the President for (Eugene L. Lyons), **1960–61:** 26, 28
Memorandum, **1960–61:** 27
Personnel system, Federal, statement, **1954:** 43
Persons, Maj. Gen. Wilton B., **1958:** 274; **1960–61:** 369
Peru, **1957:** 157
Beltran, Pedro G., **1960–61:** 247
Berckemeyer, Fernando, **1959:** 244n.
Demonstration during visit of Vice President, **1958:** 101
Development program, statement, **1960–61:** 247
Economic problems, **1958:** 103
Prado y Ugarteche, Manuel, **1960–61:** 247
Pescadores (Penghu) Islands.
See Penghu (Pescadores) Islands.
Petersen, Theodore S., **1955:** 51n.
Letter, **1955:** 125
Peterson, Elmer, *Big Dam Foolishness*, **1955:** 56
Peterson, Frank D., **1956:** 226
Peterson, Val, **1955:** 209
See also Federal Civil Defense Administrator (Val Peterson).
Letter, **1956:** 142
Petitpierre, Max, **1955:** 163
Petroleum.
See Oil.
Petty, Milburn, **1953:** 77; **1956:** 16; **1957:** 105; **1959:** 161

Peurifoy, Daniel, death of, statement, **1955:** 195
Peurifoy, John E., **1954:** 192
    Death of, statement, **1955:** 195
Peurifoy, Mrs. John E. **1955:** 195
Peyton, Wesley G., **1954:** 161
Pfeifer, Jean, relief of, **1956:** 160
Pfeiffer, William M., **1953:** 68, 69
Philadelphia, Pa., **1954:** 130; **1955:** 210; **1956:** 208,
    265; **1958:** 138n., 303; **1959:** 148 ftn. (p.
    490); **1960–61:** 45, 304, 305, 309n., 337,
    341
    Campaign address, **1956:** 283
    Clark, Mayor Joseph S., **1954:** 160
    Civil defense, **1955:** 56
    Display of 49-star flag on Independence Hall,
    1959: 150
    Fourth of July ceremonies, Independence Hall,
    1954: 160
    IRS Regional Office, **1960–61:** 288
Philip, Prince, **1957:** 218, 220n.; **1959:** 141; **1960–
    61:** 40
    National Geographic Society Medal presenta-
    tion, **1957:** 221
Philippine-American Day, message, **1960–61:** 359
Philippines, **1954:** 94; **1958:** 71; **1959:** 338; **1960–
    61:** 42, 80
    Ambassador Charles E. Bohlen, **1959:** 161, 167
    Ambassador John D. Hickerson, **1960–61:** 182n.,
    189
    Assistance, **1954:** 14 (pp. 127, 139); **1959:** 55;
    1960–61: 189, 341
    Bataan Day, **1957:** 69 and n.; **1958:** 69
    Campaign remarks, **1958:** 293
    Chamber of Commerce, **1960–61:** 187
    Defense treaty with United States, **1953:** 96
    Economy, **1960–61:** 189
    Elections, **1953:** 239, 243
    Garcia, Carlos P., **1957:** 56, 69 and n.; **1958:** 69,
    139, 140, 141; **1959:** 73; **1960–61:** 182,
    185, 188, 190
        Joint statements with, **1958:** 143; **1960–61:** 189
        Messages, **1960–61:** 106, 112, 359
    Independence, **1955:** 69
    Magsaysay, Ramon, **1954:** 101; **1957:** 52, 56, 166
        Message, **1956:** 80
    Malacanang, **1958:** 140n.
    Manila.
        See main heading, Manila.
    Military alliance, **1958:** 96
    Mindanao, **1958:** 140
    Moros, **1958:** 140
    Mutual Defense Treaty with U.S., **1960–61:** 188,
    189
    Mutual security treaty, **1958:** 261
    News conference remarks, **1953:** 15, 243; **1954:**
    101, 129
    Quezony Molina, Manuel, **1958:** 139
    Relations with U.S., **1959:** 36; **1960–61:** 185, 189

Philippines — *continued*
    Romulo, Carlos P., **1954:** 73, 101; **1957:** 166
    Santos, Bonifacio, claim for contribution to
    guerilla forces, **1958:** 231
    SEATO.
        See Southeast Asia Treaty Organization.
    Service of Dwight D. Eisenhower in, **1958:** 139
    Sugar quota, **1960–61:** 106
    Tawitawi Group, **1958:** 140
    Trade agreement revision, letter, **1955:** 91
    Trade with U.S., **1960–61:** 189
    U.S. bases, **1960–61:** 189
    Visit to, **1960–61:** 177, 182, 183, 184, 185, 186,
    187, 188, 189, 190, 209
    War damage claims against U.S., **1960–61:** 13 (p.
    65), 414 (p. 968)
Philippines, University of the, acceptance of hon-
    orary degree, remarks, **1960–61:** 186
Phillips, Cabell, **1955:** 10, 81
Phillips, Vice Adm. William K., **1954:** 172
Phleger, Herman, **1955:** 146 ftn. (p. 644)
Photography, aerial, **1956:** 264
Phoumi Nosavan, **1960–61:** 422
Physical examination of Presidential candidates,
    1956: 121
Physically Handicapped, President's Committee on
    Employment of the, **1953:** 192; **1954:** 96;
    1955: 103; **1957:** 93n., 94 and n.; **1960–61:**
    417
    Statement on, **1957:** 93
Physically handicapped persons.
    See Handicapped persons.
Physician to President, **1956:** 16
    Snyder, Maj. Gen. Howard McC., **1956:** 121, 155
Pibulsonggram, Field Marshal P.
    Exchange of messages, **1956:** 302
    Exchange of letters, **1957:** 36 and n.
    Legion of Merit, citation, **1955:** 87
Piccard, Jacques, Distinguished Public Service
    Award, citation, **1960–61:** 25
Piccolo, Luigi (Lou Little), **1958:** 286
Picketing, **1958:** 20, 216
    Blackmail, **1959:** 6, 22, 176
    News conference remarks, **1959:** 36, 89, 172,
    179
Pierce, Franklin, **1955:** 85, 92n.
Pierpoint, Robert C., **1958:** 56, 88, 310, 318; **1959:**
    17, 21, 29, 48, 67, 94, 123, 148, 172, 179,
    186, 191, 223, 243, 271, 277; **1960–61:** 7,
    24, 38, 103, 127, 143, 222, 228, 256, 263,
    268, 284, 422
Pierre, Henri, **1954:** 39, 73, 157; **1955:** 100; **1956:**
    155
Pietri, Uslar, **1959:** 44
Pike, Zebulon Montgomery, **1956:** 107
Pilgrim Fathers, **1953:** 155
Pilgrims, reference to, **1954:** 32, 204
Pilots, downed off Florida coast, **1957:** 107

Pinchot, Gifford, **1956:** 285

Pineau, Christian, **1956:** 229; **1957:** 38

Pinheiro, Israel, **1960–61:** 45

Pinto, Ignacio, **1960–61:** 324n.

Pioneer (space vehicle), **1958:** 295, 308; **1959:** 46, 48; **1960–61:** 264, 424

Pioneers, remarks on, **1958:** 269

Piowaty, Carl and W. J., relief of, disapproval, **1954:** 245

Pipelines
  Natural gas, **1957:** 13, 56
  Oil, **1957:** 28

Pittsburgh, Pa., **1954:** 130; **1956:** 216; **1957:** 4; **1958:** 153, 288; **1960–61:** 353, 354
  Campaign remarks, **1956:** 233, 234; **1958:** 303

Pius XII, **1954:** 345; **1956:** 230; **1958:** 286
  Death of, statement, **1958:** 281
  Illness, message, **1958:** 280
  Message, **1955:** 46
  News conference remarks on, **1955:** 47

Planning, long term vs. short term, **1959:** 154

Platform pledges, comment on, **1958:** 120

Platinum, imports, **1958:** 56, 96

Platt, Thomas C., **1953:** 105

Pleasantville, N. J., **1956:** 288

Pledge of allegiance to the flag, amendment, approval, **1954:** 140

Plowden, Sir Edwin, **1957:** 226n.; **1958:** 21

Plowing matches, national field days and, **1956:** 211

Plowshare project, **1960–61:** 143

Plutonium, **1960–61:** 34
  Production reactor, approval, **1958:** 193
  Purchase abroad, **1956:** 299

Plymouth Rock, **1954:** 204, 297; **1958:** 305

Po Sun Yun, message, **1960–61:** 273

Poage, Repr. W. R., **1956:** 171

Poats, Rutherford M., **1959:** 67, 102, 154, 172; **1960–61:** 21, 93, 127, 268, 284

Poinsett, Joel, **1960–61:** 73

Point 4 program, **1959:** 55; **1960–61:** 53

Poland, **1956:** 260, 282; **1957:** 17, 50, 62, 118, 230
  Ambassador Jacob Beam, **1958:** 261
  Assistance, **1956:** 282; **1958:** 141
  Campaign remarks, **1956:** 259, 272, 279, 283, 292
  Kosciuszko, Tadeusz, **1960–61:** 310
  Letters to Premier Bulganin re, **1958:** 7, 31
  News conference remarks, **1956:** 298
  Peace proposal of Woodrow Wilson re, **1960–61:** 310
  Poznan trials, statement, **1956:** 215
  Relations with Germany, **1959:** 191
  Representation at foreign ministers conference, question of, **1959:** 102
  Stepinac, Cardinal Aloysius, **1956:** 292
  Technical conference, Geneva, **1958:** 131
  Visit of Vice President Nixon (1959), **1960–61:** 310

Poland — *continued*
  Warsaw, U.S.-Communist China talks, **1958:** 257, 261, 263
  Wyszynski, Cardinal, **1953:** 235

Polar ice cap, cruise of *Nautilus* beneath, **1958:** 15, 201, 210, 211

Polaris (IRBM).
  See Missiles.

Police, Washington, D.C.
  Arrest books, inspection, approval, **1954:** 207
  Handling of transit emergency, **1955:** 149
  Incident at Lincoln Day box supper, **1954:** 33
  Increase in benefits, disapproval, **1959:** 239

Police Chiefs, International Association, 67th conference, remarks, **1960–61:** 314

Police force, Federal, **1957:** 232

Police force, international, **1960–61:** 330

Police functions, international, **1958:** 89

Police power, **1956:** 198; **1958:** 288
  Federal Government, **1957:** 17

Police state, **1954:** 128

Poling, Daniel A., **1954:** 170

Poliomyelitis, **1953:** 4, 17
  Citation to National Foundation for Infantile Paralysis, **1955:** 78
  Vaccine, **1955:** 79; **1956:** 205, 303; **1957:** 231
    Budget message, **1956:** 12 (p. 120)
    Citation to Dr. Jonas E. Salk for development of, **1955:** 77
    Distribution, **1955:** 78, 90, 112, 113
    Fifth anniversary of development, statement, **1960–61:** 105
    News conference remarks, **1955:** 81, 90, 95, 100, 112, 119
    Statements, **1955:** 113; **1958:** 109

Poliomyelitis Vaccine, National Advisory Committee on, **1955:** 81, 90, 113

Poliomyelitis Vaccine Evaluation Center, University of Michigan, **1955:** 113n.

Polish-American Congress, remarks, **1960–61:** 310

Polish armed forces in exile, **1954:** 112

Political agreements with Soviet Union, comment on, **1959:** 21

Political appointees, tasks, **1956:** 22

Political philosophy, President's, **1959:** 7
  Comment on, **1958:** 11, 318

Political revolution, **1959:** 55

Politics
  Comment on, **1955:** 112
  Public interest in, **1960–61:** 174

Poll tax abolishment, proposed, **1960–61:** 24

Pollack, Daniel, **1958:** 78

Polls of public opinion, **1957:** 92
  Government spending, **1959:** 172
  High school students, **1956:** 94
  News conference remarks, **1956:** 94, 155, 189
  Summit conferences, **1958:** 70
  Vice Presidential candidates, **1956:** 189

Polo, Marco, **1959:** 84

Pontius Pilate, **1959:** 67

Pony Express, centennial of inauguration, **1959:** 270

Poole, Jerry W., **1954:** 347

Pope, Fortune, **1958:** 284n.

Population growth, **1954:** 308; **1957:** 223; **1958:** 5 (p. 56), 110; **1959:** 6, 7, 55, 258, 288

Pork, purchase of, **1956:** 12 (p. 130), 20

Portal, Sir Charles F., **1959:** 7

Porter, H. J. (Jack), **1955:** 47; **1958:** 37

Portland, Oreg., **1956:** 252n.

　Campaign remarks, **1956:** 254, 255, 256

Portrait of the President, acceptance, **1954:** 167

Portsmouth (Ohio) atomic energy facility, **1954:** 14 (p. 128)

Portsmouth, N.H., **1960–61:** 230

　Naval shipyard, wage rates, **1958:** 191

Portugal

　Armed forces, **1960–61:** 161

　Lisbon.

　　See main heading, Lisbon.

　Salazar, Antonio de Oliveira, **1960–61:** 160, 161

　Thomaz, Americo D. R., **1960–61:** 157, 159, 160, 161

　U.S. Ambassador C. Burke Elbrick, **1960–61:** 157n.

　Visit to, **1960–61:** 157, 158, 159, 160, 161, 162

Post exchange and commissary privileges, **1955:** 100

Post Office Department, **1954:** 3, 139, 208; **1957:** 13, 75, 112; **1960–61:** 89, 217

　Airline subsidies, transfer of functions re, **1953:** 94

　"Atoms for Peace" postage stamp, **1955:** 177

　Barnes, Bert V., **1960–61:** 389n.

　Budget messages, **1954:** 14 (p. 177); **1955:** 17 (pp. 103, 164, 171); **1956:** 12 (pp. 139, 143, 144, 151); **1958:** 5 (pp. 55, 72); **1959:** 10 (pp. 76, 82); **1960–61:** 13 (pp. 65, 71, 104, 110), 414 (p. 977)

　Christmas mail, **1955:** 246

　Lease-purchase contracts, **1958:** 5 (p. 72)

　McKibbin, John M., **1959:** 18n.

　News conference remarks, **1957:** 56, 62, 72, 115, 169

　Physical plant, **1956:** 2, 32 ftn. (p. 237); **1958:** 29, 33, 43, 49, 70, 110, 117

　Postal bill, statement on signing, **1958:** 117

　Postal field service compensation bill, veto, **1955:** 102

　President Magsaysay Champion of Liberty stamp, **1957:** 166

　Reorganization, **1953:** 6

　Report, **1960–61:** 385

　Seizure of copies of *Izvestia* and *Pravda*, **1955:** 59

　Small business purchases, **1956:** 263

　Stamp in honor of American labor, **1956:** 194

Post Office Department — *continued*

　Treasury-Post Office Appropriation Act, 1958, **1957:** 99

Postal deficit, **1954:** 3, 14 (p. 87), 208; **1955:** 4, 9; **1956:** 2, 32 and ftn. (p. 237); **1957:** 13, 50, 56, 62; **1960–61:** 89, 217, 222

　Budget messages, **1955:** 17 (p. 103); **1956:** 12 (pp. 143, 144); **1958:** 5 (pp. 53, 55); **1960–61:** 13 (p. 71), 414 (pp. 938, 941, 977, 978)

Postal employees, **1954:** 139

　Budget message, **1960–61:** 13 (p. 104)

　Disapproval of salary increase, **1957:** 185

　Pay, **1954:** 43, 313, 349; **1955:** 4, 9, 59, 90, 100; **1960–61:** 13 (p. 104), 217

　　Approval of Postal Field Service Compensation Act, **1955:** 120

　　Disapproval of bill, **1954:** 208

　　Rates, **1958:** 169

　　Salary increase, **1958:** 5 (pp. 25, 55, 71), 117, 120; **1959:** 10 (pp. 50, 81)

　　Veto of pay bill, **1955:** 102

　Uniforms for, **1955:** 9

　Wage and incentive plan, **1956:** 2

Postal mail service, **1957:** 56, 62, 72

Postal Policy Act, **1960–61:** 89

　Amendment proposed, **1959:** 10 (p. 82)

Postal rates, **1954:** 3, 14 (pp. 177, 178), 139, 208; **1955:** 4, 9, 247; **1956:** 32 and ftn. (p. 237), 121; **1957:** 13, 62, 75, 169; **1959:** 10 (pp. 49, 50, 81, 82); **1960–61:** 133, 423

　Approval of bill, **1958:** 117

　Budget messages, **1955:** 17 (pp. 93, 103, 171); **1956:** 12 (pp. 84, 139); **1958:** 5 (pp. 45, 53, 55); **1960–61:** 13 (pp. 39, 71), 414 (pp. 937, 938, 941, 978)

　Budget (1960) statement, **1958:** 324

　Commission on, **1955:** 9, 17 (p. 171)

　　Proposed, **1954:** 3

　Increase, **1955:** 17 (pp. 103, 171)

　Meeting on, **1956:** 318

　Message to Congress, **1960–61:** 89

　News conference remarks, **1956:** 32, 121

Postal Savings System

　Liquidation, **1958:** 5 (p. 55)

　Proposed discontinuance, **1957:** 112

Postal service, **1954:** 14 (pp. 173, 174, 176–178); **1955:** 9; **1956:** 12 (pp. 82, 143); **1958:** 117; **1959:** 225, 270; **1960–61:** 385, 410

　Budget messages, **1955:** 17 (pp. 170, 171); **1958:** 5 (p. 53); **1959:** 10 (pp. 81, 82); **1960–61:** 13 (pp. 65, 71), 414 (pp. 938, 977, 978)

　Table, **1958:** 5 (p. 54)

Postal Union, Universal, **1959:** 270

Postmaster General (Arthur E. Summerfield), **1953:** 6, 269; **1954:** 43, 76; **1955:** 9, 90 ftn. (p. 475), 102, 138, 177; **1956:** 194; **1957:** 56, 62, 72, 166; **1958:** 29; **1959:** 270

　Chairman, Red Cross campaign, **1954:** 1

Postmaster General (Summerfield) — *continued*
 Pay scale for postal employees, **1954:** 349
 Report relating to postal rates, **1956:** 32 ftn. (p. 237)
 Resignation, letter, **1960–61:** 385
Postmasters
 Appointment, **1957:** 150
 New Hampshire conference, remarks, **1955:** 138
 National Association of, remarks, **1959:** 270
Potato industry, aid to, **1955:** 24
Potomac River
 Construction of bridges, approval, **1954:** 224
 Pollution, **1959:** 197
Potsdam, **1958:** 318
Potsdam papers, **1960–61:** 268
Potter, Sen. Charles E., **1954:** 157; **1958:** 213
Potter, Chester M., **1954:** 341
Potter, I. Lee, **1959:** 94
Potter, Philip, **1957:** 157
Poultry and eggs, price supports, **1954:** 4
Powell, Repr. Adam C., Jr., **1956:** 32; **1957:** 228; **1958:** 11
 Telegram to, **1957:** 191 and n.
Powell, Mrs. Hannah Mae, bill for relief of, **1957:** 179
Powell, Gov. Wesley, **1959:** 113
 Letter, **1959:** 112
Power, Gen. Thomas S., **1960–61:** 24
Power, sale of, **1956:** 12 (p. 138); **1958:** 5 (p. 68)
Power Authority of the State of New York, **1959:** 141n.
Power and influence, misuse, comments on, **1960–61:** 421, 422
Power projects, **1953:** 171, 187; **1954:** 3; **1955:** 4; **1960–61:** 410
 Amistad Dam, Rio Grande, **1960–61:** 13 (p. 83), 303, 334, 335, 414 (p. 995)
 Atomic, **1956:** 43, 256, 263; **1958:** 5 (p. 33), 292; **1959:** 10 (pp. 67, 68); **1960–61:** 13 (pp. 58, 59)
  Appropriations, **1958:** 193
  Foreign, **1956:** 299
  Monroe, Mich., **1956:** 198
  Shippingport, Pa., **1956:** 263; **1958:** 113
 Budget messages, **1954:** 14 (pp. 164, 167–169, 175, 176); **1955:** 17 (pp. 91, 93, 120, 121, 156–161); **1956:** 12 (pp. 134–137); **1958:** 5 (pp. 33, 68, 70); **1960–61:** 13 (pp. 58, 59), 414 (pp. 994, 995)
 Campaign remarks, **1956:** 256; **1958:** 292, 294
 Colorado River, **1954:** 62
 Columbia River Basin Development, **1960–61:** 331, 410, 414 (p. 994), 416, 419
 Cost of Federal projects, **1956:** 193
 Euratom Cooperation Act of 1958, **1958:** 236
 Fort Randall Dam, **1954:** 53
 Fryingpan-Arkansas, **1957:** 13
 Garrison Dam, **1953:** 100

Power projects — *continued*
 Hydroelectric, **1953:** 77; **1954:** 14 (pp. 167–169), 271; **1955:** 17 (pp. 158–161); **1959:** 10 (p. 95); **1960–61:** 402, 410
 Joint statement with President Lopez Mateos on, **1955:** 257
 Libby Dam, **1954:** 271
 McKenzie River, **1954:** 34
 McNary Dam, **1954:** 271
 Memphis, Tenn., area, **1955:** 56, 146, 149
  See also Dixon-Yates contract.
 Middle East, **1953:** 217
 News conference remarks, **1953:** 15, 22, 31, 54, 77, 88, 128, 208, 265; **1954:** 39, 50, 138, 172; **1955:** 10, 33, 56, 146, 149; **1956:** 96, 193, 198
 Niagara Falls, **1953:** 31, 77, 88, 128, 208, 265; **1954:** 138; **1955:** 10; **1956:** 96; **1957:** 13
 North Counties Hydro-Electric Co., damages claim, **1958:** 229
 Nuclear, **1954:** 38, 172; **1955:** 17 (pp. 91, 120, 121), 228
  Abroad, **1955:** 121
  Europe, **1958:** 145
  New England, **1955:** 223
  Shippingport plant, **1954:** 260
 Private vs. public, **1953:** 31, 77, 128; **1954:** 138, 271
 Reactor projects, **1957:** 13, 125, 159
 St. Lawrence River, **1953:** 15, 22, 31, 54, 70, 77, 246, 247; **1954:** 14 (pp. 175, 176)
 Snake River, **1953:** 77
 Southwestern Power Administration rates, **1956:** 178
 Transmission facilities, **1954:** 14 (p. 169)
 Trinity River project, **1959:** 194
 TVA area.
  See Tennessee Valley Authority.
Power resources, **1957:** 16
Powered flight, 50th anniversary, **1953:** 267
Powers, Francis G., **1960–61:** 263, 268 and ftn. (p. 648)
Poznan, Poland, **1956:** 215
Prado y Ugarteche, Manuel, **1960–61:** 247
Prasad, Rajendra, **1959:** 310, 315, 316, 317, 318
 Message, **1959:** 281
 Toast to, **1959:** 312
Prasad, Mrs. Rajendra, **1959:** 312
Prather, S. H., and S. H., Jr., relief of, disapproval, **1954:** 229
Pratt, Mrs. Thomas, **1958:** 93n.
Pravda, postal ban, **1955:** 59
Prayer, Inauguration (1953), **1956:** 28
Prayer, National Day of, **1958:** 274
 Statement, **1954:** 269
Prayer, World Day of, message, **1954:** 47
Prayer breakfast, International Christian Leadership, remarks, **1953:** 8

Praying Colonels, football team, **1960–61:** 395

Presbyterian church document on foreign policy, **1958:** 153

Presentation ceremonies, addresses or remarks. *See* Addresses or remarks at presentation ceremonies.

Presidency, **1960–61:** 354
  Comments on, **1953:** 15, 141; **1958:** 37, 88
  Duties of, effect on health, **1956:** 48
  First two years in office, comment on, **1955:** 18, 112
  Leadership in foreign and domestic matters, comment on, **1959:** 179
  News conference remarks, **1954:** 9, 129, 149; **1956:** 5, 47; **1960–61:** 34, 284
  Prestige, **1959:** 186
  Problems of future, comment on, **1960–61:** 34
  Succession to, **1956:** 47
  Woman in, comment on, **1954:** 9

Presidency, The (Lorant), **1958:** 288

President, criticism of, **1956:** 88

President of the Senate. *See* Vice President (Richard M. Nixon).

President of the United States, 1972-1976, letter to, **1958:** 314

Presidential Advisory Committee on Transport Policy and Organization, report, **1955:** 33, 62, 90 and ftn. (p. 475); **1960–61:** 21

Presidential authority
  Continuation until inauguration of successor, joint statement with President-elect Kennedy, **1960–61:** 369
  Foreign affairs, **1960–61:** 246

Presidential candidates, news conference remarks, **1957:** 124

Presidential commissions, comment on, **1960–61:** 268

Presidential disability
  Agreement with Vice President Nixon re, **1958:** 37, 40, 42
  News conference remarks, **1957:** 56, 62, 115

Presidential documents published in Federal Register, Appendix B, **1953:** p. 879; **1954:** p. 1132; **1955:** p. 877; **1958:** p. 884; **1959:** p. 902; **1960–61:** p. 1086

Presidential nomination
  Democratic, **1960–61:** 93
  Republican, comments on, **1960–61:** 7, 24, 93, 103

Presidential office space, **1956:** 16; **1957:** 45, 105, 135 and n.
  Commission on, message, **1956:** 131

Presidential power to use Armed Forces in peacetime, **1957:** 17

Presidential power re use of nuclear bombs, **1959:** 154

Presidential Railroad Commission, **1960–61:** 343n.
  Appointment of members, statement, **1960–61:** 378

Presidential reports to Congress, list, Appendix C, **1953:** p. 885; Appendix C, **1954:** p. 1138; Appendix C, **1955:** p. 884; Appendix C, **1958:** p. 889; Appendix C, **1959:** p. 908; Appendix C, **1960–61:** p. 1091
  See also Congress, reports to, messages transmitting.

Presidential responsibility, comment on, **1954:** 48, 92
  In case of attack, **1954:** 57
  Foreign affairs, **1953:** 41

Presidential Unit Citation, presentation to crew of U.S.S. *Nautilus*, **1958:** 201

President's Action Committee for Traffic Safety, **1954:** 336

President's Adviser on Personnel Management (Philip Young)
  Fund-raising campaigns, policy, **1956:** 132n.
  Report on personnel and civil service, letter, **1956:** 22
  Resignation, **1957:** 33 and n.

President's Advisory Commission on Presidential Office Space, **1957:** 45, 105, 135 and n.; **1960–61:** 414 (p. 1017)
  Proposed, **1956:** 131

President's Advisory Committee on Energy Supplies and Resources Policy (Flemming Committee), report, **1955:** 33 and ftn. (p. 259), 41, 56

President's Advisory Committee on Government Organization, **1953:** 6; **1960–61:** 349
  News conference remarks, **1953:** 37, 62
  Report, letter, **1960–61:** 433
  Study of Federal civil defense, **1956:** 142

President's Advisory Committee on a National Highway Program, **1954:** 346n., 349; **1955:** 4, 146
  Report, **1955:** 39

President's Advisory Committee on Water Resources Policy, **1956:** 12 (p. 133), 16, 170
  Report, message, **1956:** 13

Presidents of American Republics, Panama meeting, **1956:** 145, 146
  News conference and campaign remarks, **1956:** 96, 121, 155, 272, 278

Presidents of American Republics, representatives, **1957:** 64, 96

President's Award for Distinguished Federal Civilian Service, **1960–61:** 68, 389

President's Citizens Advisory Committee on the Fitness of American Youth, **1956:** 96, 128; **1957:** 45, 104 and n.

President's Commission on Increased Industrial Use of Agricultural Products, **1958:** 5 (p. 67), 12

President's Commission on Veterans' Pensions, **1956:** 267n.
  Budget message, **1955:** 17 (p. 134)
  Letter, **1955:** 51

President's Committee on Education Beyond the High School, **1956:** 85, 222, 277
President's Committee on Employment of the Physically Handicapped, **1957:** 93n.; **1960–61:** 417
  Remarks, **1953:** 192; **1954:** 96; **1955:** 103; **1957:** 94; **1958:** 99
President's Committee on Government Contracts, **1960–61:** 410
  Budget message, **1960–61:** 414 (p. 1023)
  Report, statement, **1960–61:** 407
President's Committee on Government Employment Policy, **1960–61:** 410
  Report, **1960–61:** 217 ftn. (p. 545), 394
President's Committee for Hungarian Refugee Relief, **1957:** 25, 250
  Report, **1957:** 85
President's Committee on International Information Activities, **1953:** 230n.; **1960–61:** 332 ftn. (p. 789)
  Establishment, statement, **1953:** 2
  Report, **1953:** 126, 128 and ftn. (p. 472)
President's Committee on Scientists and Engineers, **1957:** 241 and n.
  Report, letter, **1958:** 327
  Study of pay problems, **1958:** 169
President's Committee to Study the U.S. Military Assistance Program (Draper Committee), **1959:** 6, 55; **1960–61:** 36
  Budget messages, **1960–61:** 13 (p. 57), 414 (p. 962); **1959:** 10 (p. 69)
  Letter to Chairman, **1958:** 316
  News conference remarks on, **1959:** 53, 94, 154, 288
  Reports, **1959:** 53, 90, 136, 137, 170, 183, 288
President's Committee for Traffic Safety, **1954:** 37n.; **1955:** 111, 243; **1956:** 36, 37
  Letter to Harlow H. Curtice, **1956:** 305
  Letter to William Randolph Hearst, Jr., re appointment, **1955:** 124
  Letter to T.S. Petersen re appointment, **1955:** 125
  Regional conferences, message, **1958:** 45
  Report, **1957:** 14 and n.
President's Conference on Administrative Procedure, **1953:** 59
  Letter to Chairman, **1960–61:** 275
President's Conference for Benefit of Small Business, remarks, **1957:** 196, 227
President's Conference on Fitness of American Youth, message, **1955:** 217; **1956:** 128
President's Conference on Occupational Safety, **1956:** 55, 104
  Remarks, **1954:** 100; **1958:** 55
President's Council on Youth Fitness, **1956:** 128; **1957:** 104 and n.
President's Disaster Relief Fund, **1954:** 99
President's emergency fund, **1957:** 2, 152n.
President's Materials Policy Commission, **1953:** 228

President's papers, **1960–61:** 21
  Disposition, **1957:** 134
  Offer as gift to U.S., **1960–61:** 118
  Privileged communications, **1957:** 22, 115
  Relating to second term decision, **1956:** 47
President's party responsibility, **1954:** 128
President's plans after 1961, **1959:** 172
President's Science Advisory Committee, **1959:** 107; **1960–61:** 143, 400
  "Introduction to Outer Space," **1958:** 56, 57, 74
  News conference remarks, **1958:** 56, 74, 141; **1959:** 267
  Report on availability of scientific and technical information, **1958:** 326n.
  Report "Strengthening American Science," statement, **1958:** 326
  Reports, **1959:** 56, 67 ftn. (p. 294), 118
  Statement, **1960–61:** 363
  Transfer to White House, **1957:** 230n.
President's Science Advisory Committee Chairman (James R. Killian, Jr.), **1958:** 57, 64, 141
President's Special Committee to Investigate Crude Oil Imports, **1957:** 145 ftn. (p. 581)
Press Center, Memorial, New York City, dedication, remarks, **1954:** 350
Press Club, National, golden anniversary celebration, remarks, **1959:** 7
Press Club, Overseas, **1954:** 350
Press conferences.
  See News conferences.
Press releases, partial list, Appendix A, **1957:** p. 855
Prestige abroad, U.S., **1960–61:** 245, 332, 341
Preston, Dickson J., **1955:** 56
Preston, John Basil, **1956:** 226
Prettyman, Judge E. Barrett, **1953:** 59
  Letter, **1960–61:** 275
Price controls, **1953:** 216; **1954:** 21, 317, 318; **1956:** 2, 224; **1959:** 15, 267; **1960–61:** 346, 410
  Government, **1957:** 119
  News conference remarks, **1953:** 12, 22, 41, 225; **1957:** 28, 169
  Responsibility of business and labor, **1956:** 298; **1957:** 8, 16, 119, 124
Price fixing, **1954:** 165
Price freeze, **1955:** 26
Price of Peace, inaugural address, **1957:** 15 and n.
Price predictions on apples, prohibition of Government publication, veto, **1955:** 147
Price stability, **1959:** 225; **1960–61:** 117
  Economic report, **1959:** 15
Price Stability for Economic Growth, Committee on, **1959:** 6
  News conference remarks on, **1959:** 17, 36 and ftn. (p. 197), 67
  Reports, statements, **1959:** 144; **1960–61:** 117
Price Stabilization, Office of, **1953:** 12 ftn. (p. 46)

[References are to items except as otherwise indicated]

Price supports, **1953:** 6, 101, 216; **1954:** 3, 4, 21, 49, 139, 162, 196, 291, 317; **1955:** 62, 90, 127; **1956:** 6, 35, 82, 83; **1957:** 8; **1958:** 12, 16, 26, 295; **1959:** 6, 15, 23, 104, 144n.; **1960–61:** 32, 391

See also specific commodities; Agriculture.
Administrative determination, **1958:** 12
Budget messages, **1954:** 14 (pp. 86, 158–160); **1955:** 17 (pp. 93, 94, 103, 106, 150–153); **1956:** 12 (pp. 127, 128); **1958:** 5 (pp. 63–65); **1959:** 10 (pp. 49, 88, 91); **1960–61:** 13 (pp. 77, 79), 414 (pp. 985–988)
Campaign remarks, **1956:** 214, 250, 268
Corn, **1957:** 13, 16, 17, 169
Dairy products, **1958:** 60
Escalator clause in basic law, **1958:** 12
Farm "freeze" bill, veto, **1958:** 59, 60
Flexible, **1954:** 221
Hogs, **1956:** 16
Letter to Sen. Aiken, **1956:** 35
News conference remarks, **1954:** 9, 18, 25, 39, 143, 157, 161, 165, 172; **1956:** 16, 20, 47, 62, 78, 88, 171, 216; **1958:** 37, 56; **1959:** 123, 132; **1960–61:** 38, 127
Surplus crops, ban on cultivation on leased Government lands, **1956:** 111
Tobacco, veto of bill, **1955:** 140
Price undercutting, **1958:** 83
Price and wage controls, **1953:** 6, 12 and ftn. (p. 46); **1955:** 112, 146; **1958:** 120, 308; **1959:** 21, 94, 124
See also under Controls, government.
Moratorium on prices, **1958:** 103
Price-wage spiral, **1959:** 67, 123
Prices, **1953:** 6, 30, 101, 216, 227; **1954:** 21, 194; **1959:** 6, 144, 188; **1960–61:** 4, 17, 23, 143, 423
See also specific commodities.
Campaign remarks, **1960–61:** 350, 354
Coffee, **1954:** 18, 25, 39, 50, 57; **1960–61:** 111n.
Consumer, **1956:** 20, 269; **1958:** 63, 110; **1959:** 15, 76, 244
  Economic report, **1958:** 16
  Statement, **1958:** 298
Cotton, **1959:** 257
Farm products, **1954:** 261
  See also Farm economy.
Food, **1954:** 172; **1958:** 56
News conference remarks, **1953:** 12, 22, 41, 225, 230, 249; **1958:** 56, 70, 103, 120, 213; **1959:** 7, 17, 29, 42, 53, 67, 123, 148
Oil, **1957:** 28; **1959:** 67
Responsibility of business, **1957:** 8, 16, 119, 124
Rise in, **1956:** 289; **1957:** 8, 134, 195; **1959:** 7, 17, 29, 53; **1960–61:** 245
Steel, **1956:** 71, 229; **1957:** 124, 134; **1958:** 120, 213; **1959:** 42, 67, 172

Prices and Costs, Committee on Government Activities Affecting, establishment, statement, **1959:** 18
Priest, Mrs. Ivy Baker, **1955:** 187
  Letter, **1955:** 186
Priest, Repr. J. Percy, death of, statement, **1956:** 240
Priest Rapids project, Wash., **1955:** 4, 17 (p. 158); **1956:** 12 (p. 134)
Primary elections
  California, **1956:** 47
  Expenditures, **1956:** 94
  Indiana, **1956:** 96
  Maine, **1956:** 205
  Massachusetts, **1956:** 88
  Minnesota, **1956:** 62, 117
  New Hampshire, **1956:** 15, 16, 47, 56, 117
  Oregon, **1956:** 121
  Pennsylvania, **1956:** 88; **1958:** 30, 103
  President's reaction to support of electorate, **1956:** 96
  Southern states, **1956:** 155
  Wisconsin, **1956:** 47, 78, 121
Prina, L. Edgar, **1954:** 157; **1960–61:** 7, 93, 222, 422
Prince Albert, Saskatchewan, Canada, **1959:** 125n.
Prince Albert Radar Laboratory, Canada, official opening, message, **1959:** 125
Princeton University, **1960–61:** 21
Printing press, invention of, **1960–61:** 58
Prio Socarras, Carlos, **1954:** 25
Prison institutions, **1956:** 12 (p. 124)
Prisoners of Korean war, **1953:** 87, 96, 210; **1954:** 40, 94
  Agreement on, **1953:** 102
  Dean, Maj. Gen. William F., **1953:** 225, 265
  Exchange of sick and wounded, **1953:** 41, 54
  Forced repatriation, question of, **1953:** 88
  News conference remarks, **1953:** 41, 54, 88, 225, 265
  United States
    Disaffection under Communist indoctrination, **1953:** 225
    Treatment of, **1953:** 54
Prisoners of war
  Code of conduct, **1955:** 207
  German, **1954:** 314
  U.S., **1954:** 50, 94, 101
    Held by Communist China, **1954:** 161, 342, 345, 347
Prisoners of War, Defense Advisory Committee on, report, **1955:** 207n.
Prisoners of World War II
  Held by Soviet Union, **1953:** 50
  Returned to Soviet Union, **1960–61:** 268
Private bills for relief of hardship cases.
  See also Approval of acts of Congress; Legislation, vetoes and memorandums of disapproval.
  Immigration cases, **1956:** 33, 121

Private enterprise.
See Enterprise system.
Privileged documents, **1956:** 16; **1957:** 22, 115; **1958:** 11; **1960–61:** 422
  Certification forbidding disclosure to Congress of documents re aid to South America, **1960–61:** 380
  Directive of 1954, reference to, **1959:** 277
  Directive to Secretary of Defense re congressional investigation, **1954:** 113
    Comment on, **1954:** 115
  Memorandum of Attorney General re, **1954:** 113n.
  News conference remarks, **1959:** 36, 148, 161, 277
  Reports of Killian and Gaither panels, withholding of, letter, **1958:** 19
Probation and Parole Association, National, **1954:** 207
Problems of Leninism (Stalin), **1953:** 109; **1956:** 62
Proclamations, **1953:** 105, 182n.; **1954:** 285, 287; **1959:** 3, 51, 91n., 117n., 167 ftn. (p. 536), 184, 262n., 333n.; **1960–61:** 374, 383, 432
  Civil War Centennial, **1960–61:** 370
  List, Appendix B, **1953:** p. 879
  Appendix B, **1954:** p. 1132
  Appendix B, **1955:** p. 877
  Appendix B, **1956:** p. 1150
  Appendix B, **1957:** p. 868
  Appendix B, **1958:** p. 884
  Appendix B, **1959:** p. 902
  Appendix B, **1960–61:** p. 1086
  Martial law during civil defense text exercise, **1955:** 149
  National Day of Prayer, remarks on, **1958:** 274
Procter and Gamble, **1957:** 150
Proctor, Mrs. Mortimer R., **1955:** 132
Procurement, Government, **1958:** 96
Procurement, military.
See Defense procurement.
Procurement, Task Force, **1957:** 132
Production, decline in, **1960–61:** 423
Production controls (farm products), **1960–61:** 32
Professional persons, social security coverage, **1953:** 155
Professional and Technical Compensation, Defense Advisory Committee on, **1958:** 169; **1959:** 10 (p. 59)
  Budget message, **1958:** 5 (p. 31)
Profits of business and industry
  Control of, **1959:** 94
  News conference remarks, **1959:** 42, 94
Progressive moderation, comment on, **1954:** 347
Project Defender, **1960–61:** 414 (pp. 953, 954)
Project Mariner, **1960–61:** 414 (p. 972)
Project Mercury (man-in-space), **1960–61:** 13 (p. 66), 414 (p. 972)
Project Rover, **1960–61:** 414 (p. 960)

Project VELA, **1960–61:** 143 ftn. (p. 410)
Proletariat dictatorship through the Cominform, **1956:** 78
Promotions and assignments, military officers, **1958:** 80
Propaganda
  Inflammatory propaganda, United Nations address on, **1958:** 207
  Soviet, **1959:** 48
    Use of international diplomacy, **1958:** 74
  Support of mutual security program, **1959:** 154
Property, Federal, **1954:** 14 (pp. 187, 188); **1955:** 17 (pp. 95, 179–181); **1959:** 10 (p. 108); **1960–61:** 410
  See also Buildings, Federal.
  Budget messages, **1958:** 5 (pp. 45, 72); **1960–61:** 13 (pp. 101, 102, 105), 414 (pp. 1017, 1019)
  Declaration of Taking Act, amendment, **1958:** 250
  Sale of, **1958:** 5 (p. 45)
Property, Hoover Commission recommendations, **1957:** 112 and n.
Property improvement loan insurance, **1959:** 153, 208
Property management, **1956:** 12 (pp. 84, 151)
Providence, R.I., **1954:** 22n.
Proxmire, Governor William, **1957:** 150
"Prussian" general staff, **1958:** 80
Psychological Operations Coordinating Committee, **1953:** 92
Psychological Strategy Board, **1953:** 33
Psychological warfare, **1953:** 22, 128
Psychological Warfare Board, news conference remarks, **1958:** 63
Public Advisory Board for Mutual Security, report, **1953:** 22 and ftn. (p. 86)
Public assistance programs, **1954:** 10, 14 (pp. 142, 143); **1956:** 158; **1959:** 10 (pp. 46, 96–98, 102, 103); **1960–61:** 127 and ftn. (p. 362)
  Budget messages, **1955:** 17 (pp. 103, 143, 144); **1956:** 12 (p. 118); **1958:** 5 (pp. 46, 47, 51, 52); **1960–61:** 13 (pp. 87, 95), 414 (pp. 1001, 1010, 1011)
  Medical care, **1955:** 25
  Social Security Amendments of 1958, **1958:** 234
Public debt, **1957:** 13, 86
  See also Debt, national.
Public Debt, Bureau of the, **1954:** 14 (p. 187)
Public Education, Committee for, Charlottesville, Va., letter to chairman, **1958:** 267
Public enterprises, **1959:** 10 (pp. 52, 53)
Public facility loan program, **1958:** 224; **1960–61:** 13 (p. 72)
Public funds
  Accounting for, **1957:** 22
  Use for congressional travel, **1956:** 205, 216, 235

Public health, **1955:** 25; **1956:** 256; **1960–61:** 13
    (pp. 87, 93, 94), 414 (pp. 1006–1009)
  Budget messages, **1954:** 14 (pp. 140, 143–145);
      1955: 17 (pp. 142, 143); **1956:** 12 (pp.
      119–121); **1959:** 10 (pp. 101, 102)
    Tables, **1954:** 14 (pp. 141, 145)
  Officials, training for assignments abroad, **1959:**
      6
  Research and training, **1959:** 181
  Training of personnel, **1956:** 161
Public Health Service, **1953:** 28, 116; **1954:** 11, 137;
      1955: 17 (p. 142), 25, 119; **1956:** 161;
      1960–61: 13 (p. 94), 414 (pp. 1007, 1008)
  Budget message, **1954:** 14 (p. 143)
  Career incentives for medical and dental officers,
      approval, **1956:** 91
  Criteria for research projects and training pro-
      grams, **1959:** 181
  Overtime pay for quarantine inspection person-
      nel, disapproval, **1954:** 218
  Salk vaccine, **1956:** 303
Public Health Service, Surgeon General (Leonard
      A. Scheele), **1955:** 95, 112, 113, 119
Public Health Service Act, amendment, veto, **1954:**
      137
Public Health Service Commissioned Corps, sur-
      vivor benefits, **1955:** 25
Public housing, **1953:** 54; **1954:** 3, 17, 68, 168, 179,
      182, 349; **1955:** 4, 176, 194; **1959:** 153,
      208; **1960–61:** 13 (pp. 72, 73), 414 (p. 980)
  See also Housing.
  Budget messages, **1954:** 14 (pp. 150, 151); **1955:**
      17 (p. 174); **1956:** 12 (p. 145); **1959:** 10
      (pp. 46, 84)
  Low income families, **1956:** 2, 3
  Minority groups, **1954:** 101, 182
  News conference remarks, **1954:** 68, 168, 182
Public Housing Administration, **1956:** 12 (p. 145)
  Budget message, **1958:** 5 (pp. 58, 59)
Public lands, **1953:** 153; **1956:** 12 (pp. 133, 137,
      138); **1959:** 10 (p. 95); **1960–61:** 133
  Budget messages, **1954:** 14 (pp. 164, 169, 170);
      1955: 17 (pp. 162, 163); **1958:** 5 (pp. 68,
      69)
  Conveyance of lands to Jake Alexander, veto,
      1954: 156
  Highways, **1955:** 39
  Mining claims, restrictions, **1955:** 172
  Oregon, administrative jurisdiction over certain
      lands in, **1954:** 152
  Public Roads.
      See Public Roads, Bureau of.
Public morality, comment on, **1959:** 277; **1960–61:**
      34
Public opinion, **1959:** 274; **1960–61:** 17, 50, 94
Public opinion, foreign, **1956:** 235
Public opinion polls, **1957:** 92
  High school students, **1956:** 94

Public opinion polls — *continued*
  News conference remarks, **1956:** 94, 155, 189
  Vice Presidential candidates, **1956:** 189
Public Papers of the Presidents, rules governing
      publication, Appendix D, **1956:** p. 1157
  Appendix D, **1957:** p. 876
Public Roads, Bureau of, **1954:** 14 (p. 176); **1955:**
      39; **1956:** 186n.
Public utilities, **1956:** 32
  Controls over gas and oil producers, **1957:** 13,
      56, 105
Public works, **1953:** 268; **1954:** 21; **1955:** 4
Public works, **1958:** 29, 43, 223, 292; **1959:** 11, 225;
      1960–61: 410
  Appropriation Act, approval, **1955:** 157; **1958:**
      244
  Appropriation bills, vetoes, **1959:** 194, 213
  Budget messages, **1954:** 14 (pp. 124, 151, 189);
      1958: 5 (pp. 42, 68); **1959:** 10 (p. 45)
    Table, **1959:** 10 (p. 46)
  Cure for recession, comment on, **1960–61:** 422
  District of Columbia, **1954:** 3, 14 (p. 189)
  Letter to minority leaders, **1958:** 85
  Military, **1954:** 14 (p. 124)
    Spending authority reduction, **1957:** 75
  News conference remarks, **1958:** 37, 74, 103
  Planning, report, **1956:** 309
  Projects, expenditures for, **1957:** 13
  Rivers and harbors bill
    Approval, statement, **1958:** 155
    Veto, message, **1958:** 73
  Stimulus to economy, **1959:** 15
Public Works, Office of Coordinator, proposed,
      1955: 4, 19
  Appointment of Maj. Gen. John S. Bragdon as
      coordinator, **1955:** 203
Public Works Administration, **1958:** 43
Publicity activities of military services, **1958:** 80, 96
Puerto Rico, **1959:** 36; **1960–61:** 42, 80
  Dorado, **1960–61:** 86
  Gubernatorial election, **1960–61:** 93
  Meeting of Joint Chiefs of Staff, **1956:** 53
  Munoz Marin, Gov. Luis, **1954:** 48; **1959:** 102;
      1960–61: 43, 86
  Nationalists of, shooting incident in U.S. House
      of Representatives, **1954:** 48
  San Juan, **1953:** 260; **1959:** 174; **1960–61:** 43
    Governors' Conference (1959), **1960–61:** 229
  Statehood, question of, **1959:** 102; **1960–61:** 93
  Sugar quota, **1960–61:** 167n.
Puget Sound, College of, **1956:** 253
Pulaski, Count Casimir, **1956:** 265
Pulaski Day Parade, **1956:** 227
Pulitzer, Joseph, death of, statement, **1955:** 63
"Pump-priming" schemes to aid economy, **1958:**
      43; **1959:** 225
Punic War, second, **1958:** 93

Purdue University, **1953:** 97; **1954:** 291n., 335n.; **1957:** 156; **1958:** 128n.
Pusan, Korea, **1957:** 91
    Fire, statement, **1953:** 258
PWA.
    See Public Works Administration.
Pyle, Ernie, tablet honoring, dedication, **1953:** 204
Pyle, Howard, **1957:** 138
Pyle, James T., **1959:** 18n.

Quarantine inspection personnel, overtime pay, disapproval, **1954:** 218
Quarles, Donald A., **1956:** 96
    See also Defense, Deputy Secretary of.
    Death of, statement, **1959:** 97, 102
Quarles, Mrs. Donald A., **1959:** 97
Queen Mary, S.S., **1955:** 42n.
Queens Syndicate, Inc., **1957:** 184
Quemoy, **1955:** 21; **1956:** 16; **1957:** 62; **1959:** 55, 267; **1960–61:** 143, 410
    Broadcastre, **1958:** 261
    Campaign remarks, **1958:** 293, 295, 296
    Letter to Sen. Green, **1958:** 277
    Letter to Premier Khrushchev re, **1958:** 263
    Message to Vice President Nixon, **1958:** 289
    News conference remarks, **1955:** 26, 62, 90, 112; **1958:** 222, 274, 288
    Statement by Secretary Dulles, **1958:** 257
Quesada, E. R., **1958:** 9, 135, 194; **1959:** 26
    Appointment, Administrator, Federal Aviation Agency, **1958:** 272
    Aviation facilities planning, report, **1959:** 74
Quezony Molina, Manuel, **1958:** 139; **1959:** 36; **1960–61:** 183, 185
Quie, Repr. Albert H., **1960–61:** 330
Quinn, Gov. William F., **1959:** 184n.; **1960–61:** 205, 206
    Letter, **1959:** 61
Quintos, Juan D., and others, relief of, disapproval, **1960–61:** 224
Quintos, Perfecta B., **1960–61:** 224
Quito, Ecuador, **1958:** 101n.
Quotas, immigrant, **1956:** 2, 33

Raab, Julius, message to, **1957:** 5, 186
Rabat, Morocco, **1957:** 84; **1959:** 277
Rabb, Maxwell M., **1955:** 181
Rabi, I. I., **1955:** 191n.
Racketeering, **1957:** 17, 72, 77; **1958:** 20, 216, 222, 235; **1959:** 6, 10 (p. 101), 21, 123, 176, 223
    Campaign remarks, **1958:** 292, 294, 296, 303, 308
Racketeers, deportation of, **1953:** 95

Radar, **1958:** 93
    See also Distant early warning system.
    Air navigation, **1956:** 12 (p. 141)
    Sites, **1956:** 12 (p. 96)
    Storm detection, **1956:** 12 (p. 152)
Radar Laboratory, Prince Albert (Canada), official opening, message, **1959:** 125
Radar screen.
    See Warning systems.
Radford, Adm. Arthur W., **1954:** 92; **1955:** 56, 81; **1959:** 89
    See also Joint Chiefs of Staff, Chairman (Adm. Arthur W. Radford)
Radhakrishnan, Sarvepalli, **1959:** 311n., 314n., 315n.
Radiation, peaceful uses, **1955:** 121
Radiation Council, Federal, **1959:** 68n.; **1960–61:** 410
    Report, **1960–61:** 268 and ftn. (p. 654)
Radiation from natural resources and X-ray, **1956:** 266; **1957:** 105
Radiation safety standards, determination by Federal agencies, **1960–61:** 268 and ftn. (p. 654)
Radio, gift to the President, **1958:** 99
Radio, Ste. Mère Église incident, **1956:** 96
Radio astronomy center, **1956:** 12 (p. 123)
Radio broadcasts, inflammatory, in Near East, **1958:** 207
Radio Free Europe, **1955:** 32; **1956:** 66
Radio liberation, **1955:** 81
Radio Month, National, statement, **1956:** 87
Radio Moscow, **1959:** 288
Radio networks
    American Forces Network anniversary, remarks, **1958:** 158
    NBC radio-TV facilities, dedication remarks, **1958:** 111
Radio and television
    Addresses.
        See Messages to the American people.
    Equal time for appearances by candidates for public office, **1954:** 50; **1959:** 216; **1960–61:** 268 and ftn. (p. 647)
Radio and Television Broadcasters, National Association, remarks, **1955:** 105
    See also National Association of Radio and Television Broadcasters.
Radio and Television Farm Directors, National Association of, remarks, **1955:** 127; **1957:** 114 and n.
Radio Week, **1956:** 96
Radioactive fallout, **1954:** 63; **1956:** 142, 230, 266; **1957:** 230; **1959:** 81; **1960–61:** 34
    AEC report, comment on, **1955:** 41, 56
    Budget message, **1959:** 10 (p. 88)
    Clean and "dirty" bombs, **1958:** 70, 88
    Exchange of messages with Prime Minister Kishi, **1957:** 208 and n.

[References are to items except as otherwise indicated]

Radioactive fallout — *continued*
  Injury to Japanese fishermen, **1955:** 330
  Joint statement with Prime Minister Macmillan,
    1957: 55
  Letter to Premier Khrushchev, **1958:** 67
  News conference remarks, **1955:** 33; **1956:** 113,
    229; **1957:** 105, 124; **1958:** 56, 74, 88
  Soviet atomic test, **1958:** 74
  Statement, **1959:** 68
  Strontium **1956:** 90, 266
  United Nations Committee, **1957:** 208
  White House release, **1959:** 68n.
Radioactive waste disposal, **1959:** 161
Radioactivity in outer space, **1959:** 48
Radioisotopes, uses of, **1955:** 228
Radiological Health, Division of, **1960–61:** 413
Radiological health control activities, **1960–61:** 13
    (p. 94), 414 (p. 1008)
Raffo Fravega, Juan Carlos, **1960–61:** 80n., 81n.
Railroad, Louisville and Nashville, strike, **1955:** 90,
    95
Railroad Commission, Presidential, **1960–61:** 343n.
  Appointment of members, statement, **1960–61:**
    378
Railroad employee benefits, **1954:** 145; **1959:** 10
    (pp. 104, 105), 123
  Budget message, **1958:** 5 (pp. 51–53)
  Claim of William J. Kaiser, veto, **1960–61:** 113
  Retirement, **1955:** 17 (p. 145); **1956:** 168; **1960–
    61:** 13 (pp. 95, 96)
Railroad Retirement Act, amendment, approval,
    1954: 145
Railroad Retirement Board, **1958:** 53; **1960–61:**
    113
Railroad Unemployment Insurance Act, **1960–61:**
    410
Railroads
  Alaska Railroad, **1960–61:** 225, 414 (p. 1023)
  Commuter services, **1958:** 82n.
  Decline, comment on, **1960–61:** 21
  Excise taxes, **1958:** 88
  "Help Korea" trains, **1954:** 78
  Labor dispute, report of emergency board, **1954:**
    39
  Labor-management agreement, statement,
    1960–61: 343
  Mail transportation charges, **1958:** 5 (p. 55)
  Oregon and California Railroad, **1954:** 152
  Presidential Railroad Commission, **1960–61:**
    343n.
  Recommendations on, **1958:** 82 and n.
  Reduced rates in drought disaster areas, **1956:**
    236, 237
Railroads, Association of American, **1954:** 78 n.
Railway Express Agency, **1954:** 39
Railway and Steamship Clerks, Brotherhood of,
    1954: 39
Rainbow Bridge National Monument, **1960–61:**
    414 (p. 993)

Rakotomalala, Louis, **1960–61:** 324n.
Rama Road, **1954:** 102
Rambouillet, **1959:** 207n., 330
Ramsay, Adm. Bertram H., **1954:** 133
Ramser, Harold, **1960–61:** 23n.
Rand, William M., **1953:** 111n.
Randall, Clarence, **1953:** 176, 190n.; **1954:** 18, 351;
    1957: 110 and n.
  Appointment, Special Assistant to the President,
    1956: 139
  Letter, **1953:** 177
Randall (Clarence B.) Commission.
  See Commission on Foreign Economic Policy.
Randall, John D., **1960–61:** 276
Rangeley, Maine, remarks at fawn presentation
    ceremonies, **1955:** 141
Ranger moon exploration program, **1960–61:** 414
    (p. 972)
Rangoon, Burma, Buddhist Synod, **1955:** 148
Rankin, Karl L., **1954:** 168
Rankine, Paul S., **1953:** 208, 225, 243; **1954:** 63,
    328; **1955:** 26; **1956:** 53, 78, 94, 171, 198,
    216
Rao, V.K.R.V., **1959:** 314n.
Rapid City, S. Dak, **1953:** 103
Rardin, Harry, **1960–61:** 330
Rastovorov, Yuri A., **1954:** 25
Ratna Rajya Lekshmi, **1960–61:** 128, 129
Ravdin, Dr. Isidor S., **1956:** 155; **1957:** 216
Ray, Kay, **1956:** 205, 229
Ray, Philip A., report, **1960–61:** 176n.
Rayburn, Repr. Sam, **1953:** 141; **1954:** 57, 157, 341
  See also Speaker of the House of Representatives
    (Sam Rayburn)
Raymond, Jack, **1960–61:** 34
RB-47 plane incident, **1960–61:** 255, 284, 302, 313
  Statement, **1960–61:** 231
  Telegram to Senator Mansfield, **1960–61:** 232
REA.
  See Rural Electrification Administration.
Reactors, **1955:** 228
  See also Reactors, nuclear.
  Budget message, **1958:** 5 (p. 33)
  Gas cooled power reactor, **1958:** 193
  Geneva installation, **1955:** 100
  Idaho testing Station, **1956:** 12 (p. 101)
  Industrial power, **1955:** 17 (p. 121)
  International agreements for use of, **1955:** 89,
    121, 123, 165
  Merchant ship, **1955:** 79
  Naval vessels, **1955:** 17 (p. 121)
  New England, **1955:** 223
  Pennsylvania State University, **1955:** 121
  Plutonium production reactor, **1958:** 193
Reactors, nuclear, **1954:** 38, 260; **1955:** 17 (p. 143);
    1956: 43, 190, 256; **1957:** 13, 125; **1958:**
    204, 236; **1960–61:** 13 (pp. 58, 59), 414
    (pp. 959, 960)

Reactors, nuclear — *continued*
  Atomic Energy Commission appropriation,
      1957: 159
  Budget messages, **1956:** 12 (p. 101); **1959:** 10 (pp.
      67, 68)
  Construction, **1954:** 14 (p. 129)
  Foreign programs, **1956:** 190
    Europe, **1958:** 145
    Japan, request to IAEA for uranium, **1959:**
      189
  Merchant ship, **1956:** 243
Reading, Pa., **1958:** 303
Reading, the President's
  Abilene *Reflector-Chronicle*, **1954:** 149
  Big Dam Foolishness (Peterson), **1955:** 56
  Clark, Grenville, **1958:** 153
  Davis, Richard Harding, **1958:** 88
  Lorant, Stefan, *The Presidency*, **1958:** 288
  Mutt and Jeff cartoon, **1954:** 151
  Newspapers, **1960–61:** 143
  U. S. News and World Report article, **1958:** 274
  West Point Plebe (Reeder), **1955:** 117
Real Estate Boards, National Association of,
      remarks, **1960–61:** 19
Real estate investment trusts, special taxation,
      disapproval, **1956:** 183
Real property.
  See Buildings, Federal; Property, Federal.
Recession, **1958:** 49; **1959:** 225; **1960–61:** 4, 422
  Campaign remarks, **1958:** 287, 292, 293, 295, 296,
      303, 308
  Decline of, **1959:** 6
  Economic mobilization conference, address,
      1958: 110
  Effect on foreign relations, **1958:** 70
  Federal program, **1958:** 42, 63, 303
  Need for confidence, **1958:** 83
  News conference remarks, **1958:** 28, 42, 56, 63,
      70, 74, 83, 88, 103, 120, 153
  1953–1954, **1958:** 83
  1957–1958, **1959:** 15, 223, 244
  Prevention, **1956:** 19
  Psychological factors, **1958:** 37
  Question of, **1954:** 25, 26, 33, 129
  Recovery from, **1959:** 76
  Telegram to Gov. W. Averell Harriman, **1958:** 33
Rechnitzer, Andreas B., Distinguished Civilian
      Service Award, citation, **1960–61:** 25
Reciprocal trade agreements, **1957:** 32, 61
  Lead and zinc tariffs, **1957:** 157, 160
Reclamation, Bureau of, **1953:** 153; **1954:** 256, 258;
      1956: 12 (pp. 134–136); **1957:** 105; **1958:**
      37; **1959:** 194; **1960–61:** 410
  Budget messages, **1954:** 14 (pp. 167, 168); **1955:**
      17 (pp. 158–160); **1958:** 5 (pp. 68, 69);
      1959: 10 (pp. 94, 95); **1960–61:** 13 (pp. 38,
      83, 108), 414 (pp. 993, 995–997, 1025)
  Commissioner, filling of vacancy, **1953:** 128

Reclamation, Bureau of — *continued*
  Construction starts, **1955:** 157
  News conference remarks, **1953:** 37, 126, 128
  Water storage projects, **1958:** 155
Reclamation projects, **1955:** 4, 180; **1956:** 44, 165,
      256; **1958:** 49; **1959:** 42
  Appropriation, **1958:** 244
  Budget messages **1956:** 12 (p. 133); **1959:** 10 (p.
      45)
  Letter to minority leaders, **1958:** 43
Reconstruction era, **1957:** 134
Reconstruction finance Corporation, **1954:** 18;
      1955: 17 (pp. 92, 176)
  Abolition, **1957:** 78
  Budget message, **1954:** 14 (pp. 150, 178–181)
  Business loan program, liquidation, **1954:** 14 (p.
      181)
  Liquidation under Reorganization Plan 2 (1954),
      1954: 95
  Loan to Elkins, W. Va., **1956:** 163
  Production programs, **1954:** 14 (pp. 179–181)
  Real property, Sedgwick County, Kans., **1956:**
      112
  Synthetic rubber facilities disposal
    Recommendations, **1953:** 22
    Report, **1953:** 49
Records.
  See also Information.
  FBI, **1957:** 134, 169
  Federal Housing Administration, **1954:** 81
  Presidential papers, disposition, **1957:** 134; **1959:**
      179
  Privileged, **1957:** 22, 115
Records management, **1954:** 14 (pp. 187, 188);
      1955: 17 (pp. 179–181); **1956:** 12 (pp. 84,
      151); **1958:** 5 (p. 72); **1959:** 10 (p. 108);
      1960–61: 13 (pp. 101, 102), 414 (p. 1019)
  See also Information.
Recreational resources, **1958:** 5 (p. 69); **1960–61:**
      414 (p. 998)
  Outdoor Recreation Resources Review Commis-
      sion, **1958:** 268; **1959:** 10 (pp. 95, 96)
Red Cross, **1953:** 118; **1954:** 183, 204, 310; **1955:**
      210; **1956:** 138, 185, 315; **1957:** 62, 118,
      121, 140, 154, 203; **1958:** 136, 144, 184;
      1959: 156, 159, 238; **1960–61:** 153, 175,
      210, 293
  Campaigns, **1956:** 11, 47, 53; **1957:** 30, 39, 62;
      1958: 3, 38, 270; **1959:** 20
    Memorandums, **1953:** 4; **1954:** 1, 356; **1960–
      61:** 37
    Remarks, **1953:** 17; **1955:** 45
    Statements, **1954:** 46; **1959:** 45; **1960–61:** 65
  Convention, remarks, **1953:** 117; **1957:** 89
  Disaster relief in Chile, **1960–61:** 214
  District of Columbia Chapter House, dedication,
      remarks, **1953:** 201
  Flood relief in the Northeast, **1955:** 208, 209

Red Cross — *continued*
  Greek earthquake disaster, **1953:** 172
    Statement, **1953:** 173
  Harriman, E. Roland, letter, **1953:** 3
  Hungarian relief, **1956:** 304
  International, **1957:** 39
  Italian, **1954:** 315n.
  Korea, **1953:** 17; **1954:** 48
  London meeting (1942), **1953:** 117, 201
  News conference remarks, **1956:** 47, 53
  President (Gen. Alfred M. Gruenther), letter,
    1960–61: 214
Red Cross, American Junior, remarks, **1958:** 144
Red Cross Societies, League of, **1954:** 175, 182 ftn.
    (p. 678); **1955:** 37, 49; **1957:** 39
Red Feather agencies, funds for, **1956:** 138; **1957:**
    140
Red Feather campaign.
    See Community Chest campaign.
Red River flood control project, approval, **1955:**
    184
Red Wing, Minn.
  Hiawatha Bridge dedication, remarks, **1960–61:**
    330
  Rardin, Mayor Harry, **1960–61:** 330
Redevelopment Land Agency, **1956:** 4n.
Redstone Arsenal, Ala., **1959:** 267
Redstone missile (short-range).
    See also Missiles.
Reece, Repr. B. Carroll, **1959:** 77n.; **1960–61:** 403n.
Reed, Repr. Chauncey W., **1953:** 269
Reed, Repr. Daniel A., **1953:** 31, 41; **1954:** 48
Reed, Harry, **1953:** 97; **1954:** 291; **1958:** 128
  Appointment as coordinator of rural develop-
    ment program, **1957:** 156
Reed, Stanley F.
  Resignation as Supreme Court Justice, **1957:** 24
    and n.
  Withdrawal from Civil Rights Commission,
    1957: 242 and n.
Reed, Mrs. Stanley F., **1957:** 24
Reeder, Red, *West Point Plebe*, **1955:** 117
Reenlistment bonuses for military personnel, ap-
    proval of bill, **1954:** 166
Rees, Repr. Edward H., **1953:** 269
Referendum on civil rights program, **1957:** 124
Refugee Relief Act, **1953:** 208; **1954:** 63; **1955:** 109
  Approval, **1953:** 160
  Budget message, **1955:** 17 (p. 131)
  Letter to Gov. Dewey, **1954:** 188
  Letter to Governors, **1954:** 187
Refugee Relief Act, Administrator (Scott
    McLeod), **1956:** 296
Refugee Year, World, **1959:** 115; **1960–61:** 133
Refugees and escapees, **1955:** 76, 81; **1957:** 150;
    1958: 32; **1959:** 55
    See also Hungarian refugees.

Refugees and escapees — *continued*
  Admission to United States, **1953:** 187; **1954:** 92;
    1955: 17 (p. 131); **1960–61:** 96, 133, 414
    (p. 1022)
  Certain refugees, approval, **1960–61:** 233
  American voluntary societies cooperating in
    escapee program, remarks, **1955:** 60
  Arab, **1953:** 217; **1955:** 17 (p. 131); **1956:** 12 (p.
    107), 26, 58, 298; **1957:** 6, 35; **1958:** 207
  Budget message, **1958:** 5 (p. 40)
  Cuban, **1960–61:** 410
    Letter to Cardinal Spellman on aid, **1960–61:**
    371
    Report, statement, **1960–61:** 431
  East German, **1953:** 146
  Governors' Committee proposed, **1954:** 187, 188
  Immigration policies, **1956:** 2, 33, 213, 275, 306
  Indochinese, **1954:** 273
  Intergovernmental Committee for European Mi-
    gration, **1956:** 58, 213n., 306
  "Iron curtain" countries, **1956:** 12 (p. 107)
  Joint statement with Prime Minister Eden, **1956:**
    26
  Letter to President of the Senate and Speaker of
    the House, **1953:** 52
  Letter to Queen Juliana, **1953:** 53
  Message to Congress, **1955:** 109
  New York State committee on, **1954:** 188
  Palestinian, **1953:** 89
  U.N. activities, report, **1958:** 8, 148
  U.N. High Commissioner, **1956:** 58
  U.N. program, **1955:** 17 (p. 131), 156
  U.S. assistance, **1953:** 257; **1960–61:** 13 (p. 63)
  U.S. contributions to U.N. for, **1957:** 90
  Vietnamese, **1957:** 83; **1958:** 36
  White House Conference, **1959:** 115
Refugees, United States Committee for, **1959:** 91
Regina, Saskatchewan, **1960–61:** 281
Registration for election, **1956:** 206, 235
Registration of foreign agents, **1953:** 95
Regulatory agencies, Federal, **1957:** 13, 132; **1958:**
    42
    See also specific agencies.
  Acceptance of favors by members, **1958:** 28, 74
  News conference remarks, **1957:** 72
  Pending cases, reduction, **1956:** 12 (p. 84)
Regulatory agencies, State, **1957:** 72
Regulus missile.
    See Missiles.
Releases, White House, partial list, Appendix A,
    1957: p. 855
Religion, teaching of, **1956:** 241
Religion in American Life, Committee on, radio
    and television program, recorded state-
    ment, **1953:** 236
Religion of candidates and officials, comment on,
    1959: 154
Religion as political issue, comments on, **1960–61:**
    127, 143, 268, 284

Religious Action in the Social and Civil Order, Foundation for, **1954:** 327n.
Religious leaders
  Civil rights views, **1957:** 228
    Consultation on civil rights, **1957:** 207
    News conference remarks, **1956:** 62
Religious liberty, **1958:** 285
Religious Organizations, Commission on, National Conference of Christians and Jews, message, **1953:** 132
Relocation exercises, Federal.
  See Civil defense.
Remagen Bridge, remarks to participants in seizure of, **1955:** 52
Remagen Bridgehead, Society of the, **1955:** 52
Remon Cantera, Jose A.,
  Assassination, statement, **1955:** 2
  Joint statement with, **1953:** 200
Remon, Senora, **1955:** 2
Renegotiation Act of 1951, extension, **1954:** 3; **1955:** 50; **1958:** 5 (p. 32); **1959:** 10 (p. 66)
Renegotiation Board, **1957:** 132; **1960–61:** 150
Rensselaer, Ind., **1959:** 4n.
Rent controls, **1953:** 6
Reorganization Act, extension, **1955:** 4; **1959:** 10 (p. 111)
Reorganization Act of 1958, Department of Defense, approval, **1958:** 199
Reorganization and Defense Production Acts, extension proposed, **1954:** 349
Reorganization Plan No. 11 of 1939, modification, veto, **1959:** 86
Reorganization Plans, extension of period for transmitting, **1957:** 58
Reorganization Plans, messages
  1953
    No. 1, Department of Health, Education, and Welfare, establishment, **1953:** 28
    No. 2, Department of Agriculture, **1953:** 35
    No. 3, Executive Office, organization, **1953:** 40
    No. 4, Department of Justice, **1953:** 51
    No. 5, Export-Import Bank, **1953:** 60
    No. 6, Department of Defense, **1953:** 61
    No. 7, Foreign Operations Administration, establishment, **1953:** 90
    No. 8, United States Information Agency, establishment, **1953:** 91
    No. 9, Council of Economic Advisers, **1953:** 93
    No. 10, Air carriers, payments to, **1953:** 94
  1954
    No. 1, Foreign Claims Settlement Commission, **1954:** 94
    No. 2, Reconstruction Finance Corporation, **1954:** 95
  1956
    No. 1, research and development, Defense Department, **1956:** 105
    No. 2, Federal Savings and Loan Insurance Corporation, **1956:** 108

Reorganization Plans, messages — *continued*
  1957
    No. 1 (RFC), **1957:** 78 and n.
    No. 2 (RFC), **1957:** 78
  1958, No. 1, Federal and civil defense, **1958:** 84
  1959, No. 1, Departments of Interior and Agriculture, **1959:** 101
Reporters.
  See Newsmen.
Reporting, labor organizations, on welfare and pension plans, **1958:** 20, 235
Reporting for income tax and social security payroll tax purposes, simplification, **1958:** 5 (p. 52)
Reporting requirements, Government
  Budget message, **1956:** 12 (p. 151)
  Hoover Commission recommendations, **1956:** 110
  Small business concerns, **1956:** 263
Reports to the Congress.
  See Congress, reports to, messages transmitting.
Reports of the Killian and Gaither panels, withholding of, **1958:** 19
Reports to the President
  Air Coordinating Committee, **1954:** 123, 200
  Air safety actions, **1958:** 135n.
  Airline equipment investment program, **1958:** 194
  Anderson, Robert B.
    Department of the Treasury, letter, **1960–61:** 415
    Integration in civilian facilities at naval installations, **1953:** 243, 244
  Aviation facilities planning, implementation, **1959:** 74
  Benson, Ezra Taft, Department of Agriculture, **1960–61:** 391n.
  Board of Inquiry on labor dispute at atomic facilities, **1954:** 193
  Board of Inquiry on steel strike, **1959:** 265
  Cabinet Committee on Price Stability for Economic Growth, statement, **1960–61:** 117
  Carey, Archibald J., Jr., President's Committee on Government Employment Policy, letter, **1960–61:** 394
  Civil Service Commission, Federal employees training program, **1960–61:** 149
  Commission on Civil Rights, **1959:** 288
  Commission on Foreign Economic Policy, **1954:** 16, 18, 67, 68, 90, 101, 209, 349, 351, 353
  Committee on Energy Supplies and Resources Policy, comment on, **1955:** 33, 41, 56
  Committee to Study the U.S. Military Assistance Program, **1959:** 90, 136, 137, 170, 183, 288
  Department of Justice record of action on subversives, **1954:** 129, 130
  Douglas, Lewis W., financial and economic mission to United Kingdom, **1953:** 176, 177

Reports to the President — *continued*
  Dulles, John F.
    Agreements with Germany on settlement of debts and claims, **1953:** 46
    European visit, **1955:** 99
    ILO conventions and recommendations, **1955:** 107
    Mutual Defense Treaty with China, **1955:** 5
    Mutual Defense Treaty with Korea, **1954:** 6
  Eisenhower, Milton S., Latin American visit, **1953:** 48n., 198 and ftn. (p. 624)
  Federal agency relocation exercise, **1955:** 149 ftn. (p. 672)
  Federal Radiation Council, **1960–61:** 268 ftn. (p. 654)
  Flemming, Arthur S.
    Department of Health, Education, and Welfare, letter, **1960–61:** 413
    President's Advisory Committee on Government Organization, letter, **1960–61:** 433
  Food-for-peace program, statement, **1960–61:** 242
  Gates, Thomas S., Department of Defense, **1960–61:** 397n.
  Gray, Gordon, final report, letter, **1960–61:** 412
  Gruenther, Gen. Alfred M., disaster relief in Chile, letter, **1960–61:** 214
  Herter, Christian A., Department of State, **1960–61:** 409n.
  Hoegh, Leo A., Office of Civil and Defense Mobilization, letter, **1960–61:** 384
  Improvements in budgeting, **1959:** 300
  Johnston, Eric, Middle East mission, **1953:** 217n.
  Joint Federal-State Action Committee, letter, **1960–61:** 115
  Low income farmers, problems of, **1955:** 82
  Mitchell, James P.
    Department of Labor, letter, **1960–61:** 401
    Effectiveness of Labor-Management Act, letter, **1960–61:** 316
  Mueller, Frederick H.
    Department of Commerce, **1960–61:** 387
    New York World's Fair 1964–65, U.S. participation, letter, **1960–61:** 376
  National Advisory Council on International Monetary and Financial Problems, **1959:** 32
  National Monument Commission, proposed Freedom Monument, **1960–61:** 152
  North Atlantic Treaty Organization, report on, **1953:** 265 ftn. (p. 843)
  President's Advisory Committee on a National Highway Program, **1955:** 39
  President's Committee on Government Contracts, statement, **1960–61:** 407
  President's Committee on International Information Activities, **1953:** 126

Reports to the President — *continued*
  Public Advisory Board for Mutual Security, **1953:** 22 and ftn. (p. 86)
  Ray, Philip A., labor surplus areas, **1960–61:** 176
  Reconstruction Finance Corporation, synthetic rubber facilities disposal, **1953:** 49
  Rogers, William P.
    Deceptive practices in broadcasting media, letter, **1960–61:** 1
    Department of Justice, letter, **1960–61:** 411
  Rural development program, statement, **1960–61:** 322
  Science Advisory Committee, **1959:** 56
    Availability of scientific and technical information, **1958:** 326n.
    Statement, **1960–61:** 363
  Seaton, Fred A., Department of the Interior, letter, **1960–61:** 402
  Stans, Maurice H.
    Bureau of the Budget, letter, **1960–61:** 406
    Government operations, letter, **1960–61:** 435
  Steel wage negotiations, **1959:** 211
  Strauss, Lewis L., nuclear tests in Pacific, **1954:** 68n.
  Summerfield, Arthur E., Post Office Department, letter, **1960–61:** 385
  Tariff Commission, wool imports and price supports, **1954:** 49
  Transportation survey of Washington area, **1959:** 157
  Veterans facilities, elimination of segregation, **1954:** 309n.
  Voorhees, Tracy, Cuban refugee problems, statement, **1960–61:** 431
  Waterman, Alan T., National Science Foundation, letter, **1960–61:** 393
Reports to the President, letters, statements, etc., in response to
  Air Coordinating Committee, U.S. aviation policy, **1954:** 123
  Anderson, Robert B., integration in civilian facilities at naval installations, **1953:** 244
  Benson, Ezra Taft, rural development program, **1958:** 313
  Cabinet Committee on Price Stability for Economic Growth, **1959:** 144
  Commission on Foreign Economic Policy, **1954:** 16
  Committee on Scientists and Engineers, **1958:** 327
  Committee to Study the U.S. Military Assistance Program, **1959:** 137
  Committee for the White House Conference on Education, **1956:** 103
  Conference for the benefit of small business, **1957:** 227
  Department of Agriculture, rural development program, **1959:** 273

Reports to the President, responses to — *continued*
Department of Justice record of action on sub-
versives, **1954:** 130
Director, Office of Defense Mobilization, tanker
contracts, **1956:** 239
District of Columbia Auditorium Commission,
1957: 21
Douglas, Lewis W., financial and economic
mission to United Kingdom, **1953:** 176
Federal Council on Aging, **1959:** 280
Federal Highway Administrator, financing of
interstate highway system, **1959:** 138
Great Plains program, **1956:** 7
Inter-American Committee of Presidential Rep-
resentatives, **1957:** 96
Mitchell, James P., welfare of workers, **1956:** 196
National Security Training Commission, reserve
forces, **1954:** 7
President's Committee for Hungarian Refugee
Relief, **1957:** 85
President's Committee on Scientists and Engi-
neers, **1957:** 241
President's Committee for Traffic Safety, **1957:**
14
Public works planning, **1956:** 309
Science Advisory Committee, **1958:** 326; **1959:**
118
Small business, **1956:** 176
Special Committee to Investigate Crude Oil
Imports, **1958:** 54
Veterans Affairs Administrator, segregation in
VA facilities, **1954:** 309
Representation allowances, **1956:** 12 (p. 84)
Embassies, **1957:** 50
Republic Day, Pakistan, **1956:** 65
Republic Steel Corporation, **1959:** 211n.
Republican candidates (congressional), remarks to,
1960–61: 278
Republican Committee of New York State
Addresses, **1953:** 68, 69
Remarks, **1954:** 298
Republican committees' campaign book,
Eisenhower-Nixon, **1956:** 216
Republican Congressional Committee, **1957:** 108n.
National, **1960–61:** 278n.
Republican Congressmen, dinner honoring,
remarks, **1959:** 127
Republican convention (1960)
News conference remarks, **1959:** 29, 48
Question of site, **1959:** 29
Republican "Dinner with Ike" rallies, address,
1960–61: 23
Republican doctrine, **1960–61:** 245
Republican legislative conference, statements,
1953: 266, 268, 269
Republican Looks at His Party, A, **1956:** 193
Republican National Committee, **1953:** 68; **1954:**
22n., 77n.; **1957:** 108; **1959:** 127; **1960–61:**
7

Republican National Committee — *continued*
Agricultural Division, **1956:** 133
Chairman, vacancy in office, **1953:** 41
Chairman (Meade Alcorn), **1957:** 28, 50, 63, 105,
108n., 214n., 248; **1958:** 83, 96, 223, 274,
287, 310; **1959:** 21
Resignation, letter, **1959:** 69
Republican National Committee
Chairman (Leonard W. Hall), **1953:** 68, 69,
105n.; **1954:** 33, 50, 92, 161, 311, 322, 347;
1955: 47, 247; **1956:** 18, 62, 121, 206n.,
209n., 290, 294n.
See also Hall, Leonard W.
News conference remarks on, **1953:** 238, 249
Resignation, **1957:** 9
Chairman (Sen. Thruston B. Morton), **1959:** 75,
132; **1960–61:** 23, 245n., 309n., 395
Republican National Committee
Chairman (C. Wesley Roberts), **1953:** 37
Resignation, statement, **1953:** 38
Dinner honoring Republican members of
Congress, address, **1958:** 96
Leadership training school, **1956:** 122n.
Meetings, addresses, remarks, **1955:** 35; **1958:** 26,
223; **1960–61:** 246, 395
News conference remarks on, **1954:** 33, 50, 311,
347
Panel discussion, **1958:** 293, 295
President's position re, comment on, **1954:** 33
Recruitment of Government employees, **1954:**
311
Thornton, Dan, **1956:** 133
Republican National Conference, address, **1957:**
108
Republican National Convention (1952), **1960–61:**
38, 107
Republican National Convention (1956), **1955:** 10,
47; **1956:** 84
Acceptance address, **1956:** 190
Arrival at San Francisco, remarks, **1956:** 188
News conference remarks on, **1956:** 171, 189
Republican National Convention (1960), **1960–61:**
93, 222
Address, **1960–61:** 245
Republican National Federation, Young, **1960–61:**
18n.
Republican National Finance Committee, remarks,
1955: 35
Republican National Leadership Training School,
Young, remarks, **1960–61:** 18
Republican Organization, National Young, ad-
dress, **1953:** 101
Republican Party, **1957:** 28; **1960–61:** 245
Choice over Democratic Party, news conference
remarks, **1956:** 171
Comments on, **1953:** 68, 266, 268, 269; **1954:**
304, 345, 347; **1955:** 35

Republican Party — *continued*
 Middle-of-the-road philosophy, **1960–61:** 246
 100th anniversary, **1953:** 187
 Platform, **1957:** 92, 108, 215; **1960–61:** 256, 346
 Presidential nomination, comments on, **1960–61:** 7, 24, 93, 103
 President's role in restoring, **1959:** 21
 Record, remarks, **1960–61:** 107
 Role in, after retirement, **1960–61:** 422
 Strength of, **1959:** 123
 Vice Presidential nomination, **1960–61:** 38
Republican Rally, Minneapolis-St. Paul International Airport, remarks, **1960–61:** 329
Republican Rally, Pennsylvania, remarks, **1953:** 212
Republican Senatorial Committee, **1957:** 108n.
Republican State chairmen, remarks to, **1955:** 213
Republican State finance chairmen, **1957:** 105
Republican Victory Fund Rally, address, **1960–61:** 309
Republican Women, National Conference of, remarks, **1953:** 57; **1954:** 77; **1955:** 94; **1956:** 50; **1957:** 63; **1959:** 75; **1960–61:** 107
Republican Women, National Federation of, **1954:** 273
Republican Women's Finance Committee of the District of Columbia, remarks, **1955:** 104
Republican workers, New Orleans, remarks, **1953:** 220
Republicanism, modern, news conference remarks, **1957:** 17, 22, 50, 87
Republicans; A History of Their Party, **1956:** 198
Reschke, Oscar W., **1953:** 128, 243; **1954:** 172; **1956:** 20, 229
Research, **1954:** 21; **1956:** 12 (pp. 79, 82, 115); **1958:** 2
 Aeronautical, **1954:** 14 (p. 174); **1955:** 17 (p. 92); **1958:** 5 (p. 60), 64, 105, 135, 185, 246
 Agricultural, **1953:** 95; **1954:** 4, 14 (p. 163), 221, 291; **1955:** 17 (pp. 94, 155); **1956:** 6, 12 (pp. 125, 130, 132), 214, 250; **1958:** 12, 49, 292, 295; **1959:** 10 (p. 92); **1960–61:** 13 (p. 82), 32, 391, 410, 414 (p. 992)
 Basic, **1954:** 14 (pp. 151–153, 155); **1956:** 12 (pp. 122, 123); **1957:** 230, 234; **1958:** 5 (pp. 30, 33, 46, 48); **1959:** 10 (p. 98), 107; **1960–61:** 13 (pp. 39, 87, 89, 91), 393, 410, 414 (pp. 939, 959, 1004)
 Coal production, **1960–61:** 13 (p. 85), 133, 402, 414 (p. 998)
 Educational, **1956:** 8, 12 (p. 122), 222, 277
 General Motors Research Center, **1956:** 107
 Market, **1958:** 110
 Medical and health, **1954:** 3, 11, 14 (p. 143), 301, 318; **1955:** 247; **1956:** 2, 12 (pp. 116, 120), 21; **1959:** 10 (pp. 68, 102), 55, 102, 181, 238; **1960–61:** 13 (pp. 93, 94), 23, 280, 410, 413, 414 (p. 1007)

Research — *continued*
 Mental health, **1956:** 161
 Meteorological, **1960–61:** 104
 Minerals, **1954:** 14 (p. 171)
 Oceanographic, **1960–61:** 13 (p. 91), 25, 414 (p. 999)
 Public health, **1959:** 181
 Rubber, **1956:** 90
 Scientific, **1954:** 14 (p. 174), 57, 60, 92, 308; **1955:** 19; **1956:** 12 (pp. 101, 116, 122, 123); **1958:** 5 (pp. 20, 46, 48), 326n.; **1959:** 10 (pp. 44, 68), 107; **1960–61:** 363, 386, 393, 414 (pp. 959, 1003, 1004), 421
 Seismic, **1960–61:** 143 ftn. (p. 410)
 Social welfare, **1956:** 2
 Space.
  See Space research and exploration.
 Utilization of farm products, **1958:** 5 (p. 67)
 Water conversion, **1959:** 10 (p. 94); **1960–61:** 13 (pp. 84, 85)
 Weather, **1956:** 12 (p. 152); **1957:** 11, 92
Research and development, **1957:** 8, 17, 210, 230, 234; **1958:** 16, 29, 65, 105, 135
 Budget message, **1958:** 5 (pp. 33, 60)
 Joint statement with Prime Minister Macmillan, **1957:** 226
 Military, **1954:** 14 (p. 124); **1955:** 4, 17 (p. 118); **1956:** 32, 88; **1958:** 2, 80, 96; **1959:** 125, 288
  Budget messages, **1956:** 12 (pp. 81, 97, 100); **1958:** 5 (pp. 18, 19, 26, 29, 30)
  Campaign remarks, **1958:** 292, 293, 308
  Missiles, **1958:** 5 (pp. 19, 26, 29)
  News conference remarks, **1958:** 63, 74
  Reorganization plan, Defense Department, **1956:** 105
  Role of Secretary McElroy, **1959:** 286
  U-235 for, statement, **1957:** 125
  U.S.-Euratom joint program, **1958:** 145, 236
Research and Development Board (Department of Defense), **1953:** 61
 History, **1956:** 105
Research facilities, medical and dental, **1956:** 12 (pp. 116, 120), 21, 151
Reserve forces bill, **1955:** 176
 Approval, **1955:** 192
 News conference remarks, **1955:** 90, 100, 119, 146, 149
 Segregation rider, **1955:** 119
Reserve Officers Association, **1953:** 11
Reserve Officers Training Corps, Baylor University, remarks, **1956:** 114
Reserve program, **1953:** 144; **1954:** 7, 14 (p. 124), 225, 351; **1955:** 3, 4, 12
 Budget message, **1955:** 17 (p. 91)
 News conference remarks, **1954:** 200, 353
 Six-month, **1956:** 51
 White House release, **1955:** 192n.

Reserves, military, **1960–61:** 410
  Budget messages, **1960–61:** 13 (pp. 48, 49), 414
    (p. 950)
Reservoir projects, Texas, reconveyance of certain
    reservoir project lands to former owners,
    1955: 199
Reservoirs, Federal, water storage for local com-
    munities, approval, **1958:** 155
Residential construction.
  See Housing.
Resignation of commission by the President upon
    nomination, **1958:** 288
Resignation of the President, rumors of, **1957:** 62;
    1958: 11, 88
Resignations of administration personnel, com-
    ment on, **1960–61:** 263
Resignations from officials of preceding admin-
    istration, comment on, **1953:** 54
Resignations or retirements, letters
  Adams, Sherman, **1958:** 266
  Alcorn, Meade, **1959:** 69
  Anderson, Robert B., **1960–61:** 415
  Benson, Ezra Taft, **1960–61:** 391
  Brownell, Herbert, Jr., **1957:** 224
  Brundage, Percival F., **1958:** 46
  Burns, Arthur F., **1956:** 297
  Burton, Harold H., **1958:** 279
  Dodge, Joseph M., **1954:** 65
  Dulles, John Foster, **1959:** 79
  Durkin, Martin P., **1953:** 184
  Eisenhower, Milton S., **1960–61:** 349
  Flemming, Arthur S., **1957:** 29; **1960–61:** 413
  Folsom, Marion B., **1958:** 97
  Gates, Thomas S., Jr., **1960–61:** 397
  Gray, Gordon, **1960–61:** 412
  Herter, Christian A., **1960–61:** 409
  Hobby, Mrs. Oveta Culp, **1955:** 152, 153
  Hoegh, Leo A., **1960–61:** 384
  Hughes, Rowland R., **1956:** 17
  Humphrey, George M., **1957:** 102
  Kistiakowsky, George B., **1960–61:** 400
  Lodge, Henry Cabot, **1960–61:** 266
  McElroy, Neil H., **1959:** 285
  McKay, Douglas, **1956:** 67
  Minton, Sherman, **1956:** 202
  Mitchell, James P., **1960–61:** 401
  Mueller, Frederick H., **1960–61:** 387
  Reed, Stanley, **1957:** 24 and n., 242 and n.
  Roberts, C. Wesley, **1953:** 38
  Rogers, William P., **1960–61:** 411
  Seaton, Fred A., **1960–61:** 402
  Stans, Maurice H., **1960–61:** 406
  Stassen, Harold E., **1958:** 30
  Strauss, Lewis L., **1959:** 147
  Summerfield, Arthur E., **1960–61:** 385
  Warren, Lindsay C., **1954:** 69
  Weeks, Sinclair, **1958:** 299
  Wilson, Charles E., **1957:** 206 and n.
  Wright, Adm. Jerauld, **1959:** 350

Resignations or retirements, letters — *continued*
  Young, Philip, **1957:** 33
Resources for the Future, Inc., **1953:** 25
Reston, James B., **1953:** 22, 41, 88, 265; **1954:** 18,
    33, 92, 129, 138, 157, 172, 182, 311, 347,
    353; **1955:** 47, 59, 81, 95, 100, 112, 119,
    146, 149; **1956:** 20, 47, 53, 62, 78, 88, 94,
    96, 113, 121, 155, 189, 235; **1957:** 22, 28,
    45, 50, 56, 70, 72, 80, 87, 105, 124, 134,
    150; **1958:** 11, 28, 37, 74, 120, 141, 213,
    222; **1959:** 42, 48, 89, 132, 179, 223, 243,
    271, 277, 288; **1960–61:** 21, 103, 127, 256,
    268
  Interview of Nikita S. Khrushchev, **1957:** 210
Restricted data in atomic energy program, **1954:** 38
Retail Federation, American, remarks, **1953:** 23
Retail Grocers, National Association of, remarks,
    1954: 144
Retail sales, **1960–61:** 143, 256, 263
Retailers Association, **1954:** 320
Retaliatory power in case of attack, **1955:** 3
Retired persons
  Campaign remarks, **1956:** 241; **1958:** 293
  Effect of inflation, **1958:** 120, 308
  Letter, **1956:** 289
Retirement
  Benefits for retired D.C. policemen, firemen, and
    other specialized personnel, **1959:** 239
  Duff, Harry N., service disability claim of, **1958:**
    248
  Government employees, **1954:** 10, 14 (p. 189), 43,
    145; **1955:** 4, 17 (pp. 96, 106, 145, 181,
    182); **1958:** 5 (pp. 51, 52); **1960–61:** 410
    Civil service fund, **1960–61:** 13 (pp. 101–103),
      414 (p. 1020)
  Military personnel, **1955:** 4, 17 (p. 145); **1958:** 5
    (pp. 51–53); **1960–61:** 414 (p. 956)
    Credits for service, **1960–61:** 13 (pp. 95, 96),
      414 (p. 1011)
    Naval officers, **1959:** 178
    Temporary grades, rights, **1956:** 81n.
  News conference remarks, **1959:** 7, 179
  Railroad employees, **1954:** 145; **1955:** 17 (p.
    145); **1958:** 5 (pp. 51–53); **1959:** 10 (pp.
    104, 105); **1960–61:** 13 (pp. 95, 96)
    Benefits, **1956:** 168
  Women at age 62, **1956:** 158
Retirement, State and local systems, social security
    coverage, **1953:** 155
Retirement Board, Railroad, **1958:** 53
Retirement fund for civilian employees, **1956:** 12
    (pp. 150, 152)
  Veto message, **1958:** 192
Retirement plans, comments on, **1960–61:** 24, 93,
    422
Retirement Policy for Federal Personnel, Commit-
    tee on, **1954:** 10, 43, 145
  Budget message, **1954:** 14 (p. 189)
  Report, **1955:** 17 (p. 181)

[References are to items except as otherwise indicated]

Retirement system, civil service, **1956:** 2
Reuter, Ernst
 Death of, statement, **1953:** 197
 Letter, **1953:** 185
Reuther, Walter P., **1953:** 128; **1956:** 198, 216;
  1957: 157; **1959:** 36
 Letters, **1953:** 248; **1954:** 26
 Message, **1953:** 130
Revercomb, Sen. Chapman, **1958:** 302
Revere, Paul, **1956:** 87
Revolutionary War, **1953:** 8; **1954:** 50; **1960–61:**
  336
Reynolds, Dorothy S., **1960–61:** 327n.
Reynolds, James A., **1955:** 95
RFC.
 See Reconstruction Finance Corporation.
Rhee, Syngman, **1953:** 147, 159; **1954:** 6; **1957:** 80
 Exchange of toasts, **1954:** 171, 174
 Joint statement with, **1954:** 178
 Letters, **1953:** 96; **1960–61:** 141
 News conference remarks on, **1953:** 109, 128,
  141, 225; **1954:** 165, 168, 172; **1960–61:**
  127, 143
Rhee, Madame, **1954:** 171, 174
Rhine River, World War II crossing, **1960–61:** 405
Rhineland, **1958:** 201, 274
Rhode Island
 Del Sesto, Gov. Christopher, **1959:** 112, 113
 Fogarty, Repr. John E., **1957:** 62
 Green, Sen. Theodore F., **1956:** 184; **1957:** 176
  and n.; **1958:** 277
 Newport, **1957:** 176, 177, 178n., 186n., 187n.,
  188n., 189n., 191n., 193n., 197, 200n.,
  201n., 228; **1958:** 239n., 240, 242n., 243n.,
  244n., 245n., 246n., 247n., 248n., 249n.,
  250n., 251n., 252n., 253n., 254n., 255n.,
  256n., 257n., 260n., 262n., 263n., 264n.,
  265n., 266n.; **1960–61:** 228, 239
   Releases from, **1960–61:** 227, 229–238, 240–
   243, 248–254
 Pastore, Sen. John O., **1959:** 113
 Providence, **1954:** 22n.
 Roberts, Gov. Dennis J., **1955:** 222, 223; **1957:**
  138
Rhodes scholars appointed from West Point
  (1955), **1955:** 117
Rice, John S., **1959:** 71n.
Rice
 Acreage allotments, **1956:** 115; **1958:** 12, 59
 Acreage reserve (soil bank), **1956:** 6
 Agricultural surpluses, **1955:** 148
 Exports, **1958:** 58
 Price supports, **1954:** 4; **1956:** 82; **1958:** 12; **1959:**
  23
Rice University, address, **1960–61:** 336
Richards, Ernest V., Jr., **1953:** 219n.

Richards, Repr. James P., **1956:** 20; **1959:** 271
 Amendment, military assistance bill, **1953:** 265
 Middle East mission, **1957:** 17, 46, 72
Richards, Robert W., **1953:** 31, 37, 208, 225; **1954:**
  33, 73, 172, 192, 322, 328; **1955:** 90; **1956:**
  32, 94, 121, 171, 189, 235; **1957:** 50, 124;
  1958: 88; **1959:** 191
Richards, Mrs. Rose, letter, **1956:** 289
Richland, Wash.
 Self-government, **1955:** 17 (p. 121)
 Termination of Federal ownership and opera-
  tion, proposed, **1954:** 14 (p. 130)
Richmond, Va., campaign remarks, **1956:** 280
Rickey, Branch, **1958:** 88
Rickover, Adm. Hyman G., **1959:** 179
 Education, **1958:** 153
Ridder, Walter T., **1953:** 254; **1954:** 73, 161; **1955:**
  59; **1957:** 50; **1958:** 310
Riddleberger, James W., **1959:** 154; **1960–61:** 315
Ridgway, Gen. Matthew B., **1953:** 41; **1959:** 16
 See also Supreme Allied Commander, Europe
  (Gen. Matthew B. Ridgway).
 Distinguished Service Medal, citation, **1955:** 144
 News conference remarks on, **1955:** 26
 Nomination as Chief of Staff, Army, **1953:** 72, 73
  Letter, **1953:** 71
Ridgway, Mrs. Matthew B., **1955:** 144n.
Ridgway, Matthew B., Jr., **1955:** 144n.
Riefler, Winfield W., **1954:** 39
Riess, Walter, **1957:** 207
Rieve, Emil, **1956:** 198
Riggs, Robert L., **1953:** 198, 230, 243; **1954:** 18, 39,
  73, 107, 172, 328; **1955:** 33; **1956:** 88, 171,
  198, 216; **1957:** 56, 105; **1959:** 102
"Right to work" laws, **1954:** 63, 347, 353; **1957:** 72;
  1958: 274
 Campaign remarks, **1958:** 293
 States rights upheld, **1958:** 274
Rio, Sotero del, **1960–61:** 77
Rio Branco, Baron de, **1960–61:** 51
Rio de Janeiro, **1954:** 340, 345, 351; **1958:** 133;
  1960–61: 42n., 54
 Address to Congress of Brazil, **1960–61:** 49
 Collision of U.S. Navy and Brazilian planes,
  1960–61: 55, 64
 Conference in, **1955:** 4
 Meeting of ministers of finance and economy,
  1954: 345, 351
  Message, **1954:** 340
 Remarks at Naval Ministry, **1960–61:** 48
 Remarks to Supreme Court, **1960–61:** 50
 Statement on departure, **1960–61:** 55
 Toast to president Kubitschek, **1960–61:** 51
Rio Grande River, **1954:** 243; **1957:** 150; **1958:**
  137n.; **1960–61:** 335
 Amistad Dam, **1960–61:** 13 (p. 83), 303, 414 (p.
  995)
  Joint statement on, **1959:** 257
 Diablo Dam, joint statement on, **1959:** 38

Rio Grande River — *continued*
  Falcon Dam construction, **1953:** 221
  Flood, **1954:** 158
Rio Pact, **1954:** 225
Rio treaty.
  See Inter-American Treaty of Reciprocal Assistance.
Ripon, Wis., birthplace of Republican Party, **1953:** 187
River basin development, **1953:** 153; **1955:** 17 (pp. 156–161); **1958:** 155
River drainage areas, **1957:** 8
River Grange Company, Inc., **1958:** 48
River and Harbor Act, approval, **1954:** 249
Rivers, Repr. Ralph J., **1959:** 3n.
Rivers and harbors, **1955:** 17 (pp. 168, 169)
  Appropriation, **1958:** 244
  Appropriations, veto, **1959:** 194
  Development, **1954:** 14 (pp. 164, 166, 167, 175)
  Disapproval of bill, **1956:** 180
  Letter to minority leaders, **1958:** 43
  News conference remarks, **1956:** 235
Rivers and Harbors Act
  Approval, statement, **1958:** 155
  Veto, message, **1958:** 73
Rivers and Harbors Congress, National, remarks, **1954:** 120
Riverside Lumber Company, **1958:** 212
Rizal, José, **1960–61:** 186, 188
Rizley, Ross, **1955:** 106
  Letter to, re Pan American World Airways use of Great Circle route, **1956:** 14
Roa, Raul, **1960–61:** 268
Roach, Lucian, tax refund claim, veto, **1958:** 212
Roads.
  See Highways.
Robbins, Hilda H., **1960–61:** 337n.
Roberts, B. J., **1959:** 141
Roberts, C. Wesley.
  See Republican National Committee, Chairman (C. Wesley Roberts).
Roberts, Chalmers M., **1953:** 54, 77, 88, 109, 128, 208, 230, 249, 254, 265; **1954:** 9, 115, 129, 143, 157, 161, 165, 168, 192, 311, 341, 347, 353; **1955:** 10, 18, 26, 33, 41, 47, 59, 62, 90, 95, 100, 119, 146, 149, 185; **1956:** 16, 20, 32, 56, 62, 78, 88, 96, 113, 121, 155, 171, 193, 198, 205, 216; **1957:** 17, 45, 56, 62, 70, 72, 80, 87, 92, 105, 119, 134, 145, 169, 207, 210; **1958:** 28, 37, 56, 63, 74, 83, 88, 103, 120, 198, 222, 288, 310, 318; **1959:** 17, 36, 48, 53, 67, 123, 154, 172, 173, 271; **1960–61:** 21, 24, 34, 93, 103, 143, 256, 263
Roberts, Charles W., **1956:** 20, 47, 78, 94, 96, 171, 189, 193, 198, 235; **1957:** 28, 50, 62, 72, 92, 157, 169; **1958:** 11, 37, 70, 83, 198, 222, 318; **1959:** 36, 48, 67, 132, 179, 191, 223, 243, 267, 288; **1960–61:** 34, 38, 143, 222, 228, 284

Roberts, Clifford, **1957:** 236 and n.
Roberts, Gov. Dennis J., **1957:** 138
  Letters, **1955:** 222, 223
Roberts, Frank N., **1953:** 33
Roberts, Gilroy, **1955:** 244n.
Roberts, Owen J., **1958:** 153
Robertson, Sen. A. Willis, **1953:** 78; **1960–61:** 340
Robertson, David B., **1953:** 33n.
Robertson, James M., **1953:** 79n.
Robertson, Walter S., **1953:** 141; **1955:** 81; **1956:** 280; **1959:** 132
Robertson, Wishart, **1953:** 246n.
Robie, Merle S., **1960–61:** 187
Robsion, Repr. John M., Jr., **1956:** 226
Rochester, N. Y., **1956:** 263
Rockefeller, John D., Jr., death of, **1960–61:** 144
Rockefeller, John D., 3d., **1957:** 81; **1959:** 106
Rockefeller, Laurance, **1958:** 268
Rockefeller, Nelson A., **1954:** 347; **1958:** 305, 306; **1960–61:** 306
  Appointment as Special Assistant to the President, letter, **1954:** 354
  Chairman, President's Advisory Committee on Government Organization, **1953:** 62
  Meeting with, **1959:** 277
  Meeting with Vice President Nixon, **1960–61:** 256
  News conference remarks on, **1958:** 153, 222, 310; **1959:** 26, 48, 67, 94, 148, 167, 277; **1960–61:** 7, 103, 222, 256
  Presidential candidacy, **1958:** 310
  Under Secretary of Health, Education, and Welfare, **1953:** 269
  U.S. vs. Soviet position, **1960–61:** 222
Rockefeller family, **1953:** 81
Rocketry, **1957:** 210, 245
  Joint study with United Kingdom, **1957:** 226n.
  Military.
    See Missiles.
  Satellite, statement, **1957:** 211
Rockets, **1957:** 210, 230; **1960–61:** 4, 245
  See also Satellites, earth; Space exploration; Space vehicles.
  Budget messages, **1960–61:** 13 (pp. 59, 66), 414 (p. 960)
  Campaign remarks, **1958:** 292, 293, 295
  German V2, **1958:** 293
  Jupiter-C, **1958:** 27
  Manned rocket, remarks, **1958:** 74
  Moon probe, **1958:** 28, 57n., 295
    Pioneer, **1958:** 308
  Pershing, **1959:** 267
  Soviet, **1957:** 86, 245
  Soviet moon probe, **1959:** 89
Rockne, Knute, **1960–61:** 174
Rocky Beach project, Wash., **1955:** 17 (p. 158)
Rodes, Harold P., **1956:** 214
Rodopoulos, Constantine, **1959:** 325
Rodriguez, Eulogio, **1960–61:** 183n.

Rogers, Gov. C. J., **1954:** 257
Rogers, Repr. Edith Nourse, **1953:** 269
Rogers, James T., **1954:** 129, 341
Rogers, Warren, Jr., **1959:** 132, 243, 277
Rogers, William P., **1954:** 161; **1957:** 224n.
  See also Attorney General (William P. Rogers)
Role of President
  Congressional leadership, **1957:** 92
  Leader of party, **1957:** 105
Rollman, Heinz, **1960–61:** 350
Rolston, J. Albert, letter, **1958:** 267
Romagna, Jack, **1954:** 63; **1960–61:** 422
Rome, **1954:** 311; **1956:** 113, 207n., 264; **1958:** 144
  Ancient civilization, **1960–61:** 328
  Arrival, remarks, **1959:** 291
  IGY conference, **1957:** 210
  Joint statement with President Gronchi, **1959:** 293
  Remarks on departure, **1959:** 294
  Remarks at U.S. embassy, **1959:** 292
  Treaties signed at, **1957:** 100
Rommel, Erwin, **1959:** 96
Romualdez, Daniel Z., **1960–61:** 183n.
Romulo, Carlos P., **1954:** 73, 101; **1957:** 166
Roosevelt, Mrs. Eleanor, meeting with Khrushchev, **1958:** 318
Roosevelt, Franklin D., **1954:** 27, 28, 29, 50, 149n.; **1955:** 78; **1956:** 113, 235; **1957:** 105, 239n.
  Decision on Germany, **1958:** 318
  Use of veto, **1959:** 161
Roosevelt, John, **1956:** 272
Roosevelt, Theodore, **1953:** 6, 25, 105, 153; **1954:** 113n., 201; **1956:** 238; **1957:** 105, 150; **1958:** 119, 305, 320; **1959:** 7; **1960–61:** 100
  Centennial of birth, **1958:** 100, 303
Roosevelt (Theodore) Home at Sagamore Hill, dedication, remarks, **1953:** 105
Roosevelt (Theodore) Week, **1953:** 105
Root, Elihu, **1957:** 28
Rose, Frank A., **1954:** 89
Rose, H. Chapman, **1960–61:** 350
Rosellini, Gov. Albert D., **1958:** 312
Rosenberg (Julius and Ethel) case, **1953:** 22
  Statements, **1953:** 10, 114
Rosenwald, William, **1955:** 115n.
Rosh Hashana, statement, **1956:** 200
Rossides, Zenon, **1960–61:** 324n.
Roszak, Theodore, **1959:** 148 ftn. (p. 490)
Rotarians, Chula Vista, Calif., **1960–61:** 333
Roth, Philip, **1956:** 256
Roth, Robert, **1955:** 56, 119; **1958:** 103
Rothman, Stuart, congressional action on appointment, **1959:** 102
Rotunda frieze, Capitol, dedication, remarks, **1954:** 106
Rountree, William, **1959:** 299n., 301n., 304n., 305n.
  Meeting on Syria, **1957:** 157n.
Rover project, **1960–61:** 414 (p. 960)

Royal Danish Academy of Science, **1957:** 225n.
Royall, Kenneth C., **1960–61:** 143
Royalty taxes paid in United Kingdom, tax credit for, disapproval, **1956:** 181
Royer, Paul H., **1959:** 259n.
Rozmarek, Charles, **1960–61:** 310
Rubber Committee, ODM Ad Hoc, **1956:** 90
Rubber imports, **1959:** 55
Rubber plants, synthetic
  Disposal of, **1957:** 13
  Sale of, **1955:** 17 (p. 92)
Rubber producing facilities, Government owned, disposal
  Message to Congress, **1953:** 49
  News conference remarks, **1953:** 22, 198
Rubber producing facilities disposal, **1955:** 17 (p. 175)
Rubber Producing Facilities Disposal Commission, **1954:** 57; **1956:** 90
Rubber production program, **1954:** 14, (pp. 179–181)
Rubber requirements and resources report, message, **1956:** 90
Rubottom, Roy R., Jr., **1958:** 133; **1960–61:** 51, 69
Ruiz Cortines, Adolfo, **1953:** 222, 223, 225; **1956:** 53; **1959:** 21
  Exchange of messages, **1956:** 70
  Letter to, **1955:** 229
  Messages, **1954:** 158; **1955:** 216
  News conference remarks on, **1958:** 153
  Toast to, **1953:** 221
Rules governing this publication, Appendix D, **1953:** p. 886; Appendix D, **1954:** p. 1139; Appendix D, **1955:** p. 886; Appendix D, **1958:** p. 891; Appendix D, **1959:** p. 910; Appendix D **1960–61:** (p. 1093)
Rumania, **1956:** 282, 283
  Compensation claims of U.S. nationals, **1954:** 94
  Georgescu (Valeriu C.) case, **1953:** 88
Rummel, Archbishop Joseph F., **1953:** 219
Rural, Letter Carriers Association, National, remarks, **1959:** 177
Rural development program, **1958:** 12, 59; **1959:** 23; **1960–61:** 32, 140, 391, 410, 414 (p. 992)
  Appointment of coordinator, **1957:** 156
  Conference in Memphis, statement, **1958:** 128
  Low-income farm families, **1956:** 2, 3, 6, 19
    Budget message, **1956:** 12 (pp. 131, 132)
    Campaign remarks, **1956:** 214, 250
    Pilot projects, **1956:** 6, 250
    Report on, statement, **1956:** 217
  Report, letter, **1958:** 313
  Statements, **1959:** 273; **1960–61:** 322
Rural Development Program, Committee for, **1959:** 273; **1960–61:** 5
  Budget message, **1960–61:** 414 (p. 993)

Rural Electric Cooperative Association, National, remarks, **1959:** 30

Rural electric cooperatives, **1956:** 193; **1959:** 10 (p. 91)

Budget message, **1958:** 5 (p. 67)

Rural electrification, **1954:** 278, 291; **1955:** 17 (pp. 153, 154); **1959:** 30; **1960–61:** 410

Budget messages, **1954:** 14 (p. 162); **1958:** 5 (pp. 66–67); **1959:** 10 (p. 91); **1960–61:** 13 (p. 80), 414 (pp. 989, 990)

Campaign remarks, **1956:** 214

Letter to Secretary Benson, **1958:** 51

Rural Electrification Administration, **1953:** 100; **1954:** 33; **1955:** 17 (p. 153); **1956:** 193, 250; **1957:** 157; **1958:** 12; **1959:** 30; **1960–61:** 410

Budget messages, **1956:** 12 (p. 130); **1959:** 10 (pp. 51, 53, 91); **1960–61:** 13 (pp. 80, 108), 414 (pp. 989, 990)

Loan approval authority, veto, **1959:** 86

Rural Electrification Administrator (David A. Hamil), **1957:** 157

Rural Electrification Administrator (Ancher Nelsen), letter, **1954:** 278

Rural industries, **1958:** 12

Rural development program, **1958:** 313

Rural telephones.

See Telephone service, rural.

Rus de Mello Juqueira, Potado, **1960–61:** 52n.

Rush, Dr. Benjamin, **1957:** 216

Rusk, Dr. Howard A., **1953:** 15 and ftn. (p. 59); **1954:** 78n.

Russell, Sen. Richard B.

Bipartisan meeting on Suez Canal, **1956:** 184

Defense reorganization bill, **1958:** 178

News conference remarks on, **1957:** 124, 145

Telegram, **1957:** 200 and n.

Russia.

See Soviet Union.

Ruth, Robert W., **1953:** 238; **1956:** 5

Rutland, Vermont, remarks at Dairy Festival, **1955:** 131

Ryerson, Edward L., **1953:** 45; **1956:** 10n.

Ryukyu Islands

High Commissioner (Lt. Gen. Donald P. Booth), **1960–61:** 197

Joint statement with Prime Minister Kishi, **1957:** 117

Joint statement with Prime Minister Yoshida, **1954:** 330

Ota, Seisaku, **1960–61:** 197

Visit to Okinawa, **1960–61:** 177, 197, 209

Saar, French-German agreement, **1954:** 307, 337

Sabotage.

See Subversive activities.

SAC.

See Strategic Air Command.

SACEUR.

See Supreme Allied Commander Europe.

Sacido, Osiris, **1960–61:** 62, 67

SACLANT.

See Supreme Allied Command Atlantic.

Sacramento, Calif., **1959:** 270

Sadr, Mohsed, **1959:** 320

Safe driving, statements, **1954:** 255, 336; **1955:** 111, 243

Safe Driving Day

Message, **1954:** 352

News conference remarks, **1954:** 347, 353

Safety, occupational, **1957:** 13

Standards for workers, **1960–61:** 410

Safety codes for longshoremen and harbor workers, **1959:** 10 (p. 101)

Safety Council, National, **1958:** 45; **1960–61:** 410

Remarks, **1958:** 297

Sagatelyan, Mikhail R., **1960–61:** 284

SAGE.

See Semiautomatic ground environment (SAGE) system.

Saginaw, Mich., **1953:** 242n.

Saigon, Vietnam, **1954:** 168, 306; **1955:** 48

St. Andrews, Scotland, **1958:** 91

Saint Charles, **1954:** 297

St. Elizabeths Hospital, **1957:** 232

Dr. Winfred Overholser, **1960–61:** 68n.

St. George, Repr. Katharine, testimonial dinner, remarks, **1960–61:** 173

St. George Hotel, Brooklyn, N. Y., refugee reception center, **1957:** 250

St. James, Manche, France, **1956:** 102

St. John's Church (Washington, D.C.), **1960–61:** 243

St. John's College, Francis Scott Key Memorial Auditorium, dedication, **1959:** 116

St. Joseph, Mo., **1959:** 270

St. Laurent, Louis S., **1953:** 208, 246; **1956:** 53

Exchange of messages, **1956:** 71

Joint statements with, **1953:** 70, 247

St. Laurent (Omaha Beach), France, **1956:** 102

St. Lawrence power project, **1953:** 246

Joint statements with Prime Minister St. Laurent, **1953:** 70, 247

News conference remarks, **1953:** 15, 22, 31, 54, 77

St. Lawrence Seaway, **1953:** 268; **1954:** 3, 139, 209, 221, 291, 318; **1955:** 47; **1958:** 26, 110, 163; **1960–61:** 341, 350, 410

Approval of bill, **1954:** 110

Budget messages, **1954:** 14 (pp. 166, 167, 175, 176); **1955:** 17 (pp. 164, 168)

Campaign remarks, **1956:** 214, 224, 226, 251; **1958:** 292, 296

Dedication ceremonies, remarks, **1959:** 141

St. Lawrence Seaway — *continued*
    Joint statement with Prime Minister St.
        Laurent, **1953:** 247
    Letter to Secretary Weeks, **1958:** 299
    Letter to Sen. Wiley, **1953:** 56
    News conference remarks, **1953:** 15, 22, 31, 54,
        208; **1954:** 57, 63, 107; **1959:** 36
St. Lawrence Seaway Authority of Canada, **1959:**
        141n.
St. Lawrence Seaway Development Corporation of
        the United States, **1958:** 5 (p. 69); **1959:**
        141n.
St. Louis, Mo., **1953:** 57, 193; **1954:** 130
    Tornado, **1959:** 29
St. Luke, **1959:** 70
St. Marie, Mrs. Josette L., relief of, veto, **1954:** 142
Ste. Mere Eglise, France, **1954:** 131
Ste. Mere Eglise incident, World War II, **1956:** 96
St. Patrick, **1959:** 58, 59n.
St. Paul, Minn., **1956:** 229
    Campaign remarks, **1956:** 249
    Remarks at Republican Rally, **1960–61:** 329
Saint Paul, U.S.S., **1960–61:** 190n., 191
St. Paul's Protestant Episcopal Church, Rome,
        1959: 294n.
St. Thomas, Virgin Islands, **1953:** 260
Salaries.
    See Pay.
Salazar, Antonio de Oliverira, **1960–61:** 160, 161
Salerno, Italy, floods and landslides, statement,
        1954: 315
Sales, retail, **1960–61:** 143, 256, 263
Sales Executives Club, Cleveland, remarks, **1956:**
        223
Sales tax, Federal, question of, **1953:** 198
Salesmanship by business concerns, **1958:** 56, 83
Salk, Dr. Jonas E., **1955:** 78, 79, 113
    Citation, **1955:** 77
Salk vaccine.
    See Poliomyelitis vaccine.
Salpeter, A. Eliyahu, **1954:** 92, 157; **1955:** 26, 90;
        1956: 198
Saltonstall, Sen. Leverett, **1953:** 187; **1954:** 100,
        325; **1956:** 292; **1959:** 113
    Bipartisan meeting on Suez Canal, **1956:** 184
    Constitutional amendment on treatymaking
        powers, **1954:** 33
    News conference remarks on, **1954:** 33, 92
"Salute to Eisenhower" dinner, address, **1956:** 18
Salvadori, Max W., lecture by, **1956:** 62
Salvation Army, **1959:** 156, 238; **1960–61:** 153, 210
Samoa, American, **1954:** 125, 126
    Labor standards, **1956:** 172
Samos satellite, **1960–61:** 143, 255
Samuelson (Paul) economic report to President-
        elect Kennedy, **1960–61:** 422
San Agustin, Bienvenida, **1960–61:** 224
San Antonio, Texas, **1960–61:** 336

San Carlos de Bariloche, Argentina, **1960–61:** 42n.,
        64n.
    Joint declaration with President Frondizi, **1960–
        61:** 66
    Mayor Osiris Sacido, **1960–61:** 62, 67
    Remarks on arrival, **1960–61:** 62
    Remarks on departure, **1960–61:** 67
    Toast to President Frondizi, **1960–61:** 63
San Diego, Calif., **1960–61:** 333
    Dail, Mayor Charles C., **1960–61:** 333
San Francisco, Calif., **1955:** 126, 131; **1956:** 188,
        193; **1958:** 288; **1959:** 24, 89; **1960–61:**
        320n., 332
    Birthday celebration, **1957:** 215 and n.
    Campaign remarks, **1958:** 293, 294
    Christopher, Mayor George E., **1960–61:** 332
    Conference on world organization, **1958:** 7
    News conference remarks, **1955:** 47, 81, 112, 146;
        1956: 189
    Regional conference on traffic safety, **1958:** 45n.
    Republican Convention, **1956:** 190
    U.N. conference (1955), **1956:** 143
    U.N. establishment (1945), **1960–61:** 332
    U.N. 10th anniversary meeting, **1955:** 81, 112,
        146, 156
    Veterans hospital construction, **1954:** 14 (p. 134)
San Jose, Costa Rica, OAS foreign ministers meet-
        ing, **1960–61:** 228, 263, 267, 268
San Juan, Puerto Rico, **1953:** 260; **1960–61:** 43
    Governors' Conference (1959), **1960–61:** 229
    Message, **1959:** 174
San Luis Unit, Central Valley Project, **1960–61:**
        133
    Approval of bill, **1960–61:** 168
San Martin, Jose de, **1960–61:** 58, 60, 69
Sanchez Martinez, Mayor Lucina, **1960–61:** 334
Sandstrom, Emil, letter, **1955:** 37
Sandys, Duncan, **1957:** 28
Santa Margarita River, water storage facilities,
        approval, **1954:** 173
Santangelo, Repr. Alfred E., **1959:** 167
Santiago, Chile, **1960–61:** 42n., 99n.
    Address before Congress of Chile, **1960–61:** 73
    Declaration of Santiago, **1960–61:** 76
    Foreign ministers meeting, 1959 (OAS), **1960–61:**
        73, 76
    Inter-American Foreign Ministers Conference,
        1959: 172; **1960–61:** 228
    Joint statement with President Alessandri,
        1960–61: 76
    Remarks on arrival, **1960–61:** 69
    Remarks on departure, **1960–61:** 77
    Remarks on receiving medal from Congress of
        Chile, **1960–61:** 74
    Remarks at U.S. embassy, **1960–61:** 70, 72
    Toasts to President Alessandri, **1960–61:** 71, 75
Santos, Bonifacio, relief of, **1958:** 231

Sao Paulo, Brazil, **1960–61:** 42n., 49, 55
  Address at luncheon, **1960–61:** 53
  Mayor Adhemar de Barros, **1960–61:** 52
  Remarks on arrival, **1960–61:** 52
  Remarks on departure, **1960–61:** 54
Sarasin, Pote, **1960–61:** 164
Saratoga, Battle of, **1960–61:** 124
Sarayba, Felididad G., **1960–61:** 224
Sarmiento, Domingo Faustino, **1959:** 16
Sarnoff, David, **1958:** 111
  Letter to, **1957:** 57
  Recommendations on cold war strategy, **1955:**
    95
Sarr, Ibrahima, **1960–61:** 324n.
Saskatchewan, Canada, **1959:** 125n.; **1960–61:** 281
Satellite, earth, **1955:** 47 ftn. (p. 308); **1956:** 12 (p.
    123); **1957:** 8, 211, 234; **1958:** 64, 223;
    1959: 6; **1960–61:** 4
  See also Rockets; Space research and explora-
    tion; Space vehicles.
  Atlas (Score), **1958:** 321, 322; **1959:** 10 (p. 57)
  Budget messages, **1958:** 5 (p. 30); **1959:** 10 (pp.
    57, 76); **1960–61:** 414 (pp. 953, 970, 972,
    1021)
  Campaign remarks, **1958:** 292, 308
  Communications, **1960–61:** 264, 410, 414 (pp.
    970, 972), 424
  Commercial use, statement, **1960–61:** 386
  Courier, **1960–61:** 414 (p. 970), 424
  Discoverer, capsules recovered from, **1960–61:**
    264, 424
    Remarks upon inspection, **1960–61:** 261
  Echo, **1960–61:** 261, 264, 410, 414 (p. 970), 424
    Message recorded for transmission via, **1960–
    61:** 258
  Explorer, **1958:** 308; **1960–61:** 287, 424
    Explorer I, orbiting of, **1958:** 27
  Launching proposed during International Geo-
    physical Year, **1957:** 122
  Midas, **1960–61:** 143, 414 (p. 953)
  Navigation, **1960–61:** 264, 424
  News conference remarks, **1957:** 70, 210; **1958:**
    28, 274, 308; **1960–61:** 21, 143
  Reconnaissance, **1958:** 80
  Samos, **1960–61:** 143, 255
  Soviet, **1956:** 121, 265; **1957:** 210, 211, 230
    Sputniks, **1958:** 56, 70, 120, 141, 274, 287
  Tiros, **1960–61:** 143, 264, 410, 414 (p. 972), 424
    Launching, statement, **1960–61:** 104
  Transit, **1960–61:** 264, 424
  Vanguard project, **1957:** 210, 211, 234; **1958:** 28,
    308; **1959:** 267; **1960–61:** 11, 424
    Launching of test vehicle, statement, **1958:** 47
  Weather, **1960–61:** 143, 410, 414 (pp. 970, 972,
    1024), 424
    White House statement, **1958:** 57n.

Satellite countries, Soviet, **1953:** 6, 50, 121, 146,
    160, 205, 256; **1954:** 72, 143; **1955:** 12, 33,
    37n., 119, 146, 175; **1957:** 17, 150; **1958:** 2,
    32
  See also Communist bloc; *specific countries.*
  Congressional resolution on subjugation, **1953:**
    6, 14, 15, 22
  Information program, **1955:** 17 (p. 131)
  Joint statement with Western leaders, **1953:** 255
  Military strength, **1959:** 55
  News conference remarks, **1953:** 15, 22, 126, 254;
    1958: 11, 141; **1959:** 167, 172, 186
Saturn project, **1959:** 277; **1960–61:** 10, 12, 24, 287,
    410
  Budget messages, **1960–61:** 13 (pp. 47, 66), 414
    (pp. 972, 973)
Saud, King of Saudi Arabia, **1957:** 6
  Exchange of greetings with President, **1957:** 23
    and n.
  Joint statement with President, **1957:** 31
  News conference remarks on, **1957:** 17, 22, 28,
    45, 207
  Turkish-Syrian crisis, **1958:** 148
Saudi Arabia, **1956:** 53, 94, 96, 113; **1957:** 91;
    1960–61: 21
  Abdul Aziz Ibn al Saud, **1953:** 18
    Death of, **1953:** 245
  Al-Khayyal, Sheikh Abdullah, **1957:** 120 and n.
  Joint statement with King Saud, **1957:** 31
  King Saud.
    See Saud, King of Saudi Arabia.
  News conference remarks, **1957:** 56, 207
  Prince Faisal, **1953:** 18
  Saud ibn Abd al-Aziz al-Saud, message, **1953:**
    245
Saulnier, Raymond J., **1960–61:** 21
  See also Council of Economic Advisers, Chair-
    man (Raymond J. Saulnier).
  News conference remarks on, **1958:** 37
  Telegram from, **1958:** 296
Saunders, David, **1954:** 273
Savannah River atomic energy facility, **1954:** 14 (p.
    128)
Savannah, NS, **1959:** 10 (p. 80), 48
Savings accounts, insurance, **1960–61:** 13 (p. 73)
Savings bond campaign, **1958:** 70
Savings Bond Conference, remarks, **1959:** 43
Savings bonds, U.S., **1953:** 189; **1959:** 225
  Budget message, **1954:** 14 (p. 187)
  Interdepartmental Savings Bond Committee,
    1954: 15
  Interest rate increase, **1959:** 126, 188
    Letter, **1959:** 230
    Statement, **1959:** 231
  Payroll savings plan, **1955:** 186, 187
  Sale through medium of cartoons, **1954:** 151
  Series E and H, interest rates, **1957:** 76

Savings and Loan Corporation, Federal, premium
    rate increase proposed, **1960–61:** 13 (p.
    73), 414 (p. 980)
Sawyer, Roland, **1953:** 109
Saylor, Repr. John P., **1956:** 234
Sayre, Charles R., **1956:** 187n.
Sayre, Dean Francis B., Jr., letter, **1959:** 91
Scali, John, **1954:** 311; **1956:** 171, 193, 205, 298;
    1957: 17, 22, 62, 72, 87, 92, 105, 115, 124,
    134, 145, 207, 210; **1958:** 28, 37, 42, 56, 63,
    70, 74, 83, 88, 103, 153, 198, 213, 222, 288,
    310, 318; **1959:** 17, 21, 26, 42, 48, 53, 67,
    89, 94, 123, 132, 148, 154, 161, 243, 271,
    277; **1960–61:** 24, 34, 38, 93, 103, 143, 284,
    362
Scarce materials, controls, **1958:** 5 (p. 33)
Scelba, Mario, joint statement, **1955:** 61
Scelba, Signora, **1955:** 61
Scharnikow, William F., **1953:** 59
Scheele, Leonard A., **1955:** 95, 112, 113, 119; **1956:**
    137, 303
Scheibel, Kenneth M., **1953:** 230; **1954:** 9, 25, 39,
    50, 57, 73, 92, 101, 115, 129, 157, 161, 165,
    168, 172, 200, 311, 341, 347; **1955:** 10, 33,
    47, 81, 90, 112, 149; **1956:** 20, 47, 78, 121,
    171, 216, 298; **1957:** 45, 56, 115, 134, 210,
    228; **1958:** 28, 37, 56, 213, 222, 310; **1959:**
    48, 67, 102, 148, 167, 172; **1960–61:** 222,
    284
Scherer, Ray L., **1953:** 141, 225, 238; **1954:** 18, 25,
    33, 63, 68, 138, 143, 157, 182, 192, 311,
    347; **1955:** 10, 62, 81, 95, 100, 112, 119,
    146, 176; **1956:** 5, 32, 47, 53, 88, 96, 121,
    189, 193, 198, 216, 229, 235; **1957:** 17, 28,
    50, 62, 92, 115, 145, 210, 228; **1958:** 37, 63,
    70, 83, 88, 103, 213, 222, 288, 310; **1959:**
    17, 94, 102, 148, 154, 161, 167, 191, 271,
    277, 288; **1960–61:** 7, 24, 38, 103, 127, 222,
    263, 268, 284, 422
Schine, G. David, **1954:** 92
Schnitzler, William F., **1955:** 245
Schoeppel, Sen. Andrew F., **1956:** 235; **1957:** 108
    and n.; **1958:** 42
Scholarships, **1958:** 24, 28
    See also Fellowships.
    American countries, **1957:** 96
    Budget message, **1958:** 5 (p. 49)
    Federal, **1957:** 234n.
    Fulbright, **1957:** 222
    National defense education bill, **1958:** 195
        Approval, **1958:** 243
        Letter to Repr. Wainwright, **1958:** 162
    Students from Guinea, **1959:** 272
School Boards Association, National, **1955:** 96
School construction, **1955:** 19, 247; **1958:** 203;
    1960–61: 4, 284, 341
    Addresses, messages, etc., **1956:** 2, 3, 8, 19, 103,
        222, 277; **1957:** 8, 13, 16, 19, 68, 86, 118

School construction — *continued*
    Anti-segregation amendment to bill, **1955:** 149;
        1956: 20, 32
    Areas affected by Federal activities, **1957:** 170
        Approval, **1958:** 203
    Basic principles for, proposed legislation, **1957:**
        19
    Budget messages, **1955:** 17 (p. 147); **1956:** 12 (pp.
        82, 88, 116, 122); **1958:** 5 (pp. 42, 46, 50);
        1960–61: 13 (p. 90), 414 (pp. 939, 1002,
        1003)
    Campaign remarks, **1956:** 226, 234, 253, 256, 272
    Federal aid, **1954:** 3, 14 (p. 154), 182; **1960–61:**
        13 (p. 90), 23, 133, 255, 414 (pp. 939, 1002,
        1003)
    Legislative recommendations, **1956:** 8
    Meeting on, **1956:** 318
    Message to Congress, **1955:** 31
    News conference remarks, **1955:** 18, 33, 47, 119,
        149; **1956:** 20, 32, 62, 94, 121, 171, 229,
        235; **1957:** 17, 56, 62, 92, 145, 228
School districts in Federally affected areas, aid to,
        1953: 6, 95; **1954:** 14 (pp. 153, 154);
        1956: 2, 8, 12 (p. 122), 222; **1958:** 203;
        1959: 10 (pp. 98–100), 27, 181; **1960–61:**
        13 (pp. 87, 89, 90), 414 (pp. 1001–1003)
    Budget message, **1958:** 5 (pp. 46, 50)
    News conference remarks, **1959:** 17
    Norfolk, Va., **1959:** 17
School integration, **1956:** 69, 241; **1957:** 8, 198
    See also Integration; Integration public schools;
        Little Rock, Ark.
    Army posts, **1956:** 229
    Interposition resolutions on Supreme Court de-
        cision, **1956:** 47
    Louisville, Ky., **1956:** 205
    Manifesto by certain members of Congress,
        1956: 56
    News conference remarks, **1956:** 20, 32, 47, 56,
        62, 113, 171, 193, 198, 205, 229; **1957:** 124,
        134
    Texas (Texarkana), **1956:** 198, 205
    University of Alabama, **1956:** 32
School lunch program, **1954:** 14 (pp. 87, 144); **1958:**
        59; **1960–61:** 127 ftn. (p. 362)
    Budget messages, **1956:** 12 (p. 124); **1960–61:** 13
        (p. 96), 414 (pp. 989, 1012)
    Campaign remarks, **1956:** 214
School milk program, **1955:** 17 (p. 144); **1956:** 6, 83,
        214; **1958:** 12, 59
    Approval of bill, **1956:** 72
    Budget message, **1958:** 5 (p. 66)
Schools.
    See Education; Integration, public schools.
Schools abroad, American sponsored, **1959:** 55
Schorr, Daniel, **1953:** 249, 254; **1954:** 9, 18, 33, 39,
        63, 353; **1955:** 10, 47, 59, 62; **1958:** 120
Schowalter, Lt. Edward R., Jr., Medal of Honor,
        citation, **1954:** 8

Schriever, Lt. Gen. Bernard A., on missiles, **1959:** 172

Schroth, Thomas N., **1956:** 62, 94, 155, 171, 205; **1957:** 17; **1958:** 11, 74, 310; **1959:** 36, 53, 89, 94, 148, 167, 172, 186, 223, 288; **1960–61:** 21, 93, 143, 284, 422

Schuck, Arthur A., **1960–61:** 166

Schultz, Henry E., **1953:** 252

Schuman plan.
See European Coal and Steel Community.

Schurman, Wilbur M., **1955:** 137n.

Schwable, Col. Frank H., **1954:** 50

Schwartz, Lloyd M., **1953:** 41; **1954:** 9, 48, 63, 165; **1955:** 26, 33, 56, 81, 90, 112, 119, 176; **1956:** 32, 56, 94, 193, 216; **1957:** 17, 45, 50, 70, 115, 119, 157; **1958:** 63, 103; **1959:** 17, 21, 29, 36, 67, 94, 102, 123, 154, 161, 167, 271; **1960–61:** 93, 222, 263

Schweitzer, Dr. Albert, **1957:** 28
Cablegram, **1955:** 15

Schwengel, Repr. Fred, **1959:** 31n.

Science, **1959:** 56; **1960–61:** 393, 410, 429
Address on, **1959:** 107
Budget messages, **1960–61:** 13 (pp. 63, 87, 89), 414 (pp. 1003, 1004)
Cooperation with Mexico, **1959:** 257
Federal programs, **1954:** 57
Statement, **1954:** 60
NATO program, **1960–61:** 13 (p. 63)
Use for military purposes, **1955:** 3

Science, Department of, news conference remarks, **1958:** 141

Science Advisory Committee.
See President's Science Advisory Committee.

Science Board, National, **1958:** 24

Science education, **1958:** 2, 5 (pp. 18, 20, 42, 46, 48, 49), 24, 223; **1959:** 107; **1960–61:** 13 (p. 89), 414 (p. 1002)
Budget message, **1959:** 10 (pp. 46, 98, 99)
Federal scholarships for, **1954:** 328
Science Advisory Committee report, **1959:** 118

Science Foundation, National, **1955:** 17 (p. 148); **1958:** 64
Coordination of scientific information activities, **1958:** 326n.
Education programs, **1958:** 24
Funds for, **1958:** 2
International Geophysical Year Office, **1958:** 27

Science and mathematics teachers, **1957:** 230, 234n.
Conference at Defiance College, **1957:** 251

Science and security, broadcasts, **1957:** 230, 234

Science teaching, **1958:** 2, 5 (pp. 48, 49), 24

Science and Technology, Federal Council on, **1960–61:** 13 (p. 91), 349
Establishment, statement, **1959:** 56
Establishment proposed, **1958:** 326

Science and Technology, Special Assistant to President, James R. Killian, Jr., **1957:** 230
Advisory Committee, **1957:** 230

Science and Technology, Special Assistant to the President for (George B. Kistiakowsky), **1959:** 132 ftn. (p. 463)

Science Youth Month, National, statement, **1960–61:** 299

Sciences, physical (Bureau of Standards)
Budget message, **1958:** 5 (p. 48)

Scientific, cultural, and athletic exchanges, letter to Premier Bulganin, **1958:** 7

Scientific advancement, **1960–61:** 58

Scientific Advisory Committee for Office of Defense Mobilization, **1957:** 228

Scientific committee on research within NATO, proposed, **1957:** 230

Scientific cooperation
Allies, **1958:** 2
Euratom, **1958:** 145, 236

Scientific education, **1957:** 234
U.S.S.R., **1957:** 234

Scientific expeditions in Antarctic, message, **1959:** 135

Scientific research, **1954:** 60, 308; **1955:** 19; **1956:** 12 (p. 122); **1958:** 326n.; **1959:** 107; **1960–61:** 363, 386, 393, 421
Budget messages, **1954:** 14 (p. 174); **1958:** 5 (pp. 20, 46, 48); **1959:** 10 (pp. 44, 68); **1960–61:** 414 (pp. 959, 1003, 1004)
Table, **1959:** 10 (p. 45)
News conference remarks, **1954:** 57, 92

Scientific teaching, **1956:** 12 (p. 123)

Scientific and technical information exchange, **1958:** 2, 83
U.S.-Euratom agreement, **1958:** 145, 236
U.S.-Soviet Union, **1958:** 22

Scientists, **1956:** 85n.; **1957:** 105, 134, 228
British and American collaboration, **1957:** 226
Budget message, **1958:** 5 (pp. 19, 46, 49, 71)
Campaign remarks, **1958:** 293, 295
European, contacts with, **1958:** 145
Interdepartmental committee on education and utilization, **1956:** 76, 77
Morale, comment on, **1954:** 311
News conference remarks on, **1956:** 32, 88
Soviet, **1958:** 274

Scientists and Engineers, National Committee for the Development of, **1956:** 76, 277
Letter to Dr. Bevis, Chairman, **1956:** 77

Scientists and Engineers, President's Committee on
Letter, **1958:** 327
Report, **1957:** 241 and n.
Study of pay problems, **1958:** 169

Score (Atlas satellite)
Message from, **1958:** 322
Orbiting of, statement, **1958:** 321

Scotland
Carnoustie, **1953:** 140n.
St. Andrews, **1958:** 91
Visit to, **1959:** 193n., 198

Scott, Repr. Hugh, **1958:** 303; **1959:** 150; **1960–61:** 176, 354
Sea control forces, **1959:** 10 (p. 61); **1960–61:** 13 (pp. 55, 56)
Sea resources, joint statement with President Lopez Mateos on, **1959:** 257
Searcy, R. B., **1960–61:** 287
Searsport, Maine, **1959:** 250
Seashores, conservation, **1960–61:** 133
SEATO.
    See Southeast Asia Treaty Organization.
Seaton, Fred A.
    See Interior, Secretary of (Fred A. Seaton).
Seattle, Wash., **1953:** 156; **1954:** 130; **1957:** 118
    Campaign remarks, **1956:** 251
    Colombo Plan meeting, **1958:** 312
Seawolf, U.S.S., **1954:** 14 (p. 129); **1955:** 17 (p. 121); **1958:** 274
Second Continental Congress, **1956:** 283
Second Supplemental Appropriation Act, 1956, approval, **1956:** 109
Second term, the President's.
    See Candidacy for second term.
Secrecy, executive, **1956:** 216
Secret Service, **1960–61:** 38, 145, 166
Securities and Exchange Commission, **1955:** 146
    Barr, Andrew, **1960–61:** 68n.
    Budget messages, **1956:** 12 (p. 149); **1960–61:** 414 (p. 984)
    Exemption of certain corporate securities from registration, **1956:** 263; **1957:** 132
    Intervention by Sherman Adams, comment on, **1955:** 176
Security, collective.
    See Collective security.
Security, Commission on Government, **1957:** 119
Security, future, broadcasts, **1957:** 230, 234
Security, national.
    See National security.
Security clearance cases
    Ladejinsky, Wolf, **1955:** 10, 56
    News conference remarks, **1955:** 10, 18, 56, 81
    Personnel in atomic energy program, **1954:** 38
    U.S. employees of United Nations, **1955:** 156
Security Committee, National, **1956:** 51
Security Council, National.
    See National Security Council.
Security Council U. N., veto power, **1956:** 121 ftn. (p. 556)
Security information.
    See Information.
Security pacts.
    See Collective security.
Security policy statement, national, preamble quoted, **1956:** 114
Security program, industrial, Supreme Court decision on, **1959:** 148

Security program for Government employment, **1953:** 6, 95, 101; **1954:** 3, 209, 273, 317; **1960–61:** 284
    See also Loyalty program.
    Budget message, **1956:** 12 (p. 153)
    Comment on, **1955:** 10, 18, 26, 41, 81, 146
    Hatkin case, **1956:** 96
    News conference remarks, **1953:** 249, 254, 265; **1954:** 9, 18, 25, 39, 48, 311, 341, 347; **1956:** 96, 113
Security system, U.S., **1957:** 119
Security Treaty of 1951, joint statement with Prime Minister Kishi, **1957:** 117
Sedgwick County, Kans., Board of Commissioners, tax claim, **1956:** 112
Segni, Antonio, **1955:** 208n.; **1959:** 291, 293, 294
    Joint statement with, **1959:** 203, 248
    Meeting with, comment on, **1959:** 186, 214
    News conference remarks on, **1959:** 186, 243
    Toast to, **1959:** 247
Segni, Mrs. Antonio, **1959:** 247
Segregation.
    See Civil rights; Integration; Little Rock.
Seidman, J. S., **1960–61:** 304
Seismic Improvement, Panel on, **1960–61:** 143 ftn. (p. 410)
    Report (Berkner report), **1959:** 132 and ftn. (p. 463)
Seismic research, **1960–61:** 143 ftn. (p. 410)
Selective Service System, **1954:** 14 (p. 184); **1959:** 53
    Continuance of draft
        Campaign remarks, **1956:** 210, 234, 241, 258, 268, 272
        News conference remarks, **1956:** 205, 235
        Statement, **1956:** 232
    Extension, **1955:** 4, 12
Semiautomatic ground environment (SAGE) system, **1959:** 10 (p. 60)
Semmes, Gen. Harry H., letter, **1956:** 51
Senate Office Building, **1956:** 12 (p. 150)
Senegal, Republic of, Ibrahima Sarr, **1960–61:** 324n.
Senior civil service, **1956:** 22
Sentner, David P., **1953:** 31, 37, 41, 54, 88, 126, 208, 230, 238, 254; **1954:** 9, 25, 39, 63, 115, 341, 347; **1955:** 26, 81, 112, 149, 185; **1956:** 16, 32, 62, 88, 121, 155, 298; **1957:** 50, 72, 80, 92, 124, 150; **1958:** 11, 70, 198, 288; **1959:** 36, 48, 67, 89, 161, 167, 277; **1960–61:** 127, 222, 268, 284, 422
Seoul, Korea, **1960–61:** 250n., 274
    Address to National Assembly, **1960–61:** 201
    Joint statement with Prime Minister Huh Chung, **1960–61:** 203
    Mayor Kee Young Chang, **1960–61:** 198n.
    Remarks on arrival, **1960–61:** 198
    Remarks on departure, **1960–61:** 204

Seoul, Korea — *continued*
  Remarks at headquarters of Korean Army Sixth
    Corps, **1960–61:** 202
  Remarks at U.S. embassy, **1960–61:** 199
  Toast to Prime Minister Huh Chung, **1960–61:**
    200
Separation of judiciary and politics, **1956:** 32
Separation of military and civil powers, **1956:** 20
Separation of powers of Government, **1953:** 126;
    1955: 155; **1956:** 141, 165; **1958:** 83; **1959:**
    342
  Legislative and executive branches, **1954:** 113,
    115, 121, 129; **1958:** 19; **1959:** 171, 172,
    278
  News conference remarks, **1954:** 25, 115, 129;
    1959: 172
  Statement re TVA bill, **1959:** 175
Sergeant missile, **1958:** 293
  See also Missiles.
Serrano, Felixberto, **1960–61:** 187
Service, Robert, **1960–61:** 178
Service credits for medical and dental officers,
    1956: 91
Servicemen.
  See Armed forces, U. S.; Military personnel;
    Veterans.
Services, Government.
  See Charges.
Services, rise in cost, **1958:** 70
  See also Cost of living.
Seventh Fleet, remarks to officers and men, **1960–**
    61: 191
Sewage disposal at Dulles International Airport,
    1959: 197
Sewage treatment works, construction, **1960–61:** 44
  Federal grants, **1956:** 137
Shackamaxon, **1956:** 120n.
Shackford, Roland H., **1955:** 47
SHAEF.
  See Supreme Headquarters, Allied Expedition-
    ary Forces.
Shakespeare, William, **1954:** 293
Shanahan, Eileen, **1957:** 17
Shanley, Bernard M. (Special Counsel to the Pres-
    ident), **1953:** 268; **1954:** 129
Shannon, Donald H., **1954:** 48; **1955:** 90; **1956:**
    171; **1958:** 56, 213; **1959:** 161, 179; **1960–**
    61: 21, 93
Shannon, William V., **1954:** 50, 182; **1955:** 26;
    1956: 47, 53, 56; **1957:** 22; **1958:** 56
SHAPE.
  See Supreme Headquarters of Allied Powers in
    Europe.
Shapiro, Moshe, **1957:** 228
Sharm ash Shaykh (Sharm el Sheikh), U. N.
    emergency force in, **1958:** 8, 148
Sharma, Trilok Chand, **1959:** 316n.
Sharp, Dudley C. (Secretary of the Air Force),
    1960–61: 38

Sharples, Philip T., **1953:** 212
Shaw, Martha, **1957:** 68 and n.
Sheehan, James A., letter, **1956:** 267
Sheehy, Maurice S., **1956:** 98
Sheepherders, nonquota immigrant visas for, ap-
    proval, **1954:** 250
Shepley, James R., **1953:** 62; **1956:** 16
Sherard, T. D., letter, **1959:** 149
Sheridan, Monsignor John L., **1956:** 123
Sherman Anti-Trust Act, **1957:** 215
Shinkman, Paul A., **1954:** 50; **1955:** 146
Ship construction
  Merchant, **1956:** 12 (pp. 96, 141, 142)
    Nuclear-powered, **1956:** 12 (p. 142), 243
  Military program, **1956:** 12 (pp. 96, 97, 100)
  Nuclear-powered peace ship, **1956:** 12 (p. 142)
  Tankers, **1956:** 239
Shipbuilding program, **1954:** 308
Shipowners, Greek, discussions with congressional
    committee on trade embargo with Com-
    munist bloc, **1953:** 41
Shippingport, Pa., **1956:** 263
  Atomic power plant, **1959:** 10 (p. 67)
    Dedication, remarks, **1958:** 113
    Ground-breaking ceremony, remarks, **1954:**
      260
Ships
  Aircraft carriers, **1960–61:** (pp. 55, 56), 255
  Andrea Doria-Stockholm collision, statement,
    1956: 149
  Atka, icebreaker, **1955:** 47
  Barbara Anne, **1960–61:** 244n.
  Barry, **1956:** 208
  Budget messages, **1958:** 5 (pp. 18–20, 29, 59, 60);
    1960–61: 13 (pp. 51, 55, 56, 69, 91), 414
    (pp. 949, 954, 955, 975, 976)
  Des Moines, **1959:** 327n., 328n., 330n., 331
  Dorchester, **1953:** 5; **1954:** 32
  Empress of Britain, **1955:** 146
  Essex, **1959:** 331
  Federal Boating Act, amendment, disapproval,
    1959: 228
  Guided missile, **1960–61:** 245
  Hospital ship, mercy mission, **1959:** 29, 167
  Kearsarge, **1960–61:** 97
  Letter to Secretary Weeks, **1958:** 299
  Mayflower, **1954:** 32
  Merchant marine, **1954:** 14 (p. 174), 213; **1955:**
    17 (pp. 167, 168)
  Midway, **1955:** 18
  Missile destroyers, **1959:** 10 (p. 64)
  Missile ships, **1958:** 2, 5 (pp. 19, 29)
  Mortgage loans, **1960–61:** 13 (p. 69), 414 (p. 976)
  Naval, **1955:** 17 (p. 117)
  Carriers, **1958:** 292; **1959:** 10 (p. 64)
  Naval forces of allies, **1959:** 55
  Nieuw Amsterdam, **1953:** 260

Ships — *continued*
  Nuclear-powered.
    See Ships, nuclear-powered.
  Saint Charles, **1954:** 297
  Saint Paul, **1960–61:** 190n., 191
  Submarines.
    See main heading, Submarines.
  Subsidies, **1954:** 14 (p. 174); **1955:** 17 (pp. 92,
    167, 168); **1958:** 5 (pp. 59, 60); **1959:** 10
    (pp. 79, 80); **1960–61:** 13 (p. 69), 414 (p.
    975)
  Superliners, **1959:** 10 (p. 80), 21
    Construction, **1958:** 103, 120, 170
  Tanker fleet, **1954:** 191
  Trading with Israel, **1960–61:** 38
  War, **1958:** 5 (p. 20)
  Williamsburg, **1953:** 118
Ships, nuclear-powered, **1956:** 2, 12 (pp. 97, 142);
    1958: 11, 292; **1959:** 57; **1960–61:** 245, 410
  Budget messages, **1958:** 5 (pp. 18, 29); **1960–61:**
    13 (pp. 51–56, 58), 414 (pp. 938, 949, 951,
    952, 954, 955)
  Cruisers, **1958:** 2
  Enterprise, **1960–61:** 414 (p. 954)
  Frigate, **1958:** 5 (p. 29)
  Ice breaker, veto, **1958:** 204
  Long Beach, **1960–61:** 13 (p. 55), 414 (p. 954)
  Merchant ship, **1955:** 79, 81, 112, 121, 146; **1956:**
    243; **1958:** 204
    NS *Savannah*, **1959:** 10 (p. 80), 48
  Navy carrier, **1959:** 10 (p. 64)
  Soviet icebreaker, **1959:** 217n.
  S.S. *Queen Mary*, **1955:** 42n.
  Submarines, **1958:** 2, 65, 204, 292; **1959:** 6, 10 (p.
    64), 57; **1960–61:** 4, 7, 13 (pp. 51–55), 244,
    245, 255, 410, 414 (pp. 938, 949, 951, 952,
    954, 955)
    Abraham Lincoln, **1960–61:** 360
    Based in United Kingdom, **1960–61:** 360n.
    George Washington, **1960–61:** 360
    Nautilus, **1954:** 14 (p. 129), 38; **1955:** 17 (p.
      121), 81; **1956:** 243; **1958:** 15, 201, 210,
      211
    Patrick Henry, **1960–61:** 244, 360
    Seawolf, **1954:** 14 (p. 129); **1955:** 17 (p. 121);
      1958: 274
    Triton, **1960–61:** 142
Shivers, Gov. Allan, **1953:** 156; **1954:** 35n., 85n., 99,
    172; **1956:** 94, 96, 198, 298; **1957:** 228
  News conference remarks on, **1953:** 15, 62
Shollenberger, Lewis W., **1959:** 179
Short, Repr. Dewey, **1953:** 266
  Bipartisan meeting on Suez Canal, **1956:** 184
Short, Laurence E., **1954:** 77
Shotwell, James T., **1953:** 249
Shriro, Aron, bill for relief of, **1957:** 184
Shumaker, Lt. Lawrence A., Navy Commendation
    Ribbon with Metal Pendant, citation,
    1960–61: 25

Shuman, Charles, **1958:** 35n.
Shutt, Charles E., **1954:** 347; **1955:** 41, 56, 59, 90,
    95, 100, 146, 149, 185; **1956:** 16, 20, 32, 47,
    53, 62, 88, 121, 189, 193, 198, 205, 216,
    229, 235, 298; **1957:** 17, 28, 45, 70, 207;
    1958: 74, 88, 120, 222, 310; **1959:** 21, 29,
    186, 271; **1960–61:** 38, 103
Siberia, **1957:** 87
  Soviet nuclear tests, **1956:** 191n.
  Underground explosions in, **1959:** 288
Sibley, Harper, **1959:** 87
Sibley Memorial Hospital and Nurses Home site,
    approval of bill, **1957:** 175
Sicily, **1953:** 234; **1960–61:** 355
Siegel, Isadore, **1956:** 241
Sigma Delta Chi, freedom of information reports,
    1959: 288
Signal flags, **1956:** 93
Siler, Repr. Eugene, **1956:** 226
Silk yarn for cartridge cloth, **1955:** 155
Silva, Manuel, mining claim, disapproval, **1956:**
    179
Silver, Charles, **1954:** 301n.
Silver, Rabbi Abba Hillel, message, **1955:** 239
Silvercruys, Baron, **1957:** 231 and n.
Simanck, Robert E., Medal of Honor award, **1953:**
    175, 229n.
Simmons, John F., **1954:** 20n.
Simmons, R. C., **1954:** 308
Simpson, Repr. Richard M., **1953:** 41, 54, 141;
    1954: 157; **1956:** 234; **1957:** 108 and n.;
    1959: 127n.
  Death of, **1960–61:** 3
Simpson, Repr. Sid, **1953:** 269
Sims, Edward H., **1953:** 15; **1954:** 18; **1955:** 149;
    1956: 20; **1959:** 17
Singapore, **1958:** 213
Sino-Soviet bloc
    See Communist bloc; Soviet bloc.
Sirikit, Queen, **1960–61:** 209, 211, 213, 218
Sisavang Vong, messages, **1954:** 82, 117
"Sit-in" demonstrations.
    See Civil rights.
Sitting Bull, **1957:** 215
Siviero, Rodolfo, **1956:** 45n.
Sixth Fleet, landing in Beirut, **1958:** 174n.
Sixth Protocol of Supplementary Concessions to
    GATT, **1956:** 123n.
Skowhegan, Maine, remarks, **1955:** 142
Slaughter of livestock, humane methods, **1958:** 222
Slevin, Joseph R., **1953:** 54, 62, 128; **1954:** 33, 39,
    115, 182; **1955:** 81, 90, 185; **1956:** 20, 53,
    113, 298; **1957:** 45, 56, 70; **1958:** 56, 70,
    120
Slichter, Sumner H., **1954:** 129
Sloan, Alfred P., Jr., **1956:** 107; **1959:** 107
  Lahey Memorial Award, **1957:** 223
Sloan (Alfred P.) Foundation, Inc., **1957:** 223n.;
    1959: 107

Slum clearance, **1954:** 3, 14 (p. 148), 17, 179, 333; **1955:** 194, 247; **1956:** 12 (pp. 144, 145); **1957:** 13, 118; **1958:** 123
  Budget message, **1955:** 17 (pp. 171, 172)
  News conference remarks, **1954:** 73, 345; **1957:** 70, 80, 115
Small, Repr. Frank, Jr., letter, **1954:** 313
Small business, **1953:** 6; **1956:** 2, 19, 190; **1957:** 13, 16, 132, 169; **1958:** 16; **1959:** 10 (pp. 86, 87); **1960–61:** 410
  Budget messages, **1958:** 5 (pp. 23, 60); **1960–61:** 13 (pp. 65, 75), 414 (p. 983)
  Campaign remarks, **1956:** 226, 234, 241, 268, 272; **1958:** 292, 293, 295, 302, 303, 308
  Disaster loans, **1956:** 236
  Federal procurement, **1958:** 295
  14-point program, **1956:** 190
  Letter to Arthur F. Burns, **1956:** 118, 176
  Letter to minority leaders re, **1958:** 43
  Meeting on, **1956:** 318
  President's conference on, **1957:** 132, 196, 227; **1958:** 299
  Recommendations of Cabinet Committee, **1957:** 132
  Taxes, **1958:** 5 (p. 23), 43, 120, 293, 295, 302, 303
  Telegram to Fred Herman, **1956:** 263
Small Business, Cabinet Committee on, **1956:** 263; **1957:** 13, 132
  Budget message, **1958:** 5 (p. 23)
  Establishment, **1956:** 118
  Report, letter, **1956:** 176
Small Business Act of 1953, extension, **1955:** 4; **1957:** 13, 132, 145
Small Business Administration, **1954:** 95, 349; **1955:** 4, 208n.; **1956:** 234, 263; **1959:** 10 (p. 87); **1960–61:** 5, 146, 410
  Budget messages, **1954:** 14 (pp. 178, 181); **1956:** 12 (p. 148); **1958:** 5 (p. 60); **1960–61:** 13 (p. 75), 414 (pp. 983, 992)
    Table, **1958:** 5 (p. 54)
  Campaign remarks, **1958:** 293, 295, 303
  Conference for benefit of small business, **1957:** 132, 196, 227
  Continuance, **1957:** 13, 132, 145 and ftn. (p. 574)
  Disaster loan program, **1957:** 41
  Letter to minority leaders re, **1958:** 43
  Letter to Reuben Cummings re, **1956:** 288
  Loans and disaster relief, **1954:** 14 (p. 181); **1955:** 17 (p. 176); **1956:** 263
  Management counseling, **1956:** 263
  RFC functions, **1957:** 78
  Rural development program, **1957:** 156
  Taxes, **1954:** 14 (p. 96)
Small Business Administrator (Wendell B. Barnes), **1956:** 288; **1957:** 227
  Committee on Small Business, letter, **1956:** 118
  Federal Council on Aging, **1956:** 74
Small business taxes, **1955:** 4

Small Businessmen for Ike, telegram, **1956:** 263
Small nations, letter to Premier Khrushchev re, **1958:** 189
Smaller War Plants Corporation, **1957:** 78
Smathers, Sen. George A., **1955:** 62
  Secretary Weeks' letter to, **1958:** 82 and n.
Smedberg, Adm. William R., **1958:** 3d, 125
Smith, A. Robert, **1954:** 9, 50, 165, 347; **1956:** 155
Smith, Adam, **1953:** 109
Smith, Alfred E., **1954:** 298, 301; **1956:** 283; **1959:** 154
  Memorial Dinner, address, **1954:** 301
Smith, Mrs. Dorothy, **1956:** 278
Smith, Gov. Elmo, **1956:** 256
Smith, Sen. H. Alexander, **1953:** 266; **1954:** 9, 25; **1958:** 23
  Bipartisan meeting on Suez Canal, **1956:** 184
  Letter to, **1956:** 63
Smith, James H., Jr., **1958:** 316; **1959:** 26, 154
Smith, Kingsbury, interview of Molotov, **1955:** 26
Smith, Sen. Margaret Chase, **1954:** 48; **1955:** 142
  News conference remarks on, **1955:** 47, 95
Smith, McLellan, **1954:** 48; **1956:** 193, 235; **1958:** 103
Smith, Merriman, **1953:** 12, 15, 22, 31, 37, 41, 54, 62, 77, 88, 109, 126, 198, 208, 225, 230, 238, 243, 249, 265; **1954:** 9, 18, 25, 33, 48, 50, 63, 68, 73, 92, 138, 143, 157, 165, 168, 172, 182, 192, 200, 311, 322, 345, 347, 353; **1955:** 10, 18, 26, 33, 41, 47, 56, 59, 62, 95, 100, 112, 119, 146, 149, 176; **1956:** 5, 16, 20, 32, 47, 53, 56, 62, 78, 88, 94, 96, 113, 121, 155, 189, 193, 198, 205, 216, 298; **1957:** 17, 22, 28, 45, 50, 56, 62, 70, 72, 80, 87, 105, 134, 145, 150, 152, 157, 169, 207, 210, 228; **1958:** 11, 28, 37, 274, 288, 310, 318; **1959:** 17, 21, 36, 42, 48, 53, 67, 89, 94, 102, 123, 132, 148, 154, 161, 167, 186, 191, 223, 243, 267, 271, 277, 288; **1960–61:** 7, 21, 24, 34, 93, 103, 127, 143, 222
Smith, Walter Bedell, **1953:** 88; **1954:** 143, 157, 165; **1957:** 57n., 124; **1959:** 48
Smith-Mundt Act, 10th anniversary, remarks, **1958:** 23
Smithsonian Institution, **1954:** 167n.; **1955:** 22n.
  Funds, **1956:** 12 (p. 124)
Smithsonian Institution, Secretary (Leonard Carmichael), **1955:** 22
"Smokey Bear" statuette awards, **1958:** 100n.
Smoking, **1957:** 145
Smoot, Vice Adm. Roland N., **1960–61:** 192n.
Smylie, Governor Robert E., **1957:** 138
  Letter, **1960–61:** 115
Snake River development, **1953:** 77
Snark missile, **1957:** 230
Snyder, Maj. Gen. Howard McC., **1953:** 254 ftn. (p. 800); **1956:** 121, 155; **1957:** 80
Snyder, John W., **1954:** 115

Snyder, Marty, **1954:** 200
Snyder, Murray, **1954:** 101; **1956:** 113
  See also Defense, Assistant Secretary of.
  Editor's note on President's illness, **1955:** p. 822
Sobeloff, Simon E., **1956:** 113
  Delay in Senate confirmation, **1955:** 176
Sobolev, Arkady A., **1958:** 83
Social security, **1953:** 6, 16, 268; **1954:** 3, 139, 209,
    308; **1955:** 247; **1956:** 19; **1957:** 22; **1958:**
    18, 26, 96; **1959:** 280; **1960–61:** 127 ftn. (p.
    362), 413
  See also specific programs.
  Budget messages, **1954:** 14 (pp. 140–145); **1955:**
    17 (pp. 140, 141, 143–146); **1958:** 5 (p.
    51); **1959:** 10 (pp. 102, 103); **1960–61:** 13
    (pp. 87, 95), 414 (pp. 1009, 1010, 1017)
    Tables, **1954:** 14 (pp. 141, 145); **1955:** 17 (p.
      146)
  Campaign remarks, **1954:** 273, 286, 316, 317,
    318; **1956:** 214, 226, 251, 256, 268, 272;
    1958: 292, 303, 308
  Claim of estate of Margareth Weigand, **1954:** 59
  Deductions, **1954:** 18
  Extension of coverage, **1953:** 57, 155, 187; **1954:**
    273, 275, 286, 291, 308, 316, 318; **1956:** 2,
    3, 158, 251, 256; **1957:** 13; **1960–61:** 341,
    410
  Farm operators, **1956:** 158, 250
  Hadnot, Mr. and Mrs. John R., relief of, **1958:**
    238
  ILO standards, **1954:** 126
  Income earned by pensioners, **1954:** 353
  Messages to Congress, **1953:** 155; **1954:** 10
  News conference remarks, **1953:** 15, 109; **1954:**
    18, 353; **1956:** 155, 235
  Railroad workers, **1954:** 145
Social Security, Commissioner of, **1953:** 28
Social Security Act, **1953:** 155
  Amendment proposed, **1960–61:** 24
Social Security Administration, **1953:** 28
Social Security Amendments, approval, **1954:** 235
Social Security Amendments of 1956, **1956:** 155
Social Security Amendments of 1958, approval,
    1958: 234
Social Security Financing, Advisory Council on,
    1958: 5 (p. 52)
Socialism
  Comments on, **1953:** 109, 208
  News conference remarks, **1957:** 105
Socialized medicine, **1960–61:** 103
  Opposition to, **1954:** 165, 301
Society for Personnel Administration Conference,
    remarks, **1954:** 108
Society of the Remagen Bridgehead, **1955:** 52
Socrates, **1960–61:** 187
Sohn, Louis B.,
  World Peace Through World Law, **1958:** 153

Soil bank, **1956:** 2, 3, 82, 83, 115, 190; **1957:** 8, 75;
    1959: 23
  See also Agriculture.
  Acreage reserves, **1956:** 6, 20, 214; **1958:** 5 (p.
    66), 59, 60; **1959:** 10 (p. 49, 89)
    Termination proposed, **1958:** 12
  Approval of bill, **1956:** 115
  Budget messages, **1956:** 12 (pp. 126, 131); **1958:** 5
    (pp. 64, 66)
  Campaign remarks, **1956:** 214, 241, 250, 256, 268
  Conservation-reserve program, **1956:** 6; **1958:** 5
    (p. 66), 12
  Grazing on reserve acreage, **1956:** 236
  Legislative recommendations, **1956:** 6, 83
  Letter to Senator Aiken, **1956:** 35
  News conference remarks, **1956:** 20, 62, 78, 171;
    1959: 50, 92
  Payments, **1956:** 6, 83, 171, 214, 216
  Veto of bill, **1956:** 82
Soil conservation, **1953:** 100, 153, 234; **1954:** 3, 4,
    201, 291, 308; **1955:** 17 (pp. 154, 155);
    1956: 205, 211; **1958:** 5 (pp. 64, 66); **1959:**
    10 (pp. 91, 92); **1960–61:** 410
  Budget message, **1956:** 12 (pp. 125, 131, 137)
  Great Plains, program for, approval, **1956:** 169
  News conference remarks, **1953:** 15, 22
  Tax deductions, **1954:** 14 (p. 96)
Soil Conservation Service, **1954:** 14 (p. 162); **1956:**
    12 (p. 131)
  Reorganization, **1953:** 238
Soldatov, A., **1959:** 218
Solicitor General
  Functions, **1953:** 51
  Vacancy in office, **1953:** 249
Solomon, **1960–61:** 187
Somali Republic
  Independence, message to President Osman,
    1960–61: 219
  Issa, Abdullahi, **1960–61:** 324n.
Somervell, Gen. Brehon B., on retirement, **1959:**
    179
Somoza, Anastasio, death of, statement, **1956:** 219
Song, "I Believe," **1958:** 305
Songs of Solomon, reference to, **1958:** 63
Soper, Judge Morris A., **1953:** 59; **1955:** 149
Soraya, Empress of Iran, **1954:** 353; **1955:** 42
Soto, Hernando de, **1959:** 338
South Africa
  Capetown, **1955:** 18
  Racial problems, **1960–61:** 103
South America, **1957:** 92, 157
  See also American States; Inter-American; Latin
    America; *specific countries.*
  Argentina's Aviation Week, **1957:** 233
  Representatives of Presidents, report, **1957:** 96
  Student scholarships, **1957:** 96
  U. S. private investments, **1957:** 62

South Carolina
   Aiken, **1955:** 73
   Byrnes, Gov. James F., **1953:** 15; **1954:** 115, 164
   Candidates for public office, **1954:** 311
   Charleston, **1955:** 70; **1959:** 13
   Maybank, Sen. Burnet R., death of, **1954:** 233
   Richards, Repr. James P., **1953:** 265; **1956:** 20
   Thurmond, Sen. Strom, **1955:** 73, 149
South Dakota
   Anderson, Gov. Sigurd, **1953:** 101, 103; **1954:** 53
   Berry, Repr. E. Y., **1953:** 101
   Case, Sen. Francis, **1953:** 101, 269; **1954:** 138
   Lovre, Repr. Harold O., **1953:** 101
   Mundt, Sen. Karl E., **1953:** 101; **1954:** 157; **1958:** 23
   Rapid City, **1953:** 103
Southeast Asia.
   See Asia, Southeast Asia, and South Asia; *specific countries.*
Southeast Asia Collective Defense Treaty (Manila Pact), **1954:** 297, 337, 351; **1955:** 4, 5, 35; **1956:** 2; **1957:** 91
   Fourth anniversary, statement, **1958:** 260
   Joint statement with President Diem, **1957:** 83
   Joint statement with Prime Minister Macmillan, **1957:** 226
   Message, **1954:** 329
   Sixth anniversary, message, **1960–61:** 286
Southeast Asia Treaty Organization, **1955:** 4, 47; **1956:** 26, 58, 210, 218; **1957:** 111, 213, 230; **1958:** 32, 96; **1959:** 55; **1960–61:** 132, 133, 183, 188, 209, 212, 245, 410
   Bangkok conference, **1955:** 41
   Budget messages, **1960–61:** 13 (p. 58), 414 (p. 959)
   Council of ministers meeting, **1960–61:** 189, 286
     Remarks to delegates, **1960–61:** 164
   Fourth anniversary, statement, **1958:** 260
   Joint statements
     King Bhumibol Adulyadej, **1960–61:** 218
     President Garcia, **1958:** 143; **1960–61:** 189
     President Ayub Khan, **1959:** 303
     Prime Minister Suhrawardy, **1957:** 131
   Message for SEATO Day ceremonies at Bangkok, **1960–61:** 286
   New Zealand, membership, **1960–61:** 286
   News conference remarks, **1959:** 186
   Pakistan, membership, **1960–61:** 286
   Philippines, membership, **1960–61:** 286
   Secretary-General (Pote Sarasin), **1960–61:** 164
   Thailand, membership, **1960–61:** 286
   United Kingdom, membership, **1960–61:** 286
Southeast Asia Treaty Organization, proposed, **1954:** 320
   Membership of Korea and Republic of China, question of, **1954:** 168
   News conference remarks, **1954:** 101, 107, 115, 165, 168

Southeastern Drilling Corp. and H. P. Lambert Co., Inc., relief of, disapproval, **1960–61:** 292
Southeastern Power Administration, **1954:** 14 (p. 168); **1956:** 12 (p. 136); **1959:** 10 (p. 95)
Southern Bell Telephone Co., strike of employees, **1955:** 90, 95
Southern Governors and Attorneys General, Conference of, proposed, **1956:** 69
Southern Methodist University, **1954:** 12n.
Southern States, **1956:** 53
Southwest, drought disaster, **1957:** 11, 12, 41
Southwestern Power Administration, **1954:** 14 (p. 168); **1959:** 10 (p. 95)
   Budget message, **1956:** 12 (p. 136)
   Rates, **1956:** 178
Southwest Research Institute, relief of, **1958:** 247
Soviet attack on Western Powers, disarmament proposals, statement on, **1957:** 165
Soviet bloc, **1956:** 87, 230; **1958:** 2, 32, 58
   See also Communist bloc; Satellite countries; *specific countries.*
   Letter to Premier Bulganin, **1958:** 7
   Trade with, **1956:** 53
Soviet-China trade, **1957:** 70
Soviet de-Stalinization, **1957:** 228
Soviet disarmament proposal, **1957:** 115
Soviet nuclear tests, **1957:** 105, 115
Soviet Union, **1953:** 6, 50, 61, 95, 101, 159, 256; **1954:** 128, 139, 223; **1955:** 12, 99, 161; **1956:** 2, 75, 266, 282; **1958:** 2, 8, 148, 286; **1959:** 57, 70, 130, 200n.; **1960–61:** 4, 36, 42, 209, 410
   Agreement on cultural, technical, and educational exchanges, **1958:** 22
   Agreements with International Atomic Energy Agency, **1959:** 189
   Agricultural specialists, question of U.S. visit, **1955:** 47, 95
   Aircraft, **1955:** 112
   Ambassador Charles E. Bohlen, **1953:** 22, 31, 37, 41, 265; **1954:** 328, 345, 353; **1955:** 146 ftn. (p. 644)
   Ambassador Llewellyn E. Thompson, **1958:** 11, 78; **1959:** 94 and ftn. (p. 361), 218
   Amerika, distribution of, **1960–61:** 410
   Amtorg, **1955:** 10
   Anniversary, message, **1955:** 233
   Antarctica, proposed conference on, **1958:** 92
   Anti-Semitism, **1953:** 22
   Arctic inspection agreement proposed, **1958:** 163
   Armed forces, **1960–61:** 93
     East Germany, **1953:** 88, 121n.
     Reduction, **1956:** 113
   Arms shipments
     Egypt, **1956:** 282, 298
     Middle East, **1956:** 26, 53, 298; **1960–61:** 38

Soviet Union — *continued*
  Aswan Dam construction (Egypt), assistance,
      1960–61: 7
  Atheistic dictatorship, **1958:** 290, 295
  Atomic icebreaker, **1959:** 217n.
  Attacks on U.S. planes, **1953:** 31
  Automobile production, **1960–61:** 346
  Berlin issue.
      See main heading, Berlin.
  Bombers, **1956:** 94; **1960–61:** 21
  Bulganin, Nikolai A., **1955:** 62, 95, 146, 161, 164,
      166n., 185; **1956:** 16, 32, 53, 56, 78, 88, 96,
      287; **1957:** 3, 226; **1958:** 1, 11, 28, 37, 165
      Letter released in Moscow, **1956:** 291n.
      Letters to, **1955:** 220; **1956:** 23, 52, 166, 262,
          291; **1958:** 7, 17, 31
  Campaign remarks on, **1956:** 210, 283; **1958:** 290,
      295, 296; **1960–61:** 346, 348, 350
  Communist China, relations with, **1955:** 33
  Cultural exchange with U.S., **1959:** 223; **1960–
      61:** 410, 414 (p. 969)
  Cultural exhibit in New York City, **1959:** 102
  Diplomatic break with Israel, **1953:** 15
  Disarmament, **1956:** 88, 143, 266
      See also main heading, Disarmament.
      Soviet proposals, **1956:** 2, 52, 78, 166, 266;
          1960–61: 93, 245
  Downing of U.S. aircraft and detention of crew
      Air Force RB–47 plane, **1960–61:** 231, 232,
          255, 284, 302, 313
      U–2 plane, **1960–61:** 143, 154, 162, 163, 231n.,
          263
  Earth satellites, **1957:** 210, 211, 230, 234
  East-West contacts, **1956:** 23, 96, 166, 190, 204;
      1958: 2, 7, 36
  Economic activities in foreign countries, **1956:**
      53, 56, 87, 113, 198, 210
  Economic development, **1956:** 210; **1958:** 25
  Economic offensive, **1955:** 6; **1958:** 2, 5 (p. 20),
      25, 32, 36, 58, 95, 96, 290
  Economy, **1954:** 72; **1959:** 55, 271
  Education in, **1958:** 295
  Espionage activities, **1960–61:** 154, 163
  Far East, warning to U.S. re, **1958:** 261
  Farm production, **1958:** 290
  Fissionable materials production for weapons,
      cessation, U.S. proposal, **1960–61:** 302
  Four-power conference on Germany and Aus-
      tria, rejection of proposal, **1953:** 238
  Geneva conferences.
      See main heading, Geneva conferences.
  German prisoners of war held by, question of
      release, **1954:** 314
  Gromyko, Andrei A., **1957:** 92; **1958:** 28, 63, 83,
      88, 152; **1959:** 123 ftn. (p. 425), 148, 218,
      242; **1960–61:** 143
  Hydrogen bomb, **1954:** 73
      Possession of, **1953:** 198, 208; **1960–61:** 422

Soviet Union — *continued*
  Ideological offensive, **1960–61:** 2
  Interference in internal affairs of U. S., **1956:** 262
  International Tchaikovsky Piano Contest, **1958:**
      78
  Intervention in Egypt, proposed, **1956:** 291n.
  Izvestia and *Pravda,* U.S. postal ban, **1955:** 59
  Joint statements
      Chancellor Adenauer, **1954:** 314; **1955:** 122;
          1957: 100; **1959:** 192
      Prime Minister Macmillan, **1957:** 55, 226
      Prime Minister St. Laurent, **1953:** 70
      Western leaders, **1953:** 255
      Khrushchev, Nikita S., **1955:** 95, 146, 149; **1956:**
          20, 53, 78, 88, 96; **1957:** 105, 210, 226;
          1958: 1, 11, 31, 37, 56, 70, 83, 103, 141,
          181, 196, 198, 222, 261, 274, 318
      See also main heading, Khrushchev, Nikita S.
      Letters to, **1958:** 67, 86, 112, 131, 152, 165, 177,
          179, 189, 263
      TV interview, **1957:** 105
  Kozlov, Frol R., **1959:** 132, 148, 154, 161, 162,
      167
  Lebanon situation, **1958:** 172, 173, 177, 179, 189,
      198, 207
  Lend-lease, repayment of, **1959:** 243
  Lenin, Nikolai, **1956:** 78, 87
  Litvinov Assignment (1933), **1954:** 94
  Loans to, **1959:** 243
  Malinovsky, Rodion L., **1959:** 26
  Malenkov, Georgi M., **1953:** 41, 187, 208; **1954:**
      157, 311; **1955:** 33, 95; **1956:** 56; **1957:**
      228
  May Day celebrations, **1955:** 95
  Menshikov, Mikhail A., **1958:** 22, 37; **1959:** 218
  Messages, broadcasts, etc., **1957:** 8, 15, 35, 86, 90,
      230, 234, 245, 249
  Microphones concealed in U.S. embassy, **1959:**
      271
  Middle East, **1956:** 53, 56, 62, 298
      Actions in, **1954:** 68
  Mikoyan, Anastas I., **1959:** 7, 17, 21, 48
  Military action in Congo, **1960–61:** 284
  Military bases in Cuba, question of, **1960–61:**
      222
  Military establishment, information exchange
      with U.S., **1956:** 2, 23, 166, 266
  Military strength, **1954:** 14 (p. 119); **1956:** 87;
      1958: 295; **1959:** 55, 120; **1960–61:** 21, 36
  Minsk, **1958:** 31
  Missile development, **1956:** 32, 88
  Missiles, **1958:** 2, 141, 177, 222, 296, 318; **1959:** 6,
      7, 26, 172; **1960–61:** 7, 24, 34, 245
  Molotov, Vyacheslav M., **1953:** 254, 265; **1954:**
      18, 128, 314; **1955:** 26, 33, 146; **1957:** 6,
      228
  Moscow, **1958:** 189
  Moscow conference on agenda for summit meet-
      ing, **1958:** 177

Soviet Union — *continued*
Moscow Manifesto of Communist representatives (1957), **1958:** 31
NATO conference remarks, **1957:** 245, 249
New Year's greetings, **1958:** 1; **1959:** 1; **1960–61:** 2
News conference remarks, **1953:** 12, 15, 22, 31, 41, 54, 62, 77, 88, 109, 126, 198, 208, 238, 243, 254, 265; **1954:** 9, 25, 50, 68, 73, 101, 115, 138, 143, 157, 182, 192, 311, 322, 328, 341, 345; **1955:** 10, 33, 41, 47, 59, 62, 81, 95, 100, 112, 119, 146, 185; **1956:** 16, 20, 32, 53, 56, 62, 78, 88, 94, 113, 121, 198, 229, 298; **1957:** 17, 28, 50, 56, 70, 72, 80, 87, 105, 115, 124, 134, 150, 210, 228; **1958:** 11, 37, 56, 70, 74, 83, 141, 198, 274, 310, 318; **1959:** 7, 17, 21, 36, 42, 94, 102, 132, 191, 223, 243, 267, 271, 277, 288; **1960–61:** 7, 21 and ftn. (p. 131), 24, 34, 38, 93, 103, 127, 143 and ftn. (p. 410), 222, 256, 263, 268 and ftn. (p. 648), 284, 422
Non-aggression pacts, **1959:** 42
Nuclear power, **1958:** 177
Nuclear-powered aircraft, **1958:** 318
Nuclear tests, **1955:** 185; **1958:** 74, 311; **1960–61:** 143 and ftn. (p. 410)
Nuclear tests suspension, **1958:** 56, 67; **1959:** 42, 81, 277; **1960–61:** 34, 101
Annex to experts' report, **1959:** 348
Inspection proposal, **1959:** 110; **1960–61:** 38
Rejection of U.S. proposal, **1958:** 300
Nuclear weapons, **1953:** 6, 12, 198, 205, 208, 246, 256; **1955:** 33, 47; **1960–61:** 103, 422
Nuclear weapons production, **1958:** 56
Nuclear weapons tests, **1953:** 109, 208; **1954:** 68, 311; **1956:** 191, 193, 229
Paris summit conference.
See Paris summit meeting.
Participation in U.N. action in Congo, **1960–61:** 248n.
Pasternak, Boris, **1958:** 310
Peace treaty with East Germany, question of, **1960–61:** 24, 256
Peaceful coexistence with, **1954:** 157, 341
Poland, **1956:** 215, 260, 282
Political agreements with, **1959:** 21
Political changes, **1953:** 31, 50
Comment on, **1955:** 33, 59, 62, 146
Position on Germany, **1954:** 314
Prisoners of war held by, **1953:** 50
Productivity, **1960–61:** 328
Propaganda, **1959:** 48; **1960–61:** 328, 341
Rastovorov, Yuri A., Soviet agent in Tokyo, **1954:** 25
Reconnaissance flights over western territory, question of, **1960–61:** 143
Repression of Hungary, **1960–61:** 410

Soviet Union — *continued*
Satellite countries, **1954:** 72, 143; **1955:** 12, 17 (p. 131), 33, 37n., 119, 146, 175; **1958:** 2, 11, 32, 141; **1959:** 55, 167 and ftn. (p. 536), 172, 186
Satellite countries.
See also Satellite countries, Soviet.
Science education, **1954:** 328; **1957:** 234
Scientific achievements, **1958:** 274
Scientists, **1958:** 274
Sobolev, Arkady A., **1958:** 83
Soldatov, A., **1959:** 218
Soldiers, rescue by U.S. Navy, **1960–61:** 97
Soviet Zone of Germany.
See Germany, East
Space exploration, **1959:** 2, 89, 217n., 223, 267; **1960–61:** 13 (p. 66), 21, 24, 350
Sputniks, **1958:** 56, 70, 120, 141, 274, 287
Stalin, Joseph, **1953:** 15, 20, 22, 31, 50, 109; **1955:** 95; **1956:** 62, 78, 87; **1957:** 6, 228
Death of, message on, **1953:** 24
Statement re attack on Western disarmament proposal, **1957:** 165
Student exchange with U.S., **1960–61:** 38
Submarine activities, **1959:** 26
Technical conference on nuclear test detection.
See Geneva conferences.
Trade, **1954:** 9, 50, 101, 143; **1955:** 6
With Cuba, **1960–61:** 223
With U.S., **1955:** 33; **1958:** 7, 165; **1959:** 243
Treaty with East Germany, **1959:** 67
Treaty of friendship and cooperation with U.S. proposed, **1956:** 23
Trial of Francis G. Powers, **1960–61:** 268 and ftn. (p. 648)
Troops in East Germany, **1959:** 53
U.K.-Soviet talks on air safety over Germany, **1953:** 41
U.N. activities, **1955:** 156
U. N. Security Council, use of veto, **1958:** 7, 8, 31, 63, 148, 177, 198, 207; **1959:** 110n.
Underground explosions in Siberia, **1959:** 288
U.S. cultural exhibition (1959), **1960–61:** 410
See also Moscow.
U.S. flights over
Suspension of, **1960–61:** 154, 163
U–2 incident, **1960–61:** 143, 154, 162, 163, 231n., 263
U.S. plane crash in Armenia, **1958:** 310; **1959:** 94 and ftn. (p. 361)
U.S. plane shot down over Habomai Islands, **1954:** 328, 345
U.S.-Soviet discussions on atomic energy pool, **1954:** 9, 18, 39, 129
U.S.-Soviet lend-lease talks, **1960–61:** 24
U.S.-Soviet relations, **1953:** 31; **1959:** 202; **1960–61:** 2, 163

Soviet Union — *continued*
  U.S.-Soviet diplomatic relations, termination,
      question of, **1954:** 192, 345
  U.S. vs. Soviet progress, comments on, **1960–61:**
      24, 34, 222
  U.S. visitors to, **1958:** 318
  Vishinsky, Andrei Y., **1953:** 230
  Visit to, proposed, **1960–61:** 21 and ftn. (p. 131),
      127, 143
    Cancellation, **1960–61:** 163, 209
  Visit of President Eisenhower (1960), **1959:** 179,
      186, 191, 223, 242, 243, 267, 293, 340
    Announcement, **1959:** 173
  Visit of President Gronchi of Italy, **1959:** 293
  Visit of Prime Minister Macmillan, **1959:** 36, 42,
      48
  Visit of Vice President Nixon, **1959:** 17, 80, 132,
      148, 161, 162, 167, 172 and ftn. (p. 550),
      173, 179, 214, 271
  Visitors from, comment on, **1960–61:** 37
  Voroshilov, Kliment E., **1955:** 233; **1958:** 1;
      1959: 1
    Message, **1960–61:** 2
  Weapons, **1957:** 169, 230
  World War II agreements, **1953:** 12, 14, 15
  World War II prisoners of war returned to,
      1960–61: 268
  Yalta conference, **1958:** 1945.
    See also main heading, Yalta conference.
  Yemelyanov, Vasily S., **1959:** 243
  Yugoslavia, **1956:** 248
  Visit of Soviet leaders, **1955:** 100
  Zaroubin, Georgi N., **1954:** 9, 18, 39, 322; **1956:**
      23
  Zhukov, Marshal Georgi, **1955:** 33, 47, 81, 90, 95,
      100, 146, 176; **1956:** 78, 121, 298; **1957:**
      134, 150, 210, 228
Soybean exports, **1958:** 58
Soybeans, price support, **1956:** 6, 20
Spaak, Paul-Henri, **1957:** 228, 243 and n.; **1958:**
    274; **1959:** 70
  Discussions with the President and Prime Min-
      ister Macmillan, **1957:** 226
  Meeting with, comment on, **1959:** 186, 214
Spaatz, Gen. Carl, **1955:** 52
Space, outer, **1957:** 8, 230, 234; **1958:** 57, 64, 105,
    185, 295
  See also National Aeronautics and Space (Agen-
      cy) Administration; Rockets; Satellites,
      earth.
  "Introduction to Outer Space," **1958:** 56, 57
  Letter to Premier Khrushchev, **1958:** 67
  Letters to Premier Bulganin, **1958:** 7, 31
  Military application of space technology, **1958:**
      64
  News conference remarks, **1957:** 210, 228; **1958:**
      28, 56, 63
  Peaceful and scientific uses, **1958:** 7, 36, 57, 63,
      105, 148

Space platforms, news conference remarks, **1957:**
    210
Space research and exploration, **1959:** 11; **1960–61:**
    4, 10, 11, 100, 104, 245, 255, 258, 261, 287,
    302, 350, 410
  See also Rockets; Satellites, earth; Space vehi-
      cles.
  Budget messages, **1959:** 10 (pp. 44, 76, 78);
      1960–61: 13 (pp. 38, 59, 65, 66, 68), 414
      (pp. 938, 939, 960, 970, 972, 973)
    Tables, **1960–61:** 13 (p. 67), 414 (p. 971)
  News conference remarks, **1959:** 48, 89, 172, 267,
      277; **1960–61:** 21, 24
  Reports, **1959:** 25; **1960–61:** 47, 424
  Saturn project, **1959:** 277
  Soviet, **1959:** 2, 89, 217n., 223, 267; **1960–61:** 13
      (p. 66), 21, 24, 350
  U.S. achievements, statement, **1960–61:** 264
Space vehicles, **1959:** 266, 267; **1960–61:** 10
  See also Rockets; Satellites, earth; Space re-
      search and exploration.
  Budget messages, **1958:** 5 (pp. 30, 60); **1960–61:**
      13 (pp. 47, 59, 66, 68), 414 (pp. 939, 960,
      970, 972, 973)
  Centaur project, **1960–61:** 13 (p. 68), 414 (p. 972)
  Development, **1958:** 105
  High altitude test, **1958:** 295
  Letter to T. Keith Glennan, **1960–61:** 12
  Pioneer IV, **1959:** 46, 48; **1960–61:** 264, 424
  Saturn project, **1960–61:** 10, 12, 13 (pp. 47, 66),
      24, 410, 414 (pp. 972, 973)
  Soviet, **1959:** 223
    Statement, **1959:** 2
  Unmanned, proposed launching, **1958:** 64
Spagnola, Rosaline, insurance claim, disapproval,
    1954: 239
Spain, **1959:** 116
  See also Madrid.
  Ambassador John Lodge, **1959:** 338n.
  Assistance, **1955:** 76; **1956:** 58; **1959:** 55, 200, 340
  Atomic research agreement, **1955:** 121
  Castiella, Fernando Maria, **1959:** 200
  Defense agreement, **1953:** 198
  Economic and defense agreements with United
      States, **1959:** 340
  Franco, Francisco, **1959:** 200, 338, 339, 340, 341
  NATO question, **1959:** 191
  U.S. bases, **1953:** 198; **1959:** 200
  Visit to, **1959:** 338, 339, 340, 341, 346
  Visit of John Foster Dulles, **1957:** 249
Spanish-American War, **1954:** 72, 111; **1955:** 56;
    1959: 179
  Military service of Stephen S. Ogletree, **1955:** 197
  Subject of frieze in Capitol rotunda, **1954:** 106n.
Sparkman, Sen. John, **1959:** 42
Speaker of the House of Representatives (Joseph
    W. Martin, Jr.), **1953:** 6, 187, 190n.; **1954:**
    12n., 87, 106, 157, 274, 286

Speaker of the House (Martin) — *continued*
Appointment of members of Hoover Commission, **1953:** 145n.
Letters
Department of Agriculture, supplemental appropriation, proposed, **1953:** 136
Foreign economic policy, **1953:** 63
Refugees, admission to United States, **1953:** 52
Resolution on subjugated peoples, **1953:** 14
News conference remarks on, **1953:** 15, 41
Speaker of the House of Representatives (Sam Rayburn), **1955:** 90 ftn. (p. 471); **1958:** 36, 134n.; **1959:** 6, 77, 151, 184n.; **1960–61:** 4, 88, 422
Bipartisan meeting on Suez Canal, **1956:** 184
Birthday greetings, **1955:** 4; **1958:** 2
Budget, letter, **1957:** 75
Hoover Commission recommendations, letter, **1957:** 112 and n.
Letters
Air carriers equipment investment program, **1958:** 194
Assistance to Yugoslavia, **1956:** 248
Corporate and excise taxes, **1958:** 114
Debt limit increase, **1958:** 183
Defense reorganization, **1958:** 75
Federal-State Action Committee recommendations, **1958:** 106
Great Plains program, **1956:** 7
Inter-American highway, **1955:** 64
Military assistance program, **1959:** 90, 136, 170, 183
Military career incentives, **1956:** 81
Mission 66, national parks, **1956:** 29
Mutual Security appropriations, **1960–61:** 272
News conference remarks on, **1958:** 42, 70
Philippines trade agreement revision, **1955:** 91
Presidential office space, **1956:** 131; **1957:** 135 and n.
Telecommunication systems, **1959:** 47
Transportation survey of Washington area, **1959:** 157
Virgin Islands Corporation, **1955:** 14
Water resources policy, **1956:** 13
News conference remarks on, **1955:** 41, 95; **1957:** 15, 45, 80; **1959:** 42, 94, 161, 186
Presidential appointments, **1955:** 95
Special Assistant to the President for Personnel Management (Eugene L. Lyons), **1960–61:** 26, 28
Memorandum, **1960–61:** 27
Speeding, news conference remarks, **1957:** 62
Spellman, Cardinal Francis J., **1954:** 301n.; **1957:** 223 and n.; **1959:** 212; **1960–61:** 263, 306
Letter, **1960–61:** 371
Spencer, Samuel, President, D. C. Board of Commissioners, letter, **1956:** 37n.
Spencer, Samuel R., Jr., **1960–61:** 340n.

Spencer, Susie Lee, estate, veto of bill for relief of, **1956:** 134
Spending by business, **1954:** 21
Spending by Government, **1953:** 6, 39, 57, 84, 95, 98, 101, 159, 187; **1954:** 21, 203, 209, 275, 291; **1955:** 4, 19; **1958:** 110; **1959:** 11, 15, 43, 56, 63, 71, 75, 83, 116, 124, 126, 129, 143, 177, 188, 225, 300n.; **1960–61:** 4, 19, 23, 350, 410
Campaign remarks, **1954:** 273, 286; **1958:** 292, 293, 295, 296, 302, 303, 308
Congressional authorization vs. Treasury payments, **1959:** 36
Election campaign remarks (1958), **1959:** 67
Housing bill vetoes, **1959:** 153, 208
Letters
Heads of agencies and departments, **1953:** 165
Minority leaders, **1958:** 43
Repr. Halleck, **1959:** 34
News conference remarks, **1953:** 12, 31, 37, 54, 62, 109, 198, 249, 254; **1954:** 18, 192, 311, 353; **1955:** 18, 41; **1958:** 42, 213, 288, 310; **1959:** 29, 36, 67, 102, 148, 172, 223; **1960–61:** 7, 24, 34, 222, 256, 422
Public information re administration policies, **1959:** 172
Spierenburg, Dirk, **1953:** 111n.
Spiritual Foundations of American Democracy Conference, remarks, **1954:** 327
Spivack, Robert G., **1953:** 15, 31, 37, 41, 54, 77, 243, 265; **1954:** 9, 18, 25, 33, 48, 50, 57, 63, 68, 73, 107, 115, 129, 165, 172, 341; **1955:** 10, 26, 41, 59, 62, 95, 112, 146; **1956:** 16, 32, 56, 62, 96, 113, 121, 155, 189, 198, 216; **1957:** 17, 28, 45, 50, 70, 80, 92, 124, 134; **1958:** 28, 42, 70, 83, 198, 213, 222; **1959:** 21, 42, 94, 123, 148, 161, 223; **1960–61:** 21, 38, 284, 422
Spivak, Alvin A., **1958:** 37, 42, 63, 70, 83, 88, 222
Splinter political groups, **1956:** 229
Sports, **1956:** 155, 193
Boxing, **1958:** 287
Fishing and hunting, **1958:** 288
Football, **1958:** 286
Football Hall of Fame, remarks, **1958:** 307
Golf, **1958:** 11, 91, 198, 288
Sprague, J. Russel, **1953:** 68, 69
Sprague, Maj. Gen. John T., **1955:** 235
Sprague, Mansfield D., **1960–61:** 332 ftn. (p. 789)
Springfield, Ill., **1954:** 22, 203, 205n.; **1959:** 31
Sputniks, **1957:** 234; **1958:** 287
News conference remarks, **1958:** 56, 70, 120, 141, 274
Squires, Paul, **1955:** 181n.
Squirrels on White House lawn, **1955:** 62
Sreitas, C. Arreiro de, **1960–61:** 157n.
S.S. *Queen Mary*, **1955:** 42n.
Staats, Elmer B., **1959:** 18n.

Stack, James R., **1956:** 253
Stackman, Samuel, bill for relief of, **1957:** 184
Stadium for Washington, D. C., **1956:** 121; **1957:** 45
Stahl, Steve, letter, **1959:** 63
Stalin, Joseph, **1953:** 50; **1955:** 95; **1956:** 87; **1957:** 6, 228; **1960–61:** 328
    Death of, message to Soviet Government, **1953:** 24
    Decision on Germany, **1958:** 318
    Illness, statement, **1953:** 20
    News conference remarks on, **1953:** 15, 22, 31, 109; **1956:** 62, 78; **1960–61:** 222, 268
    Problems of Leninism, **1953:** 109; **1956:** 62
Stamp album, presentation to the President, **1960–61:** 178n.
    "In God We Trust," **1954:** 77
        Ceremony on issuance, remarks, **1954:** 76
    In honor of American labor, remarks, **1956:** 194
    President Magsaysay Champion of Liberty, **1957:** 166
Standard of living, U.S., **1954:** 21; **1955:** 4, 19
Standards, Bureau of, **1955:** 17 (p. 148); **1956:** 12 (p. 123, 151); **1958:** 5 (p. 48)
Stanford, Neal A., **1953:** 37, 141; **1954:** 200
Stanford University, accelerator, **1959:** 89, 107
Stanley, Governor Thomas B., **1957:** 118 and n.
Stans, Maurice, **1957:** 18
    See also Budget, Bureau of the, Director (Maurice H. Stans)
Stansgate, Viscount, **1953:** 209n.
Stanton, Edwin M., **1955:** 31
Starved Rock Dam, Illinois River, **1958:** 229
Stassen, Harold E., **1955:** 60n., 94; **1957:** 22, 56, 80; **1958:** 30n.
    See also Foreign Operations Administration, Director; Mutual Security, Director for.
    Campaign badge, **1958:** 56
    Leave from White House office, **1956:** 155, 189
    London disarmament conference, **1957:** 72 and ftn. (p. 286), 115, 169
    News conference remarks on, **1955:** 10, 47, 62, 146, 185; **1956:** 88, 96, 113, 155, 189; **1958:** 28, 37, 56, 70
    Report on disarmament talk with Khrushchev, **1956:** 88
    Special Assistant to the President on Disarmament, **1955:** 57; **1956:** 266
        Resignation, **1958:** 30
    Support of Herter for Vice President, **1956:** 155, 189
    Visit to New Delhi, **1955:** 47
State, Assistant Secretary of (William M. Rountree), **1957:** 157n.
State, Department of, **1954:** 94; **1955:** 57, 74; **1956:** 30; **1957:** 157; **1958:** 165; **1959:** 67 ftn. (p. 292), 132 ftn. (p. 463), 191 ftn. (p. 615); **1960–61:** 57n., 246, 247, 358, 386, 431

State, Department of — *continued*
    Agreement with Soviet Union on cultural, technical, and educational exchanges, **1958:** 22
    Ban on entry of newsman into Communist China, **1956:** 193
    Bowie, Robert R., **1953:** 254 ftn. (p. 800); **1955:** 146 ftn. (p. 644)
    Budget messages, **1954:** 14 (pp. 126, 136, 138, 160); **1955:** 17 (pp. 131, 132); **1956:** 12 (pp. 108, 109, 151); **1958:** 5 (p. 41); **1959:** 10 (pp. 73, 75); **1960–61:** 13 (p. 64), 414 (pp. 968, 969)
        Table, **1958:** 5 (p. 69)
    Cabot, John M., **1953:** 48, 213n.
    Conduct of foreign affairs, **1954:** 14 (p. 138)
    Coolidge, Charles A., **1959:** 186, 243
    Corsi, Edward, **1955:** 62
    Cuban policy, **1960–61:** 263
    Cultural exchange program with Soviet Union, **1959:** 223
    Delegation to 4-power conference, Geneva, **1955:** 146 ftn. (p. 644)
    Dillon, C. Douglas, **1959:** 82n., 121, 130, 174, 243, 261n.; **1960–61:** 127, 263, 362 and ftn. (p. 864), 365
    Diplomatic personnel, reduction, **1960–61:** 362
    Educational exchange programs, **1953:** 89; **1955:** 17 (p. 132)
    Flag of the United States, display with flags of other nations, **1953:** 133
    Foreign policy development, **1953:** 89, 92
    Funds for foreign travel, **1956:** 205
    Gifts, **1957:** 228
    Hoover, Herbert, Jr., **1954:** 185, 345; **1955:** 94
    Hungarian refugees, funds for, **1956:** 307
    Information programs, **1953:** 89
    International Educational Exchange Service, **1959:** 222n.
    International Information Administration, **1953:** 89, 128 ftn. (p. 477)
    International Labor Organization, **1957:** 72
    Israel, memorandum on, **1957:** 34 and n.
    Jackson, William H., **1956:** 96
    Joint Disarmament Study Group, **1959:** 191 and ftn. (p. 611), 243
    Kohler, Foy D., **1959:** 218
    Ladejinsky case, **1955:** 10
    Langelle, Russell A., **1959:** 271
    Latin American mission of Milton Eisenhower, **1956:** 216
    MacArthur, Douglas, II, **1953:** 254 ftn. (p. 800); **1955:** 146 ftn. (p. 644)
    Mann, Thomas C., visit to Venezuela, **1958:** 323
    McLeod, Scott, **1954:** 48
    Merchant, Livingston T., **1953:** 254 ftn. (p. 800); **1955:** 61, 146 ftn. (p. 644)

State, Department of — *continued*
  Military assistance responsibilities, **1959:** 136, 137
  Murphy, Robert, **1954:** 284n.; **1959:** 9n., 277 ftn. (p. 766), 293, 297, 308, 322, 327
  News conference remarks on, **1953:** 54, 77, 88, 109, 126, 128 and ftn. (p. 477), 198, 208; **1954:** 57, 107, 129, 345; **1955:** 10, 62, 81; **1960–61:** 21, 127, 143, 228 and ftn. (p. 569), 263, 284, 362
  Overseas libraries, **1953:** 109, 126, 128
  Philippines, economic discussions, **1958:** 143
  Phleger, Herman, **1955:** 146 ftn. (p. 644)
  Position on arrest of Cardinal Wyszynski of Poland, **1953:** 235
  Refugee relief program, **1954:** 187
  Reorganization, **1953:** 54
  Report, **1960–61:** 409n.
  Robertson, Walter S., **1953:** 141; **1955:** 81; **1956:** 280; **1959:** 132
  Rubottom, Roy R., Jr., **1958:** 133; **1960–61:** 51, 69
  Smith, Walter Bedell, **1953:** 88; **1954:** 143, 157, 165
  Special Assistant for the Coordination of International Educational and Cultural Relations, **1959:** 24
  Status of Forces agreements, **1957:** 92
  Technical Cooperation Administration, **1953:** 89
  U–235 for peaceful uses, **1957:** 125
  U.S. aid to South America, documents re, **1960–61:** 380
State, Deputy Under Secretary (Loy W. Henderson), **1957:** 157n.; **1959:** 19, 91
  Award for Distinguished Federal Civilian Service, **1958:** 13
State, Secretary of
  Passport control, **1958:** 161; **1959:** 10 (p. 75)
  Responsibility for foreign affairs, memorandum, **1953:** 92
State, Secretary of (John Foster Dulles), **1953:** 2n., 24n., 48, 57, 71, 111n., 129, 176, 268; **1954:** 139, 178, 225, 266, 294, 303, 346; **1955:** 26 ftn. (p. 231), 54, 94, 98n., 126, 143, 146 ftn. (p. 644), 148, 173, 204n.; **1956:** 97, 260, 262, 276; **1957:** 35; **1958:** 31, 39, 261, 316, 317n.; **1959:** 19
  See also Dulles, John Foster.
  Address on Palestine cited, **1957:** 6
  Admission to U.S. of adopted orphans, **1956:** 275
  Agreements with Germany on settlement of debts and claims, report, **1953:** 46
  Ambassadorial appointments, **1957:** 70
  Appraisal, **1954:** 87, 101; **1958:** 11
  Arab-Israeli frontier, conditional guarantee, **1956:** 298
  Arms for Israel, **1956:** 56
  Assistance to less developed areas, **1958:** 312

State, Secretary of (Dulles) — *continued*
  Atomic energy for defense, U. S.-U. K. agreement, **1958:** 157
  Australian trip, **1957:** 45
  Bangkok conference, **1955:** 41
  Bipartisan conferences, **1954:** 336, 349, 351; **1956:** 62; **1957:** 2
    Geneva conference of heads of state, **1955:** 174
  Bolivian relief, transferral of agricultural commodities for, memorandum, **1953:** 206
  Campaign remarks on, **1954:** 273, 286, 304, 317, 318, 319, 320
  China policy, **1958:** 274
  Communism, **1959:** 57
  Disarmament, **1957:** 72 ftn. (p. 286)
    Nuclear test suspension proposal, **1957:** 158
  Discussion with Canadian leaders, **1953:** 70
  Discussion with French leaders on Indochina, **1954:** 165
  Discussions with Soviets on atomic energy pool, **1954:** 9, 18, 39, 129
  East German food shortage, U.S. assistance, **1953:** 134, 138
  Election issues, **1956:** 20
  European storm disaster relief, **1953:** 7n.
  Far East policies, **1954:** 68
  Fiftieth anniversary of first service in foreign affairs, **1957:** 111
  Flood relief
    Central and Eastern Europe, memorandum, **1954:** 195
    Italy, **1954:** 315
  Foreign aid programs, **1954:** 323
  Foreign ministers meetings (1954)
    Berlin, **1954:** 18, 25, 39, 128
    Geneva, **1954:** 128
    London, **1954:** 282, 332
    Paris, **1954:** 297
  Foreign policy statement, **1958:** 289
  Formosa Strait situation, **1958:** 274, 288
    Statement, **1958:** 257
  Geneva conferences (1955)
    Foreign ministers, **1955:** 226, 227
    Heads of government, **1955:** 161, 175
  Hungarian refugees, **1957:** 25
  Hungary, discussion with President on, **1956:** 287
  Illness, **1958:** 318; **1959:** 29, 36, 42, 48, 67, 78
    Statement re, **1959:** 35
  ILO conventions and recommendations, report, **1955:** 107
  Immigration study, **1956:** 33
  International Atomic Energy Agency, **1957:** 54
  Iranian oil situation, **1953:** 129n.
  Israeli-Egyptian dispute, **1957:** 35
  Letter re Committee on Narcotics, **1954:** 343
  Letter re transfer of FOA functions, **1955:** 74

State, Secretary of (Dulles) — *continued*
 Meeting on Syria, **1957:** 157n.
 Meetings with
  Chancellor Adenauer, **1956:** 125n., 129; **1957:** 100
  Dag Hammarskjold, **1955:** 18
  Foreign ministers of Great Britain and France, **1953:** 146
  King of Morocco, **1957:** 240
  King Saud, **1957:** 31
  Madame Pandit, **1953:** 210
  Premier Mollet, **1957:** 38
  President Diem, **1957:** 83, 97n.
  President Garcia, **1958:** 143
  President Rhee, **1954:** 172
  Prime Minister Daud, **1958:** 150
  Prime Minister Fanfani, **1958:** 186
  Prime Minister Kishi, **1957:** 117
  Prime Minister Macmillan, **1957:** 55, 226 and n.
  Prime Minister Scelba, **1955:** 61
  Prime Minister Suhrawardy, **1957:** 131
  Prime Minister Yoshida, **1954:** 330
 Middle East situation, **1955:** 234
 Mutual Defense Treaty, U.S.-Korea, report, **1954:** 6
 Mutual security appropriations, **1953:** 143
 NATO
  Conference, Paris, **1957:** 249
  Meeting, **1956:** 88
  Report on, **1953:** 265 ftn. (p. 843)
 News conference remarks on, **1953:** 12, 31, 37, 41, 62, 109, 126, 225, 230, 254 and ftns. (pp. 800, 801), 265; **1954:** 9, 18, 25, 39, 48, 50, 57, 68, 73 and ftn. (p. 384), 92, 101, 107, 115, 129, 138, 143, 157, 165, 172, 182, 322, 341, 345, 347; **1955:** 18, 41, 47, 59, 81, 100, 119, 146; **1956:** 16, 20, 56, 62, 78, 88, 113, 121, 189, 205, 229, 235, 298; **1957:** 22, 28, 45, 62, 70, 80, 87, 115, 124, 134, 145, 210; **1958:** 11, 28, 42, 56, 63, 70, 274, 288, 310, 318; **1959:** 29, 36, 42, 48, 67, 78
 Newsmen in China, **1957:** 45, 80
 North Atlantic Council meeting, **1958:** 318
 Nuclear tests, **1958:** 63, 70
 Oil supply study, **1956:** 239
 Pageant of Peace ceremonies, **1957:** 248
 Pakistan drought relief, **1953:** 97
 President Magsaysay Champion of Liberty Stamp ceremonies, **1957:** 166
 Recovery from operation
  News conference remarks on, **1956:** 298
  Statement on, **1956:** 286
 Refugee Relief Act, **1955:** 109
 Report on Berlin situation, **1959:** 29
 Report on negotiations in Europe, **1954:** 307, 308
 Resignation
  Letter, **1959:** 79
  News conference remarks, **1959:** 78

State, Secretary of (Dulles) — *continued*
 Retaliation in case of aggression, **1954:** 9, 57
 Science Adviser and Science Attaches, proposed appointment of, **1957:** 230
 Shepley, James R., article, **1956:** 16
 Southeast Asia Collective Defense Treaty, report on, **1955:** 5
 Soviet summit proposal, **1958:** 42, 56
 Suez situation, **1956:** 189, 205, 229, 235
  Bipartisan meeting, **1956:** 184
  Report on, **1956:** 164, 192
 TV report on European visit, **1955:** 99
  Comment on, **1955:** 100
 U.S. airmen imprisoned in Communist China, **1955:** 18
 Visit to Asia, **1955:** 100
 Visit to Brazil, **1958:** 133, 197
 Visit to Formosa, **1955:** 47
 Visit to Middle East and Asia, **1953:** 101, 217
 Waiver of fingerprinting requirements, **1956:** 53
 "Your Government and You" broadcast, **1956:** 246
State, Secretary of (Christian A. Herter), **1959:** 82n., 110n., 123 ftn. (p. 425), 191 ftn. (p. 611), 200n., 332n., 351; **1960–61:** 22, 46n., 51, 69, 125, 132, 154, 162, 171n., 209, 294, 307, 339n., 349, 365, 369, 370, 410, 419n., 420
 See also Herter, Christian A.
 Chairman, National Advisory Committee for Inter-American Affairs, **1959:** 287n.
 Inter-American Foreign Ministers Conference, **1959:** 172
 Medal of Freedom, citation, **1960–61:** 428
 Meetings with
  Chancellor Adenauer, **1959:** 192; **1960–61:** 92
  Premier Khrushchev, **1959:** 218, 242
  President de Gaulle, **1959:** 202
  President Lleras, **1960–61:** 111
  President Toure, **1959:** 272
  Prime Minister Kishi, **1960–61:** 16
  Prime Minister Segni, **1959:** 203, 248
 NATO Ministerial Council Meeting, **1959:** 277 ftn. (p. 766)
 News conference remarks on, **1959:** 89, 94, 123, 148, 154, 161, 172, 271; **1960–61:** 21, 93, 103, 127, 143, 228
 Report, **1960–61:** 409n.
 Resignation, letter, **1960–61:** 409
 Termination of U.S. relations with Cuba, **1960–61:** 388
State, Under Secretary of (Christian A. Herter), **1957:** 22, 50, 62
 Ratification of Statute of International Atomic Energy Agency, **1957:** 144 and n.
State, Under Secretary of (Herbert Hoover, Jr.), **1956:** 287
 Acting Secretary of State, **1956:** 286

State, Under Secretary of (Hoover) — *continued*
Letter to, on departure from Federal Government, **1957:** 20
Term of service, **1957:** 20n.
State, War, and Navy Building, proposed demolition, **1957:** 105
State and community conferences on education, statement, **1955:** 96
State Highway Officials, Western Association, **1959:** 149
State of the Nation, broadcasts, **1954:** 2, 72
State Planning and Development Agencies, Association of, remarks, **1959:** 8
State of the Union, annual message to Congress, **1953:** 6; **1954:** 3; **1955:** 4; **1956:** 2; **1957:** 8; **1959:** 6; **1960–61:** 4, 410
Broadcast on, **1956:** 3
News conference remarks, **1956:** 16
State University of New York Medical Center, dedication, remarks, **1954:** 300
Statehood
Alaska, **1953:** 15, 77; **1954:** 9, 33, 50, 73, 165, 311; **1957:** 13; **1958:** 5 (p. 73), 28, 42, 120; **1959:** 21, 174; **1960–61:** 4, 13 (p. 104), 402, 410
Approval of act, **1958:** 159
Letter to Gov. Stepovich, **1958:** 160
Remarks, **1959:** 3
Hawaii, **1953:** 6, 15, 77, 268; **1954:** 3, 33, 50, 73, 161, 349; **1955:** 4, 56, 95, 247; **1956:** 2, 205; **1957:** 13; **1958:** 5 (p. 73), 28, 42, 120, 159; **1959:** 10 (p. 109), 53, 174, 225; **1960–61:** 4, 13 (p. 104), 205, 206, 402, 410
Admission into Union, remarks, **1959:** 184
Approval of act, **1959:** 60
Letter to Gov. Quinn, **1959:** 61
Letter to Maurice H. Stans, **1959:** 62
Puerto Rico, question of, **1959:** 102; **1960–61:** 93
States
See also specific states.
Atomic energy for peaceful uses, regulatory responsibilities, **1960–61:** 116
Authority over labor cases, **1959:** 176
Bills to close schools in integration situation, **1958:** 222
Candidates for public office, **1957:** 87
Civil defense directors, remarks, **1953:** 202
Control over schools, **1959:** 21
Drought disaster relief, **1958:** 12
Education, conferences on, **1954:** 3, 14 (p.153), 268
Education beyond high school, funds, **1957:** 19
Election expenditures, **1956:** 94
Employment offices, **1958:** 53
Federal aid.
See Federal aid to States.
Federal-State Action Committee, **1958:** 5 (p. 43); **1959:** 10 (pp. 68, 98); **1960–61:** 115, 116
Federal-State-local governmental responsibilities, **1957:** 8, 11, 19, 75, 118, 223

States — *continued*
Governors, letter to, **1955:** 29
Grants and loans, **1957:** 86
Health services, responsibility re, **1954:** 301
Highway commissioners, **1959:** 138
Indian reservations, jurisdiction over cases arising on, **1953:** 166
Interposition resolutions on school integration decision, **1956:** 47
Interstate highway system.
See Highway system, interstate.
Jurisdiction in labor disputes, **1954:** 5, 39, 101
Local flood control works, participation, **1953:** 153
Narcotics problem, **1954:** 343; **1956:** 31
Natural resources, conservation and development, **1953:** 153
News conference remarks, **1958:** 56, 222, 274
Polio vaccine.
See Poliomyelitis vaccine.
Public assistance, **1958:** 5 (p. 52)
Public vs. private power, **1954:** 138, 271
Responsibilities, remarks, **1953:** 156
Restoration of lands, **1957:** 75
Retirement systems, **1953:** 155
"Right to work" laws, **1954:** 63, 347, 353; **1958:** 274, 293
River basin development, **1953:** 153
Southern States, two-party system, **1953:** 220; **1954:** 322
Taxes, **1953:** 67; **1954:** 144
Tidelands dispute.
See Tidelands, Federal vs. State claims.
Traffic safety, letter, **1956:** 37
Treaties affecting.
See Bricker amendment.
Voting laws standardization, **1954:** 3
Water resources conservation, **1953:** 153
Western States, growth, **1953:** 153
States rights, **1957:** 119; **1960–61:** 335, 340
News conference remarks, **1956:** 32, 47
Statistical and economic services, **1959:** 10 (p. 100); **1960–61:** 13 (pp. 91, 92), 414 (pp. 1004, 1005)
Statistics, educational, **1958:** 5 (p. 49)
Statue of Liberty, **1953:** 252; **1954:** 77; **1959:** 190n.
Status of Forces Agreement, **1954:** 18; **1955:** 119; **1957:** 105, 134
News conference remarks, **1956:** 121; **1957:** 92, 105, 124, 134, 150
President's work on, **1957:** 105
Status of U. S. forces abroad, **1957:** 139
Staunton, Va., **1960–61:** 340
Hassett, Mayor Thomas E., **1960–61:** 340n.
Staunton Military Academy, **1960–61:** 340
Steel industry, **1959:** 142, 160, 265
Fact paper on, **1959:** 132, 172
Labor contract, **1956:** 190, 229

Steel industry — *continued*
  Labor dispute settlement, statement, **1956:** 150
  Letter to leaders, **1959:** 211
  Profits, **1959:** 94, 132
  Talks with officials, statement, **1959:** 246
Steel and Iron Institute, **1960–61:** 315
Steel prices, **1956:** 171, 229; **1957:** 124, 134; **1958:** 120, 198, 213; **1959:** 42, 53, 67, 94, 132, 172; **1960–61:** 4
Steel production, **1958:** 292, 303; **1960–61:** 222, 256
Steel strike (1959), **1960–61:** 4
  Board of Inquiry, **1959:** 264, 271
    Report, **1959:** 265
    Statement on, **1959:** 253
  Effect on national economy, statement, **1959:** 268
  Fact-finding board, question of, **1959:** 142, 223
  Fact-finding by Secretary Mitchell, **1959:** 167
  Government intervention, question of, **1959:** 142, 223, 243, 271
  Injunction under Taft-Hartley Act, **1959:** 264
    Court decisions on, **1959:** 265n.
    Letter to Attorney General Rogers, **1959:** 265
  Khrushchev visit, **1959:** 179
  Letter to leaders of steel industry, **1959:** 211
  Letters to David J. McDonald, **1959:** 142, 211
  News conference remarks, **1959:** 67, 123, 154, 161, 167, 172, 179, 186, 223, 243, 267, 271, 288; **1960–61:** 7, 21
  Settlement, comment on, **1960–61:** 7
  Statements, **1959:** 160, 243, 246, 264
  Threat of renewal, **1959:** 288, 290
Steel Training and Education Program, Indian, **1960–61:** 315n.
Steel wage negotiations, **1959:** 160
  News conference remarks, **1959:** 42, 94, 123, 132, 154, 172
  Report of Secretary Mitchell, **1959:** 211
  Role of Government, **1959:** 132
Steele, John L., **1956:** 47, 56, 94, 96, 121, 155, 193, 198, 205, 229, 298; **1957:** 17, 22, 72, 80, 87, 115, 124, 152, 157, 169, 207, 228; **1959:** 167, 191
Steele, Robert H., **1958:** 294n.
Steelman, John R., **1959:** 161
Stennis, Sen. John C., **1954:** 33, 50
Stephens, Thomas E., **1953:** 254 ftn. (p. 800)
Stephenson, Francis M., **1953:** 198, 249; **1954:** 68, 92, 341; **1955:** 62, 90; **1956:** 5, 53, 56, 216, 229; **1957:** 45, 56, 119; **1958:** 83, 141
Stepinac, Cardinal Aloysius, **1956:** 292
Stepovich, Michael A., **1959:** 3n.
  Letter, **1958:** 160
Sterns, Robert L., **1953:** 207
Stevens, Robert T.
  See Army, Secretary of the (Robert T. Stevens).
Stevenson, Adlai E., **1954:** 50; **1956:** 229, 233, 255; **1957:** 17, 22, 80, 150, 228

Stevenson, Adlai E. — *continued*
  Briefing on international situation, telegram, **1956:** 197
  Meeting with Khrushchev, **1958:** 318
  News conference remarks on, **1953:** 12, 208; **1956:** 88, 198, 205, 216, 235; **1958:** 222, 318
  Nonaggression pacts, **1953:** 208
Stewart, J. George, **1959:** 151
Stewart, J. Harold, **1954:** 12n.
Stiebeling, Hazel K., Award for Distinguished Federal Civilian Service, **1959:** 9n.
Stock market, **1955:** 18, 56; **1957:** 228
  Margin requirements, **1955:** 81
  Reaction to announcements regarding President, **1956:** 5, 32
Stockholm
  International Confederation of Free Trade Unions meeting, **1953:** 128, 130
  Reports on radioactive fallout, **1958:** 74
Stockholm, collision with *Andrea Doria*, **1956:** 149
Stockpile of nuclear weapons, **1956:** 266
  NATO countries, **1957:** 134
  Reduction, NATO meeting remarks, **1957:** 245
Stockpiling of acid-grade fluorspar, **1958:** 206
Stockpiling of strategic and critical materials, **1953:** 40; **1954:** 308; **1955:** 3, 4; **1959:** 10 (p. 68); **1960–61:** 13 (p. 59), 414 (pp. 960, 961)
  Broadcast on cost of Government, **1957:** 86
  Budget messages, **1954:** 14 (pp. 85, 86, 108, 118, 130, 180, 181); **1955:** 17 (pp. 108, 122); **1956:** 12 (pp. 80, 81, 101–103); **1958:** 5 (pp. 26, 28, 33)
  Natural rubber, **1956:** 90
  Priorities and allocations, **1958:** 5 (p. 33)
  Tin, **1954:** 14 (p. 180)
Stone, Lt. James L., Medal of Honor award, **1953:** 229n.
Stone, John, **1956:** 241
Stone, Mrs. John, **1956:** 241
Stone, William E., disability retirement claim, **1956:** 135
Storage of agricultural surpluses, cost of, **1959:** 108, 122, 139
  News conference remarks, **1959:** 102, 132
Storey, Robert G., **1954:** 12n.; **1958:** 318
Storm disasters in Western Europe, **1953:** 8
  Messages, **1953:** 7
Stover families, **1956:** 251
Strasbourg Conference, **1953:** 6
Strategic Air Command, **1955:** 13, 17 (p. 117); **1956:** 94; **1957:** 230, 234; **1958:** 2; **1959:** 55, 57; **1960–61:** 245, 255
  Bases, **1958:** 32
  Budget message, **1958:** 5 (pp. 29, 30); **1959:** 10 (p. 60); **1960–61:** 13 (pp. 52, 53)
  Campaign remarks, **1958:** 292, 296
  Effect of missile development, **1957:** 210

Strategic Air Command — *continued*
LeMay, Gen. Curtis E., **1957:** 72
News conference remarks, **1957:** 72, 210; **1959:** 26, 48; **1960–61:** 24, 256
Visits to headquarters, **1958:** 88
Vulnerability, question of, **1960–61:** 24
Strategic Air force, **1955:** 52n.
Strategic Army Corps, **1959:** 57
Strategic materials, joint statement with Prime Minister Kishi re, **1957:** 117
Strategic and critical materials, stockpiling.
See Stockpiling of strategic and critical materials.
Stratemeyer, Lt. Gen. George E., **1955:** 112
Stratford, Va., **1958:** 93
Stratton, Gov. William G., **1954:** 192, 203; **1956:** 198, 214, 216; **1957:** 124, 138; **1958:** 296; **1960–61:** 246
Strauss, Lewis L.
See also Atomic Energy Commission, Chairman (Lewis L. Strauss); Commerce, Secretary of (Lewis L. Strauss).
Congressional action on appointment, **1959:** 89, 223
Medal of Freedom citation, **1958:** 166
News conference remarks on, **1959:** 89, 148, 223
Street, Allen M., **1957:** 234 and n.
Streibert, Theodore C.
See United States Information Agency, Director (Theodore C. Streibert).
Strikes.
See Labor disputes.
Stringer, William H., **1957:** 50, 72; **1958:** 28, 120, 222
Stritch, Cardinal, death of, statement, **1958:** 115
Strom, Else, **1953:** 225
Strontium **1956:** 90, 266
Strout, Richard L., **1954:** 9
Stuart, Roger, **1954:** 107
Studebaker Corp., **1954:** 274
Studebaker Local 5 (UAW), **1954:** 203n., 274n.
Student exchange program.
See Exchange of students.
Student loan program, loyalty oath requirement, comment on, **1959:** 288
Students
American countries, scholarships, **1957:** 96
American Field Service students, remarks to, **1957:** 137
Atomic studies of foreign students, **1955:** 53, 165
Chinese, in United States, **1954:** 192
Eisenhower Fellowships, **1957:** 222
Exchange.
See Exchange of students.
Fulbright scholarships, **1957:** 222
Incentives for scientific and professional studies, **1957:** 234
U. S. students in Communist China, **1957:** 157

Students Federation of Chile, **1960–61:** 72n.
Students of Korea, message, **1960–61:** 250
Sturgis, Maj. Gen. Samuel D., Jr., **1953:** 100; **1954:** 271
Submarine nuclear propulsion plant, transfer to United Kingdom, **1958:** 156
Submarines, **1957:** 234
Budget messages, **1960–61:** 13 (p. 51), 414 (pp. 949, 955)
Furnished Egypt by U.S.S.R., **1957:** 124
Guided nuclear missile, **1957:** 230
Missile-based, **1958:** 5 (p. 29)
Submarines, nuclear-powered, **1957:** 230; **1958:** 2, 65, 204, 292; **1959:** 6, 10 (p. 64), 57; **1960–61:** 244, 245, 255
Budget messages, **1960–61:** 13 (pp. 51–55), 414 (pp. 938, 949, 951, 952, 954, 955)
Nautilus, **1954:** 14 (p. 129), 38; **1955:** 17 (p. 121), 81; **1956:** 243; **1958:** 15, 201, 210, 211
Polaris missile-based, **1960–61:** 4, 7, 13 (pp. 51–55), 244, 245, 255, 410, 414 (pp. 938, 951, 952, 954)
Abraham Lincoln, **1960–61:** 360
Based in United Kingdom, **1960–61:** 360n.
George Washington, **1960–61:** 255, 360
Patrick Henry, **1960–61:** 244, 360
Regulus missile-based, **1960–61:** 13 (p. 51)
Seawolf, **1954:** 14 (p. 129); **1955:** 17 (p. 121), 81; **1958:** 274
Triton, **1960–61:** 142
Submarines, Soviet, in U.S. waters, **1958:** 83; **1959:** 26
Submerged lands, **1956:** 56
See also Tidelands.
Submerged Lands Act, approval, **1953:** 86
Subsidies, Government, **1959:** 10 (pp. 79, 80)
Airlines, **1953:** 94; **1955:** 17 (p. 169), 30, 33, 106; **1958:** 5 (p. 60), 246; **1960–61:** 13 (p. 68), 414 (p. 974)
Airmail, **1954:** 14 (pp. 173, 174)
Budget messages, **1956:** 12 (pp. 82, 141–143); **1958:** 5 (pp. 45, 59, 60)
Foundation livestock, **1956:** 236
Payment to lead and zinc producers, disapproval, **1960–61:** 280
Ships, **1954:** 14 (p. 174); **1955:** 17 (pp. 92, 167, 168); **1958:** 5 (pp. 59, 60); **1960–61:** 13 (p. 69), 414 (p. 975)
Subversive activities, **1953:** 57, 69; **1954:** 3, 139, 210, 211, 225, 291; **1956:** 2; **1960–61:** 143, 154, 163
Campaign remarks, **1954:** 273, 286, 316
FBI jurisdiction, **1953:** 95, 263
News conference remarks, **1953:** 243, 254; **1954:** 9, 48, 129
Record of Department of justice in dealing with, **1954:** 129, 209
Statement, **1954:** 130

Subversive Activities Control Board, **1956:** 96, 155
  Tenure of office, **1955:** 189
Sudan, assistance, **1959:** 55
  Richards mission, **1957:** 72
  U.N. membership, **1958:** 8
  Proposed, **1956:** 143
Sudetenland, **1958:** 274
Suez, **1955:** 35
Suez Canal, **1954:** 157, 203, 209, 325; **1956:** 87, 164,
    184, 192, 282, 295; **1957:** 6, 28, 35, 37;
    1960–61: 302, 330, 341
  Bipartisan meeting on, **1956:** 184
  Boycott of Israeli shipping, **1960–61:** 38, 127
  Cairo discussions, **1956:** 205
  Campaign remarks, **1954:** 273, 286, 317, 319,
    320; **1956:** 210, 241, 268, 283, 290; **1958:**
    293
  Clearance, U.N. action, **1958:** 148
  Report, **1958:** 8
  Constantinople Convention of 1888, **1956:** 184,
    192, 205, 216
  Invasion (1956), **1960–61:** 21, 410
  Joint statement with Premier Mollet, **1957:** 38
  Joint statement with Prime Minister Macmillan,
    1957: 55
  London conferences
    18-nation proposal, **1956:** 184, 192, 198, 205,
      216, 235
    3-power (U. S., U. K., France), report, **1956:**
      164
  NATO forces in, **1957:** 34
  News conference remarks, **1956:** 155, 171, 189,
    193, 198, 205, 216, 229, 235; **1957:** 62, 70,
    72, 87, 228; **1960–61:** 21, 38, 127
  Oil shipments through, **1956:** 239n.
  Reports on, **1956:** 164, 192
  U.K.-Egyptian agreement, **1954:** 172, 192, 226,
    297, 316
  U.S. shipping, **1957:** 72
  White House statement on, **1957:** 34
Suez Canal Company, **1956:** 164, 282
Suffrage.
  See Voting.
Sugar, liquid, trade agreement concession, **1956:**
    123
Sugar Act, **1956:** 6; **1958:** 5 (p. 64); **1960–61:** 223n.,
    374
  Amendment and extension of, **1956:** 116; **1959:**
    10 (pp. 88, 91); **1960–61:** 106, 133, 267,
    418
  Budget messages, **1960–61:** 13 (p. 79), 414 (p.
    989)
  News conference remarks, **1960–61:** 38, 93, 222
Sugar program, **1954:** 4
Sugar quotas
  Budget message, **1960–61:** 414 (p. 989)
  Cuba, **1960–61:** 21, 38, 93, 167n., 222, 267
    Approval of bill, **1960–61:** 223
    Proclamation, statement, **1960–61:** 374

Sugar quotas — *continued*
  Dominican Republic, **1960–61:** 374, 418
    Message to Congress, **1960–61:** 267
  Letter to Sen. Bennett, **1960–61:** 167
  Philippines, telegram to President Garcia, **1960–
    61:** 106
Suhrawardy, Huseyn Shaheed, joint statement
    with, **1957:** 131
Sukarno, Achmed, **1956:** 87, 107
  Exchange of messages, **1956:** 120
  Exchange of toasts, **1956:** 106
  Letter, **1960–61:** 313
Sullivan, John J., **1957:** 176 and n.
Summerfield, Arthur E., **1959:** 270
  See also Postmaster General (Arthur E.
    Summerfield).
Summerfield, Mrs. Arthur E., **1954:** 273
Summit conferences.
  See Heads of state and governments.
Summit meeting, news conference remarks, **1957:**
    80
Sun Yat-sen, **1959:** 31; **1960–61:** 193
Superior National Forest, **1960–61:** 414 (p. 998)
Superliners, Federal loans for, **1959:** 10 (p. 80), 21
Supersonic bomber (B-58), **1957:** 230
Supplemental Appropriation Act, approval, **1959:**
    197
Supreme Allied Commander, Atlantic (Adm.
    Robert L. Dennison), designation, letter,
    1959: 351
Supreme Allied Commander Atlantic (Adm.
    Jerauld Wright), **1955:** 100
  Appointment, statement, **1954:** 36
  Retirement, letter, **1959:** 350
Supreme Allied Commander Europe, **1954:** 332;
    1956: 317; **1957:** 70
Supreme Allied Commander Europe (Gen. Lauris
    Norstad), **1957:** 28, 72, 246 and n.; **1959:**
    206
Supreme Allied Commander, Europe (Gen.
    Matthew B. Ridgway), **1953:** 72, 74, 75
  Letters, **1953:** 71, 73
Supreme Commander, Allied Powers Europe,
    former (General Gruenther), **1958:** 118
Supreme Court, U.S., **1953:** 101; **1960–61:** 50, 93
  See also Chief Justice of the United States;
    Courts, Federal.
  Appointments to, policy, **1956:** 205, 216
  Chief Justice, proposed annual address to the
    Congress, **1957:** 13
  Congressional subpoenas for Justices, question
    of, **1953:** 243
  Constitutional powers, **1956:** 47
  Decision of 1896 (separate but equal facilities),
    1956: 56, 62, 171
  Decisions
    Feres vs. United States, **1958:** 251
    Food and Drug Administration, factory in-
      spections, **1953:** 6, 95

Supreme Court, U.S. — *continued*
  Decisions — *continued*
    Industrial security program, **1959:** 148
    Jurisdiction of States in labor disputes, **1954:** 5
    Military negligence claim, **1954:** 230
    Power to deny passports, **1958:** 161
    Rosenberg case, **1953:** 114
    School integration, **1954:** 115, 192, 341; **1955:**
      149; **1956:** 20, 32, 47, 56, 69, 113, 171, 198,
      235, 241; **1957:** 124, 178, 198, 207; **1958:**
      222, 262, 274, 275, 295; **1959:** 17, 21, 102
    State "right to work" laws, **1954:** 63
    Subversion, **1959:** 42
    Taxation of disability payments, **1958:** 232;
      1959: 234; **1960–61:** 291
    Tidelands ownership, **1953:** 58
    Water diversion, **1954:** 253
  Filling of vacancies, comment on, **1954:** 311
  Jenner-Butler legislation, **1958:** 83
  Justice Harold H. Burton, retirement, **1958:** 279
  Justice Sherman Minton, resignation, **1956:** 202,
    205
  Justice Stanley Reed, resignation, **1957:** 24 and
    n.
  Meeting with Prime Minister Daud, **1958:** 150
  News conference remarks on, **1954:** 63, 115, 192,
    311, 341, 353; **1956:** 20, 32, 47, 56, 62, 113,
    171, 198, 205, 216, 235; **1957:** 28, 115, 119,
    124, 134, 169, 207; **1958:** 83, 222, 274;
    1959: 17, 21, 42, 102, 148, 277
  Nomination to fill vacancy, comment on, **1955:**
    26
  Steel strike injunction case, **1959:** 265n., 277
Supreme Court of Texas, **1956:** 56
Supreme Headquarters, Allied Expeditionary
  Forces, **1953:** 88
Supreme Headquarters of Allied Powers in Europe,
  1954: 167n., 347; **1956:** 257, 317; **1957:**
  134, 246 and n.; **1958:** 120; **1960–61:** 86,
  91n.
  Address to Chaplains (1952), **1954:** 103
  Chief of Staff, **1953:** 71, 74
  News conference remarks, **1959:** 94
  Remarks at headquarters, **1959:** 206
Surface-to-air missiles, **1957:** 230
Surgeon General, **1953:** 28
Surgeon General, Public Health Service (Leonard
  A. Scheele), **1956:** 137, 303
Surgeons, College of, **1959:** 129
  Message, **1957:** 216
Surplus agricultural commodities.
  See Agricultural surpluses.
Surplus aluminum, expenditures for, **1957:** 169
Surplus copper, expenditures for, **1957:** 169
Surplus crops, price-supported, cultivation banned
  on leased Government land, **1956:** 111
Surplus Disposal Administrator, Agricultural, ap-
  pointment, **1956:** 6
Surplus Federal land, restoration to States, **1957:**
  75

Surplus military airport facilities, **1958:** 246
Surplus real property disposal, **1957:** 13
Surrender by United States in nuclear war, news
  conference remarks, **1958:** 222
Survivor benefits.
  See Old-age and survivors' insurance.
Swanson, Henry A., Jr., **1960–61:** 330n.
Swanstrom, Bishop Edward E., **1960–61:** 371
Swarthmore College, **1959:** 116
Sweden, **1960–61:** 321n.
  Question of summit conference in, **1955:** 119
  Stockholm, **1953:** 128, 130
Swimming, **1956:** 193
Swing, Joseph M., **1956:** 229, 235; **1959:** 161
  See also Immigration and Naturalization, Com-
    missioner of.
Switzerland, **1959:** 75
  Atomic research agreement, **1955:** 121
  Basel, **1960–61:** 279
  Geneva, **1955:** 37n., 168n., 169n.
    See also Geneva conferences.
  Lausanne, **1955:** 112, 119
  Petitpierre, Max, **1955:** 163
  U.S. tariffs on Swiss watches, **1954:** 172
Sylvester, Arthur, **1953:** 22, 77, 230, 238; **1954:** 92;
  1956: 198
Symington, J. Fife, Jr., **1958:** 308
Symington, Sen. Stuart, **1953:** 31; **1956:** 32, 113;
  1959: 7, 94
  Investigation of report of Communist infiltration
    into Italian aircraft plants, **1954:** 39
  News conference remarks on, **1954:** 39, 129
Symms, Marion S., tax refund claim, **1958:** 232
Synthetic rubber, **1956:** 90
Synthetic rubber facilities, Government-owned
  Disposal, **1953:** 49; **1957:** 13
  News conference remarks, **1953:** 22, 198
  Sale of, **1955:** 17 (p. 92)
Syracuse, N.Y., **1956:** 263
Syria, **1957:** 157n.; **1958:** 177
  See also United Arab Republic.
  Lebanese situation, **1958:** 173
  News conference remarks, **1957:** 56, 134, 157,
    207
Syrian-Turkish crisis, **1958:** 148

Taber, Repr. John, **1953:** 266
Tachen Islands, **1955:** 21 36
  Evacuation, **1955:** 33
  News conference remarks, **1955:** 18, 26, 33, 47
Tacoma, Wash., campaign remarks, **1955:** 253
Taft, Sen. Robert A., **1953:** 159, 215; **1954:** 317;
  1956: 224; **1959:** 77
  Death of, statement, **1953:** 154
  Illness, **1953:** 98
  Korean war, **1953:** 88

Taft, Sen. Robert A. — *continued*
  News conference remarks on, **1953:** 15, 22, 41, 88
  Statement on budget (1952), **1959:** 21
Taft (Robert A.) Memorial Bell Tower, dedication,
    remarks, **1959:** 77
Taft (Robert A.) Memorial Foundation, **1959:** 77
Taft, Mrs. Robert A., **1953:** 154
Taft, William Howard, **1953:** 154; **1954:** 322
  Jury trials, **1957:** 105
Taft-Hartley Act, **1953:** 203; **1954:** 5, 193; **1957:** 17,
    50; **1958:** 20, 216, 293; **1959:** 142, 265
  See also Labor-management relations.
  Adequacy of, comment on, **1959:** 267
  Campaign remarks, **1956:** 241
  News conference remarks, **1953:** 109, 198; **1954:**
    9, 101, 192, 353
  Revision proposed, **1953:** 6, 109, 193, 198, 248,
    266; **1954:** 3, 9, 101, 209, 275, 349
Taft Sanitary Engineering Center, **1954:** 301
Taipei
  Address at mass rally, **1960–61:** 193
  Joint statement with President Chiang Kai-shek,
    1960–61: 195
  Remarks on arrival, **1960–61:** 192
  Remarks on departure, **1960–61:** 196
  Toast to President Chiang Kai-shek, **1960–61:**
    194
Taiwan (Formosa), **1953:** 6; **1956:** 210, 283; **1957:** 6
  See also China, Republic of; Formosa; Formosa
    Strait Situation.
  Assistance, **1956:** 12 (p. 104)
  News conference remarks, **1956:** 16, 56, 235
Taj Mahal, visit to, **1959:** 316n.
Talbot, Joseph E., **1953:** 54
Talbott, Harold E.
  See Air Force, Secretary of the.
Talbott, Philip M., **1958:** 90
Talent, waste of, **1958:** 24
Tallamy, Bertram D., report, **1959:** 138
Talle, Henry O., **1959:** 18n.
Talos missile, **1956:** 141
Tamerlane, **1960–61:** 58
Tampico, Mexico, flood relief, **1955:** 229
Tanker fleet modernization, approval, **1954:** 191
Tankers, construction, **1956:** 239
TAPline oil deliveries, **1957:** 28
Tariff Act of 1930, amendment, disapproval,
    1960–61: 285
Tariff Commission, **1953:** 141; **1954:** 67; **1955:** 6;
    1958: 25, 28
  Effect of wool imports on price support program,
    report, **1954:** 49
  Escape clause cases, **1958:** 132
  Investigation of certain imports, **1956:** 123
  Lead and zinc, production, consumption, and
    importation, investigation, **1953:** 228
  News conference remarks, **1954:** 48, 143, 172,
    200

Tariff Commission — *continued*
  Talbot, Joseph E., **1953:** 54
  Tariff recommendations
    Lead and zinc, **1954:** 143, 200
    Watches, **1954:** 172, 217
  Wool imports, effect on price support program,
    investigation, **1953:** 131
Tariff Commission, Chairman (Edgar B. Brossard),
    1953: 131
Tariffs, **1954:** 67
  Canadian clover, **1954:** 172
  Duty on imports, revised valuation procedures,
    1956: 162
  Lead and zinc, **1954:** 143, 200; **1957:** 157
    Letter re, **1957:** 160
  News conference remarks, **1954:** 9, 138, 143, 172,
    200
  Reduction of, **1955:** 4
  Watches, **1954:** 172, 217
  Wool, **1954:** 9
Tariffs and Trade, General Agreement on, **1954:**
    67; **1955:** 6, 72; **1956:** 2, 123, 310; **1958:**
    163; **1960–61:** 95
  See also Trade, international; Trade Agreements
    Act.
  Geneva negotiations, **1956:** 94 and ftn. (p. 452)
  Hat bodies, fur-felt, **1956:** 123
  Joint statement with Western leaders, **1959:** 335
  News conference remarks, **1956:** 94, 216
  Ninth Session, letter to Chairman of U.S. dele-
    gation, **1954:** 324
  Sixth Protocol Supplementary Concessions,
    1956: 123n.
  Sugar, liquid, **1956:** 123
  Tariff concessions, **1958:** 25, 58
    Seed wheat, **1958:** 217
    Textiles, **1955:** 149
  U. S. Advisory Committee, **1956:** 94
  Woolen textiles, tariff increase, **1956:** 216
Tarrytown, N.Y., **1960–61:** 346
Tassigny, Marshal Jean de Lattre de, **1954:** 133,
    198
Tawes, Gov. J. Millard, **1959:** 116
Tawitawi Group, **1958:** 140
Tax Court of the United States, **1960–61:** 150
  Survivorship annuities for widows and children
    of judges, **1960–61:** 414 (pp. 1020, 1021)
Tax laws, **1957:** 41
  Letter on small business, **1957:** 132
Tax returns, investigation by Congressional Com-
    mittees, **1955:** 90
Tax treaties, **1955:** 6
Tax write-off allowances, **1958:** 88
  Depreciation of facilities, **1957:** 80, 92, 115, 124
  Oil depletion, **1957:** 92, 145; **1958:** 28
Taxes, **1953:** 69, 83, 98, 159; **1954:** 149; **1957:** 13,
    16; **1960–61:** 80, 354, 410
  Alexander, J. Don, refund claim, **1953:** 107

Taxes — *continued*
  Broadcast, **1954:** 54
  Budget (1954), **1953:** 82
  Budget messages, **1954:** 14 (pp. 87, 88, 90–99);
    1955: 17 (pp. 87, 97–99, 145); **1956:** 12
    (pp. 88–90, 150, 151); **1958:** 5 (pp. 22–23,
    43, 45); **1959:** 10 (pp. 39–42, 79); **1960–61:**
    13 (pp. 39, 40, 42–44, 64, 69, 70, 101, 105),
    414 (pp. 937, 940, 941, 943, 944, 975, 977,
    1005, 1017, 1022)
    Tables, **1956:** 12 (p. 89); **1958:** 5 (p. 22)
  Campaign remarks, **1954:** 273, 286, 290, 316,
    318; **1956:** 214, 224, 250, 268, 279; **1958:**
    292, 293, 296, 302, 303, 308
  Collection procedures, **1955:** 17 (p. 145)
  Cooperatives, **1960–61:** 414 (p. 943)
  Corporate, **1953:** 84, 254; **1954:** 3, 14 (pp. 88,
    94–99), 54, 67, 353; **1955:** 4, 6, 17 (pp. 87,
    97, 98), 41; **1956:** 2, 183, 268; **1958:** 5 (p.
    22), 114, 120; **1959:** 10 (pp. 39, 41);
    1960–61: 13 (pp. 39, 42), 414 (pp. 937,
    940, 943, 944)
  Cuban-American Sugar Co., tax refund claim,
    1954: 244
  Enforcement programs, **1960–61:** 13 (p. 101), 414
    (p. 1017)
  Excess profits, **1953:** 12, 31, 82, 84, 95, 157, 268;
    1954: 3, 68, 290
  Excise, **1953:** 82, 84, 198; **1954:** 3, 14 (pp. 88, 99),
    48, 68, 353; **1955:** 4, 17 (pp. 87, 97, 98),
    41; **1956:** 5 (pp. 22, 45), 114, 120; **1959:** 10
    (p. 39)
    Admissions tax on motion picture perform-
      ances, **1953:** 157
    Alcoholic beverages, **1960–61:** 414 (p. 940)
    Automobiles, **1954:** 3, 14 (pp. 88, 99); **1958:**
      56; **1959:** 104, 187; **1960–61:** 414 (pp. 940,
      977)
    Cigarettes, **1960–61:** 414 (p. 940)
    Continuation, **1956:** 2
    Gasoline, **1954:** 3, 14 (pp. 88, 99), 33, 102, 165,
      273; **1958:** 5 (p. 45), 324; **1959:** 10 (pp. 41,
      42, 79), 94, 102, 104, 149, 187, 227, 252;
      1960–61: 13 (pp. 39, 43, 44, 69, 70), 133,
      222, 255, 410, 414 (pp. 941, 975, 977), 423
    Liquor, **1954:** 3, 14 (pp. 88, 99)
    Telephone service, **1959:** 10 (p. 42); **1960–61:**
      13 (p. 43), 414 (p. 940)
    Tobacco, **1954:** 3, 14 (pp. 88, 99)
    Transportation, **1958:** 88; **1960–61:** 13 (p. 43),
      414 (p. 940)
  Farmers, **1954:** 14 (p. 96), 221
  Federal-State division of functions, **1953:** 15, 16,
    67
  Federal-State revenue adjustment, **1957:** 118, 138
  Foreign business investments, **1954:** 14 (p. 97)
    Double taxation, **1956:** 2
  Gasoline for farm use, tax relief, **1956:** 6, 12 (p.
    127), 20, 72, 83, 214, 250

Taxes — *continued*
  Goldfine, Bernard, investigation of tax returns,
    1958: 153
  Grand Teton National Park, property in, **1954:**
    222
  Idaho Power Co., **1957:** 80
  Improvement in tax structure, **1958:** 110, 120,
    308; **1959:** 7
  Income, **1953:** 31, 82, 84, 95, 268; **1954:** 3, 14 (pp.
    91–94), 68, 192, 301, 313; **1955:** 41; **1958:**
    5 (p. 52), 103; **1959:** 7; **1960–61:** 13 (pp.
    39, 64), 151, 169
    Constitutional limitation proposed, **1956:** 94
    Dividends, **1954:** 165
  Increase, **1958:** 222, 324
  Knipp, Howard F., tax claim, disapproval, **1959:**
    240
  Lending institutions, **1960–61:** 414 (pp. 943, 944)
  Local taxation of Federal property, **1960–61:** 13
    (p. 105), 414 (p. 1022)
  Message to Congress, **1953:** 84
  News conference remarks, **1953:** 12, 15, 31, 41,
    62, 77, 109, 198, 208, 249, 254; **1954:** 33,
    39, 48, 50, 57, 63, 68, 165, 192, 311, 347,
    353; **1955:** 18, 41, 47, 56, 112; **1956:** 20,
    88, 113; **1957:** 56, 62, 80, 87, 92, 169;
    1958: 11, 28, 37, 42, 56, 63, 70, 74, 83, 88,
    103, 120, 153, 222, 310; **1959:** 7, 26, 94,
    102, 167; **1960–61:** 24, 222
  Oil depletion allowances, **1957:** 92, 145
  Poll, **1960–61:** 24
  Real estate investment trusts, special taxation,
    disapproval, **1956:** 183
  Reduction, **1953:** 6, 12, 30, 31, 57, 62, 82, 84, 95,
    109, 268; **1954:** 3, 14 (pp. 87–89), 21, 39,
    54, 68, 144, 169, 192, 199, 273, 275, 286,
    290, 291, 308, 311, 316, 318; **1955:** 4, 18,
    19, 41, 47, 112; **1956:** 2, 3, 12 (pp. 90, 154,
    155), 19, 20, 88, 113, 224, 229, 268, 279;
    1957: 13, 16, 22, 56, 62, 87, 92, 118, 132;
    1958: 18, 26, 28, 37, 42, 49, 63, 70, 74, 83,
    88, 96, 103, 120, 293, 308; **1959:** 7, 167
    Congressional agreement on, **1958:** 56
    Recession, **1959:** 15
Refund claims
  Abbott, Harold W., and others, disapproval,
    1959: 237
  Barkout, Raymond, **1960–61:** 288
  Boutwell, William A., **1958:** 228
  Browne, Mary M., **1958:** 230
  Caesar, George P. E., Jr., **1958:** 245
  Continental Hosiery Mills, Inc., veto, **1958:**
    187
  Eber Brothers Wine and Liquor Corp., veto,
    1959: 215
  Estes, Lourene O., disapproval, **1959:** 234
  Gregg, Mrs. Frank C., estate, **1958:** 237
  Hall, Mr. and Mrs. Robert B., disapproval,
    1958: 253

Taxes — *continued*
  Refund claims — *continued*
    Hanzal, Alfred, veto, **1958:** 34
    Haun, Cale P. and Julia Fay, **1958:** 48
    Hjerpe, Eric and Ida Mae, **1960–61:** 291
    Laney, D. S. and Elizabeth, veto, **1958:** 205
    Malowney Real Estate Company, Inc., **1958:** 227
    Moore, Duncan and Marjorie, **1958:** 256
    Peony Park, Inc., and others, disapproval, **1959:** 229
    Roach, Lucian, veto, **1958:** 212
    Ryan, Mary K., **1958:** 228
    Symms, Marion S., **1958:** 232
    Toley's Charter Boats, Inc., disapproval, **1958:** 249
    Universal Trades, Inc., **1960–61:** 150
    Woods, Nathaniel H., estate, disapproval, **1959:** 233
  Retail sales, question of, **1953:** 198
  Revision, **1953:** 6, 31, 82, 84, 157, 249, 254; **1954:** 3, 14 (pp. 87, 88, 90–99), 21, 139, 144, 165, 201, 203, 209, 273, 286; **1960–61:** 4, 13 (pp. 40, 43), 410, 414 (pp. 943, 944), 415
    Approval of bill, **1954:** 199
  Sedgwick County, Kans., unpaid balance for 1947 **1956:** 112
  Settlements in cases of fraud, disclosure of, **1953:** 95
  Small business, **1954:** 14 (p. 96); **1956:** 263, 268; **1958:** 5 (p. 23), 43, 120, 293, 295, 302, 303
  Social security payment, **1956:** 158
  State and local, Federal immunity from, **1953:** 169
  Tax credit for certain taxes of United Kingdom, disapproval, **1956:** 181
  Tax reform, **1959:** 6, 10 (pp. 41, 42), 63, 144n.
  Telephone service, **1958:** 5 (p. 43)
  Unemployment payroll, **1960–61:** 414 (p. 1005)
    Credits of successor employers, **1960–61:** 170
  U. S. companies abroad, **1957:** 13, 72, 80
Taxpayers Conference, National, **1959:** 63
Taylor, Dean P., **1956:** 94
Taylor, Rear Adm. Edmund B., **1954:** 289n.
Taylor, Henry J., **1957:** 70
Taylor, Henry N., **1957:** 45; **1958:** 63, 70, 74, 83, 288, 310; **1959:** 67, 154, 161, 186; **1960–61:** 143
Taylor, Gen. Maxwell D., **1953:** 159; **1957:** 127 and n.; **1960–61:** 7
Taylor, Gen. Maxwell D., Distinguished Service Medal, citation, **1959:** 145
Tchaikovsky Piano Contest, International, **1958:** 78
Tchichelle, Stephane, **1960–61:** 324n.
Teacher development program, remarks, **1959:** 222
Teachers, **1953:** 237; **1954:** 308; **1956:** 8, 103, 222, 277; **1957:** 68; **1958:** 24, 28, 320
  Addresses, messages, etc., **1957:** 19, 68, 230, 234
  Educational exchange program, **1954:** 128

Teachers — *continued*
  Exchange program, **1959:** 222
  Need for, **1958:** 5 (p. 46)
  Pay, **1959:** 6, 7, 118
  Science and mathematics, **1957:** 234, 251
  Science training, **1958:** 5 (p. 48); **1959:** 10 (p. 99)
  Secretary Folsom's memorandum, **1957:** 234n.
  Shortage of, **1955:** 31
Teaching, **1958:** 2
  Foreign languages, **1958:** 5 (p. 49), 24
  Improvement of, **1956:** 85n.
  Science and mathematics, **1956:** 12 (p. 123); **1958:** 2, 5 (pp. 48, 49), 24
Teamsters' Union, **1957:** 50, 87, 150, 207
  News conference remarks, **1958:** 56
Teamsters, International Brotherhood of, **1955:** 232
Teapot Dome, **1959:** 17
Technical assistance agreement with Guinea, proposed, joint statement with President Toure, **1959:** 272
Technical assistance to less developed countries, **1953:** 66, 89, 92, 213; **1954:** 67, 150, 204; **1955:** 4, 6, 76, 167; **1956:** 2, 58, 87, 121, 282; **1957:** 56, 86, 90, 91; **1958:** 36, 49; **1959:** 55, 189; **1960–61:** 4, 36, 39, 109n., 132, 133, 279
  See also Economic assistance; Foreign assistance; Mutual security program.
  Budget messages, **1954:** 14 (pp. 137–139); **1955:** 17 (p. 130); **1958:** 5 (pp. 26, 34, 36, 37, 40); **1959:** 10 (pp. 74, 75); **1960–61:** 13 (pp. 61–63), 414 (p. 967)
  Campaign remarks, **1958:** 290, 294
  Colombo Plan meeting, remarks, **1958:** 312
  Funds for, **1958:** 32
  International Bank for Reconstruction and Development, **1959:** 32
  Joint statements
    King of Morocco, **1957:** 240
    Prime Minister Eden, **1956:** 27
    Prime Minister Nkrumah, **1958:** 180
  News conference remarks, **1956:** 121
  Thailand, arrival in U. S. of 1000th participant, **1957:** 36
  U.N. activities, report, **1958:** 148
  White House statement, **1957:** 152n.
Technical assistance, U.N., **1955:** 4, 76, 156
  Budget message, **1958:** 5 (p. 40)
  U.S. contributions, **1953:** 143; **1954:** 150; **1955:** 126; **1956:** 12 (p. 106), 58, 88; **1958:** 32, 312; **1959:** 55
Technical assistance program, Organization of American States, U.S. contributions, **1959:** 55
Technical Cooperation Administration, **1953:** 89
Technical experts conference, Geneva.
  See Geneva conferences.
Technological ability, U.S., **1956:** 76

Technological aid for small business, **1956:** 263
Technological development, **1953:** 82; **1954:** 308
  Budget message, **1958:** 5 (p. 22)
  Campaign remarks, **1958:** 296
  Farming, **1958:** 12
  Funds for, **1958:** 2
Technological improvements, benefits of, **1957:** 8
Technological revolution, **1960–61:** 421
Tedder, Air Marshal Arthur W., **1954:** 133
Teheran, Iran, **1956:** 113
  Arrival, remarks, **1959:** 319
  Departure, remarks, **1959:** 323
  Joint statement with Shah of Iran, **1959:** 322
  Luncheon given by the Shah of Iran, toast, **1959:** 321
  Parliament, address to, **1959:** 320
Telecommunication systems, letter re, **1959:** 47
Telecommunications, Commission on
Proposed, report, **1959:** 47
Telephone service, rural, **1954:** 291; **1955:** 17 (pp. 153, 154); **1956:** 12 (p. 130), 214; **1959:** 86; **1960–61:** 13 (p. 80), 414 (pp. 989, 990)
  Budget messages, **1954:** 14 (p. 162); **1958:** 5 (pp. 66, 67)
  Federal-State Action Committee recommendations, **1958:** 106
  Letter to Secretary Benson, **1958:** 51
Telephone service tax, **1958:** 5 (p. 43); **1959:** 10 (p. 42); **1960–61:** 13 (p. 43), 414 (p. 940)
Telephone strike, Southern Bell Telephone Co., **1955:** 90, 95
Telephones, REA loans, **1957:** 157
Televised news conference, first, editor's note, **1955:** 18 (p. 185)
  Comment on, **1955:** 26
Television, educational, **1957:** 28
Television appearances, question of makeup, **1956:** 229
Television Committee for Nixon and Lodge, Independent, **1960–61:** 344
Television facilities, NBC, dedication, remarks, **1958:** 111
Television quiz investigation (1959), **1960–61:** 34
  Comment on, **1959:** 267, 277
Television and radio, equal time for appearances by candidates for public office, **1954:** 50; **1959:** 216; **1960–61:** 268 and ftn. (p. 647)
Television and radio, ultrahigh frequency study, **1960–61:** 13 (p. 76)
Television and radio addresses.
  See Messages to the American people.
Television and radio broadcasters, remarks, **1955:** 105
Teller, Edward, **1957:** 119, 124
Tello, Manuel, **1954:** 33
Ten-Nation Disarmament Conference.
  See Disarmament.

Tennessee, **1956:** 53, 293
  Baker, Repr. Howard H., **1957:** 124
  Cancellation of meeting, telegram, **1956:** 281n.
  Clement, Gov. Frank G., **1953:** 208, 225; **1954:** 161; **1956:** 198; **1957:** 205,n., 207
  Clinton, **1958:** 288
  Cooper, Repr. Jere, **1954:** 57, 322; **1955:** 90 ftn. (p. 471), 160; **1957:** 132, 160
  Eastern Tennessee District Court, **1954:** 193n., 281
  Evins, Repr. Joe L., **1955:** 112
  Gore, Sen. Albert, **1959:** 252
  Kefauver, Sen. Estes, **1953:** 15; **1955:** 146, 149; **1956:** 62, 78, 198, 205; **1957:** 124; **1959:** 42
  Memphis, **1954:** 39; **1955:** 56, 146, 149; **1958:** 128
  Nashville, **1960–61:** 143
  Oak Ridge, **1955:** 17 (p. 121); **1954:** 14 (pp. 30, 128), 161 and ftn. (p. 622), 192, 193, 281
  Power projects, **1955:** 56
  Priest, Repr. J. Percy, death of, **1956:** 240
  Reece, Repr. B. Carroll, **1959:** 77n.; **1960–61:** 403n.
Tennessee Valley Authority, **1953:** 109, 208, 225; **1956:** 109; **1960–61:** 13 (pp. 83, 84), 414 (pp. 995, 996)
  Appropriations, **1955:** 157
  Approval of bill re, **1959:** 175
  Budget messages, **1954:** 14 (pp. 87, 169); **1955:** 17 (pp. 161, 162); **1958:** 5 (p. 70)
    Table, **1958:** 5 (p. 69)
  Contract with British firm, comment on, **1959:** 42
  Dixon-Yates contract.
    See main heading, Dixon-Yates contract.
  Expansion, question of, **1954:** 328
  Fertilizer production, **1954:** 14 (p. 169); **1957:** 112n.
  Financing of, **1959:** 172
  Jones, Arnold R., **1957:** 124
  News conference remarks, **1954:** 39, 50, 63, 157, 161, 165, 168, 182, 200, 311, 328; **1955:** 26, 56, 100, 149; **1957:** 22, 56, 62, 80, 105, 124; **1959:** 29, 42, 161, 172
  Power facilities, **1956:** 12 (p. 136)
    John Sevier plant, **1956:** 12 (p. 136)
    Johnsonville plant, **1956:** 12 (p. 137)
  Public works, appropriation, **1956:** 136
  Vetoes, **1959:** 194, 213
  Sale of revenue bonds proposed, **1959:** 10 (p. 95)
  Steam plant, **1955:** 56, 149
  Welch, Frank J., **1959:** 29
Tennessee Valley Authority, Chairman (Gordon R. Clapp)
  News conference remarks on, **1954:** 33, 101, 107, 115, 328
Tennessee Valley Authority, Chairman (Herbert D. Vogel), **1954:** 328; **1955:** 146 ftn. (p. 646)
  See also Vogel, Brig. Gen. Herbert D.
Tennyson, Alfred, **1955:** 35; **1956:** 193

Ter Horst, J. F., **1958:** 222, 310; **1959:** 29, 36, 48, 67, 132, 148, 186, 223, 288; **1960–61:** 103

Territories and possessions, **1958:** 5 (p. 72)

Testimony of Federal employees in Congressional hearings, **1956:** 216

Testing and counseling services, **1958:** 5 (p. 49), 24

Texas, **1956:** 235, 293; **1957:** 28, 62, 234; **1958:** 123, 307; **1959:** 67 ftn. (p. 297), 75, 338

   Baylor University, **1956:** 114, 121

   Bell, Repr. John J., **1955:** 95

   Brownsville, **1959:** 250

   Cancellation of meeting, telegram, **1956:** 281n.

   Candidates for public office, **1956:** 298; **1957:** 22, 56

   Cooper Dam and Reservoir, approval, **1955:** 184

   Dallas, **1955:** 10

   Daniel, Price, **1953:** 54; **1954:** 161, 168; **1955:** 47; **1957:** 138

   Del Rio, **1959:** 257

   Denison, **1956:** 242n.; **1959:** 179, 186

   Dies, Repr. Martin, **1954:** 143

   El Paso, **1953:** 265

   Falcon Dam, **1953:** 221, 222, 223

   Houston, **1956:** 216; **1960–61:** 336

   Johnson, Sen. Lyndon B., **1954:** 63, 92, 353; **1955:** 81, 90 ftn. (p. 471), 146; **1956:** 20, 88, 184; **1957:** 50, 105; **1958:** 19, 36, 70, 83, 88; **1959:** 42, 67, 148, 161, 186; **1960–61:** 222, 236, 256, 271, 272, 356

   Kilday, Repr. Paul J., **1958:** 83

   Lackland Air Force Base, **1957:** 124

   Livestock, **1956:** 236

   Mahon, Repr. George H., **1953:** 62

   Poage, Repr. W. R., **1956:** 171

   Rayburn, Repr. Sam, **1953:** 141; **1954:** 57, 157, 341; **1955:** 4, 14, 41, 64, 90 ftn. (p. 471) 91, 95; **1956:** 7, 13, 29, 81, 131, 184, 248; **1957:** 45, 75, 80, 112, 135; **1958:** 2, 36, 42, 70, 75, 116, 114, 135n., 183, 194; **1959:** 6, 42, 47, 77, 91, 94, 136, 151, 157, 161, 171, 183, 184n., 186; **1960–61:** 4, 88, 272, 422

   Republic of, **1960–61:** 336

   San Antonio, **1957:** 22, 124; **1960–61:** 336

   School integration case, **1956:** 198, 205

   Shivers, Gov. Allan, **1953:** 15, 62, 156; **1954:** 35n., 85n., 99, 172; **1956:** 94, 96, 198, 298; **1957:** 228

   Supreme Court decision on conformity of laws with U. S. Constitution, **1956:** 56

   Texarkana, school integration, **1956:** 215

   Texas City, **1956:** 62

     Disaster, **1955:** 112

     Tin smelter, **1954:** 14 (p. 181), 63, 92

   Texas Control Board, oil, **1957:** 22

   Thompson, Repr. Clark W., **1954:** 63

   Tidelands, **1953:** 58

     Oil question, **1954:** 168

   Waco, **1956:** 114

   Wright, Repr. James C., **1958:** 74

Textile industry, interagency committee proposed, **1959:** 102

Textiles

   Import quotas, **1955:** 185; **1956:** 32; **1959:** 267

   Japanese imports, **1956:** 216

   Tariff concessions, **1955:** 149

   Wool, **1954:** 9, 48; **1959:** 67, 161, 196

     Tariff increases, **1956:** 216

Thailand, **1954:** 129

   Ambassador John E. Peurifoy, **1955:** 195

   Armed forces in Korea, **1960–61:** 212

   Assistance, **1954:** 15 (p. 127); **1959:** 55

   Bangkok conference, **1955:** 41; **1960–61:** 296

   Bhumibol Adulyadej, **1960–61:** 219, 211, 212, 213

     Joint statement with, **1960–61:** 219

   ICA program, evaluation, **1959:** 352

   Pibulsonggram, Field Marshal, **1955:** 87; **1956:** 312; **1957:** 36 and n.

   Prince Wan, **1958:** 159

   Queen Sirikit, **1960–61:** 219, 211, 213, 219

   Relations with U.S., **1960–61:** 211, 219

   Social and economic development, **1960–61:** 219

   SEATO.

     See Southeast Asia Treaty Organization.

Thanksgiving Day, **1958:** 319

   Plans, comment on, **1953:** 259

   Remarks in Augusta, Ga., **1953:** 253

Thayer, Sylvanus, Award, presentation to Dr. Lawrence, **1958:** 52

Theis, William, **1955:** 19, 51, 119, 156, 195; **1956:** 47, 99, 171

Theoklitos, Archbishop, **1959:** 325

Thermonuclear development, news conference remarks, **1956:** 95

Thermonuclear power, **1958:** 21

Thermonuclear reactions, controlled, **1956:** 12(p. 111)

Thimayya, Lt. Gen. Kodandera S., **1954:** 41

Third party

   Comment on, **1954:** 357

   News conference remarks, **1956:** 229

Third term, news conference remarks, **1958:** 311

Third term amendment to the Constitution, President's attitude on, **1959:** 17, 29, 95, 112

Thomas, Charles A., **1953:** 33n.; **1954:** 89

Thomas, Charles S., award by military chaplains, **1956:** 99

Thomas, Essell P., Jr., **1956:** 199

Thomasville, Ga., **1955:** 33; **1956:** 42n., 53; **1957:** 32n., 35; **1958:** 31n., 33n.; **1959:** 29n., 29ftn. (p. 173)

Thomaz, Americo E. R., **1960–61:** 157, 161

   Toasts to, **1960–61:** 159, 161

Thomaz, Madame, **1960–61:** 159

Thompson, Repr. Clark W., **1954:** 63

Thompson, Glenn, **1953:** 22; **1954:** 33, 165

Thompson, John S., **1955:** 51n.

Thompson, Llewellyn E., **1955:** 146 ftn. (p. 644); **1959:** 218
  Cablegram, **1958:** 78
  Interview with Premier Khrushchev on U.S. airmen, **1959:** 94 and ftn. (p. 361)
  News conference remarks on, **1958:** 11
Thompson, Col. Percy W., **1960–61:** 38
Thompson, R. Franklin, **1956:** 253
Thomson, Ga., **1957:** 182
Thomson Contracting Company, Inc., relief of, veto, **1958:** 208
Thor (IRBM).
  See Missiles.
Thorat, Maj. Gen. Sankarrao P., **1954:** 40
Thornton, Gov. Dan, **1953:** 62, 77; **1954:** 85n., 99, 256, 286; **1956:** 189, 259
  Letters, **1954:** 35; **1956:** 133
  News conference remarks on, **1954:** 39, 165
Thornton, Brig. L. W., **1960–61:** 164n.
Thorpe, James F. (Jim), **1960–61:** 395
Thuringia, Germany, Gen. Eisenhower's recommendation on, **1958:** 318
Thurmond, Strom, **1954:** 311
  News conference remarks on, **1955:** 149
  Telegram, **1955:** 73
Thurston, Lorrin, **1959:** 184n.
Thye, Sen. Edward J., **1954:** 200; **1955:** 33; **1956:** 249, 250
Tibbetts, Candy, **1955:** 141
Tibbetts, Mr. and Mrs. Verde, **1955:** 141n.
Tibet
  Communist aggression, **1960–61:** 410
  Revolt in, **1959:** 67
Tidelands, Federal vs. State claims, **1953:** 101
  Letter to Sen. Anderson, **1953:** 58
  News conference remarks, **1953:** 22, 54, 77
  Submerged Lands Act, approval, **1953:** 86
Tidelands oil question, **1954:** 168
Tieken, Robert, **1958:** 103
Timber, **1958:** 5 (p. 68), 12
  Land exchanges, **1960–61:** 13 (p. 86), 414 (pp. 997, 998)
  Sales, **1956:** 12 (pp. 133, 138)
Time article on Bolivia, **1959:** 89
Timgad, Algeria, ruined city, **1953:** 234
Timmons, Jack, **1957:** 114 and n.
Tin imports, **1958:** 58, 96; **1959:** 55
  From Bolivia, **1953:** 213
Tin production program, **1954:** 14 (pp. 179, 180)
Tin smelter, Texas City
  Budget message, **1954:** 14 (p. 180)
  News conference remarks, **1954:** 63, 92
  Report on, **1956:** 62
  Termination of Government operations, **1956:** 62 ftn. (p. 336)
Tin supply, effect of Indochina war on, **1953:** 156
Titan (ICBM).
  See Missiles.

Tiradentes (Jose Joaquim Xavier), **1960–61:** 45
Tiros weather satellites, **1960–61:** 143, 264, 410, 424
  Budget message, **1960–61:** 414 (p. 972)
  Launching of Tiros I, statement, **1960–61:** 104
Tito, Marshal Josip Broz, **1953:** 31; **1955:** 119; **1957:** 17, 22, 157
  Letter, **1960–61:** 313
  Message, **1954:** 284
Tjaden, Brenda Ann, **1960–61:** 123n.
Tobacco
  Acreage allotments, **1958:** 12; **1959:** 140
  Excise tax on, **1954:** 3, 14 (pp. 88, 99); **1955:** 41; **1957:** 13
  Exports, **1955:** 6; **1958:** 58
  Price supports, **1954:** 4; **1958:** 12; **1959:** 23
  Referendums, **1956:** 82, 83
  Veto of bill, **1959:** 140
Tobin, Maurice J., **1954:** 125, 126
Toboada, Diogenes, **1960–61:** 56n.
Tobruk, Libya, **1959:** 96
Tocqueville, Alexis de, **1959:** 214
  Journey to America, **1959:** 107
Todd, Jane, **1953:** 68, 69
Togo, Republic of, Paulin Freitas, **1960–61:** 324n.
Togoland, Trust Territory of, **1958:** 8, 148
Tokyo, Japan, **1956:** 313; **1959:** 31
  Disappearance of Soviet agent Rastovorov, **1954:** 25
Toley's Charter Boats, Inc. and others, tax refund claim, **1958:** 249
Tolstoy, Count Leo, **1959:** 31
Tombalbaye, Francois, message, **1960–61:** 257
Tompkins, William F., **1955:** 10
Tondreau, Aime A., **1955:** 139n.
Tongass National Forest, **1959:** 101
Topeka, Kans., veterans hospital construction, **1954:** 14 (p. 134)
Tornado disaster in Massachusetts, **1953:** 117
Totalitarianism, **1953:** 222; **1955:** 76
Toulon, France, remarks on arrival, **1959:** 332
Toura Gaba, Jules, **1960–61:** 324n.
Toure, Sekou
  Exchange of toasts, **1959:** 269
  Joint statement with, **1959:** 272
  Messages, **1958:** 309; **1960–61:** 364
Toure, Madame, **1959:** 269
Tours, France, Atlantic Treaty Association, message, **1959:** 204
Trade, international, **1953:** 1, 6, 44, 50, 63, 68, 69, 82, 95, 98, 101, 131, 159, 161, 187, 219; **1954:** 3, 4, 67, 91, 139, 146, 162, 209, 226, 297, 308, 324; **1955:** 4, 6, 19, 72, 79, 167; **1956:** 2, 19, 58, 87, 114, 310; **1957:** 8, 13, 32; **1958:** 2, 18, 25, 26, 32, 36, 49, 95, 96, 102, 110, 163, 165, 215, 217; **1959:** 15, 84, 87, 116; **1960–61:** 4, 72, 73, 95, 103, 131, 132, 246, 410
  See also Tariffs and Trade, General Agreement on; Trade Agreements Act, extension.

Trade, international — *continued*
 Address to Canadian Parliament, **1958:** 163
 Broadcast with Prime Minister Macmillan, **1959:**
  196
 Budget messages, **1955:** 17 (pp. 128, 132); **1956:**
  12 (p. 107); **1958:** 5 (p. 36); **1959:** 10 (pp.
  71, 73)
 Colombo Plan meeting, remarks, **1958:** 312
 Communist bloc, **1953:** 88; **1954:** 9, 67, 138, 143,
  149; **1955:** 18, 100; **1956:** 53; **1957:** 70,
  105
  Embargo, congressional discussions re, **1953:**
   41
  U.S. policy, **1959:** 48
 Conference on, address, **1958:** 58
 Foreign markets, expansion, **1958:** 29
 Japan, **1954:** 73, 90, 149; **1958:** 37, 70; **1959:** 71
 Joint statements
  Chancellor Adenauer, **1960–61:** 92
  President Lopez Mateos, **1959:** 38
  Prime Minister Churchill, **1954:** 155
  Prime Minister Eden, **1956:** 26
  Prime Minister Huh Chung, **1960–61:** 203
  Prime Minister Kishi, **1957:** 117; **1960–61:** 16
  Prime Minister Macmillan, **1957:** 55, 226
  Prime Minister St. Laurent, **1953:** 70, 247
  Prime Minister Suhrawardy, **1957:** 131
  Prime Minister Yoshida, **1954:** 330
  Western leaders, **1959:** 335
 Less developed countries, **1958:** 32
 News conference remarks, **1953:** 15, 22, 31, 41,
  54, 88, 141, 249; **1954:** 9, 50, 68, 73, 101,
  115, 138, 143, 157, 172; **1955:** 18, 33, 41,
  100, 149; **1956:** 32, 53; **1958:** 37, 70, 103,
  141; **1959:** 42, 48, 67, 243, 271
 Relation to national security, **1953:** 156
 Relation to U.S. agriculture, **1954:** 262, 263
  Statement, **1954:** 261
 Remarks to Advertising Council, **1955:** 58
 Restraint on, lessening of, **1954:** 3
 Soviet-Cuban, **1960–61:** 223
 Soviet-Mexican, **1954:** 101
 Soviet Union, **1955:** 33; **1958:** 7, 141, 165; **1959:**
  243
 Trade restrictions, **1959:** 271
 U.S.-Brazil, **1960–61:** 54
 U.S.-Canada, **1959:** 141
 U.S.-Japan, **1960–61:** 16
 U.S.-Latin America, **1960–61:** 80
 U.S.-Liberian, **1954:** 293
 U.S.-Philippines, **1960–61:** 189
 U.S.-Soviet, **1954:** 50; **1959:** 242
 U.S.-U.K., **1959:** 67, 196
Trade Agreements Act, **1954:** 67, 324; **1959:** 42;
 1960–61: 410
 See also General Agreement on Tariffs and
  Trade; Trade, international.

Trade Agreements Act — *continued*
 Extension, **1955:** 6, 79, 81; **1958:** 2, 5 (pp. 36, 38),
  25, 49
 Approval, **1955:** 129
 Conference on trade policy, address, **1958:** 58
 Escape clause and peril-point procedure, **1958:**
  58
 Letter to Repr. Mills, **1958:** 132
 News conference remarks, **1955:** 26, 41, 59;
  1958: 28, 56, 70, 103, 198, 213
 Remarks to National Trade Policy Committee,
  1955: 83
 News conference remarks, **1954:** 101, 138
Trade Agreements Extension Act (1953), **1953:** 6,
 15, 41, 54, 70, 141, 187, 190n.
 Approval, statement, **1953:** 161
 Lead and zinc tariffs, **1957:** 157, 160
 Message to Congress, **1953:** 44
Trade Agreements Extension Act of 1958, **1958:**
 217, 299
 Approval, **1958:** 215
Trade agreements program, **1957:** 32, 61
Trade with Communist Areas, Coordinating Com-
 mittee on (COCOM), **1956:** 53
Trade Cooperation, Organization for, **1955:** 248;
 1956: 2, 19, 87, 310; **1957:** 2, 8, 13, 61, 110
 and n.
 Budget message, **1956:** 12 (p. 110)
 News conference remarks, **1956:** 94 and ftn. (p.
  452)
 U.S. membership proposed, **1955:** 129, 160
  Message, **1955:** 72
Trade and Economic Affairs, Committee on, U.S.-
 Canada, **1953:** 246
 Joint statement with Prime Minister St. Laurent,
  1953: 247
Trade fairs, **1956:** 12 (p. 109)
 International, **1955:** 59; **1958:** 5 (p. 41)
 Bangkok (1954), **1955:** 6
Trade mission to Guinea, joint statement on, **1959:**
 272
Trade negotiations, Geneva, **1956:** 94 and ftn. (p.
 452), 123
Trade Policy, Committee for a National, **1957:** 110
Trade Policy Committee, **1958:** 25
 Budget message, **1958:** 5 (p. 38)
Trade unions.
 See Labor organizations.
Trade Unions, International Confederation of
 Free, meeting in Stockholm, **1953:** 128,
 130
Traffic, air, budget message, **1956:** 12 (p. 140)
Traffic accidents, **1954:** 37, 336; **1955:** 39, 243;
 1956: 2, 19, 36, 37; **1958:** 45; **1959:** 129,
 185
 Budget message, **1956:** 12 (p. 139)
 Safe Driving Day, **1954:** 347, 352, 353

Traffic accidents — *continued*
  Statements on safe driving, **1954:** 255, 336; **1955:**
    111; **1956:** 316
Traffic courts, **1959:** 185
Traffic safety, **1957:** 118; **1959:** 187
  Letter to Governors, **1956:** 37
  Letters to Harlow H. Curtice, **1956:** 36, 305
  President's Action Committee for, **1954:** 336
  President's Committee for, **1954:** 37n.; **1955:** 111,
    243; **1956:** 36, 37, 305
    Letter to William Randolph Hearst, Jr., re
      appointment, **1955:** 124
    Letter to T. S. Petersen re appointment, **1955:**
      125
  Regional conferences, message, **1958:** 45
  Report, **1957:** 14 and n.
Training
  Government employees, **1955:** 8; **1958:** 5 (p. 71)
  Military, **1953:** 144
  Public health, **1955:** 25; **1959:** 6, 181
  Veterans, **1955:** 17 (p. 136)
Trans-Atlantic Cable, centenary, message, **1958:**
  209
Trans-Pacific air carrier case, **1960–61:** 436
Trans-Pacific certificate renewal case, letter, **1956:**
  14
Transit navigation satellites, **1960–61:** 264, 424
Transit strike, Washington, D.C., **1955:** 149, 176
Transition period between administrations, **1960–**
  61: 422
  Joint statement with President-elect Kennedy,
    1960–61: 369
Transport Policy and Organization, Committee on
  Establishment, **1954:** 163
  Report, **1955:** 33, 62, 90 and ftn. (p. 475);
    1960–61: 21
Transportation, **1954:** 3; **1960–61:** 410
  Advisory Committee on Federal Policies, **1956:** 2
  Budget messages, **1954:** 14 (pp. 119, 171–176,
    178); **1959:** 10 (pp. 76–81); **1960–61:** 13
    (pp. 68–71, 104), 414 (pp. 939, 973–977)
    Table, **1954:** 14 (p. 172)
  Common carriers, contracts with Federal Gov-
    ernment, **1954:** 246
  District of Columbia, **1955:** 149, 176, 206
    Public transportation, **1954:** 252
  Excise tax on, **1955:** 41; **1960–61:** 13 (p. 43), 414
    (p. 940)
  Facilities, **1956:** 12 (pp. 138–143)
  Federal policies on, **1955:** 4
  Industry, recommendation on, **1958:** 82 and n.
  Letter to Secretary Weeks, **1954:** 163
  National Capital area, **1960–61:** 13 (p. 104)
  Survey of Washington area, report, **1959:** 157
  System, expenditures for, **1957:** 13
Transportation, Department of, proposed, **1960–**
  61: 414 (p. 946)

Transylvania College, 175th anniversary, address,
  1954: 89
Trapnell, Maj. Gen. Thomas J., **1954:** 39
Travel
  Abroad, passport control, **1958:** 161
  Abroad by the President, **1955:** 119
  Allowances for Federal personnel, **1955:** 8
  Americans abroad, **1960–61:** 362
  Expenses of military and civilian personnel,
    1960–61: 414 (p. 950)
  Freedom of, **1955:** 6, 167; **1958:** 63
  Immigration policies, **1956:** 33
  International, **1954:** 67, 323
  Interstate, racial discrimination, **1954:** 63, 143,
    161
  Joint statement with President Lopez Mateos,
    1959: 38
  Members of Congress, news conference remarks,
    1956: 205, 216, 235
  President's plans for, **1959:** 172
  Tourist, to U.S., **1960–61:** 95, 362
Treasurer of the United States (Mrs. Ivy Baker
    Priest), **1955:** 187
  Letter, **1955:** 186
Treasury, Department of the **1953:** 208, 228; **1954:**
    21, 94, 95; **1955:** 19; **1956:** 162; **1958:** 48,
    117, 143; **1960–61:** 289, 358, 362
  Bartelt, Edward F., **1954:** 15
  Budget messages, **1954:** 14 (pp. 88, 90, 99, 181);
    1955: 17 (p. 98); **1956:** 12 (pp. 90, 91);
    1958: 5 (p. 32); **1959:** 10 (pp. 41, 53, 54,
    108); **1960–61:** 13 (pp. 43, 70, 72, 74, 75,
    80, 100, 108, 110), 414 (pp. 942–944, 990,
    1005, 1016, 1017, 1024)
  Claim of Mrs. Hannah Mae Powell, veto, **1957:**
    179
  Credit controls, **1957:** 169
  Customs procedures, review of, **1954:** 67
  Debt extension program, **1953:** 6
  Development Loan Fund, financing of, **1957:** 90
  Federal sales tax proposal, study of, **1953:** 198
  Folsom, Marion B., **1955:** 112
  Indians, cooperative study with, **1953:** 166
  Interest rate on series E and H bonds, **1957:** 76;
    1960–61: 6, 133, 255, 414 (p. 942), 423
  Investigation of personnel connected with pre-
    vious administration, **1954:** 353
  Liquidation of RFC business loan program,
    administration of, **1954:** 14 (p. 181)
  Mutual security appropriations, **1953:** 143
  News conference remarks, **1954:** 129, 353; **1958:**
    11
  Overby, Andrew N., **1953:** 33, 213n.
  Report, **1960–61:** 415
  Retirement claim of Margaret P. Copin, dis-
    approval, **1960–61:** 234
  RFC functions, **1957:** 78
  Savings Bonds Division, **1959:** 43n.

Treasury, Department of the — *continued*
Savings bonds sales, **1954:** 151
Tax system review, **1953:** 6, 82, 84, 159; **1954:** 14
(pp. 90, 99), 199
Treasury-Post Office Appropriation Act, **1957:**
1958, 99
War Damage Corporation, **1957:** 78
Treasury, Secretary of the (Robert B. Anderson),
1957: 138 and n., 236; **1958:** 114; **1959:**
33, 43, 83, 126; **1960–61:** 336, 344, 369
See also Anderson, Robert B.
Budget surplus details, **1960–61:** 237
Chairman, United Givers Fund campaign, Na-
tional Capital area, **1960–61:** 153
Governor of Inter-American Development
Bank, **1959:** 261n.
Interest rate increase on savings bonds, **1959:**
231
Letter, **1959:** 230
Joint Federal-State Action Committee, letter,
1960–61: 115
Meeting of World Bank and International Mon-
etary Fund, **1958:** 278n., 312
Mission to Germany on U.S. balance of pay-
ments, **1960–61:** 362 and ftn. (p. 864), 365
News conference remarks on, **1958:** 37, 56, 70,
83, 222; **1959:** 7, 123, 186
Resignation, letter, **1960–61:** 415
Savings bond campaign, **1958:** 70
Tax agreement with Congressional leaders, **1958:**
83
Tax structure revision, **1959:** 7
Treasury, Secretary of the (George M. Humphrey),
1953: 57, 189, 268; **1954:** 169, 349, 351;
1955: 44, 90 ftn. (p. 475); **1957:** 17, 60
Anglo-American Financial Agreement of 1945,
amendment, **1957:** 44
Appraisal, **1954:** 151
Broadcast with the President, **1953:** 95
Budget, **1957:** 45
Campaign remarks on, **1956:** 224, 241
Congressional meeting, **1956:** 318
Discussions with Prime Minister Kishi, **1957:** 117
Federal Council on Aging, **1956:** 74
Foreign aid programs, **1954:** 323
Income earned by social security pensioners,
1954: 353
Meeting of Ministers of Finance and Economy
in Rio de Janeiro, **1954:** 340, 345
Meeting with Prime Minister Yoshida, **1954:** 330
NATO, report on, **1953:** 265 ftn. (p. 843)
News conference remarks on, **1953:** 15, 62, 109,
249, 254; **1954:** 33, 48, 107, 345, 353;
1955: 33, 47; **1956:** 32, 88, 94, 155; **1957:**
17, 72, 80
Oil supply study, **1956:** 239
Resignation, **1957:** 102 and n.
Resignation of Mrs. Oveta Culp Hobby, **1955:**
153

Treasury, Secretary of (Humphrey) — *continued*
Tax write-offs, **1957:** 92
Testimonial dinner honoring, message, **1953:** 242
Vice-Chairman, United Community Campaigns,
1953: 179; **1954:** 183; **1956:** 185
"Your Government and You" broadcast, **1956:**
246
Treasury bonds, flexibility of interest rates, **1959:**
30, 126, 188, 225
Treasury payments to Government agencies, **1959:**
36
Treaties.
See International agreements.
Treaty of friendship and cooperation between
U.S.S.R. and U.S., proposed, **1956:** 23
Treaty-making powers, news conference remarks,
1956: 53, 78, 96
Tree-planting ceremony on President's birthday,
remarks, **1960–61:** 325
Tree-planting in honor of Theodore Roosevelt,
1958: 100
Trieste, **1954:** 325, 337; **1955:** 18, 35; **1956:** 16, 87,
117, 198, 210, 224; **1958:** 80; **1959:** 89;
1960–61: 23, 341, 410
Campaign remarks, **1954:** 304, 316, 317, 319,
320; **1958:** 287, 290, 293, 302
Italian-Yugoslav agreement, **1954:** 286, 297, 316
Letter to Marshal Tito, **1954:** 284
Letter to President Einaudi, **1954:** 283
Trinity College, **1954:** 295
Trinity River project, **1959:** 194
Tripartite Declaration on Middle East (1950),
1955: 234, 239
Trippitt, Oscar, **1954:** 273
Triton, U.S.S., **1960–61:** 142
Troast, Paul L., **1953:** 230, 238
Trout, foreign-produced, labeling of packages, dis-
approval, **1954:** 248
Trucking industry, **1957:** 207
Trujillo, Gen. Hector B., **1956:** 88; **1960–61:** 263,
267
Truman, Harry S., President, **1954:** 27, 28, 29;
1955: 18, 33, 81; **1956:** 96, 198; **1957:** 105;
1958: 207
Action on Formosa, **1958:** 201
Congressional subpoena, **1953:** 243
Grandson, **1957:** 105
Increase in White House staff, "My View of the
Presidency," **1958:** 310
Mutual security bill, **1958:** 37
News conference remarks on, **1953:** 31, 37, 41,
54, 109, 243, 249; **1954:** 18, 33, 50, 107,
322, 328, 353; **1958:** 37, 74, 83, 213, 310,
318; **1959:** 21, 94; **1960–61:** 7, 143, 422
Order re security information, **1953:** 54, 109
Summit meetings, **1960–61:** 7
Testimony on recession, **1958:** 74
Turkey and Greece, **1958:** 295
22d amendment to Constitution, **1959:** 94

Truman Doctrine, **1958:** 36 173, 207
Trust funds, **1955:** 17 (pp. 101, 106, 107, 139, 145, 178); **1956:** 158
  Budget messages, **1954:** 14 (pp. 133, 135, 144, 145, 184, 185); **1956:** 12 (pp. 91, 92, 115, 117, 118, 125, 154); **1958:** 5 (pp. 23, 45, 51); **1959:** 10 (pp. 80, 81, 100, 101, 105); **1960–61:** 13 (pp. 44, 45, 69–71, 74, 87, 92, 95, 96), 414 (pp. 937, 941–943, 977, 999, 1005, 1009, 1011)
    Tables, **1954:** 14 (p. 102); **1955:** 17 (pp. 107, 178); **1956:** 12 (p. 92); **1958:** 5 (p. 24)
  Employment security program, **1960–61:** 414 (pp. 937, 1005)
  Highway, **1958:** 77; **1959:** 10 (pp. 80, 81), 104, 138, 149, 187, 227n., 252; **1960–61:** 13 (pp. 44, 69–71), 133, 414 (pp. 941, 977), 423
  Net accumulations in, **1957:** 13
  Old-age and survivors insurance, **1953:** 82, 84; **1954:** 14 (p. 144); **1960–61:** 13 (p. 96), 414 (pp. 942, 943, 1009, 1011)
    Statement, **1958:** 234
  Unemployment, **1954:** 14 (pp. 184, 185); **1958:** 53; **1959:** 10 (pp. 100, 101); **1960–61:** 13 (p. 92)
  Veterans insurance, **1954:** 14 (pp. 133, 135)
Trust Territories, U. N. action, reports, **1958:** 8, 148
Trust Territory of the Pacific Islands, **1954:** 125, 126
  Budget message, **1954:** 14 (p. 190)
Tsatsos, Constantine, **1959:** 327
Tsiranana, Philibert, message, **1960–61:** 207
Tuanku Syed Putra (Supreme Ruler of Malaya), **1960–61:** 339
  Message, **1960–61:** 390
Tuberculosis victims
  Admission to U.S., **1959:** 10 (p. 110)
  Recommendations re under Refugee Relief Act, **1955:** 109
Tubman, William V.
  Exchange of toasts, **1954:** 293
  Letter, **1959:** 224
  Remarks of welcome, **1954:** 292
Tuck, Chester H., **1957:** 123
Tucson, Ariz., **1957:** 10n.
Tully, Andrew F., Jr., **1953:** 12, 15, 77, 230, 243; **1954:** 39, 161; **1955:** 18, 81, 95, 100; **1956:** 20, 155, 193, 229; **1957:** 28, 72, 80, 150, 157; **1958:** 70, 88, 120, 213, 222, 310; **1959:** 29, 172, 186, 243; **1960–61:** 143, 268
Tung nuts, price supports, **1954:** 4
Tungsten alloys, imports, **1956:** 123
Tungsten supply, effect of Indochina war on, **1953:** 156
Tunis
  Arrival, remarks, **1959:** 328
  Departure remarks, **1959:** 330
  Joint statement with President Bourguiba, **1959:** 329

Tunisia
  See also Tunis.
  Ambassador Walter N. Walmsley, **1959:** 328n.
  Assistance, **1959:** 55
  Bourguiba, Habib, **1958:** 74; **1959:** 328, 330
    Joint statement with, **1959:** 329
  King Mohamed Lamine, message, **1957:** 101 and n.
  U. N. committee on Hungary, **1958:** 8
  U. N. membership, **1958:** 8
  Visit to, **1959:** 328, 329, 330
Turkey, **1954:** 18; **1955:** 4; **1956:** 2, 78; **1958:** 207, 295
  See also Ankara.
  Agreement with U.S. on civil uses of atomic energy, **1955:** 89, 112, 121
  Ambassador Fletcher Warren, **1959:** 295n., 297
  Assistance, **1955:** 76; **1956:** 12 (p. 104); **1957:** 6, 90, 91, 136, 152, 157, 169; **1958:** 32; **1959:** 55, 297; **1960–61:** 132, 133
  Atomic energy for mutual defense, U.S.-Turkey agreement, **1959:** 119n., 120
  Bayar, Celal, **1954:** 18, 19, 20, 23; **1958:** 174; **1959:** 282, 295, 296, 298
    Joint statement with, **1959:** 297
    Message, **1957:** 49
  Cyprus agreement, **1959:** 39, 40, 41
  Esenbel, Melih, **1959:** 297
  Gursel, Gen. Cemal, message, **1960–61:** 399
  Joint statement with Prime Minister Macmillan, **1957:** 226
  Menderes, Adnan, **1954:** 129; **1959:** 36, 41, 283, 297, 298
  Military agreement with Pakistan, **1954:** 44, 45
  Opening of Constituent Assembly, message, **1960–61:** 399
  Participation in Korean war, **1954:** 23; **1960–61:** 202
    Joint statement on, **1959:** 297
  Visit to, **1959:** 277, 288, 295, 296, 297, 298
  Zorlu, Fatin R., **1959:** 41, 297
Turkish-Syrian crisis, **1958:** 148
Turney, John R., **1953:** 59
TVA.
  See Tennessee Valley Authority.
Twenty-second amendment to Constitution, **1957:** 22
Twining, Gen. Nathan F., **1959:** 94, 102; **1960–61:** 24
  See also Joint Chiefs of Staff, Chairman.
  Visit to U.S.S.R., **1956:** 121
Two Nations (Disraeli), **1959:** 196
Two-party system, **1956:** 47, 268, 298
  Comment on, **1954:** 322
Two-term limitation, **1956:** 229; **1959:** 17, 29, 94, 102
  News conference remarks, **1957:** 150, 157

U-2 plane incident, **1960–61:** 154, 162, 163, 231n.
  News conference remarks, **1960–61:** 143, 263
U.A.R.
  See United Arab Republic.
Udall, James M., **1960–61:** 19
Ugly American, The (Lederer and Burdick), **1960–61:** 184
Ulinski, John A., **1953:** 41
Umatilla, Oreg., bridge at, **1954:** 271
Umstead, Gov. William B., **1954:** 92, 114
UMT.
  See Universal Military Training.
Uncommitted countries, **1958:** 32
Underwood, Gov. Cecil H., **1958:** 302
  Letter, **1960–61:** 176
UNEF.
  See United Nations Emergency Force.
Unemployment, **1953:** 249; **1954:** 21, 26, 54, 72,
    194, 308; **1955:** 4, 19; **1956:** 195; **1958:** 2,
    29, 33, 35, 49, 68, 110; **1959:** 15, 76;
    1960–61: 410, 423
  Area assistance, **1953:** 273; **1954:** 9, 18, 33; **1956:**
    2, 3, 19, 121, 155, 226, 279, 318
  Budget messages, **1956:** 12 (pp. 117, 139, 145,
    148, 149); **1960–61:** 13 (pp. 75, 76, 92),
    414 (pp. 939, 983, 1005)
  Campaign remarks, **1954:** 316, 317, 318, 319,
    320; **1956:** 224, 234, 251, 272, 279; **1958:**
    292, 294, 296, 303, 308
  Chronically depressed areas, **1957:** 13, 16; **1958:**
    5 (p. 53), 43, 120, 294, 308; **1959:** 167;
    1960–61: 5, 13 (pp. 75, 76), 133, 143, 176,
    414 (pp. 939, 983)
    Area redevelopment bill, veto, **1958:** 258;
      1960–61: 146
  Decline in, statement, **1958:** 283
  Economic report, **1958:** 16
  Federal aid, **1960–61:** 414 (p. 983), 423
  Manufacturing, **1954:** 107
  News conference remarks, **1954:** 9, 18, 33, 39, 63,
    73, 101, 107, 129, 311; **1955:** 33, 119;
    1958: 37, 42, 70, 88, 120; **1959:** 29, 36, 67,
    167; **1960–61:** 127, 143, 263
  Payroll tax, **1960–61:** 414 (p. 1005)
  Tax credits of successor employers, veto, **1960–
    61:** 170
  Trust fund.
    See Unemployment trust fund.
  West Virginia, **1960–61:** 127
Unemployment compensation, **1957:** 80
  Government employees, **1956:** 12 (p. 152)
  Veterans, **1956:** 12 (p. 112)
Unemployment insurance, **1954:** 3, 21; **1955:** 19;
    1956: 2, 234, 235; **1958:** 18, 26, 49, 96,
    110; **1959:** 15; **1960–61:** 170, 410
  Budget messages, **1954:** 14 (pp. 132, 133, 182–
    185, 188); **1955:** 17 (pp. 136, 176, 177,
    182); **1956:** 12 (p. 117); **1958:** 5 (pp. 50,

Unemployment insurance — *continued*
  Budget messages — *continued*
      51, 62); **1959:** 10 (pp. 46, 48, 49, 96, 100,
      101); **1960–61:** 13 (pp. 87, 92, 93, 97–99),
      414 (pp. 1005, 1006, 1009, 1019)
  Budget (1960), statement, **1958:** 324
  Campaign remarks, **1954:** 273, 286, 316, 317,
      318; **1958:** 292, 303, 308
  District of Columbia, approval, **1954:** 227
  Emergency program, **1954:** 73; **1959:** 10 (pp. 48,
      49, 96, 101), 53
  Extension of coverage, **1953:** 266; **1954:** 14 (p.
      182), 139, 273, 286, 308; **1957:** 13, 16, 22;
      1958: 53, 56, 83; **1959:** 123
    Approval of bill, **1954:** 236
  Federal aid, temporary, **1960–61:** 422
  Government employees, **1954:** 14 (pp. 182, 188),
      43, 313; **1955:** 17 (p. 182); **1960–61:** 414
      (p. 1019)
  Herlong amendment, **1958:** 103
  News conference remarks, **1954:** 73, 143; **1955:**
      56, 112, 119; **1958:** 56, 83, 103; **1959:** 36,
      53, 123
  Temporary, **1958:** 83, 103, 110
    Message, **1958:** 53
    Statement, **1958:** 72
  Veterans, **1954:** 14 (pp. 132, 133); **1955:** 17 (p.
      136)
Unemployment trust fund, **1954:** 14 (pp. 184, 185);
      1955: 17 (p. 178); **1958:** 53; **1959:** 10 (pp.
      100, 101); **1960–61:** 13 (p. 92)
  Table, **1954:** 14 (p. 185)
UNESCO.
  See United Nations Educational, Scientific and
      Cultural Organization.
Unfair competition, small business problems, **1956:**
      263
UNICEF.
  See United Nations International Children's
      Emergency Fund.
Union Carbide and Carbon Corp., **1954:** 193, 281
Union of Soviet Socialist Republics.
  See Soviet Union.
Unions.
  See Labor organizations.
United Arab Republic, **1958:** 177
  See also Egypt.
  Aswan Dam construction, **1960–61:** 7
  El Alamein, **1959:** 96
  Iraq, **1959:** 89
  Lebanon, **1958:** 172
  Nasser, Gamal Abdel.
    See main heading, Nasser, Gamal Abdel.
  News conference remarks, **1958:** 198; **1959:** 89,
      94
  Participation in U.N. action in Congo, **1960–61:**
      248n.

United Automobile Workers of America, **1954:** 26; **1956:** 198; **1957:** 157
  Studebaker Local 5, **1954:** 203n., 274n.
United Brotherhood of Carpenters and Joiners of America, **1953:** 224
  Anniversary, letter and remarks, **1956:** 86, 265
United Catholic Organizations for the Freeing of Cardinal Mindszenty, **1954:** 30
United Church Women, address, **1953:** 205
United Community campaigns, **1956:** 185, 221; **1958:** 184
  Letter to Harvey S. Firestone, Jr., **1954:** 276
  Memorandums, **1953:** 115, 179; **1954:** 183; **1955:** 168; **1960–61:** 210
  Recorded message, **1953:** 196
  Statements, **1955:** 218; **1957:** 203; **1958:** 270; **1959:** 238; **1960–61:** 293
United Community Defense Services, **1954:** 132
United Daughters of the Confederacy convention, remarks, **1953:** 240
United Defense Fund, **1954:** 132, 183; **1955:** 27
  Campaign, **1953:** 115, 179, 196
    National Capital area, **1953:** 127
  Citation, presentation to Gen. Doolittle, **1954:** 93
  Letter to Governors, **1954:** 55
  Meeting, remarks, **1953:** 45; **1954:** 93
United Fruit Co., **1958:** 288
United Fund campaigns, **1954:** 183, 276; **1956:** 185; **1957:** 154; **1958:** 184; **1959:** 159; **1960–61:** 293
United Gas, Coke and Chemical Workers, **1954:** 193
United Givers Fund campaign, **1956:** 138; **1957:** 140; **1958:** 136; **1959:** 156
  Memorandums, **1960–61:** 210
  National Capital area, **1960–61:** 153
United Jewish Appeal, citation of the President, **1955:** 115
United Kingdom, **1953:** 256; **1955:** 4, 18, 54n., 112 ftn. (p. 548); **1956:** 2, 276, 278; **1958:** 5 (p. 36), 8, 293; **1960–61:** 311
  See also London.
  Agreement with Egypt on Suez Canal, **1954:** 172, 192, 226, 297, 316
  Agreement with U.S. on civil uses of atomic energy, **1955:** 123
  Agreements with International Atomic Energy Agency, **1959:** 189
  Aircraft accident near London, **1959:** 36 and ftn. (p. 191)
  Ambassador Winthrop W. Aldrich, **1953:** 34n.; **1955:** 244n.
  Anglo-American Financial Agreement of 1945, **1957:** 44
  Armed forces on Continent, commitment on, **1954:** 314
  Armed forces in Korea, **1960–61:** 202
  Atomic Energy Authority, **1958:** 21

United Kingdom — *continued*
  Atomic energy for mutual defense, U.S.-U.K. agreement, **1958:** 156, 157; **1959:** 119n., 120n.
  Atomic information exchange with United States, **1954:** 73; **1956:** 26
  Attitude on summit conference, **1959:** 148
  Austrian Treaty, question of, **1954:** 128
  Bermuda Conference, **1957:** 53, 55, 70
    See also Bermuda meeting of Western leaders.
  British Empire Service League, **1955:** 119
  Butler, Richard Austen. **1953:** 128
  Churchill, Winston, **1953:** 22, 77, 88, 126, 128, 187, 198, 208, 230, 254; **1954:** 50, 63, 73, 143, 148, 157, 161, 164, 192, 297, 311, 345; **1955:** 47, 65, 244; **1956:** 78, 216; **1958:** 288, 318; **1959:** 7, 93, 94, 96; **1960–61:** 287
  Joint declaration, **1954:** 155
  Joint statement with, **1954:** 154
  Joint statement with Western leaders, **1953:** 255
  Message, **1954:** 344
  Coronation ceremonies, **1953:** 109 and ftn. (p. 439)
  Currency convertibility, **1954:** 67
  Cyprus agreement, **1959:** 39, 40, 41
  Defense paper, **1957:** 72
  Disarmament proposal, **1957:** 158, 165, 208 and n., 210, 226, 244
  Disarmament proposal in U.N., **1959:** 243
  Douglas (Lewis W.) financial and economic mission, **1953:** 176, 177
  Economy, **1959:** 196
  Eden, Anthony, **1953:** 22, 254; **1954:** 143, 148, 157; **1955:** 41, 66, 208n.; **1956:** 26, 27, 32, 53, 78, 155; **1957:** 7
  Elizabeth II, **1953:** 109 ftn. (p. 439); **1955:** 208n.; **1958:** 163, 209, 318; **1959:** 96, 141, 193, 196, 198n., 214; **1960–61:** 40, 171
  Messages, **1953:** 7, 34
  Four-power conference on Germany and Austria, proposed, **1953:** 238
  Geneva conferences.
    See main heading, Geneva conferences.
  Glubb, Lt. Gen. John B., **1956:** 53
  Home, Lord, **1960–61:** 307
  Income tax convention, **1956:** 181
  Iranian oil dispute, **1953:** 129
  Jay Treaty (1794), **1954:** 113n.
  Joint statements with Prime Minister Eden, **1956:** 26, 27
  Joint statements with Prime Minister Macmillan, **1957:** 55, 226
  Jordan, troops in, **1958:** 213
  Labor Party leaders, question of U.S. visit, **1954:** 200
  Leadership in cold war, comment on, **1959:** 48

United Kingdom — *continued*
  Letter to Premier Bulganin re, **1958:** 7
  Lloyd, Selwyn, **1956:** 78, 229; **1957:** 55, 226n.;
    1958: 293; **1959:** 39, 123 and ftn. (p. 425)
  Machinery for U.S. Department of Defense,
    British bids on, **1953:** 54
  Macmillan, Harold, **1957:** 10, 17, 28, 50, 53, 55,
    119, 219, 226, 228, 230; **1958:** 130, 141,
    293; **1959:** 36, 39, 42, 48, 67, 81, 102, 110,
    123, 179, 191, 193, 196, 198, 214, 271,
    337n., 349; **1960–61:** 103, 147, 154, 162,
    163, 313, 360n.
    East-West summit conference, agreement with
      Western leaders on, **1959:** 337
    Joint declaration, **1960–61:** 102
    Joint statements, **1960–61:** 101, 155, 307, 312
    Joint statements with Western leaders, **1959:**
      335, 336
  Meeting (U.S., France), **1956:** 298
  Membership in Western European Union, ques-
    tion of, **1954:** 307
  Missiles and rocketry, joint study, **1957:** 226n.
  Mountbatten, Vice Adm. Louis, **1955:** 119
  News conference remarks, **1954:** 73, 92, 107, 115,
    129, 143, 157, 165, 172, 192, 200; **1956:** 32,
    53, 78, 155, 229, 235, 298; **1957:** 28, 56, 70,
    72, 119, 124, 157, 228; **1958:** 56, 83, 213,
    318; **1959:** 48, 67, 89, 148, 191, 243;
    1960–61: 7, 21, 34, 38, 143 and ftn. (p.
    410)
  Non-aggression pact, proposal, **1954:** 157
  Nuclear relationship, joint study, **1957:** 226n.
  Nuclear test suspension, **1958:** 300, 311
    Inspection proposals, **1959:** 48, 89, 102, 110;
      1960–61: 102
  Nuclear tests, **1960–61:** 143 and ftn. (p. 410)
  Nuclear weapons, **1953:** 256
  Paris summit conference.
    See Paris summit meeting.
  Participation in U.N. action in Congo, **1960–61:**
    248n.
  Plowden, Sir Edwin, **1957:** 226n.; **1958:** 21
  Policy on Berlin, **1960–61:** 38
  Prince Anthony, birth of, statement, **1960–61:** 40
  Prince Philip, **1959:** 141; **1960–61:** 40
  Princess Margaret, **1953:** 34
  Queen Mother Elizabeth, **1954:** 39, 311, 322
  Queen Mother Mary, death of, **1953:** 34
  Royalty taxes paid in, tax credit for, disapproval,
    1956: 181
  Sandys, Duncan, **1957:** 28
  Scientific contributions, **1957:** 230
  SEATO.
    See Southeast Asia Treaty Organization.
  Soviet-U.K. talks on air safety over Germany,
    1953: 41
  Storm disaster, **1953:** 7, 8
  Suez Canal problem.
    See Suez Canal.

United Kingdom — *continued*
  Suez invasion (1956), **1960–61:** 21
  Technical conference on nuclear detection.
    See Geneva conferences.
  Trade with United States, **1959:** 67
  Tripartite Declaration, 1950, re Middle East,
    1956: 26, 53, 56, 62, 276
  U.N. action, **1957:** 34
  U.S. nuclear submarine bases, **1960–61:** 360n.
  U.S. relations with, **1953:** 109; **1954:** 143, 297;
    1959: 196
  Visit of President Eisenhower, **1959:** 179, 186,
    193, 196, 198, 214
  World War II cemetery, Cambridge, **1956:** 102
  Yalta conference.
    See main heading, Yalta conference.
United Mineworkers, **1957:** 215
United Nations, **1953:** 1, 6, 26, 50, 89, 98, 191, 209,
    210; **1954:** 3, 23n., 44, 45, 72, 87, 90, 91,
    155, 225, 297, 325; **1955:** 16, 20, 21, 24,
    167, 179, 239, 248; **1956:** 2, 27, 114, 191,
    218, 314; **1957:** 2; **1958:** 18, 36, 80, 94,
    173, 189, 261; **1959:** 6, 70, 72, 115, 152;
    1960–61: 4, 49, 72, 73, 78, 80, 157, 177,
    183, 193, 195, 219, 334, 410
  See also Disarmament conference, London; Dis-
    armament Subcommittee.
  Address before General Assembly, **1960–61:** 302
    Comments on, **1960–61:** 268, 284 and ftn. (p.
      682), 336
  Aerial surveillance, proposed, **1960–61:** 154, 163
  Africa, new nations
    Admission, **1960–61:** 336
    Assistance, **1960–61:** 263, 302
    Remarks to delegates, **1960–61:** 324
  Appraisal, **1954:** 192
  Arms inspection, U.S. proposal, **1960–61:** 302
  Atomic energy for peaceful uses, **1955:** 4; **1958:**
    188; **1960–61:** 330
    Conference on (1955), **1958:** 240
    President's address, **1953:** 256, 265; **1954:** 38,
      63, 129, 223, 322, 337, 347; **1959:** 302;
      1960–61: 209, 301
    President's proposal for international organi-
      zation (1953), **1955:** 59, 121; **1958:** 67
    Technical conference, Geneva, **1955:** 100, 123,
      149, 156, 176, 191, 228
    U.S. proposal for international pool, **1954:** 3,
      297, 325; **1960–61:** 302
  Budget messages, **1960–61:** 13 (pp. 62, 63), 414
    (pp. 965, 967)
  Campaign remarks, **1958:** 293, 295, 302
  Commission on prisoners of war, **1954:** 314
  Communist China
    Admission to U.N., question of, **1953:** 77, 254;
      1954: 161, 182; **1958:** 274; **1960–61:** 410
    U.S. position in case of admission, **1953:** 88
    U.S. prisoners, U.N. responsibility toward,
      1954: 345

United Nations — *continued*
  Complaint to, against violation of human rights
    and freedom of association in East
    Germany, proposed, **1953**: 130n.
  Congo situation, **1960–61**: 248, 263, 284, 339
    Emergency fund, **1960–61**: 302
    Joint statement with Prime Minister
      Macmillan, **1960–61**: 307
    U.S. position, **1960–61**: 364
  Contributions to programs by U.S., **1957**: 90
  Cyprus delegation, remarks, **1960–61**: 324
  Declaration of Jan. 1, 1942, **1958**: 177
  Disarmament, **1959**: 191, 320
    See also Disarmament Commission and sub-
      committee, U.N.
    Proposal by Premier Khrushchev, **1959**: 223,
      243
    Proposal by United Kingdom, **1959**: 243
  Distribution of agricultural surpluses, proposed,
    1960–61: 255, 279, 302
  Economic and social activities, report, **1958**: 8
  Egypt, action on, **1957**: 6, 34
  Emergency force, **1960–61**: 330
  Establishment (1945), **1960–61**: 332
  Exchange of messages with Prime Minister
    Kishi, **1957**: 208
  Flag, display of, **1953**: 133
  Forced Labor, Ad Hoc Committee on, **1955**: 156
  Forces in Middle East, **1957**: 13, 35
  Formosa Strait, question of action on, **1955**: 18
  Freedom-from-hunger campaign, statement,
    1960–61: 221
  Gaza Strip, U.N. force in, **1958**: 89
  General Assembly.
    See United Nations General Assembly.
  Guatemala, meeting on, **1955**: 156
  Hungary
    Action on, **1956**: 283, 291; **1957**: 3, 6
    Committee on, **1958**: 148
    Joint statement with Prime Minister Fanfani,
      1958: 186
    Resolution on, **1958**: 222
  International Atomic Energy Agency, **1957**: 8,
    13, 16, 54, 144 and n., 150, 169, 204, 245
  International police force, proposed, **1960–61**:
    330
  Ireland, Permanent Representative to U.N.
    (Frederick H. Boland), **1960–61**: 302n.
  Israeli-Egyptian dispute, **1957**: 35
  Joint statements
    King Bhumibol Adulyadej, **1960–61**: 218
    King Mohammad Zahir, **1959**: 308
    King Saud, **1957**: 31
    Premier Mollet, **1957**: 38
    President Ayub Khan, **1959**: 303
    President Bayar, **1959**: 297
    President Garcia, **1960–61**: 189
    President Gronchi, **1959**: 293

United Nations — *continued*
  Joint statements — *continued*
    Prime Minister Diem, **1957**: 83
    Prime Minister Huh Chung, **1960–61**: 203
    Prime Minister Kishi, **1957**: 117; **1960–61**: 16
    Prime Minister Macmillan, **1957**: 55, 226;
      1960–61: 307, 312
    Prime Minister Menzies, **1960–61**: 312
    Prime Minister St. Laurent, **1953**: 247
    Prime Minister Segni, **1959**: 248
    Shah Mohammad Reza Pahlavi, **1959**: 322
    Western leaders, **1953**: 255
  Korea
    Action on, **1954**: 168, 178, 345
    Assistance to victims of fire in Pusan, **1953**:
      258
    Conference on.
      See Geneva conferences.
    Police action (1950–53).
      See Korean war.
    U.N. Command, **1960–61**: 108, 202, 203, 212
    U.N. force in, **1958**: 89; **1959**: 311, 325
    U.N. membership, question of, **1960–61**: 203
  Laos, observers in, **1959**: 214
  Lebanon, crisis in, **1958**: 141, 176, 181, 186, 196,
    198, 291
  Letter to President Kubitschek, **1958**: 181
  Letters to Premier Bulganin, **1958**: 7, 31
  Letters to Premier Khrushchev, **1958**: 177, 189
  Membership, **1956**: 143; **1958**: 8
    Japan, **1956**: 2, 143, 313
  Messages, addresses, etc., **1957**: 3, 6, 8, 15, 35, 37,
    54, 79, 90, 198, 213
  Middle East situation, **1955**: 234; **1956**: 53, 143,
    276, 282, 287
    Action in. **1960–61**: 330
  Military forces, stand-by arrangements, Presi-
    dent's proposal, **1960–61**: 302
  News conference remarks, **1953**: 12, 77, 88, 128,
    230, 254, 265; **1954**: 73, 101, 143, 161, 168,
    172, 182, 192, 341, 345, 347; **1955**: 18, 26,
    33, 41, 59, 81, 100, 112, 146, 176; **1956**: 32,
    53, 88, 94, 205, 229, 298; **1957**: 28, 45, 50,
    62, 72, 87, 150, 169, 207; **1958**: 37, 56, 141,
    153, 213, 222, 274; **1959**: 21, 191, 223,
    243; **1960–61**: 7, 21, 38, 263, 268, 284 and
    ftn. (p. 682)
  Nuclear test observers, **1958**: 37, 56
  Operational and Executive Personnel Program,
    1960–61: 302
  Peace force, proposed, **1958**: 207, 213
  President's address on atomic power for peace
    (1953), **1956**: 52n.
    Quoted, **1956**: 266
  Refugee assistance program, **1955**: 17 (p. 131),
    76, 156; **1958**: 148
    U.S. contribution, **1954**: 14 (p. 139)

United Nations — *continued*
  Regional surveys and training institutes, **1958:** 5
    (p. 40)
  Resolutions on fomenting of civil strife, **1958:**
    207
  Scientific committee on hazards of nuclear
    testing, **1957:** 208
  Security Council.
    See United Nations Security Council.
  Space development, President's proposal, **1960–
    61:** 302
  Special projects, U.S. contribution, **1959:** 55
  Statute of International Atomic Energy Agency,
    conference, **1956:** 273
    Statement, **1956:** 274
  Suez Canal problem, **1956:** 205, 229, 241, 283,
    295
    Action on, **1957:** 38; **1960–61:** 341
  Technical assistance program, **1953:** 89, 143;
    1955: 4, 17 (p. 130), 76, 126, 156; **1958:** 5
    (p. 40); **1959:** 189; **1960–61:** 320, 410
    U.S. contribution, **1954:** 14 (p. 139), 150, 172;
      1959: 10 (p. 75), 55; **1960–61:** 13 (p. 62),
      36, 414 (p. 967)
  Tenth anniversary meeting, San Francisco, **1955:**
    81, 112, 126, 146; **1956:** 143
  Universal Declaration of Human Rights, **1953:**
    43; **1956:** 308
  U.S. contributions to programs, **1956:** 12 (pp.
    106, 107), 58, 88, 94; **1958:** 32
    Special Projects Fund, **1958:** 148, 312
  U.S. deputy representative (James J.
    Wadsworth), **1958:** 39
  U.S. employees, security clearance, **1955:** 156
  U.S. participation, reports, **1955:** 156; **1956:** 143;
    1958: 8, 148
  U.S. Representative (Henry Cabot Lodge, Jr.),
    1953: 187; **1954:** 73, 322; **1955:** 156; **1958:**
    148, 196; **1959:** 21, 218; **1960–61:** 238,
    302, 309, 348
    See also Lodge, Henry Cabot.
    News conference remarks on, **1960–61:** 268,
      284
    Resignation, letter, **1960–61:** 266
  U.S. support of, **1954:** 14 (p. 138); **1960–61:** 163,
    255, 302, 330
    Joint declaration with Prime Minister
      Churchill, **1954:** 155
  Vietnam, action on, **1957:** 83
  World Refugee Year, **1960–61:** 133
United Nations, Secretary General (Dag Ham-
    marskjold), **1953:** 256, 272n.; **1955:** 179;
    1956: 62, 96; **1957:** 50, 62; **1958:** 8, 112,
    148, 179, 207; **1960–61:** 302n., 307
  Arab-Israeli mission, **1956:** 143
  Lebanon, mission to, **1958:** 172, 173
  Meeting with Secretary Dulles, **1955:** 18
  Middle East peace mission, **1956:** 96

United Nations, Secretary General — *continued*
  Negotiations with Communist China on release
    of prisoners, **1955:** 4, 18, 156
    Statement re, **1955:** 16
  News conference remarks on, **1956:** 62, 96, 298;
    1960–61: 127, 256
  Peiping mission, **1956:** 143
United Nations Charter, **1953:** 43, 256; **1954:** 168,
  297; **1955:** 4, 26, 126, 148, 156; **1956:** 23,
  114, 121 ftn. (p. 556), 270, 291, 298; **1958:**
  89, 171, 172, 173, 174, 207, 260, 289; **1959:**
  24, 192; **1960–61:** 90, 188, 204, 209, 231,
  232, 286, 302, 303, 332, 364
  Campaign remarks, **1958:** 290, 294, 296
  Joint statements
    President Ayub Khan, **1959:** 303
    President Bayar, **1959:** 297
    President Garcia, **1958:** 143; **1960–61:** 189
    President Gronchi on, **1959:** 293
    President Rhee, **1954:** 178
    Prime Minister Daud, **1958:** 150
    Prime Minister Huh Chung, **1960–61:** 203
    Prime Minister Karamanlis on, **1959:** 327
  Letter to President Chamoun, **1958:** 182
  Letters to Premier Bulganin, **1958:** 7, 31
  Letters to Premier Khrushchev, **1958:** 112, 177,
    179, 189
  News conference remarks, **1960–61:** 21, 284, 422
United Nations Children's Fund, **1955:** 156; **1960–
  61:** 279
  U.S. contributions, **1955:** 76; **1956:** 58; **1958:** 5
    (p. 40), 32; **1959:** 10 (p. 75), 55; **1960–61:**
    13 (p. 63)
United Nations Commission on Human Rights,
  message, **1953:** 43
United Nations Day, **1960–61:** 330, 336
  United States Committee for, remarks, **1953:** 191
United Nations Disarmament Commission, **1953:**
  238, 256; **1956:** 266; **1957:** 55, 158, 165;
  1960–61: 302
  See also Disarmament Subcommittee, U.N.,
    London.
  Membership, **1958:** 148
  Need for meeting, statement, **1960–61:** 238
United Nations Economic and Social Council,
  1959: 189
United Nations Educational, Scientific and Cul-
  tural Organization, **1953:** 77; **1955:** 156;
  1960–61: 72
United Nations Emergency Force, **1958:** 8, 148
  U.S. contribution to, **1959:** 55
United Nations Food and Agriculture Organiza-
  tion, **1960–61:** 221, 279, 302
United Nations General Assembly, **1958:** 2, 312;
  1959: 91n.; **1960–61:** 255
  Action on detention of U.S. and U.N. prisoners,
    1955: 4

United Nations General Assembly — *continued*
  Addresses by the President, **1953:** 256; **1955:** 79,
    156, 177n., 228; **1959:** 302; **1960–61:** 209,
    301, 302
    Comments on, **1960–61:** 268, 284 and ftn. (p.
      682), 336
  Disarmament question, technical studies pro-
    posed, **1958:** 67, 86
  Heads of state and government attending, U.S.
    responsibility towards, statement, **1960–
    61:** 296
  Hungary, action on, **1958:** 7
  Joint statement with Prime Minister Menzies,
    1960–61: 312
  Joint statements with Prime Minister Macmillan,
    1960–61: 307, 312
  Near East crisis, emergency meeting on, state-
    ment and address, **1958:** 196, 207
  News conference remarks, **1960–61:** 256, 268,
    284 and ftn. (p. 682)
  President (Frederick H. Boland), **1960–61:** 302n.
  President (Madame Vijaya Pandit), **1953:** 210,
    256
  Resolutions
    Cooperation in peaceful uses of atomic energy
      (1954), **1955:** 156
    Nuclear tests, **1958:** 311
    "Peace through Deeds," **1958:** 173, 179
    Proposed meeting of President with Chairman
      Khrushchev, letter, **1960–61:** 313
United Nations High Commissioner for Refugees,
  1958: 148
United Nations International Children's Emergen-
  cy Fund, **1953:** 89, 143; **1960–61:** 36
United Nations Korean Reconstruction Agency,
  1953: 89, 148
United Nations peace force, **1958:** 207, 213
  News conference remarks, **1958:** 213
United Nations Refugee Fund, contributions to,
  1956: 12 (p. 107)
United Nations Relief and Works Agency, **1953:**
  217; **1958:** 8
  Contributions to, **1956:** 58
United Nations Scientific Committee on the Effect
  of Atomic Radiation, **1958:** 56
United Nations Security Council, **1953:** 256; **1954:**
  68; **1958:** 196, 261
  Arab-Israeli dispute, action on, **1953:** 230
  Congo, resolution on, **1960–61:** 248n., 256
  Discussion of RB-47 plane incident, proposed,
    1960–61: 231, 232, 255
  Lebanon, **1958:** 177, 179, 198, 207
    Observers in, **1958:** 172, 173
    Report of U.S. action, **1958:** 171
  Letters to Premier Bulganin, **1958:** 7, 31
  Letters to Premier Khrushchev, **1958:** 86, 112,
    177, 179, 189
  Soviet use of veto, **1959:** 110n.

United Nations Security Council — *continued*
  U.S. Representative (Henry Cabot Lodge), **1958:**
    148, 172, 179, 189, 196
  Veto, use in Council, **1958:** 8, 63, 148, 198, 207
    Letter to Premier Bulganin, **1958:** 7, 31
    Letter to Premier Khrushchev, **1958:** 177
United Nations Special Fund, **1960–61:** 302, 328
  Budget message, **1960–61:** 414 (pp. 965, 967)
United Nations Sub-Committee on Disarmament,
    1957: 80, 158, 165, 226
  See also Disarmament conference, London.
United Nations Truce Supervision Organization
  Findings re Israeli-Arab Jordan River devel-
    opment dispute, **1953:** 230
  Joint statement with Prime Minister Eden on,
    1956: 26
United Negro College Fund Luncheon, remarks,
    1953: 81
United Republican dinner, remarks, **1958:** 18
United Service Organizations, **1953:** 45, 115, 127,
    179, 196; **1954:** 55, 132, 310; **1955:** 130;
    1956: 138, 185; **1957:** 140, 154, 203; **1958:**
    136, 184, 270; **1959:** 156, 159, 238; **1960–
    61:** 153, 210, 293
  Defense Fund Dinner, message, **1955:** 27
  National Council, remarks, **1956:** 57
  President's acceptance of honorary
    chairmanship, **1955:** 80
United States Air Force Academy, **1954:** 9
  Appointment of son of Capt. Kincheloe, letter,
    1958: 314
  Commencement address, **1959:** 109
United States Capitol, cornerstone laying cere-
    mony, remarks, **1959:** 151
United States Chamber of Commerce
  Improvements in Federal budgeting, letter, **1959:**
    300
  Remarks, **1954:** 90; **1955:** 85; **1959:** 87; **1960–61:**
    131
United States Committee for Refugees, **1959:** 91
United States Committee for United Nations Day,
    remarks, **1953:** 191
United States Court of Appeals, Chicago, news
    conference remarks, **1958:** 103
United States District Courts
  Challenges in civil cases, **1958:** 250
  Little Rock, Ark., **1957:** 169, 178, 197, 205, 207
  School integration cases, **1956:** 32, 47, 171, 198,
    205; **1958:** 98, 274
United States European Command, **1956:** 317
United States Government, comment on form of,
    1959: 21
United States Government life insurance, **1957:** 73
United States Information Agency, **1953:** 89, 92,
    230; **1955:** 248; **1956:** 2, 87; **1957:** 86;
    1958: 5 (pp. 37, 41); **1959:** 10 (p. 75);
    1960–61: 349, 358, 410
  Broadcasts, **1957:** 37 and n., 42n.

United States Information Agency — *continued*
  Budget messages, **1954:** 14 (p. 140); **1955:** 17 (p. 131); **1960–61:** 13 (p. 65), 414 (pp. 968, 969)
  Career service for overseas foreign service officers, **1957:** 8
  Establishment under Reorganization Plan 8, message, **1953:** 91
  Increased appropriation for, **1957:** 8
  Information Service, **1954:** 87
  News conference remarks, **1957:** 72, 87
  "People's Capitalism" exhibit, **1956:** 75n.
  Remarks to staff, **1953:** 241
  Responsibilities, directive, **1953:** 231
  Statement re, **1953:** 151
United States Information Agency, Director (George V. Allen), **1958:** 23, 63; **1959:** 80n.; **1960–61:** 24
  See also Allen, George V.
  Committee on U.S. art exhibit in Moscow, **1959:** 148 and ftn. (p. 490)
United States Information Agency, Director (Arthur Larson), **1957:** 18
  Bipartisan conference, **1957:** 2
United States Information Agency, Director (Theodore C. Streibert) **1953:** 151n., 230, 231n.; **1954:** 323
United States Junior Chamber of Commerce, remarks, **1954:** 338
United States Military Academy, **1953:** 80; **1954:** 335; **1957:** 27; **1958:** 123; **1959:** 129, 259; **1960–61:** 135, 173, 319, 340
  Address to graduating class, **1955:** 118
  Appointment of Dwight D. Eisenhower, **1956:** 241
  Association of Graduates, Sylvanus Thayer award to Dr. Lawrence, **1958:** 52
  Blaik, Earl, resignation, **1959:** 7
  Boxing incident, **1958:** 287
  Bryan, Maj. Gen. Blackshear M., Superintendent, **1955:** 117, 118
  News conference remarks, **1954:** 9, 341; **1959:** 7, 179
  President's reminiscences, **1955:** 70
  Remarks to alumni, **1955:** 117
United States Mint, **1957:** 216
United States Naval Academy, **1953:** 81; **1954:** 9, 341; **1959:** 116
  Admission, Dwight D. Eisenhower barred by age limitation, **1956:** 241
  Board of Visitors, **1960–61:** 349
  Commencement address, **1958:** 125
  Council on Youth Fitness, message, **1956:** 128
  Remarks to midshipmen, **1953:** 80
United States park police, increase in benefits, disapproval, **1959:** 239
United States Secret Service, increase in benefits, disapproval, **1959:** 239

United States Steel Corporation, **1954:** 57, 113n.; **1959:** 211n.
  Report on profits, **1959:** 172
United Steel Corp., Chairman, Board of Directors (David M. Blough), **1958:** 120
United Steelworkers of America, **1953:** 77; **1956:** 150, 229; **1959:** 142, 160, 211, 265
  McDonald, David J., **1958:** 120
  News conference remarks, **1959:** 94
  Talks with officials, statement, **1959:** 246
United Textile Workers of America, **1956:** 198, 216
Universal Military Training, **1953:** 15; **1954:** 353
Universal Postal Union, **1959:** 270
Universal Trades, Inc., relief of, veto, **1960–61:** 150
Universities.
  See Colleges and universities.
Unknown Americans, burial
  Arlington Cemetery, **1958:** 122n.
  At sea, **1958:** 103
Unna, Warren W., **1957:** 72, 150; **1958:** 310; **1960–61:** 38
Upper Colorado River Basin project, **1955:** 17 (p. 159); **1956:** 2, 251, 256
  Budget message, **1956:** 12 (p. 135)
  Ceremony marking beginning, remarks, **1956:** 245
  News conference remarks, **1956:** 47, 53
Upper Volta, Republic of
  Guirma, Frederic, **1960–61:** 324n.
  Independence, message to Prime Minister Yameogo, **1960–61:** 253
Uranium, **1955:** 121, 123; **1960–61:** 34, 103, 235, 284
  See also Fissionable materials.
  Available for peaceful uses, **1956:** 43, 52, 274, 299; **1957:** 13, 124, 125
  Concentrates, **1958:** 5 (p. 33)
  Isotopes, electro-magnetic method of separation, **1958:** 52
  Isotopes available for friendly countries, **1955:** 228
    Uranium 235 to Turkey, **1955:** 89n.
  Japan's request to IAEA for, **1959:** 189
  Ores and concentrates, purchase of, **1954:** 14 (p. 128); **1960–61:** 13 (p. 58)
  Prices, **1955:** 10
Uranium 233, purchase abroad, **1956:** 299
Urban development and housing, **1958:** 106
Urban expansion, **1953:** 153
Urban League, National, message, **1958:** 315
Urban planning grants, **1956:** 2
Urban renewal, **1955:** 194; **1957:** 13, 118; **1958:** 29, 33, 43, 49, 96, 110; **1959:** 6, 106; **1960–61:** 5, 410
  Budget messages, **1954:** 14 (pp. 87, 148); **1955:** 17 (pp. 171, 172); **1956:** 12 (pp. 144, 145, 146); **1958:** 5 (pp. 43, 56–58); **1959:** 10 (pp. 38, 46, 82–84); **1960–61:** 13 (pp. 65,

Urban renewal — *continued*
  Budget messages — *continued*
    72), 414 (pp. 979, 980)
    Table, **1958:** 5 (p. 54)
  Campaign remarks, **1958:** 292
  Federal aid, **1954:** 17; **1960–61:** 414 (pp. 979, 980)
  Letter to Administrator, HHFA, **1958:** 50
  News conference remarks, **1957:** 70, 80, 115; **1959:** 26, 94
  Southwest Washington, D.C. development, **1954:** 345; **1955:** 55; **1956:** 4
  State responsibility, **1958:** 5 (p. 43)
  Statement, **1958:** 224
  Veto of bills, **1959:** 153, 208
Urban Renewal Administration
  Budget message, **1958:** 5 (pp. 56, 57)
  Funds for slum clearance, **1958:** 222
Urbanization, **1959:** 8
Uruguay
  Declaration of Montevideo, **1960–61:** 84
  Economic problems, **1958:** 103
  Letter to President Echegoyen on flood disaster, **1959:** 95
  Martinez, Homero, **1960–61:** 78n.
  Montevideo.
    See main heading, Montevideo.
  Nardone, Benito, **1960–61:** 78, 79, 82, 85, 87
  Seizure of meatpacking plant, **1958:** 103
  Student and teacher exchange, **1960–61:** 80
  U.N. committee on Hungary, **1958:** 8
  U.S. Ambassador Robert F. Woodward, **1960–61:** 78n.
  Visit to, **1960–61:** 42, 78, 79, 80, 81, 82, 83, 84, 85, 87
U. S.
  See United States.
U.S.A.: Second-Class Power? (Pearson, Anderson), **1959:** 167
USIA.
  See United States Information Agency.
U.S. News and World Report, "Today's War—How the Reds are Operating in 72 Countries," **1958:** 274
USO.
  See United Service Organizations.
U.S.S. *Abraham Lincoln*, **1960–61:** 360
U.S.S. *Atka*, Antarctic mission, **1955:** 47
U.S.S. *Barry*, **1956:** 208
U.S.S. *Canberra*, **1957:** 52n.
U.S.S. *Des Moines*, **1959:** 327n., 328n., 330n.
  Remarks to ship's company, **1959:** 331
U.S.S. *Dorchester*, **1953:** 5; **1954:** 32
U.S.S. *Essex*, **1959:** 331
U.S.S. *George Washington*, **1960–61:** 255
  Entrance into sea duty, statement, **1960–61:** 360
U.S.S. *Kearsarge*, **1960–61:** 97
U.S.S. *Midway*, visit to Capetown, South Africa, **1955:** 18

U.S.S. *Nautilus*, **1954:** 38; **1955:** 17 (p. 121) 81
  Budget message, **1954:** 14 (p. 129)
  Citation to officers and crew, **1958:** 201
  Message to Chancellor Adenauer re, **1958:** 210
  Message to Commander and crew, **1958:** 15
  Message to Premier Fanfani re, **1958:** 211
U.S.S. *Patrick Henry*, **1960–61:** 360
  Firing of Polaris missile, statement, **1960–61:** 244
U.S.S. *Saint Paul*, **1960–61:** 190n., 191
U.S.S. *Saratoga*, **1957:** 107, 108
  Remarks to officers and men, **1957:** 107
U.S.S. *Seawolf*, **1954:** 14 (p. 129); **1955:** 17 (p. 121); **1958:** 274
U.S.S. *Triton*, **1960–61:** 142
U.S.S. *Williamsburg*, **1953:** 118
U.S.S.R.
  See Soviet Union.
Utah, **1958:** 37; **1959:** 21
  Bennett, Sen. Wallace F., **1955:** 119; **1960–61:** 167
  Deseret News, **1958:** 99
  Watkins, Sen. Arthur, **1954:** 347; **1956:** 213, 245n.; **1958:** 83
Utilization research program (farm products), **1960–61:** 32
Utt, Repr. James B., **1960–61:** 333

Vaerts, Charles S., **1958:** 71n.
Valley Forge, Pa., **1953:** 137, 271; **1954:** 32; **1956:** 122
Valley Forge Military School, **1954:** 304n.
Van Allen Radiation Belt, **1960–61:** 410
Van Doren, Mark, **1959:** 116
Van Fleet, Gen. James A., **1955:** 112; **1956:** 278, 279; **1959:** 259n.
  Distinguished Service Medal, citation, **1953:** 19
  News conference remarks on, **1953:** 12, 22, 41
Van Kleffens, Eelco N., **1955:** 126
Van der Linden, Frank, **1953:** 208, 230, 249; **1954:** 63, 92, 101, 115, 161, 165, 200, 322, 345; **1955:** 26, 90, 146, 176, 185; **1956:** 32, 53, 205, 298; **1957:** 17, 22, 28, 45, 56, 62, 70, 72, 80, 87, 92, 119, 124, 134, 150, 157, 207; **1958:** 11, 42, 56, 70, 103, 288, 318; **1959:** 21, 29, 67, 94, 123, 148, 161, 172, 186, 271; **1960–61:** 7, 93, 143, 256, 263, 268, 284, 422
Van Zandt, Repr. James E., **1960–61:** 31n.
Vandenberg, Gen. Hoyt S., death of, statement, **1954:** 70
Vandenberg resolution (1948), **1954:** 101
Vanderbilt University, **1953:** 230
Vandercook, John W., **1954:** 73, 157, 165, 172
Vanguard project, **1957:** 210, 211, 234; **1958:** 28, 308; **1959:** 267; **1960–61:** 11, 424
  Launching of rocket, statement, **1958:** 47

Vatican, appointment of U.S. ambassador, question of, **1954:** 311
V-E Day, 10th anniversary, comment on, **1955:** 81
Vegetable Week, National, recorded message, **1953:** 150
Vegetables, **1958:** 60
Vegetables and fruit, surpluses, **1954:** 4
Vehicles, Government, reduction in, **1954:** 345
Velde, Repr. Harold H., **1953:** 269
Venezuela, **1955:** 26; **1960–61:** 228
　Betancourt, Romulo, **1958:** 323; **1959:** 44; **1960–61:** 267
　　Message, **1960–61:** 122
　Caracas, **1953:** 260; **1955:** 4; **1958:** 133, 323; **1960–61:** 222
　Caracas conference.
　　See Inter-American Conference, 10th, at Caracas.
　Conflict with Dominican Republic, **1960–61:** 267
　Economic problems, **1958:** 103
　Field hockey team, **1960–61:** 319n.
　Lepervanche Parparcen, Rene, **1953:** 48n.
　Oil
　　Discussions on, **1959:** 51
　　News conference remarks, **1957:** 28, 145
　Presentation of Simon Bolivar statue to United States, **1959:** 44
　Sesquicentennial of independence, **1960–61:** 122
　Visit of Vice President Nixon, **1958:** 103
Venus, **1960–61:** 287
Vergara, German, **1960–61:** 73n.
Vermont, **1957:** 108
　Aiken, Sen. George D., **1953:** 187, 268; **1954:** 143, 192, 196; **1955:** 131; **1956:** 35; **1957:** 134
　Chittenden, **1955:** 132
　Election of Congressman-at-Large, **1958:** 310
　Flanders, Sen. Ralph E., **1953:** 77, 187; **1954:** 50, 165, 168, 182; **1955:** 131, 149
　Johnson, Joseph B., **1953:** 187; **1955:** 131
　Rutland, **1955:** 131
Versailles Treaty, **1958:** 261
Vessels.
　See Ships; Ships, nuclear-powered.
Veterans, **1953:** 6, 144
　See also Armed Forces, U.S.; World War II.
　Civil service rights, **1956:** 22
　Disabled, **1956:** 12 (p. 113)
　Gift from Burma to children of U.S. veterans, **1955:** 169
　Insurance, **1956:** 12 (p. 114), 267
　Last trip of U.S.S. *Williamsburg,* remarks, **1953:** 118
　Naturalization, **1956:** 33
　Ogletree, Stephen Swan, **1955:** 197
　Readjustment benefits, **1956:** 12 (p. 111)
Veterans Administration, **1956:** 267; **1957:** 13; **1959:** 146

Veterans Administration — *continued*
　Budget messages, **1955:** 17 (pp. 132, 136, 138, 139, 173); **1956:** 12 (pp. 111, 114, 147); **1958:** 5 (pp. 53, 63); **1959:** 10 (pp. 51, 84, 85, 107); **1960–61:** 13 (pp. 74, 97, 100, 108), 414 (pp. 981, 1013, 1015, 1016, 1019, 1025)
　Claims
　　Bond, Virginia, **1960–61:** 114
　　Carlson, Theodore W., **1954:** 134
　　Cash, Elba H., **1959:** 236
　　Cochran, Carlos M., estate, **1954:** 230
　　D'Agostino, Mary, **1959:** 235
　　Denninger, Mary B., **1954:** 216
　　Harry, Ralston E., **1954:** 159
　　Hill, Raleigh, **1954:** 240
　　Hines, Fred P., **1953:** 139
　　Holder, Anna, **1954:** 42
　　Kaczmarczyk, Mrs. Rose, **1954:** 141
　　McQuilkin, Anna K., **1954:** 228
　　Morrison, Ethel H., **1953:** 162
　　St. Marie, Josette L., **1954:** 142
　　Spagnola, Rosaline, **1954:** 239
　　Webb, Mary Thaila W., **1953:** 163
　Erosion control, Madeira Beach, Fla., **1959:** 232
　Home mortgage funds, **1958:** 49
　Hospitals, elimination of racial discrimination, **1960–61:** 410
　Hospitals and domiciliaries, integration, **1954:** 309
　Interest rates on loans, **1957:** 16, 169
　Loan guaranty program, **1958:** 43
　Medical and Surgical Service, **1958:** 169
　News conference remarks on, **1953:** 22, 62
　Pay adjustments, **1955:** 8
　Regional office and hospital managers, remarks, **1960–61:** 318
　Reorganization, **1954:** 3, 14 (p. 132)
　Small business purchases, **1956:** 263
　U.S. Government life insurance, **1957:** 73
Veterans Affairs, Administrator of (H. V. Higley), **1953:** 269
　Chairman, Community Chest campaign, **1955:** 130
　Chairman, Veterans Day National Committee, letter, **1954:** 285
　Federal Council on Aging, **1956:** 74
　Integration in VA facilities, letter, **1954:** 309
Veterans Affairs, Administrator (Sumner G. Whittier), **1960–61:** 318
Veterans benefits, **1955:** 4, 51; **1956:** 2, 81n., 157, 267; **1957:** 86; **1960–61:** 318, 410
　Approval of bill, **1954:** 220
　Budget messages, **1954:** 14 (pp. 86, 130–135); **1955:** 17 (pp. 94–96, 102, 106, 132–140); **1956:** 12 (pp. 110–115); **1958:** 5 (pp. 24, 41, 51, 61–63); **1959:** 10 (pp. 105–107); **1960–61:** 13 (pp. 97–100), 414 (pp. 938, 1012–1016)

Veterans benefits — *continued*
  Budget messages — *continued*
    Tables, **1954:** 14 (pp. 131, 135); **1955:** 17 (pp.
      135, 140); **1958:** 5 (p. 62); **1959:** 10 (p.
      106); **1960–61:** 13 (p. 98), 414 (p. 1014)
    Duff, Harry N., **1958:** 248
    O'Brien, Peter J., **1958:** 251
  Compensation to Mr. and Mrs. Wright, approv-
    al, **1956:** 24
  Increase in service-connected disability compen-
    sation and dependency allowances, **1957:**
    163
  Loans, approval of bill, **1959:** 146
Veterans Day, persons receiving citizenship papers,
  remarks, **1954:** 326
Veterans Day National Committee, **1954:** 285
Veterans Federation, World, **1953:** 26
Veterans of Foreign Wars, **1953:** 13; **1955:** 169
  Norwalk, Conn., **1954:** 18
  Memorial Building, dedication, remarks, **1960–
    61:** 31
Veterans hospitals, **1956:** 21
  Budget message, **1956:** 12 (p. 114)
  Letter, **1956:** 267
  Segregation ban, **1956:** 224
Veterans housing, **1953:** 62; **1955:** 17 (pp. 136, 173,
  174); **1957:** 16; **1958:** 49, 62, 63; **1959:**
  146; **1960–61:** 13 (p. 74), 414 (pp. 981,
  982, 1014)
  Bill to extend direct loan program, **1957:** 172
  Budget messages, **1956:** 12 (pp. 112, 146, 147);
    1958: 5 (pp. 53, 59); **1959:** 10 (p. 85)
    Table, **1958:** 5 (p. 54)
  Housing Act of 1957, statement, **1957:** 129
  Letter to minority leaders, **1958:** 43
  Meeting on, **1956:** 318
  News conference remarks, **1959:** 26
Veterans pension bill, **1959:** 186
Veterans Pensions, Commission on, **1956:** 2, 267n.
  Budget messages, **1955:** 17 (p. 134); **1956:** 12 (p.
    111)
  Letter, **1955:** 51
Veto, President's use of, **1959:** 17, 132, 154, 161,
  167
Veto of items in legislation, **1958:** 5 (p. 73)
Veto Messages, **1957:** 45
  See also Memorandums of Disapproval.
  Alaskan oil and gas leases, **1959:** 182
  Alexander, J. Don, tax refund claim, **1953:** 107
  Alexander, Jake, conveyance of lands to, **1954:**
    156
  Apple price predictions, prohibition of Govern-
    ment publication, **1955:** 147
  Area redevelopment bill, **1958:** 258; **1960–61:**
    146
  Camp Blanding Military Reservation, Fla., con-
    veyance of lands within, **1954:** 121
  Crow Indian Tribe claim, **1956:** 124

Veto Messages — *continued*
  Coinage of 50-cent pieces for commemorative
    events
    Louisiana Purchase, sesquicentennial, **1954:** 29
    New York City, tercentennial, **1954:** 28
    Northampton, Mass, tercentennial, **1954:** 27
  Court of Claims jurisdiction in overtime com-
    pensation case, **1954:** 41
  District of Columbia, certain gasoline filling
    stations, **1953:** 149
  District of Columbia, regulation of election of
    delegates to national political conven-
    tions, **1954:** 206
  Farm bill, **1956:** 82
  Farm "freeze" bill, **1958:** 59
  Federal employees
    Defense of suits against operators of Gov-
      ernment motor vehicles, **1960–61:** 180
    Salary increase, **1960–61:** 217
  Federal National Mortgage Association, income
    tax treatment of nonrefundable capital
    contributions, **1960–61:** 151
  Federal Water Pollution Control Act, amend-
    ment, **1960–61:** 44
  Housing bills, **1959:** 153, 208
  Importation of seed wheat, **1958:** 217
  Income tax deductions for certain charitable
    contributions, **1960–61:** 169
  Independent Offices Appropriation Act, **1958:**
    192
  Military installations, housing, **1956:** 141
  Minerals program, **1958:** 206
  Natural Gas Act, amendment, **1956:** 41
  Nuclear-powered ice breaker, **1958:** 204
  Postal field service compensation bill, **1955:** 102
  Public Health Service Act, amendment, **1954:**
    137
  Public works appropriation bills, **1959:** 194, 213
  Relief of
    Axelroad, Colonel Benjamin, **1957:** 123
    Berry, Walter H., **1957:** 155
    Board of Commissioners, Sedgwick County,
      Kans., **1956:** 112
    Bond, Virginia, **1960–61:** 114
    Brennan, Mrs. John William, **1957:** 73
    Carlson, Theodore, W., **1954:** 134
    Compton, Mr. and Mrs. Thomas V., **1956:** 126
    Continental Hosiery Mills, Inc., **1958:** 187
    Cowan, Roy, and others, **1956:** 79
    Dew Hong-to, **1958:** 124
    Eber Brothers Wine and Liquor Corp., **1959:**
      215
    Engelbert, Wilhelm, **1954:** 58
    Glaser, Kurt, **1955:** 116
    Grand Lodge of North Dakota, **1960–61:** 181
    Gruhl, Helmuth W., **1953:** 108
    Hanzal, Alfred, **1958:** 34
    Harry, Ralston E., **1954:** 159

Veto Messages — *continued*
  Relief of — *continued*
    Haun, Cale P. and Julia Fay, **1958:** 48
    Hines, Fred P., **1953:** 139
    Holder, Anna, **1959:** 42
    Kaczmarczyk, Rose, **1954:** 141
    Kaiser, William J., **1960–61:** 113
    Kilpatrick, Shirley Leeke, **1958:** 61
    Klyce Motors, Inc., **1954:** 181
    Laney, D. S. and Elizabeth, **1958:** 205
    Nakamura, Harry H., **1959:** 155
    Our Lady of the Lake Church, **1960–61:** 179
    Roach, Lucian, **1958:** 212
    St. Marie, Josette L., **1954:** 142
    Spencer, Susie Lee, estate, **1956:** 134
    Thomson Contracting Co., Inc., **1958:** 208
    Universal Trades, Inc., **1960–61:** 150
    Weigand, Margareth, estate, **1954:** 59
  Rivers and harbors bill, **1958:** 73
  Rural Electrification Administration, loan approval authority, **1959:** 86
  Stone, William E., claim of, **1956:** 135
  Tobacco price support bill, **1959:** 140
  Unemployment tax credits of successor employers, **1960–61:** 170
  Wage rates, Portsmouth (N. H.) naval shipyard, **1958:** 191
  Wheat bill, **1959:** 139
Veto right in nuclear test inspection, Soviet proposal, **1959:** 42
Veto of specific items
  Proposed, **1959:** 6, 10 (p. 52), 300n.; **1960–61:** 13 (p. 107), 24, 414 (p. 1026)
  Question of, **1954:** 9, 57
Veto in U.N. Security Council, Soviet use, **1959:** 110n.
Vice President, **1957:** 62
  Additional, comment on, **1959:** 161
  Administrative, **1956:** 16
  Eligibility of President, comments on, **1960–61:** 7, 21
  Oath of office, **1958:** 42
  Official residence, **1957:** 13, 105
  Position in Government, **1959:** 167
  Republican nomination for, **1960–61:** 38
  Role, **1957:** 28
Vice President (Richard M. Nixon), **1953:** 6, 33, 54 ftn. (p. 205), 190n., 193; **1954:** 12n., 31, 106, 171n., 273, 286; **1955:** 4, 104, 217n., 230n., 236; **1956:** 128n., 190, 312n.; **1958:** 36, 80, 134n.; **1959:** 6, 31, 77, 82n., 100, 151n., 184n., 210; **1960–61:** 4, 23, 107, 132, 177, 208, 209, 407, 410
  See also Candidacy for second term.
  Acheson foreign policy, **1954:** 157
  Activities re price stability.
    See Committee on Price Stability for Economic Growth.

Vice President (Richard M. Nixon) — *continued*
  Administration decisions, participation in, **1960–61:** 268
  African visit, **1957:** 28, 43n., 50, 84 and n., 101 and n., 124
  Air carriers equipment investment program, letter, **1958:** 194
  Appointment of members of Hoover Commission, **1953:** 145n.
  Appraisal by the President, **1956:** 53, 56, 155, 190, 206, 241, 258
  Approach to national problems, **1960–61:** 38, 93, 103
  Assistance to Yugoslavia, letter, **1956:** 248
  Authority as acting President re nuclear bombs, **1959:** 154
  Bipartisan meetings
    Report on Hungarian refugees, **1956:** 318
    Suez problem, **1956:** 184
  Birthday greetings, **1958:** 2
  Birthday party, remarks, **1960–61:** 403
  Brazilian mission, **1956:** 20
  Broadcast for Radio Liberation, **1955:** 81
  Campaign contribution, letter, **1954:** 312
  Campaign remarks on, **1958:** 292, 294; **1960–61:** 290, 309, 344, 345, 346, 347, 348, 350, 353, 354, 355
  Candidacy for President, **1960–61:** 7, 24, 93, 103, 256, 263, 284, 290, 309, 337, 341, 344, 345, 346, 347, 348, 350, 353, 354, 355
    Post election telegram, **1960–61:** 357
    Television debates, **1960–61:** 268, 422
  Conference on Equal Job Opportunity, letter, **1955:** 225
  Congressional campaign, news conference remarks on, **1958:** 288
  Consultations with, **1960–61:** 256
  Corporate and excise taxes, letter, **1958:** 114
  Criticism of, **1955:** 10
  Death of father, **1956:** 199
  Debt limit increase, letter, **1958:** 183
  Defense reorganization, letter, **1958:** 75
  Disclosure of public sentiment on China policy, **1958:** 274
  Editor's note on President's illness, **1955:** p. 822
  European visit, **1958:** 103
  Farm program, **1960–61:** 34, 93
  Foreign policy, telegram, **1958:** 289
  Governmental position in Executive branch, **1958:** 63
  Governors Conference, Lake George, **1954:** 164; **1960–61:** 330
  Great Plains program, letter, **1956:** 7
  Honorary member of NAACP, **1956:** 216
  Hungarian refugees, report, **1957:** 2, 25
  Inauguration, **1957:** 15
  Inter-American highway, letter, **1955:** 64

Vice President (Richard M. Nixon) — *continued*
  Latin American visit, **1958:** 133n., 137, 197
    Anti-American demonstrations, **1958:** 101, 103
    Greeting on return, **1958:** 107
    Letters to, **1955:** 14, 64, 91, 225, 226; **1956:** 7, 13,
      29, 81, 131; **1957:** 112 and n., 135 and n.;
      1958: 75, 101, 114, 183, 194, 289; **1959:**
      47, 90, 136, 157, 170, 183
    Foreign economic policy, **1953:** 63
    Refugees, admission to United States, **1953:** 52
    Resolution on subjugated peoples, **1953:** 14
  Meeting with
    Congressional Medal of Honor holders, **1958:**
      122
    Governor Rockefeller, **1960–61:** 256
    Premier Khrushchev, **1959:** 218
    President Garcia, **1958:** 143
    President Lleras, **1960–61:** 111
    Prime Minister Macmillan, **1960–61:** 103
  Military assistance program, letters, **1959:** 90,
    136, 170, 183
  Military career incentives, letter, **1956:** 81
  News conference remarks on, **1953:** 198, 254,
    265; **1954:** 50, 57, 157, 200; **1955:** 10, 47,
    59, 81, 90, 112; **1956:** 20, 47, 53, 56, 88, 94,
    96, 155, 216, 229, 298; **1957:** 17, 28, 45, 50,
    56, 62, 105; **1958:** 42, 63, 88, 103, 274, 288,
    310; **1959:** 7, 17, 21, 36 and ftn. (p. 197),
    67, 89, 94, 132, 148, 154, 161, 167, 172,
    173, 179, 186, 271; **1960–61:** 7, 24, 34, 38,
    93, 103, 127, 143, 222, 256, 263, 268, 284,
    422
  Opening of U.S. exhibition in Moscow, **1959:** 80
  Pageant of Peace ceremony, **1957:** 248
  Philippines trade agreement revision, letter,
    1955: 91
  President Magsaysay Champion of Liberty
    Stamp ceremony, **1957:** 166n.
  Presidential inability, agreement on procedures,
    1958: 37, 40, 42
  Presidential office space, letter, **1956:** 131
  President's birthday celebration, **1957:** 214
  President's role in selection, **1955:** 112
  Question of summit conference attendance,
    1959: 89; **1960–61:** 127, 143
  Role, **1958:** 310
  "Salute to Eisenhower" dinner, **1956:** 18
  Steel strike settlement, role in, **1960–61:** 7
  Task of Secretary Dulles at foreign ministers
    conference, Geneva, letter, **1955:** 226
  Telecommunication system, letter, **1959:** 47
  Transportation survey of Washington area,
    letter, **1959:** 157
  Virgin Islands Corporation, letter, **1955:** 14
  Visits
    Asia, **1953:** 254, 265; **1954:** 57
    Latin America (1958), **1960–61:** 38

Vice President (Richard M. Nixon) — *continued*
  Visits — *continued*
    Soviet Union, **1959:** 17, 80, 132, 148, 161, 162,
      167, 172 and ftn. (p. 550), 173, 179, 214,
      271
  Water resources policy, letter, **1956:** 13
Vice Presidential nominees, comment on, **1955:** 112
Vicksburg National Military Park facility, **1958:**
  226
Victoria, Queen of England, **1958:** 209
Videla, Hernan, **1960–61:** 73n., 74n.
Vienna, **1955:** 98n., 114; **1957:** 25; **1959:** 121
  International Atomic Energy Agency confer-
    ence, **1957:** 204; **1960–61:** 301n.
  Meeting on Austrian treaty, **1955:** 81, 95
Vietnam, **1955:** 18, 81; **1956:** 117, 210; **1958:** 80,
    261, 274; **1960–61:** 183, 245
  See also Dien Bien Phu, battle of; Indochina;
    Indochina war.
  Anniversary of Republic, letter, **1956:** 271
  Assistance, **1954:** 306; **1955:** 17 (p. 129), 48;
    1957: 83, 90, 91, 136, 152; **1958:** 32, 36;
    1959: 10 (p. 69), 55, 71; **1960–61:** 36, 341
  Bao Dai, **1955:** 48
    Messages, **1954:** 83, 105
  Campaign remarks, **1958:** 290, 293, 302
  Diem, Ngo Dinh, **1955:** 48, 81; **1956:** 87, 271;
    1957: 81 and n., 82 and n., 83, 97 and n.
    Letter, **1954:** 306
    Message, **1960–61:** 338
  Fifth anniversary of independence, **1960–61:** 338
  Hanoi, **1960–61:** 338
  ICA program, evaluation, **1959:** 278
  Indochina war, U.S. assistance, **1953:** 66
  Joint statement with President Diem, **1957:** 83
  Joint statement with Western leaders, **1953:** 255
  Membership in defense alliance, question of,
    1954: 107
  News conference remarks, **1954:** 25, 101, 107,
    157, 168
  Partition, **1954:** 157
  Refugees, **1958:** 36
  Saigon, **1954:** 168, 306
  U.N. membership
    Proposed, **1956:** 143
    Soviet veto, **1958:** 8, 148
Vietnam, North, **1954:** 165; **1955:** 17 (p. 130); **1956:**
    87; **1959:** 71
  Communist military forces, **1957:** 83
  Joint statement with President Diem, **1957:** 83
  News conference remarks, **1958:** 198, 274
  Troop training by Communist China, **1958:** 274
Villegas Basavilbaso, Benjamin, **1960–61:** 60n.
Vimy ridge, France, **1959:** 7
Vinson, Repr. Carl, **1955:** 149
  Defense reorganization bill, **1958:** 178
  Letter to, **1958:** 108

Vinson, Fred M.
  See Chief Justice of the United States (Fred M.
    Vinson).
Violins and violas, imports, **1956:** 123
Virata, Enrique, **1960–61:** 186n.
Virgin Islands, St. Thomas, **1953:** 260; **1954:** 125,
    126
  Congressional representation, proposed, **1960–
    61:** 13 (p. 104), 133, 414 (p. 1021)
Virgin Islands Corporation, **1954:** 14 (p. 190)
  Property management, **1955:** 14
Virginia, **1959:** 75, 117n.
  Almond, Gov. J. Lindsay, Jr., **1958:** 198, 213,
    222; **1959:** 17
  Arlington, **1958:** 222; **1959:** 130n.; **1960–61:**
    138n.
  Battle, Gov. John Stewart, **1953:** 79
  Birthplace of President's mother, **1953:** 78, 79;
    1960–61: 340
  Broyhill, Repr. Joel T., **1954:** 313; **1958:** 198
  Byrd, Sen. Harry Flood, **1953:** 78; **1954:** 115;
    1955: 81, 90 ftn. (p. 471); **1956:** 280; **1957:**
    56, 80, 92; **1959:** 67, 138; **1960–61:** 340
  Candidates for public office, **1956:** 280
  Chantilly, **1958:** 9
  Drought, **1953:** 230
  Fort Myer, **1953:** 150
  Gubernatorial election, **1953:** 128, 225, 230
  Jamestown, **1957:** 118; **1959:** 259
  Mt. Sidney, **1960–61:** 340n.
  News conference remarks, **1956:** 53; **1958:** 103,
    198, 213, 222, 274
  Norfolk, **1957:** 50; **1959:** 17
  Old Rag Mountain, **1960–61:** 340
  Potomac River bridge construction, **1955:** 224
  Richmond, **1956:** 280
  Robertson, Sen. A. Willis, **1953:** 78; **1960–61:**
    340
  School integration, **1958:** 103, 198, 213, 274;
    1959: 26
    Court decisions, **1959:** 17
    Letter to J. Albert Rolston, **1958:** 267
  Stanley, Gov. Thomas B., **1957:** 118 and n.
  Staunton, **1960–61:** 340
  Stratford, **1958:** 93
  Williamsburg, **1953:** 78; **1957:** 115, 118, 119, 124,
    138; **1958:** 5 (p. 42), 106; **1960–61:** 115n.
Virginia Declaration, **1953:** 79
Virginia Military Institute, **1959:** 133
Visale, Antonio de, **1960–61:** 53n.
Visas, **1957:** 25
  Hungarian refugees, **1957:** 250
Vishinsky, Andrei Y., **1953:** 230
Visitors, foreign.
  See also specific heads of state or government.
  Adenauer, Konrad, **1954:** 311; **1960–61:** 91, 92,
    93

Visitors, foreign — *continued*
  Akihito, Crown Prince, **1960–61:** 140, 209, 308
  Albert, Prince, **1960–61:** 317
  Baudouin I, **1959:** 99, 100, 105
  Bayar, Celal, **1954:** 18, 19, 20, 23
  Bhumibol Adulyadej, **1960–61:** 209, 211, 212,
    213, 218
  Castillo Armas, Carlos, **1955:** 230
  Churchill, Winston, **1954:** 143, 157, 161, 164;
    1959: 93, 94, 96
  De Gaulle, Charles, **1960–61:** 120, 121, 124, 125,
    127
  Eden, Anthony, **1953:** 22; **1954:** 143, 157
  Educators, **1959:** 222
  Elizabeth, Queen Mother, **1954:** 39, 311, 322
  Eqbal, Manuchehr, **1959:** 251
  Frederik IX, **1960–61:** 209, 320, 321
  Frederika, Queen, **1953:** 230, 232, 233
  Frondizi, Arturo, **1959:** 13, 14, 16, 28
  Haile Selassie I, **1954:** 124, 129
  Hussein I, **1959:** 66
  Ingrid, Queen, **1960–61:** 209, 320, 321
  Khrushchev, Nikita S., **1959:** 21, 154, 161, 172,
    179, 186, 191, 196, 198n., 200, 202, 203,
    214, 217, 218, 219, 223, 242, 243, 248, 271
    Announcement of visit to U.S., **1959:** 173
  Kozlov, Frol R., **1959:** 132, 148, 154, 161, 162,
    167
  Lemus, Jose Maria, **1959:** 50, 52, 54
  Lleras Camargo, Alberto, **1960–61:** 108, 109, 110,
    111
  Lopez Mateos, Adolfo, **1959:** 243, 254, 255, 256,
    257
  Macmillan, Harold, **1959:** 67; **1960–61:** 103
  Magloire, Paul, **1955:** 23
  Mahendra Bir Bikram, **1960–61:** 128, 129
  Malayan Prime Minister, **1960–61:** 339
  Massey, Vincent, **1954:** 101
  Mayer, Rene, **1953:** 37
  Menderes, Adnan, **1954:** 129
  Mendes-France, Pierre, **1954:** 311
  Michiko, Crown Princess, **1960–61:** 140, 209, 308
  Mikoyan, Anastas I., **1959:** 7, 17, 21, 48
  News conference remarks, **1956:** 53, 56, 62;
    1957: 17, 22; **1958:** 318
  Newsmen, **1954:** 33, 157, 328
  Nu (U), **1955:** 148
  O'Kelly, Sean T., **1959:** 58, 59, 64
  Pahlavi, Mohammad Reza, **1954:** 353
  Paola, Princess, **1960–61:** 317
  Paul I, **1953:** 230, 232, 233
  Pibulsonggram, Field Marshal, **1955:** 87
  Ratna Rajya Lekshmi, **1960–61:** 128, 129
  Rhee, Syngman, **1954:** 165, 168, 171, 172, 174,
    178
  Ruiz Cortines, Adolfo, **1953:** 221
  St. Laurent, Louis S., **1953:** 208, 247
  Segni, Antonio, **1959:** 203, 243, 247, 248

Visitors, foreign — *continued*
  Sirikit, Queen, **1960–61:** 209, 211, 213, 218
  Soviet agriculturists, **1955:** 95
  Soviet leaders of thought, **1958:** 31, 36
  Toure, Sekou, **1959:** 269, 272
  Tubman, W.V.S., **1954:** 292
  Waiver of fingerprinting requirement, **1956:** 2, 33, 53
  Yoshida, Shigeru, **1954:** 311, 322, 328
  Zhukov, Marshal, question of visit, **1955:** 33, 47
Visits to foreign countries, **1960–61:** 245
  Africa, Asia, Europe (Dec. 1959), **1960–61:** 4, 7, 16, 21, 24, 38, 73, 93, 98, 121n., 127, 208, 209, 260n., 381
    Broadcast on departure, **1959:** 290
    Broadcast on return, **1960–61:** 209
    China, Republic of, **1960–61:** 177, 192, 193, 194, 195, 196, 209
    Japan, proposed.
      See Japan.
    Korea (1952), **1954:** 174n.
    Korea (1960), **1960–61:** 21 ftn. (p. 131), 93, 127, 143, 177, 198, 199, 200, 201, 202, 203, 204, 209, 250, 274
    News conference remarks, **1959:** 277, 288
    Objectives of trip, comment on, **1959:** 288
    Okinawa, **1960–61:** 177, 197, 209
    Philippines, **1960–61:** 177, 182, 183, 184, 185, 186, 187, 188, 189, 190, 209
    Remarks at Pageant of Peace, **1959:** 347
    Remarks on return, **1959:** 346
    White House statement, **1959:** 277 ftn. (p. 766)
  Canada, **1953:** 246, 247
    News conference remarks on, **1953:** 208, 243
  Great Britain, France, and Germany, **1959:** 196
    Broadcast on return, **1959:** 214
    France, **1960–61:** 147, 154, 155, 156, 162, 163
    Great Britain, **1957:** 228
    News conference remarks, **1959:** 173, 179, 186, 191
    Remarks on return, **1959:** 210
  Latin America, **1960–61:** 38, 86, 93, 98, 109n., 228
    Argentina, **1960–61:** 42, 56, 57, 58, 59, 60, 61, 62, 63, 64, 66, 67, 87
    Brazil, **1960–61:** 42, 45, 46, 48, 49, 50, 51, 52, 53, 54, 55, 87, 119
    Broadcast on departure, **1960–61:** 42
    Broadcast on return, **1960–61:** 87
    Chile, **1960–61:** 42, 69, 70, 71, 72, 73, 74, 75, 76, 77, 86, 87
    Uruguay, **1960–61:** 42, 78, 79, 80, 81, 82, 83, 84, 85, 87
  Mexico, **1959:** 36, 254; **1960–61:** 333, 334, 335
  Portugal, **1960–61:** 157, 158, 159, 160, 161, 162
  Soviet Union (1960), **1959:** 217n.; **1960–61:** 21 and ftn. (p. 131), 127, 143, 209
    Announcement, **1959:** 173

Visits to foreign countries — *continued*
  Soviet Union — *continued*
    Cancellation, **1960–61:** 163, 209
    Joint statement with General Franco, **1959:** 340
    Joint statement with King Mohammad Zahir on, **1959:** 308
    Joint statement with Premier Khrushchev on, **1959:** 242
    Joint statement with President Gronchi, **1959:** 293
    News conference remarks, **1959:** 173, 191, 223, 243, 267
Visits to small cities, news conference remarks on, **1958:** 74
Vistula River, **1957:** 124
VMI.
  See Virginia Military Institute.
Vocational education, **1954:** 14 (p. 153); **1956:** 222; **1957:** 207; **1959:** 10 (p. 98); **1960–61:** 13 (p. 89), 414 (p. 1015)
  Budget message, **1958:** 5 (pp. 43, 46)
  Federal-State Action Committee recommendations, **1958:** 106
  Rural development program, **1958:** 313
  Training program in farming areas, **1958:** 12
Vocational rehabilitation, **1954:** 3, 10, 11; **1955:** 25; **1956:** 19, 158; **1959:** 10 (pp. 46, 104); **1960–61:** 410
  Budget messages, **1954:** 14 (pp. 132, 142, 144); **1955:** 17 (pp. 94, 144); **1956:** 12 (p. 124); **1960–61:** 13 (pp. 96, 99)
  Disabled, **1954:** 14 (p. 142)
  Veterans, **1954:** 14 (p. 132); **1960–61:** 13 (p. 99)
Vocational Rehabilitation Amendments, approval, **1954:** 180
Vogel, Herbert D., **1955:** 146 ftn. (p. 646); **1957:** 62
  See also Tennessee Valley Authority, Chairman (Herbert D. Vogel).
Voice of America, **1954:** 47n.; **1959:** 10 (p. 75), 152n.; **1960–61:** 13 (p. 65), 414 (p. 969)
  Anniversary broadcast, **1957:** 37
  Congressional investigation, **1953:** 15, 22
Voluntary foreign aid for Hungarian refugees, **1957:** 250
Voluntary Home Mortgage Credit Committee, **1960–61:** 414 (p. 982)
Voluntary Home Mortgage Credit Program, continuance proposed, **1959:** 153
Voluntary organizations, refugees and escapee program, **1955:** 60, 76
Voluntary relief agencies, **1956:** 58
Von Braun, Wernher, **1958:** 28; **1960–61:** 287
  Award for Distinguished Federal Civilian Service, **1959:** 9n.
  News conference remarks on, **1959:** 267, 277
Von Brentano, Heinrich, **1956:** 20; **1959:** 192; **1960–61:** 92
Von Clausewitz, Karl, **1953:** 31

[*References are to items except as otherwise indicated*]

Von Fremd, Charles S., **1953:** 109; **1954:** 18, 25, 50, 73, 107, 129, 143, 157, 165, 200, 311, 328, 345; **1955:** 10, 33, 41, 47, 56, 59, 81, 90, 95, 112, 119, 146, 149, 185; **1956:** 32, 47, 53, 56, 62, 78, 88, 94, 96, 113, 155, 171, 193, 205, 229, 235, 298; **1957:** 17, 22, 28, 45, 62, 72, 80, 92, 105, 115, 124, 134, 150, 157, 169, 210, 228; **1958:** 213; **1959:** 89

Von Herberg, Mary Philomene, **1958:** 103, 120, 274, 318; **1959:** 21, 89

Von Karman, Theodore, letter, **1957:** 238

Von Neumann, John, **1956:** 40; **1959:** 107

Voorhees, Tracy, **1957:** 250; **1960–61:** 371
    Hungarian relief activities, **1956:** 307
    Report, **1960–61:** 431

Vorbeck, Frederic L., letter, **1954:** 30

Voroshilov, Kliment E.,
    Cablegram to, **1958:** 1
    Messages, **1955:** 233; **1959:** 1; **1960–61:** 2

Vorys, Repr. John M., bipartisan meeting on Suez Canal, **1956:** 184

Voss, Earl H., **1956:** 205; **1958:** 37; **1959:** 123, 132, 288; **1960–61:** 34, 93

Voting
    Campaign remarks, **1956:** 206, 212, 228, 278, 280, 290
    Importance of individual vote, **1954:** 317, 318, 320; **1960–61:** 310
    Standardization of laws, **1954:** 3

Voting, women, in previous election, **1956:** 268

Voting age, lowering of, **1956:** 225, 226, 235, 241, 268, 318
    Bipartisan meeting, **1956:** 318
    Proposed, **1954:** 3, 146, 349
        News conference remarks, **1954:** 107, 129, 168

Voting rights, **1957:** 8, 13; **1959:** 6, 27; **1960–61:** 4, 137, 410
    Absentee voting rights, **1955:** 29
    Alabama, **1958:** 318
    Armed forces, **1956:** 228
    Budget messages, **1960–61:** 13 (p. 105), 414 (p. 1021)
    Campaign remarks, **1958:** 295, 308
    District of Columbia, **1954:** 3, 349; **1955:** 4; **1956:** 2, 32, 318; **1957:** 13; **1959:** 36; **1960–61:** 24, 414 (p. 1021)
    Labor union members, **1956:** 198
    Lowering of age for Federal elections, **1957:** 13
    Negroes, **1956:** 2; **1958:** 102
    News conference remarks, **1957:** 134, 150, 157; **1959:** 7, 17, 36, 167; **1960–61:** 7, 24, 93
    Overseas personnel, **1955:** 4
    Statements on civil rights bill, **1957:** 133, 147

WAC.
    See Women's Army Corps.

Wachuku, Jaja, **1960–61:** 324n.

Waco, Texas, **1956:** 114

Wadsworth, James J., **1960–61:** 34
    Letter, **1958:** 39

Wage boards for Federal employees, **1958:** 169

Wage freeze, **1955:** 26

Wage-hour law
    Applicability in public works construction, **1956:** 2
    Minimum wage, extension, **1956:** 2, 3

Wage and price controls, **1953:** 6, 12 and ftn. (p. 46); **1954:** 21, 318; **1955:** 112; **1956:** 2; **1957:** 28, 119, 124; **1958:** 120, 308; **1959:** 21, 94, 124; **1960–61:** 346, 410
    See also Controls, government economic.

Wage-price spiral, **1959:** 6
    News conference remarks, **1959:** 67, 123

Wage reporting, **1957:** 13, 132
    Small business, **1956:** 263

Wages, **1954:** 308; **1955:** 4; **1956:** 196n.; **1960–61:** 17, 410
    See also Pay.
    Campaign remarks, **1954:** 318, 319; **1958:** 303, 308
    Economic report, **1958:** 16; **1959:** 15
    Federal blue collar employees, **1958:** 169
    Guaranteed annual wage, **1953:** 77; **1955:** 56, 112, 119
    Increase in, **1954:** 194; **1957:** 8, 28, 119, 124; **1958:** 103, 110, 120, 198, 310; **1959:** 15, 17, 42, 161; **1960–61:** 341
    Minimum, **1953:** 230, 265; **1954:** 25, 353; **1955:** 4, 19, 26, 81, 90, 112, 119, 149, 176; **1956:** 12 (p. 116), 229, 241; **1957:** 45; **1958:** 5 (p. 51); **1959:** 10 (p. 46), 17, 161; **1960–61:** 133, 255, 284, 414 (p. 1006)
        American Samoa, **1956:** 172
        Naval shipyard, Portsmouth, N. H., **1958:** 191; **1960–61:** 230
        News conference remarks, **1953:** 77, 230, 265; **1955:** 26, 56, 81, 90, 112, 119, 149, 176; **1956:** 224, 226, 229; **1958:** 120, 198, 310; **1959:** 17, 42, 67, 123, 161, 172
    Statement on, **1956:** 269
    Steel industry, **1959:** 42, 67, 172

Waging peace, **1955:** 146
    Cost of, statement, **1958:** 154

Wagner, Edward F., **1958:** 285n.

Wagner, Robert F., **1954:** 301; **1959:** 106; **1960–61:** 306

Wailes, Edward T., **1959:** 319n., 322

Wainwright, Repr. Stuyvesant, **1958:** 195
    Letter, **1958:** 162

Walker, Eric A., **1957:** 196 and n.

Walker, Ross V., **1956:** 234

Walker, William O., **1958:** 102

Wall Street Journal, **1958:** 42

Walla Walla, Wash., McNary Dam dedication, address, **1954:** 271

Wallis, W. Allen, **1959:** 144n.

Walmsley, Walter N., **1959:** 328n.
Walsh, Lt. Don, Legion of Merit, citation, **1960–61:** 25
Walsh, Edmund A., School of Foreign Service, dedication, remarks, **1958:** 286
Walter, Repr. Francis E., **1955:** 59, 62
Walter Reed Medical Center, **1955:** 108; **1957:** 50; **1958:** 274; **1959:** 35, 48, 114n., 262
Wan Waithayakon, Prince, **1958:** 148
War, **1954:** 72, 87, 111; **1958:** 7, 295
  See also Eisenhower, Dwight D., personal reminiscences; Indochina War; Korean War; World War I; World War II; World War III.
  Congressional power to declare, **1954:** 57, 92; **1959:** 48, 179
  Letter to Premier Khrushchev, **1958:** 177
  Letters to Premier Bulganin, **1958:** 7, 31
  News conference remarks, **1953:** 62, 208; **1954:** 57, 92, 168, 192, 311, 345, 347, 353; **1956:** 16, 32, 53, 78, 113, 216; **1958:** 120, 222
  Nuclear, **1953:** 50, 95, 114, 208, 256; **1955:** 33, 79, 175; **1958:** 32, 222; **1959:** 10 (p. 67), 55, 57, 70, 167, 223; **1960–61:** 4, 147, 163, 185, 193, 409
    Europe, **1959:** 53
  Presidential responsibility in case of attack, **1954:** 57
  Preventive war, **1959:** 48
    Comment on, **1954:** 192
  Small wars, comment on, **1954:** 353
War assets, **1957:** 145
  General Aniline and Film Corporation, **1957:** 72
War assets in United States
  German, **1954:** 50, 189, 251, 314
    Claim of Col. Harry F. Cunningham, **1953:** 168
  Japanese, **1954:** 330
  Subject of frieze in Capitol rotunda, **1954:** 106n.
War Assets Administration, **1954:** 181
War Between the States, **1954:** 22, 31; **1959:** 129, 255, 333; **1960–61:** 171n.
  Centennial
    Proclamation, **1960–61:** 370
    Statement, **1960–61:** 392
War claims, **1954:** 314
War Claims Commission, **1953:** 265
  Termination, **1954:** 94
War College, **1958:** 286
War criminals, Japanese, joint statement with Prime Minister Yoshida, **1954:** 330
War Damage Corporation, **1957:** 78
War Department, **1958:** 65
War and Peace in the Space Age: A New Approach (Gavin), **1958:** 222
War production administration, **1953:** 41
Warburton, Repr. Herbert B., **1954:** 320
Ward, J. Carlton, Jr., **1960–61:** 283

Wards Island, New York City, **1954:** 299
Waring, Fred, **1953:** 212
Warner, Emily Smith, **1954:** 301
Warning system for missile and aircraft detection, **1954:** 14 (p. 120); **1955:** 17 (p. 116); **1956:** 12 (p. 97); **1957:** 17, 230, 234; **1958:** 5 (pp. 19, 30), 163, 292; **1959:** 6, 57; **1960–61:** 245
  Ballistic Missile Early Warning System, **1960–61:** 414 (p. 953)
  Budget messages, **1959:** 10 (pp. 57, 60, 61); **1960–61:** 13 (pp. 54, 55), 414 (pp. 953, 954)
  News conference remarks, **1959:** 26
  Project Defender, **1960–61:** 414 (pp. 953, 954)
Warren, Earl, **1953:** 109 ftn. (p. 439); **1958:** 288
  See also Chief Justice of the United States (Earl Warren).
  Candidate for Presidency, news conference remarks on, **1956:** 20, 32
  Designation as Chief Justice of the United States, **1953:** 198
Warren, Mrs. Earl, **1956:** 87; **1959:** 255
Warren, Fletcher, **1959:** 295n., 297
Warren, Lindsay C.
  See Comptroller General of the United States (Lindsay C. Warren).
Warren, Lucian C., **1953:** 31, 54; **1954:** 9, 138; **1955:** 95
Warren, Matthew, **1955:** 56, 95; **1956:** 96; **1957:** 62
Warren, Shields, **1955:** 191n.
Warrior River, barge service, **1954:** 14 (p. 175)
Warsaw, Poland, U. S.-Communist China talks on Formosa area, **1958:** 257, 261, 263
Warsaw Pact, letter to Premier Bulganin, **1958:** 7
Warsaw Treaty of 1955, **1957:** 6
Washburn, Abbott, **1953:** 2n.
Washington, Booker T., **1956:** 283
Washington, George, **1953:** 11, 240, 271; **1954:** 32, 54, 72, 86, 88, 113n., 301; **1955:** 40; **1956:** 12 (p. 78), 107, 280; **1957:** 87, 115, 150; **1958:** 269; **1959:** 31, 107, 151; **1960–61:** 80, 246
  Defense posture, **1955:** 56
  News conference remarks on, **1953:** 31, 41; **1954:** 33, 50
  Quoted, **1958:** 163, 285
Washington, **1953:** 150
  Anderson, Lt. Gov. Emmett T., **1956:** 251, 253
  Candidates for public office, **1956:** 251, 253
  Claim by State of, disapproval, **1957:** 171
  Forest areas, construction of access roads to, **1954:** 14 (p. 170)
  Fort Lewis, **1956:** 253
  Holmes, Repr. Hal, **1954:** 271
  Langlie, Gov. Arthur B., **1953:** 156; **1954:** 271; **1956:** 31, 189, 251, 253
  Richland, **1954:** 14 (p. 130); **1955:** 17 (p. 121)

Washington — *continued*
Rosellini, Gov. Albert D., **1958:** 312
Seattle, **1953:** 156; **1954:** 130; **1956:** 251; **1957:** 118; **1958:** 312
Tacoma, **1956:** 253
Walla Walla, **1954:** 271
Washington, D.C.
See District of Columbia.
Washington Board of Trade, stadium project, **1956:** 121
Washington College, **1954:** 136
Washington Hebrew Congregation Temple, dedicatory remarks, **1955:** 92
Washington International Center, **1959:** 222n.
Washington National Airport, **1955:** 17 (p. 170); **1960–61:** 414 (p. 974)
Washington Real Estate Board, **1956:** 4n.
Washita River Basin reclamation project, Oklahoma, **1956:** 44
Waste treatment facilities, **1958:** 5 (pp. 43, 46, 47), 106; **1959:** 181; **1960–61:** 13 (pp. 87, 94), 414 (p. 1008)
Budget message, **1959:** 10 (pp. 45, 98, 102)
Watches, tariffs on, **1954:** 217
Swiss, **1954:** 172
Water, saline, **1957:** 11
Water conservation, **1955:** 17 (pp. 154, 155); **1957:** 11; **1958:** 5 (p. 66); **1959:** 10 (pp. 91, 92)
Water conversion, **1960–61:** 402, 410
Budget messages, **1960–61:** 13 (pp. 84, 85), 414 (p. 995)
Research on, **1959:** 10 (p. 94)
Water diversion, Lake Michigan, **1954:** 253
Water Facilities Act, amendment, **1954:** 221
Approval of bill, **1954:** 201
Water fluoridation, **1957:** 45
Water pollution, **1955:** 25; **1956:** 12 (p. 119); **1957:** 70, 207; **1958:** 106, 294; **1959:** 181; **1960–61:** 410, 413
Budget messages, **1960–61:** 13 (p. 94), 414 (pp. 996, 1008)
Conference proposed, **1960–61:** 44
Potomac River, **1959:** 197
Water Pollution Control Act Amendments, **1956:** 137
Veto, **1960–61:** 44
Water resources, **1956:** 2, 6, 44, 136, 170, 205, 245, 251, 256; **1957:** 8, 11, 13, 16, 75
Budget message, **1956:** 12 (pp. 125, 131–138)
Disapproval of certain projects, memorandum, **1956:** 180
Meeting on, **1956:** 318
Projects, **1956:** 2, 47, 251, 256
Water Resources Board, **1954:** 172
Water resources development, **1953:** 153, 234, 268; **1954:** 53, 120, 139, 201, 221, 249, 258, 271, 291, 308; **1955:** 4, 19, 247; **1958:** 49, 85, 110; **1959:** 6, 194; **1960–61:** 36, 402, 410

Water resources development — *continued*
Amistad Dam, Rio Grande, **1960–61:** 13 (p. 83), 303, 334, 335, 414 (p. 995)
Budget messages, **1954:** 14 (pp. 161–163, 166–169); **1955:** 17 (pp. 158–162); **1958:** 5 (p. 68); **1959:** 10 (pp. 38, 45, 94, 95); **1960–61:** 13 (pp. 38, 82–85), 414 (pp. 993–996)
Colorado River project, **1954:** 62, 101, 172
Columbia River, **1960–61:** 331, 410, 414 (p. 994), 416, 419
Indus River, **1959:** 288; **1960–61:** 36, 284, 297
India Pakistan Pact, statement, **1960–61:** 297
Jordan River, **1953:** 217, 230
Letter to minority leaders, **1958:** 43
Letter to Secretary McKay, **1954:** 122
Loans to farmers for, **1954:** 14 (p. 161)
Local responsibility for, **1958:** 155
Middle East, **1954:** 68
Near East, **1958:** 207
News conference remarks, **1954:** 68, 101, 157, 172, 341; **1955:** 56
Palestine, **1955:** 76
Policies on, **1954:** 122
Public Works Appropriation Act, **1958:** 244
Rivers and harbors bill, veto, **1958:** 73
Santa Margarita River, **1954:** 173
Water Resources Policy, Advisory Committee on, **1954:** 120, 122; **1956:** 170
Budget message, **1956:** 12 (p. 133)
News conference remarks, **1956:** 16
Report, message, **1956:** 13
Water shortages, **1957:** 16
Water Supply Act, approval, **1958:** 155
Water supply projects, **1954:** 3
Water transportation, **1956:** 12 (pp. 141–143); **1958:** 5 (pp. 54, 59); **1959:** 10 (pp. 79, 80); **1960–61:** 13 (pp. 69, 70), 414 (pp. 975, 976)
Water treaty, U.S.-Mexico, **1960–61:** 335
Water use, **1957:** 8, 11
Cabinet Committee report, **1957:** 8
Waterman, Alan T., **1957:** 134, 210; **1958:** 47; **1959:** 267
Federal Council on Aging, **1956:** 74
Waters, U.S.-Canadian, **1958:** 153
Watershed protection
Approval, **1956:** 170
Budget message, **1956:** 12 (p. 131)
Letter to minority leaders, **1958:** 43
Watershed protection programs, **1960–61:** 13 (p. 82), 410, 414 (pp. 991, 992, 996)
Watershed Protection and Flood Prevention Act, **1954:** 201, 221
Waterways, **1956:** 12 (p. 139)
Waterways Corporation, Inland, **1954:** 14 (p. 175)
Watkins, Sen. Arthur, **1954:** 347; **1956:** 213, 245n.; **1958:** 83; **1959:** 21
Watkins, Franklin C., **1959:** 148 ftn. (p. 490)

Watson, Thomas J., **1953:** 191
Watson, Thomas J., Jr., letter, **1956:** 310
Waugh, Samuel C., **1957:** 117; **1959:** 33
  Letter, **1954:** 324
Waverly, Ohio, **1957:** 88
Way, Chester M., **1958:** 88
Wayne, John, **1959:** 127
Wayne (Anthony) Library of American Study,
  Defiance College, cornerstone laying
  ceremony, remarks, **1953:** 215
Weapons, **1953:** 50, 61; **1956:** 12 (pp. 93, 96, 97);
  1957: 8, 13, 28, 72, 86, 87, 117, 119, 137,
  169, 210, 230, 234; **1958:** 36, 80, 295, 316;
  1960–61: 135, 143
  See also Armistice Day; Bombs; Disarmament;
    Missiles; Nuclear tests; Nuclear weapons.
  Advances in, **1956:** 58, 88, 113, 155
  Anti-submarine, **1958:** 2
  Budget message, **1958:** 5 (pp. 18, 20, 21, 30)
  Development of, **1956:** 2, 3
  Letter to Premier Bulganin, **1958:** 7
  Military assistance program, **1959:** 55
  New, **1954:** 9, 14 (p. 117), 297; **1955:** 3, 4, 81,
    149; **1958:** 2, 5 (pp. 18, 26, 80); **1959:** 6, 10
    (pp. 38, 55), 11, 55, 57, 286; **1960–61:** 13
    (pp. 47, 51, 52, 56, 58), 341, 414 (pp. 948,
    955, 958, 959)
  News conference remarks, **1954:** 9, 57; **1956:** 88,
    94, 171, 298; **1959:** 154
  Scientific progress in, **1954:** 57
Weapons systems, **1960–61:** 255
Weather Bureau, **1955:** 17 (p. 183); **1956:** 12 (p.
  152); **1957:** 92; **1960–61:** 13 (p. 104), 414
  (p. 1021)
Weather forecasting, **1960–61:** 13 (p. 104)
Weather research, **1956:** 12 (p. 152); **1957:** 11, 92
Weather satellites, **1960–61:** 143, 264, 410, 424
  Budget message, **1960–61:** 414 (pp. 970, 972,
    1021)
  Tiros I launching, statement, **1960–61:** 104
Weather services, **1958:** 5 (p. 72)
Weather-station network, Department of Defense,
  1955: 17 (p. 169)
Weather stations, ocean, **1954:** 14 (p. 175)
Weaver, Patricia, **1955:** 237
Weaver, Mr. and Mrs. William G., **1955:** 237
Webb, James E., **1959:** 89
Webb, Mary Thaila W., relief of, disapproval,
  1953: 163
Webster, Daniel, **1954:** 106; **1959:** 151
Weeks, Sinclair.
  See Commerce, Secretary of (Sinclair Weeks).
Weigand, Margareth, estate, relief of, veto, **1954:**
  59
Weigle, Richard, **1959:** 116
Weis, Judy, **1953:** 68, 69
Weisbaden, Germany, **1960–61:** 91n.
Welch, Frank J., **1956:** 187n.; **1959:** 29

Welfare and pension plans and funds, labor un-
  ions, **1954:** 5, 9
  Disclosure of, **1958:** 20, 83, 216, 242, 294; **1959:**
    10 (pp. 46, 101)
Welfare and Pension Plan Disclosure Act
  Amendments proposed, **1960–61:** 13 (p. 93), 414
    (p. 1006)
  Approval, **1958:** 235
Welfare and pension funds, private, **1957:** 17, 56,
  207
Welfare and pension plans, registration, **1957:** 13,
  16, 77
Welfare programs, **1955:** 17 (pp. 94, 140–148);
  1956: 2, 12 (p. 118); **1960–61:** 13 (pp. 87,
    89–96), 414 (pp. 999, 1001–1003, 1006–
    1012)
  Budget message, **1958:** 5 (pp. 24, 46–53)
  Tables, **1954:** 14 (pp. 141, 145); **1955:** 17 (p.
    142); **1958:** 5 (p. 47); **1960–61:** 13 (p. 88),
    414 (pp. 1000, 1001)
Welfare services, **1954:** 14 (pp. 142, 143)
Wellington, Duke of, **1959:** 100
Welsh, J. Leroy, **1956:** 187n.
Wenzell, Adolphe H., **1955:** 146 and ftn. (pp. 657,
  658), 149, 176
Wesley, John, **1954:** 204
West, Ernest E., Medal of Honor, citation, **1954:** 8
West Point.
  See U.S. Military Academy.
West Point Plebe (Reeder), **1955:** 117
West Virginia
  Bailey, Repr. Cleveland M., **1957:** 150, 228
  Candidates for public office, **1958:** 302
  Charleston, **1958:** 302
  Depressed areas, Federal aid, **1960–61:** 127 and
    ftn. (p. 362), 176
  Elkins, **1956:** 163
  Hoblitzell, Sen. John D., Jr., **1958:** 302
  Mollohan, Repr. Robert H., **1956:** 229, 235
  Moore, Repr. Arch A., Jr., **1958:** 302
  Motto, "mountaineers are always free men,"
    1958: 302
  Neal, Repr. Will E., **1958:** 302
  Neely, Sen. Matthew M., **1955:** 81, 185
  Primary election, **1960–61:** 143
  Revercomb, Sen. Chapman, **1958:** 302
  Underwood, Gov. Cecil H., **1958:** 302; **1960–61:**
    176
  White Sulphur Springs, **1956:** 53, 62, 70, 71
Westchester County, N.Y., campaign remarks,
  1960–61: 346
Western Association of State Highway Officials,
  1959: 149
Western European Union
  Accession of Germany, **1956:** 2
  Joint statement with Prime Minister Scelba,
    1955: 61

Western European Union — *continued*
  Message to Prime Ministers of member nations,
    1955: 54
  News conference remarks, **1955:** 100
Western Powers disarmament proposal, **1957:** 158,
    165, 208 and n., 210, 226, 244
Western summit conference.
  See Heads of state and governments, meetings.
Wetbacks, **1957:** 70
Wexford, Ireland, **1956:** 208
Weyel, Merle C., relief of, disapproval, **1954:** 241
Weyland, Gen. Otto P., **1953:** 159; **1958:** 310
Wheat, **1954:** 192; **1956:** 6; **1958:** 60
  Acreage allotments and marketing quotas, **1954:**
    4, 24; **1958:** 12; **1959:** 108, 139; **1960–61:**
    32
  Acreage reserves (1957), **1958:** 12
  Address to Canadian Parliament, **1958:** 163
  Distribution pool, **1953:** 12
  Durum, additional acreage allotments, **1957:** 59
  Exports, **1953:** 12, 95, 101; **1954:** 4, 14 (p. 160);
    1955: 6, 17 (p. 152); **1958:** 58, 59; **1960–
    61:** 132
  International Wheat Agreement, **1953:** 101;
    1954: 4, 14 (p. 160); **1959:** 10 (p. 91);
    1960–61: 13 (p. 77)
    Budget message, **1956:** 12 (p. 129)
    Renewal, **1956:** 6
  News conference remarks, **1959:** 102, 132, 167,
    179; **1960–61:** 127, 222, 250
  Pakistan drought relief, **1953:** 95, 159
    Approval of bill, **1953:** 119
    Message to Congress, **1953:** 97
    Message to Prime Minister Mohammed Ali,
      1953: 124
  Price supports, **1954:** 4; **1956:** 12 (p. 128), 56, 82,
    83, 88; **1959:** 23; **1960–61:** 13 (p. 77), 32,
    127, 414, (p. 987)
  Shipment to Soviet Union, comment on pro-
    posal, **1955:** 41
  Surpluses, **1953:** 12; 4 4; **1955:** 41; **1958:** 153,
    163; **1959:** 102, 104, 108, 122, 132, 139;
    1960–61: 13 (p. 77), 32, 133, 246, 279, 410,
    414 (pp. 987, 988)
  Treated seed wheat imports, **1958:** 217
  Two-price plan, **1954:** 196; **1956:** 56
  U.S.-Canadian discussions, **1958:** 153
  Wheat bill, **1959:** 132; **1960–61:** 222, 256
    Veto, **1959:** 139
  Wheat growers referendum, **1959:** 167
  Wheat program, **1960–61:** 133, 255
    Statement, **1959:** 122
Wheaton, Anne, **1957:** 63
Wheeler, Mary, **1956:** 292
Wheeler Dam, **1960–61:** 13 (p. 84)
Wheeling Steel Corporation, **1959:** 211n.
Whitaker, D. A., and others, pay claims, **1958:** 255
White, Charles M., **1959:** 211n.

White, Francis, **1955:** 229
White, Gordon E., **1958:** 141; **1959:** 21, 48, 161
White, Harry Dexter, **1954:** 33
  Case, comments on, **1953:** 243, 249
White, Dr. Paul Dudley, **1956:** 5, 96
White, Gen. Thomas D. (Chief of Staff, Air Force),
    1960–61: 7, 261n.
White, W. Wilson, nomination as Assistant Attor-
    ney General, **1958:** 103
White, Walter, **1956:** 216
White, Gen. Will W., **1955:** 176, 185
White, William Allen, **1959:** 258
White, William R., **1956:** 114
White, William S., **1954:** 192; **1955:** 56, 176; **1956:**
    16, 47; **1957:** 56, 72, 115, 134, 157; **1958:**
    42
White Citizens Councils, **1956:** 113
White Company (Doyle), **1954:** 192
White House, significance, **1957:** 105
White House Conference on Aging (1961), **1959:**
    49, 280
  Budget messages, **1959:** 10 (p. 104); **1960–61:** 13
    (p. 96), 414 (p. 1012)
  Remarks, **1960–61:** 398
White House Conference on Children and Youth
    (1960), **1959:** 10 (p. 104); **1960–61:** 103
  Address, **1960–61:** 100
  Budget messages, **1960–61:** 13 (p. 96), 414 (p.
    1012)
  Letter, **1958:** 119
  National Committee for, remarks, **1958:** 320
White House Conference on Civil Rights, comment
    on, **1958:** 310
White House Conference on Education, (1955),
    1954: 273; **1955:** 31, 96; **1956:** 2, 8, 103,
    222, 234, 253, 277; **1957:** 68
  Budget messages, **1954:** 14 (pp. 152, 153); **1955:**
    17 (pp. 141, 147)
  Letter to Governors, **1954:** 268
  News conference remarks, **1955:** 18, 33, 95
  Remarks, **1955:** 242
White House Conference of Governors, remarks,
    1953: 64, 67
White House Conference on Highway Safety,
    1956: 36, 37
  Remarks, **1954:** 37
White House Conference of Mayors, remarks,
    1953: 262
White House Conference on Refugees, statement,
    1959: 115
White House Office, **1955:** 41
  Adams, Sherman, **1953:** 37; **1954:** 50, 57, 143,
    192, 311; **1955:** 119, 146; **1958:** 28, 37,
    141, 153, 166, 198, 266
  Anderson, Dillon, **1955:** 146 ftn. (p. 644)
  Appointment of woman, question of, **1954:** 33
  Aurand, Capt. E. P., **1960–61:** 142n.
  Beach, Comdr. Edward L., **1953:** 229n., 254 ftn.
    (p. 800); **1955:** 183

White House Office — *continued*
  Bragdon, Maj. Gen. John S., **1955:** 203; **1959:** 42, 227
  Burns, Arthur F., **1954:** 107, 129
  Cutler, Robert, **1953:** 2n., 33, 266; **1958:** 95
  Disclosure of information by Presidential aides, **1955:** 62
  Dodge, Joseph M., **1954:** 348; **1955:** 74
  Draper, William H., Jr.
    See main heading, Draper, William H., Jr.
  Francis, Clarence, **1954:** 262, 263n.
  Goodpaster, Brig. Gen. Andrew J., **1959:** 145; **1960–61:** 425, 426, 427, 428, 429, 430
  Gray, Gordon, **1956:** 147; **1959:** 76; **1960–61:** 8, 9, 94, 412, 427
  Hagerty, James C.
    See main heading, Hagerty, James C.
  Harr, Karl G., Jr., **1960–61:** 9
  Hopkins, William J., **1960–61:** 68n.
  Jackson, Charles D., **1953:** 2n., 33, 126, 254 ftn. (p. 800); **1954:** 68
  Kestnbaum, Meyer, **1960–61:** 208, 372
  Killian, James R., Jr., **1958:** 28, 56, 57, 64, 70, 74, 141; **1959:** 107, 267
  Kistiakowsky, George B., **1959:** 132 ftn. (p. 463); **1960–61:** 143, 363n., 400, 429
  Lyons, Eugene L., **1960–61:** 26, 27, 28
  Martin, I. Jack, **1955:** 181
  Morgan, Gerald D., **1955:** 56, 181; **1959:** 115, 161; **1960–61:** 380n., 417
  Paarlberg, Don, **1959:** 161
  Persons, Maj. Gen. Wilton B., **1958:** 274; **1960–61:** 369
  Quesada, E. R., **1958:** 9, 135, 194; **1959:** 74
  Rabb, Maxwell M., **1955:** 181
  Rockefeller, Nelson, **1954:** 354
  Shanley, Bernard M., **1953:** 268; **1954:** 129
  Snyder, Maj. Gen. Howard McC., **1953:** 254 ftn. (p. 800)
  Snyder, Murray, **1954:** 101
    Editor's note, **1955:** p. 822
  Staff organization, **1958:** 63, 274, 310
  Stassen, Harold E., **1955:** 62, 146
  Stephens, Thomas E., **1953:** 254 ftn. (p. 800)
  Strauss, Lewis L., **1958:** 166
  Willis, Charles F., **1954:** 311
White House office space, **1954:** 136; **1956:** 16, 131; **1957:** 45, 105, 135; **1960–61:** 133, 243, 414, (pp. 1017–1019)
White House Police force, increase in benefits, disapproval, **1959:** 239
White House releases, partial list, **1953:** Appendix A, p. 863; **1954:** Appendix A, p. 1119; **1955:** Appendix A, p. 863; **1956:** Appendix A, p. 1133; **1957:** Appendix A, p. 855; **1958:** Appendix A, p. 871; **1959:** Appendix A, p. 887; **1960–61:** Appendix A, p. 1067

White House tree-planting, honoring Theodore Roosevelt, **1958:** 100
White Paper on Egypt, **1957:** 157
White River, **1954:** 50
White Sulphur Springs, W. Va., **1956:** 62, 70, 71
  Meeting with President of Mexico and Premier of Canada, **1956:** 53
Whitehead, Don, **1956:** 189, 193; **1957:** 45
Whitfield, Allen, nominee for AEC, **1955:** 62, 119
Whitman, Walt, **1959:** 59n.
Whitney Museum of American Art, **1959:** 148 ftn. (p. 490)
"Whitten Amendment," repeal proposed, **1954:** 43
Whittier, Summer, **1956:** 292
  Administrator of Veterans Affairs, **1960–61:** 318
WHO.
  See World Health Organization.
Wichita conference on drought, etc., **1957:** 11, 12, 17, 41n.
Wickard, Claude, **1956:** 171
Wicker, Tom, **1957:** 157
Widows, social security benefits, **1956:** 158
Wiggins, Pat, **1957:** 145
Wildlife resources, **1953:** 153; **1954:** 3; **1955:** 4; **1956:** 2, 256; **1958:** 5 (p. 69); **1959:** 10 (p. 95); **1960–61:** 402, 410
  Approval of act, **1956:** 173
  Budget messages, **1954:** 14 (pp. 87, 164); **1956:** 12 (pp. 133, 137); **1960–61:** 13 (p. 86), 414 (pp. 998, 999)
  Effect of Colorado River Basin project, **1956:** 47
Wildlife Range, Arctic, establishment proposed, **1960–61:** 133
Wiley, Sen. Alexander, **1953:** 54, 142, 268, 269; **1954:** 33, 110n.; **1956:** 121; **1957:** 105, 145, 169
  Bipartisan meeting on Suez Canal, **1956:** 184
  Letters, **1953:** 56, 111
Wilhelm II, **1958:** 70; **1959:** 75
Wilkins, J. Ernest,
  Death of, statement, **1959:** 12
  Rumor of resignation, **1958:** 213
Wilkins, Roy, **1959:** 167
Wilkinson, Charles B. (Bud), **1957:** 234
Wilkinson, Henry C., **1960–61:** 239
Willard, Ohio, remarks, **1953:** 214
William and Mary College, inauguration of 22d president, address, **1953:** 79
Williams, Alfred H., **1960–61:** 344n.
Williams, Mrs. Clare, **1958:** 287; **1959:** 75; **1960–61:** 107n., 395
Williams, Gov. G. Mennen, **1954:** 347; **1957:** 80; **1960–61:** 328
Williams, John H., **1953:** 22
Williams, Sen. John J., **1954:** 320; **1957:** 92
  News conference remarks on, **1954:** 92, 192, 353
Williams, Mr. and Mrs. Nathan B., **1953:** 212

Williams, Walter, Under Secretary of Commerce, **1956:** 217n.
  Death of, statement, **1959:** 333
  Visit to Japan, **1958:** 70
Williams College, **1956:** 265n.
Williamsburg, Va., **1957:** 118, 138; **1960–61:** 115n.
  Governors' Conference (1957), **1958:** 5 (p. 42), 106
  House of Burgesses, remarks, **1953:** 78
Williamsburg, U.S.S. **1953:** 118
Willis, Charles F., **1954:** 311
Willkie, Mrs. Wendell L., **1954:** 78
Wilmington, Del., campaign remarks, **1954:** 320
Wilson, Benjamin F., Medal of Honor, citation, **1954:** 79
Wilson, Repr. Bob, **1960–61:** 333
Wilson, Charles E., **1959:** 21
  See also Defense, Secretary of (Charles E. Wilson).
Wilson, Mrs. Charles E., **1957:** 28
Wilson, George C., **1959:** 123
Wilson, John H., **1956:** 51
Wilson, Kenneth L., **1954:** 287
Wilson, Malcolm, **1959:** 106
Wilson, Richard L., **1953:** 12, 22, 31, 41, 54, 62, 88, 141, 208, 225, 238, 249; **1954:** 18, 50, 57, 92, 129, 157, 168, 172, 200, 347; **1955:** 10, 26, 56, 59, 62, 95, 119, 185; **1956:** 47, 56, 78, 113, 155, 205; **1957:** 17, 22, 72, 80, 105, 134; **1958:** 11, 56, 70, 74, 120, 141, 153, 213, 222, 274; **1959:** 17, 26, 36, 48, 89, 148, 167, 271; **1960–61:** 38, 103, 422
Wilson, Samuel S., **1955:** 90
Wilson, Woodrow, **1953:** 77, 88; **1954:** 86, 89, 204; **1955:** 84, 210; **1956:** 280; **1957:** 198; **1959:** 212; **1960–61:** 310
  Ceremonies honoring memory of, address, **1960–61:** 340
  News conference remarks on, **1954:** 322, 345
  Use of veto, **1959:** 167
Wilson (Woodrow) Birthplace Foundation, **1960–61:** 340
Wilson Dam Lock, **1956:** 12 (p. 137)
Winant, John, **1955:** 59
Wind-erosion,
  Conservation measures, **1957:** 11, 12
  Expenditures for, **1956:** 236
Wire tapping, **1954:** 139
Wirth, Conrad L., **1956:** 29
Wisconsin
  Candidates for public office, **1957:** 150, 169
  Congressional election, **1953:** 225, 238; **1958:** 223
  Davis, Repr. Glenn R., **1955:** 56
  Great Lakes water level discussion, **1956:** 177
  Johnson, Repr. Lester R., **1960–61:** 330
  Kastenmeier, Repr. Robert W., **1960–61:** 7
  Kohler, Gov. Walter J., **1953:** 15; **1954:** 165; **1957:** 150

Wisconsin — *continued*
  Madison, **1959:** 89
  McCarthy, Sen. Joseph R., **1953:** 15, 22, 31, 37, 41, 109, 141, 269; **1954:** 33, 48, 50, 63, 73, 92, 107, 115, 129, 182, 345, 347; **1956:** 216, 235; **1957:** 50
  Menominee Indian Tribe, **1954:** 147
  Milwaukee, **1956:** 129
  Nash, Lt. Gov. Philleo, **1960–61:** 330
  O'Konski, Repr. Alvin E., **1953:** 225
  Primary election, **1956:** 47, 78, 121
  Proxmire, Gov. William, **1957:** 150
  Ripon, **1953:** 187
  Zablocki, Repr. Clement J., **1953:** 235
  Wiley, Sen. Alexander, **1953:** 54, 56, 111, 142, 268, 269; **1954:** 33, 110n.; **1956:** 121, 184; **1957:** 105, 145, 169
Wisdom, John, **1953:** 220
Witcover, Jules J., **1959:** 89
Witnesses, immunity from self-incrimination, **1953:** 249; **1954:** 139
Witt, Richard C., **1956:** 234
Witwer, Samuel W., **1960–61:** 246
Wolcott, Repr. Jesse P., **1953:** 266; **1954:** 68
Wolfe, James, **1959:** 141n.
Wolff, George R., **1954:** 129
Wolfson, Norman, **1955:** 181
Woll, J. Albert, **1953:** 59
Woll, Matthew, **1956:** 119
Women
  Drafting of, comment on, **1954:** 107
  Employed, **1958:** 320
  Equal pay for equal work, **1956:** 2, 190, 253, 272
  Equal rights for, **1957:** 13, 150
  Executive positions, comment on, **1955:** 100
  Invitations to White House meetings, question of, **1953:** 238
  Politics, **1957:** 63
    Comment on, **1960–61:** 107
  Public life, **1959:** 55
  Role in civil defense, **1954:** 310
  Social security benefits, **1956:** 158
  Suffrage amendment, 40th anniversary, statement, **1960–61:** 269
  Votes, percentage, **1956:** 268
  White House staff, question of, **1954:** 33
  Woman as President, question of, **1954:** 9
"Women Ask the President," broadcast, **1956:** 268
Women in the Services, Defense Advisory Committee on, remarks, **1954:** 97
Women Voters, League of, recorded interview, **1954:** 91
Women's Advisory Committee on Civil Defense, National, remarks, **1954:** 310
Women's Army Corps, World War II, **1955:** 100, 152, 153
Wood, Lt. Gov. Lloyd H., **1954:** 304
Wood, Gen. Robert E., **1954:** 12n.
Woodall, Lt. Gen. Sir John, **1957:** 53n.

Woodring, Harry O., **1954:** 182
Woods, Nathaniel H., estate, tax refund claim, disapproval, **1959:** 233
Woodson, Col. Charles W., **1960–61:** 314
Woodward, Robert F., **1960–61:** 78n.
Wool, **1954:** 196
  Direct payments to growers, **1954:** 9
  Imports, **1954:** 4, 48, 49; **1958:** 58, 96
    Effect on price-support program, letter, **1953:** 131
  Incentives for growers, **1954:** 291
  National Wool Act, extension, **1955:** 5 (p. 66)
  News conference remarks, **1954:** 9, 48, 192
  Price supports, **1954:** 4, 49
  Statement, **1954:** 49
Wool Act, National, extension proposed, **1960–61:** 414 (p. 989)
Wool Growers Association, National, **1959:** 161
Woolen fabrics, tariff increase, **1956:** 216
Woolen textiles, **1959:** 196
  Imports, **1959:** 67, 161
Wooton, Paul, **1955:** 33; **1956:** 235; **1957:** 62
Worcester, Mass., Mayor Andrew Holstrom, **1953:** 117
Work-load, the president's, **1958:** 37
Workmen's compensation, **1955:** 4; **1958:** 26
  Budget message, **1955:** 17 (p. 177)
Works Progress Administration, **1954:** 231; **1958:** 43
Work-week, 4-day, **1956:** 216
World Agriculture Fair (New Delhi), **1959:** 316; **1960–61:** 136
  Joint statement with Prime Minister Nehru on, **1959:** 317
  News conference remarks, **1959:** 277
  Remarks at opening, **1959:** 315
World Amateur Golf Team Championship Conference, remarks, **1958:** 91
World Bank.
  See International Bank for Reconstruction and Development.
World Christian Endeavor Convention, remarks, **1954:** 170
World Council of Churches
  Address, **1954:** 204
  International objectives, **1954:** 341
  News conference remarks on, **1954:** 192, 341
World Court.
  See International Court of Justice.
World Day of Prayer, message, **1954:** 47
World economy, **1959:** 258
World Health Day, statement, **1959:** 72
World Health Organization, **1955:** 25; **1958:** 207; **1959:** 72, 189; **1960–61:** 13 (p. 63), 279
  Tenth anniversary commemorative session, message, **1958:** 116
  U.S. contribution, **1959:** 55
World Meteorological Organization, **1959:** 189

World Peace Award, AMVETS, presentation to the President, **1959:** 92
World Peace Through World Law (Clark and Sohn), **1958:** 153
World Refugee Year, **1959:** 115; **1960–61:** 133
  U.S. participation, **1959:** 91
World Series, **1953:** 198; **1960–61:** 284, 319
World Touring and Automobile Clubs, Organization of, remarks, **1955:** 93
World Veterans Federation, **1953:** 26
World War I, **1953:** 37, 45, 46, 50, 105, 192, 246; **1954:** 72; **1955:** 56, 118; **1958:** 31; **1959:** 71, 255, 296; **1960–61:** 80, 171n.
  Cause of, **1955:** 26
  News conference remarks, **1959:** 7, 53
World War II, **1953:** 45, 46, 50, 96, 192, 201, 216, 241, 246, 248, 256; **1954:** 103, 159, 189, 290, 291; **1955:** 4, 10, 13, 22, 29, 59, 100, 115, 166; **1956:** 282; **1958:** 65, 80, 124, 159, 163, 173, 207, 220, 261, 293; **1959:** 57, 70, 96, 133, 198n., 217n., 254n., 344; **1960–61:** 48, 49, 52, 80, 124, 171n., 194, 205, 287, 319
  See also Eisenhower, Dwight D., personal reminiscences.
  African invasion, **1953:** 234, 267; **1959:** 330
  Airport construction, **1956:** 163
  Allied landings
    Africa, **1954:** 325; **1960–61:** 355
    France, **1954:** 9, 57, 133, 198
  Anniversary of end of hostilities in Europe, **1956:** 96
  Anzio, Battle of, **1954:** 63
  Association with allied leaders, **1959:** 7
  Association with Gen. de Gaulle, **1960–61:** 120, 121
  Brazilian dead, ceremonies honoring, **1960–61:** 379
  Bulge, Battle of the, **1958:** 310
  Burial of Unknown Americans killed in, **1958:** 103, 122n.
  Campaign remarks, **1956:** 206, 228, 253, 257, 279
  Compensation to Americans for property damage, **1959:** 10 (p. 75); **1960–61:** 13 (p. 105), 414 (p. 1023)
  D-Day, **1953:** 88; **1960–61:** 354
    Anniversary, **1956:** 121, 122
  Dedication of cemeteries, letter, **1956:** 102
  Documents, disclosure of, **1955:** 81
  Kasserine Pass, battle of, **1958:** 310
  Memoirs of Field-Marshal Montgomery, comment on, **1958:** 288
  News conference remarks, **1953:** 15, 22, 37, 88, 109, 128, 265; **1954:** 9, 57, 63, 328; **1955:** 26; **1956:** 78, 96, 113, 121, 155, 229; **1958:** 103, 288, 310; **1959:** 7, 53, 191; **1960–61:** 7, 268
  Normandy, Battle of, **1960–61:** 405

World War II — *continued*
    Operation Overlord, **1959:** 7, 8; **1960–61:** 405
    Prisoners of war held by Soviet Union, **1953:** 50
    Prisoners of war returned to Soviet Union,
        1960–61: 268
    Remarks to Orthopaedic Association, **1958:** 104
    Removal of works of art from Italy, **1956:** 45n.
    Rhine River crossing, **1960–61:** 405
    Scientific collaboration, U.S.-U.K., **1958:** 157
    Treaties, **1953:** 12, 14, 15
    U.S. prisoners of war, indemnity claims, **1954:** 94
    Veterans, **1953:** 144
    Women's Army Corps, **1955:** 100, 152, 153
World War III, prevention of, **1956:** 210, 283
World's Fair 1964–65, New York, **1959:** 186
    Report, **1960–61:** 376
    U.S. participation, **1960–61:** 358, 414 (p. 984)
Worthington, Minn., **1956:** 250
Wortsman, Gene, **1956:** 189; **1957:** 157; **1958:** 288
WPA.
    See Works Progress Administration.
Wright, Mrs. Chester, **1956:** 241
Wright, Mr. and Mrs. Derfery William, relief of,
    1956: 24
Wright, J. Newman, **1953:** 198
Wright, Repr. James C., **1958:** 74
Wright, Adm. Jerauld, **1955:** 100
    Appointment as Supreme Allied Commander,
        Atlantic, statement, **1954:** 36
    Retirement, letter, **1959:** 350
Wright, Mrs. Jerauld, **1959:** 350
Wright, Loyd, **1955:** 210
Wright, Orville and Wilbur, **1953:** 267; **1954:**
    106n.; **1959:** 169; **1960–61:** 332
Wriston, Henry, **1960–61:** 30n., 86
    Letters, **1960–61:** 29, 240
Write-off allowances.
    See Tax write-off allowances.
Wyatt, Joseph W., **1953:** 59
Wyeth, Andrew, **1959:** 148
Wyker, Mrs. James D., **1953:** 205
Wyoming
    Casper, **1954:** 257
    Mining claims, disapproval, **1956:** 179
    O'Mahoney, Sen. Joseph, **1957:** 124
    Rogers, Gov. C. J., **1954:** 257
    Taxation of property in Grand Teton National
        Park, **1954:** 222
Wyszynski, Stefan Cardinal, **1953:** 198, 235

Xavier, Jose Joaquim (Tiradentes), **1960–61:** 45
X-15 research plane, **1960–61:** 264
X-ray, radiation from, **1956:** 266

Yale University, **1956:** 255
Yalta agreement, **1953:** 12
Yalta conference (1945), **1954:** 345; **1955:** 90; **1958:**
    318
    Letter to Premier Bulganin, **1958:** 7
    Release of documents, **1955:** 59
Yalu River, Korea, **1956:** 205
Yamashita, Madam Harue, **1960–61:** 14n.
Yameogo, Maurice, message, **1960–61:** 253
Yankee Atomic Electric Co., **1955:** 223
Yap, Diosdado M., **1954:** 73, 101
Ydigoras Fuentes, Miguel, message, **1960–61:** 368
Yeh, George K. C., **1954:** 345
Yellow fever, remarks on, **1955:** 108
Yellowtail Dam and Reservoir, claim in connection
    with right-of-way, veto, **1956:** 124
Yemelyanov, Vasily S., **1959:** 243
YMCA.
    See Young Men's Christian Association.
Yoshida, Shigeru
    Joint statement, **1954:** 330
    News conference remarks on, **1954:** 311, 322, 328
Yost, Charles W., **1959:** 343n.
Youlou, Rev. Fulbert, **1959:** 214
Young, Sen. Milton R., **1953:** 225; **1954:** 18
Young, Philip, **1957:** 33 and n.
    See also Civil Service Commission, Chairman;
        President's Adviser on Personnel Man-
        agement.
Young, Robert C., **1959:** 36, 191; **1960–61:** 362
Young, Spencer (President, Board of Commis-
    sioners, District of Columbia), **1953:**
    261n., 269
Young Men's Christian Association, **1958:** 307;
    1960–61: 210
Young people, **1956:** 122, 268
    Campaign remarks, **1956:** 190, 206, 253, 279
    Fitness of, **1956:** 96, 121, 128
    News conference remarks, **1956:** 94, 96, 121, 235
    Salk vaccine for, **1956:** 303
    Voting age, **1956:** 225, 226, 235, 241, 268, 318
Young Republican National Federation, **1957:** 116
    and n.; **1960–61:** 18n.
    Leadership Training School, **1956:** 122n.; **1960–**
        61: 18
Young Republican Organization, National, ad-
    dress, **1953:** 101
Young Republicans, **1956:** 268
Young Women's Christian Association, **1958:** 307;
    1960–61: 210
Younger, Repr. J. Arthur, **1958:** 294
Youngstown Sheet and Tube Company, **1959:**
    211n.
"Your Government and You," broadcast, **1956:**
    246
Youth, Republican recruitment, **1955:** 35, 213
Youth, U.S., comment on, **1953:** 265; **1960–61:** 123

Youth, White House conference on (1960), **1958:** 119, 320; **1959:** 10 (p. 104); **1960–61:** 13 (p. 96), 100, 103, 414 (p. 1012)
Youth centers, **1958:** 307
Youth for Eisenhower, **1956:** 190
Youth fitness, **1958:** 307
  Comment on, **1960–61:** 103
  Conference on, **1955:** 217; **1956:** 128
  Letter, **1957:** 104 and n.
Youth Fitness, Citizens Advisory Committee on, **1956:** 96, 128
Youth Fitness, Council on, **1956:** 128
Youth Science Month, statement, **1960–61:** 299
Ypres, Belgium, **1959:** 7
Yu Jai Heung, Lt. Gen., **1960–61:** 202
Yugoslavia, **1954:** 319; **1955:** 4; **1956:** 210; **1957:** 118, 152, 250; **1958:** 287
  Agreement with Italy on Trieste, **1954:** 283, 284, 286, 297, 316
  Assistance, **1955:** 76, 119; **1956:** 58, 121, 235, 248; **1958:** 141
  Communist Party in, **1956:** 248
  Compensation claims of U.S. nationals, **1954:** 94
  Flood relief, **1954:** 175, 182 and ftn. (p. 678)
  News conference remarks, **1955:** 100, 119
  Tito, Marshal Josip Broz, **1953:** 31; **1955:** 119
  Letter, **1960–61:** 313
  Message, **1954:** 284
  Visit of Soviet leaders, **1955:** 100
YWCA.
  See Young Women's Christian Association.

Zablocki, Repr. Clement J., letter, **1953:** 235
Zaharias, Mrs. George (Babe Didrikson), **1956:** 216
Zahedi, Fazollah, message, **1953:** 178
Zahir, Mohammad, **1959:** 306
  Joint statement with, **1959:** 308
  Toast to, **1959:** 307
Zan Acker, Achille, **1957:** 153 and n.
Zaroubin, Georgi N., **1956:** 23
  Discussions with Secretary Dulles, **1954:** 9, 18, 39, 322
Zeckendorf, William, **1954:** 345
Zellerbach, James D., **1959:** 291n., 292, 294n.
Zhukov, Marshal Georgi, **1954:** 133; **1956:** 78, 121, 298; **1957:** 134, 150, 210, 228
  Gift to the President, **1955:** 33
  Geneva conference meeting, **1955:** 176
  News conference remarks on, **1955:** 33, 81, 90, 95, 100, 146
  Visit to U.S., comment on, **1955:** 33, 47
Zielke, George R., **1955:** 47
Zinc, **1958:** 28, 153
Zinc and lead
  Joint statements on, **1959:** 38, 257
  Producers, payment of subsidies to, disapproval, **1960–61:** 280
  Production, consumption, and importation, **1953:** 228
  Tariffs, **1954:** 143, 200; **1957:** 157, 160
Zoological Park, National, **1955:** 141n.
Zorlu, Fatin R., **1959:** 41, 297
Zumwalt, Laddie, **1956:** 241
Zwicker, Brig. Gen. Ralph W., **1954:** 48, 347